COMBATTING
SOCIAL
PROBLEMS

Techniques of Intervention

COMBATTING SOCIAL PROBLEMS

Techniques of Intervention

EDITED BY HARRY GOLD, *Southern Illinois University*

FRANK R. SCARPITTI, *Rutgers University*

HOLT, RINEHART AND WINSTON
New York Chicago San Francisco Toronto London

Library of Congress Catalog Card Number: 67–11822

2627701

Printed in the United States of America

1 2 3 4 5 6 7 8 9

Preface

Collective social action and planned social change, aimed at reducing or controlling persistent social problems, are among the dominant social and political characteristics of modern urban-industrial societies. In contemporary American society, it is increasingly impossible to review and evaluate the most widely recognized social problems of this half of the twentieth century without also taking into account the many significant "techniques of intervention" which have emerged in response. More and more both teachers and students of sociology and social problems are raising pertinent questions about what is currently being done, or is being actively considered, to ameliorate some of our most visible and costly social problems. Although the nature and extent of the problems themselves are commonly reviewed in today's most widely used social problems textbooks, only rarely are questions about alternative courses of ameliorative action adequately discussed in these "conventional" sociological sources.

This book of readings is intended to meet needs such as those implied above by providing a cross-sectional view of some of the more representative "techniques of intervention," which have emerged in response to some of our society's most serious, or at least most widely recognized, social problems. In part, its purpose is to answer in descriptive terms frequently raised questions about the growing variety of "problem-solving" programs and policies which are rapidly becoming a part of our social fabric, and about which many social problems teachers and students have only very limited and impressionistic knowledge. Therefore the editors have attempted to bring together in one volume a collection of materials describing some of the major existing and emerging programs and policies in at least nine principal social problem areas. Heretofore, most of these materials have not been readily accessible to sociologists, except in a diverse variety of professional journals, government pamphlets and documents, and in many other mass media or lay publications. Many of the relevant materials, for example, are not to be found in the sociological collections of most university libraries.

The book is designed primarily to serve as a text for survey courses in social problems, but it can also be adapted as an extension of, or supplement to, any of the more conventional social problems textbooks currently in use. In addition, it should also prove to be of value in courses aimed at professional and preprofessional students of social work, city planning, nursing, education, government, and many other problem-oriented fields.

Following an introductory chapter, which spells out more fully the rationale and orientation of this book, each substantive chapter is introduced by a summary and overview of the problem being considered. Of course, none of these summaries are completely exhaustive of the vast literature on social problems, nor can they be in a collection of this nature. Rather, we have drawn upon prevailing social theory and research in order to provide what we consider to be the minimum amount of knowledge the reader must have to fully understand and appreciate the significance of the techniques of intervention discussed in the selections following the introduction to each chapter. Thus, some teachers who adopt this book as a text may wish to supplement the chapter introductions with additional readings of a theoretical or research nature.

Chapters 2, 3, 4, and 5 are concerned with what are sometimes classified as problems of "community disorganization." These include poverty and unemployment; education and educational opportunities; race relations; and urban change and development. These problems are all highly related in their causes and consequences, and the unifying sociological themes underlying the techniques of intervention discussed in this part of the book focus on developing more efficient and equitable means for allocating community resources, reducing community conflict and/or apathy, and the development of community consensus and support for long- and short-run community-wide goals.

Chapters 6, 7, 8, 9, and 10 focus on problems of deviant behavior, or what may more accurately be called problems of personal pathology. This section of the book includes chapters on mental illness, crime, juvenile delinquency, drug addiction, and alcoholism. Whenever possible, the techniques of intervention described in these chapters are divided into those focusing upon preventing the problem and those concerned with the control of the problem and the rehabilitation of deviant individuals. Although the techniques used may at times be similar, preventing deviant behavior and controlling it after it occurs are not the same problem and may well require uniquely different theoretical orientations and programs.

Chapter 11 is perhaps this book's greatest departure from conventional sociological approaches to social problems. It is concerned with the application of human skills and resources to the solution of social problems. It deals, in effect, with the problems of the problem-solvers themselves; that is, it deals with some of the difficulties faced by those who, in a wide variety of occupational roles and in a variety of organizational setting, have become "professional" problem-solvers. This chapter identifies and discusses many kinds of new social arrangements which revolve around the roles played by these newer kinds of professions, and which have important implications for the entire problem-solving process.

We wish to make it clear that this book is not intended to suggest that the techniques of intervention described herein are necessarily "solving" the problems they are aimed at, or that these techniques provide "the" best or only answers or solutions to these problems. There are many areas of honest disagreement, among so-called "experts" as well as among various segments of the lay public, with respect to the merits and faults of the action programs reviewed here. For example, the goals, the social and economic costs and consequences, and the expected impact of many action programs now under way or seriously being proposed are subject to a great deal of conflict and controversy. In this book we cannot even begin to resolve all of the issues that are involved, nor are we better prepared than anyone else to predict with any certainty the outcome of today's problem-solving efforts. Nevertheless, there are many new and significant things being done today that all students of contemporary society should be aware of, and our mission here is to bring knowledge of as many of these alternatives as possible to an interested audience. Hopefully, this book will not "indoctrinate" the reader as to the "rightness" or "wrongness" of any given course of action, but will, instead, alert him to highly fascinating mechanisms of social change and control and stimulate further sociological study and investigation.

We wish to express our appreciation to the authors and publishers who gave us permission to reprint their works. We are also grateful to the many students in our social problems courses at various universities who helped in pointing out the need for this kind of book and who stimulated our own interest in this undertaking. Special thanks go to Ronald Hansen, coordinator of the Office of Research and Projects at Southern Illinois University, for making various kinds of research support available to us; to Virginia Whitney, librarian "extraordinary," whose unique collection of relevant materials at the Urban Studies Center at Rutgers—The State University eased our task considerably; and to Bruce Runge, research aide, who assisted in the preparation of the manuscript. Among the various colleagues who read parts of the manuscript, we are most grateful to Harry C. Bredemeier and Daniel Glazer for their early suggestions and their keen professional judgments. Of course we are especially grateful to our wives, Pat and Ellen, who assisted us in ways far too numerous to list here.

Finally, we share a common responsibility for the intellectual framework and organization of this book. In the actual division of labor Gold prepared Chapters 2, 3, 4, 5, and 11, while Scarpitti prepared Chapters 6, 7, 8, 9, and 10.

H.G.
F.R.S.

January 1967

Contents

1

Introduction

The early American sociologists who were concerned with the impact of industrialization and urbanization on the social life of the community were in the vanguard of those who identified and defined social problems, or evaluated their causes and consequences. The problems that concerned the early sociologists were "latent" social problems,[1] inasmuch as they were not widely recognized or discussed as such by the general public, with the possible exception of a few socially minded novelists, journalists, and "muckrakers." These problems were fatalistically accepted by most members of the society as part of the natural order of things and, therefore, as inevitable.

In many respects social problems such as slums and urban congestion, mental disorders, alcoholism and drug addiction, and ethnic or racial conflict were not considered appropriate subjects for open public discussion, ordinary social discourse, or serious and scientific analysis. Thus, even for many college students courses in social problems taught by the early sociologists were often the first and perhaps the last or only place in which serious analytical discussions of the nature and causes of deviant behavior or social disorganization were permitted and encouraged. Inasmuch as they studied, wrote, and taught about aspects of social life that were outside the range of normal discourse, many of the early problem-oriented social scientists were also looked upon as nonconformist or radicals by their students, the larger academic community, and the public at large.[2]

Although the nature and extent of the problems have changed to some degree, as have some of their professional interests, many sociologists today are still in the vanguard of those who see in current social trends the emergence of more contemporary "latent" social problems not yet commonly recognized or "discovered" by the general public. But what has also happened is that many of the problems first identified or defined by the early sociologists, such as some of those mentioned above, are no longer hidden from public concern but have, in fact, become "manifest" social problems during the past several decades; that is, they have now become the object of widespread public concern among all major segments of American society.

No longer is the discussion of the numerous problems of individual deviance or community disorganization confined to academic circles. Rather, action-oriented discussions can now be commonly heard in political debates at the national, state, and local levels—among leaders of business and industry, among almost all ethnic or minority groups, among religious leaders—in the university or intellectual community at large and in all segments of the mass media. Perhaps the best single recent illustration of how public concern with social problems that were "latent" several decades ago has now become widespread is the degree to which crime and delinquency, poverty and unemployment, slums and urban congestion, race relations and problems of maintaining basic institutions (such as the family, education, and religion) were recognized as public issues and freely discussed during the presidential election campaign of 1964. Indeed, many of the major issues raised in proposals for the "Great Society" are those considered in the current, standard social problems textbooks!

Along with growing public awareness of the existence of persistent problem-generating behavior, there has also been a growing public recognition that the course of many current social problems can be significantly altered through strategic interventions involving various sorts of collective social action. The notion that problems ought to and can be ameliorated is closely related to acknowledgement that a problem exists; indeed, this relationship between the recognition of a problem and the desire or ability to solve it is an aspect of many common sociological definitions of a social problem: ". . . a problem is called social when it affects a large number of people and when there is a consensus that there is a problem and that something can be done to alleviate it;"[3] or a "social problem is a condition affecting a significant number of people in ways considered undesirable, about which it is felt something can be done through collective social action."[4]

These definitions of a social problem, not unlike those found in most contemporary textbooks in the field, indicate that there must be agreement by large or significant numbers of people on 1) whether or not there is a problem and 2) whether or not something should be done about it. Each of these decisions is based upon the values of the society's members and each engenders a great deal of value conflict.[5] There is seldom universal consensus on the undesirability or harmfulness of any social condition. What is an intolerable situation to one person may well be a completely desirable condition to another. Poverty may be seen as a social evil which must be eradicated at all costs or it may be seen as a justifiable situation resulting from inferiority, laziness, or the "breaks of the game." In either case, one's values dictate the perspective taken.

In order for any condition to become a social problem, then, there must be "enough" agreement that it is undesirable or harmful to have it continue unchecked. The exact amount of agreement is unknown. For some problems, such as crime or illness, agreement on their undesirability is great. For others, such as racial inequality or political extremism, agreement is not nearly so great. Changing values also affect the social definitions of particular conditions. Many conditions that were completely acceptable a century ago (child labor) or even two decades ago (separate educational facilities for Negroes) are not tolerable today. Hence our children and grandchildren are likely to be pondering problems that we never thought of or accepted as inevitable.

Values also play an important role in determining society's response to an undesirable condition. First, it must be decided that the condition should be changed. The person who believes that poverty is the just due of the poor may agree that the condition is undesirable, but he may also believe that it cannot and should not be changed. Until there is agreement that certain conditions must be changed no social problem exists and the situation continues to be viewed as inevitable. However, when there is a consensus that a condition defined as undesirable should also be changed, a second problem of values regarding society's response is raised: "What should be done about it?"

For the social problems selected for inclusion in this book the question of what should be done has not been resolved. Although one reason for this is that the professional problem solvers concerned with a particular problem do not always know enough about the condition to affect any change, it is also true that values have often limited potential ameliorative efforts or "solutions." Some years ago Fuller and Myers indicated that values "obstruct solutions to conditions defined as social problems because people are unwilling to endorse programs of amelioration which prejudice or require abandonment of their cherished beliefs and institutions, e.g., one possible 'solution' to illegitimacy would be social acceptance of contraception and abortion, practices which in themselves are now defined as violations of the mores."[6] It is thought by many that drug addiction would be a problem of far less magnitude if we would stop reacting to it as a legal problem and instead treat it as a medical problem.[7] But it appears that to do so would be contrary to the wishes of the majority of the people who have been successfully indoctrinated with an untrue "drug fiend mythology."

Other value conflicts also emerge when remedies to problems are sought. In American society, with its traditional strong emphasis on private enterprise, there is always the question of who should attempt to bring about change. Is it the proper function of the government to initiate, support, or operate programs designed to alleviate problem conditions? Or should these tasks be left to private organizations and agencies? Another conflict is created by the problem solvers themselves. Because social problems affect many aspects of human life they are the legitimate objects of study of many professional disciplines. Often these professional disciplines do not agree on the most efficacious way of remedying the problem and such disagreement gives rise to confusion, especially among nonprofessionals.

It is obvious that considering a condition as a problem and wanting to do something to ameliorate it does not mean that there is necessarily agreement on how to solve it. As Rose has pointed out, there is "seldom consensus on the procedure to alleviate or handle a social problem, but there is some degree of agreement that the problem is at least theoretically modifiable."[8] The social problems dealt with in this book are in the process of being "modified," even though many methods of modification are being employed. They have passed through an awareness stage, during which they were identified as problems, and are now in what some writers have called the policy determination and reform stages.[9] For a few of these problems the strategy for amelioration is just now being worked out. For others programs are being put into action and policy is actually being tested on the anvil of experience. These are the "techniques of intervention"—what society is doing about its problems.

Doing something about our problems was perceptively described as one of our national characteristics by Russell Baker of the *New York Times* when he observed that "once an American is faced with a problem, he cannot resist the urge to try solving it."[10] According to Mr. Baker, today we are all faced with the "problem Problem," which can be summarized by the question, "What are we going to do when the problems run out?" Whether or not the problems will ever run out is, of course, a matter of conjecture, although most sociological observers are inclined to be skeptical that this could ever happen. But regardless of the long-range outcome, large-scale intervention has become a dominant response to the more widely recognized social problems of contemporary American society.

The current widespread public demand for solutions, along with the creation of many new problem-oriented activities and organizations, can also cause a serious value dilemma for the sociologist with regard to his appropriate professional role within the problem-solving framework. The proper behavior for the sociologist in evaluating, advocating, or becoming personally involved in actions aimed at minimizing the impact of social problems in which he is professionally interested has always been and still is the source of considerable debate and controversy within the discipline of sociology.[11]

Perhaps the school of thought which is most dominant in contemporary American sociology is the one that holds the scientific aspirations of the discipline as overriding all other considerations. According to this school of thought, sociology as a science ought not concern itself with advocating normative positions about what "ought" to be, nor even with the practical applications of sociological knowledge and techniques. Other prevailing schools of thought, probably in a minority, seem to take the more permissive view that applied research or direct participation in collective social action are indeed among the legitimate concerns of professional sociologists.

Although there are many variations of these approaches, it is not our purpose here to attempt to spell out all of the alternatives, or even to choose among them. The value dilemmas involved in choosing between theoretical and applied science, or some combination of them, are quite complex and will probably not be resolved to the satisfaction of many sociologists for some time to come.

But whatever the unresolved value dilemmas of the sociologists, the generally widespread "discovery" of social problems in this decade by many college students has produced a search for solutions. This is indicated by their commonly asked questions, such as, "What is being done," or "What can we do," to help reduce these social problems? Heightened student interest, as evidenced by their participation in demonstrations and action programs, is further testimony of this growing demand for solutions involving individual or collective action.

Of course the demand for solutions and participation in action programs are not just student characteristics. Many people have come to accept the idea that man can control the conditions of his environment. No longer must he sit by passively while undesirable situations go on unchecked. Perhaps as a result of the civil rights struggle of the 1950s and early 1960s, many people have placed new and important emphasis on rational planning and remedial action to accomplish socially desirable goals. When these methods fail, or are too slow in bringing about change, a new breed of social activists have not hesitated to employ action techniques such as picketing, marches, sit-ins, rent strikes, or boycotts. But, despite the methods, the fact is that more so than a century or even a decade ago a significant number of today's citizens will not quietly accept the consequences of social problems.

Too often the teacher of social problems has failed to acknowledge and to deal directly with these concerns, whatever his own orientation might be with regard to the issue of theoretical versus applied sociology. In some respects, many students already have a greater degree of awareness of the existence and impact of certain kinds of social problems than their teachers have recognized. Such students generate discussions or debates about alternative courses of action which many teachers are too often not prepared to lead or evaluate. This may be due to a lack of specific knowledge about how society can intervene to alter the impact of its most serious problems. Yet, the very existence of attempted interventions represents a fact which cannot be ignored by sociologists, for societal responses to social problems are an essential element of the sociological analysis of social problems in contemporary American society.

An impressively wide variety of groups and organizations—at the local, state, and national levels, as well as in both the public and private sectors of our society—already are attempting to change or ameliorate those social problems which have recently caused the most public concern. These planned interventions represent a bewildering variety of programs and techniques of varying promise, about which both the teacher and student of social problems must have knowledge, in order to assess their significance. These planned interventions are rapidly becoming a part of our social fabric, and thus they become part of the empirical data upon which the scientific study of social problems is based. They are sociological facts amenable to scientific observation, description, and analysis.

One of the basic elements of a sociological orientation to social problems is "that attempts to solve one problem may promote others, and that a completely problem-free society can probably never be attained."[12] Perhaps the latter point is obvious and to think otherwise is a utopian dream. Why? Two illustrations that dramatically show how the "solution" to one problem may give rise to others also serve to demonstrate the improbability of problem-free society. In the first case let us look at Prohibition. This "noble experiment" was seen as a "solution" to the problem of alcoholism and drinking. With the passage of the Eighteenth Amendment in 1919 federal law prohibited the sale of alcoholic beverages in the United States. The law was completely unenforcible and was flagrantly violated by otherwise law-abiding people. Later, of course, it was repealed by the Twenty-first Amendment and has become somewhat of a national joke. It is only incidental here that Prohibition did not work, since many attempted "solutions" do not succeed and are abandoned. Prohibition, however, gave impetus to another problem, organized crime, that is seen by many as a far worse evil than drinking alcoholic beverages. During the Prohibition era, organized crime in the United States flourished as it never had before and grew to such immense stature that it has remained as healthy as ever long after the repeal of Prohibition. Here was a case of an attempted, if misguided, "solution" to one problem creating another.

The second illustration deals with modern society's tremendous success in prolonging life. Since the founding of our country the years of life expectation have nearly doubled. From a life expectancy of around 35 years in 1789, the figures rose to about 50 years for both males and females in 1900, and to 66 years for males and 73 years for females in 1963.[13] This dramatic rise in life expectancy can be attributed to many factors, but it is especially due to the great advances in public health and medical practices. Modern medicine is now able to prevent many illnesses and successfully treat others that once were fatal. In this sense the social problem of physical illness and early death has been greatly moderated. However, these feats have also caused problems that did not exist when people died younger. The new problems of the aged— medical care, retirement and leisure activities, social security, adequate housing, alienation, and loneliness—have been created largely because we have been successful in prolonging life. Most would agree that the net results of this accomplishment are beneficial, but we cannot deny that new problems have been created.

Planned interventions designed to reduce or ameliorate existing social problems are sociologically significant for a variety of reasons. For example, they produce new problem-oriented organizations and institutions; they create new occupations, new roles for older occupations, new occupational values and ideologies; they generate new systems of social interaction, not only between the problem solvers and those to whom programs of problem-solving are directed, but also among the problem solvers themselves. In effect these interventions produce social change not only in the social problem areas that are the intended targets of planned social change but also, in perhaps a less anticipated way, in the structural and institutional arrangements in society. In turn these new institutional arrangements are also a basic source of social change, social control, and social integration.

More specifically, the techniques of intervention reviewed in this book lend themselves to fruitful sociological analysis in at least the following five ways:

1. They often represent the application of sociological theory to the modification of social problems. For example, the Mobilization for Youth program described in the chapter on juvenile delinquency [14] is based largely on the delinquency theories of sociologists Richard A. Cloward and Lloyd E. Ohlin. Such applications test the validity of theory and provide feedback which allows the theory to be modified in the light of empirical knowledge of ongoing social processes.

2. The interventions undoubtedly have some impact on the course of social problems, whatever the direction of the eventual outcomes may be. Deliberate efforts at change may produce trends which allows us to predict, at least in gross terms, whether a particular problem is or is not capable of solution, given the action already under way. Incidentally, they may also indicate what some of the social and economic costs of change might be, and whether these costs appear to be worth the gains anticipated. Where specific programs and activities appear to be successful in reducing the extent or incidence of certain kinds of problems, we can shift our attention to those problems which appear to be the most resistant to treatment.

3. Such interventions provide insights into some of the basic social processes of our society, especially its capacity to deal with those forces that are thought to threaten its continued survival and development. Social problems disrupt the existing social structure and create a state of social disequilibrium. Negatively defined situations (problems) break down normative expectations and create personal discomfort and distress. Though interventive techniques the social group attempts either to prevent the problem condition or to alter it once it has occurred so as to return to a state of "normalcy."

4. The internal organization of those programs, agencies, and institutions which deal with social problems has itself become of great sociological interest in recent decades. The growth and proliferation of mental hospitals and clinics, community action programs, health and welfare treatment agencies, youth service organizations and community relations programs, and city planning, urban renewal and housing commissions has stimulated a growing number of sociological studies. These are concerned with the internal structure and processes of the organizations, as well as their relationships to the communities which they serve.

5. A review of the intervention programs already under way provides some guideline to the students who wish to pursue a career in one of the many service-oriented occupations which have emerged as a response to social problems, or who wish to "do something" about social problems in a

volunteer or "lay" capacity. Knowledge of the occupational changes that are produced, the new career patterns that develop, and the cooperation or conflicts that arise between rival occupations seeking some status in social problem-solving organizations is not ony sociologically worthwhile for students to possess, but it also provides them with a better understanding of occupational areas of increasing importance and to which more and more students will eventually make career commitments.

It should be apparent from this discussion that the very machinery for attacking today's commonly recognized social problems may also be the source of new kinds of problems for our society, about which we are just beginning to be aware. One of the most significant aspects of problem-oriented occupations, such as social work, city planning, nursing, and many others, is that more and more they aspire to and take on the characteristics of professionalism, with all of the attending difficulties. Thus there is a whole range of new problems which revolve around the growth, proliferation, and professionalization of these occupations, and which have an important impact on the problem-solving process. These include the following problems: (1) changing the nature or raising the quality of the services provided through improvements in the techniques and principles of practice; (2) improving or maintaining ethical standards of practice; (3) recruitment, training, and socialization of competent and dedicated professional workers; (4) role conflict and other difficulties associated with the need to coordinate professional practice with the policies and programs of complex bureaucratic organizations; and (5) conflict between competing occupational groups working in the same or similar problem areas. All of these are crucial problems for a society in which planned social change has become widely accepted. Some of these critical issues are dealt with in Chapter 11, "The Professionalization of Problem-Solving."

SOME CAUTIONARY NOTES
ON THE USE OF THIS BOOK

This volume is intended as an introductory survey of various techniques of intervention which seem to be emerging in response to the contemporary social problems discussed in each of the chapter introductions. Each selection of readings in the following chapters describes in some detail some major approaches to the amelioration of problems which have been tried, are now under way, or are seriously being considered and likely to be undertaken in the near future. Needless to say, space limitations serve to restrict the number and variety of alternatives that can be included in one volume, and, as a result, it is not possible to include discussions of many other worthwhile policies and programs. Nevertheless, the editors believe the materials selected to be reasonably "representative" of some of the more significant contemporary approaches to problem-solving. Also, an attempt has been made to include materials not as directly accessible to the social problems student or teacher through the more conventional sociological sources.

Many approaches and programs of problem-solving are too recent in origin to have yet demonstrated their effectiveness, and many of them generate considerable controversy among those who are directly affected, among the public at large, as well as among these who are professionally involved. Some of the selections to follow do attempt to evaluate critically as well as to describe the various action alternatives. Yet it should be made clear that this book is not primarily intended as a critique or evaluation of the intervention programs and policies it describes, because only time will tell which, if any, are to be successful in altering the current nature of the problems, and what the ultimate consequences for the society as a whole will be. In the opinion of the editors, much more "feedback" than has been available so far is needed before sound and effective evaluation is in order. Much current pseudosociological criticism of ongoing programs, in our opinion, is often as premature as the over-optimistic expectations of the participants in many action programs. Such premature judgements often provide the student of social problems with exaggerated and distorted views of current problem-solving efforts, without correspondingly providing an accurate description of the actual nature and purposes of the strategies involved. Thus one often finds popular criticisms of policies and programs in problem areas, such as poverty or urban renewal, which are based on much too limited or distorted sources of knowledge of what is actually involved in these efforts to be of any constructive value.

In effect this book hopes to provide a reasonably accurate and concise description of ideas, policies, and programs in selected problem-solving areas as a *point of departure* for further feedback, evaluation, and sound critical analysis. In many cases teachers using this book may wish to supplement it with critical materials *after* the basic descriptive selections have been presented.

It should also be pointed out here that this is not necessarily a volume of "applied sociology"; that is, not all of the techniques of intervention included are of a sociological nature or origin, and many of the selections are written by experts who are not professional sociologists. Although some of the selections do represent a sociological approach to problems and applications of sociological theory, it would be grandiose to assume that all formulation and implementation of problem-solving policies in the United States has been provided by sociologists, or that the sociologist necessarily has the only answers to the tasks at hand. In this respect several interesting volumes of readings in applied sociology have recently appeared and it is not our purpose to duplicate these good efforts.[15] Rather the task before us at the present time is to understand the broader range of sociological and nonsociological intervention alternatives as best we can, and to examine how these alternatives are currently being applied to the rational control of the more widely recognized social problems of our society.

REFERENCES

1. For a discussion of latent and manifest social problems see Robert K. Merton and Robert A. Nisbet, *Contemporary Social Problems*. New York: Harcourt, Brace & World, Inc., 1966, pp. 788–792.
2. A brief but informative discussion of the roles and activities of early American problem-oriented sociologists can be found in Ernest W. Burgess and Donald Bogue, *Contributions to Urban Sociology*. Chicago: University of Chicago Press, 1964, pp. 1–14.
3. Arnold M. Rose, "Theory for the Study of Social Problems," *Social Problems*, 4 (January, 1957), p. 190.
4. Paul B. Horton and Gerald R. Leslie, *The Sociology of Social Problems*. New York: Appleton-Center-Crofts, Inc., 1965, pp. 4–6.
5. For an excellent discussion of the role of values in the definition of and reaction to a social problem see John F. Cuber, William F. Kenkel, and Robert A. Harper, *Problems of American Society: Values in Conflict*. New York: Holt, Rinehart and Winston, Inc., 1964, especially pp. 35–39.
6. Richard C. Fuller and Richard R. Myers, "The Natural History of a Social Problem," *American Sociological Review*, 6 (June 1941), p. 320.
7. In reading 5 of Chapter 9, "British Narcotics Policy," Edwin M. Schur describes how this problem is handled in another society where it is seen primarily as a medical rather than legal problem.
8. Rose, p. 190.
9. Fuller and Myers, pp. 322–328.
10. *The New York Times*, April 20, 1965, p. 18.
11. An extended discussion of this dilemma is contained in William J. Goode and Paul K. Hatt, *Methods in Social Research*. New York: McGraw Hill Book Company, 1952, Chap. 3.
12. Edwin M. Schur, "Recent Social Problems Texts: An Essay-Review," *Social Problems*, 10 (Winter 1963), pp. 287–292.
13. Horton and Leslie, p. 587; *Vital Statistics of the United States, 1963*, Vol. II, Part A. Washington, D.C.: United States Department of Health, Education and Welfare, 1965.
14. See reading 2, Chapter 8.
15. See Arthur B. Shostak (ed.), *Sociology in Action*. Homewood, Illinois: The Dorsey Press, 1966; Alvin W. Gouldner and S. M. Miller (eds.), *Applied Sociology*, New York: The Free Press of Glencoe, 1965.

2

Poverty and Unemployment

Of all the social problems of this decade poverty must certainly be considered as among those causing the most active concern, if attention by the mass media and in political debate or legislation is any criterion. But when we look at the fabulous economic growth of the United States in this century, and especially in the last decade, one wonders how we can even think of poverty as one of our significant social problems. In fact, for the first time in history, a society has made the transition from one characterized by scarcity to one characterized by abundance.[1]

There is no doubt that changes in its technical and social organization have brought enormous increases in productivity to the United States. These, in turn, have made possible rapid increases in personal and family income and in the general standard of living. For the first time more Americans own rather than rent their homes, and such products as the automobile, television, a modern stove, and refrigerator are becoming widely distributed among the entire population, including many of the poor. Not only has the general level of income risen with increased productivity, but there has also been a trend toward some equalization of income, with a general leveling up of the income of those on the bottom of the economic scale, especially since the mid-1930s. There has been a growing middle class, with a shrinking portion of the population remaining at the bottom income levels, and according to some estimates, the gap between the very rich and the very poor is becoming smaller. In the midst of an unprecedented prosperous majority, the poor have become a minority.

Thus in America today we live in what has been labeled by John Kenneth Galbraith an *affluent society*—one characterized by an imposing command of physical resources, high standards of private consumption, and freedom

most of the economic uncertainties of life that have plagued man
ghout history in most parts of the world.[2] In fact there are some observ-
ho maintain that we have now attained the technological ability to wipe
poverty completely if we so desire.[3]

In the light of these remarkable economic gains in our society, it would
be reasonable to expect that the concern about poverty as a social problem
would have significantly diminished. In effect this is what actually did
happen in the period between the end of World War II and near the middle
of the 1960s, when poverty did re-emerge as a popular issue. During this
period the fortunate majority had more and more assumed that almost everyone was sharing the rapidly rising living standards, or that everyone was
prospering as they themselves were as the result of good economic conditions.
It is really not so surprising then that the remaining millions of Americans
who did not share this economic growth had become, as described by Michael
Harrington, increasingly "invisible" to the prosperous majority.[4] Of course,
this invisibility has also resulted from the fact that the very poor had become
in a variety of ways almost completely segregated from the rest of society. As
Harrington puts it, poverty is off the "beaten path," confined to certain
geographic regions or in the deteriorating slums of central cities, well isolated
from the well-to-do suburbs where most middle-class families now live.[5] In
Harrington's words, this spatial segregation has removed poverty from "the
living, emotional experience of millions upon millions of middle-class Americans. Living out in the suburbs, it is all too easy to assume that ours is, indeed,
an affluent society."[6]

At this point it becomes important to ask why, in spite of our apparent
current prosperity, has poverty so suddenly re-emerged in the middle of this
decade as such a widely discussed and debated social problem? Why are
there so many new programs and policies being proposed and undertaken
within the framework of the "war on poverty"? After all, is it not true that
there are actually fewer people suffering from absolute economic deprivation
than ever before?

This obvious paradox has not been lost on interested observers, and it has
often been pointed out by politicians, social scientists, and in various news
media such as the press and television. For example, a recent article in
Newsweek dramatically poses the problem of poverty in the midst of plenty
as follows:

Lingering poverty in the shadow of unrivaled affluence is the painful paradox
of American life today. In a single generation the richest country on earth has
banished the bleak specter of *The Grapes of Wrath* with the gilded fantasy of the
Beverly Hillbillies. But reality has hardly kept pace with the American Dream.[7]

This apparent paradox can be interpreted or explained in many ways. For
example, the fact that poverty, now confined to a minority, hidden out of
sight and out of mind, is a new kind of poverty may be considered as at least
a partial explanation. Of course, poverty has been the rule, not the exception,

for the majority of mankind throughout history. In most societies it was usually accepted with fatalism as the natural order of things, or as the natural lot of mankind. In other words, since poverty was inevitable, it was very rarely defined as a social problem about which something might be done. Even in societies where there were glaring inequities in the class structure and the distribution of wealth, poverty for the majority was usually accepted as a natural and inevitable social arrangement.

Only when it was widely believed that the problem of poverty could be alleviated through collective social action of some sort did the demands for the elimination of poverty reach significant proportions. In the United States it was not really until the major depression of the 1930s that such demands led to widespread public concern and to many of the welfare state reforms of the New Deal. Not only was poverty and the inequities in the distribution of wealth a source of political concern, but these conditions were also widely discussed in the mass media, the literature, and in the intellectual community of that period. For example, late-movie addicts may note that some of the more significant films of the 1930s dealt with poverty as a theme, and many top stars of the day played unemployed workers, hoboes, vagabonds, and the like. Many of the top gangster films portrayed poverty as one of the causes of crime, and the famous tramp created by Charlie Chaplin a decade earlier became the protagonist for some bitter satire on existing economic conditions in such films as "Modern Times."[8] Another significant and widely read indictment of the effects of the depression and a plea for reform was reflected in John Steinbeck's novel *The Grapes of Wrath*, which also was vividly recreated as a motion picture.

One might conclude that the period from the end of World War II until the middle of this decade, when poverty all but disappeared from active concern and then suddenly reappeared, simply reflects the fact that during this relatively short period of time Americans had shifted their attention to problems of re-establishing a peace-time economy and establishing some sort of stable world order. At any rate, those Americans still experiencing poverty at the bottom of the economic ladder were no longer widely featured in the mass media or popular literature. More and more the popular heroes became middle class, and the "rat race" of Madison Avenue or "sex in the suburbs" became common themes displacing the older emphases on the trials and virtues of the poor. This changing image of America and the average American man, of course, reflects changes that really had been taking place in American society during that period. Perhaps we are today merely returning to the unfinished domestic tasks of the 1930s, after the diversions caused by World War II and the postwar national and international "reconstruction."

Another partial explanation for the re-emerging interest in poverty in the midst of plenty might also be related to some belated recognition of the potential political power of the poor. Although now a minority, their heavy concentration in some of the key urban-industrial states tends to give them the balance of power in close state and national elections. This especially

applies to the Negro segment of the voting population, which is over-represented in some of the poverty-stricken areas, and which, as the result of the
civil rights movement, has also become most actively involved in generating
demands for large-scale governmental intervention in attacking the problems
of poverty.

One might further speculate that the current concern with poverty has
been rekindled by popular social critics such as John Kenneth Galbraith or
Michael Harrington. In fact, it has been reported that Harrington's book
The Other America actually did impress the Kennedy administration of the
need for more federal action in combatting poverty with its dramatic description of the magnitude and quality of the problem.[9] And of course it may be
recalled that the current so-called "war on poverty" was originally conceived
in the last year of the Kennedy administration. In addition, the mass media,
which historically has stirred up popular interest in social problems from
time to time, must also be credited with much recent activity in reporting
various aspects of the rediscovered poverty problem.

Yet none of the speculation above adequately explains the re-emerging
concern for poverty, in the light of its shrinking effects and consequences.
Perhaps a more satisfactory explanation lies within the theoretical framework
spelled out by Robert K. Merton and Robert A. Nisbet in the preface to their
textbook *Contemporary Social Problems*. The following two propositions are
most pertinent:

> 1. The same social structure and culture that in the main make for conforming
> and organized behavior also generate tendencies toward distinctive kinds of social
> disorganization. In this sense, the problems current in a society register the social
> costs of a particular organization of social life.
> 2. It can thus be seen that the sociological orientation rejects as inadequate
> the commonly held doctrine that "evil is the cause of evil" in society. Instead, it
> alerts us to search out the ways in which socially prized arrangements and values
> in society can produce socially condemned results.[10]

In short, social problems cannot be understood except in the light of what
a society holds to be good or right. It is a matter of values or goals, so to
speak, and our economic goals and values have been changing. And they have
been changing *because* of our affluence and abundance. We no sooner reach
one economic level than we raise our standards. Hence the standards which
only a few years ago were adequate, we now view as too low. The satisfaction of at least the basic food requirements on a bare subsistence level may
have been good enough for previous generations, but in our own, it is no
longer considered adequate. In modern societies such as the United States,
sheer survival has simply become far too low a standard.

There are four main aspects of the changing standards associated with
current definitions of poverty. First, there are new definitions of what man
can achieve and of what human standards of life should prevail. Modern
technology has consistently broadened man's potential by making a longer,

healthier, better life possible. Thus, in terms of what is technically feasible, we have higher aspirations.

The second important change is that psychological and sociological satisfactions have assumed a greater significance in our new standards. As standards rise progressively higher than the sheer survival level, status and prestige considerations loom larger and larger. Even though the average person in many respects lives today even better than the privileged elites of past centuries, the fact is that wherever invidious status differences exist, these status differences will be important, no matter what the over-all wealth of the society. Psychologically and sociologically the bottom economic levels of our society are dispossessed in terms of that the rest of the nation enjoys. According to Michael Harrington, "they live on the fringe or the margin of American society, and as they watch the movies or read the magazines of affluent America, they are reminded constantly of their inferior and marginal socioeconomic status."[11] It is this low status in a society of abundance that Harrington also sees as the source of the pessimism, defeat, and despair that characterizes the "culture" of the poor in the United States. And, of course, attitudes such as these tend to be at least as difficult and costly to modify as the relative economic deprivation upon which they are based.

A third aspect of changing standards has to do with the growing involvement of the federal government in establishing quantitative guidelines for defining poverty and measuring its extent and distribution. For example, the President's Council of Economic Advisor's cut-off point of a minimum income of $3000 per year for a family of four is widely used as the standard below which is classified as poverty. Also this is the level most commonly used as a yardstick for determining the eligibility of a local area for federal poverty-program intervention. Using the above figure as a criterion, almost one-fifth of the total United States population (approximately 35 million people) is classified as poor.[12]

Of course the above definition is arbitrary, and even among federal agencies there are significant variations in the standards used to measure poverty. Current federal definitions range anywhere between $1500 and $7000 in annual family income.[13] Even within the federal government itself, there is anything but a consensus with respect to the standards to be employed for defining poverty, at least in strictly quantitative terms.

But the changes that have been taking place in standards have not only been quantitative; they have been qualitative as well. Therefore the fourth major change in standards has been the emergence of a whole new ideology with respect to human suffering. Abundance has not only made a more humane attitude toward poverty possible, but it also provides new economic justifications for improving the living conditions of the poor. This shift in standards can best be described as a change from an ideology of scarcity to an ideology of abundance.

We can trace this change by first examining the scarcity ideology which was reflected in the English Elizabethan poor laws of the seventeenth century and which was generally accepted in this country well into this century.

Although the ideology of the poor laws was generally superseded by the ideology embodied in the New Deal policies of the 1930s, the core of some conservative economic thought in the United States still appears to be based on an ideology of scarcity.

The scarcity ideology underlying the poor laws maintained that those at the bottom of the economic ladder could be helped only at the expense of those above them, and that therefore all care or aid for the poor had to be as inexpensive and humiliating as possible. The theories underlying the poor laws have been summarized by sociologist Jessie Bernard as follows:

> Human nature is essentially bad, so that unless you make relief as difficult and as humiliating as possible, people will just naturally take advantage of you. There must, therefore, be means tests of some sort or other; that is, people must prove their destitution and be willing to pay the price in humiliation, or even sacrifice of civil rights, if need be. Those receiving relief must be kept below the level of self-supporting families because economy in the administration funds is a prime consideration and the taxpayer must be protected against a potential horde of chiselers, or even the more worthy and deserving poor. He must be protected against the squandering of relief funds on swindlers; most people who need relief are inferior or deserve this misfortune, therefore there should be no "coddling" of clients. Public relief must be made as disagreeable, as punitive, and as unendurable as possible in order to reduce the numbers asking for it. Generosity would inevitably lead to abuse. Economy in the use of public funds, taken for granted as a good thing, demands that the natural tendency for people to take advantage of generosity be curbed.[14]

In almost complete contrast to the scarcity ideology of the poor laws, however, there is a much different ideology implicit in modern social welfare legislation, including the current "war on poverty." The currently prevailing ideology emphasizes instead the importance and even the necessity of maintaining individual family income for all segments of the economy. Maintaining income in poor families is no longer viewed as merely charity, philanthropy, or even generosity. Instead, it has become a basic functional prerequisite of an abundant society. If our increasing production capacities are to have an outlet, there must be a population with an adequate income to buy the products that are offered. All segments of the economy must have money to spend in order to keep it functioning properly. While the ideology of abundance may be more humane, it is also firmly based on the current economic realities of our productive system.

WHO ARE THE POOR?

The most obvious of the poor are the unemployed, and many of the current programs and proposals for dealing with poverty are aimed at increasing the opportunities for employment. Technically speaking, unemployment refers to the situation in which a person is able and willing to work but cannot find a job. Of course the economic costs of unemployment are great, but there are other important social costs as well. In a society such as ours, where one's status seems to be organized around work, take away a man's job and he feels isolated, frustrated, and lost. Even when adequate income is provided by means of unemployment compensation, unemployment is socially and psychologically very disturbing. Numerous studies by sociologists and economists have documented the tremendous dependence of workers on their jobs to give meaning to their lives.[15]

Hence, very little of the unemployment that exists in our society can be viewed as a result of negative social attitudes toward work on the part of most unemployed workers. Rather, the problem of unemployment, in addition to the economic losses involved, can best be explained sociologically in terms of the positive value work has for most members of our society. In fact, most unemployment is probably caused by larger, more complex factors in the economy as a whole, quite independent of the attitudes of the individual worker or even his employer.

There are at least two major kinds of unemployment related to the structure of the larger economy. The first of these is *cyclical* unemployment, caused by periodic economic fluctuations such as recessions and depressions. These fluctuations have traditionally produced high rates of unemployment, but there now appears to be some hope that through public and private long-range planning, major economic catastrophies such as these can be avoided or minimized in the future. What is perhaps likely to become a more serious source of unemployment in the future is rapid technological changes making many jobs, skills, and occupations obsolete and superfluous. For example, new means of automatic production, feedback control devices, and electronic data processing are among the advances commonly referred to as *automation,* which already have produced some technological unemployment. The effects of automation on unemployment are not restricted to semi-skilled or unskilled industrial workers, but may be expected to have an impact on almost the entire range of occupations and professions in our society. These effects will not only determine the number of workers required, but will also drastically transform the nature of work and the kinds of skills required.

Since we can only begin to speculate at this time what the specific consequences will be for any given point in the future, there is a great deal of controversy regarding the eventual effects of automation. Those who view the effects of automation as positive in creating more jobs, as well as more wealth, tend to see these as long-run rather than short-run gains. On the other hand, those who view automation with alarm are equally concerned with its more immediate consequences—those that will effect the current labor force and perhaps the children of this generation. Since the impact of rapid technological change is already taking its toll among large numbers of workers whose skills have been rendered obsolete and whose jobs have been seriously altered or eliminated, there is enough ground here for us to consider some of the effects of technological changes already under way as serious contemporary social problems.

It should not be assumed from the above discussion that *poverty* should be equated with *unemployment,* because these two conditions are not entirely identical. A good deal of poverty in our society is not based on unemploy-ment. In fact, most of the poor of labor-force age are employed, but their poverty comes about as a result of substandard wages or earnings—earnings at a level below that necessary to provide them with the goods and services of an abundant society.[16]

Another characteristic of many of the poor in our society is that they are simply not employable. Technically speaking they are not in the labor force and are therefore not included in the official governmental statistics on em-ployment and unemployment. These poor fall into several categories. First, there are those who are not employable because of physical or mental illness. A second major category includes the aged or retired who are too old to work, or who have been involuntarily removed from the labor force because of current values and practices regarding the aged. Fatherless homes, broken by death, desertion, or divorce, represent a third important category. In these families the female head of the household is unable to seek gainful employ-ment because she must provide care for her dependent children. Finally, there are those who are too young to have entered the labor force. This group includes students, young married couples, and unattached individuals whose families, for a variety of reasons, cannot adequately support them until they become economically self-sufficient adults. All of the above groups represent special kinds of problems which cannot be solved by providing more jobs, even though some of them may be important segments of what Michael Harrington calls the "culture" of poverty. For each of these groups, the measure for dealing with their problems must vary according to their partic-ular set of circumstances.

REDUCING POVERTY AND IMPROVING EMPLOYMENT OPPORTUNITIES

In the first reading liberal economist Leon H. Keyserling spells out a comprehensive range of proposed policies and programs designed to stim-ulate the economy as a whole; to create more jobs; to indirectly redistribute more of the nation's wealth and resources among low-income groups through more liberal monetary and tax policies; to improve direct income-reinforce-ment programs for low-income groups, such as minimum wage protection, unemployment insurance, workmen's compensation, farm-income improve-ment, and old age insurance and pensions. Another set of proposals are for programs to build human resources through more education and better social planning. Many ongoing programs and policies of the federal, state, and local governments already do incorporate some of the principles spelled out by Keyserling, and many more are in the legislative process. Some of his more general proposals are also incorporated in some of the action programs dis-cussed throughout the book. Also included in the Keyserling selection is a summary of the Economic Opportunity Act of 1964, which is at the heart of the current "war on poverty."

Title II of the Economic Opportunity Act of 1964 provides financial assistance to local communities for the development of "community action" programs to combat poverty. This is probably one of the most far-reaching, innovative, and controversial federal poverty programs yet devised. The newly created U.S. Office of Economic Opportunity has issued a *Community Action Program Guide,* which provides instructions for developing, conducting, and administering a community action program at the local level. The second reading is a digest of the major parts of the *Guide.* It spells out the major provisions and requirements of Title II, including the requirements that "a community action program be developed, conducted, and administered with the maximum feasible participation of the residents of the areas or neighborhoods in which the program will be carried out and of the members of the groups that it will serve," and that a community must have "the ability to mobilize and utilize the community's resources, public or private, in an attack on poverty." The success and/or failure to meet these two basic requirements of Title II is probably at the heart of much debate, controversy, and conflict regarding the administration and implementation of local programs. However, it should be made clear that there probably is less disagreement with respect to the goal of the federal community action programs, which is to assist local communities to "help themselves" in the war on poverty.

Sociologist Harry C. Bredemeier makes some interesting and very provocative proposals for reducing poverty in the third reading. These proposals call for the mobilization of "surplus" unskilled workers in a variety of public service areas, such as welfare agencies, schools, hospitals, fire departments, and so on, where such individuals could be usefully employed and where there is currently some short supply of workers. In addition, these proposals call for a major extension of educational, recreational, and cultural services and facilities for low-income areas of large cities. According to Bredemeier, several major purposes would be served: first, these services and facilities now notoriously inadequate, could be expanded; second, the poor could be employed in large numbers to provide these services; third, the entire society would benefit from the additional amenities; and finally, "public works" of these kinds would in many cases be contracted through private enterprise, thus giving the economy an additional "shot in the arm." (These proposals are extensions of the more general ideas presented by John Kenneth Galbraith in his book *The Affluent Society.*)

The status of low-income groups as consumers is not only disadvantaged by the lack of economic resources; it is also disadvantaged because of a lack of the appropriate skills and knowledge necessary for economical and efficient utilization of these limited resources in the urban "market," and because of direct economic exploitation by unscrupulous venders of goods and services to the urban poor. It is becoming almost general knowledge that the poor very often pay "more" and get "less" for their money in the way of necessities, such as food, shelter, clothing, recreation, and credit. One way to curb some of the abuses in this area is through consumer-oriented legislation, such as requiring "honesty" in the advertising, packaging, and pricing of consumer goods and services; rent controls; and legal regulation of interest rates. Consumer pressures for legislation of this kind recently have been growing, but little has been passed so far because of much organized opposition. Another major strategy calls for more and better consumer education for low-income groups. In the fourth reading Consumers Union surveys some of the existing programs and resources in this area.

REFERENCES

1. The analysis in this chapter introduction is based on the following works: Michael Harrington, *The Other America*. (Baltimore: The Penguin Books, Inc., 1963); John Kenneth Galbraith, *The Affluent Society*. (Boston: Houghton Mifflin Company, 1958); Jessie Bernard, *Social Problems at Midcentury*. (New York: Holt, Rinehart and Winston, Inc., 1957); Margaret S. Gordon (ed.), *Poverty in America*. (San Francisco: Chandler Publishing Company, 1965); and Robert K. Merton and Robert A. Nisbet, *Contemporary Social Problems*. (New York: Harcourt, Brace & World, Inc., 1966) 2d. ed.
2. Galbraith, pp. 1–3.
3. Michael Harrington, "A Social Reformer's View of Poverty," in Gordon, p. 37.
4. Harrington, *The Other America*, pp. 11–14.
5. Harrington, pp. 11–14.
6. Harrington, p. 12.
7. *Newsweek*, February 17, 1964.
8. For an excellent review of social problem themes in the movies of the 1930s see Lewis Jacobs *The Rise of the American Film*. New York: Harcourt, Brace & World, Inc., 1939, pp. 506–559.
9. *Newsweek*, February 17, 1964.
10. Merton and Nisbet, p. vii.
11. Harrington, p. 12.
12. R. A. Gordon, "An Economist's View of Poverty," in Gordon, pp. 3–11.
13. Paul B. Horton and Gerald R. Leslie, *The Sociology of Social Problems*. New York: Appleton-Century-Crofts, Inc., 1965, 3d. ed., pp. 334–35.
14. Bernard, p. 28.
15. Merton and Nisbet, pp. 553–555.
16. For a detailed breakdown of U.S. census data on the relationship between occupation and earnings see Donald Bogue, *The Population of the United States*. New York: The Free Press of Glencoe, Inc., 1959, p. 616–626.

ADDITIONAL READINGS

Becker, Joseph M., *In Aid of the Unemployed*. Baltimore: The Johns Hopkins Press, 1965.

Bredemeier, Harry C., and Jackson Toby, *Social Problems in America*. New York: John Wiley & Sons, Inc., 1960, pp. 177–192.

Ferman, Louis, Joyce Kornbluh, and Alan Haber (ed.), *Poverty in America*. Michigan: University of Michigan Press, 1965.

Galbraith, John Kenneth, *The Affluent Society*. Boston: Houghton Mifflin Company, 1958.

Gordon, Margaret S. (ed., *Poverty in America*. San Francisco: Chandler Publishing Company, 1965.

Harrington, Michael, *The Other America*. Baltimore: Penguin Books, Inc., 1963.

Matza, David, "Poverty and Disrepute," in Robert K. Merton and Robert A. Nisbet, *Contemporary Social Problems*. New York: Harcourt, Brace & World, Inc., 2d. ed., 1966.

May, Edgar, *The Wasted Americans*. New York: Harper & Row, Publishers, 1964.

Miller, Herman, *Rich Man, Poor Man*. New York: Thomas X. Crowell Company, 1964.

Riessman, Frank, *The Culturally Deprived Child*. New York: Harper & Row, Publishers, 1962.

Wilensky, Harold L., and Charles N. Lebeaux, *Industrial Society and Social Welfare*. New York: Russell Sage Foundation, 1958.

Zald, Mayer N., *Social Welfare Institutions*. New York: John Wiley & Sons, Inc., 1966.

PROPOSED POLICIES AND PROGRAMS:
PLANNING A LONG-RANGE BALANCED EFFORT

Leon Keyserling

This chapter lists all proposals in this study, some of which have already been discussed. The listing cannot be in order of importance, for they are links in a chain no stronger than the weakest, and many of the proposed programs overlap. Nor is it feasible to list programs according to the groups which they are intended to help; many programs converge upon the same individuals. The chain is designed, in lifting people out of poverty, to improve the tone of our whole social and moral performance.

The Most General Measures:
National Fiscal and Monetary Policies

FEDERAL TAX POLICY   For economic and social reasons, any further tax reduction should concentrate upon enlarging the after-tax income of low- and lower-middle-income families and unattached individuals. This could be accomplished by lifting exemption credits in the personal income tax structure—these ought to be approximately doubled—and by reduction of federal excise or sales taxes on necessities as distinguished from luxuries.

FEDERAL SPENDING POLICIES   Increased federal spending should take high precedence over further tax reduction. Wisely directed spending is obviously more helpful to the poor. And viewing the new technology and automation, spending can also do much more to help everybody—and especially the poor—because of its much greater stimulus to those types of output which will add most to employment opportunity and economic growth. Federal *per capita* outlays for all domestic purposes should be lifted from less than $181 in the

From *Progress or Poverty*, Chapter XII, and Appendix. December 1964. Reprinted by permission of the author and the Conference on Economic Progress, Washington, D.C.

original fiscal 1965 Budget to almost $251 by calendar 1970, and to about $256 by calendar 1975. Over the same period of time, federal *per capita* outlays for all purposes should be lifted from about $483 to $639, and then to about $677. The total federal Budget should be lifted from 97.9 billion dollars to 135 billion, and then to 156 billion. With optimum economic growth, these increases would result in a *smaller* federal Budget in ratio to total national production, and a very much smaller national debt when measured similarly.

MONETARY POLICIES   The monetary policy prevalent since 1952 has been highly regressive in its income effects, as higher interest payments have penalized low-income groups. And tight money has worked severely against adequate employment and economic growth. The policies of the Federal Reserve Board should be drastically revised—by Congressional and/or Presidential intervention—toward a more liberal expansion of the money supply from year to year, with lower interest rates.

Measure To Reshape the Structure of Job Opportunity: Prime Importance of Housing and Urban Renewal

Because of the new technology and automation, the rate of productivity gains in agriculture and in many branches of industry is extremely rapid. Even though a greatly increased demand for the products of these types of economic activity is essential toward lifting the consumption standards of the poor and deprived, feasible increases in such demand are unlikely to outrun by much the further productivity gains in agriculture and in these branches of industry. This means relatively small opportunities for expansion of employment in these types of economic activity. By far the most promising opportunities to expand employment—especially among the unskilled and semi-skilled—are in the types of economic activity where our unmet nationwide needs call for expansion of goods and services far in excess of the likely technological advances in such types of activity. And in addition to the employment benefits which would result from vast expansion of such types of activity, the goods and services which such types of activity would turn out would also be exceedingly helpful to the poor as consumers. This calls for vigorous measures to reshape the entire structure of production, demand, and job opportunity.

Housing and urban renewal is by far the most important of these areas quantitatively, and as important as any qualitatively. We need to lift housing starts from 1.6 million (almost all for middle- and high-income groups) in 1963 to about 2.2 million by 1970, with almost half of these starts divided equally between lower-middle- and low-income groups. This effort will require more favorable credit terms, including lower interest rates, to stimulate private investment in housing; for the poverty-stricken people in the slums, it will require a vast increase in public outlays at all levels, especially by the federal Government This housing expansion should be accompanied by enormous programs of urban renewal. *Per capita* federal outlays for housing and community development should rise from a negative figure of $1.56 in the original fiscal 1965 Budget (when the Government is expected "to make money" on these programs) to more than $15½ by calendar 1970, and about $16½ by calendar 1975. In the aggregate, these federal outlays should rise from a negative of 317 million dollars to 3.3 billion, and then to 3.8 billion.

Conventional-type public works, to serve genuine needs and to reduce unemployment, should receive at least a billion dollars a year of additional federal support.

Direct Income-Reinforcement Programs

MINIMUM WAGE PROTECTION The glaring deficiencies in coverage under the federal Fair Labor Standards Act should be remedied promptly, and the minimum wage floor in general should be lifted to $2.00 an hour. Overtime premiums should be extended and liberalized.

UNEMPLOYMENT INSURANCE By combined State and federal action, including higher federal standards and some federal contributions, unemployment insurance should as soon as feasible become the right of all those unemployed through no fault of their own, for as long as they are unemployed, and at average benefit payments of at least half the average full-time working wage. Regular insurance benefits should be reinforced by special revolving funds and installment payments to laid-off workers. With increased federal aid, disability coverage under public assistance and OASDI should be as broad as the broadened coverage under unemployment insurance, and disability benefits should be lifted to adequate standards as to amounts and duration.

FARM-INCOME IMPROVEMENT The whole national farm program needs drastic reconstruction, to focus more effectively upon the goal of income parity rather than price parity for farmers, and to get more of the income increases to those farmers who need them most, with accent upon the family-type farm. Hired farm labor should be covered by minimum wage and unemployment insurance legislation, and should have the right to organize and bargain collectively. The highest concentration of effort should be upon expansion of domestic consumption, including surplus food distribution programs aimed toward adequate nutrition for the millions of poor Americans who still lack it. Our exports of farm products to the underdeveloped peoples still scourged by starvation should be enlarged. Special efforts should be directed toward overcoming the exceptionally large deficiencies in education, health services, and housing in those relatively poor States where agriculture and other rural living are also highly concentrated. This calls for enlarged application of the federal "equalization" principle.

OLD AGE INSURANCE AND PENSIONS These programs, almost everywhere, are woefully behind the times, and this has grave effects upon the lives of the poor. Within about five years, the average benefits under OASDI should be approximately doubled, taking into account not only retired workers but also their spouses or survivors and other dependents. Emphasis should also be placed upon earlier retirements in general, special forms of early-retirement benefits, and pension reinsurance plans. Because of the regressive nature of payroll taxes, federal contributions financed by general taxation should assume a large part of the costs of benefit payments under OASDI. With increased federal aid, the same retirement and income objectives should be sought for our senior citizens and their families who are helped by pensions rather than insurance, and for those who for one reason or another receive neither. There is room for very large improvement in those aspects of OASDI which deal, not with old age benefits proper, but with other types of help—including medical—to those in great need.

WORKMEN'S COMPENSATION There

is urgent need for very large improvements in benefits and coverage under State workmen's compensation laws; the time has come to consider federal standards and aid to expedite this process.

SPECIAL AND GENERAL PUBLIC ASSISTANCE One of the greatest tragedies of our national life is the pitiful inadequacy of all types of public assistance (both monetary and in kind) to broken families in need, to families headed by women who cannot work, and to many other types of family groups living in poverty. This calls for enlarged federal assistance to those special types of State and local public assistance now aided federally to a degree, coupled with initiation of federal aid to general public assistance. *Per capita* federal outlays for public assistance should rise from $14.15 in the original fiscal 1965 Budget to more than $21 by calendar 1970, and more than $23 by calendar 1975. In the aggregate, the increase should be from 2.9 billion dollars to 4.5 billion, and then to 5.4 billion.

Programs To Build Our Human Resources

These programs would have the same double-barrelled effects as the proposed housing programs. They would serve immediately and directly the needs of the poor. And because the needed increases in output in these areas would far exceed the rate of technological gains in these areas, these programs would do most to enlarge employment opportunity, and, in their construction aspects, would do most to increase employment opportunity for the unskilled and semi-skilled.

EDUCATION In the public schools alone, we need from now through 1970 about 100,000 new classrooms a year, compared with actual building programs averaging about 60,000. We need to recruit about 100,000 teachers a year for the public schools, or about 50 percent more than recent and current recruit-

ment levels. Teachers still need large salary increases, especially in the poorer States. Specialized programs to deal with the school dropouts should be pushed vigorously. In higher education, very large increases are needed in scholarships, student loans, and physical plant. Even if the States and localities continue to strain their resources to the utmost, and even with the highest foreseeable private outlays, federal outlays for education should increase on a *per capita* basis from $8.35 in the original fiscal 1965 Budget to more than $33 by calendar 1970, and about $39 by calendar 1975. In the aggregate, they should be lifted from 1.7 billion dollars to 7 billion, and then to 9 billion.

MEDICAL CARE Prompt enactment of "Medicare" is essential, along with expansion of other types of public medical assistance to the needy regardless of age. We need approximately to double the average annual rate of hospital construction during the next ten years, along with vast increases in the numbers of doctors and nurses, and their improved distribution throughout the country. Medical research has made great strides, but it needs far more support. On a *per capita* basis, federal outlays for health services and research should be lifted from $8.55 in the original fiscal 1965 Budget to close to $23 by calendar 1970, and more than $30 by calendar 1975. In the aggregate, they should be lifted from 1.7 billion dollars to 4.8 billion, and then to 7 billion. With more adequate health facilities and personnel as a foundation, a federal system of universal health insurance should be established, financed in part by payroll taxes and in part by general taxation.

Training and Retraining Programs

The very encouraging projection of training and retraining programs for the poor and deprived under the Economic Opportunity Act of 1964 leaves many needs untouched. Handicapped workers need more attention. Federal aid in the form of relocation allowances is essential. In the broad category of labor and manpower and other welfare services, federal *per capita* outlays should be increased from $6.07 in the original fiscal 1965 Budget to about $9.50 by calendar 1970, and increased slightly further by 1975. In the aggregate, they should be increased from 1.2 billion dollars to 2 billion, and then to about 2.2 billion.

Conservation and Improvement of Our Natural Resources

We have been experiencing a long drawn-out neglect in this whole field. In some areas, water and power supplies are lagging far behind very rapid population growth and corresponding industrial growth. The rivers flowing through some of our most congested urban areas are polluted. The air hanging over many of our industrial areas is dirty and foul. Recreational facilities and areas are inadequate and inaccessible, certainly for many of the poor and deprived. Atomic energy research and development for industrial purposes should be quickened, with more emphasis upon public control or regulation in the public interest. Such investment is an essential part of the expansion of employment opportunity, especially for the lesser-skilled who comprise so large a portion of those who are poor, young, and jobless. This is basically a national responsibility. Federal *per capita* outlays for resource development should be lifted from $12.77 in the original fiscal 1965 Budget to about $15 by calendar 1970, and more than $15.50 by calendar 1975. In the aggregate, they should be lifted from 2.6 billion dollars to 3.2 billion, and then to 3.6 billion.

Programs for the Distressed Areas

Our approaches thus far to the shocking conditions in Appalachia and elsewhere are mere nibbling on the fringes. With appropriate modifications, we need to apply to these areas the same boldness and practical imagination, and the same comprehensiveness of effort, which went into the making of TVA. Our country now sorely needs many "TVA's."

Redressing Dislocations Caused by Government Programs

Shifts in the size and location of national defense activities, as well as in Government procurement activities arising under other programs, result in major changes in employment opportunity. The Government should make every effort to reduce dislocating effects to a minimum, including placement of new plants and other activities in labor surplus rather than in labor shortage areas, and curtailment of plants and other activities in labor shortage rather than in labor surplus areas. Similarly, the international trade and tariff policies of the United States have a short-range adverse impact upon some industries and employment therein. As these international policies are in the national interest, their economic costs should be borne by the nation rather than by specific groups, and compensatory action of the proper kind should be taken to prevent these policies from impacting with excessive severity upon these particular groups.

The War against Discrimination in All Its Forms

We cannot rest on our oars with respect to civil rights and liberties. These rights and liberties are precious for their own sake; their denial in any degree is evidence of the man-made oppression and neglect which also filter through the

whole problem of poverty and deprivation in our country. Further, the whole
crusade for civil rights and liberties needs
to be allied with the whole crusade
against poverty; for even when people
become entirely free, they will still struggle to be well-fed and well-housed. Other
forms of discrimination, while less talked
about, are also on the scene. Despite
passage of highly desirable legislation by
the Congresss in 1964, women are still
grossly discriminated against—in their
education and training opportunities,
their chances to get jobs, and their pay
when on the job. Through combined action at all levels, this type of discrimination should be stamped out. The same
comments apply to the irrational and
unjust aspects of discrimination based
on age.

The Range of State and
Local Responsibilities

Superficially, it might seem that the
foregoing listing would impose too heavy
a share of the war against poverty upon
the federal Government. But to date, the
States and localities have made Hercule-
an efforts to expand their services, in
sharp contrast with inadequate action at
the federal level. In an article in the
September 1964 *Harper's*, Edmund G.
Brown, the Governor of our most popu-
lous State with one of the most intricate
combinations of every kind of social and
economic problem, sets forth courageous-
ly and admirably the fallacy of denying
that such problems as medical care,
poverty, and education are national in
scope, or asserting that they fall within
"the province of the city or State just because they occur in the city or the State."
Governor Brown points out that we live
in a time of "jet-age federalism and it is
here to stay, no matter how fervently its
detractors invoke the Founding Fathers."

Despite all this, many of the proposals
in this study involve combined action at
all levels of government. The projections
in this study urge that the annual rate
of federal outlays for goods and services
be lifted to a 1975 level about 41 billion
dollars above the 1963 level, and that
over the same period of time the annual
rate of State and local outlays for goods
and services be lifted about 36 billion.
*Thus, the proposed increases at the State
and local levels are more than six-sevenths
as large as those proposed for the federal
Budget.*

The Range of Private Responsibilities

There is nothing in this study which
indicates the prospect or desirability of
any shrinkage in the traditional role and
responsibilities of private enterprise.
While the study urges, comparing 1975
with 1963, an increase of 77.4 billion dollars in the annual rate of outlays for goods
and services by governments at all levels,
it projects an increase of 103.6 billion in
gross private investment (including net
foreign), and an increase of 335 billion
in private consumer expenditures, adding
up to an increase of 516 billion in the
annual rate of total national production.
And within the private sector, many
adjustments in prices, wages, and profits
are needed to achieve a more workable
balance between the advance of our
productive capabilities and the advance
of effective demand for ultimate products.

Further, the proposals for expansion of
social security, to the extent adopted,
would impose additional obligations in
the form of payroll taxes upon employers
and workers in the private sector, even
though federal legislation would continue
to provide the framework.

Effective implementation of these proposals would require many changes in

the methods by which national economic and social policies are developed and applied, beginning with the Employment Act of 1946.

The Need for Improved Utilization of the Employment Act of 1946

The very real problem is how we may obtain the knowledge and consents required for the best attainable blend of private and public efforts at all levels. The Employment Act of 1946 is admirably suited to this purpose. But operations under this Act, while rewarding in many respects, require further improvement.

The Economic Reports of the President should include the types of goals set forth in this study but not as yet adequately spelled out in these *Reports*. They should contain a *Job Budget,* looking at least five and probably ten years ahead. As part of their analysis of purchasing power, and of the policies needed to maximize it, they should embrace the objective of *a minimum adequacy level of living for all American families, and include goals for the rate of the reduction of poverty in America.* Only these *Reports* can carry to a logical conclusion the coordination of the war against poverty intended by the responsibilities vested in the Director under the Economic Opportunity Act of 1964; the programs under his purview are at best limited segments of a total war against poverty. The *Economic Reports* should include the equivalent of the *American Economic Performance Budget* used throughout this study to develop balanced goals. The federal Budget should become an integral part of this *American Economic Performance Budget*—for national fiscal policy is only an implement of national economic and social policy—and so should our other basic national economic

programs, such as Social Security, housing, and monetary policies.

Proper Limitations on "Planning" in a Free Society

The methods just recommended would represent neither top-heavy concentration of responsibility, nor excessive "planning" alien to our institutions and values. They do not envisage governmental encroachment upon the traditional functions of our private economic groups. They do not even envisage major additional *types* of public functions, although they would result in quantitative increases in many of these functions. And our national economic policies, under these methods, would be guided by the same managerial integration and purposefulness which mark large business enterprises; one of the important by-products would be that the Government could slough off or reduce many of its rapidly proliferating activities by doing a few essential things better.

And while this suggested procedure would not improperly mingle private and public responsibilities, the general goals embodied in it would offer extremely useful information to the private sector of the economy. The goals for employment, production, and purchasing power, accompanied by meaningful analysis of our potentials and needs, would be helpful to private enterprise in somewhat the same manner as the "Postwar Market" surveys made by the Government and others toward the end of World War II. Moreover, by providing a better *rationale* for recommended public policies, the procedure would enlarge private understanding of needed public action. This in itself would tend to reduce greatly the ultimate determination of public policies by "compromise" of competing group pressures; it would bring to the fore the long-range mutuality of real interests which should override the short-range or superficial conflicts. Developed through consultation and cooperation between private economic leadership and the government, this procedure would help toward that larger degree of unity under freedom which is the fundamental answer to the totalitarian challenge.

In many respects, this procedure—modified to comport with our own institutions—would be similar to the "indicative planning" which has sparked the remarkable performance of some countries in Western Europe during the past decade. It would help us to steer more effectively between the Scylla of doctrinaire statism and the Charybdis of doctrinaire *laissez-faire*. Nothing much short of this can meet our own needs in the second half of the 20th Century.

APPENDIX: SUMMARY OF
THE ECONOMIC OPPORTUNITY ACT OF 1964

TITLE I—YOUTH PROGRAMS

Part A of this title provides for establishment of a Job Corps, designed to enroll young people aged 16 to 21 who are out of school and out of work, or in dead-end jobs. These young people, withdrawn from the environment of poverty in which they now exist and brought together in conservation or training centers in rural or urban areas, would be accorded opportunity for general education, vocational training, useful work, and physical upbuilding. In some ways, this aspect of the program is analogous to the Civilian Conservation Corps three decades ago. Enrollees would receive living allowances, and in some cases during service a payment up to $25 a month would be made to a member of the enrollee's family. The program is intended to enlist about 40 thousand youths during the first year, and about 100 thousand during the second. It would be undertaken through agreements with federal, State, local, or private agencies. The federal expenditure which appears to be intended for fiscal 1965 is 190 million dollars.

Part B of this title is designed to extend federal financial assistance to programs sponsored by State and local public agencies and by non-profit private agencies. These programs would provide both work and training for unemployed young people aged 16 to 21, now caught up in the consequences of their low incomes or the low incomes of their families. This endeavor would place special emphasis on the types of work permitting and encouraging those now prone to become dropouts to remain in school, or encouraging and facilitating the return to school of those who have already dropped out. It is estimated that these efforts would involve directly about 200 thousand youths during the first full year. With non-federal matching up to about 10 percent contemplated generally during the first two years, the federal outlay which appears to be intended for fiscal 1965 is 150 million dollars.

Part C of this title inaugurates a work study program to assist young people from low income families to obtain higher education. Applying to both students and potential students, and administered by the institution of higher learning involved, this effort would concentrate upon both campus employment and off-campus employment through agreements with public agencies and private nonprofit agencies. The assistance would take the form of part-time jobs, beneficial in themselves and augmenting the financial resources of these young people for educational purposes. It has been estimated that this program will cover 140 thousand students in the first full year of operation. The federal financial assistance, on a 90-10 matching basis during the first two years, appears to be intended in the amount of 72.5 million dollars for fiscal 1965. It would be made available in the first instance to the States in accord with specified formulae of apportionment, and from the States would move downward to the institutions of higher learning and through them to the students. Some grants may be made directly to the educational institutions.

Title I authorizes 412.5 million dollars for fiscal 1965.

TITLE II—URBAN AND RURAL COMMUNITY ACTION PROGRAMS

Part A of this title, under the heading of General Community Action Programs, covers federal grants to public agencies and nonprofit private agencies in qualifying communities. These grants would aid programs developed at local levels, both urban and rural, to combat poverty in all its forms—whether made manifest in youth unemployment, deficient education, slum conditions, ill-health, etc. In addition, there are provisions for federal technical-assistance grants to State agencies which help communities in the development of such programs, and for grants to public and private agencies to conduct research, training, and demonstrations related to the purposes of this Part A. The federal outlays, which appear

to be intended in the amount of 315 million dollars for fiscal 1965, are designed during the first two years to cover up to 90 percent of the total cost.

Part B of this title contemplates basic educational programs for deprived adult citizens—really education and/or training programs. The federal aid is to be advanced to the States in the form of grants, and made available through them to local educational institutions. This aid appears to be intended in the amount of 25 million dollars for fiscal 1965; the small amount reflects the idea of "pilot" projects as a start.

Part C of this title provides for establishment of an information and coordination center to encourage voluntary assistance for deserving and needy children.

Title II authorizes 340 million dollars for fiscal 1965.

TITLE III—SPECIAL PROJECTS TO COMBAT POVERTY IN RURAL AREAS

Part A of this title envisages practical income-creating assistance by the federal Government to poor families engaged in agriculture, including those with some income outside of agriculture. It authorizes loans up to $2,500 to low-income rural families to help them acquire or improve real estate, reduce encumbrances, erect improvements, operate or improve farms not larger than family-sized, participate in cooperatives, and finance non-agricultural enterprises which supplement income from farming. It also authorizes loans to local cooperatives engaged in helping low-income rural families.

Part B of this title covers in very broad terms loan assistance to public agencies, private nonprofit groups, and individuals engaged in the development of programs helping farm migrants. The types of help contemplated include housing, sanitation, day-care, and education.

This title also authorizes indemnity payments to farmers for condemned milk.

Title III authorizes 35 million dollars for fiscal 1965, and also permits utilization of 15 million additional which may be transferred from authorizations under other titles.

TITLE IV—EMPLOYMENT AND INVESTMENT INCENTIVES

This title projects new forms of assistance, more liberal and in some respects different from those now undertaken by the Small Business Administration, to assist small business firms and those seeking to establish them. Such loans outstanding at any one time are not to exceed $25,000 in amount, and are to be covered by the regular funds of the Small Business Administration.

TITLE V—WORK EXPERIENCE PROGRAMS

Building further upon 1962 and 1963 legislation, this title focuses upon experimental, demonstration, or pilot projects designed to help unemployed adults to obtain employment and to enlarge their capacities for self-support and personal independence. In this connection, it appears that major stress would be placed upon achieving transfers from relief rolls and upon helping disintegrating families and working mothers. It is estimated that this effort might reach about 130,000 unemployed adults during the first full year of operation.

For this Title V, 150 million dollars is authorized for fiscal 1965.

TITLE VI—ADMINISTRATION AND COORDINATION

The Act establishes an Office of Economic Opportunity in the Executive Office of the President, headed by a Di-rector. The Director is empowered to use both paid employees and volunteers. He is authorized to recruit and train a Volunteers in Service to America (VISTA), which brings to mind the Peace Corps, and to assign these volunteers to various aspects of the war against poverty, working largely in cooperation with other federal, State and local agencies.

Serving as an overall coordinator of the war against poverty, the Director is authorized to delegate functions to other federal agencies (some are delegated by the Act itself), and is charged with coordination of all anti-poverty efforts. Toward more effective coordination, an Economic Opportunity Council is established to advise the Director—composed of the Director as Chairman, the Secretaries of Defense, Interior, Agriculture, Commerce, Labor, and Health, Education, and Welfare, the Attorney General, the Housing and Home Finance Administrator, the Small Business Administrator, the Chairman of the Council of Economic Advisors, the Director of Selective Service, and other agency heads who may be designated by the President. There is also authorized a National Advisory Council, made up of the Director as Chairman, and not more than fourteen other members to be appointed by the President as representatives of the general public.

For this Title VI, 10 million dollars is authorized for fiscal 1965.

TITLE VII—TREATMENT OF INCOME FOR CERTAIN PUBLIC ASSISTANCE PURPOSES

This title provides that assistance under the Act, up to specified amounts, shall not limit any individual's right to receive unemployment compensation or public assistance.

Thus, the Economic Opportunity Act of 1964 authorizes 947.5 million dollars for fiscal 1965. However, the federal Budget for fiscal 1965 indicates an intent to expend only somewhat more than half of this amount during the fiscal year, the excess being available to make future commitments.

COMMUNITY ACTION GUIDE PROGRAM

GRANTS FOR COMMUNITY ACTION PROGRAMS

THE PURPOSE OF THE COMMUNITY ACTION PROGRAM   The purpose of federal assistance to community action programs is to help urban and rural communities to mobilize their resources to combat poverty. Because community needs and resources differ widely, considerable latitude is allowed in the development and conduct of a community action program.

A vital feature of every community action program is the involvement of the poor themselves—the residents of the areas and members of the groups to be served—in planning, policy-making, and operation of the program.

The long-range objective of every community action program is to effect a permanent increase in the capacity of individuals, groups, and communities afflicted by poverty to deal effectively with their own problems so that they need no further assistance.

Poverty is a condition of need, helplessness, and hopelessness. It is rooted in a network of social ills that include inadequate education, unemployment, poor health, and dilapidated housing. To alleviate them requires a varied and coordinated attack. Remedial reading, literacy courses, employment counseling, homemaker services, job development and training, consumer education, vocational rehabilitation, and health services are some of the many activities that can be supported and coordinated within a community action program to attack poverty.

ELIGIBILITY OF APPLICANT

1. DEFINITION OF COMMUNITY
The "community" to be served by a community action program may be any urban or rural, or urban and rural, geographical area, including but not limited to a State, metropolitan area, county, city, town, multi-city unit, or multi-county unit. Generally, a community should be coterminous with a major political jurisdiction, such as a city or county, or with a group of political jurisdictions exercising responsibility for related public programs. In metropolitan areas, whenever feasible, the community should include all of the urbanized or urbanizing portions of the area.

A community shall cover a geographical area of sufficient size and population to allow for the effective utilization of

From *Community Action Guide*, Vol. 1, February 1965. Parts A, B, and C (abridged). Washington, D.C.: Office of Economic Opportunity.

human, physical, and financial resources in an attack on poverty. Communities containing very small populations are encouraged to combine their efforts with adjacent jurisdictions to ensure the creation of an adequate resource base.

An acceptable alternative to combining the efforts of several small communities in a single community action program is the creation of a multi-community agency that can serve as a central administrative unit and resource base for a number of smaller community action agencies.

The delineation of the community to be served should be related to the character and incidence of poverty it contains and to the type of programs or activities to be undertaken. For example, an entire State or even a number of States may constitute a community as a basis for action with respect to the problems of special groups of the poor, such as migratory workers and seasonal agricultural laborers, whose needs cannot be adequately met on a more restricted geographical basis.

2. ELIGIBLE AGENCIES   Grants for the development, conduct, and administration of community action programs may be made to a public agency or to a private non-profit agency.

To be eligible for federal assistance, an applicant agency must have:

a. Adequate authority to enter into contracts with and to receive grants from the federal Government and to carry out the program for which it is requesting assistance, either directly or by contract or agreement with other agencies. In any case where the applicant agency is required to obtain the approval of another body before making application, or before expending program funds, or in establishing its policies, it shall provide evidence in its application for federal assistance that the other body has approved the proposed community action program prior to submission of the applica-

tion. For example, if a municipal agency is the applicant and if approval of its budget and its ability to contract with other agencies is within the jurisdiction of the city council, then the city council must approve of the program before submission of the application to OEO. Or, in the case of a private non-profit agency, if a policy advisory committee has the power to establish or change policies of the applicant agency, then the committee must approve the program prior to submission of the application.

b. The ability to mobilize and utilize the community's public or private resources in an attack on poverty. The various resources of a community, and some of the means to mobilize them, are described below in Section 4.

c. A commitment to enlist the participation of residents of the areas and members of the groups to be served in the development, conduct, and administration of the proposed program. The ways in which this may be accomplished are described below in Section 5.

d. Adequate provision for participation in policy-making by the major agencies and institutions in the community, both public and private, which have a concern with poverty and by the residents of the areas and members of the groups to be served. The actions necessary to meet this requirement in the case of a broadly based community action agency which intends to carry out a coordinated program are described in Section 6 below. Requirements to be met by any agency, including single-purpose agencies seeking federal assistance for projects of limited scope, are described in Section 7.

e. The capacity to utilize efficiently and expeditiously the assistance for which application is made. Standards for the selection of program personnel are set forth in Section 8. The means for carrying out a community action program are described in Section 9.

3. SPECIAL REQUIREMENTS FOR PRIVATE NONPROFIT ORGANIZATIONS   An applicant which is a private non-profit organization, in addition to meeting the requirements stated above, must qualify for federal assistance by meeting one of the following conditions:

a. It must be an institution of higher education, as defined in Section 401(f) of the Higher Education Facilities Act of 1963 (20 U.S.C. Sec. 701).

b. It must be an institution or organization which has had a concern with problems of poverty prior to application for federal assistance under Title II-A. Any organization formed since enactment of the Economic Opportunity Act of 1964 (August 20, 1964) will be presumed in need of sponsorship (see item c.) unless a substantial involvement in anti-poverty action can be demonstrated. If the applicant agency is formed from a group having a concern with poverty prior to application, the continuity of the organization must be demonstrated. This would be required if an unincorporated association became a non-profit corporation for the purpose of applying for federal assistance.

c. It must be sponsored by a public agency, or by one or more private institutions or organizations which have had a prior concern with problems of poverty. Sponsorship must be in the form of an official act endorsing the applicant as the community action agency for the area to be served. When the applicant claims sponsorship by a private organization, it shall provide evidence demonstrating that organization's substantial concern with problems of poverty prior to enactment of the Act.

In addition, an applicant which is a private non-profit organization must provide, prior to the receipt of any grant funds, evidence that it has established an accounting system which, in the opinion of a certified public accountant or a duly registered public accountant, is adequate to meet the purposes of the grant. In any case where a component project is to be conducted by a private agency under contract, the community action agency shall take all necessary actions to ensure that the accounting system of the other agency is adequate to meet the purposes of the contract.

4. MOBILIZATION OF RESOURCES
The act provides that an applicant must

have the ability to mobilize and utilize the community's resources, public or private, in an attack on poverty.

Every community in America has agencies which provide services to the poor. Many of these agencies already receive financial assistance from State and federal governments. Mobilization of these existing resources is an essential part of a community action program.

Most agencies tend to concentrate on one basic service function, such as education, employment, health, housing, or family welfare. Where several agencies are working in the same functional area, they relate to each other in a "service system." The mobilization of resources for a community action program should bring these various service systems together in a concerted attack on poverty.

The effort should embrace all or most of the following:

a. The educational system, including the public schools and the related State educational agencies, libraries, private schools, and other private agencies providing educational services.

b. The employment system, including the State employment service, the apprenticeship agency, employers, labor unions, the educational agencies that train and retrain people for specific occupations, the vocational rehabilitation agency, and agencies that conduct special employment programs, such as for youth or the handicapped.

c. The family welfare system, including the public welfare department, school social workers and the private agencies that try to strengthen family life by providing such services as counseling, casework, budgeting and spending techniques, and income maintenance through public assistance.

d. The health service system, including the public health department, the community nursing agency, and the clinics and emergency room of the community hospital.

e. The housing system, including public agencies concerned with the enforcement of housing and building codes, fire prevention, low-rent housing, urban renewal, and mortgage insurance, and the private agencies concerned with housing and related physical improvements.

f. The economic development system, including agencies—public or private—which assist the community to retain and enlarge its level of employment opportunities.

g. The consumer information and credit system, including banks, credit unions, consumer cooperatives and consumer education groups, better business and related business organizations.

h. The legal services system including bail-bond procedures, legal aid, public defenders, administrative appeals agencies, correctional agencies, and other private and public groups protecting the legal rights of individuals.

Each of these service systems deals with only part of the complex and interrelated causes of poverty. The separate service systems need to be linked in a total network in order to mount an effective attack on poverty. Each applicant agency must demonstrate its ability and intention to mobilize community resources against poverty through the establishment of linkages among and within service systems and through other means.

5. RESIDENT PARTICIPATION The Economic Opportunity Act requires that a community action program be developed, conducted, and administered with the maximum feasible participation of the residents of the areas or neighborhoods in which the program will be carried out and of the members of the groups that it will serve. Among the means to ensure participation of residents of the areas and members of the groups served are:

a. Representation on the policy-making body and appropriate advisory boards of the community action agency.

b. Use of existing and neighborhood organizations and the creation of new representative neighborhood organizations for advice on program policy and, where appropriate, for actual conduct and administration of elements of neighborhood-based programs.

c. The provision of meaningful opportunities for residents, either as individuals or in groups, to protest or to propose additions to or changes in the ways in which a community action program is being planned or undertaken.

d. Employment, to the maximum extent feasible, of the residents of areas being served in jobs created as part of the community action program itself. Such jobs should include positions which allow residents to influence the ways in which policy decisions are made and carried out, as well as jobs in which special advantage can be taken of the residents' knowledge of and familiarity with the area. Such employment opportunities should be maximized through the identification of tasks not requiring professional status.

e. Other methods and approaches for involving the poor include:

(1) Formation of a "grass-roots involvement" committee to focus attention on problems and methods of involving the "hard-to-reach" poor and to evaluate the effectiveness of the approaches adopted.

(2) Surveys conducted by neighborhood workers.

(3) Surveys conducted by organizations concerned with poverty.

(4) Formation of citizen forums.

(5) Formation of block clubs.

(6) Block elections, petitions, and referendums.

(7) Newsletters to neighborhood leaders and potential leaders.

(8) Neighborhood newspapers.

(9) Promotional techniques, including use of films, literature, and mobile units operating from information centers.

(10) Meetings of neighborhood groups with civic and political leaders.

The requirement of resident participation applies to all stages of a community action program, from its inception on. Achievement of meaningful participation shall be a continuing objective of every community action program, since it is through their own effective participation that the residents and groups to be served can most readily achieve the objective of a permanent increase in their capacity to deal with their own problems without further assistance.

6. PARTICIPATION IN POLICY-MAKING: BROADLY-BASED AGENCIES   The most effective and desirable community action program is one which is broadly-based, organized on a community-wide basis, and involves the coordination of a variety of anti-poverty actions. A broadly-based, coordinated program should eventually embrace components in all of the major service systems and extend to all of the major concentrations of poverty within the community. While, initially, few communities may be able to undertake fully coordinated programs, priority will be given to agencies organized for that purpose and with the wide participation of existing organizations and agencies to achieve it.

To be broadly-based, a community action agency must provide ample opportunity for participation in policy-making by the major public and private agencies responsible for services and programs concerned with poverty, other elements in the community as a whole, and the population to be served by the community action program. The opportunity for representation shall include either membership by representatives of these three categories on the policy-making or governing body of the community action agency or, where such membership is not feasible, on a policy advisory committee. The functions of such a policy advisory committee shall be to assist in review and establishment of program policies, personnel policies and recruitment, and to act as a hearing board for any citizen groups who may want to propose addi-

tions to or changes in the community action program.

The minimum standards for representation, either on the governing body of the community action agency or on a policy advisory committee, are:

a. Representation from private and public agencies shall include at least one representative of the chief elected official, or officials, of the community, the board of education, the public welfare agency, and the major private social service agencies. Consideration should also be given to representation by the public health agency, the public housing and urban renewal agencies, the local office of the State employment services, any non-public school or school system responsible for the education of a substantial number of children from poor families, and private social and education agencies headquartered in low income areas, such as a settlement house.

b. Representation from the leadership of important elements in the community, such as labor, business, religious, and minority groups. Particular attention should be paid to ensuring adequate minority group representation in cases where minority group members comprise a large proportion of the population of the "target" areas or groups selected for the community action program.

c. Representation from residents of the areas and members of the groups to be served, including at least one representative selected from each of the neighborhoods or areas in which the community action program will be concentrated. In the selection process, there should be maximum possible involvement of the groups and persons to be represented. The selection process should be designed to encourage the use, whenever feasible, of traditional democratic approaches and techniques such as group forums and discussions, nominations, and balloting. This will minimize the possibility that a representative does not command the support or confidence of the group or area that he represents. (See Section 5 above for additional means of resident participation.)

Applicants which are unable to meet these standards may request a waiver, by submitting a justification and an explanation of how adequate representation will be achieved.

Community action agencies which seek to conduct broadly-based, coordinated programs must accept the responsibility of ensuring that every interested group and organization in the community has an opportunity to express its concerns, to propose activities, and—if it represents a significant element of the community—to be represented on the governing board or policy advisory committee.

ELIGIBILITY OF ACTIVITIES

1. LOCAL INITIATIVE   The applicant agency has considerable flexibility in determining what activities it will undertake, the manner in which these activities will be undertaken, and the families and individuals that will be assisted, subject to the policies and procedures in this guide and to such further policies and procedures as may be issued by the Office of Economic Opportunity.

2. CHARACTERISTICS OF ELIGIBLE ACTIVITIES   A wide variety of activities can be included in a community action program. Each community action program shall, however, display all of the characteristics listed below.

a. *Benefit to the poor.* A community action program must focus on the needs of low-income families and individuals. Where the nature of the activity requires administration by areas or groups, services and assistance shall be made available only in areas and for groups which have a high incidence of poverty. Means tests are not required to screen out individuals or families above specific income levels; however, the applicant will be required to provide adequate evidence that any proposed activity will indeed be concentrated on the needs of the poor. Where the applicant agency selects a "target" area or population group

that does not include the poorest residents of the community, adequate reasons for such selection must be provided.

In determining the incidence and location of poverty in the community, the number and proportion of low-income families, particularly those with children, shall be given significant weight. Among other factors that shall be considered are the following:

(1) The extent of persistent unemployment and underemployment.

(2) The number and proportion of persons receiving cash or other assistance on a needs basis from public agencies or private organizations.

(3) The number of migrant or transient low-income families.

(4) School dropout rates.

(5) Military service rejection rates.

(6) Other evidence of low educational attainment.

(7) The incidence of disease, disability, and infant mortality.

(8) Housing conditions.

(9) Adequacy of community facilities and services.

(10) The incidence of crime and juvenile delinquency.

The applicant may identify additional factors which indicate evidence of poverty, particularly as they relate to specific needs to be served by proposed programs.

b. *Progress toward eliminating poverty.* The program must give promise of progress toward eliminating poverty in the community, or toward eliminating one of the underlying causes of poverty. A community action program may do this through developing employment opportunities, improving human performance, motivation, and productivity, or bettering the conditions under which people live, learn, and work. The aim of community action is not merely improvement in the standards of life of the poor but the provision of opportunities to enable poor people to move into the mainstream of American life.

c. *Utilization of other programs.* A community action program must provide for the re-direction, extension, expansion, or improved utilization of existing programs and activities. It should also make maximum use of resources available under other federal programs, including other titles of the Economic Opportunity Act, as well as of previously unused community resources, public or private.

Generally, assistance under Title II-A will not be made available where it is feasible to utilize another federal aid program. Nor will aid be made available where there is evidence that existing, available community resources are not being fully utilized to meet the need in question.

d. *Sufficient scope and size.* A community action program must provide for an adequate range of activities, and for the necessary linkages among such activities, to ensure a reasonable prospect of success. Where the full scope of services and activities cannot be provided immediately, plans should be made for their inclusion at the earliest practicable opportunity (see "Building-block" approach, below).

Programs shall be of sufficient size to deal efficiently and expeditiously with the problems toward which they are directed. This need not prevent concentration on a particular "target" neighborhood or area where problems are especially severe; it does mean that programs that are too small and too limited in scope will not be assisted.

3. "Building-block" approach

Many communities, at the outset, may be unable to initiate coordinated community action programs which link different programs and service systems in an effective and efficient attack on poverty. With establishment of such a coordinated program as its goal, a community may decide to use a "building-block" approach in the development of its community action program, beginning with one or two essential projects and subsequently adding others.

Communities may combine the "building-block" approach with a program development stage, which can either precede or accompany the undertaking of the first action projects. Encouragement is given to requests for concurrent assistance for program development and for the conduct and administration of limited programs embracing those components on which early action is most feasible.

The "building-block" approach enables an applicant to start a community action program in the most expeditious manner. It should be recognized, however, that the individual initial projects must eventually become component parts of a broader coordinated effort.

4. Definition of "component project"

A community action program is made up of component projects. Each component project comprises a specific group, or bundle, of closely related activities, usually designed to be carried out by a single agency or organization and intended to serve a particular target group or sector of the population. (For examples of what a component project might include, see the list of eligible activities under Section 6 below.)

Component projects may be of four types:

a. Program development components enable an applicant to prepare sound and effective plans and programs and to organize for community action. Grants are made under Section 204 for this purpose.

b. Conduct and administration components enable the undertaking of a variety of activities attacking poverty. Conduct and administration components may provide wholly new services, extend existing services, alter current services so that they offer new opportunities, or educate and motivate individuals to use existing services and facilities which they are not aware of or do not know how to use. In any event, they must involve more than merely the continuation of activities already under way in the community. Grants are made under Section 205 for these purposes.

c. Training or technical assistance components provide for the training of personnel — professional or non-professional — who work in community action agencies or for the provision of technical assistance in situations where it may not be feasible to utilize program development funds. Grants are made under Section 206 for these purposes.

d. Preference components are projects which are to be financed under other sections of the Economic Opportunity Act or under other federal acts, but which are included in the community action program so that preference can be obtained for them.

5. ELIGIBLE PROGRAM DEVELOPMENT ACTIVITIES   Federal assistance is provided under Section 204 for the development of community action programs in order to assist communities to prepare sound and effective plans for an attack on poverty.

Program development assistance is available either for planning a coordinated community action program which includes a broad spectrum of components, or for intensive analysis and planning of a single component. Generally, assistance for detailed work in planning a single component should not be requested until the community has undertaken and completed the development of an initial, broader analysis. For communities interested in starting their efforts with a program development stage, a suggested work program has been developed by the Office of Economic Opportunity (See Exhibit VII). Applicants may use this model or may modify or change it. The work that may be done under a program development grant is not limited to the planning of actions to be financed under Title II-A. Program development activities may include consideration of other programs under the Economic Opportunity Act, other federal programs, and the use of State, local, and private resources as well. Generally, the following types of activity are eligible:

a. Investigation of the incidence of poverty, and of its characteristics.

b. Analysis of existing agencies and services in terms of the extent to which they meet the needs of the poor and how they might become more effective in achieving this objective.

c. Preparation of proposals for the organization, financing, scope, and content of community action programs.

d. Development of means by which residents of the areas and members of the groups to be served may participate effectively in community action programs. This may include initial efforts to organize neighborhood groups to aid in program development.

Work financed by program development grants must be designed to result in the completion of a plan of action for one or more components of a community action program.

6. EXAMPLES OF ELIGIBLE CONDUCT AND ADMINISTRATION ACTIVITIES   The following activities are examples of projects which may be eligible for assistance under Section 205. The list is intended to be suggestive, rather than all-inclusive. Many additional activities can be included in a community action program. The Office of Economic Opportunity is preparing, and will publish from time to time, more detailed descriptions of possible activities which can be included in a community action program.

Applicants are strongly encouraged to consider ways in which the eligible activities suggested below can be combined with an increase in the direct involvement of poor persons in the community action program. One specific way in which this can be done in virtually every case is through the employment of "target" area residents as non-professional workers.

a. *Remedial and non-curricular education.* Federal assistance to education under Title II-A is limited to remedial and other non-curricular educational activities. Eligible educational activities include:

(1) Remedial programs that empha-

size the correction of deficiencies in reading, language arts, spelling, and mathematics.

(2) Programs that enrich the school experience beyond the normal curriculum.

(3) Supportive services to increase the classroom teacher's chance for success with children from low-income areas. Such services might include specialists in psychology, school social work, speech and hearing, and health.

(4) Pre-school day care and nursery centers for three- and four-year olds.

(5) Tutoring programs in which high school or college students and adults are used to tutor pupils in need of extra educational assistance.

(6) Specialized in-service training for school personnel to make their efforts more effective in working with the child from low-income areas.

b. *Employment, job training, and counseling.*

(1) Developing job opportunities in fields directly related to community action, where there are needs for a wide variety of nonprofessional and technical aids to extend and assist the efforts of professionals in welfare, health, education, and related fields.

(2) Economic development efforts which stimulate the creation of new jobs within the community, either in public or private employment. Emphasis shall be placed on jobs for unemployed or low-income persons.

(3) Creation of supplementary business or industrial employment opportunities for farm families who wish to remain in rural areas.

(4) Establishment of a small business development center to increase opportunities for self employment and create jobs by providing advice and assistance to very small businesses. Such a center can take advantage of Title IV of the Economic Opportunity Act, which is administered by the Small Business Administration, to help small businessmen get management training and obtain loans on liberal terms.

(5) Establishment of neighborhood-oriented employment information, counseling, and placement facilities for unemployed youth. (This activity should seek the participation of Youth Opportunity Centers established by State employment services in cooperation with the Department of Labor.)

(6) The provision of supporting services, such as guidance and counseling, to young men and women engaged in various job training programs.

(7) Job training and education programs aimed at the development of specific skills required for currently available jobs or in the work habits and communication skills required in an employment situation.

c. *Health and vocational rehabilitation.*

(1) Health examinations and referral services for low-income adults and children.

(2) Rehabilitation and training of the physically or mentally handicapped.

(3) Providing health, rehabilitation, employment, educational and related services to young men rejected for military service.

(4) Environmental health programs, such as rat extermination and other actions to improve sanitation and living conditions.

(5) Health education programs directed at the entire low-income family.

(6) Expanding the range of medical and social services available at out-patient clinics to serve low-income families more effectively.

(7) Providing information on family planning. Activities of this type will be approved only if conducted in conformity with State and local law and under the supervision of medical authorities. The use of the information service must be wholly voluntary on the part of the recipients, and must not be a prerequisite to any other form of aid. Information must be made available on a variety of techniques, so that individuals can obtain information which is consistent with their ethical, moral, or religious beliefs. OEO has special conditions applicable to any program which contains family planning activities. These will be provided on request.

d. *Housing and home management.*

(1) Improving the living conditions of the elderly through homemaker ser-

vices, which can often be performed by non-professional workers.

(2) Improving home management skills through classes and through tne use of home management aides.

(3) Providing information on such matters as how to apply and qualify for admission to low rent public housing; what to look for and how much to pay for private rental or sales housing; how to go about home rehabilitation and repair and how to obtain the most advantageous financing for such improvements; and how homeowners in temporary financial difficulty may seek and obtain relief.

(4) Aiding homeowners, tenants, and landlords in obtaining enforcement of housing and construction codes.

(5) Providing instruction in "do it yourself" home maintenance and repair, stressing simple and nontechnical operations, such as repair of furniture with hand tools, refinishing of furniture, care of walls and floors, painting, preventive maintenance of electrical appliances and equipment, etc.

(6) Organizing nonprofit sponsors or cooperative organizations to plan for rehabilitation and construction of housing for low income families.

(7) Services and facilities designed to improve the quality of life for residents of low rent public housing and to expand contacts between them and the rest of the community.

(8) Aiding in the relocation of families displaced from their homes by public or private action, including assistance in making the move, finding new housing, overcoming social or psychological adjustment problems, and becoming assimilated into a new neighborhood.

e. *Welfare*

(1) Improving the level of social services and developing new services for low income families, including recipients of public welfare.

(2) Providing group and family day care services.

(3) Assistance to in-migrant families from rural areas in meeting the problems of urban living.

(4) Providing testing, counseling, and guidance for persons unable to qualify as welfare recipients because of residency requirements or other legal restrictions.

f. *Consumer information, education, and mutual aid.*

(1) Operation of consumer information and education programs to improve the ability of low income groups to maximize their resources in tne purchase of goods and services and to acquaint the low income consumer with available services and protections.

(2) Assistance in the establishment of cooperative ventures to allow low income families to maximize their resources as well as developing leadership and managerial skills.

(3) Providing budget and family financial counseling services to effect a permanent improvement in spending habits.

(4) Establishment of low-cost credit and improved patterns of spending and saving through credit unions and banks.

g. *Legal aid and information on the rights of the poor.*

(1) Preventive law counseling, including individual counseling, drafting and dissemination of model lease agreements, financial agreements, and other contractual arrangements; and preventive legal education in the rights of the accused, the rights of welfare clients, employee rights, tenants' rights, consumers' rights, and domestic relations law.

(2) Referral of persons needing legal assistance to legal aid agencies, as part of the provision of other types of service and assistance.

(3) Coordination of legal aid and public defender agencies with other social services.

(4) Improvement of legal aid agencies by extending their area of operations into the realms of welfare and housing.

(5) Improvement of existing public defender services available to the indigent.

(6) Creation of neighborhood law firms to engage in advocacy on behalf of the poor and to aid such groups as tenants' organizations and organizations of welfare recipients.

h. *Resident Participation*

(1) Establishment of services, such as recreation, tutoring, home-making, etc., which are developed, administered, and

operated by local resident organizations such as a block club, a tenants group, a neighborhood council, or a mothers club at a local church.

(2) Providing staff services and other resources, including equipment and facilities, to existing local organizations in order to enable them to advise and inform the community action agency and other institutions about the needs, problems, and concerns of the poor. Where these are absent or without the confidence of the poor, staff can be made available for the purposes of developing local autonomous associations and organizations.

(3) Establishment of a systematic and regular survey procedure, using local residents to act as interviewers, to identify the attitudes and opinions of the residents on the administration of the community action agency and the effectiveness of its program components.

(4) Formation of resident advisory groups, with staff assigned to ensure that information and materials developed by these groups is fed back to the community action agency and provides a guide for operational policies.

i. *Neighborhood centers.* Establishment of multi-service centers to coordinate and focus different service programs at the neighborhood level. From such a center, services can be extended to families in the neighborhood. A center can house as well as integrate such activities as a day care program, a health service, an employment information and testing unit, adult literacy classes, legal advice, home-makers, and a housing information clinic. Centers may be located in schools or in vacant stores, office buildings, or municipal buildings.

j. *VISTA and Job Corps activities.*

(1) Supervision of volunteer workers enlisted in the VISTA program of the Office of Economic Opportunity, established under Title VI of the Act. Applicants are encouraged to consider the use of VISTA volunteers as an effective means of accomplishing the objectives of their community action program.

Applicants interested in including VISTA volunteers in a community action program should communicate directly with VISTA, Office of Economic Opportunity, Washington, D.C. for information on application procedures.

(2) Activities performed in connection with the Job Corps of OEO, a residential training center program established under Title I-A of the Act to aid youth between the ages of 16 and 22. Areas in which community action programs can assist and supplement Job Corps facilities include: (a) acting as a Job Corps recruiting and screening agency; (b) sponsoring and coordinating community activities which play a part in the life of enrollees at near-by Job Corps facilities; and (c) identifying opportunities for employment of Job Corps graduates and aiding in the evaluation of the subsequent experience of graduates as employees.

Applicants interested in including Job Corps–related activities in a community action program should communicate directly with Job Corps, Office of Economic Opportunity, Washington, D.C., for further information.

k. *Administration of community action programs.* The administration of a community action program is eligible for financial assistance. Where administrative or overhead costs cannot be specifically attributed to one or more components of the community action program, they may be united in an administrative component. When the community action agency is carrying out a variety of activities, and receives funds from a variety of sources, administrative costs may be allocated among such sources on a reasonable basis. Rates for allocation will be provisional, pending audit.

i. Evaluation of accomplishments. Prompt and careful evaluation of accomplishments is essential to provide a feedback of information to help improve program development, conduct, and administration. Every community action program must include provision for evaluating its effects and estimating progress made in achieving its objectives.

7. TRAINING AND TECHNICAL ASSISTANCE The activities which can be assisted under Section 206 of the Act will be described in separate guide materials being prepared by the Office of Economic

Opportunity. In general, these activities include:

a. Training programs directly linked to the carrying out of a specific community action program or component. (Training of a more general nature can also be financed by OEO under Section 207 of the Act.)

b. Technical assistance for the development, conduct, or administration of community action programs. For example, a metropolitan agency might offer technical assistance in community action to local governments and private groups in its area. (Technical assistance can also be provided by State agencies under Section 209(b) of the Act. See Exhibit IV.)

8. PREFERENCE COMPONENTS   Many federal programs can be coordinated with the conduct of a community action program. Some of the many possible activities of this kind are:

a. *Education.*

(1) Projects designed to use college students from low-income families enrolled in the work-study program established in Title I-C of the Act. This program is operated through institutions of higher education and is administered by the Office of Education in the Department of Health, Education and Welfare.

(2) Adult basic education classes financed through grants to State agencies from the Office of Education under Title II-B of the Act.

(3) Vocational education programs, financed under the Vocational Education Act.

b. *Employment, job-training, and counseling.*

(1) Work-training projects for youth between 16 and 22, financed under Title I-B of the Act, administered by the Neighborhood Youth Corps of the Department of Labor. Work-training programs may be undertaken by community action agencies either directly or by subcontract to other organizations. Community action agencies can also play a coordinating role for work-training projects undertaken by other public or private

non-profit organizations by assisting in youth selection, counseling, and training, and in placement of trainees after the completion of the project.

(2) Developing work and training opportunities for unemployed parents, with their pay financed or supplemented through the work-experience program established in Title V of the Act, administered by the Welfare Administration in the Department of Health, Education and Welfare.

(3) Developing new employment opportunities through aid to small businessmen under the loan program established in Title IV of the Act, administered by the Small Business Administration.

(4) On-the-job and in-school training programs for unemployed and underemployed workers, conducted by State employment services and vocational training agencies under the Manpower Development and Training Act.

c. *Health*

(1) Community mental health centers financed under grants from the National Institute of Mental Health.

(2) Environmental health and related assistance available through the many programs operated by the Public Health Service.

d. *Housing and Home Management.* The examples of eligible activities in meeting the housing and home-management problems of low income families given above can all be more effective when used as complements to one of the existing federal housing programs. These include the public housing, urban renewal, mortgage insurance, and other programs administered by the Housing and Home Finance Agency and its constituents and the programs of aid to rural families of the Farmers Home Administration.

9. INELIGIBLE EXPENDITURES   The following activities may not be financed as part of a community action program:

a. Any program which involves sectarian instruction or religious worship or practice.

b. Any program of general aid to elementary or secondary education in any school or school system.

c. Any expenditure made prior to the effective date of a grant or contract by the Office of Economic Opportunity.

d. Expenditures for the construction of buildings and for the purchase of real property or motor vehicles except where they can be demonstrated to be essential to the carrying out of the proposed program. Any expenditure in excess of $500 for the purchase of a single item of equipment or property must be specifically approved in advance by OEO.

e. Any activity for which a fee is charged to beneficiaries or recipients of service in connection with the activity, except where the fee schedule has been specifically approved in advance by OEO.

f. Any activity which was under way prior to the extension of federal assistance, unless it is being expanded and improved.

g. Any partisan political activity intended to further the election or defeat of any candidate for public office.

NEW STRATEGIES
FOR THE WAR ON POVERTY

A PLAN TO ENLIST PRIVATE ENTERPRISE
IN THE MANAGEMENT OF SOCIAL WELFARE

Harry C. Bredemeier

When the United States went to war in 1941, victory became our only concern. Victory demanded ships and planes, radar operators and pilots. A labor force that was able to build the armaments, an army of technicians to maintain and fly the new planes, were somehow created in response to our urgent need.

President Johnson has declared that the United States is now engaged in a war on poverty. To win this war, we must use the same approach that won in World War II. We must now, as we did then, begin by defining the urgent needs of our society. If our need 20 years ago was survival under enemy attack, our needs in the mid-60's are to remedy those continuing deficiences in the nation that survived. If we start by acknowledging

our unmet needs—in education, housing, medical care, scientific research, recreation, the arts—then we can enlist the aid of all the community in meeting those needs. This will mean not only the efforts of government, but of private enterprise as well. If government and industry, working together on these projects, create an effective demand for a large, trained labor force, that force can be created. And in its ranks will serve those same, marginal Americans for whom the war on poverty is being fought.

In purely economic terms, people are poor when the only services they are able to render don't command much of a price in the market place. We have a "poverty problem" when a sizable number of people in our society are in this position. If

From *Trans-action* (November/December 1964), pp. 3–8. Reprinted by permission of the author and the publisher.

we look at the problem as one of an over-supply of such people, then the obvious solution is to reduce the supply. There are two ways to do this:

1. Some persons can be removed from the labor force, through such devices as earlier retirement, shorter work weeks, longer vacations, extension of the compulsory schooling period, or just plain "welfare" payments. Such devices, obviously, reduce poverty only if those who are removed from the market receive high enough "transfer payments" to support them at a level above poverty. This is simply taking the payment principle by which farmers are rewarded for removing land from the market and applying it to workers, who would be rewarded for removing labor from the market.

2. Over-supply could, alternatively, be reduced by giving some of the persons with over-abundant skills new and scarcer skills. Like the first solution, this one requires sizable transfer payments while the re-training is going on. In addition, it tends to decrease the bargaining power of those persons already in possession of the scarce skills. It is, in some instances, a way of reducing some peoples' poverty by reducing other peoples' affluence, and the people whose affluence is being reduced can be counted on to resist it. They will resist it the more, the less affluent they really are; and since most of the re-training programs aim at increasing the supply of those skills that hardly bring munificence to their present possessors (painters, butchers, carpenters, etc.), resentment and resistance can be counted on to be great. It is true, of course, that certain jobs requiring complex skills cannot now be filled; and that if the unemployed or underemployed could be trained to fill them, productivity as a whole would be increased. These are not likely to be the jobs for which the

poverty stricken can quickly be trained, however.

As an apparent alternative to those two ways of combatting poverty it is sometimes proposed that poverty be attacked by raising minimum wages. This is in fact not a true alternative—which is by no means to say that it isn't meritorious for other reasons. It is not, however, an alternative solution to the poverty problem.

To see this clearly, it is necessary to distinguish between two kinds of services that people might now be purchasing at "too low" wages. On the one hand are those services (rendered, for example, by hospital orderlies) that would have to be rendered, no matter what the cost. Raising the minimum wages of such persons would, therefore, help to solve their poverty problem. However, the necessity of paying them more would mean that consumers of their services would have less to spend on other services. The demand for those other services would, of course, decrease. This also amounts, then, to an attack on some peoples' poverty by reducing the affluence of others. This is by no means an argument for not doing it; there is much to be said for such redistribution of income. There is everything, however, to be said for recognizing clearly the consequences of one kind of attack on poverty as compared to another kind; and that is what this paper is all about.

A second kind of services that are now being rendered at "too low" a wage are services that many people would not buy at a higher price. Domestic service is a reasonable example. Raising minimum wages for these workers would simply mean that a few of them would now get "decent" wages and the rest, who previously had been getting something, would be fired. Their poverty problem would be exacerbated, and would have to be met by re-training or by extended relief.

Again, this is not to say that higher minimum wages are not desirable. They can be justified by the proposition that if people don't want a service badly enough to pay a decent wage for it, they should do without it. It is only to say that this is not, fundamentally, a solution to poverty.

Reduction of the supply of labor might be a solution—provided transfer payments were high enough. In the long run, indeed, as cybernation reduces the necessity for men to earn their bread by the sweat of their brow, we shall have to develop substitutes for the "job as the meaning of life" and find radically different ways of determining shares in the national income. Today, however, this is not a viable solution. We are far from being affluent in "the public sector," and the affluence of the private sector is far from being general. We are by no means at the cybernated Garden of Eden yet; and so long as most of the world is still groaning under the burden of scarcity, it hardly becomes us to think exclusively, or even primarily, in terms of supply-reduction strategies for waging the war on poverty.

STRATEGY OF INCREASING DEMAND

We must turn, instead, to the alternative strategy of increasing demand.

From the supply-reducing point of view, poverty is a problem of an over-supply of unskilled workers. People are poor, in these terms, because they don't have valuable skills. It is also true, however, that people are poor because nobody wants the skills they have. Insofar as the problem is one of insufficient demand, the solution is to increase the demand.

In fact, of course, the poverty problem involves both supply and demand. Most poverty-stricken persons are not now competitive in the labor market; they are not now eligible for positions where demand does exceed the supply; they could not qualify for jobs even if demand were to increase generally. The attack on poverty must increase both the demand for productive skills and the ability of people to acquire those skills. We must recognize that, until these objectives are achieved, the urban owners of potential productivity are at least as worthy of support as the rural owners of potential wheat acreage.

What I wish to suggest is that an emphasis on the demand aspects of the problem will be simpler, less expensive, and more productive than the usual supply approach.

The fact is that what there is *really* a super-abundance of are public needs that could easily, profitably, and in an entirely "business-like" way be turned into effective demands. All that is necessary is to escape from the notion that shooting off gun-powder or sending every nth ton of steel into orbit is the only "productive" form of public expenditure.

The educational, recreational, and cultural services and facilities for low income families in central cities are notoriously inadequate; home-making services for uneducated mothers are greatly needed; there should be nursery schools for all children over three; families and children in trouble need help in dealing with the complex bureaucracy of social service agencies; teachers need assistants; camp sites need to be established and maintained in state and national forests and parks; houses need rehabilitation; public housing projects cry out for civilized amenities; teen-age coffee houses and canteens would fill a conspicious void;

local music, dramatic, and arts groups should be organized; research needs to be done that could employ indigenous "participant observers"; and so on and on. The possibilities for profitable investment in human lives are limited only by the fertility of the imagination.

As John Kenneth Galbraith has put it, the difficulty in the way of fighting the war on poverty by this strategy is that "Alcohol, comic books, and mouth wash all bask under the superior reputation of the market. Schools, judges, and municipal swimming pools lie under the evil reputation of bad kings."

This belief system has stood in the way of the conversion of public needs into the kind of economic demand that could solve the poverty problem. The debate between "liberals" and "conservatives" has in large part consisted of assertions and counter-assertions of the order of "Public housing is a good thing"; "No, it isn't"; "Yes, it is." The result is an impasse, during which the public needs remain unmet, even though nearly everyone agrees they exist.

There is a way out of this impasse. Although "schools, judges, and municipal swimming pools lie under the evil reputation of bad kings," the manufacture of transistors for space capsules does not. Nor does the provision of food and gasoline on state-supported parkways, or the operation of ski concessions in state parks. The implication is plain: let us both stimulate and strengthen private enterprise, and meet urgent public needs in exactly the way we do in the case of defense needs.

Since housing, recreation, slum clearance, etc., are public needs, the public should pay for them. Insofar as they are services that private enterprise can provide, let private enterprise do so in the same way it meets military needs under

contract to the Department of Defense.

To some liberals this is a red flag suggestion, since they would prefer slums to having them cleared through what they would call "subsidies to private enterprise." Equally, to some conservatives it is a red flag, since they would prefer a stagnation of private enterprise to having it stimulated through what they would call "welfare statism." I hope that most liberals would be happy to see slums cleared even though private enterprise flourished, while most conservatives would be happy to see private enterprise flourish even though a few public swimming pools got built in the process.

I suggest that with not very much imagination a way can be found to make the efficient meeting of many public needs a profitable venture for the American business community. To find those ways is to accomplish three objectives at once: To stimulate the private economy; to move effectively toward the elimination to poverty; and to enlist the support, rather than the opposition, of the American business genius in the war on poverty.

To focus attention on such ways of increasing the demand for the services of the poverty-stricken is also to engage in the very business-like process of finding ways of "getting something" for our expenditures. What we do now in our feeble and self-defeating gestures against poverty is to pour out billions of dollars in welfare payments, correctional institutions, reformatories, police raids, and so on; and get nothing. If we think in terms of meeting public needs we will not only get a lot further in our war on poverty, we will also have, at the end, schools, judges, swimming pools, camp sites, recreation centers, nursery schools, improved and rehabilitated housing, and drama groups that we can be proud of and that we can even count in the Gross National Product.

Government contracts might also provide the initial impetus for new kinds of business ventures that could, once launched, be self-supporting in the private market. Among the small businesses that might seem to have a fair chance of succeeding are the provision of crews of trained yard workers and house-cleaners and maintenance people for suburban and city households. Many persons who now find it demeaning to do "housework" as individual servants would work willingly and profitably as independent contractors or employees of a business. Many a householder would willingly stop doing his own maintenance and cleaning if he could hire a service to do it for him at a reasonable fee.

The causes of poverty are twofold. One cause is the inadequacy of poor persons' environments in supplying them with motivation, skills, health, knowledge, and helping resources; the other is the dearth of employment opportunities. The way to counteract both these conditions at once is to employ poor people to remedy the handicapping environments of poor people.

The "army" in the war on poverty must consist of the poor themselves. It is not to consist of professional or semi-professional persons or middle class "volunteers." These people will be critically important guides and allies; but the intent of the program is to mobilize the resources of those who suffer most immediately from poverty, in order to improve their ability to eliminate the causes of their poverty.

THE ARMY OF THE POOR

There are many ways in which this can be done. Welfare agencies, schools, hospitals, police and fire departments— all have duties that could be done by people with minimum training, with benefit both to the newly employed and to the efficient operation of the agency. Many routine jobs that professionals are doing now could be done by relatively uneducated people, if these new employees were trained and paid for without expense to the operating agency. There are additional, routine activities which would improve the operation of the agency if they could be carried out; untrained people can increase the extent of follow-ups, provide more detailed record keeping, and so on. Most agencies have tasks with training value that low income personnel could perform while they were being trained for larger responsibilities. Men who had not graduated from high school could, for instance, perform useful work in police or fire departments while they were completing work for their diplomas. Finally, all agencies of the community could improve their service with additional programs if people were trained to operate them. All our communities need increased patrolling of streets and parks, increased sanitation collection, tutoring services for school children, home-making services for families in trouble, convalescent help and special services for the aged, nursery schools, door-to-door recruiting in health campaigns, better maintenance of recreational areas, staff for non-profit recreation centers, larger numbers of aides in hospitals and prisons. The demand for such services awaits only the creativity of the professional in devising programs and the financial aid of the government in carrying them out.

There is one other service that requires special note. This is the parental service, as caretaker and primary educator of the young. If one thing is certain about the roots of contemporary poverty, it is that poverty-stricken adults are not capable of

giving their children the skills and motivations required for success in today's
complex world. Poverty-stricken parents
themselves lack the necessary commitment to the complex, urban-industrial
system; they lack the know-how; and they
lack the resources with which to give
their children stakes in respectability.

The fact of the matter is that society
does now "employ" women to act as
mothers, through the program of Aid to
Dependent Children—but in a self-defeating manner. The program is self-defeating
in two obvious ways: It encourages desertion by husbands and/or fathers in order
for their children to receive welfare payments; and it penalizes initiative and enterprise of mothers and their teen-age
children by reducing welfare payments
in proportion to earnings.

It is also self-defeating in a more subtle
but perhaps even more important way:
By failing to define the payment straight-
forwardly as wages for the service to
society of properly caring for and socializing children, society both loses the possibility of expecting and requiring adequate socialization, and reinforces the
alienation of ADC mothers from the
mainstream of the urban-industrial world.

Parents and teen-agers in the poverty
class *are*, in fact, helping to raise the next
generation. How they do it—whether
productively or non-productively—depends on the kind and amount of help,
support, training, and acceptance they
are given. Given handouts grudgingly
and with obvious distaste, they will participate sullenly and with minimum effort.
Given valued employment in a vital enterprise, subject to the high standards
that any important enterprise deserves,
they are more than likely to respond with
effort and commitment. If poverty-
stricken parents had the duty, in return
for reasonable wages, to learn and to

practice child care and child training,
they, their children, and society would
be vastly better off.

By paying the poor to fight the causes
of their poverty—lack of parental know-
how, poor education, stifling housing,
recreational cramping, unhealthful surroundings, teacher and social worker
shortages—we accomplish several goals
at once. We combat the causes of poverty.
We generate income for the poor. But
most importantly, we combat the most
tenacious root of poverty, the apathetic
feeling of the poor that they are outside
the mainstream of American life, recipients but not participants. My recommendation is to make them participants
from the outset.

It is when we think about how best to
equip the soldiers of this army to make
their fight that we can begin to talk effectively about training. The poor need help
in retraining and in basic education, but
they need that help in forms that are
adapted to their special circumstances,
experiences, fears, and defenses. Here is
where the middle-class professional can
serve as a needed ally in the war.

To be effective allies, teachers, social
workers and bureaucrats must adapt their
techniques to the special needs of the
poor. Techniques that would work beau-
tifully if only pupils or clients were a
little different are as useless as military
strategies that would insure victory if only
this were the last war.

If the children of the poor are to be
educated to take their places as full participants in the modern world, then
schooling must be tailored to their special
needs. Teachers, social workers, psychologists, recreation workers and others who
have been actively working with poverty-
stricken youth have developed individual
techniques and insights that could be
highly effective if systematized and gen-

eralized. Behavioral scientists have been working productively on analyzing the learning difficulties and the learning strengths of the poor. Very few of these analyses and techniques have as yet been systematically tested or compared for their relative cost or effectiveness.

As part of the war on poverty, therefore, in which every school district in poverty-stricken areas is a battle scene, teachers should begin an intensive series of seminars to study the "enemy," and to learn to use the most advanced techniques for defeating it. Local universities should provide lecturers for such seminars. The nation's outstanding behavioral scientists should be mobilized in a "Manhattan Project" of youth development to provide "curricula" and perhaps to "ride circuit" through the major cities to contribute directly to the advanced education of youth-serving personnel.

In each school, the faculty and administration should put into practice the new strategies that seem most appropriate to them for their local scene; and the effectiveness of those strategies in improving academic performance and reducing antisocial behavior should be systematically evaluated and compared. In this way, the war could be waged with ever-increasing efficiency as the results from countless natural school "laboratories" permitted the successive refinement of effective methods and the abandonment of ineffective ones.

Let us shift our attention, now, from the children to their parents. Young and middle-aged adults among the poverty stricken are important foci of concern for several reasons. In the first place, they beget, socialize, and control children whose life chances are thereby drastically reduced. In the second place, they may represent to children vivid images of the futility of ambition or of effort along the lines advocated by middle class school teachers. In the third place, they are poor.

At the same time that they are important, the adult poor present the most formidable difficulties for rehabilitation. Their very existence is evidence of the failure, in their cases, of the conventional channels—the family, the schools, and the whole network of social service agencies. To think of their returning to them is, then, idle. Moreover, these people have acquired certain investments, stakes, defenses, identifications, mistrusts, and suspicions that make most of the existing entrances to the job world (correspondence school courses, night classes) impractical and far too socially and psychically costly.

In the last war ways were found to turn people wholly ignorant of radar into radar operators because radar operators were needed. It occurred to no one to think that if workmen hadn't learned radar in their "regular schooling" that was too bad for them. What automatically occurred to everyone, rather, was that if people had not learned radar in their regular schooling, whatever irregular schooling would work was exactly what should be provided.

Irregular schooling, of the kind that will recognize and adjust to the realities of the lives of the adult poor, is what we need now. The chief of those realities is the fact that they are adults. As adults, they have given certain hostages to fortune which must be reckoned into the cost of their reentering the urban-industrial occupational world. They have wives and children who must be provided for, and they themselves require food, clothing, and shelter. Any training program must provide an income sufficient to meet those commitments.

RE-ENTRY, NOT RESCUE

On a slightly more subtle but nonetheless real level, there are matters of pride and self-respect that must be taken into account. Re-entry channels that emphasize the dependence of the poverty-stricken and the need to "rescue" them from their "miserable state" add a cost to their acceptance that may be prohibitive. Welfare can be accepted with a cynical "If-they-won't-make-room-for-me-let-'em-support-me" attitude; and self-respect can be maintained *via* hostility, verbal insolence, in-group derogation of the system, real and fancied devices for cheating it. Such defenses against the loss of self-respect in training programs, however, would defeat the purpose of the training. While it is possible to sneer at the welfare system and still profit from it, it is not possible to sneer at training programs and still profit. Alienation from parents doesn't prevent living off them, but alienation from school prevents learning.

The fact is that "Uncle Sam" must "need you" if you are to invest yourself in his activities. If he merely, and grudgingly, offers you a chance to prove that you have been a failure, you can, with any intelligence and self-respect at all, find a dozen ways to remain in poverty—but with your self inviolate.

To enter into re-entry channels must be made "the thing to do"; and it must be made as easy as possible. Where to go and what to do when you get there must be made vividly clear. Training officials must learn to define potential trainees as valuable resources, whose interests, capacities, and potentials are worthy of basic respect. The training program itself—its routines, methods, locations, rhythms, and social atmosphere—must be tailored to the needs and expectations of adults. Adults are not children; and to treat them as if they were is again to threaten their precarious self-respect.

The connection between the regimen of the training program and the "payoff" in the real world of jobs must be made immediate and clear. On-the-job training has a clear superiority in this respect to orthodox classroom training; and training in the social, emotional skills required on the job, as well as in the technical skills, could contribute to a sense of reality rather than make-believe.

Above all, the need is for channels through which people can enter the world of preparation for work with a sense of being needed and respected. This is how the poor can be equipped to fight their war. In no better way could it be made clear that this is a war on poverty and not on the poor.

CONSUMER EDUCATION
FOR LOW-INCOME FAMILIES

A LIMITED SURVEY OF PROGRAMS AND RESOURCES

Consumers Union

INTRODUCTION

CU's charter, drafted in 1936, included among its purposes "to initiate, to cooperate with, and to aid individual and group efforts . . . seeking to create and maintain decent living standards."

While CU has earned its principal reputation as a testing and rating organization, it has consistently shown its concern with the problem of living standards. CU has presented testimony, on request, at legislative, investigative, and regulatory hearings; has aided consumer education of many kinds; and has financed research on consumer problems.

One research project, co-sponsored by CU, explored the dilemma of low-income families. The poor are exposed to the same pressures to buy as everyone else, but they are the least able to choose, least able to bargain, and least able to pay. "The Poor Pay More," the book that resulted from this study, documents how poor people are cheated when they buy on credit.

What is being done and what might be done to change and to improve these conditions? Do low-income families respond to consumer education? CU decided to find out and undertook the limited survey reported here. The aim of the survey was not to make a complete roster, even of the work done with urban families, but rather to see the kinds of work being done; the obstacles; the approaches; the content; and the results where these could be determined.

It became clear that—small though the total effort is when compared to the need. —more consumer education is directed toward low-income families than any one group is aware of; there is little coordination and little exchange of information; and there are great variations in methods, in content, and in overall philosophy.

President Johnson, in his 1964 "War Against Poverty" message, said: "Very often a lack of jobs and money is not the cause of poverty but the symptom." The cause is lack of skills, and one of the most important is the skill of getting fair value for dollars spent. The findings of this survey show that some progress is being made in communicating these needed skills.

WHO IS ACTIVE IN THIS FIELD?

Here are some of the kinds of organizations active in educating or organizing low-income consumers. No attempt has

Reprinted by permission of Consumers Union of U.S., Inc., (July 1964, abridged).

been made to assess their relative importance. Only organizations with local activities are considered.

Housing Authorities and Welfare Departments

The clients of housing authorities and welfare departments are, by definition, in the low-income group. We asked the directors of the 40 agencies operating in the 20 largest U.S. cities what kinds of consumer education they were doing. We received information on 28; the findings are summarized below.

some of these classes. And, as the women increase their skill in reading and arithmetic, they are better prepared to cope with their problems as consumers.

HOUSEKEEPING TEACHERS   An interesting development in Chicago, and in several other cities, is the training of welfare clients as housekeeping teachers. They are taught the fundamentals of home-making, including money management, and are assigned to go into the homes of other women who need intensive help. These teachers are variously received; the family may feel that the

	No Consumer Education	A Little Consumer Education	A Program of Consumer Education	Totals
Welfare departments	3	6	4	13
Housing authorities	5	5	5	15
Totals	8	11	9	28

In six of the 20 largest U.S. cities there is, so far as we know, not even a token attempt at consumer education by either the welfare department or the housing authority.

Chicago and New York have probably the most developed programs.

In *Chicago*, the Cook County Department of Public Aid and the Chicago Housing Authority have been cooperating with the Mayor's Committee on New Residents in a series of courses primarily on the pitfalls of credit buying; this program is now in the process of expansion. Leadership training is being given. Field trips, dramatic skits, and parties are part of the plan to bring the program to more people.

Both the Housing Authority and the Public Aid Department give classes on homemaking. Also, the Board of Education gives classes for mothers of families receiving assistance, looking to 8th-grade and even to high-school graduation. Consumer education materials are used in

teacher is a spy who will report on them to the welfare department, or it may welcome her as a friend and helper. Because she herself is receiving public assistance, she has at least the advantage of knowing what this life is like.

VARIED PROGRAM   In New York City, through its Tenant Organization Division, the Housing Authority has sponsored or aided a wide variety of programs in consumer education and financial management. Organization of tenants' associations and of credit unions is part of this plan, but also there are courses on subjects like money management, food, and clothing; model apartments with low-cost, livable furniture; a speakers' bureau; leadership training sessions, and individual counseling. Many of the city's social agencies cooperate with the Housing Authority on these programs; a number of neighborhood houses operate in the community facilities of housing projects. Family agencies, the New York City Department of Markets, and the Consumer

Frauds office of the New York State Attorney General are among the others involved. The discussions of money management mentioned on page 5, were conducted by a family casework agency. They must have had their practical aspects, since the rent-delinquent tenants who took part in it are not rent delinquent now.

The New York City Department of Public Welfare has home economists who advise the investigators (as its caseworkers are called) and also a homemaker service program. The homemakers show mothers who need such help how to keep house and take care of children. They may also go out shopping with clients who are making major purchases. Under the Mayor's "War on Poverty" proposal hundreds of women on public assistance are to receive training in homemaking, and to pass it on to others. This sounds much like the housekeeping teacher training already discussed.

RESISTANCE TO PUBLIC AGENCIES Even these comparatively developed programs reach only a small fraction of the people needing help. Also, they encounter a certain amount of suspicion and resistance. The Housing Authority and the Welfare Department exercise tremendous power over the lives of their clients since they can, respectively, evict tenants and cut off assistance. Therefore many clients fear that anything these agencies do is designed to direct their lives or snoop into their affairs. Efforts to set up credit unions in New York City housing projects were fruitless until the Housing Authority withdrew its own personnel and left the organizing to churches, neighborhood agencies, and the New York State Credit Union League.

Voluntary Social Agencies

The work of neighborhood houses and family agencies within the housing projects has been mentioned. In addition, these agencies have outside programs such as individual counseling, classes, and consumer clinics where people can come for advice and help with legal problems.

AN ACTION PLAN Also, there are some special agencies with special approaches. In East Harlem, three settlements joined forces in 1963 to set up a Consumer Action Program which works primarily with groups of people in East Harlem, helping them to do whatever they themselves want to do about their consumer problems. The help has been primarily to provide an organizer and facilities for mimeographing. The philosophy is that of self-help.

Out of this program have grown the following:

1.   Two credit unions have been established, serving three low-income housing projects. One of the credit unions is starting a consumer education program.

2.   A Consumer Protective Committee picketed a supermarket to protest price differences, inferior meats and produce, and poor shopping conditions. The picket line brought results, both in the store picketed and in other neighborhood supermarkets. It is noteworthy that people joined the picket line who had not before been involved in any consumer activity.

3.   A group of public housing tenants organized an informal food buying cooperative for meats, vegetables, and rice. It has been highly effective on a small scale, and the attempt now is to enlarge the scope and have it operate full time.

4.   At the request of many tenement dwellers, the program is exploring ways in which tenants could buy the buildings they live in, renovate them, and run them as low-income housing cooperatives. The main problem is financing.

SEWING AND SHOPPING   A quite different approach is that of the Project on
Family Urbanization conducted by the
Association for Family Living in Chicago.
Here, consumer education is part of a
plan for reaching hard-to-reach people
who have recenty come to the city.

The first approach was to Negro wom-
en in a South Side neighborhood. Nothing
was said about urbanization or education;
the women were offered free instruction
in sewing and millinery. Those who enrolled were interested in making hats,
clothes, curtains, and slipcovers.

The instructor was available several
days a week, so that the women could
come at any time that was convenient.

As they sewed, they talked, and certain
problems came out. One problem was
shopping; the instructor took them on
trips to buy fabric for a dress; to a supermarket; to a rummage sale. This was part
of a program that included also parent
education, and counseling on individual
problems.

The program has now moved to a North
Side area housing Puerto Ricans, Mex-
icans, Southern whites, and American
Indians. To enroll women, they are doing
home visiting, speaking both Spanish and
English.

REHABILITATION   In New York City
the Phoenix Project, involving a number
of agencies, will try to help 300 families
that have applied for public housing but
are not yet considered acceptable. They
will advise on buying, will have a demonstration apartment to teach home-
making and home care. As with the
urbanization project in Chicago, consumer education is part of a comprehensive plan to help the families in whatever way is needed.

A program with goals similar to those
of the Phoenix Project is under way in
San Francisco.

Health Agencies

Both health departments and visiting
nurse services in many cities advise consumers in one specific field: Nutrition.
Nurses give diet and nutrition advice, if
needed, to the families they visit. Advice
on food is given also in clinics, as for
example a prenatal clinic, a well-baby
clinic, a clinic for diabetics.

Home Demonstration Agents
(Extension Service)

There are in the United States approximately 4,000 home economists who are
known as home demonstration agents.
They work for the extension services,
which are arms of county government,
of the state land grant colleges, and the
U.S. Department of Agriculture, and
their job is to disseminate information on
home economics.

There are home demonstration agents
in rural areas and—what is less well
known—in many cities. They carry on
home economics programs under the
leadership of the land grant colleges,
and work also with other organizations.

In Boston, for example, the Cooperative Extension Service of the University
of Massachusetts, in cooperation with
the United South End Settlements,
carried on a home economics program at
the South End public housing project.
Among the activities were food demonstrations for a group of housewives, a
club for teen-age girls, and a sewing
workshop.

The first home management aides
(like housekeeping teachers— see page 9)
in Milwaukee were trained for the welfare department by home demonstration
agents. In Milwaukee also, a workshop on
home management was given for the
Urban League.

In June 1963 the Federal Extension
Service (U.S. Department of Agricul-

ture, Washington, D.C., 20250) held a seminar on work with low-income families. Since then, extension workers in most states have become more active in this field. The Federal Extension Service is bringing out a series of four pamphlets on money management, intended for low-income families.

Groups Aiding Minorities

Both voluntary organizations and official bodies concerned with minority rights have engaged in some consumer education and action. The Chicago Urban League was active in getting legislation to protect installment buyers. Part of the work of the Mayor's Committee for New Residents, also in Chicago, has already been discussed, but it can be added that they have organized two credit unions in public housing projects, and that they are active in receiving and channeling consumer complaints.

The New York City Commission on Human Rights held a conference last winter on the exploitation of minority-group consumers. It now has a continuing committee planning a consumer education campaign, one feature of which is a price check on Harlem supermarkets.

In Baltimore, the Urban League has carried on consumer education with groups of families in public housing projects. They have held four consumer conferences this year, for occupants of public housing and for social workers in public and private agencies.

Credit Unions

Credit unions can't solve all the problems of low-income consumers. People on public assistance are not supposed to belong, because they are not allowed to have savings. (The credit unions feel this policy is wrong, and are trying to get welfare departments to change it.) And very poor credit risks can't borrow because the credit union, though more willing to take a chance than other lenders, must nevertheless consider the borrower's ability to pay.

But for people qualified to belong and to borrow, the credit union can be a most valuable resource. A cash loan at a fair interest rate frees the family to shop around and compare values, instead of falling back on "easy credit" stores that charge extortionate prices.

There have been for years a fair number of credit unions in settlement houses and churches in low-income neighborhoods. Within the past year or two, there have been concerted efforts to organize them in New York and Chicago public housing projects; seven have been organized.

It is hard work to organize a credit union, because this is a complex business run by volunteers. The volunteers must learn how to run the business, and in the course of learning they may lose interest or may have to drop out. But the potential membership—and the potential for helping that membership—is tremendous.

Unions

The aim of a union is to get its members out of the low-income category. Nevertheless, there are some unions whose members must be classed as low-income consumers.

For the national and international bodies, consumer work may be limited to publishing a consumer column in the union newspaper. But local unions and local AFL-CIO Councils, often with the help of the national AFL-CIO Community Service Activities, engage in a wide variety of consumer programs.

One such activity is a citywide consumer course. In Minneapolis, for example, the AFL-CIO Community Services have for four years held a number of well-attended eight-week consumer information courses. They have also conducted programs for delegates and wives of delegates at the state AFL-CIO convention, and for other union conventions; have supplied speakers for local union meetings; and have had consumer education activities at the Minnesota State Fair.

The National AFL-CIO Community Service Activities offers a course outline on consumer education and promotes also a program of consumer counseling, designed to inform union members of alternatives in buying; to sensitize them to false advertising, unfair installment contracts and other dishonest business practices; to help union members with specific consumer problems to get professional advice. Other activities include consumer clinics on legal troubles, and one-day institutes on special topics such as medical quackery, home improvement rackets, or whatever seems to be a pressing problem in the community.

In New York City the largest volume of consumer activity—especially for unions with low-income membership—is legal aid for members in trouble with installment payments. But there are other approaches.

One local gave an intensive course in a single big shop, reached some 400 members, and counted as one concrete result the fact that they switched from industrial life insurance (sold by the week) to long-term insurance.

Two New York unions—District 65, Retail, Wholesale, and Department Store Union, and the New York Hotel and Motel Trades Council—offer buying services to their members. The District 65 store handles small items like shirts, playsuits, toys, pots and pans; the Hotel Trades store offers furniture and men's clothing. The Hotel Trades union also has centers in the boroughs, where members can go for legal counsel.

Schools

Consumer education in the schools, a lively movement in the Thirties, has dwindled today. Some work is done, under a variety of subject headings, a Consumers Union knows from the sale of *Consumer Reports* to classes in social studies, home economics, business education, economics, and consumer education, and from the many groups of students that visit CU. But this work is not beamed particularly at members of the low-income group.

There is some movement toward consumer education in the trend to classes in family living. Topics like getting one's money's worth, use of credit, and money management should be, and often are, discussed in these classes.

ADULT CLASSES   In New York, in St. Louis, and in San Diego, we have learned about adult classes for literacy in which consumer education formed part or all of the subject matter. In the St. Louis course, the topic of money management was introduced to make reading and arithmetic more interesting. Students learned to record their spending for a month, then used the record as an aid to planning their spending for a month ahead. They learned also how to figure out the real costs of credit and installment buying. They brought in newspaper advertisements, read them and discussed what the advertisements did not tell. They read and discussed a chattel mortgage.

Consumer Orientation Program of Puerto Rico

Worthy of special mention is the work of the Programa de Orientacion del Consumidor of Puerto Rico. According to information from Mrs. Amneris Diaz, the

Executive Secretary, this program works under the Economic Stabilization Administration of the Commonwealth government, but its policy is dictated by a committee representing 20 governmental agencies that are concerned in, and contribute to, its work.

The program reaches the public through discussion groups, conferences and other meetings, movies, radio and TV programs, posters, and pamphlets. It conducts three consumer columns in two widely read newspapers. It publishes materials on clothing, foods, advertising, budgeting, and the use of credit. Illiterate consumers are reached by radio and TV.

The program handles consumer complaints concerning such matters as unfair business practices, misleading advertising, and troubles with installment buying. It offers legal advice and intervenes between consumers and merchants.

3

Education and
Educational Opportunities

The process of transmitting the culture of a society from one generation to the next has been recognized as a universal necessity throughout the history of mankind. But it is only in relatively recent times that this function has become sufficiently differentiated from the family and religious institutions so as to constitute a separate social institution in its own right. Today, formal education has become a major feature of all urban-industrial societies, and its central importance as a social institution is growing by leaps and bounds.

The reasons for modern society's increasing reliance on formal education at a massive scale are varied, and many of them have been spelled out in some detail by social scientists. Sociologist Alvin Boscoff, for example, has identified at least five major needs that are served by educational systems in modern urban societies. They include: (1) the need for a quick, efficient, and meaningful communications' network among urban groups. Formal education provides the necessary tools—techniques, ideas, and acquired interests; (2) a formal educational system is necessary to transmit the skills of a vast and complex system of specialized occupations and vocations, upon which modern societies are increasingly dependent. As a result of the increasing division of labor, the family is no longer adequate to the difficult task of allocating occupational roles among members of a society; (3) modern economies increasingly rely on the cultivation of expanding tastes and desires for consumer goods and services. Formal education on a large scale generally tends to expand the appetites and preferences of the mass consumer, which leads to continually higher living standards and increased productivity in industrial societies such as the United States; (4) formal education provides the motives and values necessary to maintain and enhance the "non-economic" civic and cultural amenities of modern communities, such as parks, recreational facilities, civic centers, libraries, and museums (this argument may be somewhat circular, because formal education may in fact provide the initial needs for such amenities); and (5) changes and innovations in the technological, economic, political, and social organization of complex urban-industrial societies are increasingly dependent on a core of managers, officials, technicians, and professionals trained in and recruited from a highly developed educational system.[1]

Another important function of formal education in a pluralistic society such as ours is the transmission of skills and attitudes necessary for citizenship. In a democracy, this function is so obvious that it is often overlooked. Formal education provides incentives and means for enriching intergroup living, for regulating excessive intergroup competition and conflict, for minimizing potentialities for violence and disorder common to all large pluralistic societies, and for preserving democratic principles and procedures in the process.

One might add to the above list the "nationalistic" functions of education in today's world, as suggested by this statement:

> In the atomic era, education is no longer merely a stairway to personal advancement, but has become a weapon of national survival . . . The next war will be won—or perhaps averted—by the nation with the best schools, for the nation with the best educational system, will, in all likelihood, have the best military weapons.[2]

All of the above are the kinds of functions formal education provides for society as a whole. But in our society there is also the expectation that education will serve the individual needs of all citizens and social groups and provide the opportunities to utilize their various talents and abilities to the fullest. Putting it another way, education is expected to provide everyone in the society with an equal opportunity for social, economic, or political advancement. As our technology becomes more sophisticated and our social and economic life becomes more complex, formal education has virtually become *the* major source of social and economic mobility; conversely, the lack of adequate formal education has become the major barrier to socio-economic advancement or security.

SOME RECENT EDUCATIONAL TRENDS

Universal or compulsory public education in the United States first became firmly established about a century ago, and it has been growing ever since. First established at the elementary school level, compulsory education was gradually extended to the secondary level, and an ever larger portion of the United States population has benefited from the increased availability of a free public education. For example, only 2 percent of the total 17-year-old population had graduated from high school a century ago, whereas approximately 65 percent of the 17-year-olds had received high school diplomas in the 1957–1958 academic year (See Table 3.1).

TABLE 3.1.   HIGH SCHOOL GRADUATES 17 YEARS OF AGE, CONTINENTAL UNITED
STATES, 1870–1958

Year	High School Graduates	Percentage of Total 17-Year-Old Population
1869–1870	16,000	2.0
1889–1890	43,731	3.5
1909–1910	156,429	8.8
1929–1930	666,904	29.0
1949–1950	1,199,700	59.0
1953–1954	1,276,100	60.0
1957–1958	1,507,600	64.9

Source: U.S. Department of Health, Education, and Welfare, Progress of Public Education in the United States of America, 1959–1960, Washington, D.C.: U.S. Government
Printing office, 1960, p. 12.

At the college level, a similar trend has been emerging. At the turn of the
century, only about 4 percent of the college-age population of the United
States actually attended college, but by 1960 approximately 40 percent of the
college-age population was attending American colleges and universities.[3]
College attendance will have grown at a still more rapid rate by the end of
the present decade, and it is expected to expand even further in the foreseeable future, as larger and larger portions of Americans plan a college education for their children.

This general trend toward more formal education for more people can be
interpreted in several ways. First, it means that our population is becoming
better educated; that is, educational levels and standards are rising for the
society as a whole. Second, it means that our society is investing more heavily
in public education than ever before. Not only are total dollar expenditures
rapidly increasing, but per pupil expenditures have been rising as well. For
example, it has been estimated that per pupil expenditures increased by a
national average of 67 percent in the ten-year period between 1954 and 1964.[4]
Of course, such increases represent rising costs, but they also represent some
very real improvements in the educational facilities and resources available
to each student. Third, this trend means that the American public has a
growing faith in the utility—or the necessity—of formal education at all levels.
This faith has been growing for an increasing variety of reasons, and it has
been growing faster than the capacity of our educational system to keep itself
abreast of all the resulting new demands. This latter trend—in the face of
qualitative and quantitative improvements in our educational system—is at
the heart of many contemporary concerns about education as a major social
problem area.

SOME SOCIAL PROBLEMS OF EDUCATION

Any analysis of the social problems reviewed in this book, as well as a much broader range of contemporary social problems which could not be reviewed here, reveals that education is almost universally considered to be a strategic causal factor. For example, problems of poverty, unemployment, and racial discrimination were viewed as at least a partial result of unequal educational opportunities, or as a failure on the part of some groups to utilize existing educational opportunities to their fullest. The relationship between poverty and education in the light of current economic trends is often illustrated in terms like these:

Those who are unemployed for very long at this time are mainly the uneducated and untrained *for whom there will never again be enough jobs to go around.* In most cases, the boy or girl who leaves school early fails to learn what has been taught there, or who has no good school to attend, will be condemned to a lifetime of low wages, periodic unemployment, and relief-check living.[5]

Almost all of the personal pathologies, or other forms of deviant behavior, were seen at least in part a result of "inadequate socialization." Since the schools play an increasingly significant role in the socialization process, inadequate socialization is often viewed as a failure on the part of the educational system to perform one of its expected functions.

On the other hand, the faith that many Americans have in universal education is often based on the assumption that education can and should solve most of our major social problems. On the basis of teaching large sections of social problems courses over the past several years, this writer has observed that most of his students sincerely believed that more education was *the* major solution to the problems covered in the courses. Of course, formal education, or the lack of it, is neither the cause or the cure all of social problems that many people believe it to be, since formal education represents only one segment of our total culture, having at best only a limited impact on the larger society:

The educational system largely reflects the morals, values, aspirations, and confusions of the society of which it is an instrument. The school by itself cannot maintain values which are crumbling in the community around it, for it is subject to the same forces which are constantly reshaping society. Nor can it cure social ills like racial discrimination and juvenile delinquency whose sources and remedies lie far beyond the scope of the school.[6]

Nevertheless, as the authors of this statement also conclude, the schools in America have become the "whipping" boy for a wide range of social problems, and for much of the general discontent in contemporary society: the schools are at the center of many controversies regarding the nature of and solutions to social problems, and they are caught in the crossfires of attack generated by pressure groups representing almost every imaginable kind of interest. For example, a large sample of Massachusetts school superintendents and school board members reported in one study that they were subject to definite pressures from groups such as these: PTA and other parent groups; teachers; taxpayers associations; city councils and municipal finance committees; political, business, and commercial organizations; personal friends; the press; old-line families and other influential individuals; church or religious groups; veterans organizations; labor unions; chambers of commerce; service clubs; fraternal organizations; farm organizations; and welfare organizations.[7]

The nature of the charges directed against the schools are equally varied. Raab and Selznick have summarized some of the more common criticisms as follows:

1.   The schools fail to transmit values. They fail to teach moral and spiritual values; they are "godless" and leave their students morally rudderless. They do not check delinquency. The schools are teaching "welfare state collectivism"; they do not show enough concern for inculcating patriotic ideals.
2.   The schools fail to provide a good basic education. They do not teach the three R's properly; they are producing fads and frills in the schools . . . the scientific education of American youth lags behind that of Russian youth.
3.   The schools fail to meet the educational and occupational needs of all students. About a third of all American students who enter high school drop out before they graduate.[8]

What very often happens is that the crossfires demanding competing and incompatible policies and programs for the schools tend to cancel one another out and effectively neutralize many school systems, preventing them from moving boldly in any direction. In the Massachusetts study mentioned above, for example, 73 percent of the school board members received protests directed against school tax increases or bond proposals, whereas 67 percent were subjected to demands for more money for the general school programs. Fifty-nine percent of the superintendents were exposed to demands to restrict their curricula and place more emphasis on the three Rs, whereas 64 percent were exposed to demands that the schools should teach still more courses and subjects.[9] Under such conflicting pressures, it is hardly any wonder that the American schools in many respects fail to completely satisfy anybody!

Yet this represents an apparent paradox. As anyone with the faintest knowledge of the history of public education in the United States knows, the performance and standards of our educational system are much higher today than they have ever been before. It must be concluded that many of our current concerns with the problems of education have to do with our rapidly rising demands and expectations—demands and expectations that only could have been generated in a nation with a history of rapid educational growth and accomplishment. Once aspirations begin to rise in anticipation of major institutional change, they generally accelerate at a rate which exceeds the capacity of complex social institutions such as formal education to respond as quickly as desired. In other words, current social problems in education may be broadly defined as another case of a growing gap between social expectations and social reality.

IMPROVING EDUCATIONAL OPPORTUNITIES

It should not be concluded from the discussion so far that some innovation is nonexistent in American education today. Actually, there are many changes continually underway in instructional techniques, teacher training and recruitment, curricula planning, facilities planning, school-community relations, school financing, educational resource allocation, and educational administration at all levels, from preschool through higher education. In addition, there is a great deal of planning going on with respect to anticipating future educational needs. Amid all the educational conflicts, controversy, and intellectual ferment surrounding current educational problems, one set of new standards reflecting some consensus among educators seems to have emerged. These new standards, which illustrate the major tasks facing both public and private education today, have been summarized as follows:

Start the child in school earlier; keep him in school more and more months of the year; retain all who start in school for twelve to fourteen years; expect him to learn more and more during this period, in wider and wider areas of human experience, under the guidance of a teacher, who has had more and more training, and who is assisted by more and more specialists, who provide an ever-expanding range of services, with access to more and more detailed personal records, based on more and more carefully validated tests.[10]

Unfortunately, it is impossible to review in this short space educational strategies in all of the areas suggested above. Rather, attention here is focused on current educational programs and policies in these three major areas: (1) improving and equalizing educational opportunities for culturally deprived or racially restricted groups in low-income urban areas; (2) providing continuing educational opportunities for adults whose education has been interrupted for a variety of social and economic reasons—or whose basic skills and knowledge have been diluted or rendered obsolete by technological and social change; and (3) extending the range of higher educational opportunities to ever growing numbers, and extending the range of services available to the larger society through higher educational institutions. In this writer's opinion, these are among the most crucial educational problems currently facing our society and its members, and they are among the problem areas in which the most interesting, and perhaps the most significant, educational innovations and social experiments are beginning to appear.

The first reading in this chapter is a summary report describing the major findings, issues, strategies, and proposals that emerged in a seminar on the education of socially deprived and segregated children, held at Dedham,

Massachusetts in September 1963. The seminar was interdisciplinary, and its participants included over 60 prominent educators, sociologists, psychiatrists, writers, politicians, and representatives of other broad areas of interest. It was organized to search out new ways to educate children, who, because of poverty, segregation, or both, fail to get an adequate education. The report summarizes the full range of problems that were considered and draws up a series of major strategies. Many of the recommendations are already underway in some communities, and some of them have already been incorporated into federal programs of aid to education, such as the one discussed below. It was a general conclusion of the seminar that more federal action would be required, because of inadequate financial and political resources at local and state levels. The seminar was held under the auspices of the Bank Street College of Education, and was underwritten by the U.S. Office of Education, the U.S. Office of Juvenile Delinquency and Youth Development, and the National Institute of Mental Health.

Despite powerful opposition, the forces demanding increased federal government intervention for improving local education and local educational opportunities have been overwhelming. One of the most significant results of these pressures in recent years has been the passage into law of the Elementary and Secondary Education Act of 1965. This law has authorized more than a billion dollars in federal funds for the fiscal year 1966 to be made available among the 50 States for improving local elementary and secondary school systems. According to the U.S. Office of Education, the purpose of the new law is to: (1) strengthen elementary and secondary school programs for educationally deprived children in low income areas; (2) provide additional school library resources, textbooks, and other instructional materials for financially impoverished school districts; (3) finance supplementary educational centers and services of all kinds; (4) broaden the areas of cooperative educational research; and (5) strengthen departments of education at the state level.[11]

All of the problems of providing equal educational opportunities to culturally deprived and segregated low-income groups are disproportionately magnified in the large central cities of America's major metropolitan areas. Here, the tensions, frustrations, and militant demands for school reforms have been most dramatic, and many large cities have literally been forced to reorganize and extend their educational facilities on a large scale, with or without federal assistance. One such city is Detroit, Michigan. In the second reading Dr. Carl Marburger describes how Detroit has developed a multiple or total approach to the educational problems of the inner core of the city through its Great Cities School Improvement Program. This is but one of a series of local "great cities" projects undertaken jointly by a number of big city school systems. These have been supported in part by local financing, but they also have been generously assisted by the Ford Foundation (nongovernmental interventions such as this are becoming a crucial element of planned social change in our society, which is a fact that should not be overlooked in the light of increasing governmental involvement in the same problem areas).

The five major approaches of the Detroit "great cities" program have been summarized as follows:

(a) teacher orientation and training—attempting to modify the teachers perceptions of the culturally deprived child and to develop teaching competencies and insights in working with such children; (b) improved use of available instructional materials and equipment and the development of appropriate instructional materials and teaching aids; (c) modification of organizational patterns for greater flexibility and more efficient programming; (d) addition of such personnel as coaching and remedial teachers, visiting social workers, and school-community agents, and (e) involvement of public and private agencies in developing school-home-community activities.[12]

Marburger (former director of the Detroit "great cities" program, now Assistant Superintendent of the Detroit Public Schools) believes that the schools must provide more effective educational facilities for disadvantaged groups than necessary for middle-class groups, and that the schools are the most important single force for counteracting the poor learning climate and lack of incentives which characterize the environment of culturally deprived children in inner-city slum areas.

Many individuals tend to think of their own education as an isolated segment of their lives, to be gotten over with as soon as possible, in order to move on to adult roles which they perceive to have very little to do with the actual content of formal education. Thus, in most current discussions of educational problems, adults past the conventional school ages tend to be a neglected group. Yet, it is apparent that many adults in our society who have not previously acquired the appropriate skills, knowledge, or merely the "credentials" for the increasingly complex roles they are expected or wish to play suffer consequences at least as acute for themselves, and nearly as costly to the larger society, as problems facing today's teen-age school "dropouts." As a result, there has been a dramatic increase in recent decades in the number of adults who seek some kind of continuing adult education or retraining. Included are adults whose formal education was previously disrupted for economic, social, or psychological reasons; adults whose occupational skills have become obsolete; adults who wish to advance their social or economic status; and at least some adults for whom continuing education is an "avocation." Many employers have also contributed to this trend by encouraging or requiring employees to upgrade their educational levels, sometimes at the employers own expense.

This trend toward continuing adult education has affected all educational levels, from elementary school through college: for example, it has been estimated that between 30 and 50 million people were enrolled part time in university extension or evening college courses in the academic year 1951–1952.[13] In the third reading A. A. Liveright (Director of the Center for the Study of Liberal Education for Adults) reviews recent trends, current objectives, programs and problems, and possible future directions for continuing adult education in American colleges and universities.

Many persons reading this book probably will have experienced some of the following consequences of burgeoning college and university enrollment first hand:

. . . fewer fully qualified professors, oversize classes, impersonality, excessive dependence upon textbooks and objective tests, and the acceptance of mediocrity. Students sit, listen, fill out test forms. They never know their professors, rarely talk, rarely write. Courses are hurdles to surmount, not doorways to exciting fields of inquiry. In the elementary school, poor teaching often leads to classroom chaos; at the college level, students just go to sleep, physically and intellectually.[14]

Criticisms such as the above are frequently leveled against many large public universities. Perhaps the prototype is the giant University of California, whose Berkeley campus has been widely discussed in the mass media (and in more esoteric circles) as the scene of much recent student discontent and unrest, in addition to almost all the conditions mentioned in the above quotation. Yet, the large public universities are growing still larger every year. Enrollment in public four-year colleges grew about three times more rapidly than did enrollment in private four-year colleges in the decade between 1950 and 1960, and by 1960 about 60 percent of all college students were enrolled in public institutions. No reduction in this trend is anticipated in the foreseeable future. The large public university is here to stay, regardless of current disapproval on the part of its critics. From this writer's perspective, the land grant movement and other types of federal support for higher education, which have helped create the large public universities as we now know them, must be counted as among the more significant "strategies of intervention" for extending and equalizing higher educational opportunities for a rapidly growing college age population.

In the fourth reading Clark Kerr, President of the University of California, summarizes many of the accomplishments of the federally supported land grant universities, reviews some of their current deficiencies, and suggests ways in which they could be improved. Originally published in 1963, before much of the recent public interest in the internal affairs of the University had become evident, this essay also reveals Kerr's valuable insights regarding some of the problems inherent to the kind of educational system in which he is a leading figure.

REFERENCES

1. Alvin Boskoff, *The Sociology of Urban Regions*. New York: Appleton-Century-Crofts, Inc., 1962, pp. 245–47.
2. Paul B. Horton and Gerald R. Leslie, *The Sociology of Social Problems*. New York: Appleton-Century-Crofts, Inc., 1965, p. 297.
3. Earl Raab and Gertrude J. Selznick, *Major Social Problems*. New York: Harper & Row, Publishers, 1964, 2d. ed., p. 362.

4. National Education Association, Ranking of the States, 1964, Research Report 1964–RI. Washington, D.C.: National Education Association, 1964, p. 46.
5. Horton and Leslie, p. 297.
6. Raab and Selznick, p. 357.
7. Ronald G. Corwin, *A Sociology of Education*. New York: Appleton-Century-Crofts, Inc., 1965, p. 350.
8. Raab and Selznick, p. 356.
9. Corwin, p. 349.
10. A. Harry Passow, ed., *Education in Depressed Areas*. New York: Teachers College, Columbia University, 1963, p. 67.
11. See "A Description and Analysis of the Elementary and Secondary Education Act of 1965," *American Education* (April 1965), pp. 3–20.
12. Passow, p. 282.
13. A. A. Liveright, *Notes and Essays on Education for Adults*, No. 30, Center for the Study of Liberal Education for Adults, 1960, p. 3.
14. Horton and Leslie, p. 302.

ADDITIONAL READINGS

Chandler, B. J., Lindley J. Stiles, and John I. Kitsuse, *Education in Urban Society*. New York: Dodd-Mead & Company, Inc., 1962.
Conant, James B., *Slums and Suburbs*. New York: McCraw-Hill Book Company, Inc., 1961.
Corwin, Ronald G., *A Sociology of Education*. New York: Appleton-Century-Crofts, Inc., 1965.
Lichter, Solomon, and others, *The Drop-Outs*. New York: The Free Press of Glencoe, Inc., 1962.
Lipset, Seymour M., and Sheldon S. Wolin (eds.), *Berkeley Student Revolt*. New York: Anchor Books, 1965.
Mayer, Martin, *The Schools*. New York: Harper & Row, Publishers, 1961.
Page, Charles H., *Sociology and Contemporary Education*. New York: Random House, 1964.
Passow, A. Harry (ed.), *Education in Depressed Areas*. New York: Teachers College, Columbia University, 1963.
Sanford, Nevitt (ed.), *The American College*. New York: John Wiley & Sons, Inc., 1962.
Sexton, Patricia C., *Education and Income*. New York: The Viking Press, Inc., 1961.
Havighurst, Robert J., and Bernice L. Neugarten, *Society and Education*. Boston: Allyn and Bacon, Inc., 2d. ed., 1962.

EDUCATION OF THE DEPRIVED
AND SEGREGATED:
SUMMARY REPORT OF THE SEMINAR ON EDUCATION FOR
CULTURALLY DIFFERENT YOUTH

David Street

ANALYSIS OF THE PROBLEM

The seminar was committed to considering what things education might do for those children and youth who, because of deprivation and segregation, are not getting the kind of education that will prepare them to become effective adults in our changing world. The group sought to identify promising ways to attack the problems of "the difficult 30 per cent," as these children were called throughout the sessions.

Basic Assumptions

Several significant assumptions were involved in the planning and conduct of the seminar.

1. Despite rising standards of American education, the problem of national educational failure—whether measured through dropouts, grade retardation, evaluations of levels of literacy, unemployment of youth, or any one of a number of other indices—is becoming increasingly apparent. Parallel to the problem of the continuance of poverty in a generally affluent society is this problem of the continuance of inadequate education in an educationally upgraded nation.

2. The problem is becoming more acute because of changes in the larger society, particularly in the skill requirements for employment, which make it increasingly likely that those who fail to receive an adequate education will fail occupationally and in many other ways.

3. The problem is widespread, but it also is concentrated in certain groups and locations. Educational failure is interlaced with other social problems, such as poverty, racial discrimination, and political inequality. It is particularly acute in "pockets of poverty," among the mountain people; among the residents of the rural South, white and Negro; and among those urban groups least far along the road to adaptation to urban life, such as the Negroes and Puerto Ricans who have recently migrated to the cities. It is most dramatically apparent in the big city slums.

4. Something *can* be done. Numerous small-scale experiments—many of them reported on in the seminar—indicate that effective action *can* be taken to increase educational success with the deprived and segregated. The aim of the seminar,

From the *Summary Report of the Seminar on Education for Culturally Different Youth,* 1965, pp. 7–17. Reprinted by permission of the author and Bank Street College of Education.

therefore, should be to discover and identify the most appropriate measures of action and to conceive of them on a scale great enough to address the full extent and character of the problem. Funds and entrepreneurship are needed, and that is where the federal government can be of assistance.

5. Recent years have seen a flowering of national attention and interdisciplinary cooperation in upgrading the quality of instruction in physical science and mathematics. This effort has tended to benefit the fortunate 70 per cent and to have little impact on the difficult 30 per cent. It is time to turn the attention of persons involved in curriculum reform in science and mathematics, along with persons from the social sciences and other disciplinary, professional, or organizational spheres, to the problems of the children with whom education is making little progress.

Diagnoses of the Problem

The problem of educational failure that results from deprivation and segregation is complex. Much energy at the seminar went into the effort to diagnose the problem—to identify its major sources and to understand their dynamics—as a first step toward planning action. Four highly interrelated sources emerged as perhaps most important.

1. The quality of family and community life. For reasons of poverty, bad living conditions, uprootedness, racial discrimination, broken homes, and a variety of other causes, many of the children of the difficult 30 per cent come from an environment that does not adequately prepare them—in language skills, motivation, self-respect, and values—for the standards of the conventional school. For many slum children, the life of the streets is more compelling than the life

in the typical school room, and the moral climate of what some characterize as a corrupt society may teach the child more than the school does. At the extreme, the community and home may leave the child not only socially disabled but also psychologically damaged.

2. Social class, racial, and ethnic patterns. Because of their position in the society, lower-class children, and the children of the nonwhite lower classes in particular, are disadvantaged in a number of ways. Poverty begets poverty. The children tend to be discriminated against, stereotyped, counselled "down," and perhaps "loved but not taught." Also, lower-class culture collides with the expectations of the school, and in terms of what the school expects, these children are "culturally deprived."

3. The technological-economic factor. As a result of technological and economic changes, occupational skill requirements are being upgraded dramatically, while the demand for labor is failing to keep pace with the expansion of the economy and population. The result is an increase in the unemployment of youth, which is extreme among those who are unskilled. Among the consequences of the latter development are the high concentration of unemployment among selected groups in the society and a loss of motivation for school work in those students whose future in the labor force is bleak. It is obvious that the educational system alone cannot solve this problem, but it is also clear that the schools have not kept pace with the changes in technology and the economy. At present, vocational education generally does not provide adequate training for participation in the rapidly changing labor force.

4. The capacity of the schools for creative change. For a variety of reasons,

the schools are deficient in their capacity to meet the problems of deprived and segregated children and youth in creative ways. The following are important among these reasons.

a. A shortage and inflexibility in the use of resources, which limit many school systems in providing adequate remedial and counselling services, sufficiently decreasing or varying class size, instituting new programs, or taking other needed actions.

b. The general tendency toward traditionalism and inflexibility in school system operations. In the big cities, administrative organization and bureaucratic control often limit the possibilities for creative innovation. In all systems there is a tendency to rely on traditional practices; for example, the recruitment criteria for school personnel are defined narrowly, usually so that professional educators are the only adults allowed inside the classroom, and teachers spend almost all of their in-school time teaching, with little time for planning, contacts with colleagues, or in-service training.

c. Curricula and teaching often are inadequate. Teaching tends to be formally academic and restricted by rigid concepts of graded materials and course work, and teachers often spend their time "presenting material" rather than stimulating the development of inquiry, initiative, interest, courage, and industry among the students. Textbooks and other curricular materials frequently fail to capture the imagination of the students, many of whom simply find school a bore.

d. The school is especially inadequate in adjusting to lower-class children. The expectations of the school are middle class, involving the application of tried-and-true teaching techniques to "normal" children. Because the difficult 30 per cent are not normal in terms of the school's expectations, the result is often simply to lower standards and to assume that the school can produce only poorly with such poor students. The lower-class child may have verbal virtuosity in the language of his own culture and may have high imagination, creativity, spontaneity, and aggressiveness, but there is little opportunity for him to use these attributes in the school. When the gap between cultures is not bridged, the child often fails to have any substantial success in school as a basis for the development of attitudes of trust and self-respect.

e. The school's relationship to the community often is inadequate. Frequently there is weak coordination between the school system and those community agencies that also are involved with the child and family. Further, the school often is unable to communicate effectively to parents and help educate them in ways to make the total environment of the child more supportive of the goals of education.

STRATEGIES FOR ACTION

The seminar members were agreed that the problem of educational failure with deprived and segregated children and youth is severe and that strong and immediate remedial actions are necessary. Creative solutions will require coordinated action on many fronts because: first, adequate efforts at educational change simply are beyond the fiscal and administrative capacities of many of the local school systems; and second, many of these changes must involve not only the schools but also governmental, business, labor, foundation, university, and community groups if they are to succeed. A broad variety of strategies, involving different aspects of the problem and different agencies for action, is appropriate. Many of these strategies would involve federal action as a prime stimulant, for only the federal government seems to have both the financial and political resources needed to take the large-scale action required.

Educational Disaster Areas

A key element in formulating strategies is the assumption that the federal government and other political units must recognize educational failure as a problem of social policy of grave national proportions. The government should provide aid to what might appropriately be called "educational disaster areas." In the same way that the federal government recognizes that certain parts of the country have economic problems beyond local or state capacity for remedying, it would acknowledge the need for action in areas of high educational failure, the inner city slums, the rural South, and elsewhere where failure is evident and the need great. This view is embodied in a position paper on social policy approved by the seminar as a whole:*

This seminar goes on record as recognizing the existence of educational disaster areas of such magnitude and intensity as to constitute one of the most grave emergencies confronting the nation. In these disaster areas, poverty, often accompanied by segregation, has produced large numbers of functional illiterates, and it continues to do so in great numbers.

We are convinced that literacy is the key to educational success. We also are convinced that failure to attain this skill predicts failure in school, unemployment, dependency, and crime. At present, our only national knowledge of literacy depends on necessarily inaccurate inferences from data on students by grade level, and on the belated and presently alarming results of tests given to military draftees.

The conference believes it vital that policy makers and public alike be alerted to the facts about illiteracy and its consequences in personal tragedy and economic waste. We must be prepared to give the same priority to using the nation's wealth for educationally underdeveloped areas at home as we do abroad. It is a high crime against the nation's youth and the nation itself that we have not seen ourselves as able to afford to educate our underprivileged youth up to presently feasible levels of success.

The conference is of the opinion that on the basis of suitable criteria, including a standard test of literacy achievement, educational disaster areas should be designated. Federal funds sufficient to achieve presently attainable national educational standards should be made available to school systems in these areas. There is sufficient knowledge at present of the educational effects of such factors as teacher competence, class size, the availability of teaching materials, programs of student incentives for further education, and school-community programs for us to act. With existing knowledge, national resources can be used more effectively to remove this educational blight from our population.

The evidence presented in this seminar strongly indicates that the immediate preschool years, kindergarten, and grades one and two are critical for the attainment of reading skills that are basic to educational success. This finding indicates that for many children these years are a disaster period. As a consequence, in addition to directing resources to educational disaster areas, we need to redirect educational resources to the disaster period—the early grades—in education. There is a need for heavy emphasis on these years in education. In addition, substantial research and development efforts should be funded in dealing with the educational problems of the primary years, and in particular for problems of success or failure in reading.

Yet we would fall short of our obligations to the youth of the nation if we aimed merely for the control of disaster. The plans we have outlined above should bring to an end the failure of the schools to perform their minimum function. We know how to improve such failing schools. But their very failure provides us with a challenge to attempt to bypass many of the defects of the typical American public school. In rebuilding from disaster, bold revisions of method and organization and daring innovations of content and of attitude are possible. We need educational experiment, both research and development in action, of many kinds. For instance, we need schools in the city whose ties with community and parents are far closer and richer than the monthly meetings of the Parent-Teacher Association, where third-graders can grasp experiments in micro-biology, where seventh-graders can write, set, and perform real theater, and where high school students can learn Russian if they will. We can afford such schools. Indeed, before too many years we will be unable to afford anything less. We must move forward to revised notions of the school, and most of the work of the seminar details the investigations and trials we ought to embark upon.

Such laboratories of excellence in schools ought not to be diffuse, nor should they be concentrated where the problems are simple. Our nation should, in order to manifest its dedication to this task, select an area where problems are presently most intense. In this area it should make a showcase of its schools. There are many reasons why *the nation's capital* should constitute such a showcase, but whatever the area, the effort should be massive and concentrated where the problems are greatest.

Working Group Approaches

The above statement on social policy indicates one area in which the seminar, in the time available, was able to develop general agreement. Most of the plenary sessions were devoted to hearing expert diagnoses of the problems of educating the difficult 30 per cent and to discussing reports of various innovative programs or experiments. The major work of hammering out specific strategies and programs for action took place in working groups created among the seminar participants. These groups dealt with eight areas of potential action that had emerged as most promising in the first few days of meetings and were reported

back to the seminar as a whole at the end. Excerpts from these reports begin on page 24. The groups were as follows:

1. *Curriculum reform.* This group considered ways to apply new developments in curriculum to the schools attended primarily by the difficult 30 per cent and to stimulate experimentation and sweeping reform, liberating intellectual and artistic achievement, through revisions of curricula, materials, and teaching in these schools.

2. *Literacy.* Members of this group considered literacy, literacy tests, and ways of raising levels of literacy nationally.

3. *Model schools.* This working group was concerned with what model schools for deprived and segregated children might be like, what functions they could serve in promoting educational change generally, and how they could be developed.

4. *Early childhood education.* The initial deliberations of this group were concerned with establishing guide lines for preschool programs that would operate in areas with large numbers of deprived and segregated children. Later, the group broadened its purview to include education of children ages six to nine and developed notions of early childhood centers.

5. *Teacher education.* This group considered the desirable attributes of the teacher of the difficult 30 per cent and ways to train teachers to acquire such attributes.

6. *School, community, and society.* This group devised plans for projects aimed at mobilizing the community to help accomplish the goals of education.

7. *Strategies for organizational and administrative change.* Members of this group attempted to lay out a prototypic comprehensive strategy for massive

change in the educational systems that serve the difficult 30 per cent.

8. *Youth work and youth education.* This working group took a broad look at the premises and patterns of work and of education for work in the "new society" and developed a large number of proposals for reform.

Major Strategies

The working groups devised a variety of approaches and special programs, varying in content, emphasis, and modes of implementation. These contain a number of common elements, such as a recurrent stress on the inclusion, in whatever projects are implemented, of research and development activities concerned with the question of how to make the process of change continuous and self-generating, and an emphasis on making certain that experimentation in the schools serving the difficult 30 per cent is included in any general educational projects that are developed. There was also an emergence of a significant number of major themes that were shared in the thinking of many clusters of participants. These themes or strategies are listed below.

1. Fostering cooperation between school systems and colleges, universities, or other groups. Colleges and universities should come to the aid of the schools that serve the difficult 30 per cent, and the schools should encourage them to help. The colleges should provide consultants from many disciplines, developing educational extension services and providing task force aid in curriculum reform. Specifically, they might develop cooperative programs of instructional reform in the South, provide high-level instruction in short courses in mathematics and physical sciences to graduates of Negro colleges (which are weak in these fields) or cooperate in running demonstration centers nationally. The colleges themselves should run model and experimental schools in urban and rural slums, and they should provide teacher training and internship experience in schools for the difficult 30 per cent. Further, they should develop programs for training specialists in in-service education of teachers and middle-level and high-level administrators, orienting them to the schools for the difficult 30 per cent. Not only school systems and colleges but also business, labor, government, and other units must cooperate in restructuring education for the world of work. Finally, procedures for facilitating cooperation between schools and other child-related agencies should be discovered and implemented.

2. Developing and disseminating improved teaching techniques, curricula, and materials. Through new efforts in pre-service and in-service teacher training, demonstration projects, improved use of new and old media, and other means, ways must be found to develop and disseminate information about promising teaching techniques. These techniques might range from linguistic and other new approaches in teaching reading to a variety of innovative teaching formats, including nongrading and team-teaching. The aim would be to foster teaching that is nonbookish, intuitive, sensitive, warm, flexible, imaginative, and responsive to the child. Curricula and materials should be revised through mobilization of experts from the academic disciplines, cooperative ventures between universities and school systems, research, introduction of curriculum specialists, inclusion of the difficult 30 per cent in ongoing curriculum projects, and other techniques. Efforts to improve the teaching of reading should avoid overconcentration on the new technical systems (not

only phonics and look-and-say, but also phonovisual, programmed instruction, initial teaching alphabet, sounds by colors, and so on) that currently are flourishing. Experimentation with such systems is important, but attention must also be given to integrating the teaching of reading with improvements in other classroom experiences of the child. Deprived and segregated children often come to school with little concept of the *uses* of literacy. Reading should not be conceived of as something to be mastered only through basal readers and *before* other learning can take place. Instead, learning to read should be accompanied by, and come partially through, learning about science, social studies, literature, and other areas, learning that will provide an intrinsic motive for gaining literacy skills.

3. Stressing the early years. Special attention should be devoted to the preschool and primary school years. Deprived and segregated children often come from environments that have not prepared them for the conventional expectations of the school and so must be given special help to become ready for school. Further, the initial school years must be adapted to their needs. Specifically, preschool and nongraded primary centers should be set up, developing flexible, well-staffed, and community-oriented programs.

4. Mobilizing resources. Standardized procedures should be found for assessing needs and allocating additional resources for individual schools that have large numbers of the difficult 30 per cent. School systems would receive funds for new or rehabilitated buildings, additional teachers, nonprofessional aides, and materials for these schools.

5. Creating model and laboratory schools and experimental school systems.

All kinds of model schools (for example, public schools run by cooperating universities or colleges, demonstration centers, summer schools, schools devoted to innovation in vocational education, or prototypic experiments within whole school systems or significant segments of school systems) should be established. These experiments should be started in a great variety of settings and might use all types of formats, including those of the nongraded school, the boarding school, the tutorial school, or even the school without a principal. As much as possible, these schools should have built-in dynamics of change and great diversity and flexibility in their educational program.

6. Upgrading teacher education. Training of teachers for the difficult 30 per cent should be upgraded through a variety of techniques. These include greater use of films and display and demonstration centers, the development of training programs that give the trainee more experience with children before the period of student teaching, the creation of courses that deal with new curriculum materials, the development of a national program of summer training for teachers, and experimentation with beginning the recruitment and training of teachers while they are still in high school. Other promising techniques include providing for internships in schools and preschool study centers, giving school systems resources to release teachers from classroom duties for in-service training, and providing physical science and mathematics training, particularly for faculties of southern colleges.

7. Improving school-community relations. Most new programs of all kinds should contain, as a major element, heightened cooperation with, mobilization of, and service to the community. Community residents—adults, dropouts,

high school students, and even grade school pupils—should be recruited into the educational task, as amateur volunteers, as paid teachers' aides, or in other roles. Such programs as the proposed preschool and primary grade centers, or enlarged work-study education projects should be run under a variety of auspices involving the community. Further, specific programs using school-community agents should be initiated, along with attempts to make the schools more congenial to the parents and to establish more effective communication with them. Finally, schools should become more highly involved in cooperative efforts with other agencies that deal with children and youth, including libraries, welfare and health agencies, the police, groups that operate study centers, agencies administering the proposed national youth corps, and the military.

8. Changing the social organization of the school and the school system. The school's capacity for creative change to meet the problems of the difficult 30 per cent must be enlarged. Ways to do this include: redefining roles and recruitment criteria for staff; training and using greater numbers of specialists, volunteers, and paid subprofessionals; raising teacher incentives by increasing specialization; providing teacher resource rooms and freeing teacher energies by turning over simple tasks to aides; upgrading specialization in curriculum construction and planning; providing improved planning and research and development operations in the schools; upgrading training of administrative personnel; making the schools more accessible to the community and redefining boundaries to diminish student travel; and facilitating flexibility and experimentation through such techniques as operating model schools, having open-ended hours for attendance in preschool centers, and abolishing rigidities in vocational education requirements.

9. Revolutionizing education for work. Education must be upgraded radically if it is to provide adequately for the education of the difficult 30 per cent for the changing world of work. Promising steps include: the elimination of present rigidities; the establishment of skill centers; the more flexible teaching of a wide range of vocational and technical skills to both youth and adults; the improvement and enlargement of work-study and guidance programs; the development of training for new kinds of work; the establishment of university-run experimental and demonstration vocational schools in urban and rural slums and racially integrated regional technical schools in the South; and the development of a program to give financial support to dropouts who return to school. Changes in education for work will have to be accompanied by major programs for providing work for youth.

CONSIDERATIONS
FOR EDUCATIONAL PLANNING

Carl A. Marburger

In Detroit and other large cities across the nation are concentrated families whose children are severely hampered in their schooling by a complex of community, home, and school conditions. To engage the total problem faced by urban educators, we shall make a brief foray into the social pathology which produced it.

INTRODUCTION TO THE PROBLEM[1]

Change in the population of the inner cores of most large cities has created areas where the majority of children have extraordinary needs which the public schools are not prepared to meet. Where once the inner city population was typically "all kinds," it has now become typically stratified. The majority of upper and middle income urbanites have moved to the suburbs or to the outer rings of the city. The population that remains is predominantly unskilled or semi-skilled, low-income, racial and ethnic minorities. When representatives of other strata moved out, the vacuum was filled by southern-Appalachian white and southern Negro in-migrants similar in many ways to the low-income minority groups that had remained in the inner city.

Numbers of the city's manufacturing and service industries have followed the upper- and middle-income exodus. What remains is the glowing downtown section, a great multi-story civic and merchandising complex, serviced by expressways and surrounded by miles of slums and "transitional" or "gray" areas, still containing a few pockets of more affluent residential areas and high-rent apartment districts.

From these slums and transitional areas come one-third of the more than 3,000,000 children now enrolled in America's fourteen largest school systems. Many of them have limited backgrounds, and most of them are concentrated in the inner city schools.

The families of these children live for the most part in low-cost public housing, or in overcrowded, substandard, multiple-dwellings of every type—or in single- and two-family homes in neighborhoods which are, in reality, transitional. Some of these neighborhoods are not yet slums, but their people are often in difficult straits, and the children reflect this in school.

The families of these children may have resided in Detroit for many years;

[1] Extracted and paraphrased from Charles Mitchell (3). Mr. Mitchell is the Project Writer for the Detroit Great Cities School Improvement Project.

but most came during and immediately after the Second World War to fill industry's needs for unskilled labor, or are very recent in-migrants from rural areas, particularly rural areas of the southern states, who shifted from a land of no current or foreseeable opportunity to a land of possible—maybe—opportunity.

The in-migrant comes into a portion of the total community which is fragmented and uncohesive, which lacks trained leadership and organization, and which physically reflects the low, inconsistent income and the lack of information and skills of its inhabitants. Here, whatever booms or economic upturns may occur in other places, depression seldom ceases. A job is a will-o'-the-wisp affair.

The family of the child with limited background may have many meritable standards and values. Even when its material well-being is limited to basic necessities, the family may be close-knit with love and caring.

But always, there is a common denominator: not enough. Not enough income, information, and skills to get along successfully; no precedent for success; insufficiencies of many sorts. The child reflects this. He is poorly prepared and poorly motivated for school. School has never seemed important to his family or to him. Obviously there are some significant adjustments to be made.

With a sufficiency of income, information, motivation, and time—in short, in an ideal situation—urban life adjustment might evolve quite pleasantly. But the situation is poor, and many children have little to do except, as one teacher's report put it, "think about the hills of home, go to school each day unprepared and purposeless, and be 'sick to mah stomach from the gas stove' (quote from child) that heats a three-room flat."

The parents of these children are not against education. At worst they see no need for it, are indifferent. Many have hopes and ambitions for their children which involve obtaining a good education. They are glad if their child does well in school, but they often have little formal education themselves, know little about studies or how children learn. They feel that they cannot, in their lack of success, understand how to help the child succeed.

The child with limited background has normal intelligence. He is not different in this respect. He can grow up in school studies and in his life if reached and interested by what the school offers. And yet, the typical child with limited background in the typical classroom is indifferent and purposeless, a poor communicator who does not respond to normal teaching methods and subject matter. His capabilities remain unrealized.

Why?

The traditional responsibilities of school staff and objectives of school services are based upon a uniform "Successful American" social and economic pattern and do not obtain effectively to the non-uniform social and economic patterns which characterize the neighborhoods from which these children come.

The typical school cannot compensate for the various lacks in the lives of children with limited backgrounds. The typical school does not provide these reinforcements to school learning which, in a stable, middle-income area, are normally provided each child by his home and out-of-school life.

Many of these reinforcements are intangible. They include: an acceptable self-image; knowledge of essentials such as nutrition and health; an implicit sense of identification with a stable family in a stable neighborhood; security and freedom from want, both material and emotional; the self-confidence and motivation to achieve which rub off on the child who is surrounded by things and involved in experiences which are accepted both *at home* and *in school* either as symbols of success or significant achievements.

Such positive factors are essential in some form in the growing up of a child. If they are insufficient or lacking, and no compensation is made for them, then the child's ability to learn in school is impeded or lost.

It seems reasonable that the educator should be concerned with *all* that affects the child he is trying to educate, and in fact teachers and administrators often informally cross traditional lines and do "unorthodox" things to help children who are not doing well in school. But except through the attendance officer, the public schools, especially the urban public schools, seldom make official organized attempts to alter the "other lives" of children. If the family does little to help prepare the child for life, and the cultural environment of the child is limited and negative, then the one force left to do the necessary shaping is the school. It must provide more for the child than it normally would, at the same time attempting, with other community services, to revive the family's positive influence and to introduce portions of our culture and our society which tend to equalize the child's limited and negative environment.

In truth, we must say with Harold Taylor that,

The educator must go to the root of the matter, and he must deal with the whole child. The root is in the social and economic conditions in which the child exists. The educator must deal bluntly with those who support the residential segregation of the colored people and the poor. He must fight those who wish to profit in real estate at the expense of the children. He must think of education as a total process, in which the conditions of society deeply affect the child's mind, the level of his achievement, and the range of his possibilities. The curriculum, the classroom, the guidance office are instruments for dealing with one part of the child's life. But they do not and cannot function in a social vacuum.

Nor is it permissible any longer to say that the social environment of the child is not the problem of the educator, that it belongs to city planners, social workers, economists, housing experts, or society. It belongs to everyone, but most of all to the educator. The educator is not a personnel manager, an administrator, an organization man, although his work involves organizing, managing, and administering. He is a social and intellectual leader, and he begins to exercise his leadership when he recognizes the conditions of his society and brings to bear upon them the force of a humanitarian philosophy (5).

THE GREAT CITIES PROJECTS

The superintendents and board-of-education members of the fourteen largest city school systems met in 1957 in Atlantic City, New Jersey, to share their concerns about the problems of education in large urban areas. Their first cooperative exploration took them into the World of Work and a careful study of current and prospective youth employment opportunities. A vocational education specialist was appointed to coordinate the efforts of the Great Cities in this area. The World of Work study continues, and findings are being implemented in programs seen as appropriate by each of the cities.

Another difficulty shared by large-city educators, that of limited fiscal resources, has led to a cooperative study of fiscal policy. If educators are to equalize and expand educational opportunity, or simply to hold ground against the press of increased enrollment, from where is the money to come? Again, a consultant was secured, and along with staff persons from each city, began to study possible resources and to formulate recommendations for revision of Great Cities fiscal policies.

The third problem shared by the large-city educators was that of educating the increasing numbers of children with limited backgrounds. After intensive analysis of the factors which indicate educational deprivation—low achievement levels, lack of kindergarten experience, poor attendance, high truancy, over-agedness in grade, high rate of failure, and the range of home and community deprivation—the Great Cities teams developed what they called "The Central Hypothesis." This hypothesis states that the problems of children with limited backgrounds can be effectively and economically solved by:

1. Development of a program of education adapted to the needs of these children,
2. Modifications in the organizational patterns within the school,
3. Proper selection and utilization of personnel,
4. Improved utilization of instructional equipment and materials,
5. Involvement of parents and of the community in the educational program.

Under the leadership of Dr. S. M. Brownell, superintendent of schools, and the direction of Dr. Carl Byerly, Detroit began testing this hypothesis in September, 1959. Detroit's pilot project, involving three schools in the central city, was the first demonstration project among the Great Cities. Further, the pilot demonstration project was financed entirely by the Detroit Board of Education. In July, 1960, the Ford Foundation provided

financial support to the Detroit Project and to several other great cities as well. This initial one-year grant made it possible to "buy time," by intensifying project activities and expanding project coverage from three to seven schools. The Ford Foundation extended the initial Detroit grant for an additional three years in July, 1961. Grant extensions have also been made to other Great Cities Projects.

The Great Cities teams of superintendents and board-of-education members have recently formed the Research Council of the Great Cities Program for School Improvement to coordinate the various activities under their jurisdiction. The most current result of their concern is an investigation of pre- and in-service education of teachers. The Research Council intends to find and recommend more effective ways to prepare teachers for the demanding work of teaching not only the children with limited backgrounds, but all children.

Thus, the Great Cities are engaged in cooperative study and action programs designed to solve the many problems peculiar to large city school systems. They intend to develop, and to prove effective, a *total educational program* for large urban areas.

Although many of the difficulties encountered by urban schools ensue from "urban blight" and its effect on children and families, it is clearly recognized that educational planning needs to be for all children and all schools, and not only for the children and the schools in depressed urban areas. Certainly the central hypothesis, put forward by Great Cities educators as a viable solution for the problem of providing a good education for the child with limited background, can be used to provide a good education for all children.

THE DETROIT PROJECT—WORKING TOWARD MORE EFFECTIVE EDUCATION

The objective of the Detroit Great Cities School Improvement Project is to increase the competence of children with limited backgrounds. By competence, we mean not academic competence alone, but competence of the "whole child" in the Harold Taylor meaning of the phrase —social competence, urban living competence, and job, or work skill competence—including the ability to learn new job skills if needed. In addition to the five points of the great cities hypothesis, the Detroit Program has these special emphases:

1. A program of teacher-school-community improvement is more effective if all levels of a school system serving an area (kindergarten through grade 12) are involved. Therefore, the seven schools in the Detroit Project include three elementary schools (kindergarten through grade 6); one elementary school (kindergarten through grade 8); two junior high schools (grades 7 and 9); and one senior high school (grades 10 through 12).

2. The program should be one which can be financed within the resources of the school budget over a long period, if it can be shown (as we anticipate) that the results of the project warrant the program's continuation and extension into other areas of the city whose school populations have similar problems and needs. Therefore, the yearly budget for the five years of the demonstration project represents an increase of less than 10 per cent above normal costs per pupil for the city. Thus, the budget, including the Ford Foundation grant (30 per cent of the total budget), is realistic in terms of

the fiscal support expected for schools in the Detroit area.

3. Any program designed to solve the problem of educating the child with limited background must operate intensively for several years. Solution of the educational problem involves making long-term changes in family and community attitudes and behavior, as well as changes in a more-or-less immediate nature in the pupil-teacher relationships and services available to the pupil. Time is needed to assure that systems of change shall be functional and lasting in effect. Therefore, Detroit's is a six-year project in the three pilot project schools, and a five-year project in the remaining four. Further, there is a commitment to evaluate the working effect of the project far beyond the actual completion date of its program.

With regard to the Great Cities hypothesis, the Detroit projects makes use of several major approaches to the solution of the problems of educating children with limited backgrounds.

One major approach is our work with teachers. Improvement of schooling depends to a great extent upon more effective teaching. Therefore, we strive to modify the perceptions of the teachers of children with limited backgrounds as this perception relates to these children, their community, and their curriculum. Many teachers initially perceive these three negatively; that is, in the light of their own experiential backgrounds. Teachers may bring to their work a rigid value system different than that of the populace of depressed urban areas—a value system, for instance, which presupposes certain limits on the intelligence and ability of the child with limited background. Some teachers have been reared in a different socio-economic situation, and have difficulty in objectively assessing the child with limited background. Other teachers have, through their profession, moved up the socio-economic ladder, and may possibly (and paradoxically) reject the all-too-familiar values of the children they teach. In any case, it is not unusual to find in the classroom a critical need for belief in the universal learning ability of humankind, regardless of socio-economic condition.

Our first attempt to bring about appropriate changes was through a series of workshop experiences. Competent consultants were secured in many disciplines: education, sociology, social work, and psychology. Our experience leads us to believe that very few significant changes in the behavior of teachers take place as a result of listening to experts. Those teachers who were tuned in to hear the expert believed and behaved in terms of what they had heard. Those teachers who were not tuned in to hear the experts did not change their behavior to any noticeable degree as a result of hearing them. The key to modification of behavior seems to be involvement.

Our workshops and in-service experiences have, therefore, been structured around local school curriculum problems and have usually involved only a single school staff. We have found that curricula vary from school to school, from community to community, and from school staff to school staff. To achieve the kind of involvement that brings positive change, *each* school staff must look seriously at its unique community, the unique problems of its youth, and its own unique strengths and weaknesses as a staff. Then the school staff may search for appropriate curricular and organizational modifications to strengthen its own school situation.

Our attempts to assist staffs to do this have taken several forms. We have provided workshop experiences through the local university. If teachers and administrators wish to have a course for credit toward an advanced degree or a number of hours beyond the Bachelor's or Master's, they may pay tuition to the university for the workshop experience. If they wish to take part in the workshop but do not wish the credit, the Detroit Great Cities Project pays their tuition so that they may audit the course.

Other local school-curriculum workshops have taken place on Saturdays, and also during the summer months. As a part of the Detroit school policy, teachers involved have been paid for their time on Saturdays and during the summer. Furthermore, some released time has been devoted to in-service education. Indications are that more released time is now an essential need.

As a result of these in-service experiences, some organizational and curriculum changes have been made. We have instituted the non-graded primary in two elementary schools. Block-time and core classes are being held in the junior high schools. Team teaching is being tried in two of the schools.

Curriculum modifications come more slowly. One significant curriculum change has taken place in our early elementary reading materials—but not without difficulty. It has long been felt that children might read with greater facility if the material with which they were dealing was more nearly related to their own real backgrounds. Negro youth, for example, rarely have an opportunity to see a Negro child illustrated in the little picture books with which they learn to read. Through a series of writing workshops we set out to build a series of pre-primers which would focus on the life of a working-class family, living in a typical, racially mixed, urban neighborhood. In spite of the sophistication of the writing committee members, we now know first hand the perils of revolutionary primer writing. The artist doing illustrations for the series depicted some typical housekeeping situations (brooms leaning in the corner, a kitchen sink with exposed pipes beneath it) and this—at least relative to other pre-primers, which do not treat the realities of housekeeping quite as fully—was taken simply as poor housekeeping, and thereby as a derogation of the Negro since this was the home of a Negro family.

The first pre-primer was only one-third the length of a normal pre-primer, because we wanted each child to have the satisfaction of completing a book in a short time. Thus, we inadvertently left the father out of the first pre-primer; indeed, we did not even refer to him. This was also interpreted as a derogation, not only of the Negro family depicted, but of Negro families in general. Finally, we called the little-boy hero of the series "Sammy." It was an unfortunate choice, since it was seen by middle-class Negro families as "stereotype by insinuation."

Having gleaned some important lessons from this experience, we expanded our primer writing committee with a number of consultants, both lay and professional, and revised the series. The first three pre-primers of this series were available in four-color reproduction in September of 1962, for experimental testing.

Other minor curriculum changes have taken place at different levels. We have produced some units for block-time classes at the secondary level, which have been found to be very useful throughout the entire school system for block-time classes.

Perhaps the only significant change in curriculum is what happens when the individual teacher closes the door of her classroom. Assuming the requisite skills in teaching the basic materials, the teacher's attitude is the most crucial factor.

At this point in our project, we conceive the formula that teacher-expectations have surprising impact on pupil-achievement. Indeed we might even say that teacher expectations have a similar impact on pupil intelligence scores. The teacher who expects achievement, who has hope for the educability of his pupils, indeed conveys this through every nuance and subtlety of his behavior. The teacher who conveys hopelessness for the educability of his children usually does so without ever really verbalizing such an attitude—at least, in front of his pupils.

With regard to expectations of pupil ability to learn, a significant experiment was done recently by Robert Rosenthal and Kermit L. Fode of the University of North Dakota. In a carefully controlled experiment, twelve senior division students in experimental psychology were assigned a group of five albino rats for running through a maze ten times a day for five days. Although the rats were randomly selected, each student was informed that the rats were either "maze-bright" or "maze-dull."

Results indicated that on three of the five days and for the experiment as a whole, E's [experimenters] believing their S's [subjects] to be bright obtained performance from them significantly superior to that obtained by E's believing their S's to be dull. The S's believed to be bright appeared to be learning the problem while those believed to be dull did not. These results occurred in spite of the fact that on the level of verbal report *both* groups of E's wanted their S's to perform well. In addition, a research assistant following the identical experimental procedure, was able to obtain, without "cheating," performance from her S's superior even to that obtained by E's believing their S's were bright. Comparing the degree of correlation between what each E specifically expected to obtain from his S's and what he actually did obtain from them for the "Bright" and "Dull" groups suggested that these groups were about equally biased although, of course, in opposite directions (4).

Thus, even when dealing with non-human subjects, the experimenter's expectations seem most significant in determining the performance of the subject. Certainly the expectations of the teacher for her pupils can determine, particularly in depressed-urban-area schools, the school survival or non-survival of the youth. If nothing else, teacher expectations affect the time spent in preparing to teach, the amount of real concern for individual students, and the degree of "soul" the teacher gives to his work.

The involvement of an almost total staff, including administration, would seem then to be essential for innovation in curriculum, and for modification of behavior to insure truly effective teaching. We obviously cannot expect anything approximating 100 per cent involvement of staff, but the nearer we come to this ideal, and to the contagion of enthusiasm which results from it, the greater the possibility of creating the milieu in which youth, particularly disadvantaged youth, can learn.

In order that teachers of children with limited backgrounds may maintain enthusiasm for teaching, and hope for the educability of their children, they must be continually reinforced. The teacher needs adequate resources to combat the corrosive influences of emotional and physical poverty with which many of his students live day in and day out. The teacher needs help to teach effectively in spite of the inadequate facilities which often seem typical of inner city schools.

High transiency rates and the generally low achievement of pupils beset by out-of-school difficulties which carry over demonstrably into the classroom can overwhelm the most conscientious teacher.

The Detroit Project does provide some reinforcement to teachers. Additional personnel, whose duties are discussed at length later in this paper, provide some aid in working with children whose reading, speech and arithmetic disabilities are pronounced, in developing stronger ties and understanding between families and the school, and so forth. Referrals of children with physical or emotional difficulties can be made more readily by the classroom teacher in Great Cities Project schools. After school and evening programs, with clubs, remedial and enrichment classes, and recreational activities tend to provide a more beneficient climate for the child than street play might provide, and to orient the child more specifically to the school and the teacher than would otherwise be so. A full summer-school program involving a large percentage of the school population not only provides interesting learning and recreational experiences for the child, but helps him to carry over what he has learned, in behavior as well as in actual knowledge, from one school year into the next.

One more concrete means of reinforcement is the addition to the general fund of each school a sum ranging from $350 to $450 to be used by the staff for the purchase of small supplies and materials which are not available through normal requisition channels. Another is the provision of funds and transportation for an additional four to five hundred bus trips to farms, parks, museums, and the like for the seven schools in the project.

Significant though these additions may

be, they are basically without purpose if the teacher does not have the opportunity in his classroom to be experimental, to be innovative, to be free to do those things which are important for the children. Such freedom to do what is needed is there, or is lamentably lacking, in accordance with the administrative style of the principal of the school. Is the school's administrative staff restrictive or non-restrictive, authoritarian or democratic, legalistic or expeditious? These are knotty questions to ask, difficult questions to answer, but they are important since they are germane to the nature of the teaching and learning processes which exist in each school. It has often been stated that the most important single individual in any community is the elementary school principal. I would extend this to all levels of school administration, elementary and secondary. To illustrate, the most obvious deterrent to enthusiastic and imaginative teaching is the authoritarian who sees his school as an armed camp which admits a school population in the morning, regiments them until early afternoon, and then sends them home, five days a week. More insidious and difficult is the legalist, who represses his staff, who processes each decision with perfect logic and imperfect premises, who operates exclusively through a tight chain of command, who so dampens enthusiasm and subverts innovation that any external assistance provides only short-term palliative results.

Documentation of the statements made above regarding teacher attitude and administrative behavior is very difficult. We have considerable evidence to support these statements. However, because of the experimental nature of the project there is need to preserve a modicum of security since release of research data could indeed contaminate the results of the experiment, particularly with our control schools. Some of the methodology used in our research will be discussed later in this paper.

WORK WITH PARENTS AND COMMUNITY

The second primary focus of our attention is upon the parents and the community. Once again, this is a question of involvement. Parents who are not involved, who do not know what is taking place in the school, can certainly not reinforce what the school is doing with their children. We also see a need to involve parents and the community so that we may raise the aspirations of the parents and their children with regard to academic and social achievement. Parents in depressed urban areas typically stay away from schools. They stay away from school because their own experiences have been either unpleasant or short-lived or both. They are fearful of the institution of the school and they lack information about what is taking place in the school. They do not typically join organizations and therefore do not normally attend parent-group meetings, do not participate in adult-education classes—they generally avoid all school contacts.

We have tried to make our Great Cities Project schools true community schools. This means that the schools must necessarily be open from eight o'clock in the morning until late at night. One of our first approaches to parents was to ask them to tell us the kinds of experiences they would like to have in the afternoons and evenings for themselves and for their children. The parents so contacted were normally those who were more articulate and more solvent economically and who had higher aspirations for themselves and their youth. The so-called hard-to-reach parents were not particularly interested regardless of what the school might offer. Using those parents who could and would respond to our inquiries, we first provided free clubs and classes which were of the upgrading nature. These classes were designed to help parents gain more skills. Often parents had unrealistic expectations about these classes, believing that jobs would become available to them as a result of their classwork. A few have gained some skills through these classes and have been able to obtain, if not better employment, at least techniques which enhanced their leadership potential and communications skills. These first classes included shorthand, speech, typing, sewing, millinery, cake decorating, and the like. The parents then told us that such classes were fine, but asked if it might be possible to provide some classes in reading and arithmetic so that parents could refresh these skills and help their children in their studies. This we did.

Even more crucial than these skill classes were the informal groups, clubs, and classes which were organized around parents' newly expressed needs. Simply the opportunity to meet together, to plan for their youngsters, to take short-term enrichment classes, to learn how to budget, how to prepare food, how to repair furniture, to be more efficient and effective in household tasks and family relations—all of these provided the adults with opportunities to bolster self-esteem and to raise aspirations for themselves and their children.

These clubs and their classes have been taught by teachers on both a voluntary and paid basis and by lay persons from the local community and from the total metropolitan area. In addition, many youth from the community have been hired as baby-sitters, teacher's aides and assistants for afternoon and evening classes and clubs. Altogether there are more than two hundred after-school clubs and classes for youth and adults in the seven schools.

Each school has had to organize after-school and evening activities in terms of its own community and the needs of that community. Some of the schools have put a greater emphasis on the enrichment programs for youth in the afternoon, others on adult programs in the evening. The greatest difficulty in involvement of youth and adults has naturally come at the secondary level, where the ambivalence of youth toward their parents and the size of the school attendance area mitigate against parental participation in school functions.

We have reached not only the "parents who go to PTA meetings"; we have been able, through the skills of some of our additional personnel, to involve a great many of the so-called hard-to-reach parents. The number of people involved in these after-school and evening activities varies, because of the short-term duration of some of the classes and clubs, but it averages between fifteen hundred and two thousand youth and adults each week.

One of the dangers inherent in such involvement of parents is the over-involvement of certain parents. We found that many of our adults would attend as many as four and five evenings a week, with the result that our program tended to fragment rather than bind families closer together. We have gone a long way in solving this problem by scheduling family nights, when the entire family participates in the available activities. We further restrict the number of evenings any family may be involved. We have also experienced some difficulty as a result of the hiring of local people. The moment that one hires people from the local community, one gives them a status which then raises them above their peers and sometimes causes a degree of rejection and considerable resentment of their new leadership capacity.

A further difficulty is the tendency to develop "programs for program's sake" rather than in terms of the needs of the community. Competition often sets in between schools and results in the scheduling of classes without any inquiry into the needs, expressed and otherwise, of the local school community.

One additional hazard that is very real in this community-school sort of operation in urban depressed areas is the danger of making the parents too dependent on the school. Parents must become dependent on the school initially, if they are to be involved at all. They must see the school as a resource for helping them with their personal and community problems. This project will not succeed if it does not develop an indigenous leadership, which assumes responsibility on its own for the problems of individuals and the local community. We have no intention of relieving parents of their responsibilities as parents, but we want them to ask for help so that they can find ways of working out the solutions to their problems themselves. We attempt in this manner to revive the positive parent-child relationship which is so often lacking in the disadvantaged family.

In order to accomplish both the teacher and parent reinforcement, we must have additional help for the regular staff of each school. This we have provided by adding three additional personnel to each of the school staffs: a school-community agent, a full-time visiting teacher, and a full-time coaching teacher or language arts consultant.

THE SCHOOL-COMMUNITY AGENT

Theoretically, the school-community agent should be a trained social worker with experience in both community organization and group-work. We were not able to achieve this ideally, but have some persons with this background and others with professional training (usually in education) and considerable experience in community organization and group-work activities. The school-community agent is, simply enough, a liaison between the community and the school. This person interprets to the community the functions of the school and interprets to the staff of the school the realities of the community. One of the agent's most important functions is to work with organized block clubs, community councils, and parent groups, if these exist, and to help organize such groups if they do not exist. In addition, we have asked these agents to assume responsibility for the after-school and evening programs for youth and adults. Often these two roles are in serious conflict. The administrative and supervisory functions which are part of the after-school and evening programs do not allow the school-community agent the freedom he requires to become the detached worker; a role which we have found is essential to successful organization of a fragmented and uncohesive depressed-area neighborhood. Further, the administrative style of each school can limit the agent to a program director's capacity or free him to become a detached expert doing constructive work in the neighborhood.

The visiting teacher is the school social worker. This person has had specific training in the case-work methodology and operates primarily with children and the parents of children who have crucial school-adjustment problems. The visiting teacher is normally assigned in the Detroit schools; but she is usually assigned to six or more schools and spends perhaps half a day a week in each school attempting to handle an unrealistic case load in this fragmented fashion. In the Great Cities Project, the visiting teacher is assigned full time and is thus able to establish roots in the neighborhood and to work closely with the specific problems of the school and the community, its youth and parents. She is able to deal more successfully with fewer cases, to know and understand the school staff and politics, and to become identified with her school and hence with parents. As we examine the role of the visiting teacher in the new five-day-a-week involvement in a single school, we are asking additional questions about the training and certification of these persons. A Michigan law requires that visiting teachers be certified as teachers and, in addition, have Master's degrees in social work with emphasis in case work. We are questioning the necessity for the teaching certificate and are examining the possibility of a combination case and group-work training because the needs of the clients often dictate group-work rather than case-work therapy.

The coaching teacher is actually a language-arts teacher who is performing special remedial functions with children who are retarded in reading. She often conducts small classes ranging from five to fifteen children working on the particular skill deficiencies of children. Once again, the coaching teacher's role is changing. She often finds it more effective to work less specifically with small groups of children and more with total staff in helping all teachers gain the necessary skills to work with the reading deficiencies of children regardless of the subject matter area.

We have seen some startling results show up in achievement in the relatively short period of a semester or a year as a result of this individualized attention given to students by the coaching teachers. We cannot make any claims about this progress in achievement until we have a look at it over a long period to see if there is a retention of the gain.

SCHOOL-AGENCY COOPERATION

In addition to the use of these specialized personnel we have also had intensive public and private agency involvement. The success of any community-school venture depends in large measure on the concentrated use of available public and private agency personnel and resources. The Detroit Great Cities School Improvement Project has therefore developed these programs:

1. In cooperation with the Neighborhood Service Organization and the Detroit Behavior Project, day camps were conducted at one of our schools during the summer of 1961 for fifty-five emotionally disturbed children from the project schools.

2. We have used the YMCA and YWCA programs and facilities. In addition to the use of their busses and physical facilities, we have many YMCA and YWCA groups meeting in our after-school program with agency, school, and lay personnel involved in leadership capacities.

3. We have shared facilities and personnel with the Detroit Parks and Recreation Department. We use one of their large recreation centers, and they use the swimming pools in the school buildings. The Detroit Parks and Recreation Department, a municipal agency separate from the schools, has also provided new programs in project schools where no recreation program had existed before.

4. We have increased the school's use of public library facilities, by shuttle-bussing children in "library caravans" to inner-city libraries. Parents served as assistant librarians on these ventures.

5. We are conducting intensive research into the relationship between physical and nutritional needs of children and the learning process, in cooperation with the Detroit Department of Health, which is a separate city agency. The health examination

clinic, which was established in one of our schools by the Pilot Club of Detroit, contains all of the equipment and facilities necessary to do a complete physical examination of the school population. The Detroit Department of Health is providing funds to reimburse the examining pediatricians.

6. We have had continuing contacts with local churches as an integral part of the school-community agents' function.

Often in urban depressed areas there is a tendency for churches and both public and private agencies to move their services from that area to other areas where progress is more easily identified. The agencies which remain in the depressed area often provide overlapping services to the hard-to-reach parents of the community. This leads to the duplication of financial aid and conflicting advice being given to families.

As a result, the Detroit Great Cities Program has developed a theoretical rationale clarifying the role of the school as it relates to the agencies and social work methodologies. This rationale is dynamic, in that it changes as new insights and role definitions develop.

We feel that the public schools, particularly the elementary schools, provide the structures in which social-work functions may best be performed. The encapsulated, or limited and defined, elementary-school *population* and the inclusion within elementary school *boundaries* of a relatively fixed population, offer one of the best field situations presently available. The school has other assets. It is established, it has access to the home, and its records for each child will automatically provide information on a large percentage of the population in the school's boundaries. Such boundaries do include the families of parochial and private students and citizens whose children

have gone through school. In these cases, even though the social work contact is not as readily made, at least the boundaries are fixed and provide a localized area for social work operation. The elementary school, therefore, could provide the basis of operations for case-work, group-work and community-work functions. These functions could be operated by school personnel or by public, private, and agency personnel. Yet at the present time, exclusive of this project, Detroit's schools are involved only in limited casework through the Visiting Teacher Program.

The schools provide little in the way of group-work functions. The one best example of group-work therapy presently in the Detroit Schools is the School Behavior Project which uses "Action Teams" of school and agency personnel in work with disturbed children referred by the school. Otherwise, the only existent group-work functions are basically of a recreational and instructional nature and performed, after school, both by Detroit Public School personnel and by agency people from many organizations and institutions. In spite of the school's ideal locus, community organization functions are left almost entirely in the hands of non-school personnel, with the rare exception of the sophisticated administrator who operates in this area to a limited extent.

The Great Cities School Improvement Project is embarked upon activities in all three aspects of social-work functions. With regard to the community organization aspect, the community agent already serves as an organizer in each of the local communities. Thus the school-community agent, particularly the agent in the elementary school, can be a most effective instrument for the performance of the crucial community organization activities as the project develops from its demonstration stage into a program for all schools in depressed urban areas.

With regard to the aspect of group-work services of a recreational and instructional nature, the schools can fill many of the needs of a local community. Adult evening programs offering appropriate up-grading, training, and retraining courses might be conducted on a non-fee or "ability-to-pay" basis in the high schools and junior high schools. At all school levels, but with emphasis at the elementary, parent and youth groups and clubs, meeting informally, could partially fulfill the project's objectives by increasing parent reinforcement of the school program and raising the aspirations of the participants. In addition to organizing and operating these informal groups in the schools, the school-community agent can act as the catalyst in bringing to the schools those group-work services of a recreational, crafts, and character-building nature as already provided by agencies in the community. Further, the school could serve in a coordinating capacity with the agencies which have facilities within the school area, so that services would cover the school evenly without duplication and wasteful expenditure of time and energy.

With regard to the aspect of group work used in rehabilitation of disturbed children, it is obvious that competent, trained group workers and therapists would be more effective than school personnel. In addition, the school setting is one in which most disturbed youngsters have met defeat and failure, and often presents a block to the progress which might be made with group therapy. It may be appropriate, therefore, to use existing neighborhood facilities other than the school building. The school team needs to be involved in these kinds of activities, however, in much the same

way as it is involved presently in the work of the School Behavior Project. The school team would continue to be a source of referrals to the therapy group.

The case-work methodology has already been mentioned in the discussion of the role of the visiting teacher. We feel that the full-time utilization of this school social worker in the Great Cities Project schools adds real strength to this dimension of each school's social work functions.

The implication might be drawn, from this emphasis upon a rationale for the school as a social-work agency, that we have a dream that the school should be all things to all people. The answer to this is emphatic: certainly not! The school must concern itself primarily with the academic enhancement of children. Yet, if the school is to prepare all youth for the world of work, and for independent social, economic, and political lives, the school needs to examine its traditional role in the light of past successes and failures. Who can say we have really succeeded with educationally disadvantaged youth in the past? It would seem that both school and society must face, and work to disarm, the "social dynamite" referred to by Dr. Conant in his *Slums and Suburbs*.

Here, the implication stands: it is very possible that the school must be more effective if it expects to produce competent, well-educated young adults. The rationale for incorporation of the social-work methodologies into the school's program is an attempt to enhance the school's effectiveness in an area of great importance, particularly in depressed urban communities, where the effects of a deprived out-of-school life impinge upon the child's in-school life, and limit his ability to learn.

We propose, along with renewed and

creative efforts with staff and curriculum, the intensive use of the social work methodologies as a part of the school's daily operation. Acceptance of the concept of the school as a social work agency affords a new opportunity to do preventive rather than remedial work with problems of youth and adults in the local community; with the goal of reinforcing the academic competence of youth. There is no intent to suggest that the schools should or could do this alone. Indeed, cooperation between school and agency is the only feasible solution. The schools, however, are in a strategic position to be the case-finding agency, the referral agency, and the catalytic agency to those groups organized to render appropriate services. In addition, the school is a public facility which needs to be utilized—by individuals and agencies and by the community for the common good.

EVALUATION

The Detroit Project is unique in that a full-time evaluator, Dr. William M. Rasschaert, has been assigned to its staff. In initiating the project in Detroit, it was recognized that programs with demonstrated effectiveness should be continued and extended to schools currently uninvolved in the project—with the stipulation that an expanded program could not exceed an annual 10 per cent per student cost increase. Not every part of the project program will remain in use. To meet cost limits, project staff must analyze statistics and data computed and filed during the five-year run, and use its findings to establish a priority list, top-rating the elements of the project program which had the most significant effect in increasing school success of the child with limited background. Recommendations from this priority list will become the program

used in extended project activities.

In the original evaluation design, two types of control schools were used:

Control Type A:

These four schools (two elementary, one junior high, and one senior high school, are in generally the same geographic area of the city as are the experimental schools. The achievement and ability levels of the pupils are quite similar to those of pupils in the experimental schools.

Control Type B:

In this group there are five schools (three elementary, one junior high, and one senior high school) and these are located in obviously different geographic parts of Detroit than the project schools. As measured by Detroit city-wide testing programs, the achievement and ability scores of the pupils in these schools consistently reflect higher levels of attainment.

As part of the total evaluation design, the project staff has prepared a document entitled *A Plan for Evaluating Major Activities in Great Cities School Improvement Programs.* Nine categories of teaching-learning, school-community, and pupil-parent-teacher activities have been considered in terms of the specific (1) nature of each activity, (2) suggested treatment of data accruing from such measurement. Among the broad categories into which all activities are ordered according to their function in the program are pupil achievement, attitude changes, behavioral changes, evaluation of teaching materials and techniques, school-community relations, and school health. Activities in each of these nine categories receive careful evaluation as we attempt to determine to what degree each activity is effective relative to the total program. For instance, in the category of behavioral change, which is most effective, the workshop at which experts speak or the workshop which involves school staff in planning curriculum change? And, relative to the total program, which has proved more effective in educating the child, modification of teacher perception or a more intensive school health program? In other words, where do we put our money to get results?

The Great Cities School Improvement Program has taken advantage of data made available by the various city-wide testing programs—the *Iowa Test of Basic Skills, the SCAT-STEP,* and the various intelligence testing programs at several grade levels. In addition, results of achievement and intelligence tests administered to project and control school pupils with tests other than those used city-wide will continue to supply us with more and different kinds of measurement data. Examples of such additional tests are the *California Achievement Tests* and the *Lorge-Thorndike Tests of Intelligence, Verbal and Non-Verbal.*

In addition to comparing pupils in project schools to pupils in Control Types A and B schools, we also intend to "follow" project-school children and measure their individual growth in ability and achievement areas over the next three years. Similarly, we are evaluating the children who attend our summer schools to attempt to determine if this type of enrichment effects improvement over a full school year of pupil-work. In terms of evaluation, the over-all pattern of this project will include two methods of looking at results with children:

1. Measurement of pupil growth in project schools as interpreted relative to two different control groups; one group in a depressed area very similar to that in which the project schools are located, and one group in an area which is very substantial and middle-class.

2. Examination of growth in selected characteristics from one period to another; this could mean using subpopulations and doing individual and group measurements or using the case study method with selected individuals.

In addition to the above, school and sociological base-line data have been collected regarding attendance, failure, lack of kindergarten experience, delinquency and youth and adult crime, and population density and transiency in each school's service area. A *Pupil Information and Attitude Inventory* was also devised by project teachers and administrators and administered to the children in the project schools from grades 4 through 12. This survey, after compilation of the data, is a part of each child's cumulative record.

Two instruments have been devised to examine the crucial factors of teacher information and teacher attitude. The *Teacher Information Questionnaire* was constructed by a group of sixteen classroom teachers in the project schools. This survey has been administered to all the teachers in the experimental and control schools. Frequency distribution and second-order runs with selected questionnaire items have been tabulated at the University of Michigan Computer Center.

Dr. Henry Meyer and Miss Donna MacLeod, from the University of Michigan, School of Social Work, designed an instrument in 1959, entitled *Values Questionnaire,* for measuring the attitudes of social workers. In 1960, Drs. Meyer and Litwak and project staff members modified this instrument to make it appropriate for administration to approximately 750 experimental and control school teachers in the Detroit Great Cities Project. This modified instrument titled *What Do You Think About These Social Questions?* measures nine dimensions (see Table 1).

TABLE 1

Value Dimension Number	Value Dimension Title
I	Individual worth versus system goals
II	Personal liberty versus societal control
III	Group responsibility versus individual responsibility
IV	Security-satisfaction versus struggle-suffering-denial
V	Relativism-secularism versus absolutism-sacredness
VI	Innovation-change versus traditionalism
VII	Changeable human nature versus inherent human-fatalism
VIII	Diversity-heterogeneity versus consensus-homogeneity-conformity
IX	Interdependence versus individual autonomy

The values questionnaire's seventy-two questions, plus the information survey's eighteen questions, have been processed through the Computer Center at the University of Michigan. Although we can acknowledge that the data from these instruments have most significant implications for the project's program and perhaps for education in Detroit, any reporting of these data as such would tend to contaminate seriously the results of the projected post-tests, particularly in our control schools.

Indeed, the midpoint of a five-year demonstration project is an awkward time for reporting in detail the significant results of evaluation and research. Baseline data have been gathered and are in the process of being analyzed and interpreted. Yet we have only subjective evidence that we have increased the competence of particular individuals and groups of children, youth and adults.

We have data to indicate that IQ scores have been substantially increased in certain situations; that achievement scores have been materially affected by specialized coaching and enrichment programs; that parent participation in school and after-school programming is far beyond our expectations; that public and private agency involvement and cooperation is increasing rapidly as these agencies come to know the objectives of the project.

We know all these things, yet we do not know, at this point in time, the lasting effect of changes in IQ and achievement, nor the degree of reinforcement of the school by parents and agencies, nor the positive change in the aspirations of parents and of children. We know we are providing significant service to the children and the families of the children. But only depth evaluation over a sufficient period of time can tell us those aspects of our program which are appropriate for movement to school areas beyond the demonstration project.

In addition, therefore, to the evaluation procedures mentioned above, it is important that we examine in detail those larger educational and sociological aspects of the project which will be determinants in movement of the project through the school system. To assist us in the examination of three of these aspects, Dr. Eugene Litwak, School of

Social Work, University of Michigan, has prepared three working papers. These papers are:

1. "Notes on the Relationship Between Family, Educational Achievement and Good Citizenship," July 25, 1961.
2. "Notes on the Relationship Between Neighborhood, Educational Achievement, and Good Citizenship," July 31, 1961.
3. "Notes on the Relationship Between Administrative Behavior, Educational Achievement and Good Citizenship," August 22, 1961.

The concepts which have been delineated in these documents and reviewed and modified by project staff and Drs. Litwak and Meyer, will be tested in a research program involving the project elementary schools, two control schools and two elementary schools outside the project. With the financial support of the Detroit Area Study of the University of Michigan and funds from additional sources, interview schedules and questionnaires are being prepared and staff organized to test the hypothesis outlined in the working papers. As Dr. Litwak says.

The full and systematic exploration of these problems is a necessary prerequisete for setting up programs which will be meaningful to the Great Cities Improvement Project. The simultaneous consideration of all three memorandum involving family, neighborhood, and administrative behavior should eventually permit the establishment of better relations between school and community (2).

CONCLUSION

What are the "short-term" forecasts for the Great Cities Project in Detroit? It is believed that a considerably larger number of children attending project schools will leave them with positive self-images, higher goals, greater scholastic achievement, and improved citizenship; they are expected to be more adequately prepared for continuing school or going to work—independent rather than dependent citizens.

It should be stressed that the Detroit Great Cities Project is not unique in its premises or in its purposes. Individual teachers and schools in Detroit and across the nation are striving to meet the needs of the child with limited background. With little organized help, and no extra funds, their work has been done with dedication and enthusiasm. Such efforts are inspirational, but they are often a stopgap, and we cannot hope that they will resolve a dilemma which has grown to such proportions that it can be met only with concerted, total-community effort. Now, as the community becomes fully aware of wasted manpower, the hard core of unemployed, the high-school drop-out and his inability in most cases to compete for a place in today's overcrowded, skill-demanding job market, it will turn more and more to educators, first for explanations, and then for positive and workable solutions. And educators must be able to provide these solutions, by bridging the gap between what the schools now offer and what life with increasing technology and urbanization demands of an individual.

And that gap does exist. In spite of the fact that more youth are finishing high school and going on to college, increasing numbers of young men and women, including a good percentage of the most able and most intelligent youth, do not find what they need in school, do not learn, lose purpose and direction, and drop out. They are abetted by indecisive parents, tolerated by an apathetic community, often tacitly disestablished by the school.

Certainly we have a commitment as a society to these youth. We should live up to that commitment, preferably before the sad decision to drop out is made. We should consider ways to prevent this crisis. It is far more wasteful of human and fiscal resources to wait until rehabilitation is necessary; particularly when we know the ways we must go to reduce drastically the number of drop-outs, and to make schooling more effective as preparation for life.

Perhaps the most significant thing about the Detroit Great Cities Project, and similar projects in many great cities, is that it stands as a statement of need, as a formal attempt on the part of a superintendent and a board of education to establish a structure which has the funds, the personnel and the support to do a thorough job of proving that all children, no matter how difficult their situation may be, can be well-educated and positively motivated.

I will close with a short list of observations about youth in today's society, made by Professor Earl Kelley (1). He states that all adults, and educators in particular, need to keep always before them these points:

1. Our culture is in jeopardy unless we can adequately care for our young.
2. Our young people are all right when we get them. If all is not well with them, it is due to what has happened to them in an adult-managed world.
3. If youth have not been too badly damaged by the life that has been thrust upon them, they enjoy and desire a good society as much as we do.
4. In urban society, our young live under more difficult circumstances than they used to.
5. The amount of juvenile delinquency in any community is a measure of that community's lack of concern for its young.
6. There is really no valid, responsible place in our urban communities for youth. They are a displaced segment of our society.
7. A place must be made for them and it seems to me that the only feasible place is the school.

It is our hope that the Detroit Great Cities School Improvement Project, in consultation and coordination with other Great Cities projects, can make schools in depressed urban areas the really "feasible place" for youth to grow to independent competent citizenship.

REFERENCES

1. Kelley, Earl C., *In Defense of Youth*, Englewood Cliffs, N.J.: Prentice-Hall, 1962, p. 145.
2. Litwak, Eugene, "Notes on Relationships Between Administrative Behavior, Educational Achievement, and Good Citizenship," mimeographed working paper, University of Michigan, Ann Arbor, August 22, 1961, p. 13.
3. Mitchell, Charles, "The Culturally Deprived—A Matter of Concern," *Childh. Educ.*, May 1962, 38 (9):412–415, 419.
4. Rosenthal, Robert, and Fode, Kermit L., "The Effect of Experimenter Bias on the Performance of the Albino Rat," unpublished manuscript, University of North Dakota, University, n.d.
5. Taylor, Harold, "The Whole Child: A Fresh Look," *Saturday Review, Educational Supplement*, December 10, 1961, pp. 42–43.

ADULT EDUCATION IN COLLEGES
AND UNIVERSITIES

A. A. *Liveright*

The past twenty years have been pioneering, exciting ones in the field of college and university adult education. The period has been characterized by growth: in the number of institutions active in higher adult education; in the quantity of students enrolled in college and university adult education; in the scope of programs and offerings; and especially in an increase of imaginative innovation. A growing number of persons especially concerned about adult education and trained for it have been attracted to the field; and a new type of student—one who is interested more in continuing higher education than in remedial training—is increasingly welcomed on the evening college campus and in various extension programs.

At the same time that college and university adult education has been characterized by growth, experimentation and increase in quality, it has also faced a number of serious difficulties. College and university adult educators are still beset by a feeling among institutions that adult education is a peripheral part of higher education; and while there are clarion calls for self-development, for continuing education and for education for public responsibility at the university level, basic institutional budgets fail to provide for such education.

This state of flux—active growth, countered by penetrating questions about the legitimacy of higher adult education and reluctance to finance it—makes for an absence of institutional arteriosclerosis; thus an air of exploration and vitality to the field.

This chapter of the *Handbook* will identify some factors responsible for the development of university and college adult education, will describe the scope of activity now carried on by the institutions of higher education, and will outline some crucial problems now confronting the total field of adult education. Since many aspects of college and university adult education are dealt with elsewhere in this *Handbook*, this chapter will look only briefly at areas such as methodology and not at all at special programs described in other sections. We may also omit reference to agricultural extension, integrally related to the Land Grant Colleges, for this is also dealt with in another chapter.

BACKGROUND

The idea of university adult education is not a new one. It is rooted in the experience of European universities, and especially in extra-mural departments of British universities. In the United States,

From *Notes and Essays*, 30 (1960), pp. 1–23. Reprinted by permission of the Center for the Study of Liberal Education for Adults.

two great pace-making institutions have been the University of Wisconsin in state-wide extension.

William Rainey Harper, in his first pronouncements at the founding of the University of Chicago in 1892, asserted the importance of adult education to the University. The first class taught in the new university was an evening class, and the university opened its doors with a correspondence study department in operation.

In the field of university extension, the "Wisconsin Idea" early set a bold and vigorous philosophy. Architect and innovator in the pioneering days of extension at the University of Wisconsin was Charles Van Hise, who said:

The broadest ideal of service demands that the University, as the best fitted instrument, shall take up the problems of carrying out knowledge to the people. . . . It is apparent that this work is one of enormous magnitude and not inferior in importance or in opportunity to the functions of the university earlier recognized—those of instruction and research.

The crux of the matter is that it is our aim to take out the knowledge, whether the people ask for it or not. It strikes me that in education we ought at least to be as careful as are the brewing interests in the state, and therefore we are not going to wait for the people to come to us, we are going to take our goods to them. We are going out to the people."[1]

A host of other colleges and universities, either in basic policy statements or in more recent statements by administrative officers, emphasize the responsibility of the college and university for continuing education—that is, programs for extending the knowledge and learning

of the campus to the members of the community regardless of age.

This feeling of responsibility on the part of institutions of higher education resulted in . . . 30 to 50 million people utilizing one or more university extension or evening college services and approximately 2 million taking part in organized and continuing adult university instructional programs in 1951–52.[2] In addition, it is estimated that some 300,000 are enrolled in adult education programs of junior colleges. The majority of these adults were involved in programs run either by urban evening colleges or by extension divisions of various state universities. A few, however, were enrolled in programs offered by several hundred small liberal arts colleges reporting some kind of adult education courses. In addition, and not necessarily included in the above figures, there are many adults who participate in continuing specialized and professional classes frequently offered through professional schools.

FACTORS INFLUENCING GROWTH

A variety of forces since 1940 have influenced dramatic growth in all adult education activities in the United States. Eight factors appear to be responsible for this growth; of these the first seven apply to the growth of the entire field, whereas the eighth pertains primarily to college and university adult education. These factors are:

1. The growth in total population and in life-expectancy, which accounts for a vastly increasing number of adults who constitute a market for adult educational programs.

2. Continuing developments in industrialization, mechanization and automation provide for more leisure time, thus making

[1] Charles Van Hise, "The University Extension Function in the Modern University," National University Extension Association *Proceedings,* 1915, pp. 7–24.

[2] John R. Morton, *University Extension in the United States,* University of Alabama Press, Birmingham, 1953.

it possible for more adults to enroll in adult education programs.

3. A continuing improvement in the standard of living and in the real incomes of all workers, which make it possible for adults to pay for programs in adult education.

4. The impact of World War II and the Korean War in terms of: bringing more adults to college campuses (for engineering, science, management and technical programs financed by the Government) and thus instilling the importance of continuing education for the students, and making colleges aware of the opportunities; proving to college faculties the challenge involved in teaching highly motivated adults—such as the veterans; emphasizing the need for different kinds of education about international and world affairs.

5. A major movement of our population from farm to city, with accompanying needs for new kinds of adult education concerned with urban renewal and redevelopment, and with needs for new kinds of remedial education.

6. Large scale proliferation of the mass-media with consequent possibilities for bringing enlarged and more imaginative educational programs into the homes and living rooms of adults.

7. Vast increase in the number of voluntary organizations and in the educational programs carried on by them, thus involving in adult education hundreds of adults who might never register for a formal program.

The eighth factor, in reality a dual one, is first that more and more people in the United States are accepting the need for a college education as part of their standard equipment for a job and for life and that, therefore, there has been a staggering increase in the number of adults who now hold college degrees. (216,521 degrees were conferred in 1940 as compared with 440,304 in 1958.)

Since it is fairly well determined that college graduates are the persons in our population most interested in furthering their education and therefore constitute the large majority of persons registered in higher adult education, the result has been increasing enrollments in informal, non-credit liberal education programs offered by many colleges and universities.

OBJECTIVES

Whereas in the past almost total emphasis was placed by evening colleges on vocational or remedial education (including offerings which permitted persons unable to attend day classes to work toward a degree or certificate during late afternoons and evenings) and by extension divisions on extending regular campus offerings to persons in rural areas, more emphasis is now on the broad idea of continuing education. New objectives appear to be to help adults continue education already begun as an undergraduate rather than to permit adults to make up for college work they did not complete when they were young.

It would, however, be unfair to suggest that most colleges and universities have abandoned assistance to adults who wish to complete interrupted college training, or that universities have shifted from vocational to personal goals. It is probably more fair to suggest that a large number of these institutions now have two-fold goals: 1) those relating to college education and vocational training; 2) those relating to life-long learning, continuing education for personal development, self-fulfillment and public responsibility.

Some indications of the broadening goals which challenge college and university adult education are provided by the following remarks:

Dean Paul McGhee in an address at Michigan State University—Oakland in 1959: ". . . questions in education now trumpeted through the land as of utmost importance will fade away in a very few years in the face of an inexorable pattern of living which requires an education more embracing than any yet known, for more people than ever before and from cradle to grave."

Dean John Diekhoff of Cleveland College, Western Reserve University had this to say in *The Alumni University:* "University programs of education for adults are often described as a second chance for adults to get the education and the degree they did not get in their youth. For these people it is really a first chance, and to provide it is one of the three most important functions of the evening college. But for the adult college graduate, the evening college of an urban university can provide a first, second, third, fourth, or nth chance to keep alive or to revive the spirit of inquiry so often characteristic of youth and too often lost with youth. It is the second chance for the university to help him do it, and it is the first chance for both of them to explore together as it should be done things that are beyond the interest or beyond the grasp of youth —things far less remote than full appreciation of De Senectute. It is because the adult's mind has changed its shape since he was an undergraduate—look in the mirror at your waistline—that he needs a specially designed education."

A recent statement by the President's Science Advisory Committee (chaired by Dr. James R. Killian, Jr.) entitled, "Education for the Age of Science": "No one in the United States denies that we should have a first class system of formal education. But not everyone realizes that the strength and happiness, even the survival of our democratic society will be determined primarily by the excellence and the appropriateness of our educational patterns. Nor is everyone aware that learning, though it begins during the school years, is a life-long venture: that education is a part of life, not merely a preparation for it."

In a similar vein, C. Scott Fletcher, President of the Fund for Adult Education, in his publication, *The Great Awakening:* "The primary goal of education in a free society is to prepare people to make wise decisions. There are, to be sure, other goals to be achieved to enable this to happen. But

ultimately, the goal is education in action— namely knowledge and thought translated into wise decisions.

"The education that fosters the ability to make wise decisions should be as long as life itself and should take place in many situations."

And finally, John Gardner in his "Introduction" to the 1958 *Report of the Carnegie Corporation,* on the aims of education: "What we need first of all is a conception of individual development which far transcends any popularly held idea of education. Education in the formal sense is only a part of the society's larger task of abetting the individual's intellectual, emotional and moral growth. Learning for learning's sake isn't enough. . . . What we must reach for is a conception of perpetual self-discovery, perpetual reshaping to realize one's goals, to realize one's best self, to be the person one could be."

Despite these indications of this challenging role of higher adult education in modern society, there exists at the present no carefully conceived and generally accepted statement describing the university's role in the continuing education of adults. Lacking such a statement or some general agreement on objectives, institutional objectives vary widely as they reflect the background and attitudes of administrative officers; the power of the adult education director; his own image of what goals should be; the immediate demands of local audiences; and the influence of one or more of the powerful campus departments.

A number of evening colleges and extension divisions are now re-examining objectives[3] in an attempt to make a timely

[3] According to a study recently completed by the CSLEA under a grant from the Fund for Adult Education (by James T. Carey, the study is in preparation for publication), only 37% of the evening colleges, 30% of the extension divisions, and 16% of the small liberal arts colleges studied report that a set of formalized objectives exist for the adult education program.

statement about the function of higher adult education. A review of preliminary re-statements of objectives by the Universities of California, Wisconsin, Chicago, Syracuse, Boston and others suggests that these will be prominent among the emerging objectives of institutions:

Intellectual and aesthetic development of the individual adult.

Dissemination of newly discovered knowledge resulting from research activities within the university.

Utilization of university resources to facilitate citizen discussion and decision making in public problems.

Leadership training, program planning and educational aid to voluntary organizations.

Education about increasing problems of urbanization.

Dissemination of knowledge and information about crucial issues in the fields of local, national and world affairs.

Stimulating of adults' desire to continue their education on their own.

Upgrading of scientific and technical personnel to meet the country's growing need for professional manpower.

Professional preparation of adult educators, especially for teachers of adults in public schools.

ORGANIZATIONAL STRUCTURE AND PERSONNEL

Thanks to an intensive study of evening colleges and extension divisions recently completed by James Carey,[4] we have a fairly complete, accurate account of organizational structure and personnel in these two types of institutions. Unfortunately, similar data are lacking for small liberal arts colleges and for junior or community colleges.

The Associations and Institutions

There are two important associations operating in the field of college and university adult education, and they do much to raise sights, improve standards, and provide for effective communication within the field.

The first and oldest of these is the National University Extension Association (NUEA), which was organized in 1915. Membership in NUEA is restricted to colleges and universities in the United States which direct a variety of extension operations both on campus and away from it. Most institutions belonging to NUEA are the large state universities; in 1959 there were 79 institutional members.

The second and younger, the Association of University Evening Colleges (AUEC), includes in its membership almost all urban colleges and universities in the United States (and several in Canada) which offer evening college programs for adults.[5] The AUEC was organized in 1939, and now has a membership of 125 institutions, as compared to 88 members in 1951.

Eliminating duplications in membership in AUEC and NUEA, we find that there were 173 colleges and universities carrying on recognized evening college or extension activities in 1959; in addition, a study conducted in 1953 by James Crimi[6] suggests that another 200 small liberal arts colleges have some kind of education for adults, bringing the total to 373, a figure which does not include junior and community college programs enrolling nearly 300,000 students in offerings designated as adult education.

The age of operations varies considerably: most extension divisions (slightly over 52%) were established prior to 1929;

[4] *Ibid.*

[5] One notable exception is the New School for Social Research in New York City, which is not a member.

[6] James E. Crimi, *Adult Education in the Liberal Arts Colleges,* Chicago, Center for the Study of Liberal Education for Adults, 1957.

well over two-thirds of the separately organized evening colleges were started after that date, with about one-third of all evening colleges started between 1947 and 1959. All of the small liberal arts colleges who indicate that they have a special adult education division report that these were started after 1929, and that most did not develop before 1947. The major up-surge in the development of evening colleges came immediately after World War II, but the growth in small liberal arts colleges would still seem to be underway.

Pattern of Growth

James Carey, in the study already mentioned,[7] identified a definite pattern of growth or life-cycle, as he called it, in evening colleges and extension departments. According to Carey, there are four stages of growth: first, departmental domination, when adult education is primarily the activity of campus departments with no independent unit for adult education established; second, autonomous development, when an identifiable or separate unit exists and major emphasis is placed on differentiating this unit from regular campus operations; third, integration, when the adult education unit comes to be accepted as an equal member of the university family; and fourth, assimilation, when the adult education division and activities, although still separate, come to be considered as integral and important parts of the university.

This pattern of growth does not, of course, take place in every institution, for one stage may be completely by-passed, or an institution may never move beyond the first or second. It is important to emphasize that there is no ideal stage, and

that different ones may be appropriate for different institutions; but in general it seems that adult education programs exhibiting the greatest degree of imagination, innovation and experimentation are those in the third and fourth stages of growth. Those divisions in the second, autonomous, stage appear to be most expendable and insecure.

Autonomy, Control and Size

Viewing the pattern of growth in various kinds of institutions, we observe that almost one-fourth (23.3%) of the evening divisions are not separately organized (that is, they were not considered a separate department and had no special dean or director in charge); almost one-half of the small liberal arts colleges (48.2%) are not autonomous. But ninety-five percent of extension divisions have a separate autonomous organization, a fact to be understood in light of the relative age of these different kinds of institutions.

One finds a similar situation applying to the size of staff and operations. Evening college organization is usually smaller and less complicated than that of extension divisions; a typical evening college usually numbers one or two staff members, with no more than 10% of these institutions using more than five. About 60% of extension divisions, on the other hand, employ at least five staff members, and many of these organizations are vast and complex. In very few cases is an evening college staff divided into departments operating different kinds of activities and having different kinds of responsibilities, but in extension this is the usual pattern. As far as the small liberal arts colleges are concerned, an adult education program is largely the part-time responsibility of a regular faculty member; where a special department exists, it is

[7] See footnote 3, p. 7.

usually a one-man operation.

There are also differences in backgrounds of evening college and extension deans: fifty-eight per cent of the chief administrative officers of extension divisions, and only twenty-seven per cent of evening college directors, have degrees in education. Extension deans and directors have a much longer tenure than evening college directors, who typically stay on the job for five years or less.

Faculty Provisions and Relationships

Procurement and compensation of faculty varies widely. Evening colleges, in general, hold to a 50-50 balance between faculty recruited from campus and those recruited from the community, while extension divisions secure considerably more than fifty percent of their faculty from campus. Liberal arts colleges tend likewise to draw the majority of their faculty from regular campus departments.

Five different faculty systems are used by evening deans and extension administrators in staffing their programs:

1. *27.8%:* Use of faculty from day-time or residence department at the discretion of the departmental chairman or dean.
2. *14.4%:* Use of extra compensation faculty for over-load teaching. Responsibility for hiring and firing in the hands of the adult dean or director.
3. *11.9%:* Joint appointment system with specific load apportioned between the adult division and regular departments. Decision on hiring and firing shared jointly.
4. *1%:* Full-time adult faculty.
5. *42.8%:* Other or mixed systems, not included in the above choices.

According to Carey, there appears to be a definite relationship between the attitudes of deans and directors toward faculty arrangements and the institution's stage in the pattern of growth. Those departments at the discretion of the departmental chairmen; those in the second mix this faculty arrangement with heavy use of extra-compensation faculty; institutions in the third or integrated stage tend to combine extra-compensation and joint-appointments; those very few in fourth stage combine full-time adult education faculty with joint-appointment and extra-compensation faculty.

As far as relations with the regular on-campus faculty are concerned, we find 68.7% of extension divisions reporting that they have a regular faculty advisory committee, compared to 52.2% of evening colleges with such a committee; only 35% of the small liberal arts colleges have any kind of faculty committee responsible for adult education activities. Generally, those schools with no separate faculty advisors are the more recent arrivals to university adult education.

An increasing number of deans of evening college and extension division have become concerned with training faculty to a greater understanding of differences between the adult and the undergraduate teaching situations. Although planned programs of faculty development exist in only a minority of institutions, their variety and imaginativeness indicate growing activity in this area. Several universities (including the Universities of Syracuse and Oklahoma) have arranged either annual or continuing seminars during which campus faculty teaching in adult education programs discuss and plan these programs. Some universities (including University College, University of Chicago) provide new faculty members teaching adults with packets of relevant literature; others (including Northeastern University and the Universities of Cincinnati and Washington) provide for student ratings of professors; and in at least one case, a university supplies a teacher-counselor to work with new teaching personnel.

Financing

University adult education has become a big financial enterprise. Roughly 48% of the AUEC institutions operate on budgets exceeding $100,000; 81% of the NUEA institutions have budgets exceeding this figure. Forty per cent of the NUEA state extension services have budgets exceeding half a million dollars, and a number are multi-million dollar operations.

In general, extension divisions and evening colleges are required to pay their own way or at least to break even. In some less well endowed institutions, adult education, in fact, acts as a money-making operation for the university as a whole. Frequently a subsidized campus course when transferred to the extension division or evening college is made to pay its own way even though it bears the same title, the same content and the same instructor.

There are some exceptions to this usual attitude. Since extension division courses are looked upon as "service" programs to the state at large, there is usually some state subsidy for extension activities, a subsidy varying from 5% in some states to about 50% in others. Where, however, some subsidy is available, state aid to extension is likely to be very small as compared with aid to other units of the university. Thus, in one of the better state universities, day colleges are expected to make 20% of their budget, and receive 80% subsidy from the state; the situation is exactly reversed in the extension division, where state aid amounts to 20% and income from fees is expected to cover the remaining 80%.

The policy of "pay-as-you-go" is modified in some evening colleges and extension departments by charges to adult education activities. The manner in which "overhead" is charged varies enormously: in one or two evening colleges, no charge is made for class-room space, administration or other general "overhead" items, but in other institutions a large and onerous "overhead" burden is assigned to adult education operations.

If we look at money available for "risk-capital" (money which can be expended for experimental programs and projects) 74.5% of state extension divisions report such money available, 66.6% of the municipal evening colleges have such funds; and only 55.2% of private institutions report any risk capital.

The pressure to make money or to break even unquestionably has a deleterious effect on adult education in general and on informal and liberal education programs in particular. First, with very limited experimental funds, the tendency is merely to incorporate courses from the day departments although these may often not be suited to the adult clientele. Second, the pressure to make money leads to an emphasis on those courses certain to have a large enrollment —thus inevitably de-emphasizing non-credit and liberal education programs.

This attitude toward financing derives both from the marginal status of an adult education function in the university spectrum and from the conviction that employed adults can and should pay their own way. It is possible that this attitude will change as the adult division matures and gains recognition as a legitimate university function deserving subsidy from the parent institution. Also, present active moves to secure support for a federal extension bill providing funds for adult education in state universities will eventually result in greater financial security.

Facilities

More and more evening colleges are creating on-campus facilities more flexible and therefore suitable for adults than are the usual undergraduate class-rooms.

There has also been a remarkable increase in the development and use of residential centers for adult education. According to a recent study of continuation centers published by the University of Washington in 1958,[8] sixteen universities owned and operated some kind of residential center either on the campus or at a sylvan spot nearby. Of these institutions, Michigan State University operates two centers, and Syracuse University runs three. Only six such facilities were initially planned as residential adult centers; most of the others resulted from an unused building or an estate left to the university which was converted for this purpose.

This development of residential centers (encouraged and directly assisted by grants to five universities from the Kellogg Foundation) emphasizes the idea that adults can more effectively concentrate on education if they are away from their customary surroundings. Nor is the idea of residential education limited to the large universities, for an increasing number of small liberal arts colleges—eager to make maximum use of their facilities and to enlarge their offerings to adults—are offering summer programs in their dormitories for business men, secretaries and other groups of adults. It seems most likely that this outcropping of residential adult education may be a fore-runner of largely expanded residential programs in the future.

CLIENTELE

In 1959 most people attending adult programs in institutions of higher education were primarily vocationally oriented. In the urban evening colleges the largest number ranges in age from 20 to 35 and represents men and women who are continuing interrupted education. Hundreds of thousands of these young men and women are attending evening colleges and extension classes for special programs in business, industry or engineering, or to complete the Bachelor's degree essential for promotion in business and industry.

Second only to this group are the many teachers taking courses to qualify for promotion, or to complete state-required certificates. But John Dyer, in *Ivory Towers in the Market Place,* makes the point that there is no typical student: "Perhaps the first characteristic of the evening college is heterogeneity. One finds here many students who already have college degrees and others who have only finished high school. The age range is from eighteen to sixty-five or seventy, with the median age being thirty plus. One-third is under twenty-five; 10 per cent over forty-five."[9]

Dyer emphasizes the variety of motivation among these students, but suggests that there are two major ones: one growing from "life space" areas (the non-academic motivation) and the other from "life chance" areas (rational, economic motivations).

John R. Morton, in his study of university extension services, has identified the

[8] University of Washington Division of Adult Education and Extension Services. *A Survey of Existing and Planned Continuation Centers of Member Institutions of the National University Extension Association,* 1958.

[9] John Dyer, *Ivory Towers in the Market Place,* Indianapolis: Bobbs-Merrill, 1956, p. 7.

extension student as one who attends extension classes, resident centers, or one who uses correspondence techniques, conferences or extension library services. He observes that men constitute a slight majority, with the educational status of all students "considerably above the average for the nation as a whole. Only 5 per cent of the users of university extension service had failed to complete high school, with 37 per cent completing undergraduate college work and more than 10 per cent being engaged in graduate study."[10] Morton further reports that more than three-fourths of participants in extension activities hold full time jobs. The age of the extension student is near that of the evening college enrollee, with the median age being 34 years, although the older student (median age, 35) is more likely to be enrolled in conference and institute programs while the younger student (25 year median) registered in the correspondence program. Morton reports that one out of three students is a professional educator; the second largest group is composed of workers in business and industry.

Although no comparable data are available we know that many thousands of doctors, lawyers, engineers, teachers and other professional persons return every year to college campuses for refresher or advanced training. And even though very many of these are not registered in evening college or extension divisions, they represent a sizeable number of people who count upon colleges and universities as sources of continuing education. As far as junior college adult clientele are concerned, we have no representative figures, but it appears that these people tend to be younger and more directly interested in technical and recreational programs.

As a result of special programs and recruiting efforts it seems likely that during the next ten or twenty years these institutions will attract an increasing number of older persons interested in continuing their education; professional groups desiring to keep in touch with recent scientific and technical changes; specialists wishing a broader general education; women stimulated to continue the education they abandoned for careers as housewives; college graduates wishing to continue or renew intellectual interests.

PROGRAM AND METHODS

On the surface, the major methodological change since 1945 has been the more frequent use of discussion and group techniques and the substitution of these methods for more traditional lecture formats.

Beneath the surface (and not unrelated to the change noted above) the most important trend in methods of higher adult education has been the concern about what, if anything, is different about the teaching of adults and of undergraduates. A new body of literature and some tentative steps toward research about the teaching of adults are gradually emerging, as administrators and faculty members concerned with adult teaching look at the differences between adults and undergraduates and try to determine what implications these differences have for their teaching methods.

The implications of differing characteristics of adults, as remarked in some of Havighurst's writings[11] and by James

---

[10] John R. Morton, *University Extension in the United States,* University of Alabama Press, Birmingham, 1953, p. 89.

[11] Robert J. Havighurst and Betty Orr, *Adult Education and Adult Needs.* Chicago: Center for the Study of Liberal Education for Adults, 1956.

Whipple in his *Especially for Adults*,[12] are just beginning to be examined. Only a few colleges and universities are looking at their teaching methods in the light of adults' special motivations and experiences. But more and more universities which are developing faculty training programs are concentrating them around problems of special methods for adults.

The question of what constitutes a good teacher of adults and who is best equipped to teach adults is still a moot question, but some research is beginning in this area. That there are some differences in teaching adults and undergraduates cannot be denied; whether a teacher required to teach adults must be different from the teacher who works with undergraduates has not been reliably determined. Preliminary study suggests, however, that an *outstanding* teacher of undergraduates will also be an excellent teacher of adults, for both cases require sensitivity to the learning situation and to the needs of students, so that any good teacher is likely to recognize changes of pace and method required for teaching adults.

Another important trend which may within a decade have a real impact on method is interest in defining objectives for adult programs, along with concurrent development of instruments to measure the achievement of such objectives.[13] Once we have workable instruments and it is possible to evaluate results, institutions can in fact compare the efficacy of different methods for achieving the same objectives. Cleveland College

and Syracuse University have already launched some research to determine the relative effectiveness of residential and "spaced-learning" programs for achieving similar objectives with similar kinds of groups. It seems likely that the interest in this problem will soon provide valuable data.

Looking at the field as a whole, we find that the evening college still depends primarily on the classroom lecture for credit courses, and on the discussion method for informal, non-credit programs. However, audio-visuals are used frequently, with several evening colleges involved in television (especially Washington University in St. Louis) on a pioneering and experimental basis.

Extension divisions—as a result of the need to take educational programs to widely scattered areas—actively and widely use a greater variety of methods. In addition to regular extension classes offered primarily through lecture and discussion, extension divisions continue correspondence programs and, in a few cases, experiment with the technique. Important among these experiments is the combination of correspondence study with televised programs: lessons are given over television with papers submitted by students through correspondence. Some correspondence study programs combine group techniques and traditional correspondence methods; these, called "group" or "directed" correspondence study, encourage people to take a course together and then to submit one paper which represents discussion and conclusions of the group. The instructor of the course, from the campus, meets occasionally with the group, to answer questions and to lead discussion.

Conferences and institutes have increased markedly since 1945. According to the best available figures in 1958, ex-

[12] James B. Whipple, *Especially for Adults*, Chicago: Center for the Study of Liberal Education for Adults, 1957.

[13] Center for the Study of Liberal Education for Adults, *Conference Report*, "Evaluation of Liberal Adult Education," September, 1958, Chicago.

tension divisions offered 1,000 conferences and institutes of 3 days or of longer duration, as well as numerous shorter meetings—and this figure is undoubtedly conservative. Although a variety of methods are used within these formats, almost all bring a group of adults (usually persons involved in the same profession or association, or with similar occupational interests) to the campus or to a residential center where they live together for a period of from one day to several weeks. Whereas in the past many extension divisions acted either as innkeepers or as middle-men between the group desiring the conference and faculty members, extension now assumes a much more active educational and planning role—many universities refuse to accept conferences or institutes for which they may not help to plan the educational content.

Extension divisions are similarly more active in the field of community development. Theoretically, this field is concerned with bringing to bear the resources of appropriate campus departments and faculty members on the problems of a particular community. The community development department, ordinarily a part of extension, makes contacts with the community, helps with a community survey and, when problems have been identified, asks appropriate campus experts to work with the community in solving its problems.

A number of extension divisions also continue to provide field library service, whereby packets of material are sent on request to residents of the state. A large proportion of the material in package-library service is now sent to teachers.

Programs in liberal education—aimed at developing man as a man rather than man as a worker, and directed toward his fulfillment as an individual and citizen—have increased materially during the past twenty years. In 1951, the AUEC, knowing of the Fund for Adult Education's interest in higher liberal education, asked for funds to implement the activities of its Committee on Liberal Education. At the same time, the NUEA evidenced interest in experimental programs in liberal education for adults. In response to the AUEC's request, the Center for the Study of Liberal Education for Adults was established and has been working closely with the AUEC since 1951, with the NUEA since 1956, and more recently in a consultative capacity with the Association of American Colleges and the Association of Colleges and Secondary Schools (representing the Negro Colleges in the South). Through publications, research activities, field visits, a national clearing-house in the field of liberal education for adults and through a number of small grants, the Center has cooperated with scores of colleges and universities to stimulate new ideas in programming and in faculty development, and generally to improve the climate supporting liberal adult education. Because of the increasing audience for liberal education programs, and the existence of an organization concentrating attention on this aspect of adult education, institutions are now involved in informal seminars, institutes, study-discussion and lecture-discussion programs devoted to liberal education. In addition, a few institutions have begun to experiment with special degrees for adults, degrees which emphasize broad generalized education rather than specialized professional training.[14]

CURRENT PROBLEMS—FUTURE DIRECTIONS

The state of flux in the field of university and college adult education during

[14] New York University, University of Pittsburgh, Syracuse University, Brooklyn College, University of Oklahoma.

the recent past is still its most pervasive characteristic and is likely to remain so for the coming decade. A number of pressing problems confront those dedicated to the field of higher adult education, but within each of them are also seeds which, if properly nurtured, can make for a far more vital program than has ever existed in the past. It seems advisable, therefore, to examine a few of the most serious problems and at the same time to remark those procedures underway, no matter how hesitantly, to solve them.

The first and most widespread problem is the fact that adult education is still considered a peripheral and possibly expendable aspect of the university or college program.

To offset this attitude, which is evidenced by many administrations and faculties, some evening college and extension divisions are now making self-surveys and holding meetings with administration and faculty in an effort to re-examine the program and objectives of the adult education arm of the university. It seems likely that this self-examination and review will continue.

A *second problem,* and one which may become more serious during the next five years, results from increasing demands on faculties, space and money as daytime enrollments rise. Evening colleges, then, have greater difficulties in attracting top campus faculty, in securing adequate space for classes, and in sharing in the college budget.

Therefore, adult education administrators are: trying to achieve joint appointments of faculty who will teach both adults and youth; asking many qualified persons in the community to teach evening classes; eliminating courses which are not university-level and might better be taught by secondary schools; improving the quality of their offerings. In addition, confronted by pressures for space, some institutions have secured from private individuals and from foundations funds they use to erect buildings specifically designed for the education of adults.

A *third problem,* which both underscores the existing administrative and faculty attitudes toward adult education and also hampers expansion, is the lack of endowment or government subsidy for adult education. Whereas the Agricultural Extension Service can count on major subsidization from the federal and state governments, and whereas undergraduate and graduate courses can rely on regular endowment money, evening college and extension operations must to a large extent pay their own way, a necessity we remarked earlier in this chapter.

This problem is a most difficult one, because securing either endowment money or the kind of government support which agricultural extension enjoys requires a change in the image of continuing general education. However, the NUEA and the Extension Council of the Land Grant Association are working closely with several federal legislative committees to secure passage of a general extension bill. And at the institutional level, more top administrative officers have become aware of the public relations, community, and alumni importance of higher adult education, which encourages them to upgrade it in the institutional hierarchy.

Other financial aid has come from the foundations. The Fund for Adult Education has been of enormous help since its organization in 1951, especially in helping universities to launch study-discussion programs and others of liberal education nature; almost all of the institutions which report any sizeable activity in the field of liberal education for adults have been involved in one or more of the study-discussion activities. But at the present, other foundations might profitably be encouraged to support university adult education; moves are being made to interest them in special programs and projects.

A *fourth problem,* and one related to growth-patterns of the evening college and extension organization, is that many have considerable autonomy without achieving an accompanying integration into the university complex. Therefore, both administrative officers and faculty members look upon the adult education activities as separate and distinct, and in time of pressure or financial crisis to be easily dispensed with.

Some people in the field believe that the solution to this problem lies in the adult education operation's building up its own constituency and power base, rather than attempting closer integration with the university; and this may well be the answer for a few very secure and profitable operations. By and large, however, other action appears to be more widely effective, as where special faculty advisory committees, Boards of Visitors, special faculty-extension planning groups are set up to increase the communication and integration between adult education and other university concerns.

A *fifth problem* relates to the fact that some adult courses are not clearly appropriate for a college or university; there has been insufficient examination of what constitutes "university-level."

A difficulty involved here is that many of the academically less impeccable courses nonetheless cost very little and bring assured income, an attractive situation for the pay-as-you-go evening operation. However, present offerings are being more carefully scrutinized, faculty committees are assisting in weeding out inappropriate programs, administrators are meeting with other adult education organizations on city and state-wide bases in an effort to determine which institution should carry on what kind of adult education program.

The sixth and seventh problems are so closely related that we must examine them together: first, there is no clear-cut statement of goals and directions for higher adult education developed by the field itself; and second, the public has no clear-cut image of what adult education can offer to their personal and social welfare.

Some tentative solutions have been tried: conferences concerning themselves with the future role of college and university adult education; meetings to discuss the philosophy of adult education;[15] individual institutions, through the self-studies previously mentioned, and through faculty and administrative seminars are re-examining the role of higher adult education.[16] Several attempts have been made to set up a national commission on adult education, and the recent President's Commission on Education Beyond the High Schools has asked a committee to study the function and role of adult education.

Although these stirrings have not yet demanded a statement of goals and directions of higher adult education, such a statement is clearly indicated. Once it has been drafted, we can concentrate upon our public image, one which underscores the vital educational potentialities existing in the field of college and university adult education.

[15] Robertson Sillars, *Seeking Common Ground in Adult Education,* "A Report of a Conference on the Philosophy of Adult Education," AEA, Chicago, 1958.

[16] *New Directions for Adult Education,* Syracuse University Press, Syracuse, 1959.

THE REALITIES OF THE
FEDERAL GRANT UNIVERSITY

Clark Kerr

Two great impacts, beyond all other forces, have molded the modern American university system and made it distinctive. Both impacts have come from sources outside the universities. Both have come primarily from the federal government. Both have come in response to national needs.

The first was the land grant movement. Abraham Lincoln signed the Morrill Act in 1862. This act set the tone for the development of American universities, both public and private, for most of the ensuing hundred years. It was one of the most seminal pieces of legislation ever enacted.

The land grant movement came in response to the rapid industrial and agricultural development of the United States that attained such momentum in the middle of the last century. Universities were to assist this development through training that went beyond the creation of "gentlemen," and of teachers, preachers, lawyers, and doctors; through research related to the technical advance of farming and manufacturing; through service to many and ultimately to almost all of the economic and political segments of society. The land grant movement was also responsive to a growing democratic, even egalitarian and populist trend in the nation. Pursuing this trend, higher education was to be open to all qualified young people from all walks of life. It was to serve less the perpetuation of an elite class and more the creation of a relatively classless society, with the doors of opportunity open to all through education.

This was a dramatic break with earlier American traditions in higher education. It created a new social force in world history. Nowhere before had universities been so closely linked with the daily life of so much of their societies. The university campus came to be one of the most heavily traveled crossroads in America— an intersection traversed by farmers, businessmen, politicians, students from almost every corner of almost every state. The cloister and the ivory tower were destroyed by being thrown open to all qualified comers.

Supporting the impact of the land grant movement was the effect on American universities of the model supplied by Germany. This German model gave academic respectability and content to the "land grant" idea; and Harvard, a private university with a long academic tradition, could travel much the same path of development as Cornell, a newly established land grant institution. German intellectualism and American populism were merged in the new university.

Pure intellect and raw pragmatism made an unlikely but successful alliance.

The second great impact on the universities began with federal support of scientific research during World War II. The wartime laboratories that were the forerunners of such continuing government-financed research centers as the Lincoln Laboratory of the Massachusetts Institute of Technology, the Argonne at Chicago, and the Lawrence Radiation Laboratory at California, opened a new age. The major universities were enlisted in national defense and in scientific and technological development as never before. (In World War I the universities had only been a source of raw recruits.

Instead of Gilman, Eliot, and White, there were now such new pioneers as Conant, Compton, and Bush to guide this alliance of the federal government with the universities. Don K. Price notes that "in the hands of Vannevar Bush, James B. Conant, and Karl T. Compton the government contract became a new type of federalism." In addition to the industrial revolution there was now the scientific revolution to be served. In addition to the stimulus of Germany, there was Russia—for Russian scientific achievements both before and after Sputnik were an immense spur to the new departure. American universities have been changed almost as much by the federal research grant as by the land grant idea.

It is interesting that American universities, which pride themselves on their autonomy, should have taken their special character as much or more from the pressures of their environment as from their own inner desires; that institutions which identify themselves either as "private" or as "state" should have found their greatest stimulus in federal initiative; that universities which are part of a highly decentralized and varied system of higher education should, nevertheless, have responded with such fidelity and alacrity to national needs; that institutions which had their historical origins in the training of "gentlemen" should have committed themselves so fully to the service of brute technology.

The "federal grant" university has been emerging over the past twenty years, but until recently it has developed more by force of circumstances than by conscious design. The universities most affected have been making largely piecemeal adjustments to the new phenomena without any great effort at an over-all view of what has been happening to them. Perhaps this was just as well—the transition probably was smoother precisely because it was not subjected to critical analysis. The federal government and the leading universities entered into a common-law marriage unblessed by predetermined policies and self-surveys —but nonetheless they formed a very productive union.

All this, however, as was inevitable, is being changed. Harvard has now studied itself. So has Princeton. Brookings and Carnegie have studied us all; so have the Department of Health, Education, and Welfare; the President's Science Advisory Committee; the American Council on Education; and the American Assembly. The principal conclusion was predictable: the federal colossus had the power to influence the most ruggedly individual of universities. A paradox emerged: the better and the more individual the university, the greater its chances of succumbing to the federal embrace. Washington did not waste its money on the second-rate.

Soon there will be a national policy as well as nationwide activity, and I am at least a little concerned. All these studies have identified problems that we knew all along to exist. But now that we have publicly identified the problems, we shall be expected to deal with them; and in dealing with them we shall create new problems. Mostly, we shall have to strive for "balance" in a number of different ways. We shall have to "balance" the wishes of individual scholars with those of their institutions; New England with the South; the sciences with the humanities; research with teaching; graduate training with undergraduate education; merit with politics; the judgment of specialists with general formulae. And yet one of the more productive aspects of federal involvement to date has been its imbalance.

We are clearly entering the second phase of the "federal grant" development. The first I shall identify as the phase of "intuitive imbalance," and the new phase just emerging as one of "bureaucratic balance." It is a good time to examine where we have been and where we may be going. We are in the midst of a vast transformation of university life and none of us can be too sure where we really are going; but we can try to peer ahead.

As a basis for discussing the two phases of federal grant development, I shall briefly review the essential facts about federal involvement with universities in this country.

1. Federal interest in higher education dates from 1787. That year saw the beginning of endowment of public institutions of higher education with public lands, following the example of the Northwest Ordinance of 1785, which provided land to support public schools at the lower levels. However, this interest was not made effective until the Morrill Land Grant Act of 1862. Then the Second Morrill Act in 1890 supplemented the original land grants with federal grants of funds to support college instruction in specified subjects; these grants still continue, and, in fact, have recently been expanded. Federal interest in higher education was further made effective by the Hatch Act in 1887, establishing the Agricultural Experiment Stations, and by the Smith-Lever Act in 1914, creating the Agricultural Extension Service. During World War I, the ROTC program was established. During the Great Depression, universities were involved in the programs of the Work Projects Administration and National Youth Administration. During World War II, universities participated heavily in the Engineering, Science and Management War Training Program inaugurated in 1940. In that same year, the National Defense Research Committee (later the Office of Scientific Research and Development) was established, and leading universities became engaged in the various programs of war research which it set up.

After World War II and again after the Korean conflict, the "G.I. Bill" and the corresponding bill for Korean veterans sent a seismic shock through academic life.

Despite this long history of federal interest, however, it is evident that with the exception of the comparatively restricted areas of agriculture and military training, there was no continuing federal involvement with higher education until World War II.

2. Currently, federal support has become a major factor in the total performance of many universities, and the sums involved are substantial. Higher education in 1960 received about $1.5 billion from the federal government—a hundredfold increase in twenty years. About one third of this $1.5 billion was for university-affiliated research centers; about one third for project research within

universities; and about one third for other things, such as residence hall loans, scholarships, and teaching programs. This last third was expended at colleges as well as universities, but the first two thirds almost exclusively at universities, and at relatively few of them.

The $1 billion for research, though only 10 percent of total federal support for research and development, accounted for 75 percent of all university expenditures on research and 15 percent of total university budgets. Clearly the shape and nature of university research are profoundly affected by federal monies.

3. Federal research funds to universities flow primarily from six agencies. In 1961 the percentage distribution was as follows:

Department of Health, Education, and Welfare	39
(37 percent was from National Institutes of Health alone)	
Department of Defense	32
National Science Foundation	11
Atomic Energy Commission	8
Department of Agriculture	6
National Aeronautics and Space Administration	3
Other agencies	1

(These figures do not include funds for university-operated government research centers.)

This federal support has been almost exclusively identified with three great and somewhat interrelated national concerns: defense (40 percent of the total in 1961, including support by the Department of Defense and the Atomic Energy Commission); scientific and technological progress (20 percent—National Science Foundation, Department of Agriculture, and NASA); and health (37 percent—through the National Institutes of Health). Federal support has not been directed explicitly toward strengthening universities generally, or one or more universities specifically, in any over-all fashion—as might be said of the University Grants Committee in Great Britain.

4. Federal research expenditures have been largely restricted to the physical and biomedical sciences, and engineering, with only about three percent for the social sciences and hardly any support for the humanities.

5. Among the totality of university functions, federal support has been heavily concentrated on research and on graduate and postdoctoral training in fields of national interest.

6. The preferred approach of the federal government to the use of university facilities for research has been (a) the specialized research center — by 1963 there were fourteen major ones, and (b) the research project. Projects have been supported for relatively short terms and specific purposes; and support has been awarded, usually on the advice of qualified experts, on the basis of prospective performance.

7. Federal research expenditures have been heavily focused on a relatively few institutions. If both project research and large research centers are included, six universities received 57 percent of the funds in a recent fiscal year, and twenty universities received 79 percent. If project research alone is considered, the figures are 28 and 54 percent. As a percentage of total university expenditures for all purposes among the leading twenty recipients, federal funds have amounted to 20 to 50 percent when project research alone is counted and from 20 to 80 percent when the research centers are added. These twenty universities are only about one tenth of all universities in the United States. They constitute the primary federal grant universities.

8. Recently there has been some spreading out of federal interest from the physical and biomedical to the social sciences; from graduate to undergraduate training; from a selective few to an expanded number of universities.

PHASE ONE: INTUITIVE IMBALANCE

For about twenty years now, Congress has been deciding in which general areas the partnership between the federal government and the universities should be developed. The areas chosen have been defense, scientific and technological progress, and health. Decisions have not been based on thorough study of national priorities. They have been made pragmatically, in response to the felt needs of the nation and of the people in accord with the possibilities of the times, and also, to an extent, in response to the urgings of very powerful lobbies. The atom was split, and could be used for war and peace. The "cold war" followed World War II and necessitated further defense work. Health became a matter of great national concern. Possibilities for space exploration developed. Congress reacted quickly to each of these realities.

Once Congress initiated a program, federal administrative officers turned to those universities best able to give immediate and effective assistance on the individual programs; or rather they turned to those scientists in the best position to respond quickly and efficiently—and those scientists were principally located in a limited number of institutions. These actions were not undertaken on the basis of any general review of institutional capacity or potential capacity, but on quick and ready apprehension of possibilities and response to them. The test was who could most effectively do the job at hand. The process was more in-

tuitive than studied.

For about twenty years, universities have been accepting the research centers and projects as proposed by faculty members and government agencies, making such day-to-day adjustments as were needed and possible. In consequence, these universities have been profoundly affected. The whole process has been one of starting new endeavors, and this has changed the pre-existing "balance" in several ways. Some real and some not so real issues have arisen for the universities.

1. Federal control and federal influence. Federal control as a substantive issue is, as Sidney Hook has said, a "red herring." With a few exceptions—the generally necessary exception of secrecy in certain types of work and the unnecessary exception of the disclaimer affidavit required by the National Defense Education Act—there has been no control in any deleterious sense. By way of contrast, state control of state universities has been a real problem. The federal government has customarily put scientifically trained persons in charge of science programs and they have operated fully within academic traditions.

The real problem is not one of federal control but of federal influence. A federal agency offers a project. A university need not accept—but, as a practical matter, it usually does. One of the quickest ways to lose a faculty member is by refusing to accept the grant he has just negotiated with his counterpart in Washington. Out of this reality have followed many of the consequences of federal aid for the universities; and they have been substantial. That they are subtle, slowly cumulative and gentlemanly makes them all the more potent.

2. University control and the agency as alma mater. A university's control over its own destiny has been substantially reduced. University funds from tuition and fees, gifts and endowments, and state sources go through the usual budget-making procedures and their assignment is subject to review in accordance with internal policy. Federal research funds, however, are usually negotiated by the individual scholar with the particular agency, and so bypass the usual review process. Thus 20 to 50 to 80 percent of a university's expenditures may be handled outside the normal channels. These funds in turn commit some of the university's own funds; they influence the assignment of space; they determine the distribution of time between teaching and research; to a large extent they establish the areas in which the university grows the fastest. Almost imperceptibly, a university is changed.

The authority of the department chairman, the dean, the president are thereby reduced; so also is the role of faculty government. This may have its advantages. Scholars seem to prefer dealing with their professional counterparts in Washington rather than with their colleagues and administrators at home. Also the university's internal process of distributing funds would be generally less selective and less flexible than the federal research project approach. Within a university, the tendency is to give each faculty member about the same opportunity and once having given it to keep giving it thereafter; but the project method allows more attention to exceptional merit and has the advantage that all projects may end some time. Additionally, federal agencies are more responsive to particular national needs than the universities would be, given the same amount of money to spend according to their own priority system.

There are, however, clearly detrimen-tal effects. Some faculty members come to use the pressure of their agency contacts against their university. They may try to force the establishment of a new administrative unit or the assignment of land for their own special building, in defiance of general university policy or priorities. These pressures, of course, should be withstood; they speak well neither of the professor nor of the agency. Also, some faculty members tend to shift their identification and loyalty from their university to the agency in Washington. Their concern with the general welfare of the university is eroded and they become tenants rather than owners, taking their grants with them as they change their institutional lodgings. The university, as Allen Wallis, president of the University of Rochester, has remarked, becomes to an extent a "hotel." The agency becomes the new alma mater. The research entrepreneur becomes a euphoric schizophrenic.

It has been said that, in the face of federal aid, university presidents have "abdicated" their responsibilities for the general conduct of their institutions. I would put it differently—they have let some things go by that they would have liked to do differently; but this is often what they do anyway. There are, however, especially acute problems when the agency insists on the tie-in sale (if we do this for you, then you must do that for us) or when it requires frequent and detailed progress reports. Then the university really is less than a free agent. It all becomes a kind of "putting-out" system with the agency taking the place of the merchant-capitalist of old. Sweat shops have developed out of such a system in earlier times and in other industries.

3. *"Scientists Affluent, Humanists Militant."* Federal research support has

added a new dimension to the eternal class struggles within a university. To student versus faculty, assistant versus tenure professors, and faculty versus administrators has been added a new hierarchical point of tension—that between humanists and scientists. The scientists, by and large, in the federal grant universities, get promoted faster, get more space, get more income through summer employment and consulting, have more secretaries and assistants, have greater access to travel funds and expense accounts, and accumulate a greater sense of status within and outside the academic community. Some humanists obviously resent all this and consider it quite unfair, even though their own situation has improved, relative to what it used to be.

However, there is still another side to the story. The scientist who gets a series of projects going can become caught in his own apparatus. Graduate students and staff members become dependent upon him. He is committed to project deadlines and periodic contract negotiations. He is enmeshed in a web of obligations and it is very hard to break out. As a result, he often works hard at things he would rather not do—more often than need be true of the humanist.

There is some current tendency for the brightest of graduate students to prefer the sciences to the social sciences and the humanities, and this will have an impact on comparative faculty quality as between fields of study in the years to come. How much of this has been caused by federal aid and how much by the current liveliness of the different fields is not at all clear. My own impression is that the brightest graduate students flock to the areas with the brightest new ideas, regardless of federal aid.

All this is said to have destroyed the "balance" among fields and it is generally concluded that something should be done about it. The balance among fields, however, has never been a static thing. If it were, philosophy, theology, and the classics would still be the dominant areas of study, as they have not been for a long time. Assuming that the balance of 1942, say, was appropriate for 1942, this does not mean it would have been appropriate for 1962. It is not enough to say that the old "balance" has been destroyed. The real question is what should be the proper balance today? It is clear that the flowering of the Renaissance should have affected the "balance" in the sixteenth centry. It would seem likely that the splitting of the atom and the deciphering of the genetic code should in their turn affect the balance of the twentieth century. We should expect the most money and the brightest students and the greatest prestige to follow the most exciting new ideas. By and large they have done so, and this one way of defining the nature of balance. (Economics was exciting in the 1930's; sociology was more exciting in the 1950's.)

The real question, it seems to me, is not one of balance in any historical or monetary sense, but rather what is most appropriate to each field in each period. "All fields are equal, only some are more equal than others." There should be no effort to do the same things in the same amounts for each field. Each should receive support in accordance with its current potentialities, and potentialities vary. There are no timeless priorities.

The academic community has lived with inequities before. Agriculture in the land grant institutions has had eleven-month appointments, low teaching loads, and heavy research subsidies for decades. Law and medicine have reflected within the academic world some of the power and affluence of their professions in the outside world. These are stated as matters of fact, not as ideal situations.

Generally, I think, it is remarkable and commendable that so high a degree of internal equity has thus far been preserved within the academic world in the face of quite chaotic pressures impinging upon it.

4. *The inevitability of concentration.* The project approach almost automatically led to concentration of federal research effort in a relatively few universities. The universities best equipped to undertake the research were also those with the faculty and facilities to provide for the training of Ph.D.'s. It is no coincidence that the six universities with a little more than 25 percent of project funds graduated about 25 percent of the Ph.D.'s; and a similar situation prevails for the top twenty universities. If "only the best will do," this concentration of effort is inevitable. A different result would have been quite surprising.

This concentration of effort has undoubtedly strengthened the facilities and improved the quality of faculties of universities already in the front rank. It has probably widened the gap between those of the first and those of the second and third ranks. It may, in fact, have actually injured universities of the second and third ranks and some colleges by turning their potential faculty members into research personnel in the front-rank universities. The good are better; the poor may well be worse. And it has greatly accentuated the differences between colleges and universities.

5. *Teaching the graduates versus teaching the undergraduates.* The much-advertised conflict between teaching and research puts the problem the wrong way. The teaching of graduate students is so closely tied to research that if research is improved, graduate instruction is almost bound to be improved also. And the almost universal experience seems to be that federal research support has improved graduate instruction. There have been better facilities, more research assistantships and fellowships, more research projects in which students can work directly with faculty members—all resulting from federal funds. At the graduate level, there has been a clear gain, and fortunately so, because graduate enrollments at the federal grant universities have been increasing rapidly.

At the undergraduate level, however, the "subtle discounting of the teaching process" has been aided and abetted. Harold Orlans, who conducted the excellent Brookings study of federal aid to universities, concludes that federal research aid "has accelerated the long-standing depreciation of undergraduate education at large universities." This is my own observation, with one exception —that a very few private institutions with long traditions of very high-quality undergraduate instruction have been able to maintain their standards; and this is to their great credit.

The reasons for the general deterioration of undergraduate teaching are several. Teaching loads and student contact hours have been reduced. Faculty members are more frequently on leave or temporarily away from the campus; some are never more than temporarily on campus. More of the instruction falls to teachers who are not members of the regular faculty. The best graduate students prefer fellowships and research assistantships to teaching assistantships. Postdoctoral fellows who might fill the gap usually do not teach. Average class size has been increasing.

There seems to be a "point of no return" after which research, consulting, graduate instruction become so absorbing that faculty efforts can no longer be concentrated on undergraduate instruction as they once were. This process has been going on for a long time; federal research funds have intensified it. As a consequence, undergraduate education in the large university is more likely to be acceptable than outstanding; educational policy from the undergraduate point of view is largely neglected. How to escape the cruel paradox that a superior faculty results in an inferior concern for undergraduate teaching is one of our more pressing problems.

6. *The faculty and the un-faculty.* University scholars traditionally have both taught and conducted research. But now some scholars are added to the staff in exclusively research capacities—and increasingly with titles suggesting professorial status. They have no teaching responsibilities and are not as yet fully accepted members of the academic community. They usually are not members of the Academic Senate and they usually are not given tenure—both traditional marks of faculty status. In many institutions, however, they may use the name of the university in getting projects under their own direction.

In a far less anomalous position is the faculty member who works on a federally sponsored project during the summer months and part-time during the regular year, and receives much of his pay from the project rather than from the university. But to what extent is he really a university employee and what security of employment does he really have? Obviously, it is no longer so clear as it once was just who is the faculty.

There has been an almost frantic remaking of the rules—new titles created, new relationships established, new classes of citizenship formulated and only partially assimilated. The Harvard cata-

logue now lists more than 5,000 "Officers of Instruction and Administration," many of whom are not faculty in the traditional sense. The "faculty" in our universities becomes an ever-changing group as the definitions change. If there can still be said to be a "faculty" at all, it is most certainly a different composite than before. Much of the teaching, much of the research are done by the "un-faculty."

7. *University "aid" to the federal government.* Federal aid has been of great benefit to the universities. It has not, however, been without its costs in money and effort. Overhead allowances vary greatly from agency to agency but seldom cover all the indirect as well as the direct costs of sponsored research. Also, matching grants for construction may force a university to upset its own priority system in order to get federal funds. This, of course, is the intent.

Additionally, federal funds have placed great new administrative burdens on the universities—on faculty members, on department chairmen, on deans, on presidents. New classes of administrators have been created—the contracting officer and the research project manager. Administration becomes a much larger aspect of the total university enterprise. Julius A. Stratton has observed, "There is a basic incompatibility between the true spirit of a university and those elements of management which tend to creep into the organization of projects, the planning of programs, and the utilization of costly facilities."

8. *On the borders of temptation.* Immense sums of money have been poured into the universities by the federal government, and universities are highly atomistic entities. The university has the responsibility for but usually not the actual control of these funds. Some abuses have inevitably developed. Funds

have been diverted at times from one use to another—and the other use one not intended by the federal agency. Some faculty members make informal alliances —if you consult on my project, then I should consult on yours—and total income has been pyramided through this exchange of consultancies to occasionally astounding levels. When these same faculty members sit on the federal panels that make the grants, the whole process becomes quite involved, to say the least. Excessive amounts of expensive equipment have at times been purchased, and equipment salesmen chase grants around. Some universities promise not only a base salary but substantial supplemental personal income and allowances from federal grants as a recruiting device in a wilder and wilder upward spiral.

There have been some scandals. There will be more. The federal agencies will exercise increasingly specific controls and the universities dependent on this new standard of living will accept these controls. The universities themselves will have to exercise more stringent controls by centralizing authority, particularly through the audit process. In a few situations, self-restraint has not been enough restraint; as one result, greater external restraint will be imposed in most situations.

With all its problems, however, federal research aid to universities has helped greatly in meeting national needs. It has greatly assisted the universities themselves. The nation is stronger. The leading universities are stronger. As Nathan Pusey reported the unanimous views of the presidents of universities participating in the Carnegie study, federal aid, over all, has been a "good thing." In their turn, the federal grant universities have adapted to their new role quite quickly and effectively.

Professor Don Price has made reference to the following limerick:

> There was a young lady from Kent
> Who said that she knew what it
> meant
> When men took her to dine,
> Gave her cocktails and wine;
> She knew what it meant—but she
> went.

I am not so sure that the universities and their presidents always knew what it meant; but one thing is certain—they went.

PHASE TWO: BUREAUCRATIC BALANCE

The general policy of federal agencies in allocating research grants to universities for the last two decades has been one of "seeking excellence wherever it is," one of accepting the established pattern and following it. The new approach is to take more of an over-all view; to change the pattern to a degree. Balance is the new virtue; imbalance the old sin.

The charge, made by Logan Wilson among others, has been that "There is no federal program—merely programs." The response—in the proposed "National Education Improvement Act of 1963," for example—is to provide: "A comprehensive program of Federal aid to meet selected and urgent needs of American education on all levels from elementary school through graduate education; to promote educational quality, expand opportunity for education, and to increase the capacity of our educational institutions; to provide for the Nation's needs in skilled manpower, national growth, and national security."

The new balance calls for developing a larger number of outstanding centers of graduate instruction and research. The Seaborg report suggested an expansion from the present fifteen or twenty centers to thirty or forty over a fifteen-year period. The National Education Improvement Act envisages expansion from twenty to seventy. This demand for geographical dispersion of centers of strength follows, in part, the new realization of the role of a university as a factor influencing the location of industry. The Roswell L. Gilpatric report for the Department of Defense explained the concentration of defense contracts in California and Massachusetts by the concentration of research and development projects in these two states, which in turn was attributed to the availability of university centers of substantial strength. An educational and political effort of considerable dimensions now seeks to reorder the current pattern of distribution in the name of balance.

Under the National Defense Education Act of 1958, preference is already given to assisting *new* graduate programs in selected subject matter areas. Teaching is being emphasized along with research. Summer refresher courses for teachers of science, improvement of science textbooks, and language laboratories are programs already well established. The National Science Foundation has a large effort under way to improve and renovate equipment for undergraduate teaching in the physical sciences. Undergraduates, as well as graduate students, are being assisted by loans and scholarships. The social sciences are receiving increasing sums of money. More funds are being granted to colleges as well as to universities, and to universities of all ranks. In particular, "institutional grants," to supplement project grants, are being given by the National Science Foundation and the National Institutes of Health. And NASA, among others, makes "training" grants to institutions instead of awarding fellowships to students who may then go wherever they wish. Thus, efforts to achieve greater "balance" are already well under way.

The approach to a university "as an institution" is of particular interest. If additional universities are to be selected to become centers of strength in research and graduate instruction, then it will be necessary for the federal government to be concerned with the "general health of the institution." This will be a notable departure from historical practice, except in agriculture. The Land Grant Association, in commenting on recent recommendations by the President's Science Advisory Committee for dispersion through assistance to institutions as such, said: "The recommendations represent a return to the principles of government-institution relations laid down in the basic land grant legislation, in which the responsibility for internal administration, fiscal management, and proper direction is vested with university officers rather than with agency staffs." It should be noted that *every* state has at least one land grant institution receiving federal support on a formula basis. The parallel with agriculture is not entirely apt, however, since agriculture by its very nature is locally and regionally oriented, but national defense and space exploration are not.

If we are to move toward federal orientation to the "total function of the university," then the University Grants Committee in Great Britain is the outstanding precedent, and one that has received some support in the United States. However, there are only about thirty universities in Great Britain and it is clear what is and what is not a university. Additionally, the University Grants Committee has come to exercise more influence over the establishment of new programs, the cost and size and even the appearance of new buildings, the equalization of faculty salaries among institutions, and the determination of admission policies than would currently be acceptable if it came from the federal government in this country.

Some hard choices must be faced. The decentralized project approach of the last two decades has much to recommend it. It is selective on merit, flexible in accordance with quality of performance, and responsive to national goals. The universities and their scholars retain substantial freedom. But such dominant reliance on the project approach is no longer likely. In fact, the project is already less the chosen instrument than it once was. Productive anarchy is no longer such a politically viable solution.

It is said that support to institutions as such will "give a university the necessary autonomy," and will permit dispersion of effort and better balance in several directions. It is not clear, however, how the particular institutions will be chosen, or, once chosen, how support might subsequently be withdrawn if performance should prove inadequate. It is difficult to assess the merit of a total institution as complex as a modern university. One alternative is to rely on a formula, as in the case of agriculture in the land grant institutions. Another is to be guided by political influence; and this is increasingly happening.

It is reported that Congress already senses its loss of control to the professional personnel in the various agencies and would like to regain it. "Congress knows it has forfeited much power over science to the Executive and it does not like it." The Harvard self-study report notes the danger of political interference and "logrolling" inherent in block grants. Inter-

university competition would be taken from the quasi-academic arena of the agency committee to the legislative halls.

Additionally, the selection of designated "centers of strength" assumes a single source of designation—a single over-all federal agency or committee. A single agency means a single source of control, as against the current pluralistic situation of several agencies and several sources of influence, with opportunity to pick and choose among them. A single source of control would turn an influential relationship into a really "perilous partnership." Finally, will funds necessarily be better spent for the national interest under institutional control than through the agencies, where decisions are freer from internal rigidities and egalitarian tendencies?

In the battle over institutional versus project support, Congressmen are more likely to prefer the institutional approach than are the professionals in the agencies; the presidents of universities than the researchers within the universities; the less well-established universities than the well-established ones; the humanists than the scientists—generally, those who have less under the project system than those who have more.

It is almost obligatory in educational circles these days to support "excellence" *and* "balance." They are the two magic words. Yet "excellence" and "balance" sometimes pull in different directions. It is also quite necessary to favor "institutional integrity" and to be against "federal control." Yet the institutional grants that aid what we are supposed to favor (integrity) may also aid what we are supposed to be against (control). Turning "integrity" over to the university president may also turn "control" over to the federal government.

How can we really best secure

"aristocracy of achievement arising out of democracy of opportunity?"

SOME SUGGESTIONS

The nation does face some grave problems in the field of education. Vastly increased numbers of students are pouring into our schools. Many qualitative deficiencies exist. State and local subdivisions are caught with relatively fixed tax structures, and private endowments and gifts have their limits also. Federal support is the most obvious way out. But federal expenditures themselves are not unlimited, and there are some realistic barriers to certain types of federal involvement.

The first consideration is that the federal government need not and cannot do everything. It seems to me that the educational system of America, good as it generally is, is in the most trouble—and thus in the greatest need of federal help—at the bottom and at the top.

At the bottom is the problem of "drop-outs" from school and "drop-outs" of the unskilled from the employed labor force. Through occupational training and retraining, through counseling, guidance, and relocation, these "drop-outs" should be assisted to acquire skills valuable in a dynamic economy where skill levels are rising at perhaps the fastest rate in history. Full employment is the necessary complement to make such training effective.

At the top, the nation needs more research activity in a number of fields and more personnel of high skill—particularly engineers, scientists, mathematicians, teachers, and medical doctors. A recent Bureau of Labor Statistics survey shows that from now to 1970 the expected supply of engineers and scientists will fill only three quarters of the demand. This leaves a very large gap. The prospect is particularly critical for engineers.

Fortunately the levels where federal aid is most necessary are levels where it is most politically feasible. My suggestions will be limited to higher education, and to the university level in particular.

1. Federal research centers, whenever possible, should be located near and identified with a university. A university, with its libraries, colleagues to talk to, and graduate students to train, provides a uniquely favorable environment for such centers. In turn, such centers provide additional research opportunities for the university's faculty members and graduate students. Instead of establishing a research center in isolation and then, perhaps, having to build a new university at the same site, it seems to me best to put the center near some university—even if it doesn't happen to be our own.

2. The project system should be continued in essentially its present form as the major means of supporting the research and graduate instruction programs of universities as well as accomplishing the specific research purposes of the federal government. If project funds double or triple during the decade of the sixties, as now seems likely, it will be possible and necessary to extend more of them beyond the twenty institutions that constitute the primary group of federal grant universities at the present time. Orlans has identified about ten universities, mostly "public" ones, which already deserve considerably more project support on the basis of their existing Ph.D. programs. Other universities will soon be moving into this group in the natural course of events. The project system follows established lines of contact through disciplines and avoids the

problems of establishing a new reliance on institutional lines of contact.

The project system has resulted in a "highly successful working relationship between the government's need for long- and short-term research and the academic scientist's abilities and interests."

To the extent that institutional grants are given, they should follow the project grants. Charles V. Kidd has suggested that 25 percent might be given as free funds to institutions, as against 75 percent in project funds. Twenty-five percent appears to be an adequate figure. These institutional grants could best be used by the universities for new projects, small projects, support of young faculty members unknown in Washington, and of fields neglected in direct federal grants —all on a very flexible basis. Thus the universities' rather different evaluation of "merit" could supplement the standards for merit of the federal agencies. I would hope that the institutional grants would be assigned automatically by the agencies as some percentage of the project grants which are themselves assigned on merit. If "quality must come first," this is the best way to assure it.

Alvin M. Weinberg has recently made the interesting suggestion that the panel system of reviewing research proposals could be improved as an instrument for making scientific judgments by including on the panels representatives of related fields, as well as representatives of the field in question. "I should think that advice from panels so constituted," he says, "would be tempered by concern for larger issues; in particular the support of a proposed research project would be viewed from the larger perspective of the relevance of that research to the rest of science." The greater impartiality of the panels would also be assured.

Contract and grant overhead should cover reasonable indirect as well as all direct costs.

Federal project funds are increasingly being used to bid salaries and allowances up and to bid teaching assignments down. How much further such competition can go without raising grave policy problems for the federal agencies is problematical. The market is sufficiently active without this added inflationary stimulus; and the universities are sufficiently in trouble with internal inequities and reduction of teaching time.

There is currently arising a three-sided competitive struggle for research and development work, involving industry, the universities, and the government itself. The universities should be preferred for basic research and for such other research as is readily related to graduate instruction.

It is being suggested, and also being implemented, that federal grants and contracts be channeled increasingly into liberal arts colleges to assist faculty research and the training of outstanding undergraduate students. This process can easily subvert the colleges from their primary obligation and start them on the way to becoming quite different types of institutions. With a project-by-project approach this is almost bound to happen. Would it not be well for the governing bodies of such colleges to examine the implications of this changed role before the process of project-by-project transformation of the nature of the institution is begun? If they accept the role they should accept it by a conscious policy decision.

3. To aid the teaching function of universities during the "deficit years" of greatly swollen enrollments just ahead, federal agencies should permit, even encourage, postdoctoral fellows and research professors to teach one-quarter or

even one-third time at no cost to the institution. The present system increases the size of the "un-faculty" and widens the gap between the researcher and the student. Also, the further creation of research career professorships might well be examined. Are they really necessary from a research point of view and is it really desirable to preclude their occupants from normal participation in the full range of academic life?

The universities themselves should see to it that teaching assistantships are fully competitive with research assistantships and fellowships.

4. Federal agencies should provide space and equipment for their postdoctoral fellows and research career professors and for all contracts and most grants without the requirement of matching funds. It is very difficult to obtain space and equipment for these purposes from either endowments or state support, and also not entirely appropriate.

5. A National Foundation for Higher Education might well be created on the model of the National Science Foundation. It could serve as a focal point for the interests of higher education and make grants outside the province of the National Science Foundation. Such a foundation would need to explore carefully the areas where support would be most productive, and also the appropriate forms of support, as did the National Science Foundation with such skill and judgment in its fields of interest. Areas for possible early consideration, as examples, are the creative arts, international studies, and environmental planning. Each is at a stage of considerable activity; each carries a high degree of national interest. Additionally, a Foundation for Higher Education might well undertake the support of great regional library resources with union catalogues

made available to other university and college libraries in the region.

6. A number of other federal programs now in effect to aid higher education have generally worked well and should be continued.

The established program of the Federal Housing Authority in making loans for residence halls, student unions, and parking structures should be continued and expanded, as should the several programs under the National Defense Education Act. These programs are all widely dispersed in their efforts, and affect nearly all universities and many colleges.

Graduate fellowship programs should be expanded as there are capable graduate students to fill them. The availability of money does not by itself create a supply of competent candidates. At least half of the graduate fellowships should be transferable on a national basis, and not more than half tied to particular institutions. The practice of the Rockefeller Foundation and Woodrow Wilson Foundation of making an institutional grant to cover part of the institutional expenses for each scholar might well be more widely emulated.

The great need for curriculum reform in many fields, caused by the changing content and structure of knowledge growing out of research, should be recognized by federal agencies. They should support the efforts of universities to re-examine and improve the teaching in these areas. Some support is being given, particularly by the National Science Foundation in the physical sciences, but unfortunately some recent developments run counter to this trend. For example, the National Institutes of Health now cannot support any such efforts in the biological sciences —an area where they are greatly needed.

Foreign service projects conducted by universities for the federal government appear to be most fruitful if there is a major institutional assignment for a substantial period of time. *Ad hoc* projects accomplish little for the foreign country or for the contracting university.

7. Medical and dental doctors are in short supply and will be in shorter supply. Fellowships and facilities for their training deserve high federal priority.

8. A Council of Advisers on Education, as suggested by the American Assembly in 1960, would provide an opportunity for an over-all view of the educational system and the educational needs of the nation as no single agency can do. This would be something like the President's Council of Economic Advisers, but in the educational field. Education may well need a better-coordinated voice than it has had, as McGeorge Bundy has so eloquently argued, but the federal government also may need a more coordinated ear.

This council might assist in the preparation of a manpower budget covering the supply of, and demand for, the skills that depend on formal education. Indeed, beyond this the nation might benefit from an over-all manpower budget, supplementing its other budgets, for it would focus attention on human resources and on the importance of developing them.

The partnership of the federal government with higher education and particularly with the federal grant universities over the last two decades has been enormously productive in enlarging the pool of scientific ideas and skills. Now we are entering a new phase of widening and deepening relationships. This new phase can carry the American commitment to education to new heights of endeavor. It can also preserve the traditional freedom of higher education from excessive control. It can enlarge the horizons of equality of opportunity. It can maintain and even increase the margin for excellence. The challenge is to make certain it does all these things.

4

Race Relations

The problem of race relations in the United States may be identified or defined in a number of ways. For example, it may be viewed as one aspect of a far more general tendency for all humans to separate themselves into groups in which members are linked to one another by feelings of solidarity and a common identity. Such groups, which may vary in size from a single family to an entire society, have been labeled as "in-groups" by sociologists. In turn there is an almost universal tendency for such groups to develop unfavorable prejudices against "out-groups" consisting perhaps of all groups other than their own.[1] This tendency, which applies to groups of all types, whenever they are differentiated by religion, "race," ethnicity, economic status, or any other cultural difference, is also commonly referred to as "ethnocentrism."[2]

Another very general way to define the problem of race relations is in reference to relationships between dominant and minority groups in a given society, such as the tendency for the majority in many societies to control or restrict the behavior of minority groups within these societies in discriminatory ways. In the case of feudal or colonial societies, a minority group may dominate a subjected majority.

Race relations may also be defined in terms of the most extreme manifestations of group prejudice and hostility, that is, racism, caste, and genocide.

Racism involves the development of a rather extensive ideology centering on the assumption of significant biological differences between racial groups. Inevitably, racism attributes biological purity and superiority to some groups and biological inferiority to others. Racist ideologies generally imply the need to keep "superior" and "inferior" groups physically separated in order to protect the purity of the "superior" group from "contamination." When racism comes to dominate a culture, to the extent that it generates a rigid system of racial segregation, such a system is commonly referred to by social scientists as a *caste* system. A well developed caste system does not permit any degree of social equality between the races, nor does it permit economic or political equality. In effect, a caste system keeps subjugated racial groups "in their place" by an elaborate network of laws, rituals, and customs, usually maintained by a constant threat of violence toward those who violate the norms of the system. Thus, in a pure caste system, there is no open biological mixing of the separate races, and there is no mobility from one racial stratum to another. Actually, there have been very few examples of pure caste systems in the history of the world—perhaps the Union of South Africa today, Hindu dominated India, Nazi Germany, and the southern United States of the recent past are the closest approximations.[3]

Genocide is the most violent and destructive form of racism. It involves a systematic effort to exterminate the members of a minority group. The racial murder of over six million Jews by the Hitler regime of Nazi Germany is the most extreme example of genocide in modern history. Genocide has also been proposed as a solution to racial problems by some racial extremists in other societies, including the United States and South Africa. Needless to say, genocide has been strongly rejected as a solution to race problems by most elements of American society.

Finally, race relations may be described in terms of the responses on the part of those groups toward whom prejudice or discriminatory attitudes are directed. For example, assimilation, avoidance, submission, accommodation, and violent or nonviolent militancy have been identified as among the variety of possible responses of a minority group in relation to the dominant majority in a given society.[4] To put it another way, any realistic analysis of intergroup relations must take into account the actions and counteractions of *all* groups involved in a system of interaction. Thus problems of race relations in the United States are best defined in terms of the attitudes and behavior of both the white majority and non-white minorities.

In the United States, relations between the white Protestant majority and racial and nonracial minorities such as American Indians, Negroes, Puerto Ricans, Mexicans, Jews, Catholics, Chinese, Japanese-Americans, French-Canadians, and almost every other ethnic group have been characterized at various times by in-group—out-group hostilities ranging in intensity from verbal rejection to systematic discrimination and to overt physical attack and violence, including riots, bombings, lynchings, and murders.

This chapter will focus on problems of Negro-white relations, primarily because the Negroes are by far the largest minority group in the United States to which the more extreme manifestations of prejudice have been most consistently directed. Also, it is the majority-minority group problem which has been widely recognized as having the most significant consequences today for the United States as a whole and about which there is the greatest concern and uncertainty with respect to its future implications. However, this focus is not intended to minimize the seriousness of problems of other minority groups in the United States but merely represents the practical limitations of this chapter imposed by time and space.

Prejudice and hostility directed against the Negro has been a cruel fact throughout American history, but this is not to say that its particular manifestations and intensity have not significantly varied from time to time and from region to region. Perhaps the most consistent pattern of race relations in the United States was the dual system of racism and caste that dominated the deep South during the period beginning roughly in the last decade of the nineteenth century and lasting until World War II. Arnold Rose has described this period of Southern history as follows:

The most important thing about the caste system is that it transformed the whole culture of the southern states. It made its mark on every institution, whether of whites or Negroes, and it created suspicion, antagonism, and violence in the relations between the races. It permeated the conversation, the thought, and the literature of the South.[5]

It should be made clear that the linkage between racism and caste during this period was rather unique, having been duplicated at only several other times and places throughout world history. For example, racism taken separately had both preceded and followed the period in which the caste system dominated the South. Racism in the United States seems to have first appeared as a rationalization for the maintenance of the slave economy which increasingly took hold in the southern states, beginning with the last half of the seventeenth century.[6] Although slavery was legally abolished following the end of the Civil War, the foundations for a rather extensive racist ideology had already been established and soon became the basis for a southern "way of life" that greatly transcended the more simple economic motivations for the exploitation of Negro labor under the slavery system. It seems almost parodoxical that the half century of the closed caste system dominated the south only after it could no longer be justified along strict economic grounds.

For the Negro the worse aspects of the caste system reached their peak around 1900. The Negro's position in the South at that time is further summarized by Rose:

It was then that segregation was most complete, violence outside the courts and mistreatments within the courts most extreme, the vote for Negroes almost nonexistent, occupational restrictions most stringent, public facilities least available, the minority group most leaderless and voiceless.[7]

One important result of these arrangements was that racism, and resulting patterns of prejudice and discrimination, were introduced into other regions of the United States, where slavery or a racial caste system had never materialized.

Today various expressions of racism are still commonplace throughout the United States, but the full extent of prejudice and discrimination is difficult to measure, since its intensity and content varies so greatly from region to region, city to city, group to group, and person to person. Also, many manifestations of prejudice are disguised from direct scrutiny, such as reflected in unofficial or clandestine "gentlemen's agreements" designed to prevent Negroes from moving into all-white northern suburban communities, where overt public expressions of racial prejudice are not generally condoned.

Nevertheless, it is obvious that for the last several decades the old caste system of the South has been crumbling and that many of the racial barriers denying Negroes equal rights and opportunities in other regions are also rapidly being torn down. In fact, many of these changes are occurring so rapidly that social scientists who study them first-hand have great difficulty keeping abreast of current trends and developments. For example, Rose has made the following assessment:

What is the present state of the Negro problem and of civil rights in the United States? There is no practical answer to this question because change in the area is so rapid that any description no matter how thorough, is out of date by the time it is brought into print . . . For the Negro problem, these are unusually crowded times.[8]

For the most part the changes that have recently been taking place reflect governmental actions, either through the passage of new legislation, or administrative and judicial interpretation of existing laws.[9] Some of the most far-reaching governmental actions have been at the federal level, including civil rights laws passed by congress in 1957, 1960, 1964, and 1965. At the time of this writing recommendations for still further civil rights legislation had been received by Congress, including a proposal for an enforceable ban on discrimination in the sale or rental of private housing. Supreme Court decisions invalidating segregated public schools and public accommodations were equally significant, as were presidential orders banning discrimination in federal employment and in the armed services, in private firms working under contract for the federal government, in government-guaranteed housing loans, and almost all other activities of the executive branch of the federal government.

At the state level, legislative actions aimed at improving the legal rights of minority groups passed over the fifteen-year period immediately following World War II have been summarized by Earl Raab:

Twenty-one states passed enforceable laws prohibiting discrimination in public and private employment. . . . In the same period, sixteen states enacted a prohibition of one kind or another against discrimination in housing. At each state legislative session these housing laws are generally broadened, as are the sanctions against discrimination in public accommodations, on the books of twenty-seven states. At least eight states created over-all commissions against discrimination to enforce these networks of law, thus establishing themselves as active partisans against inequality based on racial, religious, or ethnic identity.[10]

Most of the recent changes that have taken place have meant positive social, political, and economic gains for the Negro minority. Also, some measurable differentials between Negroes and whites reflecting past restrictions imposed by racial discrimination are beginning to diminish, such as differences in life expectancy, income, education, occupation, and political participation.

What seems to have brought these recent changes about? There are many factors which have been influential, although it is difficult to assess the relative importance of each of these taken separately. One set of factors has to do with the growing affluence of the American economy as a whole, the migration of southern Negroes to "booming" northern and western industrial areas, and the gradual industrialization of some southern communities. All of these developments have led to some upgrading of the employment and economic status of the Negro, and have reduced the important traditional forms of economic exploitation and competition as rationales for racial discrimination.[11]

A second set of factors producing positive change has had to do with the shifting beliefs and values of the dominant majority. Rising levels of public education have probably produced greater tolerance for cultural diversity, and, to a certain extent, have exposed the fallacies and logical inconsistencies of many racist beliefs. Widespread public exposure to many of the worse features of racial discrimination through the mass media coverage of racial intimidation and violence—racial murders, bombings, beatings, and the brutal misuse of police power against Negroes in some communities—has led to a growing consensus that the civil rights of Negroes have in fact been badly abused. The unjust and unequal treatment of Negroes in many areas became a widely exposed fact that no longer could be denied by responsible citizens. Perhaps another characteristic reaction—sympathy for the "underdog"—has come into play as a result of greater public awareness of racial injustice.

An increasingly cosmopolitan and internationalistic outlook by many Americans has also been a significant aspect of our changing value system. The struggle against totalitarianism and Nazi racism, beginning with World War II, forced Americans to view their own racial values in a more critical light. Americans have traveled abroad more extensively than ever before during and after World War II, and the exposure to multiracial societies, to societies in which whites are an insignificant minority, and to negative reactions to American racial practices by peoples in many areas of the world have caused us to seriously challenge our own racial practices. Competition with the Soviet Union and other Communist countries for the allegiance and support of many neutral nations in the continuing cold war has produced a desire to "mend" our own racial "fences" at home. Growing presidential and congressional concern, involvement, and leadership have also probably been significant factors in changing racial attitudes.

Social scientists and other social critics have contributed most to a change in racial attitudes by pointing out the various costs associated with maintaining racial discrimination. For example, the President's Council of Economic Advisors estimates that unused Negro talent costs the nation over 17 billion dollars a year, while the cost of relief and welfare services, and other indirect costs, are more than double this figure.[12] Racial antagonisms have been politically costly, according to social scientists, because they divert attention from other important social problems and often block their solutions. Thus, social scientists point to the ways in which racial controversies block efforts to improve education, to reduce poverty, to eliminate slums and urban congestion, and so on. Due to past racial practices the South in particular has suffered economically, politically, and socially as compared to other parts of the country. Racial tensions and race riots cost millions of dollars in property damage, as well as the added costs of police protection during periods when racial tensions are high. Some of the major contributions by social scientists have been to identify the severe psychic and emotional costs of racial discrimination to whites as well as Negroes. For example, it was the Swedish social scientist Gunnar Myrdal who identified racism as "the white man's problem" by exposing the widespread guilt and internal personal conflicts associated with the mistreatment of minorities in America.[13]

Perhaps the most significant source of changing race relations in the United States has been the rising aspirations of Negro groups and their rapidly growing demands for equal rights and opportunities in all areas of American life. Negroes, with the support and direct participation of some whites, have created a growing number of protest groups and have collectively engaged in direct political action to secure their civil rights. To these ends the civil rights movement has been largely successful and may be said to be among the most significant social revolutions in recent American history. It now appears that for the first time the Negro population has become a potent force in American political life at the national, state, and local levels, and that many politicians and lawmakers at all levels of government have become increasingly responsive to Negro demands, as evidenced earlier in this chapter. As a result these victories have led to increased dignity and self-respect within Negro groups, as well as to rising hopes for still further gains in the near future. Also, "gradualism," which was primarily a white response to Negro demands and expectations, has given way to a more urgent desire to solve remaining racial problems on the part of many whites as well as Negroes.

But at the time of this writing the problems of race relations in the United States have been by no means completely solved. There are many pockets of resistance to Negro gains in many segments of the white community, in both the North and South, and there still exist extremist groups, such as the Ku Klux Klan, willing to exploit white fears and resentments in this still sensitive area. Recent elections seem to indicate that die-hard segregationist politicians have not lost favor in some states of the deep South and have been able to maintain their influence in spite of some Negro efforts to use their increased voting power to bring about political change. In the North residential segregation and de facto school segregation still serve as major barriers to full equality for Negroes, and feelings of despair, apathy, or bitterness and resentment still afflict many Negroes caught in the poverty of the racial ghettoes in most large American cities. It has been estimated that residential segregation in many northern metropolitan areas has actually increased rather than decreased during the past two decades, as Negroes continue to fill the central cities and as whites continue to flee from the central cities to all-white suburban enclaves. This condition is a source of continuous tension between whites and Negroes, and the resulting potentialities for further riots and violence generated by this condition has been referred to by some observers as "social dynamite."[14]

In addition, there is growing awareness that within many Negro communities discrimination and the "culture" of poverty have effectively destroyed the incentives among many members for acquiring the skills, knowledge, and attitudes necessary to take advantage of the opportunities for educational and occupational advancement increasingly available to Negroes. Many such Negroes have become cynical and disillusioned by past efforts of middle-class liberal outsiders from various "helping" agencies to modify their behavior, especially when these fragmentary efforts did not sufficiently alter the social and economic restrictions imposed by the larger society. Also, when many responsible whites and Negroes attempt to socially interact in today's rapidly shifting racial climate, there is still a great deal of mutual uncertainty, distrust, and suspicion in these relationships. As Arnold Rose concludes:

> Members of racial minorities and of the white majority do not know how to associate with each other; they are excessively formal and sensitive in interpersonal relations."[15]

These are some of the unsolved problems of race relations in the United States. There is no assurance that these problems will be satisfactorily resolved without greater effort and willingness than has been demonstrated so far on the part of both whites and Negroes to modify customary attitudes and relationships. However, the social problem of race relations in the United States would probably be one of the least costly to solve, if it were desired by the large majority of our citizens.

IMPROVING RACE RELATIONS

In comparison to the strategic social and political roles played by militant student activists in many societies throughout the world, students in the United States have been relatively acquiescent and detached from the larger stream of events outside the university community. Until very recently this would have applied to Negro college students in America as well. However, the sit-ins and other civil rights demonstrations originating in southern Negro colleges in the 1950s marked the beginning of the current large-scale civil rights movement, in which Negro college students have played a dominant role. In fact, it can reasonably be speculated that without direct student participation, the Negro civil rights movement would not have been nearly as successful as it has been so far. The student demonstrations set the pace and pattern for much that followed, and the techniques of civil protest that were utilized have been widely emulated by both white and Negro student protest groups throughout the country. Student demonstrations are now commonplace in the United States with respect to a wide variety of issues, going well beyond race relations and civil rights, but so far it is doubtful that any of these have had the same moral, social, and political impact as the student sit-ins, marches, and other Negro student demonstrations in the South during the late 1950s and early 1960s. At the time of this writing, many of the leaders of these earlier student movements have shifted their tactics, interests, and affiliations, and it is difficult to predict whether civil rights demonstrations, as such, will have as much significance in the future as they have had in the past. In the first reading, Charles U. Smith, Chairman of the Sociology Department at Florida A. & M. University, analyses some of the important changes that have occurred in southern Negro colleges as a result of student participation in the civil rights movement.

Morton Grodzins in the second reading has reviewed the process of residential segregation in the largest metropolitan areas in the United States, and has concluded that the dominant pattern is one of segregated Negro ghettoes or slums in the inner areas, surrounded by white suburbs from which Negroes are largely excluded. Grodzins views this pattern as negative and fraught with many evils with respect to its social, economic, and political consequences. He offers several ways of reducing residential segregation, including controlled migration of Negroes into white neighborhoods, returning white populations to central cities, the suburbanization of Negroes, and moving Negroes out of the big cities into smaller cities, where they are now underrepresented. However, Grodzins does not sufficiently identify the mechanisms through which such a massive redistribution of both the white and Negro populations can be accomplished, nor does he suggest specific ways in which much expected bitter opposition to such measures can be placated. It may be that the only agency powerful enough to bring such changes about, at this time, is the federal government, perhaps through the passage of vigorous and enforceable legislation outlawing racial discrimination in the sale or rental of all residential housing. Such legislation has been recommended to congress by President Johnson (early 1966); at this date, however, its passage seems highly improbable. But despite difficulties and uncertainties, according to Grodzins, the stakes are high, and all efforts are justified.

When racial tensions are high, the potentialities for riots and other forms of racial violence are greatly intensified. The losses in lives and property growing out of race riots are especially tragic when, as often is the case, such disturbances do not produce any significant improvements in the prevailing race relations in a given community. There are a variety of ways in which a community may seek to avoid riots and violence, many of which are based on developing and/or maintaining meaningful lines of communication between aggravated groups, and on developing mutually acceptable mechanisms for arbitrating intergroup differences and reducing tensions. A local community relations or human rights commission is one example of this kind of approach, and it is an approach that has recently been adapted in many communities across the country in anticipation of heightening racial tensions. In the third reading, Alexander F. Miller, national community relations director of the Anti-Defamation League of B'nai B'rith and chairman of the New Rochelle (New York) Human Rights Commission, describes how potential racial violence was recently averted in New Rochelle through the intervention of the Human Rights Commission. While such an approach cannot possibly solve all of the short- and long-run racial problems of a community, as Mr. Miller readily acknowledges in his article, it may at best sufficiently reduce racial tensions to the point that more lasting solutions can be worked out.

Charles E. Silberman in the fourth reading presents two highly related strategies for bringing the Negro into the mainstream of American life. The first approach can be summarized rather simply as one of Negro "self help." This strategy calls for the creation of militant Negro "community action" organizations in Negro communities, which in Silberman's terms would throw off the shackles of white "welfare colonialism" that has for too long kept the Negro in a state of "humiliating dependency" in the large urban ghettoes. The second approach calls for the intervention of militant white community organizers, such as represented by Saul Alinsky and his Industrial Areas Foundation, as catalysts for militant Negro "self-help" programs. Both of these approaches are illustrated in Silberman's brief discussion of The Woodlawn Organization of Chicago, created in 1960.[16] Elsewhere, Silberman describes The Woodlawn Organization as "the most important and the most impressive experiment affecting Negroes anywhere in the United States."[17] Naturally, any militant social action in the United States is bound to be controversial; The Woodlawn Organization and Alinsky's militant tactics are certainly no exceptions. The issue yet to be resolved is whether the results are worth the many dangers and risks that even Alinsky freely admits are inherent in his methods.[18]

The major components of the legal approach (legislative, administrative, judicial) to insuring equal rights for all citizens of the United States, regardless of race, ethnicity, or religion, have been discussed earlier in this chapter, and space does not allow us to review them all in detail here. However, one of the most significant single applications of the judicial approach in recent years was the United States Supreme Court's 1954 ruling in the Brown *v.* Board of Education case, which declared that racially segregated educational facilities are inherently unequal. In this case the court ruled that the states must end compulsory racial segregation in the public schools "with all deliberate speed." Reading 5 is an evaluation of the impact this ruling has had on school segregation through 1965. The author, Irwin Knoll, concludes that the results so far have been substantial, but that complete school desegregation is far from having been achieved in either the North or the South. Knoll also reviews more recent Supreme Court decisions that have served to step up the pace of desegregation, as well as some of the forces that continue to block the Supreme Court's intent in Brown *v.* Board of Education.

REFERENCES

1. For extended discussions of the in-group, out-group concepts, see Robert Bierstedt, *The Social Order: An Introduction to Sociology.* New York: Mc-Graw-Hill Book Company, Inc., 1957, pp. 263–68; and Jackson Toby, *Contemporary Society.* John Wiley & Sons, Inc., 1964, pp. 166–67.
2. Gordon Allport, *The Nature of Prejudice.* New York: Doubleday & Company, Inc., 1958, pp. 16–17.
3. An excellent discussion of the concepts of racism and caste is presented by Arnold Rose in Robert K. Merton and Robert A. Nisbet, *Contemporary Social Problems.* New York: Harcourt, Brace & World, Inc., 1966, 2d ed., pp. 438–449.
4. Minority group adjustments to discrimination are reviewed in Paul B. Horton and Gerald R. Leslie, *The Sociology of Social Problems.* New York: Appleton-Century-Crofts, Inc., 1965, 3d ed., pp. 422–25.
5. Rose, in Merton and Nisbet, p. 445.
6. For a brief history of this topic, see Gunnar Myrdal, *An American Dilemma.* New York: Harper & Row, Publishers, 1944, and John Hope Franklin, *From Slavery to Freedom.* New York: Alfred A. Knopf, Inc., 1956.
7. Arnold Rose, *The Negro In America.* Boston: The Beacon Press, 1956, p. xxi.
8. Rose, p. xvii.
9. Earl Raab (ed.), *American Race Relations Today.* New York: Doubleday & Company, Inc., 1962, p. 12.
10. Raab, p. 11.
11. Rose, in Merton and Nisbet, pp. 449–454. This is a more extensive discussion of some of the changes that have been breaking down racism and caste in the United States, and 13 major forces producing these changes are identified. Our discussion here crosscuts many of Rose's categories.
12. Council of Economic Advisors, *Economic Costs of Discrimination in Employment.* Washington, D.C.: Joint Economic Committee of Congress, 1962.
13. Myrdal, pp. 1–31.
14. James B. Conant, *Slums and Suburbs.* New York: McGraw-Hill Book Company, 1961, pp. 2, 33–39.
15. Rose, in Merton and Nisbet, p. 474.
16. For a more detailed discussion see Charles E. Silberman, *Crisis in Black and White.* New York: Vintage Books, 1965, Chap. X.
17. Silberman, pp. 318.
18. Silberman, pp. 357.

ADDITIONAL READINGS

Allport, Gordon W., *The Nature of Prejudice.* New York: Anchor Books, 1958.

Bettelheim, Bruno, and Morris Janowitz, *Social Change and Prejudice.* New York: The Free Press of Glencoe, 1964.

Brink, William, and Louis Harris, *The Negro Revolution in America.* New York: Simon and Schuster, Inc., 1964.

Clark, Kenneth B., *Dark Ghetto: Dilemmas of Social Power.* New York: Harper & Row, Publishers, 1965.

Glazer, Nathan, and Daniel P. Moynihan, *Beyond the Melting Pot.* Cambridge, Mass.: M.I.T. Press, 1963.

Pettigrew, Thomas F., *A Profile of the Negro American.* Princeton, N.J.: D. Van Nostrand Company, Inc., 1964.

Raab, Earl (ed.), *American Race Relations Today.* New York: Anchor Books, 1962.

Rose, Arnold, *The Negro in America.* Boston: The Beacon Press, 1956.

———, *De Facto School Segregation.* New York: National Conference of Christians and Jews, 1964.

———, "Race and Ethnic Relations," in Robert K. Merton and Robert A. Nisbet, *Contemporary Social Problems.* New York: Harcourt, Brace & World, Inc., 2d ed., 1966.

Simpson, George E., and Milton J. Yinger, *Racial and Cultural Minorities.* New York: Harper & Row, Publishers, 1958.

Van Woodward, C., *The Strange Career of Jim Crow.* New York: Oxford University Press, 2d rev. ed., 1966.

THE SIT-INS AND
THE NEW NEGRO STUDENT

Charles U. Smith

During the late 1950's and the beginning of the 1960's college students throughout the United States began to take an active interest in the affairs of the nation and the world. This was in marked contrast to their behavior in the preceding decade when they were more quiescent and nonchalant. That Negro college students became more active in community and national affairs in this same period has been viewed with alarm and surprise by much of the white South. These Southerners regard this activity on the part of Negro students as an unexpected break with traditional patterns of "good racial relations."

It is eminently clear that the Negro college student has made a clean break with his erstwhile isolated and disassociated role in the community. This is especially true with regard to civil rights militancy. The sit-in demonstrations which have been carried on largely by Negro college students seem to have resulted from a variety of circumstances which have contributed to their changed self-image. Such circumstances include international developments, court decisions, fortuitous events and the general process of social change. These factors produced an awareness of and dissatisfaction with their previous role and status, and a revision of self-estimates by Negro college students.

Within the context of a local community and a single Negro college student body this paper seeks to examine and interpret the events and the process through which this new self-image developed. Specifically, this is an evaluation

From *Journal of Intergroup Relations* (Summer 1961). Reprinted by permission of the author.

of occurences among the Florida Agricultural and Mechanical University student body which may be somewhat illustrative of developments elsewhere.

CONTRIBUTING FACTORS

One of the most important elements in the rise of civil rights militancy among Negro college students was that of *time*. In order to understand this "timeliness," one must recognize first that almost six years had elapsed since the United States Supreme Court had ruled that public education must be desegregated and during that time the "hard core" Southern states with the greatest amount of segregation were still virtually unaffected by the ruling.

Secondly, by this time the Negro was able to appreciate the full significance of the interposition declarations, pupil assignment laws, residential requirements, achievement score requirements, health requirements, school closings, and massive resistance techniques which have effectively kept segregation despite the Court's ruling.

A third reason that the sit-in demonstrations appealed to Negro college students was the fact that throughout the struggle for civil rights for the Negro, the Negro college student, unable to vote because of age and residence requirements, had never been able to find a satisfactory role to play in the contemporary struggle.

A fourth reason that these recent efforts were so timely is that they paralleled the nationalistic struggles of native Africans and the rebellion of non-white peoples throughout the world against the domination of white nations and groups.

Fifth, even though the ruling of the Supreme Court in the *Brown* case had been largely ignored throughout the South there was the prevailing sentiment among Negroes that the salutary effects of that decision as well as a number of others regarding property, transportation, recreational facilities, interstate commerce, housing, employment and education provided a climate in this nation and abroad wherein nonviolent pressure for more extensive civil rights would result in the successful achievements of their goals.

Sixth, and finally, efforts to interest the Negro student in the struggle for greater civil rights came at a time when, because of radio, television, and other communications media, changing educational philosophies and higher educational attainments, and certain fortuitous events, the Negro college student was beginning to develop a new conception of himself as a significant element in the population of America.

SELF-IMAGE

This "new conception of self" was especially significant in the activity of the students at Florida A and M University largely because of two precedent events that helped to crystallize these students' awareness and understanding of the kind of impact that they could have on local, state and national affairs.

Generally, the Negro college student had historically led a relatively sheltered life on the fringes of the white community. This sheltered existence had been tacitly forced upon the Negro college student because of segregation and partly because of the historical necessity for preserving racial "peace" and "good racial relations" by Negro college administrators seeking increased budgets, endowments and appropriations from wealthy white private benefactors and white state legislators. As a result of this situation the Negro college became a world unto itself with its own movie theater, recreational world, eating places, educational philosophy, and accommodating paternalism. In such a setting the Negro college student received little encouragement to enter into the affairs of the larger community as a private citizen, college student, and certainly as a militant exponent of civil rights.

It is reasonably safe to say that this isolated and patronizing world of the Negro college student received its greatest initial impetus from Booker T. Washington's famous Atlanta Exposition speech of 1895 and existed without serious challenge until World War II. One can hardly blame Washington for such a philosophy since it is quite likely that his time dictated such a procedure, if Negro college education was to survive at all. And it is certainly true that college educators since Washington found it the better expedient to continue along this line while hoping to advance the level of the Negro college as an institution of higher learning. Whatever the reasons for the establishment of the tradition of "sheltering" and isolation of the Negro college; and regardless of how justifiable such a practice may have been in the past, it is eminently clear that the Negro college student of today feels that this is a tradition that is not worthy of continuance and is obviously willing to work actively for its termination.

BUS BOYCOTT

The first concrete indication of change in "conception of self" on the part of the Florida A and M University student body came not immediately after the Supreme Court decision of 1954, but two years later in 1956, when two hot and tired coeds sat next to a white woman on a crowded city bus. From this unplanned and fortuitous event arose the Tallahassee Bus Protest which had vast implications in changing the role of the Florida A and M University student body.

Through mass meetings and other demonstrations the FAMU student body was able to influence the majority of the Negro community of Tallahassee to boycott the city bus service for several months. They found that the adult members of the Negro community would listen to their ideas and cooperate with their efforts. They discovered that the state, local, and national press and other communications media were interested in what was going on in Tallahassee. They soon learned that although the white community disapproved of their actions and were angered and irritated by the protest and boycott, little, if any direct action of a punitive nature could be taken against them. They found also that college students enjoyed a kind of freedom from reprisal and a tolerance that was not shared by the non-student, adult citizens of the community. Thus began the emergence of the "new conception."

During and after the Bus Protest the FAMU students began to take more active roles in the affairs of the Tallahassee community and the State of Florida. The campus chapter of the NAACP became more active, and students began to work actively in efforts to get more Negroes registered to vote. More students began to attend the churches in the community and to attend off-campus lectures, forums, and discussion groups. In general, it appeared that there was greater concern about non-campus activities and problems on the part of the student body than there had ever been before.

A "CAUSE CELEBRE"

Three years later, in the spring of 1959, another event, fortuitous in nature, served to bolster even more the changed conception of the students' role and status. On May 1, 1959 a FAMU coed was taken at gun point from her escort after a dance, by four white youths, each of whom proceeded to rape her. These four youths were apprehended the same night and confessions were obtained in less than six hours. Immediately upon learning of the situation the FAMU students held a mass meeting and vowed to see that justice was done. They discontinued attending classes for one day and used the time in speech-making and singing, and rallying more and more of the students, as well as townspeople, to support them in their demands for speedy and total justice for the crime. National wire services, representatives of television networks, local, state, and national, and international newsmen quickly gathered on the scene. The student leaders communicated by telephone, telegraph and cablegram with such faraway places as San Francisco, California, New York, Paris, France.

Because of their activity the rape of a Negro girl, historically commonplace in the South, became a local, state, national, international *cause celebre*. Subsequently, at the trial, news representatives were on hand to provide coverage from places as far away as New York and London. In a sense, the thorough prosecution and ultimate conviction of the four youths with life sentences was anticlimactic for a group of students who were now firmly convinced that their actions could influence public opinion and behavior on a local, state, national and international level.

With the prosecution of the rape case it appears that the break with the historical tradition of isolation from affairs of the larger community was complete. No longer was the FAMU student body a group of academic nonentities patiently and lackadaisically going about the business of reading, writing, and figuring. Now they were a group with status, prestige, fame, and a reputation for social and civic action to maintain. These students had found a place in the sun that was on a par with the performance of the numerous championship athletic teams and excellent musicians for which Florida A and M University had long been noted. To the proud traditions of athletic prowess and musical virtuosity was now added another—racial militancy.

Thus, by the time the sit-in demonstrations began in Greensboro in 1959 the FAMU student body were emotionally and spiritually prepared to enter into any legitimate fray on behalf of the rights of Negroes and it was only incidental to this preparedness that CORE organized a chapter in Tallahassee in the Fall of 1959. This writer is firmly convinced that even without the support of CORE it would only have been a matter of time until members of the FAMU student body started their own demonstrations.

In the interest of accuracy it must be pointed out that not all of the FAMU student body participated in or actively supported the Bus Protest, the rape demonstrations or the sit-ins. A sizable portion of the group went about the normal and routine business of campus and college life during these incidents. There is no doubt, however, that a majority of the student body supported these activities morally, financially, or by direct participation.

OTHER INFLUENCES

While the activities described above seemed to have contributed to the preparedness and willingness of the FAMU students to engage in civil rights movements, at least four other factors are presently contributing to this "readiness" and "preparedness" and in the present view, will operate to maintain this psychological state for some time in the future.

First, there is the fact that Dr. Martin Luther King and his organization devoted to leadership in non-violent resistance (The Southern Christian Leadership Conference) has enormous influence on Negro youth. Ever since the Montgomery boycott Doctor King has been the effective spiritual leader of the non-violent movement throughout the South (and perhaps the North). He is particularly well-suited to appeal to the present-day Negro college student. He is highly trained academically; beyond reproach morally; superb oratorically; youthful, determined, and equally at home with the educated and non-educated.

The Southern Christian Leadership Conference is one of the chief exponents of the passive resistance technique and conducts workshops and institutes to train persons for this type of activity. As stated above this technique provides a kind of outlet for college students to the civil rights arena which is especially appealing, in the absence of the ballot and financial resources.

Second, the activities of students abroad and the general struggles of non-white peoples in Africa and Asia, though not so significant in the early phases of activity by the FAMU students, will undoubtedly operate to maintain their interest in minority disprivileges. The de-

position of Syngman Rhee largely because of student demonstrations and protests will effectively mobilize more and more students at FAMU to the cause of civil rights as well as other students throughout the nation.

Third, the sit-in demonstrations have attracted the attention and sympathy of white students, both north and south and will certainly cause the FAMU students as well as Negro college protesters everywhere to feel that their cause is just and that they will continue to get moral and financial support from these sympathetic groups.

Fourth, the belief in the justness of their cause has been and will be reinforced by the public pronouncement of Florida's Ex-Governor Leroy Collins that while he deplored the demonstrations he felt that the students were morally right in their demand for lunch counter service. It is also significant that at least one other public figure in the state has indicated that he agrees with Collins.

Fifth, while somewhat difficult to isolate objectively, this observer feels that an element of competition between Negro colleges has become a part of the civil rights struggle as participated in by Negro collegians. A and T College in Greensboro, North Carolina; Southern University in Baton Rouge, Louisiana; Bethune-Cookman College in Daytona Beach, Florida; Florida Normal College in St. Augustine, Florida; Morris Brown College; Morehouse College; Clark College of Atlanta; Tennessee State University and Fisk University in Nashville, Tennessee; as well as others, are all colleges and universities that engage one another in various kinds of athletic, musical, dramatic, academic, scholastic contests. It now appears that some of this spirit of competition has found its way into the civil rights arena and no college or university wants to be left behind or be found wanting in this kind of courage and conviction.

As the expression "nigger-lover" is an effective deterrent to sympathetic identification with the problems of Negroes among whites, so the expression "handkerchief-head" is used among present-day Negro students to refer to those who are afraid and unwilling to join the battle for greater civil rights; and is an epithet so powerful that students will go to almost any lengths to avoid its application to them individually or collectively.

DEPTH OF FEELING

Some degree of appreciation of the depth of feeling regarding the civil rights struggle and passive resistance that exists among many of the FAMU students may be obtained by recognizing that five students, convicted on various charges after the Tallahassee sit-ins, elected to serve the sixty-day sentences rather than pay fines of $300 each. While in serving their sentences the male students were required to work on the streets of Tallahassee and the female students did cleaning and other menial chores at the jail and in other public buildings. Furthermore, because the jail sentences caused them to miss so many classes at the University they had to withdraw from school, thereby losing an entire semester's work. Admittedly, this complete adoption of the passive resistance ideal is not typical

of the entire student body but it is plainly evident that enough of the students share this feeling to the degree that they are willing to support militant activity when called upon.

Uninformed persons have raised the cry that "outside agitators" have sparked the sit-in demonstrations in Tallahassee. The facts simply do not validate this claim. Over ninety-five per cent of the entire student body at FAMU is from Florida, including the student body president and the great majority of the members of the Student Government Association. All six of the students convicted and who served the jail sentences were native Floridians. Adult, non-student participation in Tallahassee has been largely confined to arranging bail bonds and assisting with the procurement of legal counsel for the students.

However difficult the realization may be, the hard fact is that from the student body at FAMU are slowly but surely emerging representatives of a "new Negro," with attitudes and behaviors completely alien to tradition; a "new Negro" who is able to develop his own leadership and conviction. This "new Negro" is baffling and irritating to much of the white community; and the lengths to which he is prepared to go—though they may be admired and respected—are not fully understood by members of the Negro community who have lived so long with *Plessy* vs *Ferguson*.

THE METROPOLITAN AREA
AS A RACIAL PROBLEM

Morton Grodzins

Almost nothing is being done today to meet what is likely to be the nation's most pressing social problem tomorrow. The problem can be simply stated in all its bleakness: many central cities of the great metropolitan areas of the United States are fast becoming lower class, largely Negro slums.

If racial separation and segregation lead to evil consequences, the cure is obvious; the separation should be ended. For no problem is a solution more easily stated: white populations should be brought back into the central cities, and Negroes should be allowed to choose freely where they want to live in all areas of central cities and suburbs alike. No solution is more difficult to implement.

Racial exclusiveness may be conceived as an "American dilemma" in moral terms, or a Marxian problem of class antagonisms, or a Freudian expression of instinctual attractions and cultural taboos. From these perspectives the "race problem" may be solved, if at all, only through the slow marches of gradual social change. Neither laws, nor adult education, nor *ad hoc* institutional programs can be decisive.

It can certainly be assumed that for a long time for some people in some places no program of residential integration will be palatable or acceptable. Yet it is also true that people are not frozen in antagonistic attitudes, that change is possible, and that the change can best be achieved by actual successful experiences in interracial living. Most importantly, plans can be built upon the great diversity of outlook and attitude among the urban populations of mid-century America.

The most important general step to be taken is to remove the restrictions on where Negroes may live. This is, in the first place, an act of simple justice. Of greater relevance here, if non-whites possessed genuine residential mobility, it would go a long way toward eliminating the great social costs of the present population distribution. From free movement, it follows that (1) there would be less overcrowding in Negro areas; (2) there would be fewer and smaller all-Negro neighborhoods; and (3) individual Negroes would self-selectively distribute themselves, as white populations do, among neighborhoods whose social characteristics are roughly homogeneous and roughly similar to their own.

It should not be supposed that the removal of restrictions would end Negro residential concentrations. Income factors alone will confine many Negroes to the least desirable residential areas for a long time to come. Considerations of sociability are also an important concen-

From *American Race Relations Today,* edited by Earl Raab, 1962, pp. 105–123. Reprinted by permission of the University of Pittsburgh Press.

trating factor. Investments in businesses and living quarters will keep even many of those who can afford to move as residents of all-Negro areas. Yet many Negroes now live in Negro neighborhoods simply because they have no other place to go. With the occupational upgrading and increased income that Negroes are achieving in ever-growing numbers, there is no doubt that freedom to choose residences would result in a scattering of Negro families throughout the entire urban area.

That many Negroes would continue to reside in areas of all-Negro concentration, even under circumstances that permit dispersion, would, in fact, make easier the dispersion process. Only a limited number of non-whites can afford, and wish, to move to white neighborhoods. This means that there could be a relatively complete dispersion of those so inclined, without their number becoming large in any single neighborhood.

The case of non-discrimination housing laws can best be argued in these terms. Such laws would allow the widespread dispersion of non-whites. Given the limited number of non-whites who would choose in the foreseeable future to take advantage of such laws, their main impact would be in preventing the kinds of concentration that frequently turn present "open occupancy" communities into crowded all-Negro slums.

Non-discriminatory laws, however, can do more harm than good unless they are enacted in large jurisdictions. The smallest effective area is probably a very large city. In smaller areas their effect might be to create the flight of white residents to "lily-white" jurisdictions. The full effect of non-discriminatory laws can be felt only if, in a given region, there are no such areas to which to flee. Even under this circumstance, laws against

discrimination may produce a scattering of all-Negro residential pockets rather than genuine dispersions unless attempts are made to prevent the concentration of Negroes in any given neighborhood.

Panic flights of old-resident whites at the appearance of one or a few new-resident Negro families will be discouraged if the old residents know that, no matter where they move, a similar development might take place. The new residents in most cases will seek to avoid another all-Negro neighborhood. The interests of old and new residents become congruent on the points of maintaining neighborhood standards and mixed, rather than all-Negro, occupancy. Other less happy outcomes are of course possible. But non-discrimination laws, where combined with a sensitivity to the importance of not crowding Negroes into any single area, provide opportunities for giving Negroes the free residential choice they should have while simultaneously producing minimum disturbance in existing communities.

CONTROLLED MIGRATION

The case for non-discriminating laws thus rests largely on the point that they would filter non-whites in relatively small numbers to white communities. Laws of this sort are difficult to enforce. (How does one prove discrimination if a seller decides not to sell?)

Population groups are infinitely facile in frustrating unpopular laws. Public acceptance is necessary if interracial living is to be made possible.

The tipping phenomenon has meant that interracial communities in the United States (outside some slum areas) exist only where there also exist limits on the influx of non-whites. In the usual case, these limits have been economic in nature. Thus the Kenwood region of Chicago is a truly interracial one. Homes in this neighborhood are large and expensive to maintain, and municipal housing codes are rigidly enforced. Pure economic pressures, combined with community acceptance of those Negroes who can afford to live there, have produced an upper-middle class interracial neighborhood.

In other cases, control of in-migration has been consciously contrived. The developers of the Philadelphia suburbs of Concord Park and Greenbelt Knoll have announced their intention of maintaining a white-Negro ratio of 55–45. Prospective purchasers place their names on a waiting list, and a purchase is made possible only if it maintains the desired racial distribution.

It is doubtful that many population groups, other than confirmed, egalitarian Quakers, would accept a ratio of Negroes at this high a point. On the other hand, Negro political leaders in the large cities could probably not remain political leaders if they were willing to accept controlled interracialism, set at a ratio that most whites would accept.

Nevertheless, experimentation with various systems of controlled migration is highly desirable. The tip-point phenomenon is so universal that it constitutes strong evidence in favor of control. Without control there has been a total failure to achieve interracial communities involving substantial numbers of Negroes anywhere in the great urban areas of America. Where controlled migration has been achieved, so has interracial living.

Many methods can be found to implement a controlled migration. A free real estate market, accompanied by enforced, adequate housing codes, is the preferred mechanism. The direct rationing of sales,

as in the Philadelphia suburbs, is possible in a number of different forms. Community organizations of all types, including church groups, can be mobilized. Informal pressures upon real estate operators and mortgagers can be effective. The private, if not public, support of Negro leaders for controlled migration can be achieved. At Concord Park and Greenbelt Knoll, the builders found no opposition from Negroes to a balanced community pattern, once it was explained that the larger goal was to break down racial segregation. Many Negroes will support policies aimed at avoiding all-Negro communities if alternative housing opportunities are available.

The moral problem is not an easy one. It is the problem of placing limits upon Negro in-migration to particular urban and suburban areas. It means fostering a smaller discrimination in favor of scotching a larger one. Whatever the difficulties of such a position, it seems to be, for a large number of Negroes and whites alike, a preferable alternative to the present pattern of segregated population groups.

RETURNING WHITE POPULATION TO CENTRAL CITIES

Values of urbanism, other things being equal, compete easily with the suburban way of life. The other things now *not* equal include: modern, moderate priced housing; cleanliness and green space; good schools; safety against hoodlum attack; a sense of neighborhood solidarity. If such amenities were available, the attractions of urban life would almost certainly be sufficient to bring large numbers of white residents back into the cities. The cities offer a diversity of living conditions, a choice of companionship, and a range of leisure time activities that cannot be matched by the suburbs with their relatively closed and static conditions of life. The isolation of the dormitory suburbs, the large fraction of life demanded for commuting, and the social restriction of village living have already produced a swelling protest. Some segment of the metropolitan population is certainly composed of confirmed suburbanites, and no changes in the central city would attract them. But urban life would beckon large numbers if it could compete with suburbia in terms of the economics of housing, the safety and comfort of families, and the social solidarity of neighborhoods.

No precise data exist concerning the extent to which the disillusionment with the suburbs has already started a return flow to the cities. Certainly that flow has been considerable, especially among older couples, the more wealthy, and the childless. (The Chicago Gold Coast and the Manhattan luxury apartment would make important foci of research for measuring this flow.) What needs to be done is to bring into this stream the larger numbers of young and middle-aged couples who have families and who are not wealthy. Developments within the suburbs—the overcrowding of schools, the blighting of badly planned residential areas, and the full flowering of the uninhibited automobile culture—will provide an additional push toward the cities.

Whatever may be accomplished by individual home owners and real estate specialists will not be sufficient to reverse the massive population trends described earlier. The effort must be aided by governmental action. The important point is that governmental programs must be on a far larger scale than any action thus far undertaken.

The basic unit of operation must be a large site: a complete neighborhood or even a complete area of the city. The scale of urban renewal must be conceived not in square blocks, but in square miles. Destruction or rehabilitation of old urban dwellings and the building of new neighborhoods must be planned not in tens of acres but in hundreds. Whole sections of cities will have to be made over in order to attract an influx of stable white population groups.

Rebuilding on this scale is important for many reasons. And it would provide one opportunity to achieve interracial communities. Many white families affirm that they move to the suburbs not because they have Negroes for neighbors but because of the neighborhood deterioration that accompanies the high densities and rowdy behavior of the inmigrants. Large rebuilt areas, strictly controlled against over-crowding, would have the effect of removing such objections. Very large sums of public money will be required for this sort of program, but the obstacles are political rather than economic. Intricate collaborative devices among the local, state, and federal governments will be necessary. The history of urban redevelopment thus far, with few exceptions, is a history of too little, too late. Anything less than a massive program may have admirable local effects for particular population fractions, as when adequate housing is substituted for slum housing over several blocks for a few residents in New York's Harlem. These ameliorative programs are not to be criticized. But they do not attack the basic problem of the bifurcation of races on urban-suburban lines. To meet this problem, the rebuilding of entire sections of major cities is necessary.

THE SUBURBANIZATION OF NEGROES

Any extensive rebuilding of central cities will displace Negro populations who inhabit the very urban areas most in need of rebuilding. No progress is possible unless a redistribution of the Negro population simultaneously occurs. One objective must be a migration of Negroes to suburban areas.

It is widely assumed that opening suburbs to Negroes would be readily achieved if there existed a single local government whose jurisdiction covered the entire metropolitan area. This is certainly too optimistic a view of the matter. Even under a metropolitan government, the people in outlying areas would not be without ability to resist, politically and socially, the incursion of what they consider "undesirable elements" into their communities. In Chicago and in many other places, residents of "better" neighborhoods *within* the central city have successfully opposed housing measures which threatened to bring Negro residents into their areas. If the free distribution of non-white groups is not politically feasible on an inter-neighborhood basis, the creation of a metropolitan government will certainly not make it so on an inter-city one. A single government for a whole area might conceivably provide a more satisfactory political arena for the eventual solution of distributing non-white groups throughout an entire metropolitan area, but will not *ipso facto* guarantee that distribution.

Nor is it true that restrictions on the migration of Negro and other non-white groups to the suburbs is solely a class or economic matter. Any examination of the variety of suburban conditions leads to the conclusion that urban blight and the dilapidated housing and social conditions that accompany it are not uniquely characteristic of the central cities. Rather, blight exists in varying degrees of intensity in all parts of the metropolitan area, central city and suburbs alike. In all but

the very newest of planned suburban developments, many dwelling units exist which, in the terms of the Bureau of the Census, "should be torn down, extensively repaired, or rebuilt." Only a fraction of these units are Negro dwellings. In many metropolitan areas a larger proportion of dwelling units outside than inside the central city are dilapidated or lack running water.

Despite these facts, in many suburban areas the extravagances of legal restrictions covering suburban building should be examined for their effect upon maintaining Negro urban concentrations. Provisions covering lot sizes, sidewalks, streets, building setbacks, and building materials often have very little to do with the maintenance of standards of health and decency. They are, rather, frankly established to stabilize or to upgrade community levels, including the maintenance of their racial character. The effect is to make suburban housing too expensive for even the Negroes who otherwise could afford, and would prefer, suburban living. Less extravagant building and housing codes would certainly lead to some greater degree of Negro suburbanization. This can be accomplished without producing additional suburban slums. The antidote to overstringent building restrictions is not their complete abolition.

Non-discriminatory housing laws would, as we have seen, go a long way in encouraging some suburbanization of Negroes. Other discriminating practices —many of them extra-legal—should be ended. If local building inspectors cannot be trained to administer laws impartially, they should be replaced by officials who can, under state or federal supervision. If local police forces will not protect the property and lives of Negro purchasers of suburban homes, then procedures for training, replacing, or penalizing such officials must be adopted. If established realtors will not sell to Negroes, others should be encouraged, and perhaps paid, to do so.

Social attitudes change more slowly than laws, and only a moderate incursion of Negroes into established suburbs can be expected in the near future. The best chance for even this modest development is under community auspices on the basis of controlled migrations. The need for Negro suburban housing will greatly exceed the receptivity of the established suburbs, especially if central city rebuilding is undertaken on the scale that it is needed. This sharply raises the question of the desirability of encouraging all-Negro suburbs.

The negative consideration is obvious: all-Negro suburbs would simply substitute one sort of segregated life for another. On the other hand, there is much to be said on the positive side. Such suburbs would be a large factor in redressing the present imbalance in the urban-suburban population distribution. As we have seen, this in itself is a highly desirable step. Secondly, such communities, adequately planned and constructed, would provide a great improvement in living conditions, superior to both the urban and suburban slums in which so large a proportion of Negroes now reside. Thirdly, and perhaps most importantly, the all-Negro middle-class suburb could very well constitute a significant step in the direction of large-scale interracial communities. Present conditions of life of the largest fraction of the Negro population discourage, rather than encourage, the habits of thought and conduct deemed desirable by the larger white community. The middle-class Negro suburb would foster such attributes. If class, in addition to skin color,

is a principal cause of segregation, then the class differential may be overcome by the middle-class suburban life.

As in so many planned social changes, schemes for all-Negro suburban communities may produce unexpected ill consequences. One deserves mention. Grant the truth of what has been said: that good suburban housing in a good suburban neighborhood will aid in producing a Negro population of model, middle-class, social attributes, and that nothing distinguishes this group from middle-class whites except skin color. It is then easily assumed that interracial living is the next step. But the opposite assumption must also be entertained: that whites will continue to resist interracial living. In this event Negroes will all the more resent their segregation and whites will have no line except the color line on which to take a stand. If Negro-white tensions pivot exclusively on color, they may be exacerbated to a new point of bitterness.

Despite such dangers, the more persuasive evidence is that Negro-white tensions will decrease, not increase, as the populations become socially more alike. For this reason, as well as the need to meet short-run housing requirements, experiments with all-Negro suburban communities should be encouraged.

NEGROES TO SMALLER CITIES

Discussion of the possible distribution of some Negroes to points outside the larger metropolitan areas does not fall strictly within the purposes of this study. Yet it is worth noting that Negroes are greatly underrepresented in virtually all places outside the South and the larger urban areas of the rest of the country. A program of encouraging migration to these smaller cities would somewhat mitigate the large city, urban-suburban racial bifurcation and, at the same time, establish important new opportunities for integrated living. The effects of such an effort should not be overestimated. For example, if one unrealistically assumes it were possible for non-southern cities of from 10 thousand to 250 thousand population to be increased 5 per cent in total population by an in-migration of Negroes, the total number so placed would be about a million, or less than the number of Negroes in New York City at the 1960 census.

Nevertheless, attempts to locate Negroes in cities of this size—as well as in smaller urban areas—would be worthwhile. Since employment opportunities in industry constitute the most important attraction for Negro in-migrants, the success of such attempts would pivot upon the availability of such jobs for Negroes (therefore a shortage of white workers) and upon information concerning such opportunities being disseminated among potential migrants. The former factor will to a large extent depend upon further industrial growth in small- and medium-size urban areas. The factor of publicity is more immediately controllable. The information flow now directed at potential migrants from the South (by such organizations as the Urban League) could very well be focused more sharply on the existing and emerging opportunities outside the larger metropolitan areas.

No single measure will solve the problem in any single area, and the same combination of measures will not be appropriate as leverage points in any two areas. What strikes the observer is the paucity of imagination that has been brought to bear on the issue. The Quaker communities in the Philadelphia area provide a model for one kind of controlled

migration that is only slowly being taken up in other places. The investment in almost any city of, say, a million dollars in a revolving fund for the purchase of homes to foster interracial neighborhoods, with careful planning and public relations, could make a dent in the pattern of segregation. A well-staffed, resourceful office with the objective of publicizing successes of interracial residential contacts would be a valuable positive aid to enlarging those contacts and no less valuable a means of dissipating images of disagreeableness and violence that widely prevail.

Action programs of this sort are obvious needs. Beyond them there exists a wide range of more experimental possibilities for both private and public agencies. For example, there are a number of newly built areas in the central cities whose attractiveness and proximity to work and recreational facilities make them highly desirable living places. Lake Meadows, in Chicago, is a good example of this sort of development. Nevertheless, these areas tend to become all-Negro communities because of their relatively small size, or their situation close to older Negro slums, or other factors. It might be possible to make such newly built areas model interracial neighborhoods. How can white residents be attracted to them? A private foundation might bring the attractions of such developments to the attention of whites by maintaining a good small museum at such a site or by arranging concerts there (but at no other nearby place) of outstanding musical groups, or by providing superior park and swimming facilities, or indeed by partially subsidizing rental costs for limited periods. The marginal attractions needed to bring whites into such intrinsically attractive areas may in many cases be quite small; and once a pattern of interracial living is successfully achieved it may be expected to continue as subsidies are diminished. Private organizations could in a similar way reward suburban communities that make it easy for Negroes to take up residence.

The national government may not be barred from an analogous type of activity. A good case can be made for a federal program to provide suburbs with aid for community facilities they already need and will need even more in years to come: schools, parks, libraries, swimming pools, and similar amenities. It is commonplace for federal legislation to establish conditions that must be met by local governments before they qualify for financial aid. The question arises: is it possible to write a federal law that would supply aid for community facilities on a priority basis to those suburbs containing a given minimum of Negro residents? Constitutional and political questions immediately arise. Clearly no requirement based directly upon a racial classification would meet constitutional standards. Yet it is not beyond the realm of legal creativity to find another scheme of definition that would foster the end of racial distribution and yet remain within constitutional limits. The more difficult objection is political, but it is by no means insurmountable. Even southern congressmen might support such a measure if for no other reason than glee over the embarrassment of their northern colleagues. The larger point is not to argue for the desirability or feasibility of this particular measure, but rather to suggest the need for inventive action. The growing consequences of the population schism, plus the plight that many suburbs will soon find themselves in, combine to bring within the realm of probability even schemes that at first blush seem impossible of achievement.

The whole discussion of "solutions" now rests too largely upon moral terms. The wealth of the United States has historically been used to remove issues from the idealistic to a cash basis, and in this issue, too, cash may be a great salve for moral wounds. This is not meant to be a cynical statement. It is, rather, counsel for the strategy of induced social change. Payment in the form of needed community facilities should accompany other types of action.

Church, social work, and educational institutions must prepare the ground for interracial living and must be ready to act when tensions occur. Indeed, mobilization of resources must take place over a very wide range, from training police officers in problems of race relations to the establishment of special community programs for the improvement of interracial contacts; from the provision of social services for Negro in-migrants to education programs for prospective employers of Negroes; from block activity preparing the way for Negro neighbors to nation-wide programs that implement basic Negro civil rights. Every community facility—churches, schools, labor unions, recreational groups, economic organizations, and government—can be enlisted. Here, as with almost all programs of civic change, working through established institutions and existing voluntary groups is the best avenue to success.

CONCLUSION

It is frequently argued that problems created by the present distribution of Negroes in the large metropolitan areas are only transitory problems. They will solve themselves through the normal processes of acculturation. This view holds that every immigrant wave to the great cities has at least initially produced disadvantaged ethnic islands. With the passage of time, however, these islands have given way as the second and third generations have acquired cultural characteristics of the larger society and broken away from the habits of conduct of their immigrant fathers and grandfathers. This is the pattern of the Jews in New York, the Poles in Chicago, the Italians in San Francisco. There is some evidence that the Negro group is going through the same process as its members surmount social, vocational, professional, and residential barriers. All the problem needs is time. The American melting pot will work for Negroes as it has for others.

This is a hopeful view. Despite many examples of successful interracial adjustment, it is a view not substantiated by either history or available data. The example of earlier European immigrants all concern white populations. No statistically significant evidence exists indicating the inevitable dissolution of the Negro concentrations. As with Japanese-Americans before World War II, acceptance by the larger community for a relatively few Negroes is being accompanied by life within closed communities for the relatively many. (The Japanese community in Los Angeles grew continuously between 1900 and 1942.) The factor of skin color, alone, is one cause for the different course of development. The very size of the Negro concentration in the larger cities, resulting in the establishment of an entire Negro economic and social life, can also be expected to obstruct the decline of the communities in which that life flourishes. To this must be added the disinclination of many white groups to accept Negroes as neighbors and social companions. The total picture for the future, if present trends are unaltered, is the further breaking down

of some boundaries of the closed community affecting proportionately small numbers of Negroes. For the largest numbers, segregation will continue and probably increase, rather than decline.

This is almost certainly the correct prognosis for the immediate 30 years ahead. To the extent that the natural acculturation argument is one covering the distant future—say 80 or 100 years—it may have greater accuracy. But to that extent it is largely irrelevant. The central cities of the metropolitan areas dominate the nation not only in population but also in retail and wholesale sales, manufacturing, and the provision of services to individuals and businesses. They set the tone and pattern for the entire complex of community interdependence in politics, economics, and cultural life. If the analysis presented here is accurate, the whole nation is faced with a wide range of deleterious consequences. And these consequences will take their toll long before the "natural desuetude" of segregation is accomplished. This is the justification for taking all positive steps possible to end the present patterns of segregation.

Another reason for not disturbing the current population distribution might lie in the danger that dispersion would deprive Negroes of the political power they have acquired as the consequence of concentration. This is not a valid argument for two reasons.

On the one hand, it does not take into account the genuine gains that accrue to the Negro population as the consequence of dispersion. Increasing strain in race relations seems always to accompany concentrated numbers. Where a minority group is dispersed, it is less visible, less likely to be considered a unit, less feared, less subject to discrimination. Where it is concentrated and segregated, it is more likely to be relegated to a sub-ordinate position, and its members have fewer opportunities for assimilation into the larger social structure.

On the other hand, dispersion of residential areas would not necessarily lead to a decline in Negro political power. The 100 per cent Negro voting districts can be viewed as a type of gerrymandering in which political power is lost by the very concentration of voters. Negroes constituting 50 per cent of the voters in two election districts (or 25 per cent in four districts) will wield more political power than if they composed 100 per cent of a single district. What is to be avoided is the halfway house: not enough dispersion to prevent clear subordination, with not enough concentration to make numbers politically effective. Within the larger metropolitan areas this is an unlikely possibility. The gains to be made by Negroes from political action built upon concentration can never equal those that can be achieved by dispersion throughout the metropolitan areas.

The programs suggested for overcoming Negro concentrations face great obstacles. They arouse the ire of the ignorant and the prejudiced. They are disquieting to even the fair-minded and the sophisticated who live good lives and who perform their civic duties conscientiously. And they will be bitterly opposed by a wide range of people: owners, mortgagers, and others who profit from the present patterns of land use; political leaders in the central cities, including Negro leaders, who fear the dissipation of established constituencies, as well as political leaders of other areas whose tenure will be disturbed by the incursion of new voters into their districts; old residents of suburbs and the better central-city neighborhoods who hold strongly to their comfortable social situations and established shopping, social, and educational patterns. Even those with humanitarian motives will voice opposition to some plans on the grounds that they constitute an unwarranted interference in the life patterns of the poor. And Negro groups and leaders will not easily be won over to some aspects of the proposed program. They will, for example, see large-scale urban renewal as a displacement and an imposition, before its advantages will be apparent. Negroes have already in many cities distinguished themselves for their opposition to smaller-scale programs of urban renewal. Some of this opposition may be blunted, as when Negro opposition to urban renewal is placated by well-planned programs of relocation housing. But every such move, in turn, is likely to increase opposition from other sources, in the example given from areas in which the relocation housing is to be placed.

Despite difficulties and despite the uncertainty of success, all efforts are justified. The stakes are high: the preservation and further development of many facets of urban American life, for whites and Negroes alike. By building a non-discriminatory housing market in both city and suburbs, income and social attributes, not race, can be maximized as the criteria for residential location. By rebuilding large areas of central cities, white populations can be induced to return to those cities. By combating restrictions against Negro occupancy of suburbs, a flow of non-whites can be started in that direction. By attracting Negroes to jobs in the smaller cities outside the South, where they are now underrepresented, some of the present and potential city-suburban population imbalance may be corrected. By encouraging through community resources the controlled migration of Negroes into all areas of city and suburbs, a significant redistribution of Negroes and whites can take place. All these measures minimize the dangerous operation of the tip-point psychology. Here, as elsewhere, nothing succeeds like success, and a demonstra-

tion that such a program can produce results in one metropolitan area of the nation will be important for all areas. The only way to avoid the consequences of racial schism is to bridge it.

CRISIS WITHOUT VIOLENCE:
THE STORY OF A HOT SUMMER

Alexander F. Miller

THE TIME

For millions of Americans involved in the civil rights issue, the spring of 1964 proved menacingly warm; Dr. Martin Luther King was not alone in forecasting a long, hot summer. The three-month filibuster on the Civil Rights Act was itself a harbinger of crisis, all the more obvious because extremists among the filibusterers, aware that they could not stop the ultimate passage of the act, were openly looking beyond obstructionism in Washington to outright defiance at home.

Other factors contributed to a sense of crisis. Negro leaders were haunted by the possibility of Goldwater in the White House and Governor Wallace's shadow over it. By the end of May, Wallace had won the Wisconsin primary and had very nearly won in Maryland; early in June, Goldwater attained his clinching victory in California. The "white backlash" seemed very much a threatening reality.

These developments could not have

been better designed to try the patience of American Negroes, already tantalized by ten years of frustrating token compliance with the 1954 decision, nor could anything have given it a clearer sense of the implacability of the forces arrayed against it. Negro leaders and their supporters responded with massive preparations for a showdown in the South, once the act became law. And even while the filibuster continued, isolated outbreaks of violence occurred—not only in Jacksonville and Tuscaloosa, Birmingham and Canton, but also in New York, Baltimore, and San Francisco.

By the end of spring, it was abundantly clear that many Negro communities, North, East, South, and West, were on the verge of explosion.

Then, on June 21, the first day of summer, three civil rights workers disappeared in Philadelphia, Mississippi, and in New Rochelle, New York, a policeman clubbed a Negro youngster over the head.

The dark and bloody trail of the three civil rights youths from a small-town jail

From *Crisis Without Violence: The Story of a Hot Summer*, 1965, pp. 7–32. Reprinted with the permission of the Anti-Defamation League of B'nai B'rith, 315 Lexington Avenue, New York, N. Y., 10016.

cell to their common grave in a Mississippi backwater dam has become a well-thumbed page of tragic contemporary history. The New Rochelle incident has a different importance. It was the first of a series of racial crises in Northern commuities arising from charges of police brutality. But whereas the happenings in Harlem, Bedford-Stuyvesant, Rochester, Philadelphia, Newark, and other cities made national headlines, the New Rochelle incident was never more than a local story. This is what makes it worth retelling.

THE PLACE

New Rochelle is a compact, rather elongated city of 80,000 inhabitants lying twenty-five miles northeast of New York City. It has some light industry and considerable retail business, but it functions chiefly as a bedroom for thousands of commuters to New York City. As is typical for suburbs in this area, the religio-ethnic composition of its population runs counter to the national standard: the minorities are in the majority. Thus, roughly equal numbers of Catholics and Jews together make up more than 50 per cent of the population, while Protestants about 25 per cent, and Negroes the remainder.

Most of the nearly 20,000 Negroes live in a clearly defined ghetto that cuts diagonally across the heart of the community. Perhaps 12 per cent of them live in substandard housing. Two integrated districts adjoin the ghetto; in them, middle- and lower-middle-class Negroes live alongside whites on the pleasant, tree-lined streets that make up most of New Rochelle's residential areas. A handful of wealthy Negroes have bought substantial homes in the more exclusive districts.

During most of the city's history,

Negro-white relations have been peaceful enough, and in some ways rather better than average. Ten years ago, when Baltimore was having difficulty desegregating its schools, the integrated New Rochelle High School played host to a group of Baltimore youngsters to demonstrate that Jim Crow need have no place in a classroom.

The local grammar schools, however, shaped by the prevailing neighborhood-school concept, were in a different situation. For some years the Lincoln School, which had become enveloped by the growing Negro ghetto, was a point of friction between the white and Negro communities. Attempts to desegregate it had been foiled by Board of Education maneuvers. Matters came to a head in 1960-61; local integrationists, the story of Little Rock fresh in their minds, began alluding to New Rochelle as "New Rock." Negro parents instituted a desegregation suit and shortly thereafter a new and progressive-minded school superintendent moved into the picture. The court decision by Judge Irving Kauffman—an important one in civil rights annals—gave Negro parents the right to have their children transported to integrated schools; eventually the Lincoln School building, old and much deteriorated, was torn down.

The importance of the "New Rock" incident went beyond the court's decision. It hastened the development of a mature and militant local Negro leadership, moving the community into the mainstream of the social revolution begun seven years earlier by the U.S. Supreme Court decision in *Brown vs. Board of Education.* With the school problem at least temporarily settled, the leaders turned their attention to other old and burning issues: housing, job discrimination, relations with police, etc.

But since no specific municipal agency

was in a position to take an overall look into the discrimination problem, more often than not the complaints of the Negroes tended to become lost in that amorphous bureaucracy known as City Hall. That was one reason why New Rochelle's municipal administration reacted favorably when, in June of 1963, Governor Rockefeller urged mayors throughout the state to set up Human Rights Commissions in their respective communities.

THE COMMISSION

Pursuant to a City Council resolution, a nine-man Human Rights Commission was appointed in December 1963, as one of the last official acts of an outgoing Mayor. Two of the members were Negroes, both sociologists with impressive academic backgrounds. The seven white members roughly approximated the religious composition of the city's population: three Catholics, three Jews, and one Protestant (the Negro members were also Protestants). They included three clergymen (one of each major faith), a businessman, a public relations expert, a labor union official, and an experienced professional in intergroup relations.

The circumstances under which the commission began its work were not altogether auspicious. On one hand, it had to establish relations with a new City Hall administration and, more particularly, with a new Mayor who had had no hand in appointing it. On the other side, the Negro leadership, not unnaturally, tended to look upon this new arm of City Hall as part of the white "power structure," and therefore not entirely trustworthy.

It was not until some weeks after the commission had begun to function that a small office suite in City Hall was put at its disposal. And, it was the end of May,

before the commission was able to find a suitable executive director—the one paid employee, aside from a secretary, for whom provision was made in the budget.

Despite these difficulties, the first few months of operation were by no means without accomplishment. Aside from the vital preliminary work of establishing contacts, the commission made some headway in the handling of job discrimination complaints. With its institutional prestige not yet established, such successes as were achieved were due mainly to the considerable personal prestige and the dedicated hard work of individual commissioners.

Meanwhile, the group sought to define for itself exactly what pattern of procedures and attitudes was best calculated to achieve the goals outlined in its operating charter. The commissioners realized that, almost by definition, they would be identified in the public mind with the cause of minorities. But within this overall bias, justified by the laws of the federal and state governments as well as those of the municipality, they were determined to act only on facts. The commission would, and did, scrutinize Negro complaints as objectively as it examined the explanations, justifications, and/or denials of those complained against. If the commission did not want Negroes to consider it as part of the white power structure, neither did it want whites to look upon it as a partisan of the Negro community. The commissioners did not see themselves as Negro partisans; they considered themselves partisans of law, order, and the democratic ideal of equal opportunities for all citizens.

On the first day of the summer of 1963, the New Rochelle Human Rights Commission was six months old, and had been operating at full capacity—that is, with a paid executive director and secretary—

for no more than three weeks. Three days later it was plunged into the gravest racial crisis in the city's history.

JUNE 21: THE BLOW

On the evening of Sunday, June 21, Patrolman Richard Deere, a member of the New Rochelle police force for fifteen months, was patrolling the walks of Hartley Houses, a housing development in the Negro area about ten minutes' walk from City Hall. He was under orders to disperse groups of young people who might be blocking the walks or threatening to become unruly. At one point, according to testimony, he ordered a Negro boy, 17-year-old Richard Hunter, to move on. The boy did not obey the command, which was then repeated. Still Hunter didn't move. Patrolman Deere put his hand on the young Negro's arm and said, "Come along with me." When Hunter resisted, the patrolman hit him over the head with his club. Hunter fell to the ground, bleeding, and an ambulance was called. In the hospital emergency ward, the wound was treated—six stitches were required to close it. The attending physician was then ready to release the boy, but a private physician, sent to the hospital by the boy's mother, said that there was evidence of concussion and ordered his patient held for observation.

Many of the facts concerning the attack and its aftermath are still under dispute. For instance, was it really necessary for Hunter to be kept in the hospital? But some of the facts are unarguable. One is that the policeman, in his late twenties, is 5 feet 11 inches tall, and weighs 180 pounds, and that the boy on whom he used his club was nearly 4 inches shorter and weighed 45 pounds less. Another is that at no time during the confrontation did the boy strike at the officer, or even threaten to strike.

Since the attack took place in full view of scores of onlookers, news of the incident spread rapidly throughout the housing development and thence to the Negro community as a whole. The boy's mother, who had been standing nearby (how close was a matter of dispute) during the incident, called upon the Negro leadership to act in protest, forcefully and at once. The leaders were not averse to acting. Patrolman Deere's blow culminated a long series of Negro grievances, including three or four fairly well authenticated cases of police brutality within the preceding twelve months. The edginess of the Negroes was increased by the atmosphere of racial crisis that had been developing all over the country during that whole spring.

For the next two days Negro leaders met privately, consulting on the telephone, preparing a rank-and-file following to carry out the plans they had in mind. Every important Negro organization represented in New Rochelle was involved: CORE, the NAACP, the Urban League, the Negro American Labor Council, the Interdenominational Ministerial Alliance, the Hartley Tenants Council, and a county-wide federation of Negro groups called the Joint Committee for Equal Opportunity.

The total lack of communication between the Negro and white communities of New Rochelle is revealed sharply by the fact that not a word of any of this frantic activity seeped through to the city at large—not to the Human Rights Commission, not to the Mayor's office, not to the man on the street. Not only was the city unaware that its Negro citizens were aroused; by and large, it was not even aware that anything had happened to provoke them. The clubbing of the boy had rated not a line in the local newspaper.

On Wednesday afternoon, three days

after the clubbing, the Negroes' plans were finally revealed. Mimeographed fliers prepared by the leadership were distributed; they called upon Negroes to join a march on City Hall that night to protest police brutality. It was a mark of the earnestness and grim sense of responsibility of the Negro leaders that all City Hall offices, including those of the Police Department, received copies of the fliers.

The chairman of the Human Rights Commission, in New York at the time, was told of this development by telephone. He was also informed that no one—not even the police—knew for certain that the information carried by the fliers was valid. The commission's executive director, from her office in City Hall, tried in vain to reach some of the Negro leaders by telephone. Ultimately she went in person to Hartley Houses, where the demonstration was to begin, and found between 1,200 and 1,500 people gathering. When the march began, she joined the procession as it streamed toward City Hall. The atmosphere, as she later described it, was determined, but far from menacing; the marchers, many of them youngsters, were orderly and enthusiastic.

By this time the chairman had returned from New York and rushed directly to City Hall. He found the lawns and parking areas around the building gradually filling up with demonstrators. A chant began: "Badge 16 must go!" (Badge 16 was worn by Patrolman Deere.) The Chief of Police, with unusual tact, ordered that only unarmed officers of higher rank should mingle with the crowd; patrolmen were ordered to stay on the periphery, and not to move unless called upon.

The chairman and the director approached a group of Negro leaders milling around the City Hall's main entrance. "We are at the end of our rope," one of them said. "This crowd is pretty quiet now, but if we can't get some satisfaction out of tonight, they'll be uncontrollable." He added that he and his colleagues had asked to see the Commissioner of Police and had been told he was not in the building. The director assured them that the Commissioner could be recalled quickly and that a meeting could be arranged within minutes.

The Police Commissioner, new at his post, had never even heard of the Human Rights Commission, but through the intercession of the Chief of Police and others, the chairman arranged for a meeting. Some of the Negro leaders, using loudspeakers, told the crowd to quiet down, that talks would soon be in progress. Most of the chanting subsided and hundreds among the crowd sat down on the ground, determined to stay put while the talks went on.

About a dozen leaders, with the chairman and the director of the Human Relations Commission, crowded into the Commissioner's office. The talks started off badly. The Negroes were tense; the Commissioner had difficulty adjusting to a complex situation in what was for him a new environment. The Negroes wanted Deere suspended forthwith, and they wanted a civilian review board appointed to pass upon cases such as this. The Commissioner opposed both demands; he would take no action against any of his policemen, he said brusquely, without a departmental hearing.

Several times during the acrimonious exchanges, police officers came into the room to report that the situation outside was deteriorating. The crowd was restive; there were sit-downs in the street, holding up traffic. Again police action was cautious, tactful. Orders went out that the sit-downs were not to be disturbed; instead, traffic was rerouted.

Toward eleven o'clock, the Commissioner wanted to break up the meeting. "We're not getting anywhere," he said. "We're tired and hot-headed. Let's meet again in the morning at eight o'clock." When the massed demonstrators were told of this decision by loudspeaker from the City Hall steps, there were renewed shouts and catcalls, and a restlessness went through the crowd. It was obvious that the demonstrators might quickly turn ugly. The chairman urged both the Commissioner and the Negro leaders to resume their meeting and to keep at it until some agreement, no matter how preliminary or how tenuous, was reached. The Commissioner finally consented, but demanded that the Negro representation be reduced to six persons. After some debate, the Negroes complied.

The second session was more constructive. The committee was permitted to present witnesses to the attack on Hunter. The Commissioner gave repeated assurances that Deere's conduct would be reviewed. But he reminded his listeners that there were criminal charges against Hunter: disorderly conduct and resistance to arrest. These charges, he said, must be disposed of before the Police Department could review the case against the patrolman. However, he promised to do everything in his power to speed action all along the line.

The meeting broke up on this note. The Negro leaders had at least been given an opportunity to show that they had a case. The line of communication had been established; nobody had walked out on anybody. If the members of the Negro committee were not happy when they left City Hall, they were a little less unhappy than they had been when they arrived.

While the talks were proceeding, the director of the Human Relations Commission had been circulating among the demonstrators outside, urging them to go home—especially the young ones. Many had left. Now the long night ended with no indications of violence except for a few rocks thrown at passing cars, which injured no one and damaged nothing.

JUNE 25–26: KEEP TALKING

From the point of view of the commission, two things now seemed of vital importance: that lines of communication be kept open, and that the Negro community be made aware that the city administration as a whole, and not merely the police, was involved with developments. With this in mind the chairman talked with the Mayor early the next morning. As a result, the Mayor and the Corporation Counsel met that afternoon with local Negro ministers and the commission director. The clergymen were assured of the Mayor's deep and continuing personal interest in the whole problem. A statement was then drawn up by the Mayor and the Corporation Counsel, was approved by the commission chairman, and then released for publication over the signatures of the Mayor and the chairman. The statement, addressed primarily to the city's Negro citizens, read:

As city officials, we are concerned with and responsible for protecting the constitutional rights of every citizen of New Rochelle. We recognize and agree with your desire to settle the charges of alleged police brutality. The City Court has promised an immediate and speedy disposition of the case [i.e., the charges against Hunter]. Immediately following the court trial, regardless of the verdict, a departmental trial of the arresting police officer will be held.

It is our conviction that a prompt legal decision will insure a fair and final settlement of the case. This due process of law will protect the individual liberties of all concerned. We are anxious to dispose of this matter as quickly as anyone in the city.

However, it is important that we do not slight judicial process. No city official should have the power to suspend or discharge employees by whim. That is why we need hearings, a departmental trial, and due process of law.

The chairman, in signing this document, realized that the commission was taking a measurable risk in aligning itself so early against the Negro demand for the immediate suspension of Deere. Yet it seemed to the chairman, and to other members of the commission, that to argue *for* suspension involved the greater risk. The commission's charter gave it no policing or enforcement powers; its only hope of achieving results in the future was through orderly legal procedures. To flout such procedures now might set a precedent that could easily boomerang. What if a Negro policeman were to be suspended without hearing on charges leveled by some prejudiced superior?

At least the statement did inform the Negro community that the Mayor, as well as the commission, was committed to follow through on the affair. But even as the statement was under preparation, pickets were still circling City Hall demanding, "Badge No. 16 must go!"

At this point it was clear enough that a delay was unavoidable in the development of the Hunter-Deere case, enmeshed as it was in due process. No date could be set for Deere's hearing: it must wait on the disposition of the charges against Hunter, and Hunter was still in the hospital. Justice could wait patiently, but would the Negro community? It seemed to the chairman that the city administration must make some immediate move to prove its good will toward its Negro citizens; if no such move was possible in the Deere case, then one must be made in some other direction.

The commission's chairman presented this point of view, as forcefully as he could, at a meeting the next day which brought together the Police Commissioner, other city officials, members of the Chamber of Commerce, and the cooperative Mayor. The chairman urged a serious study of the feasibility of a human relations course for the police and of the creation of a civilian-staffed police review board. He stressed the need for more jobs for Negroes, especially on the city payroll, and recommended enlargement and intensification of the programs of the Youth Board and the Recreation Commission. In the latter connection, he pointed out that many of the demonstrators on June 24, and many of those who were at the moment picketing City Hall, were high school youngsters on vacation who had found neither employment nor adequate playground space.

The chairman had not expected, and did not get, any specific, affirmative response to his suggestions at this meeting. He did, however, get a thoroughly sympathetic hearing—a fact which was duly noted by newspapermen present and was subsequently reported to the public. By the next day, the Negro community knew that the city administration was giving serious consideration to a wide range of Negro grievances.

JUNE 30: THE NEGROES INDICT

Long before the Hunter-Deere incident, the commission had set up for the evening of June 30 a meeting with 150 community leaders, Negro and white, to discuss housing, education, job-discrimination, and related issues, as part of an over-all educational program designed to improve intergroup communication and to generate specific plans for alleviating the Negroes' justified complaints.

Now, in view of the emergency situation, the Mayor turned the planned conference into a town meeting. Interest in the proceedings was the only ticket needed for admission. The City Council chamber was thrown open for the purpose. The Mayor, councilmen, and the commission chairman sat on the dais; the audience, which filled the chamber, was perhaps two-thirds Negro.

In an opening statement, the Mayor explained why he had preempted the occasion and stated again the reasons why he and the Human Rights Commission had opposed peremptory suspension of Patrolman Deere. Then he laid down the ground rules for the evening:

Each speaker from an organization will have no more than five minutes, and there will not be more than two speakers from an organization. Independent speakers will be limited to three minutes. . . . The Chair reserves the right to shorten the time of any speaker if he is merely repeating what has been said by previous speakers. . . . I am certain that in two hours everybody will have had an opportunity to express himself, or hear his thoughts expressed by others.

In the next two hours, some twenty speakers were heard, all but two or three of them Negroes. In intellectual quality, they varied widely; but in sincerity, dignity, and forcefulness they were at a uniformly impressive level. Collectively, the statements added up to a formidable indictment of New Rochelle's white community. Most speakers stressed the immediate issue, i.e., the attack on Hunter, and joined in demanding the patrolman's suspension, but others ranged widely in that dark, discriminatory world in which the American Negro has his being. Perhaps the following extracts will convey the atmosphere of the evening:

The refusal of the Police Commissioner backed by the City Administration to suspend the patrolman left the Negro community in the position of always requesting relief, but never being heard. The age-old pattern of asking the Negro to wait came to the fore.

We recognize and respect the need for law and order and the responsibility of the Police Department for the preservation of law and order. But we neither respect nor recognize the need to whitewash members of the Police Department who operate contrary to the interests of any segment of our community.

We have emphasized that the portrayal of the Negro citizen as undesirable as characterized by our local newspaper would lead to an explosive situation.

I am terrified by the specter which has haunted me ever since I grew up as a little black child on 135th Street in Harlem. Policemen project their own limitations upon men, women and children. We want protection by police officers, responsible police officers. We do not want to feel that we must be protected from the police.

I lived in New Rochelle twenty-eight years and I want to say to you, I haven't slept one minute because of this race problem. The race prejudice is very bad in this town. This incident of police brutality would not be allowed to happen in any other part of town.

I think it is important that we be honest in our statements to you, that we let you know that we are angry, that we are determined and that we will do everything necessary, including being violent, to protect ourselves in the light of what is existing in New Rochelle.

We had high hopes for the Human Rights Commission. But we find that they too have come under the hammer of the Administration, and have taken sides already. Therefore, we too are suspicious of even that commission.

We know of officers now serving on the force who, when addressing our people, refer to them as niggers and black bastards. We have had it! This must stop!

If the democratic process of law and order are to prevail, there can be only one yardstick applicable to all our citizens. The business of "we" and "you" must be eliminated now.

We do not seek special treatment. We ask the same treatment.

Every time you hurt a Negro child, commissioner, Mayor and all City Councilmen, remember that you have a wife and mother. . . . Let it not come to pass that Negroes will be forced to take the position of an eye for an eye and a tooth for a tooth.

I think we are going to walk away tonight not having much faith in what's going to happen. . . . I see another twenty, thirty years of a long, up-hill struggle.

Perhaps the quiet demeanor of the city fathers, who asked no questions and betrayed no emotion, contributed to the pessimism of the final speaker. But this is traditional behavior at open hearings; it meant nothing. The Mayor, closing the proceedings, assured the speakers that their words would be weighed carefully.

Afterwards, the Human Rights Commission met in special session. It was not an easy session. Some commissioners resented the fact that the Mayor and City Council had taken over the evening; the chairman's decision to stand with the Mayor against the immediate suspension of Deere also was sharply criticized. But the debate did not result in a split; and because it did not, its constructive aspects can be emphasized. It led to some necessary thinking about what should be done if a serious and permanent disagreement did split the commission and redoubled the group's zeal to proceed in directions on which all the commissioners were more or less agreed. The commission decided to make its own investigation of the pos-

sibilities of a civilian review board and of a human relations course for the police and, if they proved practicable, officially to favor both.

UNEASY INTERLUDE

Any easing of tensions that may have resulted from the June 30 open hearing did not survive the next few weeks. In retrospect, it would seem that too little was happening in New Rochelle, and too much was happening elsewhere. Violence in Atlanta and Americus, Georgia, and in Hattiesberg and Clarksdale, Mississippi, was followed by the murder of a Negro army reserve officer on a Georgia highway and that of a Negro youth by a police lieutenant, on a New York City street. These disturbing events dominated the local press and radio during the first half of July, and almost nothing of a constructive nature emerged from City Hall to offer them any competition.

What New Rochelle's Negroes wanted most of all was action against Deere. Early in the month they won a small victory when the Commissioner of Police, who would normally be expected to preside over Deere's hearing, announced that he would not do so, that a state Supreme Court judge would preside—if one could be found to accept the responsibility. The satisfaction of the civil rights groups with this development was tempered by two factors: the Commissioner, in withdrawing as hearing officer, emphasized that he was doing so for this case only and was setting no precedent, and his withdrawal further postponed setting the date of the hearing.

While the case against the patrolman lagged, that against Hunter went ahead on schedule. Released from the hospital on July 4, young Hunter was brought before City Court on charges of disorderly conduct and resisting arrest and was bound over for grand jury action.

The Human Rights Commission became increasingly concerned with developments—or, rather, the lack of them. It was obvious that the Negro community was again becoming restless. Rumors began to fly around the city's streets: the Communists were stirring. up the Negroes; Black Muslims were agitating for riots; 500 Negroes from New York City were planning to invade New Rochelle. Week-ends, especially, brought forebodings of violence. Repeatedly, during this period, the chairman and the director of the commission urged the Mayor and other city officials to take action on the proposals for a human relations course for the police and for a civilian review board. To the latter proposal, the Commissioner of Police remained adamantly opposed; on one occasion, when the director approached him on the subject, his response was to show her a resolution adopted by a national police organization declaring that such review boards were part of a Communist plot to undermine the police.

True, all this time the Police Department was behaving with commendable caution, refusing to be stampeded by rumors. Its most experienced patrolmen, Negro and white, were stationed at potential trouble spots; every effort was exerted to avoid another "incident." But at this juncture, good police work solved no problems. Local tensions sharpened as violence erupted in Harlem, precipitated by a more tragic form of the same kind of incident that had started New Rochelle's troubles. By July 21, riots had spread to Brooklyn. The commission knew that local Negro organizations were consulting with one another on possible further action. Would the riot virus infect New Rochelle? The commission

felt that something had to be done at once and on July 23 met in emergency session to decide what.

At the meeting, the director presented the commissioners with the following report, based on a series of informal interviews she had conducted over the previous fortnight throughout the Negro areas:

The Human Rights Commission has quietly sought information in off-the-record discussions with adult Negroes, both in the professional and laboring classes, most of whom are not active participants in civil rights groups. These discussions indicate that:
1. Some of the Negroes interviewed have had personal harassment from the police in New Rochelle and feel that this is universally true.
2. Some feel that the false stereotype persists that the Negro is an inferior citizen given to immorality and lawless conduct; many policemen fail to recognize that the majority of Negroes are good citizens, intelligent, educated, cultured and responsible.
3. All Negroes interviewed were acutely aware of the problems created for the police by hooligan Negro youngsters or adult thugs who create, contribute to and reinforce the bad image of the Negro, and who are using the present over-all hostility between the Negro community and the police as an excuse and cover for their own unlawful actions. Nevertheless, they saw no justification for and resented the fact that police tend to transfer their feeling of hostility to Negro criminals to the entire Negro community.
4. Approximately 70 per cent of those interviewed doubted that any citizen would be given a fair hearing on a complaint against a police officer if that complaint were processed by other police officers. Many cited previous violations of conduct by policemen toward Negroes where complaints had been "shoved under the rug," ignored, or "whitewashed."

Appended to this report was a series of recommendations: (1) increases in police salaries to attract the best possible recruits; (2) immediate initiation of an in-service program in community relations for the Police Department; (3) a police campaign to recruit and promote Negro personnel; (4) establishment of a police advisory board to hear citizens' complaints against the police.

The commissioners, after discussing the report at length and adding further recommendations, decided that the chairman and the director should try to see the Mayor and City Manager as soon as possible in order to impress upon them the seriousness with which the commission viewed the current situation and to request an early meeting of the commission with the City Council.

The Mayor, City Manager, and Corporation Counsel met with the chairman and director the following morning. All three city officials were ready to cooperate. They agreed to arrange the session with the City Council within the next few days and in the meantime to inform press and radio of the efforts of the Corporation Counsel to secure a hearing officer for the Deere hearings. The Corporation Counsel had been unable to find a Supreme Court judge to accept the post, and he was now negotiating in other directions. The Police Department had decided to institute the long-sought course in human relations for its personnel and this decision would also be announced publicly.

A day or two later, the chairman was informed that the City Council would meet with the Human Rights Commission on July 30.

JULY 30: A PROGRAM

In opening the session with the City Council, the chairman listed the reasons for believing the situation in New Rochelle to be explosive: the delays in the Hunter-Deere affair; the lack of communication between the Negro and white communities; the absence of progress on housing, job discrimination, and other basic problems; the danger inherent in the wide publicity being given to riots all over the country. While the commission recognized that basic problems would yield only to long-term endeavors, some things could be done immediately. The need was great, the Council was reminded, to convince the city's Negro citizens that the administration really had their welfare at heart. One area in which prompt action was possible was finding constructive occupation for teenagers, on vacation from school, whose volatile temperaments and idleness made them potential troublemakers.

After a series of specific suggestions had been advanced by various members of the commission, the City Council agreed to the following:

1. The Police Department's human relations course would be given the widest possible publicity.

2. Efforts would be redoubled to get Deere's long-promised hearing under way.

3. The Council would publicly request New Rochelle's business and industrial community to initiate a program for hiring young people; further, it would take the initiative by hiring some fifty to work part-time for the city for the rest of the summer.

4. The Recreation Commission would look into the feasibility of night-lighting the city's athletic fields, and work toward increasing utilization of playgrounds and expanding its entire program through the use of church and synagogue facilities.

5. The Mayor would write to every individual who had addressed the open meeting of June 30, informing him that

his statement was being given careful consideration and outlining steps the city was taking, or had taken, in its attack on discrimination.

6. The Human Rights Commission would meet with the Youth Board and the Recreation Commission to explore schemes for year-round consecutive utilization of teenagers' time.

7. A member of the Recreation Commission, a well-known athlete, would be assigned to work with young people in potentially troublesome areas.

8. The city administration would encourage Negroes to apply for positions on the police force. (Earlier efforts in this direction had failed to elicit much response; the commission felt that another try at this time was important.)

9. The Human Rights Commission would meet with the Municipal Housing Authority to determine what more could be done to promote additional integrated housing, and to make sure that the tenants of low-cost housing were provided with recreational and cultural facilities.

10. The Mayor would explore the possibility of acquiring for the city a share of the funds being made available by President Johnson's campaign against poverty.

The only one of the commission's proposals to arouse serious opposition was the creation of a civilian review board. In view of the Police Department's hostility to the idea, the opposition came as no surprise. During the discussion, the Human Rights Commission pointed out that by virtue of its charter it could accept from any individual a complaint based on discrimination, whether the alleged discrimination was charged against a private citizen, a city official, or a police official. However, the commission's "verdict" in such a case would carry only advisory weight, since the charter bestowed no powers of enforcement.

On the whole, the commission had every reason to feel pleased with the results of the meeting, especially since a full report appeared in the next day's press. The members realized, however, that not even a Human Rights Commission could substitute adequately for direct communication between the Negro community and the city's lawmakers. Clearly, in view of the cooperative spirit that had just been shown, the time was ripe for a direct confrontation of the City Council with the leadership of the civil rights groups. The commission chairman therefore suggested such a session, and the idea was immediately approved.

The meeting took place on August 4, the commission being represented by its director. By all accounts, it was a satisfactory occasion; there was genuine give-and-take between the Negroes and the City Council. The Hunter-Deere affair occupied only a small part of the agenda. The range of subjects discussed may be gleaned from the following summary of a list of proposals presented to the Council by representatives of the Westchester County Joint Committee on Equal Opportunity:

1. That the City Administration establish a Labor and Industry Department to deal with job training and retraining; that city departments be integrated at every level, that "in order to correct the injustices to Negroes over scores of years, the administration will have to extend preferential treatment in some cases" involving employment.

2. That a Civilian Review Board be created to deal with charges of police brutality.

3. That zoning provisions be reviewed to allow for integrated low- and middle-income housing developments outside the city's cen-

ter, i.e., outside the Negro ghetto; that all appropriate government agencies, as well as all appropriate sectors of business, guarantee the goal of "open occupancy" through support and enforcement of the New York State Fair Housing Law.

In turn, the Mayor and the city fathers reviewed in detail the Administration's activities to date in counteracting discrimination. No basic problems were solved; how could they be? But an important step had been taken toward mutual understanding, and a useful account of the session appeared in the press. Of all the Negro leaders in attendance, only one subsequently denounced the meeting as a failure, and other leaders stated privately that his derogation did not represent the consensus.

Moreover, at this session the Negroes heard what they had been waiting to hear since June 21: a definite date had been set for the inquiry into Patrolman Deere's attack on young Hunter. The hearing officer would be Henry J. Smith, president of the Westchester County Bar Association; the date would be August 11. The hearing would be an open one, as the civil rights forces had demanded, and the complainant would be the City of New Rochelle. Never before in the city's history had a police hearing of this kind been conducted by anyone outside the department, nor had any such hearing ever been held in public. The Negroes had won another victory: contrary to the original fiat, the hearing would not wait upon the ultimate determination of the case against young Hunter, which was still at an early stage.

THE FOLLOW-THROUGH

The program initiated by the commission and approved by the City Council on July 30 had meaning only to the extent that it would be translated into action. The following is a summary of the steps taken during the ensuing weeks to implement the program:

THE POLICE   In September, members of the department were given a brief course in human relations; as this is written, proposals have been made for a second and more intensive course. Meanwhile, the Commissioner of Police emphasized to his personnel the need for courtesy in dealing with all segments of the public. Obviously, the ugly image of the man in blue that most Negro citizens have carried around with them for years cannot be changed overnight; it will be a long time before the stereotypes in the minds of both policemen and Negro can be replaced by more realistic images.

EMPLOYMENT   Under the auspices of the Chamber of Commerce, the Human Rights Commission had a meeting with a group of New Rochelle businessmen, which resulted in a number of job openings for young Negroes; more important, it served to awaken important members of the business community to the broad problems of job discrimination, and there is reason to hope for steady progress in this direction. A favorable trend was established by the early success of the commission in inducing certain banks which had long been citadels of job discrimination to hire Negroes in white-collar jobs.

The Commissioner of Police appointed a Negro as his private secretary, and a Negro was appointed as Assistant City Clerk—the first time in New Rochelle's history that such a position had been filled by a Negro.

From the problem of job discrimination the commission was led of necessity, into the problem of education. On more than one occasion the commission located job opportunities for Negroes and then could not find applicants who could qualify. (The commission is now encouraging the Negro leadership to try to find applicants for jobs in the Fire and Police Departments.) This situation has led to discussions with high school administrators on possible changes in the curriculum that might provide more skilled young graduates for the labor market. Here again a long-range program is involved. Nevertheless, it is a mark of progress when many white employers who, through either prejudice or thoughtlessness, had never hired Negroes, now express themselves ready to do so when an opportunity arises. The commission intends to follow up these promises.

YOUTH AND RECREATION   Collaboration with the Youth Board and Recreation Commission has led to plans—and first steps—toward the enlargement of their programs. Since expansions of this kind almost always involve money, an important test of the administration's willingness to implement its good will in these directions will be its attitude toward the budget.

ANTI-POVERTY PROGRAM   A committee appointed by the Mayor met with federal officials and, as a result, a delegation was sent to Washington with proposals that, it is hoped, will secure federal financial support. The plans involve the creation of more jobs and an increase of services to culturally deprived areas of the city.

A further point: the Mayor, in fulfillment of his promise, wrote a thoughtful and responsive letter to every citizen who had spoken at the June 30 meeting. The commission felt that this gesture was important in establishing and maintaining a feeling of direct relationship between the individual citizen and his local government, without which progress is extremely difficult.

SEPTEMBER 14: DENOUEMENT

New Rochelle's long, hot summer came to an end on September 14, when Hearing Officer Henry J. Smith gave his verdict on the brutality charge leveled by the city against Patrolman Deere.

The hearings were held, on schedule, for three days beginning August 11. With the city as complainant, an assistant corporation counsel prosecuted, while a New Rochelle attorney acted for Deere. The testimony of twenty witnesses filled 625 pages of the hearing record.

At no time was the validity of Deere's arrest of Hunter questioned. The sole point at issue was whether the patrolman had used unnecessary force in making the arrest. It would serve no useful purpose here to review the evidence; on details, much of it was conflicting. But the main facts, as they emerged during the hearing, were in no way different from those which had been widely accepted for months: a policeman had hit a youngster over the head with a club with such force that six stitches were required to close the resultant scalp wound.

After the evidence was all in, the hearing officer took almost a month to reach his verdict. Here are the operative paragraphs of his decision:

The accusation that the patrolman used more force than was necessary is, in my opinion, supported by the weight of the evidence.

Since the charges against Ptl. Deere have been established, I read . . . the Civil Service Law . . . as requiring some affirmative action and the only alternatives given are dismissal, suspension, a fine, and a reprimand.

The first three are clearly inappropriate in a case of a young policeman erring in judgment while trying to do his duty in a difficult situation. . . . I therefore recommend that the punishment of Ptl. Deere be a reprimand upon the ground that the charges made in the complaint have been sustained.

A policeman had been found guilty—a rare occurrence in cases such as this, as police department records throughout the country will show. But did the punishment fit the crime? Many thought so, but others—not all of them Negroes—vehemently thought not; they considered that Deere had gotten away with something that could easily have turned out to be murder. What, these critics asked, would have happened to a Negro policeman who had clubbed a white boy under similar circumstances?

The commission, aware of the strong resentment among Negroes at the mild punishment called for by Henry, feared that another crisis was in the making. But the Negro leadership contented itself with sharp statements criticizing the verdict and calling once more for the establishment of a civilian review board, and the Negro community refrained from physical protest.

Violence had been detoured. The commission, which had worked so hard all summer to build that detour, felt at once encouraged and challenged. On the one hand, it knew now that if racial strife should ever come to New Rochelle, the Hunter-Deere case would not be the cause, but it also knew that the potential for violence would remain as long as the basic problems brought into focus during the summer remained unsolved.*

CONCLUSIONS

The summer began with a single, specific crisis arising out of an act of

*As of this writing, the case against Hunter had not come to trial.

brutality by a policeman. Following a pattern now become familiar, the single crisis grew into many; all the long-standing grievances of New Rochelle's Negro citizens were simultaneously brought into the foreground. All these grievances were interrelated, which made it impossible to limit these pages to the history of the Hunter-Deere incident. For instance, it is reasonable to suppose that the City Council's approval of the Human Rights Commission's action-program of July 30 tended to deter a second street demonstration for Hunter. It is equally reasonable to suppose that the city administration's expressed willingness to grapple, at long last, with the accumulated grievances of the Negroes contributed to the restraint shown by the Negro community after the verdict on Deere was announced.

The interplay of the many factors involved cannot be measured in specific terms; neither, in this context, can the hole played throughout by the commission. The commission had certain factors in its favor: dedicated, hard-working, qualified personnel; a vigorous and efficient director; a sympathetic Mayor; Negro leaders who, with few exceptions, kept their eyes on the main goal; a compact community that could easily be reached when there was something to say. Other factors worked against the commission: it lacked institutional prestige because its existence had been so short; it had no enforcement powers; and, like similar bodies elsewhere, it was suspect by both sides during much of its operations.

There is less difficulty in evaluating what the commission *learned* than what it *did*. Out of the summer's experience emerged lessons which have fairly general application:

COMMUNICATION   The commission

knew from the beginning, of course, that there was a lack of communication between the Negro and white communities; what it did not at once appreciate was the *extent* of the lack. The Northern white, accustomed to rubbing shoulders with Negroes in the street, in restaurants, movie houses, subways and trains, blandly assumes a knowledge of his fellow citizen that is not really there. Physical propinquity is mistaken for communication. The truth is that, in a white crowd, a Negro frequently walks alone, and the bigger the crowd the more alone he walks.

On June 24 a white businessman stood at the outskirts of the crowd demonstrating around City Hall. He was worried that the crowd might get out of hand and begin to smash up neighborhood stores. Suddenly he said to the Human Rights Commission chairman, standing nearby, "There's Mr. B. He's a friend of mine—comes into my store all the time." "He's one of the leaders of the demonstration," the chairman responded, "Why don't you go and speak to him?" "Oh, I couldn't do that," the businessman said. "I've never talked to him about things like this." He could not discuss, with a man whom he referred to as a friend, one of the few matters in the lives of either that was of genuine concern to both.

On another occasion, the head of a trade association who has been prominent locally for many years, admitted to the commission director that he knew neither the names nor the faces of the dozen Negroes who were in the same business as he. "Sure, they're in the same business," he explained, "but in another world."

The elementary step of establishing contact between the two communities absorbed much of the commission's energies during the summer. And in the commission's long-range plans for the future, the maintenance and extension of these contacts must play a dominant role.

THE POLICE ATTITUDE   It is almost superfluous to point out the enormous influence exercised by the police in determining a community's intergroup relations. Nowadays, whenever racial violence erupts in a Northern community, one is tempted to say, "What were the police doing!" The Hunter incident would hardly have precipitated a crisis had it not been preceded by a long history of friction between the police and the Negro community: But it is idle, as well as fallacious, to hold the man in uniform exclusively to blame. When he is arrogant and too free with his club or gun, he is as often motivated by fear as by prejudice. The burning, threatening resentments of the Negro community are too much for him. Moreover, he is not responsible for the conditions which have created these resentments. He did not build the Negro slums or create the unemployment which breed crime; it is not his fault that the Negroes constitute the least privileged segment of American society. One might as well blame him because he is merely a policeman and not a psychologist, sociologist, city planner, and politician rolled into one.

Obviously, relations between Negroes and police will remain unstable until many other problems are settled or on the way to settlement—housing, employment, education, etc. But certain palliative measures are possible. Courses in human relations, when extensive and intensive enough, have been found to improve the attitudes of the police toward minorities. Employment of more Negroes by the police, emphasis on courtesy and self-restraint—these, too, can help. But it is important to remember that, in general, the behavior of the patrolman on the beat is determined more by the examples set by his departmental superiors than by anything he reads or is told.

OBJECTIVITY No human rights commission or similar body can expect to win the active, permanent support of extremists—either white reactionaries or Negro radicals. But by being objective and factual in its approach to specific problems, it can eventually gain the cooperation of the majority in both white and Negro communities. In New Rochelle, the commission's early stand against Deere's suspension lost it some Negro support at the time but allayed much of the white community's suspicion. Its subsequent upholding of other Negro demands was therefore more acceptable to the whites and at the same time persuaded the Negroes that the new organization held out some hope for them. In each instance, the commission made its decisions on the merits of the case, not with a view to possible results; but the results followed.

Objectivity does not at all mean refusing to take a position on one side or another. When the facts showed discrimination, the commission was quick to call openly for remedy. But when the facts are in dispute—for instance, whether the building of an old people's home in a certain area would tend to perpetuate the Negro ghetto—the commission takes no public position but concentrates on helping the disputants reach a compromise.

RESTRAINT One of the most important factors in the achievement of peace in New Rochelle was the self-restraint of the Negro community. This was particularly commendable—and particularly re-

markable—in view of the nationwide climate of violence at the time. By their controlled and civilized behavior, the Negroes of New Rochelle advanced the cause of equality not only there but throughout the country.

TACT To its dismay, the commission found that some of its simplest, most obvious steps were misinterpreted. When realtors were asked to meet for a discussion of open housing, many among them took the invitation *per se* as an accusation of discrimination. Similarly, some educators who had done outstanding intergroup work in their schools expected to have their accomplishments belittled by the commission when it invited them to confer on certain aspects of the race issue.

These initial reactions, the commission found, can be overcome by tact. It is often possible to question the results of a course of conduct; it is always dangerous to impugn motives. The commission found that the best way to get cooperation is to start with the assumption that there is good will all around.

Special tact is needed in dealing with leaders of organizations in any social group. Leaders have organizational loyalties as well as their overriding loyalty to a cause. Like a Congressman, a leader has a constituency whose consensus must, in the long run, determine the limits of his own actions and decisions.

THE MEANING OF CRISIS In spite of all the proverbs extolling prevention, it is, unhappily, only crisis, or the threat of crisis, that brings about the dynamic required for change. History may yet show that the attack on young Hunter marked a turning point in Negro-white relations in New Rochelle; if that proves true, it will be fortunate that the only martyr suffered nothing worse than a scalp wound.

But if the summer of 1964 did indeed mark a significant turn in the city's history and this is by no means certain as yet— the cause was not exclusively the affair of young Hunter. The violence that swept the South, and so many Northern cities, affected the local power structure to the point where it was no longer immune to change. To a human rights commission, crisis presents at once tremendous opportunities and tremendous perils. Where it can use crisis constructively, without violence, it must and will inevitably win the gratitude of *all* segments of the community.

If the resolution of the New Rochelle crisis seems to have taken an unreasonable length of time, one must remember that this was the first experience of a recently formed commission. Techniques in handling such situations must be learned. Should another crisis occur, the resolution would undoubtedly be achieved more quickly.

In delivering to the city administration the first annual report of the New Rochelle Human Rights Commission, the chairman said:

We are mindful that New Rochelle reacts not only to local conditions but to whatever goes on elsewhere in America and, indeed, in the world. If there is one lesson that comes out of the first year of existence of this commission, it is this: The social and economic equality of opportunity sought by Negroes is a war waged in every human heart. Until every white citizen subscribes, wholeheartedly, and in his actions as well as his ethics, to the ideal of equality, the revolution here will not end.

If the revolution is far from ended, it has at least begun well.

THE DEEPENING CRISIS IN METROPOLIS*

Charles E. Silberman

There are, as there always have been, any number of crises affecting the large city —transportation, for example, or air pollution. These are real problems, and I do not mean to minimize their importance. But there can be no question, it seems to me, that when we speak of *the* crisis of metropolis we are referring to only one thing—to the crisis in black and white. For whether it be poverty, the burden of welfare, juvenile delinquency, adult criminality, unemployment, the physical

deterioration of the "inner city," or the fact that the tax base is narrowing as the expenditure base broadens, the problem is inescapably bound up with race—with the explosive growth of the large cities' Negro population, the anger and frustration that Negroes are beginning to express, and the political pressures generated by the "Negro revolt" and the so-called "white backlash."

While the crisis is deepening, it seems to me that its nature is becoming clearer. I can best illustrate this, perhaps, through a small exercise in self-vindication. My object is not to demonstrate my own

*Address before the Eighteenth Annual Conference of the National Association of Intergroup Relations Officials, October 7, 1964.

From *The Journal of Intergroup Relations* 4, 3 (Summer 1965), pp. 119–129. Reprinted by permission of the author.

prescience (though I would be less than frank if I did not admit to certain feelings of self-satisfaction), but to suggest how rapid is the march of events and how quickly our whole perspective can change under their pressure.

A number of liberal and radical critics, for example, took exception to a statement in the opening chapter of my book, that "White Americans . . . are discovering . . . how deep is the store of anger and hatred three and a half centuries of humiliation have built up in the American Negro, and how quickly that anger can explode into violence." One critic suggested that I had been carried away by rhetoric; what impressed him was the absence of Negro violence, a phenomenon he seemed to attribute to the influence of Martin Luther King. And in *The Nation* of June 29th, Martin Mayer was even more pointed. "In the world of created non-news which surrounds race questions," he wrote, "Silberman is probably stuck with the idle chatter about violence that takes up a number of his pages."

Nineteen days later, the Harlem riots began, and the "non-news" became front-page news in virtually every newspaper in the land.

These riots, I submit, represent a great watershed in the history of the Negro and of race relations in the United States. I should like to explore their meaning with you, very briefly. What concerns me, let me emphasize, is not how they began or whether the police responded with too much or too little force; that is a subject for another speech. My interest here is in exploring what the riots mean for the future of the large city—every large city.

THE 1964 RIOTS AND THE NEGRO MIND

Race riots as such are hardly a novelty to the great cities of the North or South. On the contrary, they antedate the passage of the 1964 Civil Rights Act and Lyndon Johnson's accession to the Presidency. They even antedate Earl Warren's appointment as Chief Justice of the United States. The fact is that race riots have been a recurrent phenomenon throughout American history. In a seventeen-year period during the 1830's and 1840's, the City of Philadelphia, Pa., experienced no fewer than five race riots. In New York City more than 2,000 were killed and 8,000 injured during the four-day Draft Riot in July of 1863. In this century, Springfield, Ill., Atlanta, Chicago, East St. Louis, and Detroit, among others, have been the scenes of major race riots. But, until the summer of 1964, a race riot could be defined, quite simply, as mob violence by whites directed against Negroes.

This summer the definition changed: the riots were started by Negroes, and they involved violence directed against whites—or, if you prefer, against the principal symbol of white power and authority in the slums, the police.

The events of July and August, it seems to me, establish beyond any shadow of a doubt that Negroes *have* changed their minds; the day of the docile Negro is gone, and gone forever.

What is remarkable is not that this change occurred, but that whites were taken so completely by surprise. Here is one reporter's account of the reaction of the white storekeepers in Bedford-Stuyvesant (Brooklyn) after the first night of rioting.

The fear is something you can touch with your fingers. And even more palpable is the atmosphere of bitter, bewildered regret. Over and over you hear, "And we always thought we were well-liked here. . . ."

And here's another reporter's description of a merchant's frantic attempt to get his windows boarded up in preparation for the second night.

As he dialed the number (of a lumber yard), a small boy raced past laughing. "We got revenge!" the boy taunted. "We got revenge!"

"Revenge for what?" the storekeeper muttered to himself.

Revenge for what? Any white man who could ask that question—any white merchant who could say, "And we always thought we were well-liked here"—had been living in a world of fantasy. For Negro anger is not new; it has always been there. What is new is simply the Negroes' willingness to express it. As James Baldwin put it, "To be a Negro in this country and to be relatively conscious is to be in a rage almost all the time." More than that, to be a Negro is to suspect, and even to hate, white men. With those Negroes who deny their hatred, Saunders Redding has written, "I have no quarrel . . . It is simply that I do not believe them." I know whereof Mr. Redding speaks.

ANGER, HATRED AND ALIENATION

In short, the anger and the hatred are facts—uncomfortable facts, but facts nonetheless. So is the breadth and depth of the alienation from American society which a great many Negroes feel. And so long as Negroes feel excluded from American society, they are not going to feel bound by its constraints, and appeals for "responsible behavior" or "responsible leadership" are bound to be met with cynical derision. The first person narrator of Ralph Ellison's *Invisible Man* remarks, "I can hear you say, 'What a horrible, irresponsible bastard!' And you're right. I leap to agree with you . . . But to whom can I be responsible, and

why should I be, when you refuse to see me?"

What is crucial, let me emphasize, is not whether Negro anger, hatred, and alienation are justified, but whether we have the honesty and courage to face up to them. And by "we," of course, I mean blacks as well as white. They must be taken into account in any program to improve Negro-white relations; they must be taken into account in any program to help Negro youngsters or adults climb out of the slum. For the anger and hate and alienation are there; unless they find some constructive outlet, they inevitably poison and corrode the spirit and, as we saw this summer, they sometimes lead to purposeless violence.

Unless they are recognized and dealt with, they doom to failure the best-intentioned attempts at speeding Negroes' acculturation, for a great many Negroes regard doing the things that "acculturation" implies as "going along with Mr. Charlie's program." In short, we must all, black and white alike, face up to the harsh realities of what 350 years of brutality and humiliation have done to the Negro in America.

We have no other choice. There is, first, the very real danger of further violence —by Negroes against whites, and by whites against Negroes—for we are just discovering the depths of white racism; we are just discovering what Alexis de Tocqueville pointed out 125 years ago, that the United States is a racist society. The greater danger, however, is not violence but something deeper and far more corrosive: a sense of permanent alienation from American society. Unless the Negro position improves very quickly, Negroes of whatever class may come to regard their separation from American life as permanent, and so consider themselves outside the constraints and allegiances of American society. Thus the Negro district of every large city could come to constitute an American Casbah, with its own values and controls and an implacable hatred of everything white that would, in effect, destroy the metropolis. We are dangerously close to that point already.

I did not come here, however, to warn of the Apocolypse, but to suggest, in all humility, how we might avoid it—in particular, to suggest what the groups represented in NAIRO can and should do.

THE IRRELEVANCE OF LIBERALISM

We in intergroup relations think of ourselves as being in the vanguard of the fight for civil rights, for social justice, for the elimination of poverty. The truth, I fear, is that we have been falling behind, that we have gotten out of touch with present realities.

One reason, I submit, is that the political and social ideology we developed over the years as members of a broad liberal coalition is irrelevant, if not downright misleading. For example, we have developed a conception of civil rights as involving the rights of individuals; our whole attack on prejudice and discrimination rests on the demand that people be treated as individuals, not as members of a group. This philosophy, I submit, is a rationalization *after* the fact—a rationalization which ignores, or denies, the true history of ethnic groups in the United States. The plain fact is that every ethnic group that has moved into the mainstream of American life has done so in large part through the exercise of group power. As Glazer and Moynihan have demonstrated so clearly in *Beyond The Melting Pot,* the crucial thing about the melting pot is that it never happened. I think Mayor Wagner can testify to the

political muscle which the major ethnic groups in his city still use.

In any case, the essence of the Negro revolt is the fact that the Negro is no longer addressing himself to the white man's prejudice; he is no longer primarily interested in changing either the minds or the hearts of white Americans. He is, instead, trying to change white *behavior.* And in that effort, he is recognizing that the rights and privileges of an individual depend primarily upon the status achieved by the group to which he belongs—which is to say, upon the power that group is able to acquire and exercise. As my good friend David Danzig put it in the February 1964 issue of *Commentary,* "What is now perceived as the 'revolt' of the Negro amounts to this: the solitary Negro seeking admission into the white world through unusual achievement has been replaced by the organized Negro insisting upon a legitimate share for his group of the goods of American society. The white liberal, in turn, who—whether or not he has been fully conscious of it—has generally conceived of progress in race relations as the one-by-one assimilation of deserving Negroes into the larger society, finds himself confused and threatened by suddenly having to come to terms with an aggressive Negro community that wishes to enter it *en masse.*"

THE NEGRO DEMAND FOR POWER

This fact, in turn, poses another ideological problem. The whole orientation of the intergroup relations movement, or approach, traditionally has been toward an emphasis on persuasion, rationality, and the reduction of intergroup tensions. By its very nature, this approach assumes gradualism, since it takes time to rid people of prejudice or to change their minds.

It assumes that people's minds or beliefs must be changed before their behavior can be changed, whereas one of the key findings of social psychology, as Jerome Bruner has reminded us, is that men act themselves into a way of believing at least as often as they believe themselves into a way of acting. Most important of all, the emphasis on the reduction of intergroup tensions is incompatible with the main thrust and meaning of the Negro protest movement: its demand for power.

And power—not desegregated lunch counters, not integrated schools, no, not even equal (or for that matter, preferential) access to jobs—is what the Negro revolt is all about.

Indeed, the Negro revolt cannot be understood except as a long-suppressed reaction against an imbalance of power— an imbalance which whites take for granted, but which Negroes have always resented. Negroes have never had the sense of controlling their own destinies; they have never had the feeling that they were making, or even participating in, the decisions that really counted, the decisions that affected their lives and fortunes.

Equally important, Negroes' demand for power is a crucial part of the struggle to overcome the devastation that the past 350 years have wrought on Negro personality. The apathy and aimlessness— the *anomie,* to use the sociologists' term —that characterize the Negro poor, and the crisis of identity that afflicts Negroes of all classes, stem from their sense of dependency and powerlessness—their conviction that "Mr. Charlie" controls everything, Negro leaders included, and that he has stacked the cards so that Negroes can never win. Negroes cannot overcome the apathy that keeps them locked in the slum—they cannot achieve their manhood, to use the phrase that has

recurred throughout Negro protest literature for centuries—until they are in a position to make or influence the decisions that affect them—until, in a word, they have power.

At the same time, it must be admitted, the Negro demand for power has itself evoked the white backlash, bringing to the surface racist sentiments that had been hidden—in some instances, racist sentiments no one thought existed. The white backlash, no less than Negro anger, is a fact that has to be reckoned with— by civil rights groups no less than by mayors. I hope I am not being pollyanaish, however, in suggesting that the conflict may contain the seeds of its own solution. What is crucial, I think, is that, for all their antipathy, whites *are* being forced to negotiate with Negroes—which means they are forced to recognize Negro power. When whites negotiate with Negroes, therefore, it not only helps solve the Negro's "Negro problem," it helps solve the white man's "Negro problem," as well; for whites begin to see Negroes in a different light—as equals, as men.

CONFLICT, INEVITABLE VEHICLE OF POWER SHIFTS

What I want to emphasize here, however, is that conflict is inevitable; power cannot be achieved without it. Let me repeat: *power cannot be acquired without conflict.* For no group ever surrenders power voluntarily. Nor can power be received as a gift; it must be taken, for it is in the process of striving for power that people become powerful; it is in the process of fighting for freedom that they become free.

Several things follow from this. For one thing, whites will have to abandon their tradition of command and their habit of speaking for, and acting for, Negroes. Their role must be limited: to stimulate indigenous leadership and activity, to teach skills of organization, and then to retire to the sidelines—to retire to the sidelines even if the black neophytes are making mistakes. For if Negroes are to gain a sense of potency and dignity, it is essential that they take the initiative in action on their own behalf; the politics of human life do not permit of equality when one person or one group is constantly in the position of magnanimous donor and the other in the position of perennial recipient.

"We act as though taking help is about as comfortable as giving it," Elizabeth H. Ross of the District of Columbia Department of Public Welfare has said. "We have more or less convinced ourselves that accepting help is not necessarily a submission, nor an effort."

But it *is* a submission—one that erodes the dignity and destroys the spirit. At this moment of history, therefore, it is far more important that things be done *by* Negroes than they be done *for* them. For only if the mass of Negro slum-dwellers are involved in action on their own behalf will they be able to climb out of their slums en masse—which is to say, only if the mass of Negro slum-dwellers are involved in action on their own behalf can the city be saved. But can this be done?

IT CAN BE DONE

The answer, quite simply, is that it has been done—in the Woodlawn section of Chicago, under the aegis of Saul D. Alinsky of the Industrial Areas Foundation. To do the job, however, requires a radical break with a great many of the traditions and assumptions of the profession of intergroup relations. To mobilize the resi-

dents of a slum, that is to say, requires the development of indigenous leadership and, equally important, the development of a mass organization which will give the slum dwellers the power they need to force change. But this organization can be created only by appealing to the self-interest of the local residents and to their resentment and distrust of the outside world, and only by demonstrating through boycotts, strikes, picketing, and other so-called disruptive actions that the use of power *can* change things. The community organizer thus must function as a catalytic agent, transmuting hidden resentments and hostilities into open problems and persuading people to break through their apathy and develop and harness the power necessary to change the prevailing patterns. Change of this sort cannot be accomplished without conflict. "When those prominent in the status quo turn and label you an agitator," Saul Alinsky has said, "they are completely correct, for that, in one word, is your function—to agitate to the point of conflict."

Accepting the necessity and the inevitability of conflict is no easy matter. It goes against the grain of intergroup relations as a profession, since our traditional emphasis, as I have already suggested, has been on reducing conflict and tension. It also threatens—and this is much more important—it also threatens our own sense of security. While most Negroes are outside the main stream of middle-class American life, most professional intergroup relations officials are on the inside. We may think of ourselves as an embattled minority, but we really are not. Hence we have a very real and deep interest in maintaining peace and harmony.

White liberals—among whom I include intergroup relations officials—want racial change, all right, but without trouble or turmoil, and without upsetting the existing organizations and institutional arrangements. But changes of the sort Negroes now demand, at the speed which they insist upon, cannot be provided *without* considerable conflict; too many Americans will have to give up some privilege or advantage they now enjoy or surrender the comforting sense of their own superiority. Hence white liberals must develop a new theory of politics—one geared to rapid change rather than one designed to eliminate conflict. They must learn that there are far worse things than conflict; in the words of Rabbi Abraham Joshua Heschel, "So long as our society is more concerned to prevent strife than to prevent humiliation, its moral status will be depressing indeed."

OF GOVERNMENT AND REVOLUTION

We liberals must learn an even harder lesson—harder, because it requires us to abandon a crucial part of our ideology, and men cling to their ideologies even more tightly than to their status. That lesson is that governmental crash programs—and by that I mean "domestic Marshall Plans" and "wars on poverty"—can never produce the self-help that is essential if real and lasting change is to come about.

Let me make my meaning clear, lest someone confuse me with Mitchell of Newburgh or with Goldwater of Arizona. In no sense am I attacking governmental action on either the federal or the local level; on the contrary, neither the federal government nor any city or state that I know of is spending more than a fraction of what is necessary to do more than just scratch the surface. What I am attacking is the romantic notion that the government—any government—will organize a

revolution against itself. And that, with only some exaggeration, is what has to be done if the residents of Harlem, Bedford-Stuyvesant, North Philadelphia, and so on, are to break through their apathy and begin to acquire power for themselves. To assume that meaningful community organizations—my emphasis here is on *meaningful*—can be created by government or financed through government funds is, it seems to me, to betray a naiveté of tragic proportions. If logic alone is not enough to demonstrate that no government will finance attacks against itself or against the existing structure of society, we now have experience of Mobilization for Youth as proof of my thesis.

Thus, Senator Jacob Javits, who at least had the political courage to come to Mobilization's defense, suggested that the agency "trim down their social action programs so that they can carry on their essential job-training program for youth." What the Senator failed to realize, of course, was that the social action programs—not the job retraining programs—were the agency's *raison d'etre*.

City Council President Paul R. Screvane has been even more explicit. "The city government," he said, "does not sanction or agree that lawless and disruptive activities should be encouraged by any organization that is financed by public funds."

I am not criticizing Mr. Screvane; I doubt that any public official could take any other position. But I insist that if Mobilization for Youth—or Haryou, or any of the other similar agencies that are being planned—are barred from so-called "disruptive activities," they might just as well close up shop now. For the real issue in the Mobilization dispute, I submit, is whether we truly want the poor to be independent and self-reliant, or whether in fact we prefer to keep them dependent and apathetic; whether public assistance should be used to give the poor the means with which to help themselves, or whether welfare should be used to keep the poor tranquilized and non-threatening.

THE LESSON FOR INTERGROUP RELATIONS AGENCIES

In retrospect, therefore, the organizers of Mobilization for Youth were naive in assuming that they could, in their phrase, "organize the unaffiliated" with funds coming from government. With the benefit of hindsight, they appear to have made another equally fatal mistake in judgment: they took the praise they received from virtually every intergroup relations agency at face value; they naively assumed that praise meant support. They have discovered the magnitude of this error in the last six or eight weeks, when most intergroup agencies have been conspicuous by their silence.

I know all the arguments in favor of silence: you don't enter a barroom brawl when you're carrying a baby in your arms. But if you'll excuse my mixing metaphors—something my editors would never do—intergroup relations officials might ponder Harry Truman's homily that "If you can't stand the heat, get out of the kitchen." And there is bound to be heat in the kitchen of intergroup relations. As Rev. Arthur Brazier, first president of The Woodlawn Organization in Chicago, has put it,

The period of race relations, with its well-intentioned but limited possibilities, is over. The days of approaching segregation via high-level conferences, emergency spot moves of personalized social and political pressures . . . of generous financial contributions to various Negro organizations and causes, and all of the other actions which characterize the white liberal of the past period of "race relations," those days are over; they are ended . . . The struggle, and it is a struggle, has moved down into the streets, the homes, the schools, into the very political and economic centers of our society and, in short, down to the people themselves.

If they are to play a significant role in solving the racial crisis, therefore, intergroup agencies and officials will have to shift their emphasis from conferences and study to action, to involvement in the struggle. There is an old Talmudic injunction that seems to me to be relevant here: "Let not your learning exceed your deeds." The rabbis, needless to say, were not derogating learning but emphasizing that justice is neither an abstraction, nor a sentiment, nor a relationship, but an *act*. When the Prophets of old spoke of justice, their injunction was not to *be* just but to *do* justice; it is the act that counts.

AND THE LESSON FOR NEGRO AGENCIES

Negro agencies, let me emphasize, must also change. The last several years have been characterized by enormous dissipation of energies in one-shot demonstrations that are doomed to failure, and that can only result in even more frustration and bitterness, and by an almost total absence of any attempt to build mass-based organizations for the long pull. The reason, I suspect, is that Negroes, for all their experience of white prejudice and brutality, grossly underestimated the depth of white resistance; for a time, at least, after Birmingham, there was a general feeling that a few more blasts on the trumpet were all that was needed to bring the walls tumbling down.

The classic example—and I use it only

to illustrate my point, not for any invidious comparisons—was the first New York City school boycott, though the march on Washington could be substituted just as well. For the first time, the impossible was done: the Negro residents of the city were pulled together in something like a democratic, mass-based organization. It was a very considerable achievement. And for what? To boycott the schools for a single day—as if a one-day boycott (or even a week-long boycott) could have solved the enormously complex problem of providing Negro slum youngsters with the kind of education they need. And after the one-day boycott

—after the incredible effort that had gone into organizing the Negro community— the organization was simply disbanded. The result was cynicism and disillusionment, leading up, finally, to the fiasco of May 18th, when only four or five thousand people turned out for a rally which, it was announced in advance, would be a failure if any fewer than 15,000 showed up. Negro leaders, I fear, no less than white, have spent too much time on talk and too little on action. The job of building and maintaining a mass organization is a hard, mean, dirty job that must go on seven days a week, fifty-two weeks a year.

TEN YEARS OF DELIBERATE SPEED

Erwin Knoll

Does segregation of children in public schools solely on the basis of race, even though the physical facilities and other 'tangible' factors may be equal, deprive the children of the minority group of equal opportunities?"

"We believe that it does."

On Monday afternoon, May 17, 1954, the Chief Justice of the United States calmly read those words in a hushed Supreme Court chamber and ushered in a new era for race relations and for the Nation's schools. Speaking for a unanimous Court, Justice Earl Warren declared that "in the field of public education the doctrine of 'separate but equal' has no place. Separate educational facilities are inherently unequal."

When Justice Warren read the historic

decision in *Brown* v. *Board of Education* a little more than a decade ago, separation of public school pupils "solely on the basis of race" was required by law in 17 Southern and border States and in the District of Columbia. School segregation was also practiced, with or without legal sanction, in scores of Northern communities. The equity of "separate but equal" facilities, enunciated by the Supreme Court in its *Plessy* v. *Ferguson* decision (which involved facilities in trains), had stood since 1896.

The momentous significance of the Supreme Court's new ruling was therefore readily apparent. Almost as soon as Justice Warren finished speaking, the Voice of America was broadcasting the news in 34 languages to nations that had

From *American Education*, January 1965, pp. 1–3. Printed by U.S. Office of Education, Department of Health, Education, and Welfare.

been sharply critical of racial discrimination in the United States. On Tuesday morning, May 18, the *New York Times* devoted seven full pages to the decision.

"Let all the people praise the Lord," said Mary McLeod Bethune, the famous Negro educator and crusader, reflecting the jubilant response of the Negro.

The ruling was generally welcomed in the North. In the South, some predicted —accurately, as it turned out—that "blood would run in the streets" before the Court's decision was put into effect, but most initial Southern reaction, was restrained.

A decade and more after *Brown* v. *Board of Education,* only the most preliminary assessment of the decision's full impact is possible. That the South has a long way to go toward full compliance with the letter of the law is a fact that is demonstrable by simple arithmetic. That many Northern localities are only beginning to comply with the spirit of the law is self-evident even as belated progress is made.

That the Supreme Court ruling of 1954 will, in time, bring a full measure of educational opportunity to all Americans is a promise that appears, in 1965, to be moving toward fulfillment. At the rate of compliance between 1954 and 1965, it would take centuries for the public schools of the Deep South to achieve full desegregation. But such stark calculations are somewhat beside the point. Judicial, legislative, political, and social pressures are at work to quicken the pace.

A national opinion poll conducted shortly after the Supreme Court ruled found that 54 percent of the populace approved the decision and 41 percent disapproved. The national percentage of those endorsing desegregation, as gaged by subsequent polls, has grown steadily since 1954. But in the Southern and border States, the first poll found that only 24 percent approved the decision, while 71 percent disapproved, and those percentages have held steady for the past decade.

At the time of the ruling, however, neither in the North nor in the South did anyone foresee its full impact. Certainly Northerners, complacently confident that their schools had long been "integrated," did not anticipate the mass demonstrations and boycotts that would be mounted in protest against racial imbalance and substandard classroom conditions.

Few suspected, in 1954, that Southern State legislatures would enact more than 400 laws and resolutions—199 in Louisiana alone—designed to delay or delimit implementation of the Supreme Court decision, or that desegregation efforts would be attended by shootings, bombings, burnings, and riots.

It could not be foreseen, in 1954, that one of the localities directly involved in the Supreme Court's decision—Clarendon County, S. C.—would still be operating an entirely segregated school system 11 years later, or that another—Prince Edward County, Va.—would padlock its public schools for 5 years to avoid desegregation and would not reopen them until the fall of 1964, and then only under the mandate of another Supreme Court order.

In this eleventh year since *Brown* v. *Board of Education,* some desegregation has come to 583 of the 2,989 school districts in the 11 States of the Deep South. The number of desegregated districts ranges from 3 in Louisiana and 4 in Mississippi, to 292 in Texas. The South has 734 school districts with either all-white or all-Negro enrollments and 1,672 biracial districts in which no desegregation whatever has taken place. When school opened last fall, 139 districts were desegregated for the first time—about the same number that had taken the step a year earlier. In the 6 border States and the District of Columbia, 720 of the 771 biracial districts have desegregated.

But numbers of desegrated districts are deceptive, for much of the compliance has been token, at best. Though more than a fourth of the biracial districts in the 11 Southern States are listed as desegregated, well under 2 percent of the Negro pupils in these States are attending classes with white children. The percentage has been rising almost imperceptibly since 1954. This year, slightly more than 50,000 of the 2.9 million Negro pupils in the South are directly benefiting from *Brown* v. *Board of Education.* If the border region is included, the percentage is still only about 11.

Nevertheless, judicial, legislative, and other pressures have been stepping up the pace. Most telling among judicial moves was an opinion by the Supreme Court last May. The Court, which in 1955 suggested a flexible standard of "all deliberate speed" for implementation of its 1954 desegregation ruling, declared that "the time for mere 'deliberate speed' has run out."

In another decision last May, this one involving Atlanta's gradual desegregation plan, the Court observed that "the context in which we must interpret and apply this language ['all deliberate speed'] to their plans for desegregation has been significantly altered." Taking their cue from these and other recent Supreme Court comments, lower Federal courts have been insisting on more rigorous standards.

The 1954 decision was given its first statutory recognition by Congress in the Civil Rights Act of 1964.

Title IV of the act requires the U.S. Office of Education to make a survey and report to the Congress within 2 years on the progress of desegregation and conditions affecting the lack of equal educational opportunity by reason of race, religion, or national origin at all levels.

The Office also is authorized to give technical assistance and grants, if requested, to local public school systems planning or experiencing the process of desegregation. Such assistance may take the form of—

1. Technical aid, such as information or expert personnel

2. Special institutes at colleges or universities to train school personnel to deal with desegregation problems

3. Grants to school boards to pay for training programs or employment of specialists.

An $8-million supplemental appropriation for the Office of Education was approved by the Congress in October.

In addition, title IV of the act empowers the Attorney General to file suit for the desegregation of public schools and colleges if he receives a signed complaint, believes the complaint has merit, and certifies that the aggrieved persons are unable to initiate or maintain legal proceedings, and that the action would "materially further" orderly school desegregation.

Title VI of the act, which bars racial discrimination in any program or activity receiving Federal financial assistance, is also expected to accelerate the rate of school desegregation in the South—especially as it gives local officials who would like to proceed with desegregation an economic argument with which to persuade reluctant constituents.

Regulations for carrying out Title VI were approved by the President in December.

THE PERCENTAGES OF PROGRESS

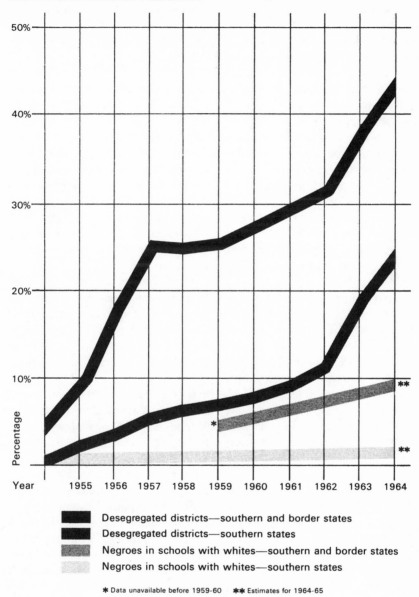

Desegregated districts—southern and border states

Desegregated districts—southern states

Negroes in schools with whites—southern and border states

Negroes in schools with whites—southern states

* Data unavailable before 1959-60   ** Estimates for 1964-65

Whatever the future pace of deseg-regation may be, the *educational* impact of the 1954 Supreme Court decision has already been substantial, and promises to produce even more sweeping changes. Even before the Court spoke, while the first legal challenges to the "separate but equal" doctrine were making their tortuous way through the lower courts, Southern school districts began moving to bring Negro schools into compliance with the 1896 *Plessy* v. *Ferguson* requirement by making them truly equal in terms of buildings, equipment, and the like. That effort continues.

"We have several decades of proof that separate facilities are seldom equal," says Syracuse University sociologist Charles V. Willie. "The only reason for separating persons in the first place is to accord them differential treatment."

Nowhere has the validity of this comment been better illustrated than in the public schools of the District of Columbia, where the "separate but equal" doctrine was firmly adhered to until the Supreme Court made its decision. It was not until the Negro and white divisions of the school system were merged that citizens learned of shocking deficiencies in the achievement levels of Negro pupils. The discovery prompted a search for new techniques of teaching and school organization, a search which has begun to show impressive results despite formidable fiscal and political obstacles.

Because *de jure* school desegregation in the South is far from an accomplished fact, the region has not yet been confronted with the even more complex issue facing the North—*de facto* segregation based on discrimination in housing. How this will be solved remains to be seen.

Two significant Supreme Court actions in the field of *de facto* school segregation were recorded in 1964. In the first, a case involving the public schools of Gary, Ind., the Supreme Court left standing a lower court ruling that school authorities are not constitutionally obligated to end racial imbalance that does not stem from assignment of pupils by race. In the second case, the Court declined to review a lower court's finding that New York City may deliberately zone a school district so as to minimize racial imbalance. The two actions, seemingly contradictory at first glance, actually point to a con-

sistent position under the Constitution: local school authorities *may* but *do not have to* take racial factors into account in seeking to promote balanced enrollments.

There are those who hold, with Dr. Willie of Syracuse, that the neighborhood school concept "cannot be justified" when it contributes to the perpetuation of segregated schools. Others contend that the cities must upgrade their slum schools, Negro or white, while preserving the principle of neighborhood attendance.

New York City, the Nation's largest school system, is pressed on the one hand by demands of militant civil rights organizations and on the other by the protests of white "parents and taxpayers." It is groping toward a policy that will encompass school rezoning, transportation of some pupils to promote racial balance, and intensive improvement of schools in the city's Negro and Puerto Rican ghettos.

In Chicago, where controversy over racial imbalances and inadequacies of predominantly Negro schools reached the flashpoint a year ago, a five-man panel headed by University of Chicago sociologist Philip M. Hauser has rebuked the school board for failing to "move earlier and more rapidly in a determined and creative manner to resolve the problem of school integration." The committee proposed enlarged elementary school zones to promote more biracial classes, "open" (citywide) enrollment in secondary schools, better integration of teaching staffs and across-the-board efforts to improve the quality of the school program.

In Portland, Oreg., a 43-man Committee on Race and Education, headed by Circuit Judge Herbert M. Schwab, addressed itself frankly last fall to the question of whether Portland's schools are providing equal educational opportunities for children of all races. It frankly answered: "No, they are not. Our studies indicate that our schools in their present educational practices are not achieving their purpose for students from culturally deprived circumstances and this is particularly true for Negro students." The Portland committee's massive 249-page report rejected proposals for transportation or school-pairing as devices for achieving racial balance. But it urged adoption of a far-reaching program of educational reforms.

In these cities, in Baltimore, St. Louis, Cleveland, and a score or more of other urban centers the past year has brought some innovations that have made "compensatory education" the year's most significant term in the lexicon of American pedagogy—prekindergarten programs, after-school classes, remedial and counseling efforts on an unprecedented scale.

Even with such steps behind them, however, the Nation's schools have an awesome amount of catching up to do. The Civil Rights Act of 1964 has provided statutory authority for the Office of Education to bring its formidable research resources to bear on the issues involved in school desegregation. Only the turmoil in the streets of the North and the endless litigation in the courtrooms of the South has brought the questions to the fore in local and State education agencies and on the college campuses.

High on the list of critical issues is the training provided for Negro teachers in the South. The Educational Testing Service, which administers the National Teacher Examination, has studied the performance of graduates of Southern Negro teacher's colleges. Arthur L. Benson, who directs the teacher testing program, said last year: "Unless the vicious circle is broken, whereby large numbers of undereducated American teachers are permitted to undereducate other generations of Americans, it is futile to hope that the gap between inadequate schooling for large numbers of children, and quality education for others, will be closed in Southern education."

The entire field of Negro higher education is just beginning to receive attention. In the South, 131 publicly supported institutions of higher learning—more than 60 percent of the total—have officially desegregated. Of 299 private institutions, at least 136 now admit students of both races. But these figures, like those for desegregated school districts, are overshadowed by the facts of actual enrollments; most Negro college students in the region continue to attend understaffed and underfinanced Negro institutions. The recent surge of interest in the plight of these schools has proved to be a mixed blessing. Some Negro educators detect a patronizing "big brother" attitude in some Northern institutions that are offering help, and ohers complain that the new demand for "instant Negroes" in student and faculty ranks of predominantly white colleges is stripping the Negro institutions of their promising scholars.

These, however, are problems of concern, not of neglect, and they point to long-range progress as well as to troublesome short-range dislocations. The same can be said of all difficulties, financial, political, practical, and theoretical, that confront education in the North and South as it attempts to come to terms with the challenge of providing equal educational opportunity.

5

Urban Change and
Development:
The Planning Approach

Rapid urban growth is perhaps one of the most important social trends of modern American society. So pronounced has been this trend in recent decades that almost all contemporary social problems, including all of those considered in this book, have been associated with the process of urbanization in one way or another. For example, the relationship between the physical dimensions of urbanization and the social pathologies they seemingly produce have been recently described by a prominent journalist as follows:

An observer of the sprawling urban scene today might be compelled to concede that the superficial monotony of physical similarity must be the least important of all the ailments of the squatting modern metropolis region whose air grows fouler and more dangerous by the day, whose water is threatened increasingly by pollution, whose mobility is undermined by accumulations of vehicles and withering transit, whose educational system reels under a growing variety of economic, social, and national emergencies, and whose entire pattern is assuming an ominous shape and sociological form, with well-to-do whites in their suburban cities ringing poverty ridden minority groups widening at the core.[1]

In another example, sociologist Alvin Boskoff identifies the major social problems associated with recent urban growth in this brief but exhaustive classification scheme:

1. Urban congestion and uncontrolled competition for urban space.
2. Personal inadequacy and insecurity.
3. The costs and dilemmas provoked by continual striving for status.
4. The absence of communal cohesion or morality, especially in crisis periods.
5. The failure to promote orderly physical and social development for the urban region as a whole.[2]

Of course, the relationship between a very broad and general social process such as urbanization and much more concrete examples of social problems such as race relations, poverty, crime, or the personal pathologies are very difficult to observe directly, and there is a very complex and indirect chain of events by which these two levels of behavior can even be remotely connected. But it is not our purpose to examine the much less direct results of urbanization here, because these are more adequately reviewed elsewhere in this book. Rather, this chapter is primarily concerned with the most direct physical, social, and economic consequences of urban growth and development, such as reflected in the general pattern and character of land use, the location of physical structures and facilities, the design of street, transit, and transportation systems, and the nature and distribution of other physical facilities and services which are considered necessary and desirable for "the economic betterment, comfort, convenience, and the general welfare" of life in urban communities. In other words, the discussion to follow is about those kinds of problems which increasingly are coming to be the technical responsibility of a wide variety of urban planning agencies in local, state, and national governments. Taken by themselves, these problems are of sufficient magnitude and complexity to warrant separate consideration.

URBAN CONGESTION

Slums, overcrowding, and congestion are among the most obvious conditions of much urban development, and they can be directly related to recent changes in the density and distribution of the American population, as well as to technological changes which have made such population shifts possible. For example, while urban growth was steady but not very rapid in the United States up to the early part of the nineteenth century, it was dramatically accelerated by the industrial revolution, which brought large numbers of rural and foreign migrants to American cities in the latter part of the nineteenth and early part of the twentieth centuries. By 1920 more than one half of the United States population lived in urban areas. This accelerated trend has continued to the present. Today, more than 70 percent of the population lives in urban areas, while only about 8 percent remain in rural farm areas. This is almost a complete reversal in the distribution of the population since the time of the first U.S. census in 1790, when only 5 percent of the population lived in urban areas and the large majority lived on farms.[3]

Much urban growth has been concentrated in our largest cities, which have been growing in numbers and density, and this trend has produced serious problems of overcrowding in residential, industrial, commercial, and public facilities. In the earliest periods of rapid urban expansion, the health and sanitation problems created by the concentration of large numbers of people in relatively small land areas often made living conditions intolerable and resulted in repeated epidemics of major proportions. Some of these conditions, as well as some of the early responses to them, have been reported as follows:

As early as 1834, a sanitary report for New York City called attention to bad housing as a cause of disease. A second report, submitted in 1842, was even more detailed and insistent in pointing out the interrelation between the two. The first tangible result of these studies and of agitation for improvement was the creation of a city health department in 1866 and the passage of the first tenement law in 1867. Buildings with no sanitary facilities beyond the privy and the gutter were being crowded together in such a way as to leave many dwellings virtually without light and air. Not until 1879 was a law passed prohibiting the building of rooms without windows. Nor were these conditions confined to New York City. None of the large cities made adequate public provision for disposal of sewage until late in the nineteenth century, and even in 1900 Philadelpia and St. Louis had twice as much street mileage as sewer mileage. In the same year Baltimore, New Orleans, and other cities were still relying on open gutters for drainage. Frequently, cities were prompted to construct sewer systems only by social catastrophe. Memphis, for example, did not take this step until after the city had been practically depopulated by a yellow fever epidemic in 1879.[4]

Throughout the last half of the nineteenth century and the early part of the twentieth, isolated efforts were made in a wide variety of American cities to ameliorate problems of urban congestion, poor housing, inadequate facilities, sanitation, and a host of other needed urban services and institutions. These efforts were successful in reducing the high death rates associated with poor sanitation and health facilities.

The fact, however, remains that not only do some of the worse conditions of overcrowding remain in our large cities today, but that such congestion has created a host of new problems, such as the contamination of the air, the growing shortage of a fresh water supply, and the traffic tie-ups and snarls that are now critical aspects of the daily life of urbanites in our largest cities.

A contributing factor, of course, has been the uncontrolled competition for scarce urban space. This often leads to the incompatible use of adjacent parcels of land, represented by the intrusion of unsightly, noisy, and congestion-producing commercial and industrial activities into residential areas, and an ever more intensive utilization of the land, without regard for such consequences as increased pressures on already overburdened transportation, sewage, water, and utility systems, recreation facilities, and so on.

Also, residential areas tend to deteriorate and become dilapidated in the expectation on the part of many land owners that eventually such properties will succumb to the inevitable pressures of more intensive and economically more productive industrial and commercial uses. In fact, much slum clearance, supposedly undertaken for the benefit of the affected slum dwellers, actually facilitates the conversion of residential areas into nonresidential uses.[5] What happens in this process is that residential land values become so high that many middle income families are either forced to live in substandard housing at excessive cost, or are forced to leave the central cities in order to find suitable housing within a reasonable price range. Of course, the housing problem becomes even more difficult for many low income and minority groups caught in the squeeze between high cost substandard housing in the central cities and the social barriers which tend to exclude them from the suburban housing market. For these groups the overcrowded slums are the only available alternative.

METROPOLITANISM AND URBAN SPRAWL

In contrast to the plight of the city dweller, the migration of those who can afford and choose to move to outlying suburban areas represents a much larger and perhaps more significant trend toward decentralization of the growing urban population. This has produced a *metropolitan* pattern of urban settlement. Recent metropolitan development not only represents a decentralization of the residential population, but also includes a redistribution of many industrial and commercial activities over an ever-expanding land area surrounding the central cities. This trend has been greatly facilitated by scientific and technological advances of this century, especially in the areas of transportation and communications. The extensive use of the automobile has eliminated the necessity of locating the place of work and residence in close proximity. Thus, those who were first able to afford the use of the private automobile were among the first urbanites to resettle in suburban residential enclaves, well separated from the more hectic, noisy and other unpleasant aspects of the central business district or the factory.

Shopping centers, factories, and other business establishments were able to decentralize as they lessened their dependence on waterways, railroads, and an adjacent labor supply. The telephone, the motor truck, and the automobile made them readily accessible to their suppliers, their customers, and their employees at almost any location within the metropolitan complex. Much of the industrial and commercial decentralization thus made possible was probably a response to the larger quantities of cheaper land in outlying suburban fringes. However, it should also be noted that this general pattern of dispersion and decentralization is also probably a result of changing values, such as industry's desire for more space, more attractive living conditions for its employees, and an increasing emphasis on visible symbols of status, such as may be afforded by the availability of green open space, pleasingly visible architecture and landscaping, adequate parking facilities, etc.[6]

It is difficult to identify the boundaries or assess the extent of metropolitan growth and development, but perhaps the most commonly accepted estimates are those developed by the U.S. Bureau of the Census. According to current Census Bureau standards, the *Standard Metropolitan Statistical Area* (SMSA) is the appropriate metropolitan unit. SMSAs are defined as counties containing at least one, or more, city of at least 50,000 population, plus adjacent counties meeting specified criteria of urban character that are economically and socially integrated with the county containing the central city.[7] So defined, many metropolitan areas ignore the political lines of cities and even of some states. According to the 1960 U.S. census, there were 212 SMSAs in the United States containing 112,885,178 inhabitants, or 62.8 percent of the total national population. In addition, the 24 largest SMSAs each had a population of more than a million inhabitants. And it is expected that existing SMSAs will contain an even larger portion of the total population in the near future.

Of course, statistics such as these do not adequately describe the full impact of urban sprawl as metropolitan development extends itself and engulfs surrounding villages, cities, towns, counties, and farmlands. For example, the sprawl of metropolitan growth has been described in these more commonly recognizable visual terms by historian Oscar Handlin:

Seen from above, the modern city edges imperceptibly out of its setting. There are not clear boundaries. Just now the white trace of the superhighway passes through cultivated fields; now it is lost in an asphalt maze of streets and buildings. As one drives in from the airport or looks out from the train window, clumps of suburban housing, industrial complexes, and occasional green spaces flash by; it is hard to tell where city begins and country ends.[9]

This sprawling metropolitan settlement pattern in urban areas vastly extends the demand for urban services, such as adequate water and sanitation systems, transportation and communication facilities for the circulation of people, goods, and messages, recreation, schools, and other public facilities, and the maintenance of public safety and order over a much larger and complex area of land and population. According to Scott Greer, it is the failure to accomplish essential urban housekeeping tasks such as these, at the level expected by most citizens, that is the major source of most "metropolitan problems."[10]

THE POLITICAL FRAGMENTATION OF THE METROPOLIS

Large metropolitan areas in the United States are characterized by their extreme fragmentation into many separate and autonomous local political units. For example, there are over 16,000 legally distinguishable separate local political units in the 212 Standard Metropolitan Statistical Areas in the United States. In the Chicago metropolitan area alone, there are over 950 separate local governments, and in the New York metropolitan area there are over 1100 separate political units.[11] This pattern is repeated to a lesser extent in every metropolitan area in the country, and as sprawling urban growth continues, this proliferation is expected to get even worse. This political fragmentation seems to result from the fact that the technological advances in transportations and communications, which have permitted and encouraged the physical and social integration of increasingly larger geographic areas, have not been accompanied by any real increase in governmental integration. The populations moving outward from the central cities have resisted annexation and have incorporated themselves into small residential enclaves, variously called cities, townships, or villages.

The lack of fit between political and social boundaries has important consequences for the decision-making structure of the metropolitan area. It means that no local government decisions applying to all parts of the area are possible. Yet many of the conditions which have been defined as the social problems of urban areas can only be controlled by an area-wide political system. As some public officials put it, air pollution does not recognize political boundaries, nor do crime, epidemics, poverty, and other conditions which require government action. Scott Greer describes the problem this way:

The vast sprawl of contiguous and overlapping sites for human activity that makes up a metropolitan complex is fragmented and incoherent in its policy. Disjunction between economic, social, and political boundaries has even led some to dismiss the term "metropolitan community," for existence side by side in space is no guarantee of social structure.[12]

It must be concluded that governmental fragmentation, if it has not actually caused problems such as traffic congestion, air and water pollution, and urban blight, has nevertheless effectively prevented any significant solutions to these kinds of problems. Perhaps this, at least in part, helps to explain the increasing involvement of the federal government in the many problems of metropolitan areas.

THE PLANNING APPROACH

Planning cities is not a new development, of course, and historically there are examples of planned cities that go back as far as several thousand years. Even in the United States planned cities were a part of its early history. For example, William Penn laid out a planned street system for Philadelphia in 1682, an important plan was prepared for Manhattan Island in 1811, and the original plan for Washington, D.C., prepared in 1802, is another significant example of early city planning in the United States.[13]

But these early planning efforts were not typical of what was to follow, inasmuch as city planning as a modern social movement in the United States can more accurately be traced back to the demands for social reforms near the middle of the last century. These demands were a response to some of the worse conditions associated with the urban-industrial revolution. That they represented a distinct departure from the earlier examples of planned cities has been evidenced as follows by Robert A. Walker:

The problem of modern city planning is one of planning new cities only to a minor degree. It is primarily a problem of replanning cities already built; also, the planning movement in the United States has followed lines which set it apart rather sharply from recent European experience. This is particularly true with respect to administrative organization for planning. The origins of modern city planning in this country must be sought in the economic, social, and political upheavals of the last century.[14]

While isolated attempts were made to ameliorate problems of congestion, poor housing, inadequate facilities for transportation, sanitation, and a host of other needed urban services, it began to be recognized around the turn of the century that these fragmentary efforts were inadequate and that there would have to be more comprehensive approaches to solving these problems. Walker has viewed this important impetus to the modern planning movement as follows:

There was a growing realization among those interested in all these problems that they were interrelated; and it is in this recognition of relationship and of the importance of positive programs for the future, as contrasted with the piece-meal corrective measures, that we find the mainspring of modern planning.[15]

Another important aspect of the early phases of the modern city planning movement was a growing concern on the part of certain civic improvement organizations with improving the appearance of their communities. Beginning in the last part of the nineteenth century and lasting roughly until World War I, this phase has been identified as the "city beautiful" movement.[16] Here, the major emphasis was on the esthetic appearance of the city, as reflected in civic centers, parks, and landscapes. Also, much of the inspiration for this movement appears to have been generated by the Chicago World's Fair of 1893. It has been reported that returning World's Fair visitors, impressed by the architectural splendor of the exhibits, stimulated popular interest in civic esthetics, and that the Fair itself helped activate the symbol of the "city beautiful." Real estate boards, private builders, and bankers were among the private civic groups which had a major influence on this phase of the planning movement, and while they may have viewed the ugliness, crowding, and lack of public facilities as physically, economically, and socially unhealthy, they were also probably seeking symbol of status and achievement through the creation of urban "monuments" which would enhance the physical image of their cities.[18]

Except for a few notable exceptions, the plans advocated and prepared by the earlier protagonists of planning received no official or legal status and were usually not implemented in practice. Most of them have been characterized as little more than broad outlines of future possibilities designed to arouse public enthusiasm.[19]

Also, planning had no official status as a part of the formal structure of local government in its earliest days, and it was not until 1907 that the first official planning commission was created at Hartford, Connecticut. Initially, the planning commissions had little or no formal authority, and they functioned primarily as separate advisory boards to the executive and legislative branches of local government, to be consulted largely at the discretion of the mayor or city council. The planning commissions, averaging in size from 6 to 9 private citizens appointed as members, theoretically represented a cross section of community interests. In practice, however, they were usually over-represented by architects, realtors, engineers, and lawyers. This was often justified on the grounds that appropriate technical knowledge of professional training contributed the most desirable qualification for membership on the planning commission. This particular occupational composition of the earlier planning commissions was crucial in spelling out their activities and technical scope. Thus, the city plans focused primarily on architectural and engineering problems. This not only stereotyped the content of the term "city planning," as physical in scope, but it also tended to partially limit planning from developing in other potential directions until much later. For example, the techniques of economic and sociological research designed to identify planning needs in these areas were introduced before World War I, but partly as a result of the architectural and engineering orientation of the leading planners of this early period, the actual use of these techniques was not widely accepted at the outset, and it was not until the very late 1920s or early 1930s that the scope of planning was broadened to include these important areas.[20]

On the other hand, this phase of the planning movement had begun to focus on the efficient function of cities and the rational coordination of municipal services. It provided a set of goals which could be incorporated into the ongoing processes of city government, such as zoning and subdivision controls, public works, and other activities that could be justified on the basis of sound financial as well as architectural or engineering considerations. The preservation and increase of property values associated with sound zoning practices, for example, was a predominant factor in the acceptance and adoption of zoning as a legitimate function of local government.[21]

Perhaps the breadth and limitations of planning in the 1920s can best be illustrated by a summary of the contents of the major city plans of that period, as reported below:

A commonly used classification divides a comprehensive city plan into six main elements: zoning, streets, transit, transportation (rail), water, and air, public recreation, and civic art, or civic appearance. Taken together, street planning, land subdivision regulations, and zoning are counted on to motivate the types of land development and housing which the city plan aims to secure, so that in many plans housing does not appear as a separate element.[22]

The 1930s saw the planning movement continuing to cumulatively broaden the scope of its goals into a more comprehensive approach to urban problems. For example, the disorganizing effects of the depression were instrumental in focusing increased attention on slums, poverty, inadequate housing, disease, and other social problems that had been glossed over in many of the architecturally oriented activities of the earlier periods. Federal and state governments were forced to assume a larger responsibility for many activities formerly considered the responsibility of local municipalities, and federal agencies such as the FHA, the WPA, and the National Resources Planning Board were created and funds were made available for dealing with these problems. The impact on city planning was as follows:

The planning commissions, responding to the stimulus of available federal funds, entered energetically into planning for slum clearance and housing. Incidental to the preparation of applications for housing projects, they collected data on such phases of city life and government as crime, disease, income, industry, the cost of rendering municipal services, and tax delinquency. Increasingly, social science materials and methods and social scientists came to play a significant role in city planning.[23]

The 1930s were also characterized by an increased interest in questions of the administration and organization of planning as an integral part of local government. By that time a number of university-trained public administrators had joined the staffs of city planning agencies, and helped generate the administrative trends in planning described below:

Municipal officials, as well as students of public administration, came increasingly to see that the city planning agency could perform many quite practical administrative tasks which would help to solve pressing problems, especially when there is much to do and few funds to do it with. The preparation of informational reports of all sorts, capital improvement programming, and capital budgeting came to be ongoing activities of many of the municipal planning agencies.[24]

Finally, another major trend in planning in the 1930s was the growing interest in planning for a wider variety of geographic and governmental units, such as counties, metropolitan areas, regions, and states. It was probably this latter trend, along with resultant debates about the most appropriate unit for planning, that led the American City Planning Institute, the representative professional association, to change its name to the American Institute of Planners in 1939, leaving the geographic and political boundaries of the units for which the planning is done open to almost all potential possibilities.[25] Thus, city planning, urban planning, city and regional planning, comprehensive planning, physical planning, land use planning, and so on are among the various labels intermittently used by the agencies and professionals involved in planning for the orderly growth and development of urban communities.

But in spite of the many advances in its technical scope and function, it was not until the period following World War II that urban planning began to make a significantly visible impact on the urban scene. The postwar population "explosion," the boom in housing and transportation, the rapidly growing suburban areas, the declining central cities, the increased social and geographic mobility of the population, and the resultant demands for higher standards in all phases of urban living were among the major forces which led to the dramatic postwar expansion of urban planning activities. The current acceptance of urban planning as a necessary and desirable function of local government is well illustrated by the fact that over 96 percent of all United States cities over 10,000 population had official planning commissions as of 1961. In actual numbers there were 1136 such commissions actively operating.[26]

The rapid growth of the urban planning profession in recent years is another good illustration of the central role of urban planning as a response to problems of urban development. This skill group has continued to grow in size and scope, with a rather marked acceleration following World War II. For example, the American Institute of Planners, the representative professional association, grew fourfold from approximately 1000 members in 1954 to over 4000 members by 1964. Growing outward from an original architectural and engineering approach, urban planning has cumulatively encompassed legal, economic, social, political, and administrative approaches and techniques. It is perhaps parodoxical that many current controversies and debates revolving around planning efforts such as urban renewal and slum clearance, transportation, and the location of schools and recreation grow out of the fact that urban planning has indeed become so effective in producing visible changes in the current urban scene.

CURRENT STRATEGIES FOR URBAN PLANNING

In the first reading, F. Stuart Chapin, Jr., spells out some of the major techniques available to planners for guiding urban growth. The general master plan, urban development policies' instruments, area-wide public works programs, urban development codes, and metropolitan area programs of civic education are among the techniques reviewed.

William L. C. Wheaton (in the second reading) reviews the recent development plans for two major metropolitan areas in the United States and suggests how current developments in operations research make it possible to establish some measurable criteria for estimating the costs and benefits of these plans and the means for their implementation.

Scott Greer critically assesses the underlying assumptions of urban renewal, and what it has accomplished to date, in the third reading. Urban renewal has become in recent years one of the most controversial and misunderstood aspects of planned urban development. Technically speaking, urban renewal is not necessarily an integral part of long-range comprehensive planning, as described in the first two selections in this chapter, because many comprehensive community master plans do not contain specific provisions for urban renewal, and because some local urban renewal projects have been undertaken without reference to the guiding framework of a comprehensive community plan. In many communities, planning agencies and urban renewal agencies are, in fact, independent, autonomous, and sometimes competing departments of local government.

The most relevant criticisms of existing urban renewal projects have to do with their impact on low-income housing. Contrary to the original goals of the federally sponsored urban renewal program, the critics maintain that urban renewal to date has materially *reduced* the supply of low-cost housing in American cities, by replacing "bull-dozed" slum housing with new "luxury" housing, or more economically profitable commercial development of a non-residential character. Much criticism points not only to the psychic and emotional burdens imposed on low-income groups (predominantly ethnic and Negro minorities) involuntarily relocated from renewal areas, but also to the fact that urban renewal has not adequately compensated the relocated groups for their losses; that is, it has not necessarily provided them with better housing or neighborhood facilities than those from which they have been evicted. Of course, this is not so much a criticism of the general concept of urban renewal itself as it is a criticism of the particular uses to which urban renewal has been put. Most critics would probably support urban renewal, if it were used to provide more and better low-cost housing for low-income groups, and if relocation problems could be minimized or handled in more helpful and humane ways than they have in the past. The fact that urban renewal nevertheless has become a widely used approach for redeveloping economically declining areas in many cities suggests that it becomes increasingly important that the programs and policies of urban renewal be more clearly understood.

Finally, some of the current major proposals and programs for relieving the problems of urban transportation systems are reviewed by the staff of *Consumers Union* in the last reading in this chapter.

REFERENCES

1. Mitchell Gordon, *Sick Cities*. New York: Crowell Collier and Macmillan, Inc., 1963, pp. 339–340.
2. Alvin Boskoff, *The Sociology of Urban Regions*. New York: Appleton-Century-Crofts, Inc., 1962, p. 298.
3. Ronald Freedman (ed.), *Population: The Vital Revolution*. New York: Anchor Books, 1964, pp. 124–125.
4. Robert A. Walker, *The Planning Function in Urban Government*. Chicago: University of Chicago Press, 1950, pp. 6–7.
5. See Herbert J. Gans, "The Human Implications of Current Redevelopment and Relocation Planning," *Journal of the American Institute of Planners* (February 1959) pp. 15–25.
6. Boskoff, p. 121.
7. For a useful summary of the more detailed Census Bureau definitions, see John C. Bollens and Henry J. Schmandt, *The Metropolis*. New York: Harper & Row, Publishers, 1965, pp. 7–8.
8. Bollens and Schmandt, pp. 10–14.
9. Oscar Handlin and John Burchard (eds.), *The Historian and the City*. Cambridge, Mass.: Harvard University Press, 1963, p. 1.
10. Scott Greer, *The Emerging City*. New York: The Free Press of Glencoe, 1962, p. 169.
11. Gordon, p. 333.
12. Greer, p. 168.
13. Harry Gold, "The Professionalization of Urban Planning," unpublished doctoral dissertation, University of Michigan, 1965, p. 24.
14. Walker, pp. 5–6.
15. Walker, p. 10.
16. Harvey S. Perloff, *Education for Planning: City, State, and Regional*. Baltimore: Johns Hopkins Press, 1957, p. 55.
17. Perloff, p. 55.
18. Perloff, pp. 9–11.
19. Walker, pp. 13–14.
20. Perloff, pp. 12–15.
21. Gold, pp. 29–31.

22. T. K. Hubbard and H. V. Hubbard, *Our Cities Today and Tomorrow*. Cambridge, Mass.: Harvard University Press, 1929, p. 109.
23. Perloff, p. 15.
24. Perloff, p. 16.
25. Gold, pp. 37–38.
26. *The Municipal Year Book 1961*. International City Managers' Association, 1961, p. 271.

ADDITIONAL READINGS

Altshuler, Alan A., *The City Planning Process*, Ithaca, N.Y.: Cornell University Press, 1966.
Bollens, John C., and Henry J. Schmandt, *The Metropolis*. New York: Harper & Row, Publishers, 1965.
Boskoff, Alvin, *The Sociology of Urban Regions*. New York: Appleton-Century-Crofts, Inc., 1962.
Chapin, F. Stuart, Jr., and Shirley F. Weiss, *Urban Growth Dynamics in a Regional Cluster of Cities*. New York: John Wiley & Sons, Inc., 1962.
Gist, Noel P., and Sylvia Fava, *Urban Society*. New York: Thomas Y. Crowell Company, 5th ed., 1964.
Glaab, Charles N., *The American City*. Homewood, Ill.: The Dorsey Press, 1963.
Gordon, Mitchell, *Sick Cities*. Baltimore: The Penguin Books, 1965.
Greer, Scott, *The Emerging City*. New York: The Free Press of Glencoe, 1962.
———, *Urban Renewal and American Cities*. Indianapolis: The Bobbs-Merrill Company, Inc., 1965.
Jacobs, Jane, *The Death and Decline of American Cities*. New York: Random House, Inc., 1961.
Perloff, Harvey S., (ed.), *Planning and the Urban Community*. Pittsburgh: University of Pittsburgh Press, 1961.
Rossi, Peter H., and Robert A. Dentler, *The Politics of Urban Renewal*. New York: The Free Press of Glencoe, 1961.
Smerk, George, *Urban Transportation*. Bloomington, Indiana: Indiana University Press, 1965.

TAKING STOCK OF TECHNIQUES
FOR SHAPING URBAN GROWTH

F. Stuart Chapin, Jr.

The implications of the steady drift of population to urban regions, coupled with trends toward larger families and an extended life span, have become a favorite subject of speculation. Certainly the take-off base for this growth is incontrovertible: there is no mistake about the expansion under way in metropolitan areas today. What proportions this build-up will reach one, two, or three decades ahead is anybody's guess, but under the most conservative view, the physical impact is likely to be staggering. How well equipped is the planning profession for the task ahead? Quite apart from the never-ending quest for new and improved techniques, what tools do we now have for shaping growth, and are we getting optimal performance out of them?

This paper seeks to take stock of the situation by reviewing the range of techniques available to urban planners today and then exploring ways of making more effective use of them. "Techniques" is used to refer to means for prescribing, regulating, or in other ways influencing the course of events in urban areas so as to produce an intended pattern of land development. Urban growth or expansion is taken to mean the physical extension of urban areas by growth. Though related to urban growth, the renewal of devel-

oped areas is not specifically treated here.

In focusing on techniques, this paper by definition is not directly concerned with goals. Yet in some respects, a goal image of the form of the city as it may develop and assume a semblance of reality in the consciousness of the community constitutes a technique in itself—in the long run, perhaps the most powerful technique of all. The Center City image of Philadelphia indicates how an idea can achieve momentum of this kind. While there is thus power to an idea that in effect makes it a technique, for purposes of this discussion goals per se are not considered.

Techniques in use in urban areas today are a curious patchwork of devices, many an outgrowth of special-purpose efforts to meet particular problems and needs of their time, and many bearing the mark of the fragmented governmental situations that have prevailed during the period when the techniques evolved. We do not have to look far to see that urban growth problems have been with us for some time, but only in the post-World War II period of growth have we begun to see the serious proportions that these problems can reach in the years immediately ahead. Until recently it was common to find techniques developed and

From *Journal of the American Institute of Planners*, 29, 2 (May 1963). By permission of the author and the American Institute of Planners.

administered on an individual basis, each serving a purpose with respect to a problem or need and each treated unilaterally for that purpose alone. The "Balkanization" of governmental jurisdictions in metropolitan areas has greatly complicated the situation, and until improved mechanisms of intergovernmental collaboration are developed and put into practice, this situation is likely to continue to be a source of difficulty and confusion.

Many of the techniques were pioneering developments of their time and came into being with much travail. The persistence of a technique—its ability to weather change and resist attack through the ensuing years and, indeed, repel modernization and readaptation—appears to bear some relationship to the extent of baptismal fire it faced in the beginning. Zoning offers a classic illustration of a war horse which has achieved great strength by dint of the battles it has been through. Acceptance was slow to develop, and even after its initial validity as a technique was established, it went through many tests. To survive, therefore, techniques such as zoning have become so thick-skinned that they seem to have an immunity to re-evaluation and modification. Families and businesses which made location decisions on the basis of these measures view their modernization with suspicion—sometimes with justification. Further, the custodians of these techniques sometimes add to the climate of resistance. Local officials frequently are unable to free themselves from the memories of the battles encountered in getting acceptance of the technique and behave in ways which slow up the readaptation of old techniques to mesh with new ones.

Thus the evolution of techniques one at a time and in segmented jurisdictions, and the resistance to change that goes with the hard-won acceptance of a technique, have all contributed to the patchwork inheritance we have today. But the climate is changing. Now that the magnitude of growth and the outlines of the problems that lie ahead can be seen more clearly, there is a willingess to try new techniques which were unheard of before World War II. There is also a greater emphasis on positive measures, a deepening interest in pinning down goals of urban growth and expansion and in defining alternative land development and transportation patterns for fulfillment of these goals. To reach decisions where choices must be made forces local officials and groups into a wider scope of approach to problems and needs of expansion. This enlarged perspective in turn makes for a more favorable climate for acceptance of new techniques and adaptation of old ones. It permits an approach that looks beyond the present or even the decade ahead, and views urban expansion in terms of a whole sequence of growth stages where techniques are utilized in varying matched combinations at different points in time. This dynamic approach is fundamental in evaluating techniques for guiding urban development.

What are the techniques that have been used to date in regulating, directing, or in other ways influencing urban expansion, and what are the objectives implicit in each? How might they be used with greater effectiveness? Techniques in use today might be classified in any number of ways, but for purposes of this discussion they are listed on a basis that will fit into the guidance system approach proposed at the end of this paper:

1. A general plan for the metropolitan region
2. The urban development policies instrument

3. A metropolitan area public works program
4. An urban development code
5. An informed metropolitan community

Implicit in this listing is an over-all organizing force which is customarily embodied in the general plan. But in performing this organizing role, the plan functions as a technique through the medium of the other techniques which succeed it on the list. Also implicit is the mutual reinforcement that the last four groups of techniques supply to one another and the notion that techniques can be employed in strategic and linked combinations. These interrelationships among techniques will be taken up in the last part of this paper.

The general plan—variously known as the comprehensive plan, master plan, guide plan, development plan—is perhaps the oldest of the techniques for guiding urban expansion in use today. The use of a plan for organizing the structure and form of urban settlements goes back well before the Christian era. In recent times, especially in the Western World, the effectiveness of a plan in guiding development has been dependent on how well-related it is to the decision-making process of governing bodies. This dependence has given rise to the emphasis that today is placed on the planning process and the function of planning in government.

Acceptance of the general plan concept is not universal. Indeed, the concept has been under heavy attack in the past few years. Much of the criticism can be expected as a normal outgrowth of the first large-scale test of the concept, for until the 701 Program came along, the instances where the general plan was used as an instrument of decision-making by local governments were not many.

Under the spotlight, the fly specks of the general plan suddenly assume enormous proportions. There are also whole new legions of "experts" on the scene who provide a considerable claque in the politics of finding fault with a concept. But with all the growing pains of a concept undergoing its first widespread test, it is well to note some of the more basic criticisms that lie beneath the smoke.

There are many worthy of note. One very fundamental and often repeated criticism is the Rip Van Winkle history of the general plan concept in many communities—a failure to follow through on the original legislative grant of authority to develop and adopt the general plan, often resulting in a decimation of the concept by the use of such techniques as zoning and subdivision control without first preparing the plan on which they were supposed to be based. A whole series of criticisms focus on the nature of the plan itself. One of these sources of criticism points to the mechanistic and unimaginative character of plans, a complete blackout in the area of urban design. Another points to the absence of any consideration of attitudes and preferences of people living in the urban area, and another singles out the blind spot in plans with respect to the tensions and pace of modern-day living patterns, a seeming lack of consideration of their adverse effects.

Another group of criticisms is leveled at some of the old concepts of planning. For example, the neighborhood unit concept came under fire in the early 'fifties on grounds that it had become an over-romanticized concept being perverted to selfish ends and used as an instrument of segregation. Now, ten years later, still in a cloud of doubt, the concept is under attack on other grounds. The new criticism maintains that the concept is rendered obsolete by technological change and altered living patterns, and suggests that not only are many neighborhood concepts obsolete but that many other long-accepted principles and standards of planning must be re-examined and adapted to the present-day character and locus of activities of the average metropolitan area household. It is pointed out that these changes have stretched out distances and changed the whole scale of the general plan. Such criticisms indicate some of the pressures that the planning field is facing in updating the general plan concept and keeping it in a central position as a technique for shaping urban growth.

These very criticisms indicate an underlying strength that the general plan concept possesses, and this strength will undoubtedly increase as more research and study are focused on these problems. The strength of the general plan as a technique derives from the perspective it gives of the interrelationships between functional, time, and spatial components of urban development. In a functional context, it provides an overview of the structural relationships among land use, transportation, and community facilities and services. In a time context, it provides for sequence or scheduled progression of public action in relation to urban expansion, and in a spatial context it establishes the pattern and form of urban expansion.

In recent years there has been a tendency for the general plan to be set forth in three levels of detail. First, there is the "horizon" concept of urban expansion in the larger region, usually expressed in a very generalized pattern as a "goal form" for growth and development. It has no time schedule and no price tag attached. Second, there is the traditional version of the plan—a coordinated set of proposals for development over a 20- to 25-year period, with its recommended

general priority schedule, financial program, and various actions needed in effectuating the plan. As a plan which may be formally adopted, it frequently focuses on a particular jurisdiction. The third concept involved in the general plan is short-term, often a five-year scheme, essentially a first stage to the 20-year plan which becomes the basis for the capital budget of the governing body. A more extended form of this kind of improvement program, called the "Community Renewal Program," has been stimulated by federal aid in recent years.

Implicit in the general plan concept is the necessity for relating plans to the flow of time and for progressive refinement of the more distant-horizon proposals so that they may be introduced into the decision-making process at the proper time and carried forward from the 20-year docket to the five-year schedule. There is also the necessity for re-evaluation of proposals in the pipeline against the unpredictable changes that emerge and alter the validity of the basic premises of the general plan.

While the concept is therefore well defined, this does not insure that the plan will be used to guide growth. There are several fundamental requirements which must be fulfilled if the plan is to have force and effect. First, the effectiveness of the general plan as a technique is dependent on the imaginativeness of the plan itself and its power to inspire wide support. Second, it is dependent on the technical practicability of the plan and its power to inspire confidence. Finally, it is dependent on the extent to which planning is in the mainstream of decision-making.

The imaginativeness of the plan is directly related to its success in dealing with the living qualities of cities, the extent to which it recognizes how the city affects man's sense and his satisfactions with his surroundings, and thus his out-look and behavior generally. Few general plans have been based on considerations that go deeply into livability and the psychological adjustments that residents must make to emerging forms of urban society; few have given much considera-tion to the ways in which urban design may serve to alleviate stress in day-to-day activities and make the urban environ-ment more satisfying. To remedy this situation a great deal more attention must be given to carrying the general plan beyond the somewhat mechanistic func-tional stage that has characterized plans in the past, to a conception of the city as it may be experienced by residents once proposals take form on the ground. Not only must studies of livability and the follow-through in urban design be an integral part of the general plan prep-aration, but they must be a continuing part of the planning activity.

The practicability of the plan is a function in part of how feasible the pro-posals are and in part of how competent they are. Feasibility is usually measured in terms of the financial reasonableness of proposals and how sensitive they are to human considerations and the over-riding political factors. Boldness and imagination do not mean that a plan is unfeasible. Indeed, a plan may be un-feasible unless it is bold and imaginative. But even with the widespread appeal that comes with a truly creative plan, the cost-benefit aspects of the proposals con-tained in the plan cannot be slighted.

The technical competence of the gen-eral plan must be judged by the extent to which the plan considers underlying interrelationships among the structural elements of the city—relationships over time and in space between activity cen-ters, movements of people and goods between these centers, and availability of essential facilities and services for the various activities. As the plan becomes a greater force in decisions, pressures for improving techniques of analyzing these relationships will increase. More and more, planning agencies in large met-ropolitan areas will turn to machine methods of data handling and systems analysis approaches in their analytical work. At this moment most metropolitan planning agencies are still struggling with obsolete techniques of a craftsman's era, totally inadequate for the kinds of demands which urban areas are even now experiencing. In this respect, research is of crucial importance in updating plan-ning techniques so that the general plan can assume a more effective role as an instrument for organizing urban growth.

Yet advances in design and analysis are not enough to insure that the general plan will become an organizing force in urban expansion. To be a force, it needs to be something more than a phrase in the enabling legislation or a collection of proposals in a handsome spiral-bound report with fold-out color maps and acetate overlays. The general plan is a politically dynamic concept, influencing the governmental decision-making proc-ess and responsive to it. No matter how imaginative and well-conceived the plan may be, it is unlikely to achieve success as an organizing force unless planning is a well established and an astutely direct-ed function of local government, situated in the mainstream of the decision-making process. For planning to be effective at the metropolitan level, governmental ar-rangements are needed which give plan-ning direct access to decision-making channels encompassing the entire urban-izing region. In sum, a well-conceived plan has a greater chance of becoming an organizing force when there are estab-lished channels for handling plan proposals on a metropolitan-wide basis and when proposals introduced into these channels are imaginative and practical.

It is increasingly recognized that where public policy is closely keyed to the general plan, it can be an extremely effective technique for guiding urban expansion. "Public policies" is considered here to refer to consciously derived guides that governing bodies, commissions, or administrative officials of government develop to achieve consistency of action in the pursuit of some public purpose or in the administration of particular public responsibilities. In this sense, policies may exist in a great many spheres of urban affairs not directly or even indirectly germane to urban expansion. However, a great many policies do have significance for the physical setting of cities, and it is this sphere of policy formulation that is of concern here.

Illustrative examples come to mind. Policy on the degree of commitment by city administrations to support various forms of transportation is an illustration. The establishment of a sewer extension policy or the adoption of an annexation policy are familiar examples of policies that city councils may develop to insure a consistent and equitable approach in actions they take on these needs as they arise from time to time. Although not covered here, tax policy should certainly be listed as a policy area of profound importance to urban expansion. Many other examples could be mentioned.

The potentialities of using public policies as instruments for guiding expansion have passed virtually unnoticed until relatively recently. But public bodies are beginning to recognize the cumulative impact that consistency of action can have in achieving particular goals: planning and transportation agen-cies, for example, are increasingly concerned with the impact that various public policies may have on the patterns of urban growth. There is rising interest in the effect that the service level policies for water and sewerage systems, expressway and transit systems, and schools and recreation systems may have on patterns of land development. Similarly state policies on such matters as stream sanitation, air pollution, reforestation, and other state resource-use programs may exert direct or indirect influences on patterns of urban expansion.

The impact of federal programs on localities is a particularly critical area of policy co-ordination. Federal grants and loans for various public works have long been recognized as a force that directly or indirectly influences local decisions on growth and development. The policies that are established in administering mortgage insurance, small business loans, defense plant location, programs for distressed areas, or programs relating to such national resources as land, water, and forests all may have an indirect effect on the form of urban development. Thus, if FHA policies are administered so that in addition to enforcing underwriting standards they provide for direct and continuous co-ordination with local land use objectives, these policies, in unison with local public works policies, can be expected to complement and reinforce efforts at guiding land development. Similarly, policies on small business loans and assistance to distressed areas can become positive influences when fitted to a policies instrument at the local level. The accelerated tax amortization incentives for defense plants which meet certain local criteria have been used in the past to implement certain defense policies. Water control policies for protection against floods, soil conservation, or recreation, all may profoundly affect the patterns of urban expansion. If systematically co-ordinated with local public works and other policies, such federal policies can be made to function in concert with local techniques for guiding urban growth.

So long as policies grow out of one responsible agency there is some likelihood of deliberation and reasoned co-ordination. The further removed the administration of policy is from the point of application, the less likely it is that policies relating to urban expansion will be enmeshed in one coordinated policies instrument on any spontaneous basis. State policies are likely to be unilateral in their application in urban areas, each administered for the special purpose for which it was established, often without reference to other state policies or to local policies. The same may be said of federal policies. In programs where grant and loan provisions call for administrative co-ordination at the point of application—such as the workable program requirement for HHFA housing and renewal assistance—substantial progress is being made to relate public policies that impinge on urban expansion at the local level. But as yet there is no comparable mechanism to insure that all relevant state and federal programs are coordinated with local development policies at the point of impact in local areas.

Clearly the effectiveness of policies as a means for shaping urban growth is dependent on whether the relevant policies can be brought together in one *modus operandi*—a framework for steering public policy—and whether such a framework becomes a recognized basis of co-ordinated action by all levels of government in policy decisions relating to urban development. What is suggested here is a follow-through on the notion that Henry

Fagin advanced a few years ago for codifying urban policies in one *urban development policies instrument.*[1]

As noted above, individual policies are often adopted initially for quite different purposes. But if a policy is adopted to achieve some consistency and equitableness in the expenditure of public funds for sewer extensions and to keep expenditures in this area within the fiscal capabilities of local government, conceivably it could at the same time take into account *where* the sewers are extended and the implications this may have for watermain extension, street improvements, and school construction. The thought here is to achieve co-ordination in policy formulation and thereby accomplish a sounder result from an over-all fiscal point of view and achieve a better pattern of growth in the bargain.

For the urban development policies instrument to be an effective technique, it must be sufficiently concrete and acceptable to the governing bodies concerned to be adopted by resolution. Whether it is adopted initially may be dependent on political considerations—and it is beyond the scope of this paper to go into problems of intergovernmental relations—but ultimately there will need to be a formal statement of policy with concurrence by all participating metropolitan area governing bodies. This

[1] See Henry Fagin, "Organizing and Carrying Out Planning Activities Within Urban Government," *Journal of the American Institute of Planners,* XXV (August, 1959, 109–114. Note my suggested term "urban development policies instrument" as opposed to Fagin's "policies plan." The purpose of this distinction is to narrow the area of concern to a more pragmatic usage of "policy," to limit the focus to land development policies within the full gamut of public policies, and to get away from a potential source of confusion for planners in attempting to explain to local groups the difference between a "policies plan" and a "general plan."

kind of collateral action is beginning to develop on a formal basis (for example, the Metropolitan Regional Council in the New York area), and there are numerous instances of informal understandings between units of local government. Such an instrument could become quite common if formal joint agreement on an urban development policies instrument were a requirement in order to qualify for various federal and state financial aids.

The exact content of the instrument will be determined in each metropolitan area from the general plan, its guiding statement of goals for urban expansion, the proposals set forth for achieving these goals, and the timing of the development proposals. In implementation of these concepts, the policies instrument brings together relevant existing policies that impinge on urban expansion, identifies appropriate new ones, and ties the old and new into a related series of statements. Thus it considers current policies for transportation, utilities, schools, recreation, fire and police protection, and other public services to insure that such matters as levels and intensity of service, areas to be served, and method of financing are working in harmony and not at cross purposes with the general plan. In addition, tax policies, debt policies, annexation policies, and so on, would be examined as they affect land development. Similarly, policies on which regulatory measures are based would be taken into account.

Along with content, timing is important. The policies instrument will need to recognize general growth stages identified in the plan. Accordingly, it may group policy positions into a graded series of "policy bundles" consonant with particular growth stages. Under such an approach, policy bundles may be organized according to the extent of emphasis on development called for during a particular period of time. To take a very simple illustration, policies conceivably could be grouped into these four bundles: Condition I bundle might contain policies which would tend to inhibit development; Condition II bundle, policies which would tend to postpone development; Condition III bundle, policies which would tend to initiate development; and Condition IV bundle, policies which would tend to push development. Such policy bundles might then be applied to particular planning or development areas identified in the general plan. The foregoing example is hypothetical, for it is clear that how these bundles are actually organized and what is finally set down in statement form within each bundle will vary with every metropolitan area.

Finally, recent research on land development models indicates that it will soon be possible to test the implications for land development of putting into effect different policy combinations. Much more research is needed, but studies made to date suggest that it is possible to establish a connection between a particular mix of public policies and particular patterns of land development. These relationships are complex. It is difficult to isolate the impact of policies from other forces that influence the direction and intensity of land development, and it is difficult to evaluate the lag differentials and take into account technological factors that will modify the effect of policy combinations. But this work suggests that an urban development policies instrument, especially when it is coupled with public works programming, has great potentiality as a technique for guiding development.

Public policy formulation and public works programming go hand in hand.

While public policy establishes the conditions under which public facilities and services will be extended, the public works program constitutes a means of follow-through once a policy has been adopted. It identifies specific improvements for specific locations and gives them a priority. If day-to-day decisions of governing bodies can be related through a policies instrument to achieve a more rational pattern of urban expansion, a public works program related to the general plan and attuned to the policies instrument can have an infinitely stronger influence on urban development.

Somewhat parallel to the situation with respect to policy formulation, there are three problems in making public works programming an effective mechanism for shaping urban growth: 1) co-ordination among functional elements of the overall public works program, 2) co-ordination of public works programming among local governmental jurisdictions, and 3) co-ordination of federal and state with local programs. The first kind of co-ordination is typically achieved through the public works and the capital budgeting mechanism. The second is a metropolitan area problem, requiring some form of intergovernmental collaboration within the metropolitan area and the surrounding region. The third requires mechanisms for intergovernmental co-operation in the planning and the scheduling of state and federal works which are to be constructed in or near metropolitan areas.

The programming of public works properly grows out of the general plan and is an important link between planning and the decision-making process. As a mechanism for guiding growth, the scheduling of public works provides a means of influencing the location, timing and intensity of development in an urban area. The development of an expressway system in a particular quadrant of the metropolitan area will draw growth into this quadrant and along tributary systems of major streets that feed into this expressway. If properly co-ordinated with the construction of sewage disposal facilities and trunk sewer lines, expansions in the water treatment plant and water mains, and the development of school facilities in this sector, these measures can have considerable cumulative effect in channeling growth to particular areas, and in dispersing or concentrating it. Therefore, to insure that these facilities are located and timed in harmony with other techniques used in shaping urban growth, the programming of public works will need to be done in project combinations, probably with the make-up of these combinations changing with each growth stage.

But public works programs frequently involve decisions made at other levels of government. If HHFA's Community Facilities Administration makes loans to local sanitary districts without consideration of the metropolitan-wide water and sewerage problem, and of the effect that unco-ordinated small systems may have on a metropolitan land policy, an important means of guiding urban expansion will be dissipated. As the President recognized in his message to Congress in April of last year, the importance of co-ordinated programming is particularly critical in the transportation field. Programs for improvement in commuter and mass transportation fully co-ordinated with expressway building programs constitute a powerful technique for shaping the growth patterns of cities.

The list of public works that involve intergovernmental patterns of co-operation extends to many other fields of concern—urban renewal, public housing port development, river and harbor improvements, airports, and including soon in all likelihood, public school and college facilities. Can any one decision be divorced from other public works decisions? If the intent is to exercise some consistent and rational guidance over urban expansion, logic will surely argue for some form of co-ordinated public works programming in an intergovernmental framework for joint action.

While policy direction and public works spending have been underused as tools for guiding urban expansion, control by regulation has been widely used, often overworked, as a technique for steering urban growth. Here too, we encounter problems resulting from the fragmented governmental situations that often prevail in large metropolitan areas. Under zoning, there is frequently an absence of uniform criteria for the establishment of zoning districts and a lack of uniform standards for use, density, and bulk requirements from one municipality to another in a metropolitan area. Enforcement practices may also vary considerably. Moreover, within single jurisdictions, a problem results from the proliferation of regulatory measures that have been adopted one by one without being related to regulations already on the books.

So far there has been no extensive involvement of the federal government in regulatory measures and only limited involvement of state governments. Indirectly, through HHFA's workable program requirement, for example, the federal government has sought to strengthen the effect of urban renewal programs by requiring as a condition for federal aid that localities put into effect or upgrade such regulatory measures as zoning, housing, and building codes. Up to the present time, the state has entered the picture mainly in providing enabling leg-islation, in enforcing statewide standards in certain areas (building codes, stream sanitation requirements), and in providing assistance in drafting ordinances. However, as metropolitan areas spread territorially and coalesce from one part of a state to another and across state lines, we can expect an increasing state participation in regulatory activity.

To achieve a broader approach to urban expansion and to insure more effective and expeditious regulation, metropolitan areas increasingly will need to devise and experiment with new ways of collaborating on a metropolitan-wide basis. Such ordinances as zoning, subdivision control, building, housing, fire and other similar codes, regulation of open space easements and airport approaches, and rules governing mapped streets and future transportation corridors will need to be brought together and reorganized into one *urban development code*.

The urban development code would reorganize and codify in one metropolitan area instrument the regulations presently scattered through different ordinances in each jurisdiction that relate to land development and the construction, use, and occupancy of structures on the land. Such a code would also include controls in the use of land, water, and air in the larger region. If the image of the general plan for urban growth in an entire metropolitan area is to become an effective consideration in the thinking of the many households, firms, and institutions that take up the land and develop it, a single metropolitan code with some measure of order and simplicity is essential. Developers work in many jurisdictions, and individual location decisions are constantly made without reference to municipal or county boundaries. With the profusion of regulatory measures and the continual tinkering with these ordinances, even the most imaginative metropolitan area plan loses its organizing force and the image becomes blurred in skirmishes with the rules.

Simplification is needed to make regulatory requirements intelligible to the general public as well as easy to administer. In the process of codifying, parts of ordinances dealing with similar matters would be brought together. Thus, site planning features of group housing developments might be brought together in one place in the code, construction requirements in another, and the occupancy requirements in still another. Parts of ordinances which define districts (building use zones, fire zones, density zones) might be brought together so as to minimize confusion for the citizen as well as for the administrator.

In addition to the emphasis on coordination and simplification, the urban development code would be designed to function as a positive influence in shaping growth. Assuming legislative authorization for development timing, the code would seek to define in matched combinations varying development requirements corresponding to particular development stages identified in connection with the policies instrument discussed above. Thus, for the newly developing areas, one set of requirements may be featured; and for older established areas, another combination may be employed. Over time, according to some kind of performance criteria, the combination of requirements would be modified. This kind of flexibility might be a built-in feature of the code.

This final technique relies on the persuasive power of a sound and logical approach to urban expansion. It depends on a broad and continuing program of civic education and assumes that the residents of the metropolitan area—the households, the industrialists, the businessmen, and the institutional groups—will see the wisdom of planned urban expansion. While other techniques seek to guide the location decisions of these groups by plans, policies, public works, and regulation, this is a direct-appeal technique built around the notion of keeping people informed about the general plan and of achieving public objectives of urban expansion through the cumulative effect of general adherence to sound principles and standards of land development.

While directed to many of those whose decisions to move or locate in the future will account for a substantial part of the expected urban expansion, civic education is an extremely elusive guidance technique. A broadly conceived and continuing program of civic education utilizing a variety of communications media will probably exert some influence on location decisions of households, firms, and institutions over time, but there is unlikely to be a groundswell of spontaneous conformance without some reinforcement from other techniques.

There are at least four complementing areas of emphasis in a civic education program. One is more direct than the other three and is the most familiar of the civic education techniques. It involves a carefully worked-out continuing program of public information, reporting on problems and needs and the steps necessary to meet them as they arise in the future. It utilizes mass media of all kinds—the press, radio, television, public forums, illustrated talks, exhibitions, printed brochures, leaflet reminders. A second technique of civic education utilizes the principle of participation to inform individuals and groups. It seeks to guide actions by developing a sense of responsibility. Thus, technical and citizen advisory committees assist in various ways in studying, advising, and publicizing approaches to such problems as traffic, housing, and stream or air pollution. A third technique seeks to educate through demonstration projects of self-help and mutual co-operation. This technique has been successfully used in urban renewal programs in several cities, showing how private effort can be related to public actions in upgrading residential areas. The fourth technique is directed to school children and, by means of field studies and school projects, seeks to develop interest and understanding on the part of children through group investigation and study of their community. Such a technique has a dual role—it reaches the parents through the child's interest in local problems, and it has long-range implications in developing a more informed citizenry for the 10- to 20-year pull ahead.

Like policy planning and public works programming, civic education is a relatively underdeveloped technique in most metropolitan areas today. Direct media such as newspapers, radio, television, and printed reports have been used widely, but much more can be done in relating these efforts to a carefully structured continuing program of civic education. To achieve maximum effectiveness in the use of these four civic education devices, a general long-range civic education program would need to be organized and timed in close relationship to the other techniques, and to key stages in the general plan.

The individual civic education techniques would need to be used in differing combinations, with some designed for use in particular stages during the preparation of the general plan and others for particular stages in implementation of the plan, in effect backstopping other techniques. Some combinations may be grouped for use in particular areas to deal with particular stages of growth. Thus the civic education program, like the other techniques, has possibilities for much wider application in guiding urban growth.

So far, emphasis has been placed on a broadened approach and a fuller use of existing techniques. I have suggested that by making better use of the techniques we have, we can make urban expansion follow more rational patterns. We may also hope to achieve greater economy, convenience and attractiveness of development through the conscious and purposeful use of these techniques. But I have also tried to stress the fact that much of the positive benefit to be gained from these techniques will depend on how well co-ordinated they are, whether they augment or work at cross purposes with one another. Thus we come finally to the notion of *urban development guidance systems*. The terminology is used advisely. While this is obviously an area where methods of systems analysis can be introduced to advantage, the term is also being used in a pragmatic sense. Thus, each of the five classes of techniques that have been discussed may be viewed as a subsystem to the larger guidance system.

The concept is a simple one. A guidance system draws upon the general plan of the metropolitan area for the underlying rationale in the location and timing of urban expansion—land development, the construction of essential links in the transportation networks, and the provision of required community facilities. In serving as an organizing force, the general plan thus becomes a key technique for steering both public and private actions so that they produce the desired pattern of development in the metropolitan landscape. But at the same time an urban development policies instrument that specifies under what conditions public services will be extended to new areas of development, and a public works program that sets forth the schedule under which facilities will be built in order to supply these services, become the key techniques for formalizing actions in the public sector. By the same token, an over-all urban development code and a broad-gauge civic education program become key techniques for regulating and insuring more informed action in the private sector. Thus the techniques we have been reviewing are interrelated, and if they are to achieve their fullest potential their relationships must be recognized and given conscious direction through one co-ordinated framework.

In the abstract, then, the guidance system is an operations plan. Theoretically, modern systems analysis techniques can cope with such a complex of techniques. In practice, there may be strong political reasons that would militate against utilizing it in any complete sense of the meaning suggested above. Regardless of the degree to which such a systems approach is achievable, the underlying principles have an urgent and immediate applicability. This is no long-range proposal. Both public and private decisions are being made today which require the organizing force of a well-conceived plan and a programmed use of techniques aimed at shaping urban growth. Without a guidance system to give urban expansion patterns a more rational form, metropolitan areas face problems which will be truly staggering by today's standards.

OPERATIONS RESEARCH FOR
METROPOLITAN PLANNING

William L. C. Wheaton

The dominant feature of American society today is the steady and rapid concentration of our population in urban areas. Virtually 100 per cent of our future national population growth will occur in these areas, as a result of both natural increase and migration. Our national productivity and standard of living will depend in considerable degree upon our ability to plan for this future development and for the necessary redevelopment of existing cities in ways which will overcome the congestion, the problems of health and welfare, and the high costs occasioned by deficiencies in our present cities.

Two recent metropolitan master plans, the plans for Denver and Washington, D.C., illustrate the problems of planning for this growth. In different ways they are among the best of recent metropolitan plans have received some acclaim in the city planning profession. They reflect adequately the state of practice in this field and the philosophical and scientific foundations of that practice.

Both plans are relatively brief—about 100 pages in length—and consist largely of maps and charts. They are addressed to government officials and informed civic leaders. The underlying studies, to the extent that they exist, are not presented, summarized, or referenced. Thus, in both

cases, there is no published basis for judging the adequacy of the analysis behind the plans. One aspect of these plans appears to reveal underlying issues most clearly: the distribution of population, activities, and land uses within the metropolitan area.

The Washington metropolitan area plan[1] was prepared by the National Capital Planning Commission in 1961. The population of the metropolitan area is projected to grow from a present level of 2,000,000 to an estimated 5,000,000 by the year 2000. Since federal employment bulks large in the metropolitan total, a separate projection has been made for it. In the past, this employment has been concentrated largely in the center of the metropolitan area. The plan assumes that it will become federal policy to create sub-centers of federal employment on the fringes of the metropolitan area, as has been done in recent years with several major agencies. This decentralization of federal employment will presumably be accompanied by a comparable and contiguous growth of other employment on a decentralized basis. The plan further assumes that any scattered pattern of

[1] *A Policies Plan for the Year 2000: The Nation's Capital,* National Capital Planning Commission, 1961.

From *Journal of the American Institute of Planners,* 29, 4 (November 1963). Reprinted by permission of the author and the American Institute of Planners.

development is uneconomic and socially and aesthetically bad. Finally, it assumes that the reservation of large amounts of open space in the form of greenbelts is a desirable goal and can be achieved through a combination of planned transportation systems and public controls.

Upon these assumptions, the plan briefly examines the following alternatives:

First, the restriction of metropolitan growth by a combination of federal policy, which would move future federal employment centers to other cities, and local policy, which would restrict areas available for urban growth. The effect of these policies would be to increase the density of the remaining areas and deter the movement of people and enterprises to metropolitan Washington. This alternative is rejected as neither feasible nor desirable. In all the other alternatives presented, the rate of population growth is assumed to be exogenous, beyond the control of the public policy.

Second, a pattern which would accommodate present growth in new independent cities. This alternative is described as attractive but difficult to attain, particularly in view of its dependence upon the co-operation of the areas affected and the difficulties of channeling growth into such cities.

Third, a pattern called "planned sprawl." This alternative assumes that the present pattern of residential expansion will proceed, but that sub-centers for community services, commercial services, and federal employment will emerge, linked by highways; and that these will form a sprawling but partially nucleated suburban pattern. This alternative is rejected on the grounds that it would be undesirable, would increase journeys to work, would reserve no open space, and would limit housing and employment choices to those now available in the suburban areas.

Fourth, the emergence of a number of dispersed cities. This alternative differs from the second only in that several more proposed cities of smaller size are suggested.

Fifth, a ring of cities. This pattern would have certain communication and transportation advantages over the dispersed city pattern, but, like it, would tend to generate pressures for development in the greenbelt and would tend to deemphasize the importance of the metropolitan center.

Sixth, peripheral communities. This alternative is not essentially different from the preceding two, but it poses another possible pattern of growth with narrower open spaces and slightly more concentrated radial transportation routes. Again it assumes less control over the pattern of development than would be the case in preceding alternatives.

Finally, the radial corridor plan, based upon the establishment of major radial transit and expressway systems. This plan assumes that such transit axes can be built, usually in advance of population growth, that employment and community service centers will be generated along them and lead to the development of a fairly high-density core along each corridor and surrounding the stops in the transit system. It is claimed that this pattern would provide a wider choice of housing types, including single family detached homes, garden apartments, and elevator apartments along each corridor. This pattern would supposedly facilitate employment choices by providing employment centers along each linear axis and in the center. The report argues that this plan would lead to the growth and renewal of the metropolitan center as a major business and employment district. Growth could thus be restricted in the interstitial green spaces, preserving access to the countryside at convenient distances from most of the population. A radial transit system and a radial and ring highway system are conceived as the most important development forces to effect the plan.

Needless to say, the radial corridor plan is the pattern of development which is recommended for adoption by the National Capital Planning Commission and the adjoining states, counties, and municipalities.

The plan itself shows a static future state for the year 2000. In this respect it is similar to almost all past master plans, which usually show a condition forecast or proposed for 25 years hence. There is no indication of the intervening states, even little discussion of the processes necessary for their achievement, although one of the alternatives presented is, in effect, a forecast of the results of continued "normal" growth under the normal planning, regulatory, and market forces now operative.

The Washington plan is one of the first to try to present alternatives for public choice. It does so, however, in a totally sketchy fashion, without any analysis of the economic, social, or other implications of the choices offered, or any calculation of the costs or benefits of any alternative. Nevertheless it is an important advance in posing the issues.

The Denver Metropolitan Plan,[2] produced in 1961 after several years of effort, projects the growth of that metropolitan area to the year 2000. It estimates that the population will grow from 880,000 in 1960 to 2,450,000 by the year 2000. The growth rate is assumed to be largely autonomous, the result of regional and national market forces, and therefore, beyond the control of the metropolitan planning agencies. It is rare for any metropolitan plan to examine or even consider whether metropolitan population growth is controllable, or should be the subject of public policy.

Metropolitan employment is derived from estimated population in the Denver plan. From these estimates of population and of employment—broken down at least into industrial, commercial, and other categories—requirements for different land uses are estimated. Such estimates are derived empirically from existing average land use ratios as they appear to be modified by current trends. Marginal

rates are rarely used in forecasting land requirements.

Since residential land uses comprise about half of all land uses, and since the housing market is one of the most autonomous of the forces shaping the metropolitan area, the residential land use plan becomes a major element in any metropolitan plan. The usual approach is to estimate the future holding capacity of land based upon existing or prospective zoned densities, and to assume that development will be more or less contiguous to existing development despite the evident fact that current residential development is widely scattered and follows no evident systematic pattern. This procedure leads to an estimated distribution of resident population and residential land uses.

In a similar way, industrial land uses are estimated from the projected industrial employment multiplied by prospective employment density. Sites not clearly usurped for residential use are identified for industrial purposes. Estimates are prepared of the amount and type of land required for commercial and community facility uses, and located by ordinary market area delineation in each community or sub-region.

Given these estimates and locations of residential, industrial, commercial, and institutional or public land uses, transportation requirements are estimated for the major patterns of movement, notably the journey to work, and a transportation system is derived from such estimated requirements. In the Denver case, it is a highway system placing little reliance upon public transit facilities.

In addition, the Denver plan shows space requirements for schools, parks, police and fire stations, libraries, health and welfare facilities, and the other public facilities occupying space. Finally, the plan takes account of such sub-surface

[2] *Metro Growth Plan 1970–2000*, Master Plan Report No. 16, Inter-County Regional Planning Commission, Denver (undated), 1961.

facilities as sewer and water systems.

The Denver plan assumes that growth will follow a contiguous pattern, with the edge of the developed area pushing steadily outward during the next forty years.

A 50 per cent residential land vacancy rate is assumed from 1960 to 1980 and 30 per cent thereafter. In the last two decades of the forecast period, an almost inconceivable shift to apartment house living is assumed. In combination, these assumptions serve to restrict the area of growth, and to take some account of scatteration. The Denver Plan is unique among American plans in this attempt to project the rate and location of growth through time, and the plan has an interesting although relatively fragmentary basis for analyzing the forces at work which will produce such a pattern and rate of expansion.

The Denver plan also divides the metropolitan area into communities and neighborhoods. Each of these is assumed to contain a resident population, local public and private facilities—such as schools and shops—required to service that population, and some employment opportunities.

In the plan, these communities are separated from each other by a system of parks, parkways, and expressways. No means presently exist for the reservation of these separations as public open spaces or as reserved sites for future expressways. In fact, the aerial photographs upon which these community plans are superimposed reveal that many of the planned open spaces or separation strips are fully developed for housing or other land uses today.

Finally, the plan assumes that a large proportion, if not all, of the growth of the Denver area can be contained within delineated metropolitan boundaries. Again, no effective means exist for such containment, since our present zoning powers, as they are operated by local governments, have proven incapable of long withstanding normal market forces. It is possible, of course, to hold development within limits by ultra-low-density zoning which raises the cost of houses and thus reduces the size of the market. Such a policy would probably be illegal, however, and would in any case have very serious adverse effects upon metropolitan growth if pursued as a major means of containing development.

The type, quantity, and timing of community facilities—particularly highways, and water and sewer lines—affect the rate and location of urban development, but means do not presently exist for programming such facilities on a metropolitan basis to guide development in conformity with the master plan. Some of the better governed central cities do engage in capital programming. But even within such single-government jurisdictions, systematic consideration of the effect of programmed actions upon development rates and patterns is rare. One of the most common assumptions in modern planning is that the location and character of highway and transit facilities will affect the rate and character of development in the areas served by such transportation facilities. Nevertheless, comparatively little is known about the actual effects involved, and this subject is only beginning to be explored in a systematic way.

In short, the Denver plan proposes to organize the region's future expansion in stages and on a contiguous basis. It assumes that the forces affecting the rate of aggregate expansion are autonomous. It proposes a distribution of population and industry into separated communities, but no very effective means of implementation are presently available to achieve this distribution. Its major contribution is the presentation of the idea of an evolving process of growth, and preliminary notions of the factors that might affect rates of growth in different areas.

The Washington and Denver plans provoke these questions: What grounds are there for the choice of any of these patterns of development, as opposed to whatever pattern will evolve from normal market forces as they are influenced by normal regulations and the usual imperfections in the market? Is any of these patterns more efficient than any other, more economic? Does any one of these patterns really offer a higher level of "amenity," however defined? How many would support such judgments? Which of these plans most nearly conforms to the preferences of the American public regarding housing, employment, the journey to work, recreation, and community facilities?

The planners' biases are quite clear. They regard the present pattern of scattered development as inherently evil. Often in planning literature this needs no demonstration: like natural law, it is obvious to all right-thinking people. Elsewhere it is claimed that scatteration reduces open space; leads to longer journeys to work; minimizes the efficiency of providing community facilities; reduces choice in housing types and residential location, shopping, and access to community facilities; uses far more land than is necessary for urban growth; usurps land that should be retained in agricultural use; destroys the countryside; is "undemocratic." In extreme cases, such as Spectorsky's *The Exurbanites* and Gordon's *The Split-Level Trap*, the suburban pattern is blamed for excessive

drinking, loose moral behavior, and neurotic or psychotic disorders. The case against scatteration, in short, is a popular one with very weak underpinnings.[3]

A second universal planners' bias is one in favor of the preservation of open space. This view is derived directly from the middle-class suburban background of many planners and the traditional American and British view which associates the country and the rural life with virtue and rectitude, and the city with sin and evil. Somehow, if open space can be preserved and if people will but go to see it, their lives will be elevated and mankind will be the better. In this line of reason, of course, it is rare that we find any calculations of how many people want how much open space or are willing to pay how much to have it. Nor do we often find calculations of what the price of preserving such open space might be to the community, to the social, geographic, and economic patterns of urban growth, or to our productive capacity.

A third traditional bias of the planner favors the maintenance of a strong central business district and the preservation of the density pattern of past cities. Here it is assumed that the city must have a high-density core, containing a high proportion of the area's shopping, banking, commercial, managerial, civic, public, educational, and cultural functions. Because central districts have in the past provided for a large proportion of the cities' tax revenue, it is argued that they must do so in the future. Again, there is much evidence that the central city functions survive as well or better when

[3] For a contrary view, however, see Jack Lessinger, "The Case for Scatteration: Some Reflections on the National Capital Region *Plan for the Year 2000*," *Journal of the American Institute of Planners*, XXVIII (August, 1962), 159–170.

located elsewhere, that new and vigorous cities are developing without such high-density central business districts, and that the present trend in the location of many if not all of these functions is toward other than central locations.

The fourth planners' bias is that the journey to work should be reduced by shortening the distance between places of residence and places of employment. It is assumed that this reduction of work distance for primary wage earners will not be accompanied by any corresponding increase in work distance or reduction in job choice for secondary wage earners. It is further assumed that people desire to economize in travel time, distance, and cost. Again there is some evidence to the contrary.

Finally, planners usually assume that the American people desire a wider range of choice in the types and locations of dwellings. Most planners will express a greater preference for row houses, garden apartments, and elevator apartments than for single-family houses, and most will express a greater preference for central or urban locations as opposed to suburban locations. It is assumed that the American public has similar preferences but is deprived by the operation of the housing market of opportunities to express them in the purchase or rental of homes. Again there is much evidence to the contrary.

Other equally important objectives might guide metropolitan plans, but rarely emerge in primary roles. The provision of full employment would probably be chosen by many of the American people as a first objective of any public policy. Perhaps today so few are directly affected by the spectre of unemployment that this has become an objective of over-whelming importance for only a minority. Maximizing opportunity for individual growth and productivity is a classic liberal goal and certainly continues to deserve consideration. Our society may operate fairly smoothly to maximize such opportunities for the majority, but certain minority and underprivileged groups continue to suffer relative deprivation in these fields. Unfortunately we have no means for measuring the effect of any metropolitan growth patterns upon full employment or individual opportunity.

Could a system of planning analysis and projection indicate which plans would maximize gross regional product? In the case of the Washington, D.C. and Denver plans, which of these would accomplish that goal? This generation of planners has no answer to such a question. Few would know how to approach it. Even more difficult might be the analysis of plans in terms of their effect upon individual consumer income, presumably involving some objective of maximizing aggregate consumer income under the constraint of providing some minimum income for each individual and a relatively free market distribution of income above the subsistence level. Again the difficulties are formidable. Both these objectives would have wide public appeal, and might reduce particularist local pressures as the public, business leaders, and government officials gain confidence in the accuracy of the analysis systems being used. However, both objectives also show the fundamental lack of both data and analytic concepts for linking such broad social or economic goals to the physical plans of metropolitan areas.

The problem of establishing feasible goals for metropolitan planning is not merely one of matching objectives to the level of present analytical competence. It also requires coming to grips with the nature of the systems which comprise metropolitan areas.

First, the agents of metropolitan decision-making are widely varied in size, influence, intelligence, and location. In many respects, each of them is autonomous. They include in the typical metropolitan area from 300 to 900 units of local government, plus super-imposed layers of county, state, and federal agencies. Other major decision agents are thousands of business firms, large and small, often acting autonomously and sometimes irrationally. Furthermore, the individual decisions of hundreds of thousands of people in their choice of a place of employment, a journey to work, or a place to live deeply affect the structure of growth of the metropolitan area. Manifestly no one can directly command or influence more than a fraction of the decisions involved in metropolitan growth. Even the largest and most powerful agents of government are unlikely to have direct influence over more than one or two per cent of investment decision-making. The most important single agent in most metropolitan areas is likely to be the central city municipal government, and after that, the major electric utility.

Second, the values and motivations of these agents have an equally wide range of variation. A small group of a few hundred people directly affected by the location of a major expressway serving millions of other people can halt a major highway location decision for a whole generation. Yet the millions whose desire for an adequate transportation system is but dimly felt, and in conflict with their desire to hold taxes to a minimum, may not be influential in securing a reasonably efficient package of transportation services in any form. The whole structure of government and our political traditions, plus the fact that 75 per cent of the gross national product is spent privately, tend to permit the intensely felt desires of interests of small fractions of the population to dominate the less intensely felt desires of the majority. Any realistic analysis of the operative meaning of welfare under these circumstances must take cognizance of a wide range in the marginal utility of income, and of an equally wide range in the marginal utility of other forms of benefits offered by our society. It must weigh the interests of hundreds of different groups and the effort which they are prepared to expend on behalf of segmental goals, and it must take note of the often conflicting goals of all individuals and most institutions.

Beyond economic considerations, the metropolitan area is a system for conferring status or prestige, a system for producing and receiving communications, a system for the distribution and use of power. Values in any one of these systems often substitute for values in one of the overlying systems. The analytical system required to reproduce the most important of these effects will be complex indeed.

Third, our understanding of the forces which are operative in the growth, development, and change of the metropolitan area is comparatively primitive. The housing market is among the most influential forces at work, but there are still only fragments of a theory of housing market behavior, only fragments of a systematic analysis of the migration of people within a metropolitan area, and there is little knowledge of the reasons for their behavior. Similarly, we have only a partial understanding of the factors affecting industrial and other employment location, and only fragments of theories regarding transportation and movement patterns. Our knowledge of the influence of major public decisions is even more limited. We know comparatively little about the influence of transportation systems on the development of land uses. We know little about the influence of changing land uses on transportation systems. We know little about the actual influence of zoning, sub-division regulations, and building codes upon the pattern or character of urban growth.

Fourth, any attempt to plan for urban growth involves the development and implementation of policies affecting the rates and direction of change in the urban system. It is, therefore, essential to develop measures of these rates of change as they exist under present market conditions and public policies. This is a comparatively new concept among city planners; yet until we know what the existing rates of change are and what the character of these changes is, we can scarcely influence the system in any rational, projectable, or effective way. It is possible now, for instance, to estimate crudely the net rate of investment occurring in newly developing suburban areas. It is obvious that our worst slum areas are the result of net dis-investment over long periods of time. We can infer that between these extremes sub-areas will have varying net rates of investment or dis-investment which will ultimately lead to the improvement or decline of these parts of the city. In some situations, net dis-investment proceeds for some years and then is reversed, as when a former slum area becomes a prestige area for rehabilitation. Yet even so elementary a measure as the net rate of investment is not presently available to city planners. Other rates of change in the urban system have scarcely been conceived.

Fifth, planning requires relatively long-range projections of future conditions. Investments in highways, utilities, housing, and factories typically have a physical life of 30 to 50 years. Their economic life may be considerably shorter. Depending upon the type of investment involved, the accuracy of projections of future population growth, for instance, may seriously affect willingness to invest or the types of investment made. Yet, our ability to forecast future conditions in society is notoriously poor. The record of population forecasts is a dismal one. The record of land use forecasting is far worse and no one correctly foresaw such a major innovation as the automobile or its consequences for urban growth. Since investments continue to be made and must be made, it is obvious that all investors discount the future very heavily and therefore make investments only under the most favorable circumstances or where large losses are tolerable. Presumably, if more reliable forecasts could be made, many new types of decisions would follow. Until some radical change in the quality of forecasts becomes possible, only a system of continuously revising projections and of continuously calculating the consequences of current investments can provide the best possible degree of knowledge for current or future decisions.

Despite these difficulties, there are reasons for expecting real progress toward a systematic and scientifically based approach to metropolitan planning.

The current vast expansion of urban populations, the proliferation of public services to them, recent rapid advances in computer technology, and the economies involved in handling all kinds of records and accounts electronically, all combine to make possible data systems which will yield knowledge never before available. Recently, the City of Los Angeles proposed the establishment of a central data library extracted from the operating records of over a hundred government agencies. While even a superficial analysis suggested that no single system could serve the multitudinous needs of city agencies, it became obvious that the city was perfectly capable of establishing a persons file and a properties file which would produce dramatically useful current data and make possible a real breakthrough in planning.

A persons file could show the demographic composition of all areas at any time, and, through school-transfer and other records, could show the movement of people and families from district to district, together with the economic, social, and educational characteristics of the movers. It would thus be possible to know annually whether the average income of an area was increasing or decreasing, by knowing the characteristics of those moving into or out of the area. Such trends projected over time could give advance information to private realtors, individual property owners, and municipal officials, of the prospective qualitive improvement or decline of residential areas. It could warn school administrators of changes in prospect for the child population, and enable them to anticipate required adjustments in curriculum. It could forecast major changes in consumer buying patterns for retailers.

The properties file in this same system would contain information on activities concerning each parcel of property, including employment, traffic generation, net profits derived from gross receipts, tax payments, and net investment or disinvestment derived from current property assessments. Thus, the properties file could be used to appraise current conditions in an area and forecast future ones from trend data. It could be used to estimate changing transportation requirements, the changing location of employment, and even the changing character of employment or other economic activity in different parts of the community.

Such a data system could be established at reasonable cost, for it would be based largely on accounting and record-keeping machinery now required for departmental operating purposes. With minor adjustments, such a system could extract vital information for planning purposes.

To benefit from area data systems, planners must know for what purposes they will use the data other than for a description of current trends. We presently lack definitions of goals, measures of efficiency, measures of correlation, theories of urban growth, and the other analytical insights needed to use potentially available data.

In the absence of means for linking broad societal goals to metropolitan plans, planners might well fall back on such simple objectives as the provision of a balanced package of municipal services within the tax resources of the metropolitan community or its component parts. This is beginning to be recognized as a serious subject. Some parts of every metropolitan area are tax-deprived and others are tax-rich. Some parts have excessively low levels of municipal service and others have perfectly adequate ones. Thus, in the Philadelphia metropolitan area, certain school districts spend as little as $300 per child per year and others spend as much as $1,000 per child per year. With some comparable efficiency in dollar expenditures for education, it is apparent that some children are being deprived of educational opportunity, opportunity for self-advancement, or even opportunity for future employment, in contrast to others. Thus, planning for the equalization and raising of standards of municipal services may become a vital link to broader social objectives. Here is a limited goal but one which the public could understand and might regard as sufficiently important to affect public policy. With attainable analytical tools, it should be possible to devise plans which would provide a relatively balanced package of public services at a reasonable tax cost to the affected public under present or revised tax systems, grants-in-aid from higher levels of government, and public service patterns. Here the effect of alternative physical patterns of urban growth, the mix of housing, industry, stores, and public facilities, the tax revenue consequence of each alternative mix, and the municipal cost consequences of alternative mixes should be readily measurable. True, local public services do not affect as much as 10 per cent of consumer expenditures, and the variation between alternatives on the service output side might not exceed 30 or 40 per cent of the average. But this is a sensitive area in public policy and one which often motivates people to action.

A system of analysis which would estimate the alternative transportation costs of different patterns of urban growth might exercise a similar influence on public thinking. At the present time, most people spend from 10 to 20 per cent of their income for various forms of transportation. Expenditures for goods shipment are considerably lower in aggregate national income accounts but vary widely with industry and location. If people's time were measured as a cost, aggregate expenditures for transportation would be substantially higher.

It is apparent, however, that most consumers spend about 9/10 of their transportation dollar on equipment—the automobile—and less than 1/10 on the facilities on which they drive the car—roads and highways. Out of this proportional distribution of transportation expenditures they get poor transportation services involving incredible delays, excessive operating, maintenance, and repair costs, and the most tedious, if not psychologically unhealthy, experiences. Presumably, a shift in the distribution of transportation expenditures to increase outlays for facilities through a few cents increase in gas tax for highways, and a corresponding reduction in outlays for new cars, could produce fairly efficient, pleasant, and rapid transportation systems in most cities, with no increase in aggregate expenditures at all. Combining the greater efficiencies possible through reallocation of resources with those which might be realized with different patterns of urban growth, we might point to measurable costs and measurable benefits for alternative systems. The influence of alternative patterns upon aggregate and sub-area transportation expenditures should be readily calculable.

This kind of analysis is under way at the Penn-Jersey Transportation Study in the Philadelphia area and has recently been completed in a fairly well-rounded way for one growth pattern in the Chicago region. Many facets of the analysis remain for further development, but this is a manageable subject.

In combination, these two types of analysis, the costs of municipal services and the costs of transportation, cover nearly a third of consumer expenditures. This order of magnitude is surely sufficient to provide the American people with a basis for choice between alternative patterns of metropolitan growth. It is probably sufficient, if certain patterns appear clearly preferable in these terms, to motivate Americans to create the means for their achievement.

These are two avenues of exploration in which operations research might provide early help for city planning. Beyond this level there are problems of the efficiency of the city as a system of production and distribution of goods and services. It is entirely possible that we can develop measures with which to test these aspects of metropolitan plans, but in the more distant future. Perhaps the emergence of the affluent society is shifting the public concern from such measurable goals to less tangible ones, such as equality of opportunity. Here the need is to develop measures of change in social and economic status, and a clearer understanding of the effects of public actions. At present, we are only on the threshold of the analysis of social policy and its consequences.

URBAN RENEWAL AS A THEORY

Scott Greer

The movement to clear the slums had its origins during the Great Depression of the 1930's. It rested upon accumulated dissatisfaction with some of the social consequences of city life, as well as the desire to get people to work, "builders to building, lenders to lending." Those who pressed for attention to such matters were not, however, slum dwellers themselves; they were self-selected members of middle-class society concerned with social welfare and the public interest. Such people try to represent both the interest of the poor and the society's interest in the consequences of urban slums. Ashworth speaks of English slums in the early nineteenth century:

Their inhabitants were in no position to obtain the constitution of any additional (governing) body, and for a time no one from outside felt much interest in discovering what their problems were or, indeed, that they had any special problems of their own. But the societies of the new congested districts were not discrete entities and more and more people outside them gradually become aware of the pressure of their novel, powerful, and alarming qualities. Even if he were not his brother's keeper, every man of property was affected by the multiplication of thieves; everyone who valued his life felt it desirable not to have a mass of carriers of virulent diseases too close at hand. . . . It was morality (or, more exactly, criminality) and disease that were causing concern. Overcrowding and congestion, poverty, crime, ill-health and heavy mortality were shown to be conditions found together.[1]

Concern with slums as centers of poverty, crime, and ill-health is still with us.

In America the accelerating growth of urban concentrations during the nine-

[1] William Ashworth, *The Genesis of Modern British Town Planning* (London: Routledge and Kegan Paul Ltd., 1954), pp. 47–48.

teenth century had also produced these enormous neighborhoods of the poor. Here, too, investigators and reformers began to define them as major urban problems. Some reformers even defined the city itself as the cause of evil and attempted to recapture the agrarian virtues—going so far as to export slum children to the hinterland.[2] In time, the effort changed toward the settlement house movement, the growth of private charities, and pressure for public aid. These efforts were illuminated by social surveys that defined the poor neighborhoods of the city as "problems"—and type-cast *places* as villains. Poverty, crime, disease, broken families, and the like were linked together in certain geographical areas of the city where housing was deteriorated and rents low; these neighborhoods were given the summary name, "the slums."

Slums were seen as threats to the larger society. As the centers of concentration for criminals and diseased persons, they were "contagious," for their effects were apt to spill over into the city as a whole. Then too, as aggregations of the most unfortunate, speaking foreign languages and living in different worlds, they were suspected as aliens, seditionists, and possibly anarchists. Some observers, like Jane Addams, considered the development of children in such environment as grounds for anxiety; what kind of equity was this—and what kind of new generation was being reared in the "city within a city," as Robert Park called it?

The complex interaction of poverty, the housing market, and the layout of the city were all lumped together in the term,

[2] Cf., Anselm Strauss, *Images of the American City* (New York: The Free Press of Glencoe, 1961), pp. 178–179. See also the discussion of rural values in urban America found in Robert Wood, *Suburbia* (Boston: Houghton-Mifflin Co., 1959).

slums. Poor people lived in certain houses on certain streets, mostly through necessity. And poor folks have poor ways. Yet these observations were combined and reified, and slums were thought of as things in themselves, having malignant powers and spreading like cancer. Buildings infected buildings and the latter, in turn, infected people. Thus the physical environment took on an overweening importance in the minds of reformers: Out of all the important consumer goods, *housing* became a major focus, for housing was considered the key to the elimination of slums.

THE PROGRAM TO ELIMINATE SLUMS: 1937

The New Deal launched many new programs aimed at achieving certain social goals immediately, as well as contributing to the long-run aim of "priming the pump" of the economy. One major goal was the improvement of housing, which resulted in the Housing Act of 1937. For those who could afford to buy or build if they could obtain money, this act provided help with mortgages; for those who could not afford decent housing, it provided public housing. Thus the first slum-clearance effort consisted simply of tearing down the offending slums and replacing them with publicly subsidized housing. The program had the anticipated effect of stimulating the construction industry and it eventually produced nearly three million public-housing units for the poor. In the process, an approximately equal number of dilapidated houses in crowded city neighborhoods was demolished. Tall public-housing apartment buildings took their place.

The program might be called, indifferently, public housing or slum clearance. Few public-housing units were ever built in the middle-class areas of the outer city because citizens protested vigorously at the threat of public housing nearby; they were built on the site of slums. Then, as housing became more plentiful, public housing became increasingly a service for the bottom dogs—broken families, the aged poor, the ill, and, especially, residentially restricted Negroes. Objections to public housing now combined distaste for Negroes with distaste for the poor as neighbors. As a result of citizen pressure on local politicians, public housing was more and more often sited in the center of the Negro districts and, to avoid a net decrease in available housing, the structures grew taller.[3]

This public housing has been called, with some justice, "minimal charity." Those with no choice were housed in apartments high up in tall buildings, in the center of the city. This was the exact opposite of the housing preferred by Americans who had a choice—the single family unit surrounded by its own yard, convenient for the surveillance of children and offering a degree of privacy. Public housing was operated by managers who carried over criteria of the real estate business to what was essentially a welfare program, men whose pride was in high collection rates and low vacancies, low breakage and minimal costs. These are all useful rules for real estate management no doubt; they are not so relevant to the problems of maintaining order, safety, and community among the concentrated mass of the poor who make up public housing's clientele.

Thus, as typical public housing became slab towers filled with poor Negroes in the middle of Negro working-class

neighborhoods, it developed its own critics among the liberals who once fought for it. They spoke of it as "immuring the slums," or "slums with hot running water."[4] Some spoke of it as a way of increasing segregation in the slums. As the social climate of the Depression evaporated in the economic sun of the postwar years, the program steadily lost popularity.

URBAN REDEVELOPMENT: 1949

Disenchantment with the public-housing kind of slum clearance was caused by more than its unpopularity as a housing program. It was becoming clear that, at the then current rate of development, public housing could never rebuild all the neighborhoods that had deteriorated during the decade of the Depression and five years of war. And, in the post-Depression climate of thought, continued large-scale investment in public works did not appear politically unpopular. Thus a bipartisan coalition developed the legislation that eventually became the Taft-Ellender-Wagner Bill, the Housing Act of 1949. A portfolio bill including provisions for public housing and mortgage insurance as well, it provided the basic charter for urban redevelopment.

This bill was a center of controversy for several years before its enactment.[5] It was felt to be popular because of the severe housing shortage resulting from

[4] See, for example, Jan Jacobs, *The Death and Life of Great American Cities* (New York: Random House, 1961); also Catherine Bauer, "The Dreary Deadlock in Public Housing," *Architectural Forum*, CVI (May 1957), 140–142, 219–222.

[3] Martin Meyerson and Edward C. Banfield, *Politics, Planning, and the Public Interest* (Glencoe: The Free Press, 1955), describe in convincing detail the struggle over public-housing sites in Chicago.

[5] See the excellent brief history of urban renewal law in Ashley A. Foard and Hilbert Fefferman, "Federal Urban Renewal Legislation," *Law and Contemporary Politics*, Vol. 25, No. 4 (Autumn 1960), pp. 635–684.

depression and war. On the other hand, "Objections to the comprehensive housing legislation as a whole, and particularly bitter objections to the public housing provisions, were expressed by every national trade organization whose members were primarily engaged in producing, financing, or dealing with residential property."[6] Foard and Fefferman believe that the public housing provision acted as a stalking horse for urban redevelopment: In the intensity of opposition to public housing, the program to clear land and sell it on the market escaped radical censure. As one conservative critic put it, "I am in favor of the slum elimination section. I am opposed to the public housing section."[7] This schism between the support for public housing and that for urban development continues to the present, and is one of the important horns in several dilemmas.

The new program was popular with a wide range of supporters, and those concerned with rebuilding the cities had high hopes for it. The bill was still primarily focused upon housing and the neighborhood, however, and required that any area redeveloped should be predominantly residential—that is, over half the acreage should be devoted to residential uses. As the Taft subcommittee report put it: "The Subcommittee is not convinced that the federal government should embark upon a general program of aid to cities looking to their rebuilding in more attractive and economical patterns."[8]

Senator Taft argued that the over-all structure of the urban areas should be

[6] *Ibid.*, p. 650.
[7] Senator John Bricker, quoted in *ibid.*, p. 648.
[8] Quoted in Foard and Fefferman, "Legislation," p. 663.

taken as given. The program should be aimed at a constant improvement of housing within the existing layout of cities—a concentration upon "spot removal." The planners, with whom he argued in the hearings on the bill, tended to see "spots" as symptoms of the larger system. This dichotomy runs throughout the history of the urban renewal program.

URBAN RENEWAL: 1954

The urban redevelopment program created by the 1949 Housing Act was criticized on several counts. Many were distressed at the problems created for the very poor who were displaced by projects in a time of severe housing shortage. Others pointed out the impossibility of financing over-all redevelopment, when evidence accumulated to show that "blight" was growing faster than redevelopment. The weakness of housing codes and their enforcement seemed to some an obvious contributory factor in the problem; the continued unplanned development of cities bothered others. In response to a wide range of criticisms, the Housing Act of 1949 was amended in 1954 with support from a bipartisan coalition and a Republican administration.

The major innovation in redevelopment was the Workable Program. As described earlier, it is a logical answer to many, if not all, of the Acts' criticisms. It was so written as to increase the contributions of private enterprise, the responsibility of local government, and the participation of private citizens in the neighborhoods to be conserved or rehabilitated. In sum, these changes were expected to produce more results with fewer federal dollars. The amendments allocated funds for more public housing, needed for the displaced, but they also allowed the use of 10 per cent of grants-in-aid for areas not primarily residential or not to be redeveloped as residential. The overwhelming emphasis upon housing was moderated for the first time.

The slum clearance programs of 1937 had evolved into the urban renewal program of 1954. The program was now focused upon much more than the redevelopment of deteriorated neighborhoods; it was assigned the task of conserving the existing stock of housing, rehabilitating that which was beginning to deteriorate, and planning that which was to be built. It was to result in the clarification and enforcement of housing standards as statutory acts. Cities had to be planned in a comprehensive fashion, nonresidential areas redeveloped, rehabilitated, or conserved, and the private real estate market controlled through indirection.

The planners won with a vengeance, and Senator Taft lost. If "slums and blight" are but symptoms of a larger whole, whoever defines that whole and its proper nature is defining the program. The Housing Act was further amended in 1961; again the emphasis was upon nonresidential redevelopment. The percentage allowed was extended to 30 per cent, while the major intellectual innovation was the provision for a comprehensive renewal program, to encompass the entire city in one plan for the future.

The reader has probably noticed how few definitions have been given. This is partly because in the universe of discourse definitions are very rare, and partly because the problem is so basic to an understanding of the way urban renewal is practiced that it deserves systematic discussion.

DEFINITIONS, ARGUMENTS, AND MEASURES: THE BONES OF THEORY

A blueprint for social action can be broken down usefully into three kinds of components. First, there are *definitions* that are used to identify the important elements in the situation to be changed and the useful tools for changing it. Secondly, there are ideas about *cause* used to explain the existence of the problem, and thus the conditions for changing it. These are linked together in arguments that support the use of some given treatment for a given problem. Finally, and very important, there are *measurement* concepts, used to translate the definitions (of problem and of treatment) into precise identifications in a concrete situation. The importance of these measurement concepts lies in the actor's practical dependence upon them. In practice the definition gets simplified to *whatever the measurements measure.*[9]

The most important definitional concept used in the urban renewal program is that of "slums or blighted areas." When one reads the legislation to find the target of the program, the phase turns up repeatedly; it is the key term in the program's *raison d'être.* Yet nowhere in the law is the phrase defined. In the Declaration of National Housing Policy we are told that the purpose of the act is "the elimination of substandard *and other*

[9] For example, if one's measure of intelligence is a child's response to a Stanford-Binet intelligence test, the child's IQ score, for practical purposes, is his intelligence: All that is not measured by the test is irrelevant to decision. No concepts are more important than those we use for identification and measure of the world. For a lengthy discussion of this matter, see Aaron Cicourel, *Method and Measurement in Sociology* (New York: The Free Press of Glencoe, 1964).

inadequate housing," and "the goal of a decent home and a *suitable* living environment for every American family" [my italics].

Such lack of definition is not unusual in the law. It is to be expected whenever a term or phrase is so widely known and has such a standard connotation and denotation that all will agree on its meaning. This, however, is far from true where the words "slum" and "blight," are concerned. Allen A. Twichell, in charge of the American Public Health Association's work in formulating housing standards and measures, has this to say about blight:

It usually refers to an area or district of some size. It refers to no one characteristic or condition, nor even to any one set of conditions or characteristics that are always found in the same combination. Instead, it covers a fairly wide range of conditions and characteristics that from example to example are found in differing combinations, and with or without certain secondary features.[10]

Such a definition is extremely difficult to apply, since it cannot specify necessary and sufficient conditions for proving that blight exists. There is a considerable likelihood that the terms "blight" and "nonblight" will not be mutually exclusive. Thus, one man's blight may be another man's nonblight, depending upon how important he thinks a given condition or characteristic to be. Yet people's homes are condemned and destroyed because they fall in the blight category, and billions of dollars are spent in blight removal. The problem is a crucial one; it is no less than that of defining the official norms of housing in American society. How is the term "decent" to be changed

from a subjective reaction to one that is objective, one that can be consistently applied and, therefore, allow an equitable public policy? A just policy cannot be based upon a rubber measuring stick, for then the law would not apply equally to all.

As we have noted, the term "slum" was applied to areas where certain people and structures were concentrated. As Ashworth notes, these areas were defined as problems of the public because criminality and disease were widespread among their residents. The general meaning of slums has not changed much since 1842: Slums are neighborhoods where the "social pathologies" of alcoholism, disordered family life, prostitution, and the like, are common occurrences. In addition, slums are neighborhoods with given structural characteristics. They are old, the houses are esthetically displeasing to the slum definer, the rents are relatively low, the houses are crowded. Since the two kinds of attributes—the social and the physical—coexist in given areas, the attack of public policy on slums has been implemented in the Housing Act. But in that Act the negative, "slums," is vague, and it is accompanied by an equally vague positive, "decent homes."

Decent homes are whatever structures are acceptable among the relevant social group. Standards vary greatly. Sergei Grimm, the planner, tells of his determination to find out what "substandard" meant to the man on the street. After a certain amount of questioning, he reported, "I found out. Substandard is whatever is worst *in our neighborhood!*[11] Decency is an open-ended definition: As consumption norms move upward and the average aspiration for housing moves with them, a proportion of houses built to earlier

---

[10] "Measuring the Quality of Housing," in *Urban Redevelopment; Problems and Practices,* ed. Coleman Woodbury (Chicago: University of Chicago Press, 1953), p. 11.

[11] In personal communication.

design becomes "indecent." The open-ended definition of good neighborhoods allows an open-ended definition of slums.

The government, to implement its program for slum elimination and prevention, must define decent housing. But "decent" is a value judgment, and it can-not be a definition which is empirically and logically coercive. "Blight" is not just an aspect of things; it is also a judgment of them. Where such a situation holds, agreement is not possible through investigation and test; it is produced by persuasion and compliance. The concept of blight is translated into fact by fiat.

This crucial judgment results then from the application of administratively framed housing standards. Twichell resolves the problem in these terms: "Without trying to make this definition too fine, it would probably be agreed that the two basic characteristics of blighted areas are substandardness and either stagnation or deterioration." But these two notions are really one, for "stagnation or deterioration" is defined by progressive "substandardness."

In the past, once districts have started downhill (i.e., *have begun to fall below minimum standards,* either because of physical or economic change in the district itself or in its vicinity *or because the standards have risen* over a period of time), most of them have continued downward and often at an increasing rate.[12] [Italics mine.]

Whoever is framing the housing code, then, is creating "blighted areas" by definition. If "standards have risen," in Twichell's terms, an area goes "downhill."

There are several "model" housing codes in general use. One is that of the American Public Health Association, created by Mr. Twichell; another is the

Uniform Housing Code, developed in the San Francisco Bay Area and required for the acceptable Workable Program in western cities. The codes spell out minimally acceptable space and occupancy standards, light and ventilation, sanitation, heating, electrical, and structural conditions. The codes spell out a type of housing that is modest by American standards, though wildly utopian for most of the remainder of humanity. They include the all-American bathroom, hot running water, and other amenities of middle-class, urban life. The codes have been very influential and their influence has been increased by the Workable Program requirement, for the Urban Renewal Administration has the power to judge codes for "acceptability."

Nevertheless, the arbitrary nature of the codes is clear from a comparison of those enacted by different cities.[13] Of fifty-six cities listed in one study, fifteen had no requirements for minimal space, and in the other forty-one cities, it ranged from fifty to one hundred square feet per occupant; most cities had requirements for light and ventilation, but they ranged from 6 per cent of the wall area in Norfolk to 12½ per cent in Los Angeles; similarly, only four persons might share a water-closet in Denver, but twenty might do so in Los Angeles, and there was no limit in Baltimore. The same variation occurred with every requirement of the codes. Decent housing was not uniformly defined, even among housing officials of large American cities.

A slum or blighted area is, for purposes of urban renewal, an areally con-

---

[12] Twichell, in Woodbury, *op. cit.,* pp. 11–12.

[13] *Provisions of Housing Codes in Various American Cities* (Washington, D.C.; Housing and Home Finance Agency, Urban Renewal Administration, 1956). The codes are probably becoming more uniform as a result of pressure from the URA.

centrated collection of substandard dwellings. This administrative definition does not say anything at all about the causes of such conditions. Causal theory is important, however, for action aimed at changing them. Looking at the literature on the subject, including the technical bulletins of the URA, one can only conclude that "blight" is thought of as a social disease. Thus:

Blight does not stand still. It has a way of spreading from house to house, from block to block, from neighborhood to neighborhood.

Caught early enough, blight can be arrested and the downward trend reversed. On the other hand, once an area has reached an advanced stage of deterioration, nothing short of the major surgery of clearance and redevelopment will suffice. Start to work now on the areas in the early stages of blight that have strength and vitality enough to enable them to respond to the preventative and corrective therapy of conservation.[14]

However, at a more mundane level, blight is due to either (1) substandardness in original construction, (2) lack of maintenance, or (3) a substandard use— i.e., crowding and the like. The first case reflects either a discrepancy in housing norms between builder and code-writer or a change in standards over time; the second reflects lack of capital investment; the third usually indicates a different use of the building than that originally planned.

As William Grigsby has recently remarked, the naive belief is that most substandardness is produced by lack of maintenance.[15] Lack of maintenance is, then,

assumed to flow from lack of commitment to either the house or the neighborhood. (In the technical guide quoted in footnote[14], administrators are advised to choose areas in which most homes are owned, in districts that people like.) This emphasis upon maintenance as the key to substandardness results in a tripartite classification of problem areas. First, there are the "rock bottom slums," adjudged to be so far gone in substandardness that nobody would want to rehabilitate them; here clearance is required. Secondly, there are neighborhoods which can be "spot redeveloped" and rehabilitated through code enforcement and the private action of owners. Thirdly, there are the neighborhoods that are judged "basically sound," requiring only increased capital input by the owners in the form of renovation and better maintenance. The first areas are called *clearance areas*, the second *rehabilitation areas*, the third, *conservation areas*. They are defined, basically, by the proportion of units which are substandard and the probable individual cost of bringing the units up to code requirements. If the cost is so high as to represent a poor investment (if it is greater than the market value of the house will be after rehabilitation) it is judged fit only for demolition.

Thus the maintenance and improvement of the *existing* housing stock is a basic aim of urban renewal. The reasoning behind this emphasis upon the existing stock is very simple:

Existing dwellings constitute the greatest housing resource at our disposal. It is this supply of older housing that must be preserved if we are to meet the housing requirements of the large segment of the American people who cannot afford, or do not desire, new housing. . . .

Our cities cannot be renewed nor blight eliminated and potential blight arrested by

---

[14] *Selecting Areas for Conservation*, Urban Renewal Service Technical Guide 3 (Washington, D.C.: Urban Renewal Administration, September 1960), p. 1.

[15] William Grigsby, *Housing Markets and Public Policy* (Philadelphia: University of Pennsylvania Press, 1964), p. 229. In fact, some two-thirds is due to plumbing, reflecting in most cases the standards used in original construction.

clearance and redevelopment alone. Only by utilizing conservation and rehabilitation as well as clearance can we be successful. . . .[16]

And, since substandard houses tend to cluster by area, substandard *areas* are the focus of efforts at rehabilitation and conservation. Such areas are defined by their present conditions and by the possibility of their being upgraded at the cost of the owners. How is this to be done?

The Workable Program for the elimination and prevention of slums is based on certain assumptions about how people can be controlled. It will work only if those assumptions hold. Those assumptions may be grouped around the various subgoals of the program: (1) the destruction of existing slums and their replacement with standard structures, (2) the rehousing of ex-slum dwellers in standard housing, (3) the enforcement of housing codes so as to bring existing houses up to code standards, and, (4) the use of the local capital budget to improve public facilities in substandard areas.

Clearance of existing slums and replacement. One must assume that local governmental officials will designate "rock bottom slum" areas for projects, that the local political process will allow this designation (i.e., slum dwellers and owners will comply), and that private real estate interests will bid for the land and build standard dwellings on it.

Re-housing of ex-slum dwellers in standard housing. One must assume that a supply of such housing exists at a price the slum dwellers can and will afford to pay; that they have knowledge of such housing; that they are willing and able to move into it.

[16] *Home Improvement*, Bulletin 2, Urban Renewal Service (Washington, D.C.: Urban Renewal Administration, October 1960).

The enforcing of housing codes. One must assume that the codes do indeed define "non-slum" housing individually and in the spatial aggregate, that local governmental officials can and will apply the same measure to all areas alike, that the owners of structures can be forced (or persuaded) to comply with the code requirements, and that this can be done rapidly enough to bring about a net decrease in number of substandard dwellings.

The use of local capital budget. One must assume that capital improvements in public services will improve the "decency" of neighborhoods, that local officials will allocate larger resources to the substandard areas, that the local political process will support such increased use of tax money, and that this will occur at a pace that is related to the general private improvement of dwelling units.

These assumptions are all questionable. The present substandard use of a space is no guarantee that it has attractions on the private land market: Substandard use would create a presumption to the contrary. Nor does the fact that given populations now live in slums necessarily indicate any overriding desire to live in standard housing and standard neighborhoods. Insofar as self-selection was involved in their original choice, it would presumably still operate. Those who choose other consumer goods over more expensive housing would still do so. The dubious quality of housing as defined by local codes has led to administrative control from URA; nevertheless, the assumption that codes can be enforced against the will of the population requires that we ignore the role of the coerced citizens as voters and taxpayers. Finally, urban renewal is a federal program largely because of the fiscal straits of the municipalities; this argues a very moderate increase in public capital investment for the neighborhoods inhabited by the poorest and politically least effective citizens.

However, the Urban Renewal Administration has very weak tools for testing the degree to which the assumptions indeed hold. The Workable Program is a document summarizing local actions taken in each category prescribed. This document is prepared by the LPA and is rarely based upon adequate information. Many relocatees are "lost"; little is known about the quality of code enforcement; alternative sites for redevelopment are rarely discussed; the over-all use of public capital budget is not critically evaluated in terms of the commitment presumably made by the municipality. In short, a document of good intentions is substituted for other measures of the program. The next chapter shows that there are good administrative reasons for using this particular "measure" to determine compliance with the Program.

THE AUGMENTED PROGRAM: 1961

The Workable Program was never popular with most LPA officials. Its emphasis upon housing and relocation together forced a commitment to public housing. Its emphasis on code enforcement led agencies into very complex and emotion-generating public policy. And, as housing became in many cities a problem chiefly among Negroes, support for housing programs in general dwindled. At the same time, other interests pressed for more concern with the problems of the central business district of the city. The central city mayors were worried about tax bases, for, as downtown property declined, shopping centers grew by leaps and bounds in the suburbs. The mayors

pressed for general programs of city redevelopment and for smaller local contributions to the program. Arguing that the local tax base is inadequate and regressive, the United States Conference of Mayors lobbied for an increase of the federal contribution from 66-2/3 per cent to 80 per cent.[17] They were joined by influential allies; as Foard and Fefferman said in 1960:

Foremost among these are department store owners and mortgage and other lenders concerned about large outstanding investments in downtown retail properties now suffering competition from suburban shopping centers. Redevelopment to provide downtown commercial centers with parking space and attractive surroundings is a business necessity to them and a source of increased tax revenue to the city.[18]

To these interests was joined the steady pressure of those theorists who had always felt that urban renewal should be concerned with the entire urban structure, that slums and blight are merely symptoms of weakness in the general pattern. For the directors of the various LPAs, such a change in orientation meant divorce from the unpopular issue of housing and an opportunity to enlist wide support for a program of community redevelopment. The propaganda of the deed is important to a new and unestablished program: What better propaganda was possible than the creation of new malls and tall towers in the CBD? The "city beautiful" appeals to the general public; a changed locational order, encouraging the "city profitable," appeals to downtown businessmen.

The mayors did not get their increased federal contribution. However, increas-

17 Foard and Fefferman, "Legislation," p. 675. Some mayors wanted the federal government to pay 90 per cent.
18 *Ibid.*, p. 672.

ing laxness in the interpretation of public capital improvements as local contributions means that the local cash contribution has now shrunk to approximately 14 per cent.[19] They did get an increase in the nonresidential allowance, to 30 per cent of total grant funds. (This is approximately half again the percentage of the total urban area devoted to commercial uses.) When one remembers that 49 per cent of "predominantly residential" can be in truth non-residential, it is clear that as much as 64 per cent of the program can be devoted to improving non-residential properties in a city. The planners got a provision for the development of total "community renewal programs," looking toward an integrated drive to rebuild and shape the entire central city.

DEFINITIONAL PROBLEMS: SLUMS VERSUS BLIGHT

We have been discussing slums and blight as though they were identical. As long as the program was limited to predominantly residential redevelopment, this identification was approximately correct. Today, with that "general program of aid to cities" which the Taft subcommittee deplored, "blight" has become the key term. Slums are merely "residential blight." The meaning of blight is not nearly as clear, even, as that of slums. Following Twichell, we can speak of it as substandard quality of structures—but "sub" what standard?

When a given space within a city is used for a given purpose—parking lot, City Hall, department store, factory—how does one determine if it is properly used? Again, the only standard possible is an administratively determined one, producing facts by fiat. In a recent and influ-

ential text on planning, for example, one author has this to say about blight:

Simple forms of blight include such physical characteristics as structural deterioration, missing sanitation facilities, structures in disrepair or lacking in elemental maintenance, presence of trash and rubbish accumulations in yards, adverse environmental influences such as noise, odors, dust, and so on, and missing community facilities such as schools, playgrounds, public water and sewerage systems, and adequate street and drainage facilities. Usually associated with simple forms of physical blight are certain social and economic indicators of blight. Social indicators of blight include presence of abnormally high rates of juvenile delinquency, venereal disease, and similar results from other health and welfare indices; and economic indicators include concentrations of tax delinquent and tax title properties, declining property values, and presence of an abnormally large number of building vacancies. *Complex forms of blight* are said to exist when an area contains a mixture of incompatible land uses (the classic illustration being the glue factory located in the residential area), obsolete or impractical layout of lots, blocks, and streets, unsafe and unhealthful conditions existing or possible when marginal land is in use, particularly land subject to floods, marshiness, or tidal flows.[20]

Most of these indicators are quite irrelevant to any given area. Some are, in fact, inevitable if an area has industrial or commercial activities. Blight, like slums, represents the parts of town that the observer finds distasteful, but in even more different ways.

The measures actually used for non-residential neighborhoods are those listed as economic indicators—tax delinquency, declining property values, and vacancies. They are usually held to occur *because* of the conditions that Chapin

[19] *Ibid.*, p. 683.

[20] F. Stuart Chapin, Jr., *Urban Land Use Planning* (New York: Harper and Brothers, 1957), pp. 232–233.

terms "complex blight." Because of mixed land uses, obsolete street layouts, and drainage problems, the area is economically less productive: The deterioration of trade and therefore of economic value results. And as this occurs, the present occupiers of the land use it in such a way that private redevelopment is discouraged.[21]

Many areas in any city are slowly losing their competitive value on the land market. How, then, is one to determine which areas are the truly blighted ones? Chapin's definition is of no use, for given attributes may or may not occur in given instances. After all, a given space may have value *only* for its present use: Hoover and Vernon have documented the case for the economic necessity and value of deteriorated commercial areas in cities. They see them as economically necessary for small, struggling enterprises, which include new starts—they are venture capital for innovations.[22] There must be cheap quarters for small businesses and they are apt to have higher vacancy rates and more tax delinquencies. There must be residential neighborhoods for the poor—they are bound to be largely made up of obsolete structures, indecent by a newer building code. In short, the "blighting" of urban areas is a logical product of a free market in land.

However, there is a criterion for the blighted area as against the simply cheap area. That is whether or not it could be rebuilt for a "higher" use. And by a higher use is almost always meant a more

profitable use—one that increases tax assessments, increases the number and wealth of consumers in the neighborhood, and increases the profits of those with a stake in the CBD. Rents and taxes go up and vacancies down, as use becomes higher. The definition of blight is, simply, that "this land is too good for these people."

As urban renewal became a program to increase the goodness, truth, and beauty of the urban capital plant, residential and nonresidential alike, blight became an ever-expandable term. Like slums, it is an open-ended value judgment, based upon an open-ended aspiration for the given city. Any area might be judged by someone to deserve a "higher use." One who cares for parks might consider open space a higher use than the Empire State Building. But the economic criterion is crucial because of the program's basic commitment to the private real estate industry. Only that land that can be redeveloped at a profit will be bidden for—and only that which is bidden for can be raised to higher uses. The augmented Housing Act of 1961 put the municipalities and the URA squarely in the local downtown real estate market, as buyers, sellers, and speculators.

RENOVATION OF THE CBD

Thus urban renewal, though embedded in the Housing Act, with a purpose said to be the elimination and prevention of slums, is also a program for the renovation of the central business district. Enormous investments are being made in the purchase and clearance of downtown property; land cleared to date has been about 85 per cent residential, but most of it is then redeveloped as commercial facilities, office buildings, or expensive high-

[21] I have telescoped a long argument into a few propositions, chiefly because it is, intellectually, this simple. There is a large literature on urban real estate dealing with the subject.

[22] Edgar M. Hoover and Raymond Vernon, *Anatomy of a Metropolis* (Cambridge: Harvard University Press, 1959), especially Chap. 2.

rise apartments. Certain assumptions are implicit in such a program.

1. It is assumed that the age and deterioration of structures produces lack of financial profitability and not vice versa. As a corollary, it is assumed that there is a large, untapped demand for CBD location among those who can afford high rentals and construction costs.

2. It is assumed that residential deterioration does not affect commercial development seriously, or that commercial redevelopment of the CBD can decrease deterioration in residential neighborhoods of the central city.

These assumptions are necessary. The first one is required because, if demand for downtown land is constant or shrinking, the development of new structures can only lead to vacancies, lower rental, and eventual tax delinquency in those which remain—in short, blight. The second assumption is required if the program does not give major and effective attention to slum elimination. It is precisely around the CBD that the most deteriorated neighborhoods now stand, and the progressive destruction of low-income housing without a complementary increase in standard low-cost housing can only shift the slums from one location to another. If the nearby existence of large substandard areas, inhabited by poor Negroes, hurts the commercial profitability of the CBD, then *commercial* redevelopment alone is no solution.

In summary, the slum clearance provisions of the Housing Act of 1937 have been slowly transformed into a large-scale program to redevelop the central city. In the process, the vague term "slum" has been subsumed under the vaguer term "blight." In this discussion, for clarity's sake, slum refers to the poor housing in which live the poor members of the society, and blight refers to a land use that is not as profitable as some alternative, in terms of general values, usually financial.

One might simplify and say: "Slum elimination requires that the housing of the poor be improved; blight elimination necessitates the movement of the right activities to the right location." Slum elimination and prevention does not make necessary any great shift in business and industrial plants or any commercial rebirth of the CBD. It does not require a better transportation system and location grid for the city in terms of efficiency, beauty, or civic pride. Contrariwise, the elimination of blight does not require the elimination of the poor housing of the poor; it simply means it must be located in the *right place*. That might very well be exactly where it is now located, given the cost to the society of acquiring the land from its present owners and writing it down to the value bidders assign it.[23]

The aims of the program are now extremely global; they are not necessarily contradictory: If the displaced poor are relocated in improved housing, if neighborhoods are maintained or upgraded, if better housing in better locations is available for all, the CBD may also be replanned and redeveloped without contradiction. However, the aims of slum elimination and blight elimination, as the terms are used here, are most certainly not identical. And, given scarce resources, to choose one is to reject the other in that degree.

There is, then, a problem of priorities. First, one must decide the relative im-

[23] This point is central to the analysis by Otis A. Davis and Andrew B. Whinston in "The Economics of Urban Renewal," *Law and Contemporary Problems*, Vol. 26, No. 1 (Winter 1961), pp. 105 ff.

portance of blight removal as against slum clearance. Secondly, within each kind of program one must decide where the action will occur. Out of all of the neighborhoods of the poor, which will be rehabilitated or redeveloped? Out of all the declining commercial and industrial areas, which will be selected for a project? How do you estimate, before commitment, the general value of a project in terms of removing slums forever, or removing generalized blight forever? The Community Renewal Programs now being developed are an effort to narrow alternatives, but such programs typically require so much action in so many places over so long a period of time that they do not yield priorities. And, in truth, too little is known about the causation of slums and blight for anyone to plan their elimination over a period of decades. The plans are at best informed guesses; at worst, they are efforts in a peculiar art form.

In the absence of an objective standard of priorities, the political process and the real estate market are the sources of a program's logic. The political response is a measure of its success. The LPAs move toward a program of downtown redevelopment and the upgrading of residential districts nearby because this is effective propaganda of the deed. They produce the positive response of relevant publics, including the political officials of the central city and the downtown businessmen. As it succeeds in this sense, it tends to set the precedent for other programs, in this and other cities. In the center of the city many persons can see the program's effects; and they are influential persons. Tall towers and green malls have a disproportionate intellectual appeal because of their esthetic effect. Meanwhile, most of the substandard houses, neighborhoods, and districts may remain exactly what they were before—substandard.

GETTING TO WORK AND BACK

Ruth and Edward Brecher

Every weekday morning between 6:30 and 7, commuters living in Pleasant Hill, Calif., 25 miles east of San Francisco, rise and dress, bolt a hasty breakfast, kiss their wives goodbye, and drive off to their jobs in downtown San Francisco. They battle traffic through the Caldecott Tunnel and over the Bay Bridge. Downtown they find a place to park, then walk to their offices. After 5 P.M. they ransom their cars and battle traffic home again.

If luck is with them, the trip takes only an hour or an hour and a quarter each way. But on days when the freeways jam up, as they often do, it may take an hour and a half or even two hours. The monetary cost, including bridge tolls, parking charges, and car expenses (50 miles at 10¢ a mile), averages about $6.15 per day.

Beginning some morning in 1969, however, if all goes according to schedule, the Pleasant Hill commuters will have available an alternative route. They will be able to rise at 7:30 A.M. instead of 6:30 or 7, eat breakfast, then drive to the new Bay Area Rapid Transit (BART) station out in the country, halfway between Pleasant Hill and Walnut Creek. There a BART parking lot, with space for 1350 cars, will be waiting for them; or their wives may drive them to the station and deposit them a few steps from the platform. Their wait will be short, for during the rush hour a BART train, dispatched and controlled by a computer, will pull out for Oakland and San Francisco every two or three minutes. There will be vacant seats waiting for them on the train—foam-padded seats, four inches wider than the usual transit standard.

Gliding along safely in quiet, air-conditioned comfort at speeds up to 80 miles per hour and averaging 50 miles per hour including the 20-second stops, they will prepare for the day's work or read their morning papers in good light for the 29 minutes it will take them to reach downtown San Francisco. At night they will reverse the route, saving another 30 minutes or more, and will arrive home relaxed and rested before 6 P.M. instead of disgruntled and grumpy at 6:30 or 7.

Their round-trip BART ticket, including parking at the BART station, will cost $1.40 instead of $6.15 by car. BART, moreover, may enable some families to get along with one car instead of two, or with two instead of three.

HOW OUR CITIES GOT SNARLED UP

In most large, traffic-plagued American cities today, a battle is raging between those who urge modern rapid transit like the BART system and those who favor more automobile freeways and expressways. Throughout the past decade or more, the freeway proponents have been victorious, for a number of reasons.

The United States entered the 1950s with a seriously inadequate urban public transportation system of buses, transit lines, and commuter railroads and an equally inadequate system of streets and highways. During the decade, conditions grew even worse. The number of autos registered rose from 40,000,000 to 61,000,000 and of vehicle miles per year from 458,000,000,000 to 719,000,000,000; but road-building did not keep pace. Passengers abandoned public transportation lines for most uses, but continued to jam the transit vehicles for the rush-hour trips to and from work in the central business districts of our large cities. Transit fares rose, and the trend to the automobile and to traffic congestion was intensified; yet peak-hour transit vehicles remained as overcrowded as ever. Our major cities seemed headed toward a monumental snafu.

Basically, there were three ways to deal with the problem: 1) modernizing and expanding our public transit systems; 2) concentrating on the private automobile and building more freeways and parking garages; or 3) creating a balanced transportation system, using each mode of travel for the job it could do best.

Here was a major public issue, with many complex engineering, economic, sociological, esthetic, and political facets. But before it could be adequately debated, the die was cast in favor of the private automobile. Congress in 1956 authorized a vast new nationwide Interstate Highway System to provide nonstop, limited-access, high-speed travel on some 41,000 miles of rural and urban freeways designed with gentle grades, broad curves, and generous interchanges. The system was to be built in 16 years at a cost of $41,000,000,000.

Why did this plan win adoption? Three reasons may be cited. One was the obvious, urgent need for *some* kind of transportation improvement. The second was the popularity of the automobile. Almost everyone was delighted by the prospect that the Interstate System would soon enable us to drive at 60 miles per hour or more almost anywhere—even to work and back.

But it was a third factor that turned the tide in favor of the Interstate System —a nationwide "highway lobby," adequately financed and equipped with the elements of a powerful strategy for obtaining political action.

Pressing for the Interstate Highway System in 1956—and pooh-poohing "old-fashioned" plans to rebuild our rapid transit facilities—were the automobile manufacturers and their 64,000 local car dealers, the gasoline companies, the tire companies, and the influential motor clubs, including the American Automobile Association. Their allies included the politically well-connected highway contractors and the highway department officials in city halls and state capitals; the trucking industry, which wanted faster roads for its trucks; the cement and asphalt companies; and the many industries that profit from cars and roads. Seldom has a single public issue mobilized such a potent lobby.

The financing of the Interstate System, which might have been the insuperable obstacle to its adoption, was a marvel of ingenuity. To circumvent the opposition of economy-minded city councilors and state legislators, the highway lobby plan provided that 90% of the $41,000,000,000 would come from Federal taxes. But Congress, too, is economy-minded. Therefore the plan also provided that the financing should be set up entirely outside the regular Federal budget. Federal taxes on gasoline, tires, and accessories and tonnage taxes on trucks would be increased

and the proceeds accumulated in a "highway trust fund." The Federal 90% would not be classed as an ordinary appropriation, but would be dispensed out of this special fund. Congress bought the entire "package." Moreover, cities wishing even more freeways than the Interstate System projected could get a 50% subsidy for them.

The plan looked foolproof in 1956. But today, with half of the 16 years of the Interstate System construction program behind us, critics are beginning to take another look. Many of them are not happy with what they see.

The rural portions of the system are relatively popular. The new rural freeways are fast and safer than ordinary roads; many people enjoy driving them, though some find them monotonous. Conservationists, of course, complain that the rural freeways sometimes invade this country's rapidly disappearing wilderness regions, wildlife sanctuaries, and other areas that should remain sacrosanct (though future invasions may be slowed down by the Wilderness Act of 1964). And other critics maintain that the billions being spent on rural freeways might better be devoted to more urgently needed public services—as though there were any assurance that if an appreciable portion of the money had not been spent on the highways, it would have been devoted to schools, health services, parks and playgrounds, or other public uses.

Far more numerous and more trenchant criticisms have been aimed at urban parts of the Interstate System.

LIMITED PEAK-HOUR CAPACITY

One major criticism concerns the freeway's limited peak-hour capacity. A single freeway lane can, in theory, carry 1500 cars an hour at high speed, with five or even six occupants in each car. Thus, if loaded to capacity, an eight-lane freeway should carry 1,500,000 persons past a given point in a day. But this is not what happens. Practical limitations reduce *usable* capacity to a comparative trickle.

The chart illustrates the most important of these limitations. It shows urban traffic divided into two main classes. First, there is a broad base of miscellaneous traffic—shopping trips, school trips, social trips, salesmen's calls, visits to the doctor and the dentist, and so on. For the great majority of these trips, the automobile has no rival. An urban freeway system adequate to handle such traffic has much to recommend it.

But superimposed upon this base is a second type of urban traffic—the journey to work and back. These work trips tend to be concentrated into a single hour or two, each morning in one direction and each afternoon in the opposite direction. Cars on such trips carry an average of only 1.3 to 1.5 occupants each, and most of them are headed for a compact, highly congested central business district, or CBD, and to other densely developed neighborhoods. Under such circumstances—and they prevail in most large cities—congestion can be avoided in an all-automobile system only by building lanes that will be needed for only an hour or two each day and will therefore carry only a few thousand cars per day.

Incredible as it may seem, capacity actually goes up when congestion slows traffic down. At 20 or 30 miles per hour, cars follow one another more closely, and one lane can therefore deliver 2000 cars or more per hour instead of only 1500. But a freeway in this congested condition—as every driver knows—is vulnerable to being blocked altogether as additional cars try to worm their way

into the stream of traffic, and as cars run out of gas, tires go flat, engines overheat, or fenders tangle. Then capacity drops to zero, while drivers gaze ruefully at road signs reading: "SPEED LIMIT—60 MPH."

True, congestion can be somewhat reduced by making middle lanes reversible so that an eight-lane freeway, for example, can carry five or six lanes in the dominant direction during peak hours. Even so, the number of lanes adequate to serve the ordinary traffic to and from a central business district may have to be doubled or even trebled to handle without congestion those mountainous rush-hour travel peaks so clearly visible in the figure shown on page 234.

The high cost of these added peak-hour-only lanes per car using them, along with the valuable downtown space they require, makes it unlikely that enough of them will ever be built. If they are built, they will fall afoul of the apparently inexorable rule that new roads soon attract enough new traffic to jam them. The Long Island Expressway in the East and the Santa Ana Freeway in the West, which vie for the title "world's largest parking lot," have become examples of the congestion they were to relieve.

PARKING GEOMETRY

It is a law of nature that once a commuter's car gets to town, it has to be parked. Here again the basic considerations are common to most large cities. It may be feasible to provide parking for CBD shoppers and miscellaneous visitors, even though it may involve costly underground or multistory garages. To provide, in addition, all-day parking for workers enormously aggravates the problem.

To allow not only for the space a car occupies but adequate maneuver-space as well ordinarily requires about 350 square feet per car—almost twice as much space as an office or work area for one worker. That leaves room for only 125 cars per acre of parking lot or garage floorspace. When such space for CBD parking needs are combined with space needs for CBD expressways, the whole function of the CBD, which needs compactness, is impaired.

THE HIGH COST OF FREEWAYS

Urban freeways look like bargains to local governments because of the 50% or 90% Federal subsidy for the capital cost. Rapid transit systems like San Francisco's BART, in contrast, look enormously expensive because the whole cost must be borne at home. However, in the absence of a Federal freeway subsidy or if both systems were similarly subsidized, the comparison would be quite different. Here are the relative lengths and costs of the urban and rural portions of the Interstate System:

	Number of miles	Total cost	Average cost per route mile
Rural	36,000	$22.5 billion	$ 625,000
Urban	5,000	18.5 billion	3,700,000

Costs for routes through congested areas, however, run much higher:

Freeway	Cost per route mile
Downtown San Diego (Calif.)	$ 5,500,000
Pasadena (East-West) Freeway (Calif.)	10,300,000
Prospect Expressway Gowanus-Prospect (N.Y.)	13,600,000
Kennedy (Northwest) and Edens Expressways (Ill.)	15,600,000

These are not extreme examples. A 1961 San Francisco study estimated that future esthetically acceptable freeways for that city would cost more than $23,-000,000 a mile. A 1½-mile downtown stretch of Boston's Central Artery cost more than $40,000,000 a mile. One estimate places the cost of a crosstown expressway in Manhattan at $100,000,000 a mile.

San Francisco's 75-mile BART system will cost $13,000,000 a mile. It will have

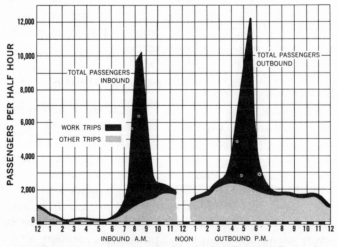

The figures came from a study done at San Francisco-Peninsula Gateway, but the pattern is typical of every metropolitan area

a peak-hour capacity of 30,000 seated passengers in each direction. Even with two lanes reversible, a comparable $13,-000,000-per-mile eight-lane freeway would have a peak-hour capacity of only 7000 or 8000 cars (10,000 or 12,000 occupants) before congestion began to slow travel down. And the rapid transit line, of course, requires a much narrower right-of-way and no costly parking facilities downtown.

Another aspect of cost is what the urban freeway does to local tax rolls. Within the city, the freeway takes valuable land off the tax rolls and thus increases the load on the remaining land. The effect can be substantial. Washington, D.C., for example, had 2100 acres of highly taxed downtown land on its rolls in 1960. Construction of all highways then proposed would have reduced the taxable downtown area by 375 acres or 17%.

The loss in city tax revenues, it is true, may in many cases be balanced, or more than balanced, by increased tax revenues in the suburbs, where undeveloped property near freeway interchanges is conve.·:ed into high-tax shopping centers, industrial sites, and homesites. This may be fine for the undeveloped suburbs and for the property owners and speculators who reap the land-boom bonanza; but it is small solace for the residents of central cities, where the tax load is already heaviest.

For ordinary travel, the freeway is a very good buy. It more than pays its own way as compared with travel on ordinary streets and highways. But its economic advantage is lost when it is expected to handle the task for which it is least fitted —carrying peak-hour traffic into and out of the densely developed portions of our large cities.

THE SOCIAL COSTS OF FREEWAYS

To the extent that freeways have indirectly produced a deterioration of public transportation, they hurt particularly those who are too old or too physically handicapped to drive. These people must depend on the substandard public transportation—and they live under the continuing threat that what little there is may be curtailed or discontinued. Many continue to drive, though they should not, because there is no other way to get around. Licensing officials tend to revoke licenses only in extreme cases if alternative transportation is not available. Fifteen per cent of the entire adult population or more may be in this group of aged or handicapped.

Other, far greater social costs of freeways are familiar to planners through the protests of families and businesses marked for uprooting. Freeway proposals for the District of Columbia, before they were scaled down, called for the displacement of 33,000 men, women, and children—almost 5% of the District's population. And additional thousands in the Maryland and Virginia suburbs were living in the paths of proposed freeway routes.

Before a Federally-subsidized housing project is approved, local sponsors must give assurance that uprooted families will be relocated. No similar assurance is required of highway departments planning Federally-subsidized roadways. Property owners ousted by a new freeway, of course, receive approximately the market value of their property—but it isn't always easy to find a new home at that price. Renters until recently got nothing, and store owners got nothing for the "going concern" value of their stores. To meet the protests, Congress in 1962 amended the Federal-Aid Highway Act to provide payments up to $200 for family moving expenses and up to $3000 to stores. But since a way of life is at stake as well as moving expenses, these payments have not provided satisfaction.

Freeways also sometimes cut suburbs in half or amputate a neighborhood from the main community. In some states, approval of the local government is required before a new route can be built through its boundaries. In such states, even a village can force a new freeway to make a costly detour; a solid phalanx of villages often can and sometimes does block a new route altogether.

The historic landmark and the public park are other frequent victims of the freeway. A study made for the Minneapolis Board of Park Commissioners in 1960 revealed that the Interstate System planned to invade 15 Minneapolis park properties and that other state and county highways were scheduled to invade an additional 13. The park territory coveted by the highway departments totaled 295 acres—or five acres of park land for every square mile within the city limits.

A 1962 amendment to the Federal-Aid Highway Act provides that no Federal grants for urban highways will be approved after July 1, 1965, unless the proposed route has been reviewed as part of a regional planning process that takes social and community values into consideration. This is surely an important and long-overdue step in the right direction; it should have been part of the original 1956 plan.

But the new planning procedures will prove beneficial only for those communities that organize promptly and effectively to make use of them. Otherwise the same old highway planners will continue to make the same old decisions from their new desks in a "regional planning office." A future article in this series will consider ways in which consumer groups can effectively participate in the new planning process.

To many freeway enthusiasts, objections based on personal or local considerations seem selfish and even perverse. Sacrifices, they urge, must be made to the common good. There is some merit in this view. Individual objections can be pressed beyond reason. In one instance a freeway was delayed, and then rerouted at an added cost of $1,000,000, because of complaints from eight families slated for relocation. But even unreasonable opposition is a fact of political life with which transportation planners must now contend, just as they must contend with rivers too broad to bridge and mountains too massive to tunnel.

Opposition can be expected to grow even more effective during the remaining years of the Interstate System construction program, as more communities experience for themselves just how a freeway affects community life—and as all the "easy" routes are completed, leaving unfinished and perhaps unfinishable the routes that dispossess the largest number of people, remove the largest amounts of taxable land from the rolls, despoil the best-loved parks and views, or otherwise rouse the ire of the local citizenry.

If the high dollar cost and the high social cost of urban freeways were necessary to achieve a fast transportation system, the benefits might be balanced against the costs. But commuters are increasingly learning that for the trip to work downtown, the new freeways are not fast.

WOULD STAGGERING WORK HOURS HELP?

All forms of transportation would work much better, of course, if everybody didn't have to get to work and home again at the same time. Hence proposals are sometimes made to stagger work hours. The main objections:

Work hours are already considerably staggered; if everyone worked from 9 to 5, conditions would be even worse than they are. Many commuters already drive in early or leave late or both to avoid the peak-hour rush. Hence half-hour or even full-hour staggering would have relatively little additional effect.

To get a major impact, staggering of work hours would have to be spread over several hours at least. Thus many people would have to report for work objectionably early, and others would be held at work objectionably late. One amenity people want is leisure hours together. Higher pay is demanded for working during hours when others are free.

A central business district exists to enable people to transact business with one another face to face. If some open late while others close early, efficiency is lost.

Despite these general drawbacks, work-staggering in particular circumstances may be worth trying, and experiments should be encouraged.

CU has examined unpublished data, for example, for a 12-mile-long stretch of Chicago's Congress Street (Eisenhower) Expressway, composed partly of eight lanes posted at 55 miles per hour and partly of six lanes posted at 60 or 65 miles per hour. When traffic is flowing freely, a driver can cover the 12 miles with ease in 13 minutes. But during rush hour, the trip over the same 12 miles may take as long as 35 minutes.

This figure, impressive though it is, seriously understates the problem. For it does not include the excess time it takes to get into or out of a parking garage in rush-hour traffic, to weave through the congested local streets to a freeway entrance, to queue up at the entrance, and then to crawl up the ramp and push a way into the moving stream of traffic.

Wasted time can be evaluated in various ways. One approach values the commuter's time at some arbitrarily chosen amount, such as $1.50 per hour. On this basis, 30 minutes wasted each way each day costs each commuter some $325 per year. More complicated calculations have also been made. None of them takes into account what it means to wife, husband, and children to be cheated out of an hour together—and to have a father arrive home fretful, grumpy, exhausted, and late for dinner after battling traffic congestion on the new freeway.

OUR CONGESTED FUTURE

Freeway proponents point out that the urban freeway system is not complete as yet. Thus laymen may be tempted to dismiss current freeway congestion as mere "growing pains"—a temporary affliction that will be cured when the rest of the Interstate System freeways are opened to traffic.

Transportation engineers know better. The ultimate inadequacy of the center-city portions of the Interstate System was revealed in 1961, in a study commissioned by the Automobile Manufacturers Association and published under the title "Future Highways and Urban Growth." This study, made by the traffic consulting firm of Wilbur Smith and Associates, considers the urban traffic situation in

1972, assuming that all Interstate System and other planned urban freeways are completed by that date. Its conclusion: the annual rate of urban freeway construction will thereafter have to be doubled!

The Interstate System plan called for building 5000 miles of urban freeway during the 16 years from 1956 to 1972; the 1961 report calls for building an additional 5600 urban miles during the eight years from 1972 to 1980.

BAN CARS OR BEAT THEM TO TOWN?

After looking at traffic-plagued cities, some critics have proposed that private automobiles be banned altogether from their congested central areas—thus forcing would-be drivers onto public transportation.

This solution is hardly popular; yet it is very close to what is actually happening—with no formal law or regulation to keep cars out—in some large cities today. Fewer than 5% of the people employed in Manhattan south of 60th Street, for example, drive their cars to work—not because many of those who don't aren't eager to drive in, but because a combination of clogged streets, bridges, and tunnels, inadequate parking facilities, and high parking charges bar their entry.

Similarly in Chicago, only about 12% of those entering the central business district in rush hour drive in. In other large cities the barriers to entry are more porous—but access is strictly rationed all the same. Though few officials will openly admit it, congestion is quietly accepted as the cheapest device for discouraging additional drivers from driving to town. Indeed, congestion is politically popular in an off-the-record way because you don't have to float a bond issue to finance it.

It is here that the true significance of San Francisco's BART system, described above, becomes apparent. The Bay Area proposes to solve its journey-to-work problems, not by banning cars or by making it excessively slow, costly, and unpleasant to drive, but by offering a cheaper, faster, more convenient, less irksome way to get to town.

Mechanical breakdowns and strikes will on occasion interrupt service along even the best-run transit system, though such interruptions should be rarer than those caused by rain, snow, and fog on the freeway systems. And even rapid transit built to BART standards, it is true, will not do for all commuting problems. Some commuters will no doubt continue to drive to town daily because they need their cars during the day, or because their destinations are not conveniently reachable by rapid transit. Others will drive on occasion when they are taking passengers along, or are planning to stop en route, or expect to return home with bulky packages. And some may continue to drive simply because they enjoy driving, even though it takes longer and costs more.

But so many people *will* use the new rapid transit systems that the question arises, can enough seats be supplied them or will rush-hour passengers be jammed indecently onto the new trains as they are onto many of our present urban transit vehicles? The answer remains in doubt. San Francisco BART plans leave considerable leeway to increase peak-hour capacity if future traffic exceeds the forecasts. Other systems, however, may not be so generously planned. And even if there is adequate capacity, the management of a transit system may cut rush-hour service below the capacity of the tracks in order to save on equipment or operating expenses. In either case, the bright new trains of tomorrow may be

CAN BUSES DO THE JOB?

Present-day urban bus systems—even "express" buses on freeways—are too slow to be worth serious consideration in planning an acceptable commuting system. A bus can move no faster than the car ahead of it.

Bus proponents, however, have suggested that enormous advantages might be gained through a properly designed bus system using a private or reserved right of way. To cite one example, a bus might circulate through a suburban neighborhood to collect passengers in the morning, then travel nonstop to town along a high-speed freeway lane reserved exclusively for buses, and deliver its passengers at stops along an elevated or underground downtown busway loop. Among the advantages cited are pickup and delivery close to your home and place of work, no transfer from one vehicle to another, and great flexibility in rerouting the vehicles as travel demand changes. The crucial disadvantage of this system is the long wait between buses. Neighborhood pickup for the no-transfer service would necessitate infrequent scheduling if the buses were to draw anything like capacity loads. Bus systems offering frequent service can be designed—but in such systems other advantages, such as pickup and delivery close to your door, must be sacrificed.

Other disadvantages of the bus are inferior comfort (as compared with good rail transit) and the high cost of supplying a driver for every 50 or 60 seated passengers. Adequate downtown bus terminal facilities and space for daytime bus storage are also costly and space-consuming.

Certainly every city planning a new rapid transit system should give full consideration to bus possibilities. Engineers and economists who have made detailed mass transportation studies for large American cities in the past decade, however, have recommended bus instead of rail transit for the trip to work in only one case—St. Louis.

Another proposal involving buses is highly ingenious. It involves placing barriers at freeway entrances and limiting access to 1500 or 1600 vehicles per lane per hour, so that traffic can flow freely at high speeds even during rush hours. When a stalled car blocks a lane, the ramp barriers would promptly reduce the flow of entering cars still further to prevent bottlenecking along the freeway. Buses would be given preferential access at the barriers, and thus could carry you to town at high speeds without requiring a costly reserved or private right of way.

But at least two problems remain to be solved: how to find room for the cars queuing up at the barriers, especially downtown in the afternoon, and how to deal with the private drivers fidgeting at their wheels in the queues as the buses roll by.

even more shockingly overcrowded than some of today's transit vehicles—for tomorrow's commuters may be prepared to tolerate even worse conditions in order to stay off the freeways and get to work at top speeds.

Transit planners should be closely questioned concerning the *excess* capacity of a new system; and the management of existing systems on which there is crowding should be asked what can be done to match seats to demand.

COMBINING TRANSIT WITH FREEWAYS

The ideal urban transportation plan, almost everyone now agrees, would combine a rapid transit system of BART quality or better with a freeway system adequate to carry the rest of the traffic. These two aspects of a sound plan are not incompatible.

Chicago's Congress Street Expressway and rapid transit line is the pioneering example of combined planning. It is, for the most part, an eight-lane expressway with a two-track rapid transit line, and space for a third track, down the median. Rapid transit requires only about one-fifth of the width of the right-of-way; yet it has a theoretical peak-hour capacity of 30,000 seated passengers in each direction per hour (60,000 in the peak direction if the third track is installed). The expressway, occupying four-fifths of the right-of-way, begins to jam up when more than 6000 cars (9000 occupants) travel along it per hour in either direction. The expressway cost about $188,500,000; the rapid transit line cost an additional $36,000,000.

Two other new Chicago expressways also have space down the median for rapid transit, but funds to build the transit lines are lacking. Los Angeles, San Francisco, and Washington, D.C., similarly plan to use freeway medians for a portion of their transit lines. The moral for other cities is clear. If a new freeway is being planned to enter your downtown area, has adequate consideration been given to provide room along it for future transit needs?

PRETTY GOOD ISN'T GOOD ENOUGH

Opponents of rapid transit make a completely valid criticism of the Congress Street transit line arrangement. They point out that even though its two-track transit line *could* carry 30,000 seated passengers per hour, it actually runs many fewer cars than its capacity would allow and thus attracts only 13,500 passengers,

including standees, during the rush hour. Hence the automobile expressway continues to jam up. To appreciate what's wrong with the Congress Street transit line, and with most other public transportation in the United States today, let's compare Chicago's Congress Street line with San Francisco's BART standards.

First and foremost, 50% of the passengers on the Congress Street line must stand during the peak hour. Even for the riders who do find seats, comfort is far below BART standards. The cars are not air-conditioned, for example. And the service is only technically "rapid" transit. Scheduled speeds range from 17 to 26 miles per hour, as compared with BART's 50 miles per hour (both including the time of stops at the stations).

Moreover, the Congress Street line is only nine miles long; much of its potential patronage lies beyond its outer terminus. Where it does reach, there are inconvenient arrangements for handling passengers driven to the train by their wives, inadequate peripheral parking for those who want to drive to the station, and inadequate "feeder" buses to bring passengers to the train. At the other end of the line, Chicago's distribution system for carrying passengers to their destinations fails to serve a number of new mid-city developments where the transportation demand is heaviest.

These shortcomings are typical of most mass transportation lines in the United States today. Indeed, many are much worse. Mass transportation is patronized mostly by people who do not own cars, by those who would prefer to drive to work but can't afford it, and by those who fear they won't be able to find a parking place or to afford those that are available.

Chicago could remedy Congress Street's transit shortcomings at relatively moderate cost—much less than the cost of an additional freeway. It could also build high-quality transit lines along its other freeways at moderate cost.

But opposition from railroad interests and the highway lobby blocked action on transit improvement in the 1961 Illinois legislature. It boils down to this: commuters are not yet organized as effectively as the highway lobby is, nor are they as sure of what fits their best interest. For instance, they are often misled when automobile club executives and other opponents of rapid transit tell them that the BART system and similar proposals will handle at most only 5% or so of the trips people want to make. The figures may be right, but the implication isn't. For the 5% of trips that modern transit can handle best are the all-important trips to and from work.

DO CAR POOLS HELP?

Car-pooling could possibly solve our urban transportation problem—if we all drove to town five or six in each car. But this is neither reliable nor convenient as a form of mass transportation. Four passengers must wait until the fifth is ready each morning and afternoon. Either time is wasted during pickups and deliveries or the advantage of door-to-door service is lost. Readers who have car-pooled will no doubt recall other shortcomings. Nevertheless, each car pool contributes its mite to easing transportation problems, and pooling should be encouraged—by receiving preferential parking privileges, for example—while cities await adequate transportation.

ROLE OF THE COMMUTER RAILROADS

Many suburban commuters face a different sort of transportation crisis.

Their communities' problem does not take the shape of a monumental traffic jam or over-crowded transit, but rather a notice posted at the local railroad station that the line proposes to raise its fares or curtail its passenger service—or discontinue service altogether.

Commuters faced with situations such as these often band together to protest, or hire lawyers to protest for them, at Interstate Commerce Commission hearings and at state public utility commission proceedings. They also petition their local officials and state legislators to "save our commuter railroads" by relieving them of taxes and by paying them tax subsidies.

Philadelphia has pioneered a better solution to the commuter railroad problem. During the 1950s far-sighted Philadelphia public officials, looking at a map of the Penn-Jersey metropolitan area, noted that the rights of way of the dozen or more commuter railroad lines fanning out in all directions from downtown Philadelphia and from Camden could be used to create a magnificent public transportation system—if the lines could be tied together and service standards raised. Hence, when the railroads serving Philadelphia began petitioning for fare increases and for permission to curtail service, the city countered with an alternative proposal.

It offered to *buy* service from the railroads in accordance with a carefully drafted contract. It would seek to supply top-speed, comfortable, air-conditioned "Silverliners"—reputed locally to be the finest electric commuter cars in the United States today. These new cars would be added to existing schedules to shorten the intervals between trains and provide seats for more passengers. The railroads would be required to lower instead of raise their fares. Stations would be improved and additional parking provided around them. The city would foot the bills, with aid from a Federal demonstration grant.

The plan was tried initially on two commuter lines and proved so successful that it has since been extended to several more. Two neighboring counties, through the Southeastern Pennsylvania Compact (SEPACT), have now joined Philadelphia and the Federal government in supplying the needed funds. Railroad commuters are getting better service for less money, and the rest of the city is benefited through fewer cars jamming the downtown streets and freeways. A similar plan has since been launched on some Boston commuter railroad lines.

The Philadelphia plan is important because of three major features that distinguish it from the usual "save our commuter railroads" pleas.

The subsidy is used directly for the benefit of railroad patrons, not to bail out railroad bondholders.

The plan does not just seek to maintain existing service. It assures more and better service at lower fares.

Every dollar spent—and this is the ingenious heart of Philadelphia's plan—brings the city and its suburbs one step closer to a consolidated, area-wide rapid transit system capable of providing service close to BART standards.

In 1964, for example, John Bailey of SEPACT submitted a report showing how railroad rights-of-way could be utilized to provide a high-speed 216-mile rapid transit system with Silverliner comfort, peripheral parking, and convenient central-city distribution at a cost of only $130,000,000. And $27,000,000 worth of this conversion program had already been completed. New cars had been purchased, peripheral parking provided, and other improvements made. As a result, Bailey's "package" could be completed

for an additional cost of only $103,000,-000—less than the cost of building eight or 10 miles of downtown freeway.

The Regional Plan Association has been developing a similar plan for New York City's commuter railroads.

WHAT'S THE ANSWER FOR YOUR CITY?

A surprising number of North American cities are now considering rapid transit proposals leading toward San Francisco-type service—and a few have already started building transit systems.

Toronto residents, for example, voted 10-to-1 for a new subway back in 1946. Trains rolled over the first 4.5 miles of the system in 1954—and success was so immediate and obvious that plans for expansion were promptly drafted. Some 6.5 miles are currently in operation—not very much, but enough to keep from 10,000 to 25,000 cars off Toronto streets each weekday. Construction now under way will provide 21 miles of transit by 1967, and future plans now call for 39 miles by 1980. Along with new transit construction, Toronto is also developing a computer-based traffic control system to handle the cars and trucks remaining on the streets with maximum efficiency.

Montreal is similarly building a new subway system—26.2 miles approved to date—after a mayor was elected on the platform: "Vote for me and get a subway."

Philadelphia voters last November approved by a substantial margin an $87,300,000 bond issue to finance subway extensions. The Philadelphia-Camden rapid transit line is being extended into the South Jersey suburbs at a cost of $50,000,000. And there is the pending proposal already described to convert 216 miles of Philadelphia's commuter railroad lines into a high-speed transit system approaching BART standards.

Atlanta has plans for a 65.4-mile rapid transit network. Voters last November approved a constitutional amendment that is the first step toward that goal.

Boston is planning major improvements with the help of state funds from a 2¢-a-pack increase in the cigarette tax, imposed following a monumental traffic tie-up in December 1963. Its old transit authority serving the city and 13 suburbs has been replaced by a new agency authorized to improve service to the city and 77 suburbs.

Los Angeles has plans for a new 64-mile system not unlike San Francisco's.

Washington, D.C. plans, submitted to Congress in 1963, called for 83 miles of high-quality transit service.

Edmonton, Alberta, with a population of only 300,000, is the smallest North American city with a rapid transit plan: six lines totalling 25 miles. "We hope to start digging in 1968," an Edmonton official reports.

New York, Chicago, Cleveland, and Pittsburgh have plans for extending and improving their existing transit systems—but these plans fall short in varying degrees of San Francisco BART standards.

A few other cities—St. Louis, for example—have transit plans gathering dust in municipal office files, and several cities, such as Baltimore and Seattle, are beginning to get ready to make transit plans.

This optimistic review of North American transit progress is subject to one major qualification: All of the plans require public tax funds to subsidize construction; but to date only Toronto, Montreal, and San Francisco have firmly committed public funds in adequate amounts. Thus a tremendous field is waiting for action—not necessarily to rally

support for BART-type public transit in every large city, but at least to examine the issues carefully and come up with reasoned support of *some* locally feasible solution to the transportation problem.

That Toronto, Montreal, and the San Francisco Bay Area should be the leaders in laying money on the line for high-quality transit is hardly coincidence. "If you would make your city loved," said an ancient Greek proverb, "you must first make her lovable." Toronto, Montreal, and San Francisco have made themselves lovable cities—and it is at least partly in an effort to preserve their inherent quality from the freeway and the parking lot that residents of these cities and their suburbs have been willing to tax themselves for rapid transit.

The presence of three Canadian cities on the list is also worth a comment. American cities facing a choice between downtown freeways and rapid transit are deterred from choosing transit, even when it makes excellent sense, by our national freeway financing program. Since 90% of the cost of new urban freeways included in the Interstate System and 50% of the cost of most urban freeways in excess of the Interstate System come out of the Federal "highway trust fund," even cities that want and need rapid transit have to date been tempted by the Federal carrot to build more freeways instead.

A change is in sight, however. The Urban Mass Transportation Act passed by Congress in 1964 establishes a national policy of aiding public urban transportation. If adequate funds are appropriated to achieve the goals set forth in the 1964 Act, cities may at last be free to plan their transportation in terms of sound engineering and public policy rather than in terms of which plan will draw the lushest Federal subsidy.

_6_

Mental Illness

DEFINING MENTAL ILLNESS

In his 1965 State of the Union address President Lyndon B. Johnson stated: "Mental illness afflicts one out of ten Americans, fills nearly one-half of all the hospital beds in the Nation, and costs $3 billion annually."[1] This would indicate that mental illness is a problem that must be reckoned with in contemporary society. Despite its dimensions and the widespread agreement that it is a social problem, mental illness and its opposite mental health are difficult concepts to define. One recent work lists four reasons why this is so:[2] (1) although some mental illnesses are the result of organic or physical impairments, it is now believed that most are not; (2) the concept mental illness is used to describe a wide range of behaviors and symptoms, from those that are relatively minor to those that are socially repugnant and personally incapacitating; (3) various schools of psychological thought define mental illness and mental health differently, some seeing practically all members of society as somewhat deviant and others reserving that classification only for those who are unable to perform minimum daily functions; (4) what is considered mental illness varies across cultures since behavior that is expected and accepted in one culture might be defined as deviant by the standards of another culture.

Many social scientists have attempted to conceptualize the factors which determine mental health and mental illness. Marie Jahoda, in a particularly lucid statement, suggests three criteria for determining the mental health of an individual:

(a) active adjustment or attempts at mastery of his environment as distinct both from his inability to adjust and from his indiscriminate adjustment through passive acceptance of environmental conditions; (b) unity of his personality, the maintenance of a stable, internal integration which remains intact notwithstanding the flexibility of behavior which derives from active adjustment; and (c) ability to perceive correctly the world and himself.[3]

The difficulty in agreeing upon a definition of mental illness is reflected in the psychiatric profession's lack of consensus on what constitutes this kind of sickness. Because of the many problems mentioned earlier, there can be no clear line of demarcation between the mentally healthy individual and the mentally ill.[4] This state of affairs is aggravated by the lack of good measures and diagnostic tools. The lack of standard measures of normal and abnormal behavior and the inability of psychiatrists to determine mental status in a quantitative fashion has contributed to the present difficulty of adequately defining mental illness. In addition, many of the attempts to derive such a definition have been colored by middle-class value judgments.[5] Mental health is thought of as synonmous with middle-class criteria and, by implication, the reverse of lower-class standards.

In 1958 a Joint Commission on Mental Illness and Health culminated an intensive study with a report on the definition of mental health and mental disorder. The report states in part:

In speaking of a person's mental health, it is advisable to distinguish between attributes and actions. The individual may be classified as more or less healthy in a long-term view of his behavior or, in other words, according to his enduring attributes. Or, his actions may be regarded as more or less healthy—that is, appropriate—from the viewpoint of a single, immediate, short-term situation.

Standards of mentally healthy, or normal, behavior vary with the time, place, culture, and expectations of the social group. In short, different peoples have different norms of appropriate behavior.

Mental health is one of many human values; it should not be regarded as the ultimate good in itself.

No completely acceptable all-inclusive concept exists for physical illness and, likewise, none exists for mental health or mental illness.[6]

From a sociological point of view, mental illness is a condition that affects the individual's ability to perform his social roles. But, it is not just that since many physical illnesses also prevent the sick person's performing his social roles fully. In addition, mental illness results in deviant behavior which is thought to be caused by an "abnormal" mental condition. Deviant behavior may be disturbing to the individual himself (delusions and anxiety feelings) or to others around him (paranoid or manic behavior). The severity of the disorder is simply the extent to which these behaviors interfere with the person's own functioning and/or the functioning of other people. Of course, this will also be related to the extent of deviation from normative standards. Great behavioral deviation is thought to manifest the most severe mental disorders.

Recently, Thomas Szasz, an American psychiatrist, has argued that mental disorders really do not exist and what has been traditionally labeled mental illness is actually the expression of the individual's struggle to handle the problems of everyday life.[7] Although Szasz does not deny the existence of certain behaviors currently labeled as mental disorders, his claim is that these are not illnesses since they deviate from psychosocial, ethical, and legal norms and not from medical standards. Hence, to treat such nonmedical deviations, defined by the individual's social context, by medical action is illogical and serves to obscure what are really problems of human relations. Although this is not a widely held view, it does serve to illustrate the changing conceptions of mental health and illness and the difficulty encountered in attempting to define them.

TYPES OF MENTAL DISORDERS

There is a wide range of mental disorders just as there are many kinds of physical illnesses. The various mental disorders are usually classified according to their seriousness. One loose classification generally used by laymen is psychotic and neurotic disorders. Psychotic disorders are severe and usually involve the patient's being out of contact with reality, disoriented, and confused. In extreme cases the patient may be incontinent, unable to communicate, stuporous, delusional, or hallucinatory. Neuroses, on the other hand, are milder disturbances and are seldom as incapacitating as the psychoses. They involve a number of symptoms which make life adjustment difficult. The vagueness of symptoms such as anxiety, psychosomatic illness, and compulsions has led to widely varying estimates of the extent of neurotic disorders.

A much more rigorous classification of mental disorders has been presented in the American Psychiatric Association's Diagnostic and Statistical Manual. According to this source, mental disorders can be grouped into four major categories: organic mental disorders, mental deficiency, psychotic disorders, and nonpsychotic disorders.[8] This classification goes beyond the psychoses-neuroses distinction and subsumes most of the diagnostic categories recognized by contemporary psychiatry.

1. ORGANIC MENTAL DISORDERS. This category is separated into *acute and chronic brain syndromes* because there are differences between the two in terms of prognosis, treatment, and course of the illness. These disorders are the result of damage to brain tissue. Such damage may be mild or severe, temporary or permanent. When damage does occur, however, impairment of orientation, memory, intellectual functions, judgment, and emotional reaction results.

Damage to brain tissue is often the result of old age—senility and cerebral arteriosclerosis. It is reported by one authority that over the past fifty years the hospitalization of patients suffering from these old-age mental disorders has increased so that they now constitute approximately 25 percent of all first admissions to mental hospitals.[9] In addition, organic mental disorders may also result from syphilis of the brain, chronic alcoholism, and persistent trauma to the brain such as is sustained by professional boxers.

2. MENTAL DEFICIENCY. This category of mental disorder refers to those who have a defect in intelligence (a lack of "brain power") which has existed since birth and which has not resulted from organic brain disease or a known prenatal cause. The intelligence defect can be classified as mild, moderate, or severe depending upon scores on standard intelligence tests and level of functioning. A mild defect entails a functional or vocational impairment (I.Q.s of approximately 65 to 75); a moderate defect refers to functional impairment which requires special training and guidance (I.Q.s of 50 to 65); a severe intelligence defect refers to functional impairment requiring custodial or complete protective care (I.Q.s of less than 50).[10] Although psychological test scores are widely used in estimating the degree of intellectual defect, an equally important criterion is the ability of the person to function in a socially adequate manner.

3. PSYCHOTIC DISORDERS. The functional psychoses are not the result of damage to the brain but, instead, are thought to be psychological in origin. These are the most severe mental disorders and constitute about 80 percent of all first admissions to mental hospitals.[11] Psychotic disorders are characterized by personality disintegration and a sharp break with reality. In addition, the psychotic has great difficulty relating effectively to other people or to his own activity. It appears that his entire personality is changed by the illness. The three major functional psychoses are *affective, schizophrenic,* and *paranoid disorders.*

Affective disorders, sometimes called manic-depressive disorders, are characterized by severe fluctuations of mood with resulting disturbances of thought and behavior. The individual may go from periods of being greatly excited and elated to periods of being depressed and withdrawn. In some cases, hallucinations and delusions may also be symptoms of this disorder. The rates of affective disorders seem to be greater for females than for males and the diagnosis is most frequently made between the ages of 30 to 55.[12]

Schizophrenia, the most common of the functional psychoses, occurs very frequently among young adults although the symptoms may be manifested at any time. The schizophrenic characteristically withdraws from reality and retreats into his own imagined world where he may feel controlled by false beliefs, voices, and other strange forces. Psychiatrists recognize many types of schizophrenic disorders, including *simple, hebephrenic, catatonic, paranoid,* and *chronic undifferentiated* subtypes.[13] Simple schizophrenia begins early in life with the person's withdrawing, daydreaming, and being unable to concentrate. Delusions and hallucinations are rarely evident, but, without treatment, deterioration is likely to occur. The hebephrenic type is characterized by isolation from reality plus unpredictable giggling, silly behavior and mannerisms, delusions and hallucinations. The catatonic type of schizophrenic reaction includes patients who have episodes of excitement and stupor. Behavior ranges from complete withdrawal including speechlessness and immobility to excitement and possible violence. The paranoid schizophrenic may be very suspicious of everyone, feeling that he is being plotted against, or he may suffer from delusions of grandeur, believing that he is God or Napoleon. Lastly, the chronic undifferentiated type is a residual category used when symptoms are not clear and the patient cannot otherwise be classified.

Paranoid disorders, unlike the paranoid type of schizophrenia, are relatively rare diagnoses and are typified by persistent delusions of persecution or grandeur. Paranoids create an elaborate delusional system focused on a few areas or perhaps on a few people, defending it with well reasoned and logical intellectual arguments. There are no hallucinations and outside of the paranoid's delusional system his thoughts and emotions are relatively normal.

4.   Nonpsychotic disorders.   Included in this grouping are *psychosomatic disorders, neurotic disorders,* and *personality disorders.* These disorders are not as incapacitating as the psychotic disorders and are usually treated in the community by private psychiatrists or other outpatient services. They are characerized by a variety of symptoms, some more serious than others, which are not as socially antagonistic as most psychotic symptoms. While psychoses often prevent the individual's performing his social roles, nonpsychotic disorders usually make role performance difficult but not impossible.

Psychosomatic disorders are responses to emotional factors which take the form of physical impairment. Disorders such as stomach ulcers, colitis, hypertension, or hives are believed to be the result of psychological factors. These emotional factors, perhaps stress, guilt, or anxiety, find expression in some people by causing physiological disorders which may be severe enough to threaten life. In such cases it is necessary to treat the patient for his physical ailment as well as its psychological roots.

Neurotic disorders, or neuroses, are characterized chiefly by anxiety which may be consciously felt and expressed or unconsciously controlled by using various psychological defense mechanisms. Neurotics generally retain a firm grip on reality and do not manifest such symptoms as delusions and hallucinations. However, when anxiety and its accompanying feelings of guilt, shame, and hostility impair the individual's ability to carry out his normal activities, a neurosis may be just as incapacitating as other types of mental disorders. The form that the neurosis takes depends upon the way that the patient has learned to handle his anxiety. The form known as *anxiety reaction* connotes diffuse and uncontrolled anxiety; *conversion reaction* represents anxiety converted into a loss of control over bodily organs—tremors, paralysis, or blindness; *obsessive-compulsive reactions* refers to the persistence of unwanted ideas and impulses to perform certain acts over which the person has no control; *phobic reactions* represent the fear of a specific idea, object, or situation.

Lastly, *personality or character disorders* include a variety of behaviors because other diagnostic categories do not seem appropriate and "the persons so described cannot tolerate stress without losing their emotional equilibrium or stability."[14] This classification is generally used to refer to persons who are emotionally immature, feel inadequate, cannot meet their obligations, and seek to escape from life's pressures. In some instances these persons are quite amoral in their conduct and, in the past, were often referred to as psychopaths or sociopaths. Unlike other mental disorders, personality disorders are not manifested by mental or emotional symptoms but by a lifelong pattern of behavior that is socially inappropriate.

EXTENT OF MENTAL ILLNESS

Since there is no precise definition of mental illness it is difficult to determine its exact extent. However, using the criterion of patients known to mental health authorities, it is generally believed that mental illness is increasing. In addition, patients who only a few years ago would have been destined to spend years in a mental hospital are now being released within months. Despite the fact that total admissions to mental hospitals are increasing at the rate of 2 percent per year, more effective treatment and earlier release has meant an actual decrease in the total number of resident patients.[15] From 1955 to 1960, the first five years of extensive use of drug therapy, the number of resident patients decreased by about 4 percent.[16] In April 1965 the number of resident patients in state and local government hospitals was 477,000 or 3.4 percent below the number in these hospitals a year earlier. This decrease occurred while admissions during the first four months of the year rose by 2.6 percent.[17]

These figures account for the great majority of all known mentally ill patients who are hospitalized in public institutions. In 1963 an additional 13,000 patients were hospitalized in private mental hospitals.[18] Further, over 300,000 patients received treatment at out-patient psychiatric clinics throughout the United States.[19]

Obviously, the extent of mental illness is most often determined by the rate of hospitalization in institutions for the care of the mentally ill. However, there are major shortcomings to the use of hospitalization rates as an indicator of the incidence of mental illness. This index is not adequate since all sick persons do not have an equal opportunity to be hospitalized. Mental hospitalization is most apt to occur when the sick person lives close to a mental hospital, when beds are available in the local hospital, when his family has some understanding of mental illness, and when there are no feasible alternatives to hospital care. The opposite of these conditions decreases the rate of hospitalization and makes this index a less adequate measure of mental illness.[20]

Many of the findings of recent research also suggest that mental hospitalization statistics are not valid measures of the amount of actual mental illness in a population. For example, in a recent study rates of mental hospitalization were compared to some noninstitutional indicators of the amount of psychopathology in the United States. It was found that rates of mental hospitalization are not closely related to such noninstitutional indicators as deaths from alcoholism, duodenal ulcer, asthma, mental disorder and suicide, narcotics arrests, and infanticide.[21]

Other researchers have compared the incidence rates of hospitalized psychosis in two communities in the Boston area and found significantly higher rates in the lower-class community (Roxbury) than in the upper level socio-economic community (Wellesley).[22] However, despite the smaller rate of hospitalization, Wellesley residents revealed a higher incidence of psychosis than Roxbury residents. The explanation of these contradictory findings lies in the differing attitudes toward the hospitalization of the mentally ill in the two communities. Residents of the higher socioeconomic community resisted hospitalization in many ways and for many reasons. Wellesley residents felt that the mentally ill person should be kept out of the state hospital at any cost. This was partly due to their attitude that state mental hospitals were "snake pits," and in part to their reluctance to use public hospital facilities since these were regarded as institutions established to serve only the very poor. Residents of Wellesley also resisted hospitalization for their mentally ill family members for the equally important reason that they had more money and better housing which made it easier for them to keep ill members of the family at home.

An important factor that is implied in this study is that middle-class individuals displaying early symptoms of mental illness are more likely to be known by and come to the attention of individuals in the community who are able to provide various kinds of assistance short of hospitalization. Among these are services rendered by physicians, clergymen, social workers, and psychiatrists in private practice. There is some evidence that middle-class individuals are more likely than lower-class indivduals to use these resources as alternatives to hospitalization.

Another study also reveals that many mentally ill persons are not hospitalized and thus not represented in our official statistics. The "Midtown" study in Manhattan selected a representative sample of 1660 persons, 87 percent of whom were asked to respond to 120 specific questions dealing with psychological symptoms of disturbance.[23] The sample was divided into six categories by number, quality, and severity of self-reported symptoms: well (no important or major symptoms), mildly disturbed (some symptoms but fairly good behavior), moderately disturbed (a greater number and more important symptoms but functioning is still reasonably good), marked disturbance (some impairment in performance), severe disturbance (performance quite impaired), and incapacitation. Only persons falling into the latter three groups were considered impaired.

The results indicated that 23.4 percent of the sample was impaired.[24] One may conclude from this that one in four people in the study area was experiencing psychological problems that interfered with their everyday functioning. However, it must be remembered that all mental disorders were included in this percentage and psychotics probably constituted only a small segment of the impaired population. Nevertheless, they were not hospitalized, a fact that lends further support to the widely held notion among mental health researchers that the prevalence of mental illness is much greater than revealed by statistical rates of hospitalization.

SOME EXPLANATIONS OF MENTAL ILLNESS

The causes of mental illness are still not known and, as a result, there are competing theories of causation. These competing theories include the organic, the psychological, and the sociocultural.[25] Organic theories assume that there is something within the individual that causes the mental illness. Psychological and sociocultural theories, on the other hand, attribute causation to factors external to the individual, inadequate socialization or environmental pressures. Although these theories may appear contradictory on the surface, it may well be that certain individuals have organic deficiencies that combine with environmental factors to produce mental disorder. A strong organic predisposition to mental illness may become manifest only when the individual is exposed to inadequate socialization experiences or environmental stress. However, since there are still no definite etiological links between the internal and external factors, we shall briefly examine each of the competing causative theories as separate entities.

Organic theories have stressed the effects of heredity, biochemical functioning, and brain pathology as causes of mental illness.[26] Since certain mental disorders are more common among persons from families with a history of the disorder, it has been concluded by some that the pathology is inherited or that the propensity for the disorder, in the form of an organic weakness or malfunction, is passed on. Others have attributed mental disorder to a toxic substance that may be produced by the body, or to certain metabolic changes in the organism. Finally, some organic theorists have offered brain and nervous system damage as the cause of functional disorders as well as the organic psychoses. None of these organic theories which emphasize internal factors as the cause of mental illness have been proved, but much research is being devoted to their testing.

The psychological theories of causation stem primarily from the early work of Freud.[27] Most psychologists and psychiatrists approach mental illness from the orientation of psychoanalytic theory which sees the individual's personality and character determined by early interpersonal experiences with parents and siblings. Personality, ego, superego, and other psychic constructs are the products of experience in the first few years of life. A person's approach to life is the result of his personality structure which develops early in interpersonal relations. Adherents to this theory usually believe that the mentally ill person is one who has developed inadequate mechanisms of internal control (ego and superego) because of faulty interpersonal experiences. Hence, he is unable to resolve the basic strivings of the id (primitive, instinctual impulses). The anxiety resulting from the conflict between man's biological nature and the restraints placed upon him by society is manifested in maladaptive behavior (neurosis) or, in severe cases, in regressive behavior (psychosis).

Contemporary "Neo-Freudians" have shifted the emphasis away from instinctual and biological motivations to the role played by culture in shaping behavior. Conflict and the resulting anxiety are not solely the products of faulty interactive experiences in early life but may result from experiences throughout life in a culture containing many conflicts.[28] The conflicts of the social environment contribute to the anxiety, tension, and guilt that characterize modern man.

Sociocultural theories of the etiology of mental illness focus on general features of the culture which are thought to contribute to individual pathology. Just why particular environmental conditions contribute to emotional illness for some people and not for others is not known, but it is believed by many social scientists that cultural factors such as social isolation, role inconsistency and ambiguity, the complexity of contemporary society, and the inconsistency of modern culture have a direct bearing upon mental illness. Several specific etiologic theories have been built upon these and other cultural factors.

Faris and Dunham's social isolation theory is one of the best known sociocultural explanations of mental disorders.[29] As a result of their work on the distribution of mental disorders in Chicago, they discovered that the highest rates of schizophrenia were in socially disorganized areas characterized by great impersonality and anonymity. In these areas the population was heterogeneous, highly mobile and overwhelmingly lower-class. Here people were permitted to withdraw from all meaningful interaction and isolate themselves from others. The researchers concluded that schizophrenia may well be a response of certain personality types to the effects of social isolation.

Inappropriate role-playing has also been seen as an explanation of mental disorder. This may take the form of one's being incapable of performing certain roles, being unable to adjust to role contradictions, or being unable to shift from one role to another as situations change.[30] In addition, industrial society does not provide a process of smooth transition from one role to another. There is often little or no preparation for the roles one is expected to play. Obviously, these role incapacities and discontinuities create stress and anxiety for the individual which may develop into a serious mental disorder.

Another hypothesized explanation of mental illness is the nature of modern society. It is a complex, mass society in which many demands for adjustments are placed upon the individual who must operate within extremely complicated and intertwined institutional settings.[31] Social change is rapid and sometimes traumatic. At the same time, the demands placed upon the individual by his wide-ranging institutional involvements and by persistent social change create conflict. When he is not able to resolve the conflict that he feels exists among institutional expectations, he may become unhappy, anxious, or emotionally ill. However, this etiologic theory, like the others mentioned, demands a great deal more research before anyone can speak of it as "the" cause of mental disorder.

WHAT CAN BE DONE?

As with most problems of personal deviance, intervention techniques have focused largely upon controlling mental illness and not upon preventing it. It appears to be the opinion of many that our present knowledge of etiology is not sufficient to result in effective preventive programs. This is especially true for the mental disorders not associated with physical disease or genetic transmission. Effective prevention of such disorders as functional psychoses or neuroses may demand changes in many of our social institutions which are not likely to undergo change easily. In the first reading Eli Bower discusses the concept of primary prevention, defined as enhancing mental health and reducing the prevalence and incidence of emotional illness in the general population, and suggests possibilities for preventive action. He postulates that normal emotional hazards occur in all areas of life activity but that they can be kept from becoming more serious problems if certain services are available to help the individual overcome them. Many mental and emotional disorders would be prevented by intervention in troubled situations before crises occurred.

Secondary prevention, on the other hand, entails the early recognition of actual or potential emotional disorders and the provision of immediate treatment to allay the condition. The second reading describes an effort to prevent mental illness through early detection and early treatment. The Montreal "Well-Being Clinic" provides those wishing to use its services with a routine mental health check-up. Although it offers no treatment services itself, it does serve to assess the state of one's mental health and to make referrals to appropriate helping agencies. But, all too often, primary and secondary preventive programs are not available or fail, but the mental disorders must be controlled.

The most frequent way of controlling mental illness is treatment in a mental hospital. Such hospitals have long been stereotyped as harsh custodial institutions where a patient has little chance of recovery. Although hospitalization may not be as successful as some might desire, today it is substantially different from what it was only a few decades ago. In the third reading an excerpt from a report by The Joint Commission on Mental Illness and Health, the role of new drugs in transforming the mental hospital into a potentially rehabilitative setting is described. Since their first introduction in 1953, the use of tranquilizers has become increasingly popular, making treatment a distinct possibility by reducing the patient's excitement or tension and making it feasible for him to participate in supplemental therapy programs. Tranquilizing the hospital population has permitted the creation of a conflict-free environment with as little stress as possible where the "outside world" can be replicated within the treatment setting. In the "new" mental hospital the patient need not be constrained and has greater opportunity to gain insight into his disability and overcome prior, unfortunate interpersonal experiences by developing new, rewarding ones.

Nevertheless, the efficacy of the large mental hospital continues to be questioned. Within the past few years these questions have been turned into action and several experimental programs have tested the feasibility of treating the mental patient outside of the hospital. Such an experimental program is described in the fourth reading. With the help of the tranquilizing drugs, these researchers were able to keep 77.2 percent of their population of acutely ill psychotics functioning in the community. This amazing result was achieved with relatively minimal therapy provided for the patients. It is possible that an enriched program of this kind, including many other community services, may result in an even more successful effort than this one.

The treatment of the mentally ill has been a neglected area for decades, partly because of a lack of concern and partly because of insufficient knowledge. Recently, however, technical breakthroughs as well as new public interest indicate that this neglect may not long be the case. Unfortunately, no solution to the problem of mental illness is in sight, but as prevention and control efforts increase, the possibility of some day solving this vexing problem becomes greater.

REFERENCES

1. "The State of the Union," Presidential Message to Congress, January 4, 1965, *Indicators*. Washington, D.C.: U.S. Department of Health, Education and Welfare, February 1965, p. 6.
2. Russell R. Dynes, Alfred C. Clarke, Simon Dinitz, and Iwao Ishino, *Social Problems: Dissensus and Deviation in an Industrial Society*. New York: Oxford University Press, 1964, p. 397.
3. Marie Jahoda, "Toward a Social Psychology of Mental Health," in Arnold Rose (ed.), *Mental Health and Mental Disorder*. New York: W. W. Norton & Company, 1955, p. 566.
4. August B. Hollingshead, "Factors Associated with Prevalence of Mental Illness," in Eleanor E. Maccoby, Theodore M. Newcomb, and Eugene L. Hartley (eds.), *Readings in Social Psychology*. New York: Holt, Rinehart and Winston, Inc., 1958, p. 426.
5. Marshall B. Clinard, *Sociology of Deviant Behavior*. New York: Holt, Rinehart and Winston, Inc., 1963, p. 365.
6. Marie Jahoda, *Current Concepts of Positive Mental Health*, Report of the Joint Commission on Mental Illness and Health, No. 1. New York: Basic Books, 1958, pp. X–XI.
7. Thomas S. Szasz, "The Myth of Mental Illness," *The American Psychologist*, 15 (February 1960), pp. 113–118.
8. *Mental Disorders: Diagnostic and Statistical Manual*, The Committee on Nomenclature and Statistics of the American Psychiatric Association. Washington, D.C.: American Psychiatric Association Mental Hospital Service, 1952, pp. 14–50.
9. John A. Clausen, "Mental Disorders," in Robert K. Merton and Robert A. Nisbet (eds.), *Contemporary Social Problems*. New York: Harcourt, Brace & World, Inc., 1966, p. 36
10. These I.Q. ranges were selected by the authors and are generally lower than those cited in the A.P.A. *Diagnostic and Statistical Manual*, p. 24.
11. Earl Raab and Gertrude J. Selznick, *Major Social Problems*. New York: Harper & Row, Publishers, 1964, p. 417.
12. Dynes, and others, p. 400.
13. Dynes, and others, p. 401.
14. Dynes, and others, p. 405.
15. Dynes, and others, p. 406.
16. *Statistical Abstract of the United States: 1963*. Washington, D.C.: U.S. Bureau of the Census, 1963, p. 84.

17. "Patients in State and Local Mental Hospitals," *Indicators*. Washington, D.C.: U.S. Department of Health, Education and Welfare, August, 1965, p. S–8.
18. *Patients in Mental Institutions*, 1963, Part III. Washington, D.C.: U.S. Department of Health, Education and Welfare, 1965, p. III–9.
19. *Outpatient Psychiatric Clinics*, 1963. Washington, D.C.: U.S. Department of Health, Education and Welfare, 1965, p. 14.
20. Clausen, p. 59.
21. Jack P. Gibbs, "Rates of Mental Hospitalization: A Study of Societal Reaction to Deviant Behavior," *American Sociological Review*, 26 (December 1962), pp. 782–792.
22. Bert Kaplan, Robert B. Reed, and Wyman Richardson, "A Comparison of the Incidence of Hospitalized and Non-Hospitalized Cases of Psychosis in Two Communities," *American Sociological Review*, 56 (August 1956), pp. 472–479.
23. Leo Srole, Thomas S. Langner, Stanley T. Michael, Marian K. Opler, and Thomas A. C. Rennie, *Mental Health in the Metropolis: The Manhattan Midtown Study*, Vol. 1, New York: McGraw-Hill Book Company, Inc., 1962.
24. Srole, and others, p. 138.
25. Dynes, and others, p. 417.
26. Dynes, and others, pp. 418–421.
27. Clinard, pp. 125–139.
28. As an example of Neo-Freudian theory, see Karen Horney, *The Neurotic Personality of our Times*. New York: W. W. Norton & Company, 1937; *Neurosis and Human Growth*. New York: W. W. Norton & Company, 1950.
29. Robert E. L. Faris and H. Warren Dunham, *Mental Disorders in Urban Areas*. Chicago: University of Chicago Press, 1939.
30. Clinard, pp. 389–394.
31. John F. Cuber, William F. Kenkel, and Robert A. Harper, *Problems of American Society*. New York: Holt, Rinehart and Winston, Inc., 1964, pp. 266–268.

ADDITIONAL READINGS

Clausen, John A., "Mental Disorders," in Robert K. Merton and Robert A. Nisbet (eds.), *Contemporary Social Problems*. New York: Harcourt, Brace & World, Inc., 1966, pp. 26–83.

Dynes, Russell R., Alfred C. Clarke, Simon Dinitz, and Iwao Ishino, *Social Problems: Dissensus and Deviation in an Industrial Society*. New York: Oxford University Press, 1964, Chaps. 14 and 15.

Goffman, Erving, *Asylums*. New York: Doubleday & Company, Inc., 1961.

Hollingshead, August B., and F. C. Redlich, *Social Class and Mental Illness*. New York: John Wiley & Sons, Inc., 1958.

Jones, Maxwell, *The Therapeutic Community*. New York: Basic Books, 1953.

Pasamanick, Benjamin, Frank R. Scarpitti, and Simon Dinitz, *Schizophrenics in the Community: An Experimental Study in the Prevention of Hospitalization*. New York: Appleton-Century-Crofts, Inc., 1967.

Rose, Arnold (ed.), *Mental Health and Mental Disorder*. New York: W. W. Norton & Company, Inc., 1955.

PRIMARY PREVENTION OF MENTAL AND EMOTIONAL DISORDERS:

A CONCEPTUAL FRAMEWORK AND ACTION POSSIBILITIES[*]

Eli M. Bower

Magic and science have had a curious and interesting alliance in the history of human societies. One specific kind of science-magic which man has developed over the years is that of word power. It is illustrated by fairy or folk tales in which discovering or using an appropriate word enables the hero or heroine to gain power over a natural, supernatural or human enemy. *Ali Baba and the Forty Thieves* and *The Story of Rumpelstiltskin,* for example, utilize such magic words to move mountains and solve a complex personal problem. Folklore and myths[†] also exemplify the solution of a problem by abstention from or disuse of an appropriate word or name. In Grimm's *The Wild Swans,* the sister's power to help her seven brothers is gained by her ability not to utter a single word. Odysseus in his adventure with the Cyclops gains power over the giant Polyphemus by telling him his name is "Noman." When Polyphemus is attacked by Odysseus he cries out, "Noman is killing me by craft and not by main force." His brother Cyclops, somewhat dismayed, answers, "Well, if no man is using force and you are alone, there's no help for a bit of sickness when heaven sends it." Odysseus continues, "With these words away they went and my heart laughed within me to think how a mere nobody had taken them all in with my machinomanations."[18]

In the Twentieth Century our "open sesame" to the solution of problems has been the word "prevention," which has found some of its magical fruition in many of man's relationships to viruses, bacteria and protozoans. The "magic bullet" and the newer "miracle drugs" are still part of the "abracadabra" of man's relationship to microbes. Dubos observes, "The common use of the word 'miracle' in referring to the effect of a new drug reveals that men still find it easier to believe in mysterious forces than to trust to rational processes. . . . Men want miracles as much today as in the past"[9] (page 132). Smallpox, however, *is* prevented by a nick on the arm and polio by several shots. The magic of prevention as a word, idea or myth remains a Twentieth Century Rumpelstiltskin in all branches of man's activities, except one. Little in the way of magic words, incantations or mystical

[*] Presented at the 1961 Annual Meeting; accepted for publication, June 6, 1961.

[†] Not surprisingly, myth is derived from the Greek, *mythos,* meaning *word.*

From *American Journal of Orthopsychiatry,* 33, 5 (October 1963), pp. 832–848. Copyright, the American Orthopsychiatric Association, Inc. Reprinted by permission of the author and publisher.

emanations exist for the prevention of the emotional and behavioral disorders of man. Indeed, one would be hard-pressed to divine the kinds of conjurations and "answers oracular" a contemporary John Wellington Wells might dream up to get the job done.

Thus it appears that the lack of creativity and action in the prevention of mental and behavioral disorders originates in forces too powerful for either magic or science. We do not need a Sherlock Holmes or an Arsène Lupin to perceive that there may be more to this conceptual and research abyss in prevention than a lack of imagination and interest. Indeed, one could make a good case for the existence of explicit and implicit cultural resistances to the prevention of emotional and behavioral disorders. Perhaps a necessary first step, then, in any preventive program is to examine the antagonism realistically, and plan strategies of action that take into account the probabilities of success in light of an understanding of the opposition.[8]

COMMUNITY ANTAGONISMS TOWARD PREVENTION

A common conception of prevention often obfuscates thinking and action, namely, that little can be accomplished short of major social overhaul. Prevention of mental and emotional disorders is seen as the exclusive result of the abolition of injustice, discrimination, economic insecurity, poverty, slums and illness. To seek less is to attempt to fell a giant sequoia with a toy axe. Any effort, therefore, that is not aimed directly at major social change is viewed as an inadequate and inconsequential attack at the problem. A corollary of this notion is that prevention involves wheels within wheels

within wheels. Thus, any possible action is perceived as if it were a combined luncheon check presented by an inexperienced waiter to a group of women at the end of an *a la carte* meal. The alleged magnitude of the complexities and the ungeared wheels within wheels perceived are also major deterrents to biological and social scientists who can, with little effort, find more digestible problems to define and solve. Other scientists who see some value in pursuing this kind of "elusive Pimpernel" search in vain for something akin to Archimedes' lever with which the whole of the problem can be moved. Many believe one should concentrate on immediate needs such as the care, treatment, and rehabilitation of mental patients. Such problems are real and specific. If one means to do anything in this field, "they" say, let's start with this problem. Small beginnings, however, need to be made on many fronts. Farnsworth, for example, notes, "Both the treatment of mental illness and the promotion of mental health are necessary in any well-conceived community program designed to reduce crippling emotional conflict. To throw up our hands and stop promoting mental health programs because we cannot define mental health or can portray results only inexactly is to show both lack of common sense and lack of courage."[11] There is a *need* and there is a *problem*. The need to care and treat the ill is our major concern, yet it is fairly obvious that all the king's horses and all the king's men will have little effect on the problem—how to reduce or curtail the development of the illness in the first place.

A second and related phenomenon that influences preventive efforts in the mental health field is the high, often impregnable, fortress of personal privacy—the right and privilege of each person, and family, in a free society to mind his own business and have others mind theirs. If prevention of any kind includes early effective intervention in the lives of persons in the population at large, then the intervention must take place prior to such time as the person is singled out for special help. Where it can be shown that such intervention is necessary, indeed, mandatory for the common good, as it is in automobile use, school attendance and physical hygiene and sanitation, acceptance may be given. Yet, in polio inoculations and water fluoridation, invasion of personal privacy is still a major issue in families or communities that decide to accept or reject these preventive programs.

"At present," Bellak writes, "the governing of men and the raising of children seem to be among the very few occupations in civilized society for which no training or certified ability are required —and for fairly sound reasons. Imposition of laws on either activity could constitute a serious invasion of personal freedom."[1] Laws providing sanctions for intervention by an agency or person in the private life of an individual are, therefore, clearly and with sound reason limited to situations that endanger the life or health of the person or his neighbors. In essence, one can only stop minding one's own business and become one's brother's keeper when "brother" is in pretty sad shape. Nevertheless, few persons would be prepared to sacrifice the values of a free society on any nebulous, preventive altar.

Yet, some primary institutions are actually mobilized and authorized to help the family in a positive and potentially preventive manner. For example, the well-baby clinic and the public

school are given informal and official sanction to interfere and meddle—the former, in relation to the child's health, the latter, in terms of the child's educational progress or lack of it. However, these institutions must also be alert to the dangers inherent in such sanctions. The school must find its leverage in its assigned task of educating children and carefully define and demonstrate the role of auxiliary services such as health examinations, psychological testing and mental health consultation as necessary in carrying out this assignment. The health and educational progress of children represent to most parents important and highly significant achievements; almost always, there is a strong motivation to do whatever is necessary to work with the school or well-baby clinic in enhancing their child's health or educational success.

Another major social resistance to prevention, pointed out by Ruth Eissler, lies in the realm of the reduction of criminal and antisocial behavior:

". . . modern society, with all its dazzling technological progress has not been able to protect itself from individual or mass aggression against property or life. Must we assume that this helplessness is accidental and has no psychological basis? If we take the standpoint that society needs its criminals in the same way as the mother of my delinquent patient needed his delinquency, then we understand the existence of two general tendencies. The first is the seduction of individuals into criminal acting-out. The second is the interference with or the prevention of anything which promises to prevent delinquency."[10]

One explanation advanced for this phenomenon is related to cultural values in which success lies with virtue and failure with sin. In a free society each person has equal opportunity with his fellows to show his mettle as a conscientious, hard-working and, therefore, successful citizen. If he chooses not to be conscientious and hard-working, he has only himself to blame for the consequences. Such competition in games, school work, business and life can only be perceived as successful for all when it is unsuccessful for some. As Don Alhambra sings it in *The Gondoliers*, "In short, whoever you may be/To this conclusion you'll agree/When everyone is somebodee/Then no one's anybodee."

To a great extent, the ritual of the TV-Western, in which good wins over evil fair and square, celebrates this notion at least once or twice each evening. On the other hand, increasing clinical and research evidence supports the notion that those individuals who find positive satisfactions and relationships in family, neighborhood and school also find these satisfactions and relationships as adults; and that those who find frustration, failure and defeat in these primary institutions also tend to be defeated in adulthood. This unconscious sponsorship and enhancement of defeat and alienation in and among groups of children and adolescents is often spelled out in terms of pseudo-Darwinian theory.[17] Yet the idea of equalitarianism is in our historical bones. How have we come to place equality for all and excellence for all as one-dimensional opposites? Gardner states the question more succinctly: "How can we provide opportunities and rewards for individuals of every degree of ability so that individuals at every level will realize their full potentialities, perform at their best and harbor no resentment toward any other level?"[14]

WHO BELLS THE CAT?

As a specific activity, prevention still has the major problem of interesting and involving members of the professions dealing with mental illness, most of whom are involved in individual relationships with patients. Clinicians trained in treatment, rehabilitation and adjunctive therapies in a one-to-one relationship naturally find this more rewarding than they find plunging into the misty arena of prevention. The physician is responsible for the health of his patient, particularly when such health is threatened. As Fox points out, "Curative medicine has generally had precedence over preventive medicine: people come to the doctor to be healed, and most practicing physicians still think of prevention as subsidiary to their main task—which is, to treat the sick. Though they subscribe, intellectually, to prevention, they really feel more at home when the disease has 'got going'."[12] Often, the mental health worker, be he psychiatric technician, nurse, psychologist, social worker or psychiatrist, is deeply impressed by the mountainous obstacles to effecting positive, healthful changes in mental patients and, consequently, finds it difficult to comprehend how other less intensive types of experiences might have prevented the illness.

Yet, one is often surprised by the range, variety and quality of human experiences and human relationships that can and do produce significant changes in personality. Sanford's experience and research lead him to conclude that marked and profound changes do occur in students during the college years.

"Some students," he writes, "undergo in the normal course of events changes of the same order as those brought about by psychotherapy. Not only may there be expansion and reorganization in the ego, with increased sophistication, broader perspective, increased flexibility of control but, also, there may be changes in the relations among the ego, the id, and the superego. The question is, what makes these changes occur and what can be done deliberately to bring them about. There is a common notion that changes so profound as to involve the relations of id, superego, and ego can be brought about after adolescence only by means as thoroughgoing as psychoanalysis or deep psychotherapy. I'm suggesting that changes of a pretty fundamental kind can be brought about by regular educational procedures or by events occurring in the normal course of events, provided we know enough about what makes changes occur."[30]

In bringing prevention into the ken of the psychiatrist, clinical psychologist or social worker, one may need to recognize and deal with the minimization or depreciation of change processes other than a depth peeling of defenses. Stevenson, in his study of direct instigation of behavioral changes in psychotherapy, finds that some patients often improve markedly when they have mastered a stressful situation or relationship and that by helping such patients manage a day-to-day problem, change is brought about.[31] In the early relationships of the mental health professions and the parents of retarded children, it was often assumed that being a parent of a retarded child necessitated intensive psychological help or mental health counseling. Yet, many such parents were more puzzled and distressed by a lack of information and skill in basic home management of the child, and were often best helped by

simple instruction in how to help retarded children learn to feed and dress themselves.

It is possible, as Sanford suggests, that our overemphasis on individual therapy as a major community resource retards to some degree our interest in or our giving priority to prevention. The fact is, primary prevention is the concern of all of the mental health professions, but the responsibility of no one group. Much preventive gold can be mined from clinicians and therapists by encouraging them to translate their clinical experiences and knowledge into programs with preventive possibilities. Such translations, however, must be within a framework of what is operationally feasible within one of the "key integrative systems" of our society. Gardner Murphy may well be right: "The ultimate keys to the understanding of mental health will come, not through exclusive preoccupation with the pathological, but with the broader understanding of the nature of life and of growth. Perhaps the understanding of resonant health and joyful adaptation to life will help us to understand and formulate the issues regarding the prevention of mental disorder."[24]

PREVENTION OF WHAT?

Lastly, there is the knotty problem of defining the goals of prevention. Do such goals include the development of individuals who can more easily be helped by community resources; a reduction in hospitalized schizophrenics; or making persons more amenable to psychotherapy? If our purpose is the promotion of emotional robustness, what exactly does this mean and how can this goal be translated into specific, positive and, hopefully, measurable objectives of health? Dubos notes, "Solving problems of disease is not the same thing as creating health. . . . This task demands a kind of wisdom and vision which transcends specialized knowledge of remedies and treatments and which apprehends in all their complexities and subtleties the relation between living things and their total environment"[9] (page 22). The lack of specificity as to what constitutes mental illness, plus the changing character of such illnesses, make this baseline difficult to define or use in evaluating programs. Yet, where living is equated with and therefore measured by degrees of illness rather than health, one can easily perceive the world as a giant hospital peopled by patients whose only health lies in discovering how sick they are. Nevertheless, reliable measures or indexes of health or illness of a community are the *sine qua non* of any preventive program.

A FRAMEWORK FOR PRIMARY PREVENTION

No single problem in primary prevention has a solution deserving of greater priority than the development of a platform or position from which one can begin to organize and act. One cannot exert leverage on any field of forces except from some fixed position. Without such a theoretical framework little can be done in developing hypotheses, testing them and further developing or, if need be, abandoning them.

Primary prevention of mental and emotional disorders is any specific biological, social or psychological intervention that promotes or enhances the mental and emotional robustness or reduces the incidence and prevalence of mental or emotional illnesses in the population at large. In this framework, primary preventive programs are aimed at persons not yet separated from the general population and, hopefully, at interventions specific enough to be operationally defined and measured.

Measured how—along what dimensions and by what value system? To be sure, some types of primary prevention can be specified in relation to specific diseases or impairments. In such illnesses as phenylketonuria or pellagra psychosis, an appropriate diet initiated at an appropriate time may prevent some of the serious complications of the illness. Other types of mental illness, however, may come about as the cumulative effect of a myriad of interacting social and biological causes and be relatively uninfluenced by any single intervention. Yet, if one assumes that emotional robustness is built on the interactive elements of a healthy organism with enhancing life experiences, one must consider how one could increase those social forces in a community that help the population at large to cope with normal problems, rather than to defend against them, to deal with stress effectively, and to be less vulnerable to illness, including the mental illnesses.

There is, of course, a basic assumption about human behavior and mental health in these propositions, namely, that those social, psychological and biological forces which tend to enhance the full development of the human characteristics of man are desirable and preventive of mental illness; those factors which tend to limit or block such development have greater illness-producing potential and are, therefore, undesirable. By human characteristics, the full development of which are sought, I mean the ability to love and to work productively (Freud's *Lieben und Arbeiten*). In this framework one might suport those social and biological forces that tend to make man an effectively functioning organism with maximum ability to adapt to his own potential as well as to the potential of his environment. One can, therefore, hypothesize that forces which increase or enhance the degrees of freedom of man's individual and social behavior are mentally healthful, whereas, those which reduce such freedom are unhealthful.

What, specifically, is meant by degrees of behavioral freedom? Behavioral freedom may be regarded as the ability of the organism to develop and maintain a resiliency and flexibility in response to a changing environment and a changing self; operationally, such freedom may be defined as the number of behavioral alternatives available in a personality under normal conditions. Such behaviorial freedom is not unlike that of a sailboat that can take full advantage of changing winds and currents by changing sails and direction, but is bound by the nature of the craft and the strength and direction of the forces driving it.

"We say of a boat skimming the water with light foot, 'How free she runs,' when we mean how perfectly she obeys the great breath out of the heavens that fills her sails. Throw her head up into the wind and see how she will halt and stagger, how every sheet will shiver and her whole frame will be shaken, how instantly she is 'in irons' in the expressive phrase of the sea. She is free only when you have let her fall off again and she has recovered once more her nice adjustment to the forces she must obey and cannot defy."[33]

In thinking of preventive action as increasing or enhancing man's behavioral degrees of freedom, one must refer to Kubie's relentless pursuit of this notion in differentiating normal behavior from neurotic behavior. His contention is that socially positive behavior can be the consequence of either healthy or neurotic processes, but that there is a basic difference in organismic elasticity or homeostasis between the normal and neurotic. This elasticity manifests itself in the individual's freedom and flexibility to learn through experience, to change and to adapt to changing external circumstances.

"Thus, the essence of normality is flexibility, in contrast to the freezing of behavior into patterns of unalterability . . . that characterize every manifestation of the neurotic process whether in impulses, purposes, acts, thoughts, or feelings. No single psychological act can be looked upon as neurotic unless it is the product of processes that predetermine a tendency to its automatic repetition."[21]

In brief, the neurotic is like the magic broom in "The Sorcerer's Apprentice"; he cannot change or curtail actions and becomes overwhelmed by the consequences of repetitive behavior. In its beginnings repetitive behavior represents an economic and ecological solution to a problem or conflict faced by the organism. Because the essence of the solution is only dimly perceived by the individual, the pursuit becomes more and more relentless and recurring. Since such goals are basically symbolic and highly masked to the individual, the chances of crossing the goal line and moving on to new patterns of behavior are slim.

Considerable clinical evidence supports the view that fixed or rigid patterns of behavior are derived from the unconscious components of personality. Despite the possibility that behavior primarily motivated by unconscious forces may be useful and valuable in maintaining the health and personality integration of the individual, such behavior is relatively unresponsive to changing environmental conditions. On the other hand,

Zonal Classification – PEOPLE

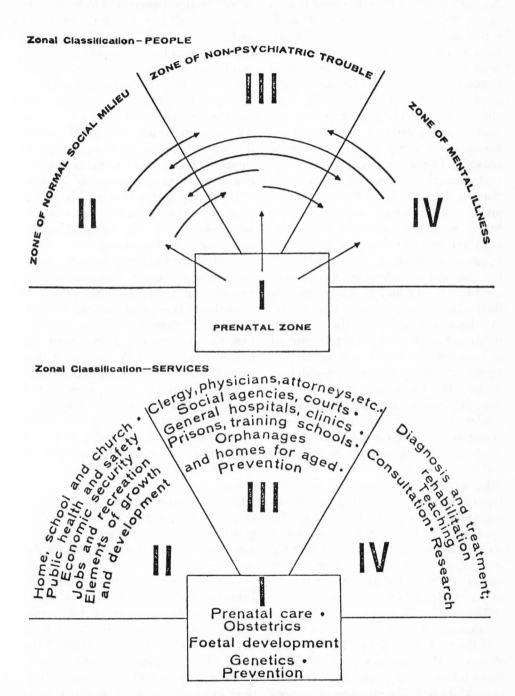

Zonal classifications of people and services. These are indicative, rather than inclusive. (From Daniel Blain, M.D. Copyright, The American Psychiatric Association. Reproduced by permission.)

behavior resulting from forces at a level of relative awareness is most often directed at goals that are reasonably attainable and, subsequently, reduces the need to continue the same pattern of behavior. The degrees of freedom or the number of behavioral alternatives available to an individual are therefore enhanced to the extent to which his behavior is the result of preconscious or conscious forces in the personality.

One might well question the assumption, as does Redlich,[28] that acts determined by conscious or preconscious forces move the individual in a more healthful direction than acts determined by unconscious forces. For example, are not unconscious defense mechanisms health-producing and health-oriented in their adaptive and ego-protective goals? To the extent to which the organism needs ego defenses to maintain himself and mediate noxious forces in his environment, such defenses are health producing. Yet, the increased use of such unconscious defenses will, in the long run, render the organism less and less able to choose alternative modes of behaving and weave into the personality an inflexible and repetitive behavior pattern.[22] It is also true, however, that repetitive, inflexible types of behavior can produce benefits in some relationships, particularly in specific vocations or jobs. Neurotic processes in individuals can and do result in *culturally defined* sucessful behavior, just as one can be a blatant failure without benefit of personality defect or neurosis.

The concept of degrees of behavioral freedom as differentiating between health and illness is utilized by Murphy[25] and Bruner[6] in their discussions of the differences between coping and defending. *In coping with problems,* one enhances and expands the resiliency and resources of the organism; *in defending against problems,* developmental blocks and distortions develop, reducing the resiliency and resources of the organism and depriving it of the freedom to act in new ways. Coping can be conceived of as integrative to personality, defending as disintegrative. Bruner points out that there is always a mixture of coping and defending in dealing with problems, but it is highly important that one distinguish sharply between the two processes, which can best be made in terms of learning effectiveness. "Let me suggest," he writes, "that effective cognitive learning in school—in contrast to the gratification-demanding, action-related, and affect-infused earlier learning—depends upon a denaturing process, if I may use such a fanciful expression. This involves at least three things. It requires, first, the development of a system of cognitive organization that detaches concepts from the modes of action that they evoke. A hole exists without the act of digging. Secondly, it requires the development of a capacity to detach concepts from these affective contexts. A father exists without reference to the thinker's feeling of ambivalence. It demands, moreover, a capacity to delay gratification so that, figuratively, each act of acquiring knowledge is not self-sufficiently brought to an end either by success or failure, and whatever happens can be taken as informative and not as simply frustrating or gratifying"[6] (page 8).

In a defensive, neurotic pattern of behavior, inflexibility or illness would reduce the effectiveness of the organism's functioning, especially as a constructive social being. Thus, one index of the health of a community or a society could be the ways people choose to spend their time, especially their uncommitted time. Meier[23] sees the possibility of compiling an index representing the variety of life in a society—specifically, ways in which people *choose* to spend their time. He proposes that an increase in variety almost always reflects an enhancement in social integration and that "human hours have allocation properties which are not dissimilar from those applied to land. Time like land can only be consumed or wasted. There are only trivial exceptions to this rule. Yet, intuitively, we have the general impression that time can be conserved. Like money income, it can be invested. Schooling and the acquisition of skills are examples of such investments of human hours. The return on the investment is not more time but an increase in the range of choice in gainful employment and in social activities. Thus, we arrive at a significant index for social progress—variety in the pattern of life"[23] (page 29). One could, therefore, conceive of *degrees of behavioral freedom* in terms of operational social indexes that would reflect changes in variety and patterns of life and could be used as a method of evaluating preventive programs. For example, one might examine the allocation of time of persons with personality disturbances or a mentally ill group in a hospital as compared to various other persons and communities.

A FRAMEWORK FOR PREVENTION

The zonal classifications of people and services in the figure above presents a framework and a functioning methodology for prevention. Primary prevention can be considered medical, social or psychological action within Zones I and II, which reduces the need for the services and institutions of Zones III or IV. The goals of such action, with respect to the institutions and services of Zone I and Zone II, are threefold:

1. To increase the biological robustness of human beings by strengthening those institutions and agencies directly involved in prenatal, pregnancy and early infant care.

2. To increase the flexibility of the agencies serving persons of Zones I and II, so that such agencies may encompass and affect a greater variety and number of persons in the general population. For example, the extension of school services for retarded or emotionally disturbed children may make it possible for a child usually needing Zone III or IV services to remain in Zone II. The utilization of prenatal medical or nursing advisory services for lower-class pregnant mothers may be significantly influenced by placing such services close to neighborhood shopping or laundry centers. Or the presence of a counseling center for workers may make the difference for a number of individuals in maintaining employment and family economic support.

3. To assist primary institutions in planning individual and social techniques by which stress immunity or manageability can become a natural outcome of their relationship to children and their families.

It is evident that, in this scheme of primary prevention, the preventive forces will be those affecting the operation, accessibility, adaptability and modifiability of the institutions and agencies found in Zones I and II. Particularly, one needs to determine: (a) which specific social and community forces tend to push Zone II persons into requiring Zone III or IV services; (b) how present medical, genetic and biological information can be translated into social action so as to reduce the number of Zone I infants entering Zones III or IV; and (c) how Zones I and II agencies and institutions can be reinforced, modified or developed to lessen the need for Zones III and IV services.

The institutions and agencies in Zones I and II can be denoted as the front-line defenses of a community. If such institutions and agencies cannot adequately serve individuals in their field, Zones III or IV services are required. Some of the forces moving people into Zones III or IV are the number and character of the emotionally hazardous situations and crises the individual has been required to mediate and manage, and how mediation and management were accomplished. The key, therefore, to movement from one zone to another lies in the quality of the mediation (coping or defending) of the emotionally hazardous situation or crisis. Klein and Lindemann[20] define an emotionally hazardous situation as any sudden alteration in the field of social forces affecting an individual so that the individual's perception and expectation of self and others undergo change. In each instance an emotionally hazardous situation or crisis is a normal life occurrence that is temporarily upsetting, not always in an unpleasant sense, but one that necessitates rapid reorganization and mobilization of an individual's personality resources. Such life situations as birth of a sibling, death of a loved one, school entrance, school failure, marriage, job promotion, divorce or inheritance of a large sum of money from a dead uncle's estate are examples of emotionally hazardous situations. The hazard in these situations is that the individual may find himself unable to manage the increased stress in a healthful way. Yet, such hazards and hurdles are part of the normal process of living and are, in large part, the cutting edges that sharpen and crystallize personality development and integration.

Whether for good or bad, emotionally hazardous crises have these aspects in common: (a) They cause a rise in inner tension and uneasiness; (b) they cause some disorganization in normal functioning; and (c) they necessitate some internal change in self to manage the situation. In baseball parlance, an individual in an emotionally hazardous situation is said to "stand loose at the plate," that is, the individual is lightly balanced to be able to move quickly in any direction. During this period of relative instability, minimal forces have their greatest effects, much like the effect of a one-gram weight at one end of a delicately balanced teeter-totter. Such a gram of weight would have little effect if the forces governing the organism were relatively stable.

The implications of the emotionally vulnerable situation or crisis as a fulcrum for preventive action is clear. To the extent to which such situations can be identified and the "crisis" institution or agency prepared and strengthened to make the most of this opportunity, to that extent can it place grams of force on the side of health and personality growth. In primary prevention one is focused on the emotionally hazardous situation that occurs in the context of the operation of each of the services or agencies in Zones I or II. Such institutions and agencies are often aware of some crises and do a great deal to help individuals deal effectively with them. Sometimes, however, the agency or service may fail to recognize relevant crises, or fail to take advantage of the health-producing potential of the situation. For example, the school may well be aware of the effect of the birth of a child on his siblings but, as an institution, it is seldom in a position to obtain and use this information systematically. Such an important and natural event in the lives of children may be sufficiently upsetting to the sibling to warrant some attention by the school. To capitalize on this emotionally hazardous situation, teachers may need to plan opportunities for the sibling to be recognized, to be helpful, to be successful—in short, to help the child, within the structure and role of the institution, to manage and mediate the crisis. In some cases, the child may need no more than an extra pat on the back from the teacher. In others, a planned conference with parents may be of some help. What is critical is the recognition by the institution of the emotionally vulnerable position of the child and a readiness to act positively upon it.

Table 1 lists some services and institutions of Zones I and II, along with some emotionally hazardous and enhancing situations or crises that occur in relation to each institution, with some possibilities for preventive action in each case. Neither the services, hazards, nor action possibilities listed are intended to be comprehensive or exhaustive. However, this conceptualization may help provide a fulcrum for the development of pilot and experimental studies and other preventive programs that can be delineated and evaluated. For example, the first emotional hazard under "family" is that of loss of father through death, divorce or desertion. With few exceptions, the burden for breadwinning is thrust upon the mother who, in turn, finds it necessary to depend upon child-caring services for her children. In part, such services are provided by relatives, friends, nursery schools, foster homes and child-care centers. In California, child-care centers were initiated during World War II to increase the labor force, and have since continued in operation to serve one-parent families of modest incomes and some families of teachers and nurses. Such a child-care facility usually serves preschool children all day and cares for school children part of the day.

There is sufficient evidence to support the hypothesis that one-parent families are more vulnerable to stress and emotional hazards than are intact families. The child-care facility, properly staffed and oriented, would then be a potentially preventive force in developing and maintaining some type of assistance and support for the mothers and children utilizing this service. Such assistance could be provided by a psychiatric social worker or another professional person hired to work with the child-care staff or families. In theory, the child-care center as a primary institution would be reinforced

TABLE 1

Zone II service	Normal emotional hazard	Possibilities for preventive action
1. Family	Loss of father through death, divorce or desertion	Reinforcement of child-care services for working mothers
	Loss of mother	Reinforcement of foster-home services
	Adolescence	Increase in staff and professionalization of high-school counselors, deans, and vice-principals
	Birth of sibling	Pediatric or well-baby clinic counseling
	Death	Management of grief—religious or community agency worker

TABLE 1 (contd.)

2. Public health	Phenylketonuria	Detection and diet
	Childhood illnesses	Vaccination, immunization
	Stress caused by children—economic, housing, etc.	Reinforcement of well-baby clinic through mental health consultation to staff
	Pregnancy	Adequate prenatal care for mothers of lower socioeconomic status
3. School	Birth of sibling	Recognition of event by school and appropriate intervention
	School entrance of child	Screening vulnerable children
	Intellectual retardation	Special classes and assistance
	Teacher concern and anxiety about a child's behavior	Consultation by mental health specialists
	School failure	Early identification and prevention through appropriate school program
4. Religion	Marriage	Counseling by clergy
5. Job or		Opportunity to define role through services of a mental health counselor
Profession	Promotion or demotion	
6. Recreation	Appropriate and rewarding use of leisure time	Active community and city recreational programs
7. Housing	Lack of space—need for privacy	Working with architects and housing developers

as a preventive agency by enlisting trained personnel to work with parents or child-care staff on the normal problems of people who are bringing up children but who are obliged to work at the same time.

Or, let us take the emotional hazard of pregnancy and birth. One of the points made by Wortis,[34] Pasamanick,[19, 27] Freedman[13] and others is that adequate prenatal and natal care is a significant and far-reaching measure in the prevention of neuropsychiatric disorders in children. In most cases, such care is available. Yet, significant numbers of mothers in lower socioeconomic neighborhoods are not normally motivated to seek medi-

cal care during pregnancy. Ordinarily they will use medical assistance only as a last resort. Many such mothers would take advantage of preventive medical services if such services were present somewhere along the paths they normally travel, or if they could be motivated to detour a few blocks for them. For example, space in empty stores near laundromats or markets could be rented for health department personnel and manned by nurses who could spend time with a mother while she was shopping or waiting for her load of wash. Such a program could be evaluated by comparing rates of premature births, birth injuries or other birth difficulties before and after the service, or with rates in neighborhoods where no such service exists.

FULCRA FOR PREVENTION

It is increasingly evident that there are three basic interrelated ingredients in primary prevention: (1) a healthful birth experience, (2) a healthful family experience, and (3) a successful school experience. Healthful birth experiences are largely the result of early medical care and advice that help prospective mothers obtain and use preventive medical care. Although the evidence is far from complete, Bowlby,[4] Brody[5] and Ribble,[29] to name only three, have emphasized the primacy of family relationships and their effect on the mental health of children. Bowlby summarized numerous studies from various countries that illustrated the emotional impact on children of early separation from their parents. Ribble and Brody studied the pivotal relationship of mothering and personality development, and Caplan[7] pointed out how a neighborhood health center can be a preventive force in enhancing and strengthening family resources for the child. Goodrich,[16] at the Bio-Social Growth Center of the National Institute of Mental Health, studied the emotional hazard of early separation of the child from the mother in a nursery school setting. He found this crisis a potentially manageable staging area for research in primary prevention and suggested some areas of developmental influences that affect how a child or family manages a crisis. Early separation anxieties in a child often mean the possibility of greater problems later on with school entrance or bereavement.

The school has become increasingly primary to a child's personality growth. Consequently it can be the prime mover for alerting parents whose children need additional help or support within the school or, in some cases, additional services outside the school. In essence, the role of the school as a preventive force is realized to the extent to which it is able to make the educational experience a successful learning experience for all children. Two studies from widely disparate sources illustrate the intertwined threads of successful school experience and primary prevention. In a 30-year follow-up study of children who had been referred to a municipal clinic because of problem behavior, the investigators included students from the files of the public schools who matched the patients in age, sex, IQ, race and residence. In addition, this group was selected on the basis of having no school record of behavior or discipline problems. Although the investigators were not studying the health of the control group, they were struck with the fact "that the simple criteria used to choose the control subjects—no excessive absences, no full grades repeated, no disciplinary action recorded and an IQ of 80 or better—have yielded a strikingly healthy group."[26] This was particularly striking since the control group was drawn largely from disadvantaged classes and a history of broken homes was found in one-third of the cases.

The other link of evidence relating school success and primary prevention is found in Ginzberg and his associates' monumental study of the ineffective soldier of World War II. They found that, while poverty, racial discrimination and lack of industrialization could help explain higher rates of emotional instability for individuals who came from certain sections of the country, each of these factors was also related to the differentially low educational achievement of the region. The study demonstrated that, although a higher level of educational attainment was no safeguard against emotional disorders, the lower the educational level, the higher the incidence of emotional disorders. As to cause, Ginzberg noted, "A disturbed childhood is likely to be reflected in learning difficulties; children who do poorly in school are likely to develop emotional problems."[15]

If the school is to become an effective preventive force, it must develop ways to identify early the children who are or are becoming learning problems, so that school and community resources can help such children most effectively and economically. The potential learning difficulty may be related to intellectual, emotional or family-centered problems; even so, the problem may first manifest itself in the school, which can, if it recognizes the problem, pave the way for early help through parent conferences, counseling or psychological or remedial service.[2, 3]

In job situations, the hazards seem to be just as numerous for going up the ladder as down. A person moving up in a large industrial or governmental agency may find it difficult to accept his new role or recast his loyalties with a particular group. He may have greater responsibility for men or production than he is able to manage. A staff-related mental health counselor in industry or work organization may provide some source of help for emotionally hazardous situations of this type.

Wilner and Walkley[32] and others have mapped out preliminary steps for studying the interrelationships of housing and mental health. In studying the mental health of families in relation to their housing, including such things as the extent of plumbing leaks or the number of rats, the general impression of these investigators based on preliminary short-term evaluations is that moving from poor to good housing does not, on the average, result in measurable improvement in the mental health of the family. In the matter of housing and related social economic problems, one must be continually reminded of the large body of research describing the high, positive relationship between the indicators of social class and the many kinds of human illnesses. As Wilner and Walkley point out, "The list of pathologies so related is long, beginning with early studies on crime and delinquency. Other examples are alcoholism, broken homes, and divorce (Beverly Hills notwithstanding) syphilis, tuberculosis, and childhood communicable diseases. New entries are being made as time goes by: Reading disability has entered the lists, as has the incidence of narcotics use among teenagers, as well as the incidence of mental illness." Housing, by and large, shows a marked negative relationship with most illnesses so that, in general, as housing deteriorates, illnesses rise. Psychoses have been found to increase with housing deterioration; neuroses, on the other hand, seem to increase with improved housing.

WHITHER PREVENTION?

Prevention is, at present, a high-status, magic word generally applicable to almost all professional endeavors in mental health. The term is applicable to newer and more effective treatment methods for schizophrenia, preventive hospitalization of suicidal patients or the use of drugs for quieting patients, or, in vague or general terms, to improved housing, better human relations, better schools, more staff, and so on. This lack of specificity in the term prevention is especially critical in a field that already has a large element of vagueness and expansiveness. If, as Freud noted, thinking is action in rehearsal, it behooves individuals interested in preventive action to get into rehearsal ideas that are primarily preventive, specific enough to be replicated in more than one locality and operational enough to be evaluated within one's lifetime. Also, it must be kept in mind that the preventive battlegrounds are the primary institutions or agencies of a society. We must determine the specific interventions or modifications these institutions can make to reduce the stress vulnerability or enhance the personality resources of the human organisms they serve.

Prevention has to do with the quality of the interactions and the degree of effectiveness of the primary institutions of a society in providing each person with increments of ego strength and personality robustness for coping with the "slings and arrows" of life. The nature of these interactions and experiences would be considered preventive to the extent to which such experiences enhance the degrees of psychological freedom of an individual to select behavioral alternatives and to act upon them. This preventive model and point of view was succinctly illustrated by an old Cornish test of insanity related by Woodward. The test situation comprised a sink, a tap of running water, a bucket and a ladle. The bucket was placed under the tap of running water and the subject asked to bail the water out of the bucket with the ladle. If the subject continued to bail without paying some attention to reducing or preventing the flow of water into the pail, he was judged to be mentally incompetent. Similarly, any society that attempts to provide more and larger buckets to contain the problems of that society, without simultaneously attempting to reduce the flow, might be equally suspect. Treatment, rehabilitation and incarceration are our necessary buckets to contain the flow. Prevention, however, deals with the tap, the sources of flow and the leverages needed to turn the faucet down or off.

REFERENCES

1. Bellak, L. 1959. Schizophrenia: A Review of the Syndrome. Logos Press. New York, N.Y. : viii.
2. Bower, E. M. 1960. Early Identification of Emotionally Handicapped Children in School. Charles C Thomas. Springfield, Ill.
3. ———, 1961. Primary prevention in a school setting. *In* Prevention of Mental Disorders in Children. G. Caplan, Ed. Basic Books, Inc. New York, N.Y. : 353–377.
4. Bowlby, J. 1951. Maternal Care and Mental Health. World Health Organization. Geneva, Switzerland.
5. Brody, S. 1956. Patterns of Mothering. International Universities Press, Inc. New York, N.Y.
6. Bruner, J. S. On Coping and Defending. Mimeographed.
7. Caplan, G. 1951. A public health approach to child psychiatry. Ment. Hyg. 35:235–249.
8. Cumming, E., and J. Cumming. 1957. Closed Ranks. Harvard University Press. Cambridge, Mass.
9. Dubos, R. 1959. Mirage of Health. Harper & Bros. New York, N.Y.
10. Eissler, R. 1955. Scapegoats of society. *In* Searchlights on Delinquency. K. R. Eissler, Ed. International Universities Press, Inc. New York, N.Y. : 228.
11. Farnsworth, D. L. 1961. The provision of appropriate treatment: hospital and community collaboration. Ment. Hosps. 12:18.
12. Fox, T. F. 1960. Priorities. *In* Steps in the Development of Integrated Psychiatric Services. Milbank Memorial Fund. New York, N.Y. : 16.
13. Freedman, A., *et al.* 1960. The influence of hyperbilirubinemia on the early development of the premature. Psychiat. Res. Reps. 13:108–123.

14. Gardner, J. 1961. Excellence. Harper & Bros. New York, N.Y. : 115.

15. Ginzberg, E., and Associates. 1959. The Ineffective Soldier: Lessons for Management and the Nation. Columbia University Press. New York, N.Y. : 118.

16. Goodrich, D. W. 1961. Possibilities for preventive intervention during initial personality formation. *In* Prevention of. Mental Disorders in Children. G. Caplan, Ed. Basic Books, Inc. New York, N.Y. : 249–264.

17. Hofstadter, R. 1955. Social Darwinism in American Thought. Beacon Press. Boston, Mass.

18. Homer. 1949. The Odyssey. W.H.D. Rouse, Trans. Mentor. New York, N.Y. : 108.

19. Kawi, A. A., and B. Pasamanick. 1959. The Association of Factors of Pregnancy with the Development of Reading Disorders in Childhood. Society for Research in Child Development. Yellow Springs, Ohio.

20. Klein, D., and E. Lindemann. 1961. Preventive intervention in individual and family crisis situations. *In* Prevention of Mental Disorders in Children. G. Caplan, Ed. Basic Books, Inc. New York, N.Y. : 283–306.

21. Kubie, L. S. 1954. The fundamental nature of the distinction between normality and neuroses. Psychoanal. Quart. 23: 183.

22. ———, 1957. Social forces and the neurotic process. *In* Explorations in Social Psychiatry. A. Lexington, *et al.*, Eds. Basic Books, Inc. New York, N.Y.

23. Meier, R. L. 1959. Human time allocation: a basis for social accounts. J. Amer. Institute of Planners. 25(Nov.): 27–33.

24. Murphy, G. 1960. The prevention of mental disorder: some research suggestions. J. Hillside Hospital. 9:146.

25. Murphy, L. B. 1961. Preventive implications of development in the preschool years. *In* Prevention of Mental Disorders in Children. G. Caplan, Ed. Basic Books, Inc. New York, N.Y. : 218–248.

26. O'Neil, P., and L. Robbins. 1958. The relation of childhood behavior problems to adult psychiatric status. Amer. J. Psychiat. 114:968.

27. Pasamanick, B. 1956. The epidemiology of behavior disorders in childhood. *In* Neurology and Psychiatry in Childhood. William & Wilkins Co., Inc. Baltimore, Md.

28. Redlich, F. C. 1957. The concept of health in psychiatry. *In* Explorations in Social Psychiatry. A. Leighton *et al.*, Eds. Basic Books, Inc. New York, N.Y.

29. Ribble, M. 1943. The Rights of Infants. Columbia University Press. New York, N.Y.

30. Sanford, R. N. 1959. The development of the healthy personality in the society of today. *In* Modern Mental Health Concepts and Their Application in Public Health Education. State Department of Public Health. Berkeley, Calif. : 8.

31. Stevenson, I. 1959. Direct instigation of behavioral changes in psychotherapy. AMA Arch. Gen. Psychiat. 1: 99–107.

32. Wilner, D., and R. Walkley. 1959. Housing environment and mental health. In Epidemiology of Mental Disorder. American Association for the Advancement of Science. Washington, D.C. : 143–174.

33. Wilson, W. 1926. The New Freedom. *In* Essays Old and New. Essie Chamberlain, Ed. Harcourt Brace and Co. New York, N.Y. : 43.

34. Wortis. H., C. B. Heimer, M. Braine, M. Redlo and R. Rue. 1963. Growing up in Brooklyn: an early history of the premature child. Amer. J. Orthopsychiat. 33(3):535–539.

THE WELL-BEING CLINIC:[1]

A Study of the Effectiveness of an Attempt to Provide Routine Mental Health Check-ups for Community Groups

A. W. MacLeod, M.D., B. Silverman, M.D., and Phyllis Poland

The department of psychiatry of McGill University in Montreal has, in the past 2 years, initiated a mental health activity which has been named the Well-Being Clinic. This project has been carried on through the Allan Memorial Institute of the Royal Victoria Hospital, the Mental Hygiene Institute, and the University Extension Department, and in collaboration with two Red Feather Agencies—the Y.W.C.A. and the Dispensary.

This preliminary report gives some details of its development, outlines the manner in which the service operates, summarizes results so far obtained, and discusses basic assumptions underlying its conception.

The name "Well-Being Clinic" was suggested by the statement in the manifesto of the World Health Organization: "Health is a state of complete, physical, mental and social well-being and not merely the absence of disease or infirmity." The primary aim of the service is to offer the ordinary citizen a routine pe-

riodic check-up of his mental health just as the earlier-established Well-Baby and Well-Woman Clinics offer routine check-ups of physical health.

There are 2 Well-Being Clinics presently in operation in Montreal. One is at the Allan Memorial Institute of the Royal Victoria Hospital, and the other at the central division of the Y.W.C.A. Both are staffed by members of the social service department of the Royal Victoria Hospital and both are served by a consultant psychiatrist from the department of psychiatry, McGill University.

Origins of the Idea

The "Well-Being Clinic" had its beginning in the interest of the Montreal Y.W.C.A. in the problem of overweight in young women. The Y.W.C.A. called in the Diet Dispensary to collaborate on a program offering keep-fit exercises and lectures on how and what to eat. It soon became apparent that obesity was often as much a psychological as a caloric problem, that many overweight girls also suffered from some degree of social mal-

[1] Read at the 112th annual meeting of The American Psychiatric Association, Chicago, Ill., April 30–May 4, 1956.

From *American Journal of Psychiatry*, 113 (March 1957), pp. 795–800. Reprinted by permission of the authors and the publisher.

adjustment or deprivation. At this stage, the Mental Hygiene Institute was asked to assume responsibility for developing the program further to include factors relating to mental health.

A series of lectures on mental health and a course of group-therapy sessions entitled "Adjustment to Living" was the next development. This, in turn, was followed by a program entitled "The Health and Charm Course," the objective of which was to provide help in the practical details of modern urban living through a series of seminars conducted by experts in such diverse fields as budgeting, hostess duties, public speaking, art appreciation, marriage counselling, clothes and hair-styling, home nursing, recreation, and community organization. During these several programs the idea of the "Well-Being Clinic" was gradually taking shape as providing an integrated needed service to normal people who are coping with the stresses and problems of normal living.

A similar educational program, organized by the extension department of McGill University under the title "Understanding Ourselves," and reaching a wider public, provided a second interest-group to which the "Well-Being Clinic" idea could be introduced as a logical extension. This McGill course currently consists of 15 weekly 2-hour periods. During the first hour, the presentation of a mental health film is followed by a half-hour lecture on the relation between the mental mechanisms demonstrated in the film and the problems of emotional interplay and adjustment in everyday life.

During the second hour, the main group is divided into subgroups of not more than 20 persons under the chairmanship of mental health experts from the department of psychiatry and the School of Social Work of McGill University. Solutions to personal emotional problems are sought through group discussion, role-playing, and psychological interpretation. Because of the content of these courses, it is hoped that those who use the clinic will bring to their first interview some understanding of the role the clinic can play in promoting better mental health.

Clinic Operation

When a person registers at the clinic he is reminded of 3 things: (1) the initial interview will not be carried out by a doctor but by a qualified psychiatric social worker; (2) the purpose of the examination will be to assess the registrant's state of health in terms of ability to live an adequate life; and (3) the clinic in itself will offer no diagnostic or treatment facilities but will accept responsibility for referral if problems are disclosed that call for further exploration or help.

In essence the Well-Being Clinic gives the individual the opportunity to sit down for an hour's private conversation with an interested, experienced worker in the mental health field. He is given the chance to hear himself as he outlines his daily activities. He is helped to assess realistically his ability to derive satisfaction and adequate financial return from his work, to handle his personal emotional problems effectively, to achieve and maintain happiness in marriage and family life, and to play a meaningful role in the community around him.

A detailed record is kept of the content of each interview. For purposes of recording, a rating scale is in the process of development. There are necessarily many theoretical and practical difficulties to be overcome before a satisfactory scale can be evolved. The organizers of the

Clinic are well aware that the present system of recording and rating leaves much to be desired but they are hopeful that, following the lead offered by the Barrabee-Finesinger Normative Social Adjustment Scale(1), further improvement will be made.

The purpose of the initial interview is appraisal, not primarily to find out whether problems exist—everybody has problems—but to see how problems are being handled. If, in the opinion of the clinic worker, the individual is grappling effectively with his personal ration of environmental difficulties and personal frustrations, his mental health is considered adequate for his needs, and he is told so.

As would be expected, some individuals have problems of personal and social adjustment that are temporarily beyond their ability to handle effectively. As such problems come to light, they are tentatively identified and the case is referred to the consultant psychiatrist (or to the agency or service) for further evaluation. Following this evaluation, it is decided how and where the individual can obtain further help.

The First Hundred Applicants

As a guide in assessing the work of the clinic and as a help in directing future planning, the first 100 cases seen have been studied and classified, and 3 broad categories established: (1) the essentially healthy, (2) the relatively healthy who are unnecessarily handicapped by personal or social problems, and (3) the seriously impaired.

CATEGORY ONE   These individuals were defined as essentially healthy. They gave evidence of having handled their problems effectively in the past, demonstrated in interview that they had a real-

istic appreciation of their present life situation, and revealed that they were actively seeking solutions and making progress in solving current difficulties. The clinic staff was able to help them define some of their problems more clearly, to evaluate their level of effectiveness in mental health terms, and to arrive at an assessment of sound mental health.

Forty-eight of the first 100 persons interviewed were classified in Category One. The percentage thus classified as essentially healthy increased progressively during the first hundred interviews. As this increase could not be traced to any relevant change in the composition of the groups to whom the service was offered, it must be attributed to a positive shift in the scale of evaluations. It has been widely observed that professional training in the health field predisposes practitioners to look for and focus on the aberrant or abnormal, to underestimate the positive terms in the equation of health. As Blau(2) has remarked: "the historical tendency of medicine to focus on disease has obscured the fact that health is the main goal of therapy and that it too is the object of treatment." This unavoidable bias in the direction of diagnosing disease rather than health of seemingly affected the techniques and rating methods of clinic staff and consultants less and less as their "well-being" orientation increased. It can be reasonably speculated that future ratings may include even higher percentages in the essentially health category.

CATEGORY TWO   The 36 individuals in this group were assessed as essentially healthy people who were unnecessarily handicapped by problems that could be benefitted by referral to available community psychiatric, medical, or social agencies. That these mental health problems came to light as a result of the clinic interview speaks in favor of its usefulness as a screening device for the early detection of treatable cases of personal and social maladjustment. The cases included states of anxiety and depression, emotional problems centering around employment where either promotion, dismissal, or retirement were expected but not planned for, family conflict over the management of emotionally-disturbed or mentally defective children, marital maladjustment, and feelings of social isolation. The following are examples:

Miss E., a 45-year-old woman, has been a Civil Service stenographer for 25 years. She has reached the top position and salary in her job with no further prospect of advancement. Her only living relative is a married sister in another part of the country. She lives alone in a small apartment and has no friends. Her usual routine is to go home after work, make her dinner, do her housework, and prepare for her next day's work. Her only outside activity is to attend a concert or a lecture once or twice a month. She gets depressed easily and feels that unless she can find some interesting social activity she can share with others, she may soon have a mental breakdown.

Mrs. C., 39, has 3 children, the eldest of whom is mentally defective. Her husband's earnings are not sufficient to pay for the treatment that has been recommended so Mrs. C. is working. She has managed to make arrangements for the daytime care of her 2 younger children. She is nervous and worried as to whether she is doing the right thing for her family and is seeking some new approach to her present dilemma.

Miss D., a 30-year-old woman, has asthma and deep emotional problems in regard to her feminine role and parental relationships. Despite her attempt to solve these problems by obtaining high educational qualifications which enable her to do work giving her status and prestige, she remains depressed and lonely and has been unable to form emotionally satisfying relationships with those around her. Up till now she has shied away from psychiatric help but wonders what she should do in the near future.

CATEGORY THREE   The 10 persons in this group appeared to be functioning on the borderline, with serious problems in nearly all major areas of their lives. Typically they presented a picture of life-long social and emotional deprivation and maladjustment. For this group, the usefulness of existing community psychiatric, medical, and social agency resources had already been exhausted.

UNCLASSIFIED   Six individuals were unclassifiable on the information available. Some decided not to reveal their problems. Others who obviously needed further psychiatric evaluation refused to seek it.

Composition of Sample

Of the 100 applicants, 85 were women, 15 men. The high percentage of women is accounted for, in part, by the fact that the popular Y.W.C.A. course in mental health provided the major field of clinic operation. Nearly 75% of the group were between the ages of 20 to 39 years. Occupations included housewives, office workers, professionals, business men and women, students, and domestic workers.

DISPOSITION OF CASES   Among the 100 cases, a total of 55 referrals were recommended. Psychiatric referral was recommended in 30 cases and acted upon in 21 cases. Of this number, 8 were directed to private psychiatrists, 8 to psychiatric clinics, and 5, who had had previous psychiatric treatment, to their own psychiatrists.

There were 6 referrals to physicians for physical complaints, and 9 to social agencies such as the marriage counselling service, the vocational guidance service, and the community recreational agencies. Another 7 were referred for group psychotherapy; 3 were advised to return to the clinic for further evaluation in a few months' time.

Basic Assumptions

It could be argued that the development of a mental health service such as the "Well-Being Clinic" must be based on inadequately validated hypotheses. As Eaton(3) insists "Mental Health as a scientific concept does not now exist" and Jahoda(4) has stated "There exists no psychologically meaningful and from the point of view of research, operationally useful description of what is commonly understood to constitute mental health." Yet, mental illness is real enough. And both the pressure of public opinion and the desire of mental health workers to undertake preventive and early-detection programs argue for new experimental services founded on present knowledge, incomplete as it is.

Few will deny that at the core of an individual's social and personal maladjustment there lie handicaps of unmastered, unconscious, intrapsychic conflicts arising from the earliest life experiences. Psychoanalysis remains the therapy of choice for the treatment of such problems. Yet what hope is there that such specialized services can be made available in the near future to the community at large? As actively expanding as our present psychiatric resources are, and as effective as psychotherapy and the physical and pharmacological methods of treatment have proved to be, it must be admitted that they frequently are unable to do as much as one would wish in the general improvement of community mental health. Thus until such services become more adequate, other hopeful approaches must be made on the basis of certain well-founded assumptions.

One such assumption underlying the work of the Well-Being Clinic is the concept that health is dynamic rather than static. The term "health" denotes a skill in maintaining desired values at biological, psychological, and social levels of human organization. This view of health as a human skill implies that it can be taught, learned, and improved through practice; it also implies that mental health can be impaired in 2 ways: (1) through failure of the community to organize itself in such a way as to provide emotionally satisfying, socially acceptable activities for a wide diversity of personalities; (2) through failure or inability of the individual to make use of such opportunities when they are provided.

Another basic assumption is that health is relative. "Healthier" and "healthiest" convey more precise meanings than "health"; no one is 100% well, and no one is 100% ill. Health is the resultant of a way of living that develops the ability to react appropriately to psychological stress and environment difficulties of all kinds. It has been pointed out, for example, that the healthier of 2 individuals is the one who has the greater ability to maintain an even temper, an alert intelligence and a happy disposition in the face of comparable frustrations. Those who face their problems squarely, perceiving them with the least subjective distortion, and who seek and implement possible solutions, show a healthier reaction than those who passively accept failure or who retain a sense of the urgency of a problem but make no adequate attempts to solve it. The more a person knows himself and is himself, the healthier he is.

Implicit in the development of the Well-Being Clinic is the conviction that mental hygiene activities must be educational and community-wide to be fully effective. They must be aimed not only at prompt detection and treatment but also at prevention. An objective must be the modifying of life conditions to lessen the incidence of ill health and to protect the health of susceptible individuals closely related to the overtly or potentially sick. The development of a Well-Being Clinic is not enough. It must be part of a network of well-organized and voluntary agencies, health and hospital services.

The concept of social isolation as an etiological factor in mental ill health is another basic assumption. Bowlby(5), in his report to the World Health Organization entitled "Maternal Care and Mental Health," conclusively documented the long-range, crippling effect of early maternal deprivation—a form of social isolation. Hebb(6) and his co-workers at McGill University have demonstrated the emergence of behavior reminiscent of that seen in cases of psychotic breakdown in normal university students subjected to marked degrees of social and sensory deprivation. Perhaps of as much importance, as far as the community is concerned, is the evidence of various psychosocial studies that social isolation in the "here and now" life of adult individuals can impair the effectiveness of the role they play in the community.

Of particular interest is the problem created by the sense of social isolation that develops in the mind of the still-active worker who has been forced into the relative inactivity of retirement because of company retirement policy. Or again, there is the problem of the aged and infirm, the returned convict, the partially cured physical or mental invalid in need of more rehabilitation than present services offer, and the relatively inadequate individuals who need help and guidance before they can become participating members of the community.

Observations from "Clinic" Experience

The staff of the Well-Being Clinic were early struck by the number of individuals who said during the interview that they felt isolated from the social life and the recreational activities of the community. In some cases, environmental difficulties did in reality exist. A young girl, an office worker, had moved into Montreal from another province with her parents a few years ago. Her parents had died; she moved to a single-room apartment in the suburbs. All she could do was to travel to work and keep going during the day. At night she was too exhausted to make the extra effort to find a suitable niche for herself in the community.

Other cases came from rapidly growing suburban areas where there had not yet been time to develop adequate, organized social and recreational facilities. In this respect the findings of the Well-Being Clinic supported Burgess'(7) view that a high degree of social organization is associated with good mental health while a low degree of social organization is correlated with a high rate of mental disorders and of social problems. However, even in communities that appeared, on the surface at least, to be well organized and to offer many emotionally satisfying, socially acceptable outlets for group activity, there were found individuals who for one reason or another were unable to find a meaningful social role for themselves without additional help. The clinic evidence pointed to the possibility of such individuals suffering in silence for a long time before their deteriorating mental health brought them to the notice of existing health resources.

SUMMARY

The existence of a Well-Being Clinic should in itself be an encouragement to people to seek help in emotional problems. The positive health orientation of the clinic lessens the likelihood of those exploring the state of their mental health being labelled "neurotic." It should help relieve chronic and often unnecessary concern about mental health derived from the public's misinterpretation of well-intentioned mental health propaganda. It should help in the early detection of mental illnesses and social maladjustment thus making early treatment possible. And it should make useful contributions to the field of psychiatric research by assisting in the assessment of the effectiveness of existing treatment resources and perhaps by identifying as yet unrecognized disturbed human relationships.

On the negative side it can be said that the clinic may bring to light many cases for whom there is at present no therapeutic resource, and that it may miss many cases of early illness. The degree of effectiveness of the initial screening interview may roughly parallel that obtained in mass radiography of the chest in the field of preventive public health. Yet compared with a community in which a Well-Being Clinic does not exist, it can be argued that Montreal has set in motion a promising venture. The idea of the Well-Being Clinic has been favorably received in Montreal. Professional and industrial organizations have shown an interest in setting up further clinics adapted to their particular needs. Outlying communities have expressed similar interest.

The clinics in Montreal have remained financially self-supporting. And the 2 group programs to which they were attached had over the past year a paying enrolment of 200 persons. The clinics, therefore, have not been a costly experiment.

Remembering that in the final analyses it is the well people of the community who must carry the burden of the ill, and this is by no means only a financial burden, it is of paramount importance that experimentation should go forward in the direction of keeping the healthy as healthy as possible.

REFERENCES

1. Barrabee, P., E. L. Barrabee, and J. E. Finesinger, *Am. J. Psychiat.*, 112:252, Oct. 1955.
2. Blau, A. Ibid., 110:594. Feb. 1954.
3. Eaton, J. W. Ibid., 108:81, Aug. 1951.
4. Jahoda, M. Toward a social psychology of mental health. *In* Problems of Infancy and Childhood, Milton J. E. Senn (Ed.), Trans Fourth Conference, Supplement II. New York: Josiah Macy Jr. Foundation, 1950.
5. Bowlby, J. Maternal care and mental health—A Report prepared on behalf of the World Health Organization as a contribution to the United Nations Programme for the welfare of homeless children. Geneva, Switzerland: World Health Organization, Monog. Ser. No. 2.
6. Baxton, W. H., W. Haron, and T. H. Scott. *J. Canad. Psychol.*, 8:70, 1954.
7. Burgess, E. W. Mental health in modern society. *In* Mental Health and Mental Disorder, A Sociological Approach. Arnold A. Rose (Ed.), New York: W. W. Norton, 1955.

NEW TECHNIQUES
IN MENTAL HOSPITAL CARE

We inherit the same problems of evaluation with the tranquilizing drugs, experimentally tested in the treatment of the mentally ill in 1953 and by 1955 in general use in State hospitals that could afford them. Estimates from various States indicate that as many as one third of all public mental hospital patients now receive these drugs, the general rule being to tranquilize patients who are hyperactive, unmanageable, excited, highly disturbed, or highly disturbing.

These drugs have revolutionized the management of psychotic patients in American mental hospitals, and probably deserve primary credit for reversal of the upward spiral of the State hospital inpatient load in the last four years. They have largely replaced the various forms of shock, as well as surgery on the prefrontal lobes of the brain (lobotomy). Unquestionably, the drugs have delivered the greatest blow for patient freedom, in terms of nonrestraint, since Pinel struck off the chains of the lunatics in the Paris asylum 168 years ago. The most noticeable effect of the drugs is to reduce the hospital ward noise level. Bedlam has been laid to rest. The debate still continues as to what precisely the drugs accomplish, physiologically and socially. Some have predicted they would empty mental hospitals, and others have dubbed them chemical strait jackets. In the surprising, pleasant effects they produce on patient-staff relationships, the drugs

might be described as moral treatment in pill form, as may be judged from the remarks of Robert H. Felix (1960), Director of the National Institute of Mental Health:

In the whole of *materia medica*, I suspect that the tranquilizers are the only substances whose responses have been measured or observed not only on the persons who receive the drugs but also on those who live and work in the same surroundings. We have known for some time that if mental hospital patients can be made aware of the staff's sympathetic perception and high expectations, the patients will tend to fit the roles which are set for them. It has also been evident that every improvement in the patient's behavior tends to enhance the staff's attitudes toward him. In the tranquilizers we have found a valuable means by which both staff and patients have been able to help each other to perform at a higher and more constructive level.

In short, we have *new hope*. Medicine long has believed that the man who feels he can do something for a patient and can impart the feeling to the patient that something *is* being done for him may "pull a patient through" conditions that would overwhelm the bored, unenthusiastic, or uncertain person. In less scientific circles, this kind of mutual enthusiasm is known as faith healing. Conversely, when the persons attending the critically ill patient feel that they cannot help him, then surely there is little hope for him. This hopelessness is an old story in our

From *Action for Mental Health*, the Final Report of the Joint Commission on Mental Illness and Health, © 1961 by Basic Books, Inc., New York.

large, overcrowded, understaffed State hospitals.

Understandably, the biases introduced by a long history of contention and doubt about the relative merits of one course of treatment or another and the question of whether we are measuring drug efficacy or enthusiasm make scientific evaluation of the effects of the tranquilizers a tricky problem.

For this final report, we have the benefit of a four-year study of the use of tranquilizers in the New York State mental hospitals (Henry Brill and Robert E. Patton, 1957, 1959). The study covers the period from March 31, 1955 to March 31, 1959. In 1955, the Department of Mental Hygiene, State of New York, under the direction of Dr. Paul Hoch, introduced chlorpromazine and reserpine for general use in the State's 18 mental hospitals, some 30,000 patients receiving drug treatment during the first year out of a total patient load of 93,300. The drug-treated portion rose to 40,000 by 1959.

Prior to 1956, the resident population of New York State mental hospitals had continually increased, having doubled itself since 1929, reflecting population growth, an increased proportion of aged persons, reduced mortality rates, and a greater use of mental hospitals. As in so many other States, the New York State mental hospital system was the victim of a population explosion following public indifference and neglect. As elsewhere, the public mental hospitals had no control over total admissions or over the suitability of patients for hospitalization; the law required that they admit all patients certified, or committed, to their care. The public and not the professional staffs thus determined the hospital's destiny.

The New York State mental patient population was 91,000 in 1954, prior to the introduction of the drugs, and rose another 2300 by 1955. Then in 1955–1956, the first year of the tranquilizers, the trend abruptly reversed itself and a net fall of nearly 500 occurred in the resident hospital population. The mental hospital systems of about three-fifths of the States witnessed the same phenomenon in 1956. As indicated in Chapter I, the reversal of trend and continued decreases have occurred in the State mental hospital population of the entire United States. In four years' time, the New York State mental hospital population declined to 89,000 in 1959, a net drop of approximately 4000.

The immediate assumption in 1956 was that this dramatic event, coming as the first ray of spring sun to a snowbound and winter-worn family, was caused by the tranquilizers. Doubters had to be satisfied. They were of two general kinds: (1) those well trained in scientific method and interpretation of data who were simply aware of the common mistake of confusing coincidental events with cause and effect; (2) those whose own orientation and prejudices opposed them to the idea that a pill could make a big difference. The latter group, it would seem, were chiefly those who preferred analytic psychotherapy of the individual or who advocated a sociological approach, but of course included some organic-minded hospital psychiatrists trained in pessimism by years of disappointed hopes in one new treatment or another.

The New York State mental hospital system appeared well suited for a state-wide analysis of the relationship between tranquilizers and the hospital population reduction. New York's public mental hospital patients constitute roughly one eighth of the total for the United States. The State was financially in a position to afford the use of drugs as needed on a wide range of patients. Importantly, the administrative and statistical controls were good, making it feasible to set up a study in all hospitals of the system and to collect and analyze large quantities of data. At the same time, the ratio of physicians and other professional staff members to patients was only a little above the national average (that is to say, rather low), minimizing the possibility of greatly increasing individual attention to patients. Most importantly, as Brill and Patton pointed out, there had been no change in methods or standards for admitting or discharging patients at the time drug treatment began. They state:

The measure of therapeutic potential has been the capacity to return patients to society. It is recognized that return to the community does not represent an end in itself and can be easily subject to changes of administrative policy. We can only say that such policy changes have not taken place. Moreover, anyone who has attempted to change the operating conditions of a large organization . . . will recognize that sweeping administrative changes are virtually impossible to achieve quickly, but require a period of years. The fact is that no effort was made to produce any administrative changes during the first year of large-scale drug therapy; during the last three, a very active program of change and liberalization has been under way.

Thus, Brill and Patton have been able to compare a year of no change in trend (1954–1955) with a year in which the introduction of the drugs constituted the only apparent innovation (1955–1956) and these with a two-year period (1956–1958) in which a number of favorable factors besides drugs were added.

The figure below is taken from their study (1959). It shows, in a graphic fashion, how the need for restraint and seclusion of patients decreased and all

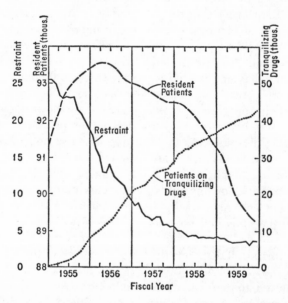

This figure shows trends in percentage of patients requiring seclusion (restraint) and in total number of patients residing in New York State hospitals in the four years following the introduction and during the increasing use of tranquilizing drugs. (From Brill and Patton, 1959, p. 498. By permission of the *American Journal of Psychiatry,* Vol. 116.)

but disappeared in inverse ratio to the increase in patients receiving tranquilizing drugs. It also shows the over-all downward trend in the resident population. The data are for the fiscal years, beginning March 31, 1954. The authors point out that there appeared to be no wearing off in the effect of the drugs on patient behavior, such as could be attributed to initial enthusiasm. However, since the physicians did not stick to chlorpromazine and reserpine but tended to try newer products in the tranquilizer group, the authors interpreted the choice of *which drug* as to be of no decisive importance. This leaves room for interpreting the drug benefits as partly psychological; that is, as patients quiet down and become less disturbing, staff morale goes up and relations with patients improve.

Brill and Patton concluded (1957) that use of the drugs largely caused the abrupt resident population fall in the first year (1954–1955). They also pointed out (1959) that in 1956 the Department of Mental Hygiene began a new program of intensified treatment for newly admitted patients, gradually extended through all institutions, and also began conversion to an open-hospital system. This more liberal philosophy brought freedom of the grounds to some 60 per cent of all cases by 1959, ten times the number who had such freedom in 1956.

The investigators, sharing the general view of the hospital staffs, were inclined to give the drugs the principal credit for making it possible to unlock wards and treat the mentally ill more like general hospital patients and less like prisoners. As an additional dividend, the number of suicides remained consistently below the average for the preceding ten years.

The New York study dealt with a variety of questions, all requiring answers in order to assess the place of the tranquilizers in the treatment of the mentally ill. Because of their pertinence, we will briefly summarize some other findings from this study.

Whereas first admissions previously exceeded discharges (all releases alive), discharges exceeded first admissions slightly for the first time in 1958–1959. About 50 per cent of the patients were maintained on drug therapy after leaving the hospital. The relapse rate (all patients returning to the hospital) was about 35 per cent, but, in contrast to the findings of some other investigators, this was no higher than in predrug days.

No sickness associated with long-term use of the drugs was identified clinically.

The greatest gain in the release of patients occurred in the age group from twenty-five to forty-four, with some reduction also occurring in the forty-five- to sixty-four-year-old group in the hospital. In contrast, there was an increase in the number of patients over sixty-five. Here, the drugs appear of little use.

From the standpoint of diagnosis, schizophrenic patients showed far greater benefit (as measured by release from the hospital within five years) than did patients with other types of psychosis or organic brain disease. The increase in releases was most marked among schizophrenics who had been in the hospital two to four years—"I would seem that we may have gained less in speed of therapy than in effectiveness in prevention of chronicity" (1959). As with the senile psychoses, alcoholic psychoses and character disorders likewise showed increases rather than reductions in the face of treatment with tranquilizers.

Brill and Patton showed the discharge rate among drug-treated patients in 1957–1958 to be twice that for patients not treated with tranquilizers—roughly 20 per cent as opposed to 10 per cent.

The New York study substantiated the general observation, as remarked to us by Jonathan Cole: "The drugs do not move mountains." The authors summarize (1959):

It now becomes important to analyze the trends for their significance with regard to future plans for mental hospitals, especially as many mental hospitals in various parts of the world have noted a decreased pressure for hospital beds or an outright fall in population. In some quarters these changes have been discounted as cyclical and unimportant and in others the attitude has been that it is now a matter of a relatively short time before mental hospitals will be empty and that the problem of hospital psychiatry has at long last been solved.

Our own data lead us to take a position somewhat between these two extremes and considerably toward the conservative side. The persistence of reduction for four successive years seems to rule out any cyclical variation and the fact that the reduction of the population is limited to functional cases and most marked in schizophrenics points to the action of a specific therapeutic influence rather than a general change of policy. . . .

If we looked only at the reduction in our population, we may forecast a rather gradual melting away of the chronic schizophrenic cases to perhaps 50 to 75% of their present number which is a humane and practical advance that would relieve New York State of a quarter of its present mental hospital population. . . .

In their appraisals, Brill and Patton did not, of course, look *only* at the reduction in the State hospital population but also at the continued increase in total admissions and in certain types of admissions—senile psychoses, juvenile-behavior disorders, adult character disorders, alcoholism—"a sort of deferred business." Here the outlook remains less cheerful.

Not mentioned in their study is the fact (cited in Chapter I) that the net decrease in State hospital inpatients, now a well-established trend, cannot be observed in the patient loads of Veterans Administration mental hospitals, general hospital psychiatric units, or private mental hospitals. Looking beyond the immediate effects of the drugs, what we seem to be witnessing is an as yet small, overall shift of the mental hospital patient load away from State hospitals and toward other types of care. Inasmuch as senile psychosis is the No. 1 reason for admission to mental hospitals and this category does not especially benefit from tranquilizers, we might predict that the effects of an aging population will become the predominant factor in determining future trends in the State hospital patient load. Unlike schizophrenia, the No. 2 reason for admission, senile psychosis can quickly flood crowded facilities for chronic patients and yet not have a long-range cumulative effect; the older patients die within a few years after admission whereas schizophrenics live on for many years.

THE NEW MENTAL HOSPITAL: A THERAPEUTIC COMMUNITY

In the typical general hospital, where there are more than two employees per patient, the approach of the doctors, nurses, and technicians in some instances may seem impersonal and routine, but the patient takes it for granted they are there to make him comfortable and to get him well; the staff, in turn, takes it for granted that they enjoy his confidence and cooperation in these objectives. Whether private or charity patient, the individual retains his rights as a citizen and acquires special rights as a sick person in need of help. He fully expects to be treated as a human being and, with few exceptions, is so treated. None of this can be taken for granted on the locked wards of the typical State hospital; here, there are three patients for every employee, physicians and nurses seldom attend the patient, he loses his rights as an individual and acquires none as a patient, he is encouraged to fade into the herdlike background, and his illness attracts attention only as it may create a disturbance and require his further restriction. The system effectively deprives him of all hope. Here, in the mass view, we are still fighting the battle of Pinel, who was among the first to observe that such hospitalization can convert an acute breakdown into a chronic state.

This negative contribution of the State hospital has been repeatedly observed, and nowhere has been better expounded than in the comments of Dr. Robert C. Hunt, Superintendent of the Hudson River State Hospital, one of the most progressive large mental hospitals in the United States:

Much of the unnecessary crippling of the mentally ill must be laid at the door of the state mental hospital both from the standpoint of how it functions internally and how it is used by the society it serves. Despite the glorious early history of our state hospitals as first-rate treatment institutions; despite recent advances in the effectiveness of treatment; despite all the propaganda to the effect that these are hospitals for the treatment of the ill; despite the dedicated zeal of treatment-minded staff, commitment to the state hospital continues, in most cases, to represent to the patient and to his family major social surgery by "putting him away." At best it is likely to be a regretful acceptance of permanent loss with family readjustments which make it difficult to reverse the process. The machinery for bringing about the admission, especially in the larger cities, does nothing to mitigate this. The police ambulance, the rapid impersonal processing in a huge psychopathic hospital, the judicial proceedings, and the mass transportation to a remote fortress, must seem to many like a casting out of the unfit.

It is a common experience that the patient who arrives at the state hospital fearful of the legendary horrors, is surprised and grateful at finding that he is treated with kindness, gentleness, and understanding, with genuine concern for his welfare. Overt cruelty is probably less common in a well-run state hospital than in the average neighborhood outside. Well-meaning kindness can itself be a cause of disability, however, when based upon false premises. The certified mental patient in our culture is traditionally regarded as one who has lost all capacity for managing his own affairs. For his own protection and welfare and for the safety of the public, his every move must be directed and supervised. He is ordered to get out of bed, is told what clothing to put on, when and where he may smoke a cigarette. He is ordered to take part in occupational therapy, to toss a medicine ball, or watch a movie. He takes a bath at the prescribed time and under the immediate supervision of an attendant. To make sure that no patient can escape from this well-intentioned coddling, all but a tiny minority spend their lives behind locked doors and barred windows with their occasional airings strictly guarded by watchful attendants. . . . In our enlightened times, most of us working in public mental hospitals have been satisfied that we were applying the lessons learned from Pinel, that at least we were not making our patients worse by medieval brutalities even though our treatment techniques left something to be desired. This smugness has been shattered by such pioneers as Macmillan and Rees [Duncan Macmillan and T. P. Rees, British pioneers of the open hospital movement] who have rediscovered the values of the open hospital. Their experiences . . . have shown beyond question that much of the aggressive, disturbed, suicidal, and regressive behavior of the mentally ill is not necessarily or inherently part of the illness as such but is very largely an artificial by-product of the way of life imposed upon them. The virtual disappearance of antisocial and irresponsible behavior when patients are treated and trusted as responsible fellow human beings is most convincing and forces us to a total re-examination of our traditional procedures. . . .

The tranquilizing drugs have brought about dramatic changes in some of the outward manifestations of the hospital culture but do not in and of themselves change the basic structure. . . .

The foregoing critical remarks should not be misunderstood as just another denunciation of that whipping boy of American psychiatry, the state hospital. I have no patience with those ostensibly well-meaning crusaders who place the blame for the custodial culture on such internal factors as too few doctors, too few nurses, too little therapy, and too few dollars. A basic assumption in many reform waves seems to be that the addition of therapeutic tools and viewpoints to the mental hospital will automatically convert it from a custodial to a treatment institution. . . . The presence of a treatment-minded staff, and of humane and enlightened administration, doubtless mitigates some of the evils of the custodial function, but does not and cannot by itself abolish the function. The point I am trying to make is that the custodial culture within the mental hospital is in large part an inevitable consequence of the expectations of the population we serve. Our society *hopes* for successful treatment, but it *demands* safe custody of those whom it rejects. The pressure for security is constant, unremitting, and a long accumulation of responses to this pressure for safe custody is embodied in hospital customs, traditions, regulations, laws, and architecture. We also live through times of acute exacerbation of these pressures, during which we are excoriated by the judiciary, crucified by the press, and harassed by litigants over our supposed lapses from security. In times like these it is a rarely courageous hospital superintendent who does not tighten his security measures and become more restrictive in release policies. The custodial function of the mental hospital is a necessary and inevitable product of the community demand and can never be abolished by measures taken within the hospital alone . . . (Hunt, 1958, pp. 12–15).

Hunt regards the open hospital as an essential factor in achieving community tolerance of the mentally ill, holding the unlocked door to be the greatest therapeutic development of the present generation, even more important than the tranquilizers. He summarizes his convictions, patterned after those of Schwartz, Greenblatt, and other experimenters in social-psychiatric treatment (the therapeutic community in a broad sense) as follows (1958, p. 21):

1. The enormous disability associated with mental illness is to a large extent superimposed, is preventable and treatable.
2. Disability is superimposed by the rejection mechanisms stemming from cultural attitudes.
3. Hospitalization as such is an important cause of disability.
4. The best of treatment-minded state hospitals perform a disabling custodial function.
5. The custodial culture within a state hospital is largely created by public pressure for security.
6. Some of the treatment functions and most of the custodial functions of the hospital should be returned to the community.
7. This can be accomplished only by a change in public attitudes and concepts of responsibility.
8. Public attitudes cannot be expected to change until hospitals demonstrate the value and safety of community care by becoming open hospitals.

REFERENCES

Brill, H., and Patton, R. E., 1957. Analysis of 1955–1956 population fall in New York State mental hospitals in first year of large-scale use of tranquilizing drugs. *Am. J. Psychiat.*, 114:509.

———, 1959. Analysis of population reduction in New York State mental hospitals during the first four years of large-scale therapy with psychotropic drugs. *Am. J. Psychiat.*, 116:495.

Felix, R. H., 1960. Psychotropic drugs: pacemakers in research and treatment. National Institute of Mental Health. (Mimeographed.)

Hunt, R. C., 1958. Ingredients of a rehabilitation program. *An Approach to the Prevention of Disability from Chronic Psychoses.* Proceedings of the 34th Annual Conference of the Milbank Memorial Fund, 1957, Part I, p. 9. Milbank Memorial Fund.

AN EXPERIMENTAL STUDY IN
THE PREVENTION OF HOSPITALIZATION
OF SCHIZOPHRENICS

THIRTY MONTHS OF EXPERIENCE*

Simon Dinitz, Frank R. Scarpitti, Joseph L. Albini,
Mark Lefton, and Benjamin Pasamanick

This paper describes an experimental study which attempted to evaluate the feasibility and effectiveness of a unique, though relatively modest, program of home care treatment for schizophrenic patients.

The study herein reported is especially timely since recent proposals in the United States and elsewhere have called for the establishment of home and community care programs to prevent hospitalization in certain types of mental illness. These proposals have been generated by the alleged failure of the traditional mental hospital as a therapeutic institution; by the desire to prevent the social stigma customarily imposed by society on the hospitalized mentally ill; by the need to prevent the alienation from family and friends often associated with prolonged institutionalization, and, most importantly, by the advent of the ataractic drugs which make such programs possible.

These proposals have resulted in the passage of legislation in the U.S. establishing community mental health centers. Once operative, these centers will theoretically function to provide patients with adequate care, supervision and treatment in the community. In view of this new emphasis, the preliminary results of this study may suggest what might reasonably be expected from the home care approach. These results were obtained during 30 months of a controlled study of the relative efficacy of maintaining schizophrenic patients at home under nursing care (with and without drug therapy) as opposed to hospitalization.

STUDY DESIGN

The design of this controlled study and the problems encountered in its implementation have been described in detail in a previous paper.[1] Only a brief

* This study was supported by a grant (MH 07874) of the Public Health Service, National Institute of Mental Health.

We wish to express our gratitude to Dr. Athan Karras and to Mr. Gene Priddy for their contrbutions.

Smith, Kline and French Laboratories and Sandoz, Inc., supplied the drugs used in this study.

From *American Journal of Orthopsychiatry*, 35, 1 (January 1965), pp. 1–9. Copyright, the American Orthopsychiatric Association, Inc. Reprinted by permission of the authors and publisher.

summary statement of the methodology will be included.[2]

In the latter part of 1961 a study center (called the Institute Treatment Center) was established in downtown Louisville, Kentucky. Staffed by a director, a part-time psychiatrist, a psychologist, a social worker and five nurses with public health nursing experience, this center was given responsibility for the conduct of the study. The establishment of this facility at some distance from Central State Hospital, located outside of Louisville, necessitated the employment on a part-time basis of a psychiatrist from that hospital to screen all newly admitted patients and to determine their eligibility for inclusion in the study. Newly admitted state hospital patients and relatives were brought to the Treatment Center and interviewed if the patients met the following criteria: a diagnosis of schizophrenia, non-suicidal or homicidal, age between 18 and 60 years, residence in Louisville or the nine surrounding counties and having a family or someone else willing to provide supervision at home. If the staff psychiatrist confirmed the diagnosis and deemed the patient suitable for the program and if the family expressed willingness to cooperate, the patient was accepted for the study. Using a deck of random cards, the director assigned the patient to one of three groups approximately as follows: home on drugs (40 per cent), home on placebo (30 per cent), or hospital control (30 per cent).

The randomly assigned hospital control patients immediately were returned to Central State Hospital. The home care patients were returned to their families. Shortly after return home the public health nurse assigned to the case visited the patient and family. The same nurse made weekly calls for the first three months, bi-monthly visits for the second

three months and monthly visits thereafter. On each visit she left the medication prescribed by the psychiatrist. She also completed a written report on the status of the patient which then was reviewed by the staff psychiatrist.

INSTRUMENTS, TESTS AND MEASURES

In order to obtain the data necessary to answer the questions about the feasibility and efficacy of home care, various instruments, tests and measures were used. These included:

Psychiatric evaluation Two instruments (a psychiatric inventory and the Lorr IMPS) were used by the staff psychiatrist to evaluate the mental status of all patients on a regular basis. Home care patients were examined at intake and at six-month intervals thereafter. Hospital control patients were evaluated at intake and again after six and 18 months whether or not they still were hospitalized.

Psychological tests All groups were studied by the staff psychologist who administered the Wechsler Adult Intelligence Scale, a reaction time test series, and the Bender Gestalt and Porteus Maze tests. Testing periods were the same as for the psychiatric evaluations.

Social history A complete social history was taken by the social worker at the time of admission of the patient to the project.

Nurses reports and ratings The public health nurse completed a mental status rating form on each visit to the home care patient. This form was the Lorr IMPS. She also completed a behavior chart checklist, a physical status rating sheet and a nursing report. The latter was submitted to the staff psychiatrist. The nurse also obtained a monthly report from the responsible relative concerning the patient's functioning.

Hospital control patients were visited by the nurse one month after hospital release, and these same instruments were administered at that time.

Under the procedures outlined above, 64 patients were assigned to the drug home care group, 45 to the placebo home care group and 54 to the hospital control or "natural" group.[2] For the purposes of this analysis, 11 patients have been eliminated from consideration. These 11 study dropouts left the project to seek private care, refused to cooperate or left the community. (Findings on an "am-

per cent of the hospital controls. In terms of education, more than one-third of the home care patients, but significantly fewer of the controls (13 per cent), were high school graduates ($p = .05$).[*] Most were Protestants. These characteristics are shown in Table 1.

At the time of admission to the study, patients in the drug group had averaged 1.9 previous mental hospital admissions, placebo patients had averaged 2.0 admissions and control patients 2.3 admissions. These differences were not statistically significant. Nearly one in five drug patients had never before been hospitalized, more than half had been institution-

TABLE 1   SOCIAL CHARACTERISTICS OF DRUG, PLACEBO, AND HOSPITAL CONTROL PATIENTS

Category	N	Mean Age	Percent Male	Percent White	Percent Protestant	Percent High School Graduates
Drug	57	35.9	35	68	32	37
Placebo	41	36.2	32	68	29	34
Hospital Control	54	37.6	30	65	41	13

bulatory" group of schizophrenics also studied experimentally will not be reported in this paper.)

SOCIAL BACKGROUND DATA

The patients in the three study groups (home on drugs, home on placebo, and hospital controls) were similar to each other in almost all social background characteristics. Their average age was 36.6 years at time of admission to the project. About a third were males. More than two-thirds were white. There was some slight, but not significant, variation in marital status. Married patients constituted 54 per cent of the drug cases, 44 per cent of the placebo subjects and 52

alized once or twice and a fifth more had been hospitalized on three or more separate occasions. In the placebo group almost a fourth of the patients were first admissions, 37 per cent had been hospitalized once or twice and 39 per cent had been institutionalized three or more times. Of the hospital controls 15 per cent had never before been hospitalized, 47 per cent had been in a hospital once or twice and 38 per cent had experienced at least three prior hospitalizations (Table 2).

All patients also were evaluated by the staff psychiatrist using the revised

* The variable of education, however, was not found to be related to case outcome. Neither were the other social background characteristics.

Inpatient Multidimensional Psychiatric Scale (the Lorr IMPS). This scale contains 10 factor syndromes; four combine to provide a schizophrenic disorganization morbidity score. The four sub-scales comprising the morbidity score are: motor disturbance, disorientation, conceptual disorganization, and retardation and apathy. According to the psychiatrist's ratings the mean schizophrenic disorganization score was 39.6 for the drug home care patients at admission, 48.6 for the placebo patients and 43.5 for the hospital controls. These scores were not

after. The results of the initial nurses' ratings were similar to those obtained by the psychiatrist. Two findings with regard to these nurses' ratings deserve mention. First, as has been found in other studies, the nurses consistently rated the same patients as significantly less impaired than the psychiatrist had rated them. Second, the nurses' ratings showed the placebo patients to be significantly more impaired than the drug home care patients (Table 3).

The psychological battery administered to the subjects at admission to the

TABLE 2   Previous Hospitalization Records of Drug, Placebo, and Hospital Control Patients

Category	N	Mean Number of Previous Hospital-izations	Percent No Previous Hospital-izations	Percent One or Two Previous Hospital-izations	Percent Three or More Previous Hospital-izations
Drug	57	1.93	19.3	54.4	26.3
Successes	44	1.75	22.7	54.5	22.7
Failures	13	2.54	7.7	53.8	38.5
Placebo	41	2.02	24.4	30.6	39.0
Successes	14	1.86	21.4	50.0	28.6
Failures	27	2.11	25.9	29.6	44.5
Hospital Controls	54	2.28	15.1	47.2	37.8

significantly different from each other, and all were higher than the one and two-rater mean scores obtained by Lorr for his norm sample of hospitalized patients. From this it may be concluded that according to the psychiatrist, at least, our patients did not constitute the more favorable risks or the less severely impaired.

The Lorr IMPS also was used by the nurses to rate the home care patients. These ratings were made on the first home visit and on specified visits there-

study and at specified subsequent intervals consisted of a sequential reaction time test, the Wechsler Adult Intelligence Scale, the Bender Gestalt and the Porteus Mazes. The results obtained in the initial administration suggest that the drug, placebo and hospital control patients did not systematically or consistently differ from each other on most of these measures.

In more specific terms, using the total of medians of 20 blocks of five trials each, the three groups did not statistically

TABLE 3   SCHIZOPHRENIC DISORGANIZATION (IMPS) MORBIDITY RATINGS BY PSYCHIA-
TRIST AND NURSES OF DRUG, PLACEBO, AND HOSPITAL CONTROL PATIENTS AT
ADMISSION

		Psychiatrist Ratings		Nurses' Ratings	
Category	N	M	σ	M	σ
Drug	57	39.6	20.3	16.9	16.6
Placebo	41	48.6	28.6	24.2*	18.1
Hospital Control	54	43.5	21.2		

* Significant at .05

differ from each other in reaction time. On the WAIS intelligence test, however, the hospital control patients scored significantly lower in IQ than the home care patients.[3] On the Bender Gestalt, with use of reciprocals of Z scores derived by Pascal and Suttell, the hospital control patients showed somewhat, but not significantly, more pathology than the home care patients.[4] Using the QE (error quotient) score on the Porteus Mazes, the controls showed significantly less pathology than the home care subjects. On the IQ score derived from the Porteus Mazes the hospital controls were found to be significantly lower in IQ than the home care patients, as would have been predicted from the WAIS. None of the groups, in other words, was loaded with the sicker patients or the poorer risks although the controls did not score quite as well as the others (Table 4).

RESULTS

HOME CARE VERSUS HOSPITAL CONTROL PATIENTS   In order to determine the effect of home care treatment as opposed to hospitalization, the experiences of the drug and placebo patients were contrasted with those of the hospitalized patients in the control group. After 30 months the findings indicated the superiority of home care treatment in terms of

TABLE 4   PSYCHOLOGICAL TEST SCORES OF DRUG, PLACEBO, AND HOSPITAL CONTROL
PATIENTS AT ADMISSION

	Log Reaction Time*		WAIS		Bender Gestalt (Reciprocal of Z)**		Porteus Mazes			
							QE†		IQ	
Category	M	σ	M	σ	M	σ	M	σ	M	σ
Drug	3.2860	166.7	81.2	16.4	107.5	24.9	61.0	16.3	80.7	32.5
Placebo	3.2965	176.8	80.1	19.1	99.9	26.3	58.4	12.8	80.8	32.0
Hospital Control	3.2748	131.5	72.6	17.2	97.0	34.8	55.7	15.2	68.0	28.9

* Composite of 20 blocks, five trials per block
** Reciprocal of Z for each patient
† Square root transformation of QE for each patient

the amount and percentage of time spent at home by home care and hospital control patients.

The 57 drug home care patients spent 28,601 days, or 90.2 per cent of their total time in the program, at home. The 41 placebo home care patients spent 18,327 days, or 80 per cent of their total days in the study, at home. The 54 hospital control patients spent 23,136 days, or 75 per cent of their project days, at home. With the experience of the hospital controls as the baseline we estimate that the placebo patients were saved 1156 days of hospitalization and the drug patients 4818 days during these 30 months. Most of these savings, of course, were a function of the prevention of initial hospitalization.

DRUG VERSUS PLACEBO HOME CARE SUCCESSFUL PATIENTS   During the period under study 44 of the 57 drug home care patients (77.2 per cent) remained continuously in the community. These 44 successful patients spent an average of 532.4 consecutive days at home. In contrast, significantly fewer of the placebo home care subjects (14 of 41, or 34.1 per cent) remained continuously at home during this period. These 14 successful placebo patients spent an average of 531.6 consecutive days at home.

Operationally defining failure as a hospital admission, the 13 drug home care failure patients experienced 30 hospital admissions and an average of 239.2 in-patient hospital days. The 27 placebo home care failures were hospitalized 45 times and spent an average of 169.2 days of in-patient hospital time. The 54 hospital control patients spent a mean of 83.4 days in initial hospitalization and an additional 59.1 days in 38 subsequent hospitalizations. Two other points deserve mention. First, the relative disparity between the percentage of successful

patients in the drug and placebo groups did not decrease significantly with time, as others studying ambulatory patients have reported.[5] Of the patients taken into the program before Dec. 1, 1962, 74.2 per cent of those in the drug and 27.3 per cent of those in the placebo group still were at home in April, 1964. Of the patients enrolled in the study after December, 1962, 80.8 per cent of those in the drug group and 42.1 per cent in the placebo group still were at home at the end of the study.

Second, as already indicated, drug failure patients spent more time in the hospital than placebo failures. This finding would lead to the conclusion that the drug failures were so very ill that medication in ordinarily adequate dosage could not maintain them at home. The placebo failures included not only such comparably sick patients but others who very probably could have succeeded in the community on drugs. These latter patients tended to reduce the average length of hospitalization of all placebo failure patients.

INITIAL PSYCHIATRIC AND PSYCHOLOGICAL EVALUATIONS AND SUCCESS   Using the initial Lorr IMPS ratings by the staff psychiatrist and the nurses of the home care patients, there was a pronounced trend for future successful patients to have been rated as less impaired than the future failures. This trend was observable in both home care groups (Table 5). Unfortunately the relatively small number of failure cases and the large intragroup variance precluded this trend from attaining statistical significance.

Except for the results on the Porteus Mazes error quotient, all of the other initial psychological test scores pointed in the direction of differentiating future successful from future failure patients in the drug group. On the sequential re-

TABLE 5   PSYCHOLOGICAL AND PSYCHIATRIC MEAN TEST SCORES OF SUCCESS AND FAIL-
URE PATIENTS AT ADMISSION

	Log Reaction Time** Mean	WAIS IQ Mean	Bender Gestalt Reciprocal of Z† Mean	Porteus Mazes		Psychiatrist Ratings IMPS Mean	Nurses' Ratings IMPS Mean
				QE‡ Mean	IQ Mean		
Drug							
Success	3.2575	81.3	109.4	60.8	83.3	38.4	14.6
Failure	3.2947	80.6	100.9	62.0	71.7	43.8	23.5
Placebo							
Success	3.2164	87.3	112.2	58.8	96.8	49.3	19.1
Failure	3.3365*	76.5	93.1*	57.5	73.1*	48.3	26.8

* Denotes statistical significance at .05
** Composite of 20 blocks, five trials per block
† Reciprocal of Z for each subject
‡ Square root transformation of QE for each subject

action time test and the Bender Gestalt the future failures were slower in reaction time and showed greater pathology. The future drug failures also were lower in IQ than the future drug successes on both the WAIS and the Porteus Mazes. In the placebo group future success and failures were significantly different from one another in reaction time on the Bender Gestalt and on the Porteus Mazes IQ.

Thus, the initial Lorr scale psychiatric evaluations were more likely to distinguish success and failure in the drug home care group, and the initial psychological evaluations were more likely to discriminate the successes and failures in the placebo home care group. By preventing the hospitalization of many patients of moderately severe initial psychiatric impairment, drug intervention probably introduced a much greater degree of variability into the psychological test scores of the successes and thereby reduced predictability. In the placebo group successes were more homogeneous in test scores measuring pathology and

therefore predictability was likely to be greater. Psychiatric ratings, being more directly focused on classical pathological symptoms, were more likely to screen out the very severely impaired for whom even drug intervention is inadequate to prevent hospitalization.

DISCUSSION

The results at the end of this controlled study indicated that an intervention program using pubic health nursing practices and psychoactive drugs can prevent hospitalization of three-fourths or more of seriously ill schizophrenics whose families are willing to supervise them at home. It should be added, however, that while we have demonstrated that it is possible to prevent hospitalization, we do not as yet know whether the successful home care patients functioned at any higher level than the discharged hospital control patients. This problem will be examined in future reports.

Experience also showed that after the drug patients had remained successfully at home for six months, their success rate did not greatly decline with additional exposure ranging upwards of two years in some instances. There were several reasons for this, but perhaps the two most important were the changes in medication available to the psychiatrist and the enormous effort expended by the field staff in conserving home care patients.

A comparison of the drug and placebo home care patients left little doubt about the importance of drug medication in preventing institutionalization. The experience of the placebo patients tended to approximate more closely that of the hospital controls than of the drug home care subjects. The combination of the public health nurse and the placebo effect became increasingly attenuated with time. Even the support, advice and services provided by the nurse on her home visits to patient and family soon proved insufficient to prevent hospitalization. This rapid waning of the "placebo effect" was clearly demonstrated by the fact that 21 of the 27 placebo failures were hospitalized within the first six months after admission to the program.

One final aspect should be mentioned at this time. This concerns the monetary cost of a program such as has been described. Without going into elaborate fiscal details, a similar home care program with a case load of 400 patients, but without research and evaluation procedures, would not be substantially less expensive than the present U.S. per capita mental hospital operating outlays of approximately $5 per patient-day. It is estimated that a clinic serving 400 schizophrenic home care patients would require the services of a full-time psychiatrist, a clinical psychologist, two psychiatric social workers and eight public health nurses as well as psychiatric aides and secretarial personnel.

The addition of any care facilities such as a sheltered workshop, family counseling services or an occupational therapy program would add substantially to the costs involved in home care treatment. An even modestly enriched program realistically would cost more per capita than present patient expenditures, but probably still less than services in state hospital admission and treatment units which average about $15 to $20 a day. In view of these cost factors if for no other reason, it becomes mandatory that the efficacy of each component in any suggested home care program be determined through careful research before it becomes permanent.

Thus, home care programs will not materially reduce the financial problems besetting mental institutions. However these home care programs will (a) prevent the hospitalization of a very significant number of schizophrenics; (b) provide continuous care for patients including regular visits from a public health nurse, contact with a psychiatrist and psychologist and community services through a social worker; (c) prevent most patients from experiencing the problems associated with hospitalization; (d) educate families to develop a more accepting stance or attitude toward the patient, and (e) reduce to some extent the need for providing ever more beds at an approximate average cost of $5000 each for the care of the mentally ill.

REFERENCES

1. Scarpitti, F. R., et al. 1964. Problems in a home care study for schizophrenics. Arch. Gen Psychiat. 10(2):143–154.
2. See also Pasamanick, B., et. al. 1964. Home versus hospital care for schizophrenics: a controlled study of the use of drugs and public health nursing care.

Jour. Amer. Med. Assoc. 187(1): 177–181.

3. The WAIS scores were prorated from six subtests. See Karras, A. 1963. Predicting full scale WAIS IQs from WAIS subtests for a psychiatric population. Jour. Clin. Psychol. 19(1):100.

4. Pascal, G., and B. J. Suttell. 1951. The Bender Gestalt Test: Quantification and Validity for Adults. Grune and Stratton, New York.

5. Engelhardt, D. M. 1964. Phenothiazines in the prevention of psychiatric hospitalization. Arch. Gen. Psychiat. 11(2):162.

7

Crime

DEFINING CRIME

As most people know, crime is the violation of a law. However, the violation
of most laws does not constitute a crime because the majority of our laws
are civil statutes. Civil or "tort" law is enforced by the courts when a person seeks compensation for an alleged injury to himself or his property.[1]
To be found guilty of the violation of civil law may mean the paying of
damages to the injured party. In such cases the court acts to arbitrate a
dispute between two individuals who are attempting to settle a private
wrong.

Unlike a civil wrong, a crime violates a criminal statute. Theoretically
criminal law embodies those norms that society cherishes most and that it
feels must be maintained for the protection of the entire group. Hence,
when a crime is committed it is the state which acts as the injured party
and seek to redress the wrong by apprehending and punishing the offender.
Four factors—politicality, specificity, uniformity, and penal sanction—characterize criminal statutes and distinguish them from other rules of human
conduct.[2]

First, criminal laws must be enacted by some group with duly constituted
political authority. Hence, only federal, state, or municipal legislative bodies
are empowered to enact criminal statutes. Although various formal groups
and associations may bind their members to specific rules and regulations,
these are not criminal laws because they are not made by the state. Second,
criminal statutes must be specific. They must specify in some detail just
what is prohibited and under what conditions particular acts constitute law
violation. Third, uniformity implies that criminal laws are applicable to
everyone within the enacting political authority's jurisdiction. What is a

crime for one person should be a crime for all who violate the rule regardless of class, position, or other such factors. Fourth, all criminal statutes include a penal sanction or the specification of punishment. Unlike civil law, criminal law always specifies the punishment to be meted out to offenders, although the court may be given the opportunity to choose from several punishment alternatives.

In addition to the violation of a criminal statute, an act must also be overt and the result of criminal intent before it can be considered a crime. No crime is committed until one actually violates a law or attempts to do so, although in certain cases conspiring to commit a criminal act is considered illegal. In combination with the criminal act there must also be criminal intent or *mens rea*. The concept of *mens rea*, commonly known as "guilty mind," means that there can be no crime without actual intent on the part of the violator. For example, a person who is not mentally responsible for his behavior is not capable of committing a crime. It is for this reason that courts recognize insanity as an exception to the *mens rea* doctrine. Under the M'Naghten rule that has been applicable in American jurisprudence for many years a person cannot be found guilty of a crime if it can be shown that at the time of the act he was unable to distinguish between right and wrong.[3] However, the ability to know right from wrong has been an unsatisfactory basis for exception from criminal responsibility since it is difficult to determine in retrospect and since it accounts for only a small number of mentally ill law violators. As a result, some states recognize irresistible impulse as a basis for exemption from criminal responsibility and, recently, the United States Circuit Court of Appeals has ruled that no criminal responsibility can be fixed if a violation is the result of mental illness or mental incapacity.[4]

Other conditions that may exclude a person from criminal responsibility even though a legal code has been violated are juvenile status, self defense, negligence, duress, or ignorance of the true facts. Many critics have pointed out that the doctrine of intent may be eroding as a condition of crime. In some states the law provides that persons may be convicted of certain crimes without criminal intent being established. This, unfortunately, has long been the situation in cases of vehicular homicide resulting from negligence or intoxication.

Crimes are usually classified on the basis of their seriousness. Major crimes, known as felonies, include such offenses as murder, assault, rape, and grand larceny and are punishable by imprisonment for more than one year. Less serious offenses, known as misdemeanors, are punishable by incarceration for less than one year. Offenses such as petty larceny, public drunkenness, and traffic violations are included in this classification.

THE EXTENT OF CRIME

Knowledge about the amount of crime in the United States comes from the annual report of the Federal Bureau of Investigation which compiles crime statistics submitted voluntarily by police departments throughout the nation. These *Uniform Crime Reports* are the only authoritative source of nationwide data regarding crimes known to the police and arrests made for violations of the legal code. The crimes of murder and nonnegligent manslaughter, forcible rape, robbery, aggravated assault, burglary, larceny of $50 or more, and auto theft are used as an index to determine the nature and extent of the crime problem. In 1964[5] there was an estimated total of 2,604,000 crimes in these categories representing an increase of 13 percent over 1963. The rate of crime per 100,000 residents of the United States was 1,361.2, ranging from a low 4.8 for homicide to a high of 508.4 for burglary.

TABLE 1. Estimated Number and Rate of Major Crimes Known to the Police, 1964*

Offense	Number	Rate per 100,000 Population
Murder and nonnegligent manslaughter	9,249	4.8
Forcible rape	20,551	10.7
Robbery	111,753	58.4
Aggravated assault	184,908	96.6
Burglary	1,110,458	580.4
Larceny ($50 and over)	704,536	368.2
Auto theft	462,971	242.0
Total offenses	2,604,426	1,361.2

*Source: *Uniform Crime Reports, 1964*, p. 49. Rates are based on a total population base of 191,334,000.

The property crimes of burglary, larceny, and auto theft accounted for 87 percent of the total major offenses, up 13 percent over 1963 and 61 percent over 1958. On the other hand, the crimes of murder and nonnegligent manslaughter, forcible rape, robbery, and aggravated assault accounted for 13 percent of the total offenses, a 15 percent increase as a group over 1963 and a 40 percent increase over 1958. Since 1958 crime has increased six times faster than the population.[6]

Statistics regarding the number of arrests made for specific violations present a similar picture of the extent of crime.[7] Although the number of arrests made is never as great as the number of crimes known to the police, the total for 1964 reported to the F.B.I. by over 3000 police agencies was in excess of three million, up 2.1 percent over 1963. However, as Table 2 shows, most of these arrests were not for the most serious personal and property offenses.

Certain uniformities are found in crime rates which help us to understand its distribution through the social system.[8] For example, rates of crime are uniformly much higher in urban areas than in rural areas. In addition, rates of crime are much higher for men than they are for women. Age is also an important factor in the crime rates since adolescents have a higher rate than

TABLE 2. Total Adult Arrest Trends for 1963 and 1964 as Reported to the F.B.I. by 3,115 Urban Police Departments*

Offense Charged	1963	1964	Percent Change
Criminal homicide	7,142	7,553	+5.4
Forcible rape	6,937	6,826	−1.6
Robbery	25,325	26,258	+3.7
Aggravated assault	53,005	61,515	+16.1
Burglary	74,026	80,187	+8.3
Larceny ($50 and over)	134,613	146,103	+8.5
Auto theft	27,805	30,666	+10.3
Other assaults	141,398	147,183	+4.1
Forgery and counterfeiting	23,731	23,908	+.7
Embezzlement and fraud	43,565	46,383	+6.5
Stolen property: buying, receiving, possessing	9,387	10,767	+14.7
Weapons: carrying, possessing, etc.	30,226	33,907	+12.2
Prostitution and commercialized advice	24,490	26,594	+8.6
Sex offenses (except forcible rape and prostitution)	42,354	40,296	−4.9
Narcotic drug laws	25,562	32,930	+28.8
Gambling	97,168	98,492	+1.4
Offenses against family and children	48,629	49,545	+1.9
Driving under the influence of alcohol	182,232	193,399	+6.1
Liquor laws	89,160	101,247	+13.6
Drunkenness	1,311,593	1,309,034	−.2
Disorderly conduct	373,027	363,131	−2.7
Vagrance	121,912	114,974	−5.7
All other offenses (except traffic)	327,080	337,499	+3.2
Suspicion	58,898	64,280	+9.1
Total	3,220,367	3,288,397	+2.1

*Source: *Uniform Crime Reports, 1964*, p. 110.

adults and middle-aged adults a much higher rate than the elderly. As one might expect, the crime rates of the lower class are a great deal higher than those of the middle class or upper class. And finally, certain ethnic and racial groups, such as Negroes, Italians, and Irish, presently have very high rates of crime while others, such as the Japanese, Chinese, and Jewish, have much lower rates.

Without a doubt, the total volume of known crimes and arrests made in the United States is increasing yearly and at a much faster rate than population increases. On the surface these statistics would lead us to believe that there is actually more lawlessness now than at any time in the past. This may not be completely accurate when the current increase in the number of known crimes is viewed in the light of improved detection methods employed by police agencies, the redefinition of formerly quasi-legal behavior as illegal, greater dependence upon criminal law as a social control technique, and similar factors that might help to explain the apparent increase.[9] We do know, however, that crimes go unreported and the official crime rate would go zooming upward were they to become part of the police record.

Two important studies give some indication of the great amount of unreported crime. In the first study,[10] a questionnaire was administered to a sample of 1698 "law-abiding" persons, 1020 men and 678 women. They were asked if they ever committed any of 49 offenses deemed illegal by New York State law. Included in the list of offenses were items such as disorderly conduct, assault, robbery, illegal possession of firearms, bribery, fraud, tax evasion, extortion, and criminal libel. Men in the sample over the age of 16 admitted to having committed an average of 18 offenses. For the female members of the sample the average number of offenses was 11 per person. In all, 64 percent of the men and 29 percent of the women admitted to having committed at least one felony.

In the second study,[11] 337 nondelinquent college students were compared with 2049 juveniles charged with delinquency by the juvenile court. The nondelinquent college students were asked if they had ever committed any of 55 offenses with which the adjudicated delinquents had been charged. The students reported that they had averaged 17.6 offenses, and for almost every offense the percentage of college students who reported the offense was greater than the percentage of delinquents charged with the same offense.[12]

Although the methodological difficulties inherent in research of this type raise questions about the accuracy of resulting generalizations, these studies do indicate that the number of law violations actually committed is far in excess of the number officially known. What the actual difference is remains unknown. The important thing to remember is that the mere violation of a law does not by itself make one a criminal. These studies suggest that while many people violate the criminal law, it is a relatively small proportion who do so repeatedly and come to be defined by themselves and others as criminals.

SOME EXPLANATIONS OF CRIME

Ever since Cesare Lombroso made the first scientific attempt to explain criminal behavior, scientists in many disciplines have evolved theories and conducted research designed to solve the mystery of this particular type of human behavior.[13] Much of the earliest work concentrated on the role of biological factors in criminality. In essence, these theories attempted to explain crime on the basis of heredity and physical constitution.[14] It was felt that certain persons possess specific constitutional weaknesses that are inherited and which predispose the individual to criminal behavior. Individuals who are born with such characteristics cannot live a normal or law-abiding life because of their innate physical and mental deficiencies. The body-type approach, a variation of the biological approach, maintains that it is the individual's general morphological structure and not specific physical characteristics which determines a predisposition to crime.[15]

Psychologists and psychiatrists have also made major contributions to the collection of etiological theories.[16] Psychologists generally attempt to explain crime by focusing on the relationship between criminal behavior and the intelligence of the offender or by probing into the criminal's personality to determine his "unique" traits and needs. On the other hand, psychiatric approaches to crime are based on psychoanalytic theory and are similar to the psychiatric explanations of mental illness mentioned in the last chapter. Specifically, crime is viewed as the symptom of a deep emotional disorder or problem resulting from inner conflicts and guilt.

The biological, psychological, and psychiatric approaches, at least in their most orthodox forms, place causal emphasis on the individual and individual characteristics. Factors external to the individual are de-emphasized if not completely disregarded. This is in sharp contrast to the sociological explanations of crime which place primary emphasis on those factors that are seen as the framework within which criminal behavior becomes meaningful. Sociological theories stress the importance of values and norms because, as Matza has indicated, ". . . values and norms serve as directives to action and that, despite the complexity involved in the emergence of beliefs, once presented they commit adherents to lines of actions."[17] The traditional sociological frame of reference has seen the social deviate as a "normal" person who is pressured into deviancy because he is influenced by a "bad environment."

The breakdown of social organization and the resulting social disorganization or anomie that characterizes many slum and transitional areas is thought to be fertile ground for the growth of norm-violating behavior.[18] But, seeing crime as an expression of social disorganization does not explain how individuals come to take up law-violating behavior. One important criticism of the disorganization theory has focused upon its inability to explain differential responses to the problems of the social structure. It does not account for individuals who experience environmental pressures toward crime but who do not become criminal. Even in the most disorganized area, many, probably most, do not violate the law and conform reasonably well to the social norms. Hence, several attempts have been made to explain the process by which cirminal behavior is derived from general environmental conditions. One of the original and most important explanations of this sort has been offered by Edwin Sutherland.[19]

Sutherland conceived of criminality as participation in a cultural tradition and as the result of association with representatives of that tradition. He believed that criminal behavior is learned just as any other type of behavior is learned and that it is learned through association and interaction with others who are already criminal. The person becomes criminal once he has internalized the criminal skills and attitudes he has been exposed to in intimate, primary associations with law violators. Sutherland's theory of "differential association" was originally stated in terms of nine principles:

1. Criminal behavior is learned, not inherited. Therefore, an individual who commits an offense has to be trained in this kind of action.
2. Criminal behavior is learned in interaction with other persons in a process of communication.
3. The learning of criminal behavior occurs primarily within intimate, primary groups. Impersonal communication is unimportant in passing on such behavior.
4. Learning criminal behavior includes not only specific techniques for violating the law, but it also includes attitudes, motives, drives, and rationalizations for law violation.
5. Learning criminal behavior also includes the division of legal codes into favorable (those that should be observed) and unfavorable (those that can be violated.)
6. A person becomes criminal when he has internalized more definitions that are favorable to the violation of law than definitions that are unfavorable to the violation of law. Since a person assimilates the surrounding culture, criminal behavior implies contact with criminal patterns and little association with noncriminal patterns.
7. Differential associations vary in priority, frequency, duration, and intensity. That is, associations vary in terms of when in life they occur, how often they occur, how long they occur, and the meaningfulness of the association to the individual.
8. The process by which criminal patterns are learned is precisely the same as the process by which noncriminal patterns are learned. It is the content of the learning and not the mechanisms by which it is learned that differs.
9. Since both criminal and noncriminal behavior patterns are motivated by the same needs and values, criminal behavior cannot be explained by them. While the motivation for each type of behavior is the same, the expression of the motivation differs.

Sutherland used his theory of differential association to account for all types of crime, regardless of the social characteristics of the offender. All law violators were seen as reflecting the behavioral patterns of the groups with which they have prolonged and meaningful relations. If the behavioral patterns learned in association with others happened to be criminal, then the individual will become a criminal. Of course, there is much more opportunity for the individual to have criminal associations in disorganized areas that have high crime and delinquency rates than in areas that are socially integrated and stable.

Impressed with Sutherland's theory of differential association and yet recognizing some of its shortcomings, Glaser attempted to establish a hypothesis that would answer some of the unsolved questions posed by this theory. Unlike Sutherland he used the personality factor as an essential causal element.[20] Glaser supplemented Sutherland's theory by including "role-taking imagery" and refers to it as a differential identification process. Glaser believed that different persons identify with deviant elements to different degrees even though the amount of association is the same. Taken into account by Glaser's theory is the effect of past identification, attitudes, and other factors. Differential identification is less rigid than differential association since identification may shift with role and status changes during social interaction.

Similarly, Cressey holds that the individual is motivated by previously conceived rationalizations that result from past interpersonal relationships.[21] When these rationalizations develop well, they give the individual justification and support for his behavior. If the individual sees himself to be subject to a particular behavioral pattern, he will automatically perform this behavior. Hence, in his study of embezzlers, Cressey states:

> Trusted persons become trust violators when they conceive of themselves as having a financial problem which is nonsharable, are aware that this problem can be secretly resolved by violation of the position of financial trust, and are able to apply to their own conduct in that situation verbalizations which enable them to adjust their conceptions of themselves as users of the entrusted funds or property.[22]

A more recent attempt to combine individual and social factors to explain behavior has been made by Walter C. Reckless. Reckless' "containment theory"[23] specifies an inner control system and an outer control system which are able or unable to work alone or together to handle the forces conducive to crime. The outer control system refers to the individual's social world, the external social structure designed to guide his behavior in a socially approved manner. Inner controls on the other hand consist mainly of self components which provide an internal buffer protecting against deviation. These two control systems should form a solid, united front against the adversities and pressures of the environment.

In industrial societies external containment resides primarily in the family and other groups in which the individual participates. When the outer controls are adequate they will contain the individual and prevent deviation. When they are inadequate and structural supports cannot contain the individual, the inner control system must serve to hold the person in line. Its ability to do this is dependent upon the presence of either a good or poor self-concept.

According to Reckless, the direction of socialization and the resulting good or bad concept of self are the chief factors responsible for a person's insulation against deviancy or his involvement in unlawful behavior. This is especially true in those areas characterized by great social disorganization. Here the outer controls on one's behavior are weak if they have not completely broken down and the direction of his actions will be dependent upon his self-image. Since the self-concept is a composite of the person's interactive experience, his chances for developing a positive self-feeling are much less in a bad environment than they would be in an adequate social environment.

Weaknesses in the two containing systems are not seen as "causes" of crime. The "causes" or contributing factors may be delinquent companions, lower-class status, unstable family life, or any other factor that has been suggested. The containing systems serve as the individual's insulation or protection against those forces that might influence him toward criminality. When these are weak the person is vulnerable and might succumb. When these are strong he is likely to remain law-abiding despite the environmental pressures.

Although rules in the form of codified laws are the ballast of social order, they are often violated and society has long been concerned about such violations. As a result, great efforts have been made to determine the causes of crime, but, as yet, they are still not entirely known. To the sociologist, most crime is viewed as one of several behavioral alternatives that may result from the tensions produced by disorganizing social conditions such as slums, poverty, unemployment, delinquent companions, or unstable families. Through the processes of differential association or differential identification or lack of containment, some people choose the criminal alternative as a way of reducing the situationally induced tensions. Preventing and controlling crime is largely a matter of influencing such choices and steering them in a nondeviant direction.

WHAT CAN BE DONE?

Crime prevention is something of a misnomer generally used to refer to juvenile delinquency-prevention programs, since there are few programs designed specifically to prevent adult crime. Instead, the emphasis is on correction and rehabilitation of the individual once he has broken the law and been convicted because the violator is now known and placed in a situation where he can be worked with regardless of his desire for "help."

In the first reading Jackson Toby examines the social control function of punishment which has been used since time immemorial as group response to norm deviation and more recently thought of as a preventive technique. He indicates that the fear of punishment does serve to control the behavior of some people. Others have developed internal control mechanisms through adequate socialization or for some reason do not fear the anticipated punishment. In addition, "punishing" or "treating" criminal offenders serves to sustain the morale of conformists because, in either case, the offender has not gotten away with his misdeed and thereby is not a role model to be emulated. Punishment, then, has more significance for conformists than for deviants since it is Toby's conclusion that as practiced today punishment is an obstacle to truly rehabilitating the offender.

In the second reading H. Ashley Weeks acquaints us with some of the history of treating criminals. He traces the development of punishment and the prison system from Beccaria and Bentham, the first to link rationally theories of crime causation with control measures, to the present, concluding that punishment still remains the basic philosophy of correction. Although techniques are more humane and less brutal today, overcrowding, lack of a professional staff, untrained nonprofessionals, and limited budgets mitigate against meaningful treatment. The large institution is also detrimental to rehabilitation. However, Weeks does offer several examples of programs that are based on "modern conceptions of changing human behavior" and he indicates that rehabilitation of offenders is not impossible under the right conditions.

In the third reading Donald R. Cressey shows the theoretical basis for using criminals in the rehabilitation of other criminals. Combining the principles of differential association and symbolic interaction, the role of verbalizations in determining attitudes and consequent social behavior, he contends that criminal conduct will change only when the criminal avoids some verbalizations and acquires others. These processes occur most readily when "criminals become active members of intimate groups whose verbalizations make all criminality as guilt-producing, shameful, repulsive, and impossible as, say, cannibalism." Criminals who have rejected deviant attitudes and behaviors are uniquely able to help others in the rehabilitative process. When so doing, they are not only agents of change, but also the target of such change and commit themselves further to anticriminal verbalizations. This approach to rehabilitation is the essence of most types of group therapy and is becoming increasingly useful in efforts to change social behavior.

Lastly, Stanley P. Grupp describes a program which was originated in Wisconsin in 1913 but has only recently found greater acceptance and applicability. Work release means that prisoners are able to work at regular jobs outside of the prison during a portion of the day. Such programs are part of the recent move to de-emphasize the institution as a cure-all and to get inmates back into the community and functioning as quickly as possible. Although most states that provide for work release extend it only to misdemenants, three states now include felons and it seems probable that this number will soon grow. As Grupp points out, the advantages of work release are numerous and it is certainly a positive alternative to the meaninglessness of incarceration.

REFERENCES

1. Edwin H. Sutherland and Donald R. Cressey, *Principles of Criminology*. Philadelphia: J. B. Lippincott Company, 1966, pp. 7–8. Chapter 1 contains an excellent discussion of "Criminology and Criminal Law."
2. Sutherland and Cressey, pp. 5–8.
3. Sheldon Glueck, "Mental Illness and Criminal Responsibility," *Journal of Social Therapy*, 2 (1956), pp. 134–157.
4. Elmer H. Johnson, *Crime, Correction and Society*. Homewood, Ill.: The Dorsey Press, 1964, p. 130.
5. Federal Bureau of Investigation, United States Department of Justice, *Uniform Crime Reports*, 1964. Washington, D.C.: Government Printing Office, 1964, pp. 1, 2–3, 49.
6. Federal Bureau of Investigation, pp. 1, 2.
7. Federal Bureau of Investigation, pp. 105, 110.

8. Donald R. Cressey, "Crime", in Robert K. Merton and Robert A. Nisbet (eds.), *Contemporary Social Problems*. New York: Harcourt, Brace & World, Inc., 1966, pp. 146–160.
9. Johnson, pp. 54–58.
10. James S. Wallerstein and Clement J. Wyle, "Our Law-Abiding Lawbreakers," *Probation*, 25 (March–April 1947), pp. 107–112.
11. Austin L. Porterfield, "Delinquency and Its Outcome in Court and College," *American Journal of Sociology*, 49 (November 1943), pp. 199–208.
12. Porterfield, pp. 201–202.
13. For a concise discussion of the early theories of crime see George B. Vold, *Theoretical Crimonology*. New York: Oxford University Press, 1958, Chaps. 1 and 2.
14. Vold, Chap. 3.
15. See, for example, Ernest A. Hooton, *Crime and the Man*. Cambridge, Mass.: Harvard University Press, 1939, and William H. Sheldon, *Varieties of Delinquent Youth*. New York: Harper & Row, Publishers. 1949.
16. Walter C. Reckless has an excellent discussion of what he calls "psychogenie explanations" of crime in *The Crime Problem*. New York: Appleton-Century-Crofts, Inc., 1961, Chap. 15.
17. David Matza, *Delinquency and Drift*. New York: John Wiley & Sons, Inc., 1964, p. 18.
18. Clifford R. Shaw and Henry D. McKay, *Juvenile Delinquency and Urban Areas*. Chicago: University of Chicago Press, 1942.
19. Sutherland and Cressey, pp. 79–98.
20. Daniel Glaser, "Criminality Theories and Behavioral Images," *American Journal of Sociology*, 61 (March 1956), pp. 433–444.
21. Donald R. Cressey, *Other People's Money*. New York: The Free Press of Glencoe, 1953.
22. Cressey, pp. 27–30.
23. Reckless, Chap. 18.

ADDITIONAL READINGS

Cressey, Donald R., "Crime" in R. K. Merton and R. A. Nisbet (eds.) *Contemporary Social Problems*. New York: Harcourt, Brace & World, Inc., 1966, pp. 136–192.

Dynes, Russell, Alfred C. Clarke, Simon Dinitz and Iwao Ishino, *Social Problems: Dissensus and Deviation in an Industrial Society*. New York: Oxford University Press, 1964, Chaps. 16, 17, 18.

Gibbons, Don C., *Changing the Lawbreaker*. Englewood Cliffs, N.J.: Prentice-Hall, Inc., 1965.

Johnston, Norman, Leonard Savitz and Marvin E. Wolfgang, *The Sociology of Punishment and Correction*. New York: John Wiley & Sons, Inc., 1962.

Reckless, Walter C., *The Crime Problem*. New York: Appleton-Century-Crofts, Inc., 1961.

Sutherland, Edwin H., and Donald R. Cressey, *Principles of Criminology*. Philadelphia: J. B. Lippincott Company, 1966.

Sykes, Gresham M., *The Society of Captives*. Princeton, N.J.: Princeton University Press, 1958.

Vold, George B., *Theoretical Criminology*. New York: Oxford University Press, 1958.

Wolfgang, Marvin E., Leonard Savitz and Norman Johnston, *The Sociology of Crime and Delinquency*. New York: John Wiley & Sons, Inc., 1962.

IS PUNISHMENT NECESSARY?*

Jackson Toby

Of 11 contemporary textbooks in criminology written by sociologists, ten have one or more chapters devoted to the punishment of offenders.[1] All ten include a history of methods of punishment in Western society and, more specifically, a discussion of capital punishment. Seven discuss punishment in pre-literate societies. Seven include theoretical or philosophical discussions of the "justification" of punishment—usually in terms of "retribution," "deterrence," and "reformation." These theoretical analyses are at least as much indebted to law and philosophy as to sociology. Thus, in considering the basis for punishment, three textbooks refer both to Jeremy Bentham and to Emile Durkheim; three textbooks refer to Bentham but not to Durkheim; and one textbook refers to Durkheim but not to Bentham. Several textbook writers express their opposition to punishment,

especially to cruel punishment. This opposition is alleged to be based on an incompatibility of punishment with scientific considerations. The following quotation is a case in point:

We still punish primarily for vengeance, or to deter, or in the interest of a 'just' balance of accounts between 'deliberate' evildoers on the one hand and an injured and enraged society on the other. We do not yet generally punish or treat as scientific criminology would imply, namely, in order to change antisocial attitudes into social attitudes.[2]

Most of the textbook writers note with satisfaction that "the trend in modern countries has been toward humanizing punishment and toward the reduction of brutalities."[3] They point to the decreased use of capital punishment, the introduction of amenities into the modern prison by enlightened penology, and the increasing emphasis on nonpunitive and individualized methods of dealing with offenders, e.g., probation, parole, psychotherapy. In short, students reading these textbooks might infer that punishment is a vestigial carry-over of a barbaric past and will disappear as humanitarianism and rationality spread. Let us examine this inference in terms of the motives underlying punishment and the necessities of social control.

* This article is a revised version of a paper presented to the 1959 meeting of the Eastern Sociological Society.

[1] Barnes & Teeters, *New Horizons in Criminology* (3d ed. 1959); Caldwell, *Criminology* (1956); Cavan, *Criminology* (1955); Elliot, *Crime in Modern Society* (1952); Korn & McCorkle, *Criminology and Penology* (1959); Reckless, *The Crime Problem* (2d ed. 1955); Sutherland & Cressey, *Principles of Criminology* (5th ed. 1955); Taft, *Criminology* (3d ed. 1956); Tappan, *Crime, Justice and Correction* (1960); von Hentig, *Crime: Causes and Conditions* (1947); Wood & Waite, *Crime and Its Treatment* (1941).

[2] Taft, *op. cit. supra* note 1, at 359.
[3] Reckless, *op. cit. supra* note 1, at 450.

THE URGE TO PUNISH

Many crimes have identifiable victims. In the case of crimes against the person, physical or psychic injuries have been visited upon the victim. In the case of crimes against property, someone's property has been stolen or destroyed. In pressing charges against the offender, the victim may express hostility against the person who injured him in a socially acceptable way. Those who identify with the victim—not only his friends and family but those who can imagine the same injury being done to them—may join with him in clamoring for the punishment of the offender. If, as has been argued, the norm of reciprocity is fundamental to human interaction, this hostility of the victim constituency toward offenders is an obstacle to the elimination of punishment from social life.[4] Of course, the size of the group constituted by victims and those who identify with victims may be small. Empirical study would probably show that it varies by offense. Thus, it is possible that nearly everyone identifies with the victim of a murderer but relatively few people with the victim of a blackmailer. The greater the size of the victim constituency, the greater the opposition to a non-punitive reaction to the offender.

It would be interesting indeed to measure the size and the composition of the victim constituencies for various crimes. Take rape as an illustration. Since the victims of rape are females, we might hypothesize that *women* would express greater punitiveness toward rapists than *men* and that degrees of hostility would correspond to real or imaginary exposure

to rape. Thus, pretty young girls might express more punitiveness toward rapists than homely women. Among males, we might predict that greater punitiveness would be expressed by those with more reason to identify with the victims. Thus, males having sisters or daughters in the late teens or early twenties might express more punitiveness toward rapists than males lacking vulnerable "hostages to fortune."

Such a study might throw considerable light on the wellsprings of punitive motivation, particularly if victimization reactions were distinguished from other reasons for punitiveness. One way to explore such motivation would be to ask the same respondents to express their punitive predispositions toward offenses which do not involve victims at all, e.g., gambling, or which involve victims of a quite different kind. Thus, rape might be balanced by an offense the victims of which are largely male. Survey research of this type is capable of ascertaining the opposition to milder penalties for various offenses. It would incidentally throw light on the comparatively gentle societal reaction to white-collar crime. Perhaps the explanation lies in the difficulty of identifying with the victims of patent infringement or watered hams.[5]

THE SOCIAL CONTROL FUNCTIONS OF PUNISHMENT

Conformists who identify with the *victim* are motivated to punish the offender out of some combination of rage and fear. Conformists who identify with the *offender*, albeit unconsciously, may wish to punish him for quite different reasons.

---

4 Gouldner, *The Norm of Reciprocity: A Preliminary Statement*, 25 Am. Soc. Rev. 161 (1960).

5 In this connection, it is well to recall that there is less reluctance to steal from corporations than from humans. See A. W. Jones, *Life, Liberty, and Property* (1941).

Whatever the basis for the motivation to punish, the existence of punitive reactions to deviance is an obstacle to the abolition to punishment. However, it is by no means the sole obstacle. Even though a negligible segment of society felt punitive toward offenders, it might still not be feasible to eliminate punishment if the social control of deviance depended on it. Let us consider, therefore, the consequences of punishing offenders for (a) preventing crime, (b) sustaining the morale of conformists, and (c) rehabilitating offenders.

Punishment as a Means of Crime Prevention

Durkheim defined punishment as an act of vengeance. "What we avenge, what the criminal expiates, is the outrage to morality."[6] But why is vengeance necessary? Not because of the need to deter the bulk of the population from doing likewise. The socialization process prevents most deviant behavior. Those who have introjected the moral norms of their society cannot commit crimes because their self-concepts will not permit them to do so. Only the unsocialized (and therefore amoral) individual fits the model of classical criminology and is deterred from expressing deviant impulses by a nice calculation of pleasures and punishments.[7] Other things being equal, the anticipation of punishment would seem to have more deterrent value for inadequately socialized members of the group. It is difficult to investigate this proposition empirically because other motivationally relevant factors are usually varying simultaneously, e.g., the situational temptations confronting various individuals, their optimism about the chances of escaping detection, and the differential impact of the same punishment on individuals of different status.[8] Clearly, though, the deterrent effect of anticipated punishments is a complex empirical problem, and Durkheim was not interested in it. Feeling as he did that *some* crime is normal in every society, he apparently decided that the crime prevention function of punishment is not crucial. He pointed out that minute gradation in punishment would not be necessary if punishment were simply a means of deterring the potential offender (crime prevention). "Robbers are as strongly inclined to rob as murderers are to murder; the resistance offered by the former is not less than that of the latter, and consequently, to control it, we would have recourse to the same means."[9] Durkheim was factually correct; the offenses punished most severely are not necessarily the ones which present the greatest problem of social defense. Thus, quantitatively speaking, murder is an unimportant cause of death; in the United States it claims only half as many lives annually as does suicide and only one-fifth the toll of automobile accidents. Furthermore, criminologists have been unable to demonstrate a relationship between the murder rate of a community and its use or lack of use of capital punishment.

Most contemporary sociologists would agree with Durkheim that the anticipation of punishment is not the first line of defense against crime. The socialization process keeps most people law abiding, not the police—if for no other reason than the police are not able to catch every

[6] Durkheim, *The Division of Labor in Society* 89 (1947).
[7] Parsons, *The Structure of Social Action* 402-03 (1939).

[8] Toby, *Social Disorganization and Stake in Conformity: Complementary Factors in the Predatory Behavior of Young Hoodlums*, 48 J. Crim. L., C. & P.S. 12 (1957).
[9] *Op. cit. supra* note 6, at 88.

offender. This does not mean, however, that the police could be disbanded. During World War II, the Nazis deported all of Denmark's police force, thus providing a natural experiment testing the deterrent efficacy of formal sanctions.[10] Crime increased greatly. Even though punishment is uncertain, especially under contemporary urban conditions, the possibility of punishment keeps some conformists law-abiding. The empirical question is: *How many* conformists would become deviants if they did not fear punishment?

Punishment as a Means of Sustaining the Morale of Conformists

Durkheim considered punishment indispensable as a means of containing the demoralizing consequences of the crimes that could not be prevented. Punishment was not for Durkheim mere vindictiveness. Without punishment Durkheim anticipated the demoralization of "upright people" in the face of defiance of the collective conscience. He believed that unpunished deviance tends to demoralize the conformist and therefore he talked about punishment as a means of repairing "the wounds made upon collective sentiments."[11] Durkheim was not entirely clear; he expressed his ideas in metaphorical language. Nonetheless, we can identify the hypothesis that the punishment of offenders promotes the solidarity of conformists.

Durkheim anticipated psychoanalytic thinking as the following reformulation of his argument shows: One who resists the temptation to do what the group prohibits, to drive his car at 80 miles per hour, to beat up an enemy, to take what he wants without paying for it, would like to feel that these self-imposed abnegations have some meaning. When he sees others defy rules without untoward consequences, he needs some reassurance that his sacrifices were made in a good cause. If "the good die young and the wicked flourish as the green bay tree," the moral scruples which enable conformists to restrain their own deviant inclinations lack social validation. The social significance of punishing offenders is that deviance is thereby defined as unsuccessful in the eyes of conformists, thus making the inhibition or repression of their own deviant impulses seem worthwhile. Righteous indignation is collectively sanctioned reaction formation. The law-abiding person who unconsciously resents restraining his desire to steal and murder has an opportunity, by identifying with the police and the courts, to affect the precarious balance within his own personality between internal controls and the temptation to deviate. A bizarre example of this psychological mechanism is the man who seeks out homosexuals and beats them up mercilessly. Such pathological hostility toward homosexuals is due to the sadist's anxiety over his own sex-role identification. By "punishing" the homosexual, he denies the latent homosexuality in his own psyche. No doubt, some of the persons involved in the administration of punishment are sadistically motivated. But Durkheim hypothesized that the psychic equilibrium of the *ordinary* member of the group may be threatened by violation of norms; Durkheim was not concerned about psychopathological punitiveness.

Whatever the practical difficulties, Durkheim's hypothesis is, in principle, testable. It should be possible to estimate the demoralizing impact of noncon-

---

[10] Trolle, "Syv Måneder uten politi" ("Seven Months Without Police") (Copenhagen, 1945), quoted in Christie, *Scandinavian Criminology,* 31 *Sociological Inquiry* 101 (1961).

[11] Durkheim, *op. cit. supra* note 6, at 108.

formity on conformists. Clearly, though, this is no simple matter. The extent of demoralization resulting from the failure to punish may vary with type of crime. The unpunished traffic violator may cause more demoralization than the unpunished exhibitionist—depending on whether or not outwardly conforming members of society are more tempted to exceed the speed limit than to expose themselves. The extent of demoralization may also vary with position in the social structure occupied by the conformist. Thus, Ranulf suggested that the middle class was especially vulnerable:

[T]he disinterested tendency to inflict punishment is a distinctive characteristic of the lower middle class, that is, of a social class living under conditions which force its members to an extraordinarily high degree of self-restraint and subject them to much frustration of natural desires. If a psychological interpretation is to be put on this correlation of facts, it can hardly be to any other effect than that moral indignation is a kind of resentment caused by the repression of instincts.[12]

Once the facts on the rate and the incidence of moral indignation are known, it will become possible to determine whether something must be done to the offender in order to prevent the demoralization of conformists. Suppose that research revealed that a very large proportion of conformists react with moral indignation to *most* violations of the criminal laws. Does this imply that punishment is a functional necessity? Durkheim apparently thought so, but he might have been less dogmatic in his approach to punishment had he specified the functional problem more clearly: making the nonconformist unattractive

as a role model. If the norm violation can be defined as unenviable through some other process than by inflicting suffering upon him, punishment is not required by the exigencies of social control.

Punishment can be discussed on three distinct levels: (a) in terms of the motivations of the societal agents administering it, (b) in terms of the definition of the situation on the part of the person being punished, and (c) in terms of its impact on conformists. At this point I am chiefly concerned with the third level, the impact on conformists. Note that punishment of offenders sustains the morale of conformists only under certain conditions. The first has already been discussed, namely that conformists unconsciously wish to violate the rules themselves. The second is that conformists implicitly assume that the nonconformity is a result of *deliberate defiance* of society's norms. For some conformists, this second condition is not met. Under the guidance of psychiatric thinking, some conformists assume that norm violation is the result of illness rather than wickedness.[13] For such conformists, punishment of the offender does not contribute to their morale. Since they assume that the nonconformity is an involuntary symptom of a disordered personality, the offender is automatically unenviable because illness is (by definition) undesirable. Of course, it is an empirical question as to the relative proportions of the conforming members of society who make the "wicked" or the "sick" assumption about the motivation of the offender, but this can be discovered by investigation.

[12] Ranulf, *Moral Indignation and Middle-Class Psychology* 198 (Copenhagen, 1938).

[13] Talcott Parsons has repeatedly suggested the analogy between illness and criminality. See also Aubert & Messinger, *The Criminal and the Sick*, 1 Inquiry 137 (1958), and Wootton, Social Science and Social Pathology 203–67 (1959).

In Western industrial societies, there is increasing tendency to call contemporary methods of dealing with offenders "treatment" rather than "punishment." Perhaps this means that increasing proportions of the population are willing to accept the "sick" theory of nonconformity. Note, however, that the emphasis on "treatment" may be more a matter of symbolism than of substance. Although the definition of the situation as treatment rather than punishment tends to be humanizing—both to the offender and to the persons who must deal with him—there are still kind guards and cruel nurses. Furthermore, it would be an error to suppose that punishment is invariably experienced as painful by the criminal whereas treatment is always experienced as pleasant by the psychopathological offender. Some gang delinquents consider a reformatory sentence an opportunity to renew old acquaintances and to learn new delinquent skills; they resist fiercely the degrading suggestion that they need the services of the "nut doctor." Some mental patients are terrified by shock treatment and embarrased by group therapy.

What then is the significance of the increasing emphasis on "treatment"? Why call an institution for the criminally insane a "hospital" although it bears a closer resemblance to a prison than to a hospital for the physically ill? In my opinion, the increased emphasis on treatment in penological thinking and practice reflects the existence of a large group of conformists who are undecided as between the "wicked" and the "sick" theories of nonconformity. When they observe that the offender is placed in "treatment," their provisional diagnosis of illness is confirmed, and therefore they do not feel that he has "gotten away with it." Note that "treatment" has the capacity to make the offender unenviable to con-

formists whether or not it is effective in rehabilitating him and whether or not he experiences it as pleasant. Those old-fashioned conformists who are not persuaded by official diagnoses of illness will not be satisfied by "treatment"; they will prefer to see an attempt made to visit physical suffering or mental anguish on the offender. For them, punishment is necessary to prevent demoralization.

Punishment as a Means of Reforming the Offender

Rehabilitation of offenders swells the number of conformists and therefore is regarded both by humanitarians and by scientifically minded penologists as more constructive than punishment. Most of the arguments against imprisonment and other forms of punishment in the correctional literature boil down to the assertion that punishment is incompatible with rehabilitation. The high rate of recidivism for prisons and reformatories is cited as evidence of the irrationality of punishment.[14] What sense is there in subjecting offenders to the frustrations of incarceration? If rehabilitative programs are designed to help the offender cope with frustrations in his life situation, which presumably were responsible for his nonconformity, imprisoning him hardly seems a good way to begin. To generalize the argument, the status degradation inherent in punishment makes it more difficult to induce the offender to play a legitimate role instead of a nonconforming one. Whatever the offender's original motivations for nonconformity, punishment adds to them by neutralizing his fear of losing the respect of the community; he has already lost it.

Plausible though this argument is, em-

[14] Vold, *Does the Prison Reform?* 293 Annals 42 (1954).

pirical research has not yet verified it. The superior rehabilitative efficacy of "enlightened" prisons is a humanitarian assumption, but brutal correctional systems have, so far as is known, comparable recidivism rates to "enlightened" systems. True, the recidivism rate of offenders who are fined or placed on probation is less than the recidivism rate of offenders who are incarcerated, but this comparison is not merely one of varying degrees of punishment. Presumably, more severe punishment is meted out to criminals who are more deeply committed to a deviant way of life. Until it is demonstrated that the recidivism rates of strictly comparable populations of deviants differ depending on the degree of punitiveness with which they are treated, the empirical incompatibility of punishment and rehabilitation will remain an open question.

Even on theoretical grounds, however, the incompatibility of punishment and rehabilitation can be questioned once it is recognized that one may precede the other. Perhaps, as Lloyd McCorkle and Richard Korn think, some types of deviants become willing to change only if the bankruptcy of their way of life is conclusively demonstrated to them.[15] On this assumption, punishment may be a necessary preliminary to a rehabilitative program in much the same way that shock treatment makes certain types of psychotics accessible to psychotherapy.

It seems to me that the compatibility of punishment and rehabilitation could be clarified (although not settled) if it were considered from the point of view of the *meaning* of punishment to the offender. Those offenders who regard punishment as a deserved deprivation resulting from their own misbehavior are qualitatively different from offenders who regard

punishment as a misfortune bearing no relationship to morality. Thus, a child who is spanked by his father and the member of a bopping gang who is jailed for carrying concealed weapons are both "punished." But one accepts the deprivation as legitimate, and the other bows before superior force. I would hypothesize that punishment has rehabilitative significance only for the former. If this is so, correctional officials must convince the prisoner that his punishment is just before they can motivate him to change. This is no simple task. It is difficult for several reasons:

1. It is obvious to convicted offenders, if not to correctional officials, that *some* so-called "criminals" are being punished disproportionately for trifling offenses whereas *some* predatory business men and politicians enjoy prosperity and freedom. To deny that injustices occur confirms the cynical in their belief that "legitimate" people are not only as predatory as criminals but hypocritical to boot. When correctional officials act as though there were no intermediate position between asserting that perfect justice characterizes our society and that it is a jungle, they make it more difficult to persuade persons undergoing punishment that the best approximation of justice is available that imperfect human beings can manage.[16]

2. Of course, the more cases of injustice known to offenders, the harder it is to argue that the contemporary approximation of justice is the best that can be managed. It is difficult to persuade Negro inmates that their incarceration has moral significance if their life experience has demonstrated to them that the police and

[15] McCorkle & Korn, *Resocialization Within Walls,* 293 Annals 88 (1954).

[16] See the interesting discussions of human fallibility in the works of Reinhold Neibuhr—e.g., *The Children of Light and the Children of Darkness* (1950).

the courts are less scrupulous of *their* rights than of the rights of white persons. It is difficult to persuade an indigent inmate that his incarceration has moral significance if his poverty resulted in inadequate legal representation.[17]

3. Finally, the major form of punishment for serious offenders (imprisonment) tends to generate a contraculture which denies that justice has anything to do with legal penalties.[18] That is to say, it is too costly to confine large numbers of people in isolation from one another, yet congregate confinement results in the mutual reinforcement of self-justifications. Even those who enter prison feeling contrite are influenced by the self-righteous inmate climate; this may be part of the reason recidivism rates rise with each successive commitment.[19]

In view of the foregoing considerations, I hypothesize that punishment—as it is now practiced in Western societies—is usually an obstacle to rehabilitation. Some exceptions to this generalization should be noted. A few small treatment institutions have not only prevented the development of a self-righteous contraculture but have managed to establish an inmate climate supportive of changed values.[20] In such institutions punishment has rehabilitative significance for the same reason it has educational significance in the normal family: it is legitimate.

To sum up: The social control functions of punishment include crime prevention, sustaining the morale of the

conformists, and the rehabilitation of offenders. All of the empirical evidence is not in, but it is quite possible that punishment contributes to some of these and interferes with others. Suppose, for example, that punishment is necessary for crime prevention and to maintain the morale of conformists but is generally an obstacle to the rehabilitation of offenders. Since the proportion of deviants is small in any viable system as compared with the proportion of conformists, the failure to rehabilitate them will not jeopardize the social order. Therefore, under these assumptions, sociological counsel would favor the continued employment of punishment.

CONCLUSION

A member of a social system who violates its cherished rules threatens the stability of that system. Conformists who identify with the victim are motivated to punish the criminal in order to feel safe. Conformists who unconsciously identify with the criminal fear their own ambivalence. If norm violation is defined by conformists as willful, visiting upon the offender some injury or degradation will make him unenviable. If his behavior is defined by conformists as a symptom of pathology they are delighted not to share, putting him into treatment validates their diagnosis of undesirable illness. Whether he is "punished" or "treated," however, the disruptive consequence of his deviance is contained. Thus, from the viewpoint of social control, the alternative outcomes of the punishment or treatment processes, rehabilitation or recidivism, are less important than the deviant's neutralization as a possible role model. Whether punishment is or is not necessary rests ultimately on empirical questions: (1) the extent to which identification with the victim occurs, (2) the extent

---

[17] Trebach, *The Indigent Defendant,* 11 Rutgers L. Rev. 625 (1957).

[18] For a discussion of the concept of contraculture, see Yinger, *Contraculture and Subculture,* 25 Am. Soc. Rev. 625 (1960).

[19] Sellin, *Recidivism and Maturation,* 4 Nat'l Probation and Parole A.J. 241 (1958).

[20] McCorkle, Elias & Bixby, The Highfields Story (1958), and Empey & Rabow, *Experiment in Delinquency Rehabilitation,* 26 Am. Soc. Rev. 679 (1961).

to which nonconformity is prevented by the anticipation of punishment, (3) what the consequences are for the morale of conformists of punishing the deviant or of treating his imputed pathology, and (4) the compatibility between punishment and rehabilitation.

TREATMENT: PAST, PRESENT AND POSSIBLE

H. Ashley Weeks

From the days of Hammurabi (ca. 1955–1913 B.C.) to the present we know pretty well how man has regarded and treated deviant behavior. We can infer from Hammurabi's code as well as from other early writings that treatment of deviant behavior (there was no distinction during those early days between mental aberration of one kind or another and delinquent or criminal behavior as it is defined today) was then essentially revengeful—"an eye for an eye, a tooth for a tooth." If a person slandered another, his tongue was cut out; if he took what did not belong to him, his fingers or hands were removed; if he killed, he was killed in turn. A large number of specific offenses were enumerated with specific punishments to go with them, and not only was the offender subject to punishment, but if he was not caught or available for punishment other members of his family could be punished in his stead.

Concurrent with such thinking was the belief that aberrant behavior was the work of the devil or evil spirits. Among many different peoples even ordinary illnesses were attributed to evil spirits, and the way to change or cure the behavior was to exorcise these evil spirits which were in possession. Christ cast out demons into swine and they were so affected that they ran into a river and were drowned. Even as late as the nineteenth century an indictment used by judges in the English courts not only accused the defendant of violating the law, but also of "being prompted and instigated by the devil and not having the fear of God before his eyes." And about the time of the War between the States, the North Carolina Supreme Court declared: "To know the right and still the wrong pursue proceeds from a perverse will brought about by the seduction of the evil one."[1]

It was not until relatively modern times that more rational and philosophical theories of crime causation, and controls resulting from such theoretical ideas, were developed. Cesare Beccaria in 1764 is credited with the first application of a theory of crime causation to punishment. Beccaria believed in a hedonistic philosophy, that man acted solely on a pleasure-pain principle. From this premise he argued that in order to control crime it was necessary to devise a system

[1] H. Shepard. *Journal of Criminal Law and Criminology*, 13 (January-February 1923) p. 486.

From *Key Issues*, 2 (1965), pp. 57–62. Reprinted by permission of the author and St. Leonard's House, Chicago, Illinois.

of punishment which would inflict at least a little more pain to an individual who committed a delinquent or criminal act than the pleasure he derived from committing the act. According to Beccaria, the exact punishment for each criminal act should be made known to all; and each person, regardless of age, wealth, social status, circumstances, sanity, or whatnot should receive the same punishment for the same crime.

Jeremy Bentham, in England, accepting the hedonistic philosophy, applied the theory to recommended legislation.[2] From England Beccaria's ideas, modified and elucidated by Bentham, spread to other European countries and to America. Although there has been some modification of the absolute equality of punishment, particularly as applied to children and "lunatics" because such persons were incapable of calculating pleasures and pains intelligently, and some small amount of judicial discretion so far as the penalties were concerned, the ideas of Beccaria and Bentham became the prevailing body of criminal law and have persisted to the present.

Even though the psychology underlying the theories is now generally questioned, the ideas are still applied almost automatically. When a particularly heinous offense is publicized there is an immediate demand to stiffen the penalty, as though this action would curtail similar offenses. Actually there has been no evidence that increased penalties of any kind have acted as deterrents of criminal or delinquent behavior. It is difficult to understand why there is still so much faith in this kind of simple expedient when there seems to be increasing evidence that very little, if any, relationship exists

between the number and nature of offenses committed and the severity of the punishment meted out. In fact, there appears to be evidence to the contrary. There is a positive relationship between the length of time a person stays in a custodial facility and the rate of recidivism. The longer the institutional stay the greater the chance of failure on parole or the greater the chance of a new offense with a return to the same or a different institution.

A striking example of this is the abolition of capital punishment for relatively minor offenses. No one argues that a person should be hanged for stealing a loaf of bread as was once the case in England. In fact, one hears more arguments against capital punishment than for it regardless of the enormity of the offense.

The more that is learned about human behavior the greater the evidence that all behavior, whether law-abiding or the opposite, results from what happens in the course of the socialization of the individual. If a child has love, understanding, good adult figures to identify with and emulate, he will usually grow into adulthood as a law-abiding citizen, whereas the reverse is likely when these elements are lacking. This is not to say, of course, that this is a simple one-to-one relationship. Behavior of any kind, at any one time, is the complex resultant of a multiplicity of interrelated factors, but the basic ingredients of socialization must be present. Much of the law enforcement machinery, in the long run, serves to hinder the socialization process.

Let us examine some of the historical theories and ideas underlying the correctional system as it has developed and exists at present. One of the earliest prison systems which was founded on a philosophy of reform, or at least attempted rehabilitation, was the so-called Pennsyl-

[2] Jeremy Bentham. *An Introduction to the Principles of Morals and Legislation*, London, Pickering, 1823.

vania system, brought about by demands by the Quakers for reform. This system held the belief that more than simple confinement or punishment must take place if an individual was to return to society at the expiration of his sentence as a law-abiding citizen. The Quakers, being a religious sect, believed that a man who was arrested, tried, and sentenced must realize that he had done wrong and must want to be better. Their way to assure his betterment was for him to be penitent. They therefore recommended and established between 1791 and 1801 in the Walnut Street Jail, Philadelphia, solitary cells where hardened inmates were incarcerated and remained alone to meditate and be penitent over their sins and wrong-doing. Although there were some other long-term prisons before this, such as the Maison de Force in Ghent and the Hospice of Saint Michael in Rome, Harry Elmer Barnes credits the Walnut Street Jail as being the "practical birth place" of the prison system, not only in the United States but throughout the world. There seems to be no doubt that it was the first institution to which the name "penitentiary" could be applied.

About the same time as the Quakers were creating their reforms, New York established a new prison at Auburn, where solitary cells were built for the oldest and most hardened criminals as a test of the Pennsylvania system. It was a dismal failure. Some Frenchmen, observing this test at first hand, condemned it outright as conducive to depression and insanity and endangering life.

As the result of the test at Auburn, prison policies were modified and inmates, although still confined in solitary cells at night, were allowed to work together and eat together though they were not allowed to communicate with one another. This latter system prevailed and became the dominant system in the United States until recently. Now, possibly because of overcrowding and newer theories, solitary confinement has been abandoned except as further punishment for some drastic violation of prison rules and regulations.

Late in the nineteenth century another innovation in the "treatment" of offenders had world-wide ramifications. The State of New York established a new institution for adolescent and young adult offenders up to the age of 30. It was a graded system. Each inmate, on admission, was placed in second grade. If he behaved and gave no trouble for six months, he graduated to first grade. After another six months in this grade without trouble, he became eligible for parole. If, at any time during his stay, there was misconduct he was placed in a third grade in which he had to demonstrate "good behavior" for a month before being returned to second grade and then again to first after the required lapse of time. In addition to the grade system, the Elmira Reformatory emphasized physical training, military training, schooling, and training for a trade. For the first time the length of stay became a function of an observable reformation, at least according to prison keepers and supervisors. Along with such reform went the indeterminate sentence and parole, so that those who made the grade got out earlier. Unquestionably, as the system developed, some inmates learned to "do time" and "keep their noses clean," and so got out quicker than others, without any fundamental change in their behavior or reformation of their characters. Nonetheless, ideally it was a step forward and influenced the establishment of the Borstal System in England where Sir Evelyn Ruggles-Brice during 1897 set apart a specialized institution at Borstal prison modeled after that at Elmira.

Reformatories and industrial or vocational schools for even younger offenders were established subsequently as the Juvenile Court idea expanded and need developed for some kind of institution to confine those who most needed "help" from the state. Many juvenile facilities, reformatories and prisons have put work programs into effect. The work was rationalized as training for outside vocations, but no one, so far as is known, ever tried to ascertain how many entered or even tried to get jobs similar to those they had engaged in while in the facility. For example, almost every state industrial school has a farm on which a high proportion of the boys work, despite the fact that most inmates are from urban environments and return to such communities upon discharge.

Although some changes have taken place over the years, which have made the punishment of offenders more humane and less brutal, the fact remains that for most adults and juveniles incarcerated in institutions there is no real program of treatment or understanding of the behavioral manifestations which brought them before the courts and into the various kinds of institutions. Punishment for wrongdoing still remains the basic philosophy with an almost blind faith that enough punishment will remold behavior, and because of fear of more punishment inmates will subsequently refrain from criminal and delinquent acts. But most institutions for juvenile delinquents and adult criminals show high recidivist rates.

We should not, however, be too quick to condemn those who manage our correctional institutions. In some ways their tasks have become almost impossible. Institutions have grown ever more crowded until today practically all of them are housing many more persons than they were built to accommodate. It is no wonder that many institutional workers ask resignedly, "What can we do? How can we carry on any treatment program under such conditions?" Treatment implies knowledge of the individual, and to get such knowledge there must be adequate professional staff. Then training or retraining of many non-professional workers is necessary so that they will be capable of carrying out a therapeutic program for the individual once knowledge of his needs is gained, and all this must be done within limited budgets.

What can we say to these persons? What can we do? Is there any hope? In very recent years there have been a few experiments which offer much promise. There have also been a number of studies which seem to indicate that perhaps we should begin to move in a different direction. First, it seems clear that a great many persons now housed in the larger maximum security institutions do not need to be kept in such places at all. It has been estimated by Robert D. Barnes, the famous Senior Architect of the Federal Bureau of Prisons, that only one-third of the prisoner population in state penal and correctional institutions need maximum security facilities, and only a small proportion of these would need to be confined in an inside cell in a walled institution.

Philosophically it can be argued that the more we confine individuals the less likely they are to make a go of it when they are released to take their places once again in society. Any large institution requires regimentation. Once an offender enters a large institution he loses most of his individual responsibility. Instead of building personal responsibility the institution removes it. The individual has no choices. He rises when a bell rings, he goes to the bathroom and to eat when other bells ring, he eats what is put on a tray, he goes to work at another bell and he does what he is told. He engages in what recreation he is allowed at a specific time. He is locked into his cell and lights are turned off according to institutional regulations. After years of such a regime is it any wonder that so many have difficulty in adjusting to the outside world?

Thus any attempts to break up the larger institutions into smaller units are all to the good. Such newer facilities as work camps, and places with more freedoms of choice and opportunities of socializing with family and friends at picnic-style visiting grounds, such as those at the California Institution for Men at Chino, seem to offer great possibilities. Parole prediction studies have shown that one of the most effective indicators of success on parole is the number of letters the inmate received from family and friends while in the institution. This shows the value of keeping up the offenders' most important social contacts.

Such short-term facilities as Highfields, established by the State of New Jersey for boys, have been demonstrated to be tremendously successful in terms of reducing the number of boys who become recidivists after their three to four months' stay.[3] Highfields is a small therapeutically oriented facility begun in 1950 for a maximum of twenty boys who voluntarily go there, at the discretion of the judge, while still on probation. There the boys engage in what are called "social group interaction sessions" five nights a week. The sessions go by this name to emphasize the fact that they attempt to

uncover the individual's social problems rather than any deep-seated psychotic ones. The boys work during the day at a nearby state institution for which they are paid a minimum amount. They are allowed at least one furlough home during their stay. While at the facility the boys discover their problems and attempt to do something about them. When this happens the boys may return home regardless of how long they have been at the facility.

The original Highfields was considered so successful that similar facilities, including one for girls, have been established in New Jersey.

Another successful experiment is the one carried out by BARO under the auspices of Kings County Court in Brooklyn, New York. Two probation officers, Drs. Alexander Bassin and Alexander Smith, undertook to conduct non-directed group psycho-therapy sessions with a randomly selected group of young adult offenders, with great success. Later they conducted similar successful sessions with groups of narcotic offenders, sex offenders and alcoholics.

A third experiment using a different method but with the same underlying philosophy was also successful. Dr. Martin Haskel carried out role-training sessions with a randomly selected group of Riker's Island inmates about to be released on parole. The role-training sessions were organized around the problems of getting and keeping a job and getting along with one's family. Not only did the tests given show an improvement for the treatment group when compared with a control group, but a follow-up study three months after release showed a much larger number of those undergoing the role-training sessions still successfully on parole than was the case in the control group.

[3] H. Ashley Weeks. *Youthful Offenders at Highfields,* University of Michigan Press, Ann Arbor, Michigan, 1958.

These three examples of successful treatment programs based on modern conceptions of changing human behavior into more socialized ways are not offered as the only ones being carried on or offering the most chance of successful outcomes. Other treatment programs could be cited. The ones discussed are those which the author of this essay has been close to in one capacity or another and therefore knows about at first hand.

It should be made clear that such programs as those discussed are not set forth as cure-alls, any more than a doctor would claim that he is successful in treating all sick patients who come to him for help. It is felt that these three examples of treatment programs do show possibilities of what can be accomplished when programs are carefully conceived and carried through. Some offenders should probably always be kept under custody. It does not make sense to release a criminal just because he has served his sentence when nothing has been done to resocialize him or change the behavior which got him into trouble in the first place. No one wants to mollycoddle offenders, or be sickly sentimental about the poor lads and lassies who get into trouble with the law. But what is being done at present in most prisons, penitentiaries, reformatories, and industrial schools is not really protecting society. It is time we tried sound treatment programs based on what we know of human behavior, and as we learn more about what works, modify the programs and keep trying.

SOCIAL PSYCHOLOGICAL FOUNDATIONS FOR USING CRIMINALS IN THE REHABILITATION OF CRIMINALS*

Donald R. Cressey

Social psychological theory has broad and significant implications for the use of criminals in the rehabilitation of criminals. However, the implications of general social psychological theory or of social psychological theories of criminal conduct have not been spelled out and have not been explicitly utilized in attempts to change criminals into noncriminals. Such theory has enabled us to learn a great deal about the processes by which men move from the status of "noncriminal" to the status of "criminal." We ought to use the same theory, and the knowledge gained by means of it, in attempts to move men from the status of "criminal" to the status of "noncriminal." Its use would be of great theoretical significance, for each attempt to change criminals could be an experimental test

* Revision of a paper presented before the Illinois Academy of Criminology, Urbana, Ill., May 8, 1964, and published in *Key Issues* (St. Leonard's House, Chicago), 1965.

From *Journal of Research in Crime and Delinquency*, 2 (July 1965), pp. 49–59. Reprinted by permission of the author and publisher.

of hypotheses derived from theory, and each such test would lead to improvement of theory.

On practical grounds, correctional agencies need theory enabling them to make maximum use of the personnel available to act as rehabilitation agents. By and large, correctional leaders of the last quarter century have subscribed to a psychiatric theory of rehabilitation—a set of theory which, unfortunately, can be implemented only by a highly educated, "professionally trained" person; they often conclude, therefore, that rehabilitation work attempted by persons not trained on the university postgraduate level is both ineffective and potentially dangerous. Despite this conclusion, there are not now and never will be enough similarly trained persons to man our rehabilitation agencies. As an alternative to louder and more desperate pleas for greater numbers of psychiatrists and social workers, there should be developed rehabilitation theory acknowledging the fact that highly educated personnel are not available to change criminals into noncriminals.

There is no shortage, in the United States or elsewhere, of average, run-of-the-mill, but mature and moral men and women of the sort making up the majority of the personnel in factories, businesses, and prisons—men and women with at most a high-school education. With increasing automation, more and more personnel of this kind will be leaving "production" occupations and will be available for "service" occupations, including that of rehabilitating criminals. The first important task in rehabilitation criminology is recognition of the availability of this tremendous manpower force. The second task, and the most difficult and crucial task that criminologists will face during the remainder of this century, is development of sound rehabilitation theory and procedures which will enable correctional agencies to utilize this reservoir of men.

Wardens and other agency administrators could then implement such a rehabilitation theory by creating an organization made up principally of men who have been trained in trade school to be skilled correctional technicians and whose occupational titles could properly be "people changers." If we have learned one thing about mental hospitals and correctional institutions since World War II, it is that change in patients and prisoners depends more on the actions of attendants, guards, and other patients and prisoners than it does on the actions of professional personnel. In the manpower pool that could readily supply the people changers we need is a copious supply of convicted persons being discharged from probation, prison, and parole each year, and of persons who are *ex*-convicts even if they are still under the supervision of a correctional agency. If we develop a theory on which to base a "people changer" occupation calling for skills somewhat comparable to those of automobile mechanics and television repairmen, the probability is high that ex-criminals will be among the most effective practitioners of the occupation. There is a basis in social psychological theory for the belief that ex-criminals can be highly effective *agents* of change and, further, that as they act as agents of change they themselves become the *targets* of change, thus insuring their own rehabilitation. Still to be accomplished is the difficult task of showing how general social psychological theory and criminological theory can be transformed into a theory of correction, and the difficult task of transforming the new theory of correction into a program of action.

"SYMBOLIC INTERACTION" THEORY AND CRIME CAUSATION

Sutherland's theory of differential association places great emphasis upon the kinds of variables that must be considered as fundamental if one is to explain delinquent and criminal behavior.[1] One can best appreciate the "individual conduct" part of this theory, in contrast to the "epidemiological" part, if he views it as a set of directives about the kinds of things that ought to be included in a theory of criminality, rather than as an actual statement of theory.[2] The variables identified as important to delinquency and criminality are the same variables considered in social psychology's general "symbolic interaction" theory as the elements basic in any kind of social behavior —verbalizations ("symbolizations") in the form of norms, values, definitions, attitudes, rationalizations, rules, etc. Moreover, the theory of differential association also directs us, as does general "symbolic interaction" theory, to a concern for the fact that the process of receiving a behavior pattern is greatly affected by the nature of the relationship between donor and receiver. In short, the theory implies that in attempts to explain delinquent and criminal conduct we should stop looking for emotional disturbances and personality traits, which are secondary variables, and start looking at the verbalizations of groups in which individuals participate, which are primary variables.

In telling us to look at people's words ("symbols") when we try to explain why most people are noncriminals and only a small proportion are criminals, Sutherland early aligned himself with a group of social scientists called, for convenience, "symbolic interactionists." The ideas of this group are quite different from the psychiatric view that "personality" is an outgrowth of the effect that the "restrictions" necessary to social order have on the individual's expressions of his own pristine needs. The "symbolic interactionists" view "social organization" and "personality" as two facets of the same thing.[3] The person or personality is seen as a part of the kinds of social relationships and values in which he participates; he obtains his essence from the rituals, values, norms, rules, schedules, customs, and regulations of various kinds which surround him; he is not separable from the social relationships in which he lives. The person behaves according to the rules (which are sometimes contradictory) of the social organizations in which he participates; he cannot behave any other way. This is to say that criminal or noncriminal behavior is—like other behaviors, attitudes, beliefs, and values which a person exhibits—the *property of groups*, not of individuals. Criminal and delinquent behavior is not just a *product* of an individual's contacts with certain kinds of groups; it is in a very real sense "owned" by groups rather than by individuals, just as a language is owned by a collectivity rather than by any individual.

"Participation" in "social relationships" and in "social organization" is, of course,

[1] E. H. Sutherland and D. R. Cressey, *Principles of Criminology* (New York, Lippincott, 6th ed., 1960), pp. 74–80. See also A. K. Cohen, A. R. Lindesmith, and K. F. Schuessler, eds., *The Sutherland Papers* (Bloomington, Ind., Indiana University Press, 1956).

[2] D. R. Cressey, "Epidemiology and Individual Conduct: A Case from Criminology," *Pacific Sociological Review,* Fall 1960, pp. 47–58.

[3] See A. H. Stanton and M. S. Schwartz, *The Mental Hospital: A Study of Institutional Participation in Psychiatric Illness and Treatment* (New York, Basic Books, 1954), pp. 37–38.

the subject matter of all anthropology, sociology, and social psychology. Nevertheless, "participation" in "social organization" is rather meaningless as an explanatory principle when it stands alone. As I have pointed out elsewhere, "[such concepts] serve only to indicate in a general way, to oversimplify, and to dramatize social interactions which are so confused, entangled, complicated, and subtle that even the participants are unable to describe clearly their own involvements."[4] Sutherland's criminological principle, like more general symbolic interactionist theory, tells us what to look for after we have moved toward consideration of the specific effects that "participation in social relationships" has on individual conduct. What Sutherland says we should study if we are going to establish a theory for explaining criminal conduct is, in a word, *words*. Values, attitudes, norms, rationalizations, and rules are all composed of symbols ("verbalizations"), and these verbalizations, of course, are learned from others, as pointed out years ago by symbolic interaction theorists like Mead, Dewey, Cooley, Baldwin, Whorf, Langer, and others.

In simplified form, symbolic interactionist theory tells us that cultures and subcultures consist of collections of behaviors contained in the use of *words* in prescribed ways. These words make it "proper" to behave in a certain way toward an object designated by the word "cat," and "improper" to behave in this same way toward an object designated by the word "hammer." They also make it "wrong" or "illegal" to behave in other ways. It is highly relevant to a theory of criminal behavior and to a theory of correction that words also make it "all right"

[4] D. R. Cressey, ed., *The Prison* (New York, Holt, Rinehart, and Winston, 1961), pp. 2–4.

to behave in some situations in a manner which also is "wrong" or "illegal."

Verbalizations, it should be emphasized, are not invented by a person on the spur of the moment. They exist as *group definitions* of what is appropriate; they necessarily are learned from persons who have had prior experience with them. In our culture, for example, there are many ideologies, contained in words, which sanction crime. To give some easy examples: "Honesty is the best policy, *but* business is business." "It is all right to steal a loaf of bread when you are starving." "All people steal when they get into a tight spot." "Some of our most respectable citizens got their start in life by using other people's money temporarily."

An anthropologist has given us an excellent example, from another culture, of the highly significant effect that words have in the production of individual conduct of the kind likely to be labeled "deviant," if not "criminal":

The Burmese are Buddhist, hence must not take the life of animals. Fishermen are threatened with dire punishment for their murderous occupation, but they find a loophole by not literally killing the fish. "These are merely put on the bank to dry, after their long soaking in the river, and if they are foolish and ill-judged enough to die while undergoing the process, it is their own fault." . . . When so convenient a theory had once been expounded, it naturally became an apology of the whole guild of fishermen.[5]

Other examples of the significant influence words have on individual conduct can be found in my study of criminal violators of financial trust,[6] in which I

[5] R. H. Lowie, *An Introduction to Cultural Anthropology* (New York, Rinehart, enlarged ed., 1940), p. 379.

[6] D. R. Cressey, *Other People's Money: A Study in the Social Psychology of Embezzlement* (Glencoe, Ill., Free Press, 1953).

noted that the embezzler defines the relationship between an unsharable financial problem and an illegal solution to that problem (embezzlement) in words, supplied by his culture, that enable him to look upon his embezzlement as something other than embezzlement. Suppose that a bank clerk with no significant history of criminality finds himself with an unsharable financial problem and an opportunity to solve that problem by stealing from his company. Suppose, further, that you said to him, "Jack, steal the money from your boss." The chances are that in response to these words he would simply look at you in horror, just as he would if you suggested that he solve his problem by sticking a pistol into the face of an attendant at the corner gas station. But suppose you said, "Jack, steal the money from your *company*." That would probably bring about less of a horror reaction,[7] but still, Jack would feel, honest and trusted men "just don't do such things." However, if you suggest that he surreptitiously "borrow" some money from the bank, you would be helping him over a tremendous hurdle, for honest and trusted men do "borrow." As a matter of fact, the idea of "borrowing" is used by some embezzlers as a verbalization that adjusts the two contradictory roles involved, the role of an honest man and the role of a crook, and hence is one of a number of verbalizations that make embezzlement possible.

A great deal of additional evidence supporting the importance of verbalizations in both criminal and noncriminal conduct is found in the literature, but it has not been systematically collected and published. Here are a few examples:

1. Lindesmith reported that if a person habituated to drugs talks to himself in certain ways, he will become an addict, while if he talks to himself in other ways, he will avoid addiction entirely. Lindesmith's most general conclusion was that persons can become addicts only if certain kinds of verbalizations are available to them.[8]

2. Becker's studies of marijuana addicts consistently showed that perception of the effect of marijuana is determined by the kinds of words given to smokers by users.[9]

3. Lane found that differences in the white-collar crime rate among New England shoe manufacturing firms was determined by the verbalizations available in local communities. For example, 7 per cent of the firms in one town violated the laws, while in another town 44 per cent violated. Lane concluded that at least one of the reasons for the differences is "the difference in attitude toward the law, the government, and the morality of illegality."[10]

4. Similarly, Clinard analyzed violations of O.P.A. regulations during World War II and concluded that businessmen violated the regulations because they did not "believe in" them; they possessed verbalizations which made the criminal law seem irrelevant.[11]

5. In a study of delinquents, Sykes

[7] E. O. Smigel, "Public Attitudes toward Stealing as Related to the Size of the Victim Organization," *American Sociological Review,* June 1956, pp. 320–27.

[8] A. R. Lindesmith, *Opiate Addiction* (Bloomington, Ind., Principia Press, 1947).

[9] H. S. Becker, "Becoming a Marijuana User," *American Journal of Sociology,* November 1953, pp. 235–43; and "Marijuana Use and Social Control," *Social Problems,* Summer 1955, pp. 35–44.

[10] R. E. Lane, "Why Businessmen Violate the Law," *Journal of Criminal Law and Criminology,* July–August 1953, pp. 151–65.

[11] M. B. Clinard, "Criminological Theories of Violations of Wartime Regulations," *American Journal of Sociology,* June 1946, pp. 258–70; and *The Black Market* (New York, Rinehart, 1952).

and Matza, following up the idea suggested in *Other People's Money,* concluded that since all youths accept conventional values to some degree, they must "neutralize" these conventional values before they can commit delinquencies. As illustrations of the "techniques of neutralization" used by delinquents, Sykes and Matza cite use of verbalizations which blame parents or misfortune for one's theft, define the victim as worthless, justify offenses as a duty toward one's friends, and note the faults of those who condemn delinquency.[12]

In a recent discussion of the research on social class and childhood personality, Sewell, who might be called a general "symbolic interaction" theorist, stressed the importance of attitudes and values (verbalizations), in contrast to emotional traits:

It now seems clear that scientific concern with the relations between social class and personality has perhaps been too much focused on global aspects of personality and possibly too much on early socialization. Therefore, it is suggested that the more promising direction for future research will come from a shift in emphasis, toward greater concern with those particular aspects of personality which are most likely to be directly influenced by the positions of the child's family in the social stratification system, such as attitudes, values, and aspirations, rather than with deeper personality characteristics.[13]

The trend noted by Sewell in general social psychological research has been noted by Glaser in criminological research and thinking. Since criminology must get at least the general direction of

its theory from the behavioral sciences, it is not surprising to find it following the general trends in theory. Glaser summarized the theoretical position in criminology as follows:

The process of rationalization reconciles crime or delinquency with conventionality; it permits a person to maintain a favorable conception of himself, while acting in ways which others see as inconsistent with a favorable self-conception. In this analysis of motivation by the verbal representation of the world with which a person justifies his behavior, sociologists are converging with many psychologists. This seems to be an individualistic analysis of behavior, but the so-called "symbolic interactionists" viewpoint is gaining acceptance, and it sees individual human thought as essentially a social interaction process: the individual "talks to himself" in thinking and reacts to his own words and gestures in "working himself" into an emotional state in much the same manner as he does in discussion or in emotional interaction with others.[14]

"SYMBOLIC INTERACTION" THEORY AND THE PROBLEM OF CHANGING CRIMINALS

If social conduct is a function of verbalization learned from membership groups and reference groups, then attempts to change it should concentrate on methods for avoiding certain verbalizations and acquiring others. Theory indicates that men conceive of themselves as a type (e.g., "criminal") when they have intimate associates who conceive of themselves as that type and when they are officially handled as if they were members of that type. Both processes have verbalizations as their content. This observation has enabled us to start working on a consistent set of "rehabilitation theory" which holds that a person can be stopped from conceiving of himself

[12] G. Sykes and D. Matza, "Techniques of Neutralization: A Theory of Delinquency," *American Sociological Review,* December 1957, pp. 664–70.
[13] W. H. Sewell, "Social Class and Childhood Personality," *Sociometry,* December 1961, pp. 340–56.

[14] D. Glaser, "The Sociological Approach to Crime and Correction," *Law and Contemporary Problems,* Autumn 1958, pp. 683–702.

as one type (*e.g.*, "criminal") and stimulated to conceive of himself as another type (*e.g.*, "square John") by isolating him from persons who conceive of themselves as the first type and refraining from handling him as if he were a member of that type, while at the same time surrounding him with intimate associates who think of themselves as the second type and officially handling him as if he were a member of the second type. The basic idea here is that a new set of attitudes, values, rationalizations, definitions, etc., must be substituted for the set that he has been using in performing the social conduct said to be undesirable, illegal, or immoral. The new set of verbalizations must be concerned with the fact that criminal conduct is *wrong.*

The infrequency of crime in our society cannot be accounted for by lack of opportunities for learning illegitimate skills or by fear of the risk attending the commission of criminal acts. The opportunity to acquire the skills of the criminal is great, and the probability of being arrested for a crime committed is low. Why, then, don't more people commit crime? Toby, who asked this question, has answered that people have learned that criminal conduct is wrong, indecent, or immoral. He points out that the tremendous amount of conforming behavior in any society can be understood only if we can see that individuals possess self-conceptions which make it impossible for them to engage in criminal or delinquent conduct without arousing feelings of guilt and shame that are incompatible with the self-conceptions.[15] "Guilt" and "shame" are contained in the verbalizations that make up a culture. In changing criminals, the basic problem is one of insuring that these

[15] J. Toby, "Criminal Motivation," *British Journal of Criminology,* April 1962, pp. 317–36.

criminals become active members of intimate groups whose verbalizations produce "guilt" and "shame" when criminal acts are performed or even contemplated. Stated negatively, the problem is one of insuring that persons do not learn to behave according to verbalizations which make crime psychologically possible.[16]

However, implementation of this basic idea is not as simple as it seems. First of all, our attempts to change a criminal's conduct might merely reinforce his use of the myriad verbalizations that have made and are making him act as he does. Or, he might be changed into a different kind of criminal. At a minimum, then, we must learn more about the process of social interaction in correctional settings, where the criminal whose change is being attempted is sometimes given words that make his criminality worse or that substitute one form of criminality for another.

USING CRIMINALS TO REFORM CRIMINALS

"Symbolic interaction" theory supports the idea that criminals can be used effectively to introduce "guilt" and "shame" into the psychological make-up of those who would commit crime and to avoid production of further criminality, or a different form of criminality, among

[16] See W. C. Reckless, S. Dinitz, and E. Murray, "Self Concept as an Insulator against Delinquency," *American Sociological Review,* December 1956, pp. 744–46; W. C. Reckless, S. Dinitz, and B. Kay, "The Self Component in Potential Delinquency and Potential Nondelinquency," *American Sociological Review,* October 1957, pp. 566–70; E. L. Lively, S. Dinitz, and W. C. Reckless, "Self Concept as a Predictor of Juvenile Delinquency," *American Journal of Orthopsychiatry,* January 1962, pp. 159–68; and S. Dinitz, F. R. Scarpitti, and W. C. Reckless, "Delinquency Vulnerability: A Cross Group and Longitudinal Analysis," *American Sociological Review,* August 1962, pp. 515–17.

the population whose change is sought. In the first place, criminals who have committed crimes and delinquencies by means of certain verbalizations, and who have rejected these verbalizations in favor of verbalizations making crime psychologically difficult or even impossible, should be more effective in changing criminals' self-conceptions than would men who have never had close familiarity with the procriminal verbalizations. In the second place, criminals used · as agents of change should be more efficient than noncriminals in avoiding the presentation of the verbalizations appropriate to a new kind of criminality or deviancy.

There are two approaches to the problem of expecting criminals to present anticriminal verbalizations to other criminals. In the first approach, the criminal-turned-reformer is viewed as the *agent* of change; in the second, he is viewed as the *target* of change.

The literature on group therapy reports many examples of groups in which the subjects served as effective agents of change. Opinion is almost unanimous that group therapy is an effective technique for treating mental patients and that its principal contribution has been reduction of social isolation and egocentricity among the subjects.[17] Arguments in favor of group therapy for criminals are less frequent; they tend to be organized around the "emotional disturbances" theory of criminality, rather than around symbolic interaction theory. One principal argument centers on the criminal's ability to establish rapport with other criminals.[18] Another centers

on the function of therapy in reducing isolation and egocentricity among criminals.[19] As I pointed out some ten years ago, neither of these is actually an argument for the effectiveness of group therapy in changing criminals.[20]

From the standpoint of the theory sketched out above, group therapy for criminals ought to be effective to the degree that the criminal-as-an-agent-of-change prevents criminals from using the "techniques of neutralization"—the verbalizations—which he, himself, used in perpetrating offenses, and to the degree that new anticriminal verbalizations are substituted. In one experiment with group therapy for female offenders, the old verbalizations were not prevented; the result was that, in the words of the therapist, "the participants would not accept the proposition that the source of their predicament was not 'bad luck' or a 'bad judge.'"[21] Another report said that delinquents "were convinced that everyone is dishonest, that even the police, the government, and the judges took bribes. Thus, they sought to convince themselves that they were not different from anyone else.... They needed persons with socially acceptable standards and conduct with whom they could identify."[22] Theoretically, at least, the degree of rapport is increased if these "persons with socially acceptable standards and conduct" are themselves criminals - turned - reformers,

[19] L. W. McCorkle, "Group Therapy in the Treatment of Offenders," *Federal Probation*, December 1952, pp. 22–27.

[20] D. R. Creesey, "Contradictory Theories in Correctional Group Therapy Programs," *Federal Probation*, June 1954, pp. 20–26.

[21] J. W. Fidler, "Possibility of Group Therapy with Female Offenders," *International Journal of Group Psychotherapy*, November 1951, pp. 330–36.

[22] C. Gersten, "An Experimental Evaluation of Group Therapy with Juvenile Delinquents," *International Journal of Group Psychotherapy*, November 1951, pp. 311–18.

[17] M. B. Clinard, "The Group Approach to Social Reintegration," *American Sociological Review*, April 1949, pp. 257–62.

[18] F. L. Bixby and L. W. McCorkle, "Applying the Principles of Group Therapy in Correctional Institutions," *Federal Probation*, March 1950, pp. 36–40.

rather than professional reformers such as social workers and prison guards. Just as men are relatively unaffected by radio and television dramatizations, they are unaffected by verbalizations presented by men they cannot understand and do not respect. On a general level, Festinger and his coworkers have provided extensive documentation of the principle that the persons who are to be changed and the persons doing the changing must have a strong sense of belonging to the same group.[23]

The implications of the social psychological ideas discussed above seem even clearer in connection with making the criminal "rehabilitator" the *target* of change. The basic notion here is that as a person tries to change others, he necessarily must use the verbalizations appropriate to the behavior he is trying to create in those others. In an earlier article, I named this process "retroflexive reformation," for in attempting to change others, the criminal almost automatically identifies himself with other persons engaging in reformation and, accordingly, with persons whose behavior is controlled by noncriminal and anticriminal verbalizations.[24] He then must assign status to others and to himself on the basis of noncriminal and anticriminal conduct or, at least, on the basis of exhibition of noncriminal and anticriminal verbalizations. When this is the case, he is by definition a member of law-abiding groups, the objective of reformation programs. At the same time, he is alienated from his previous procriminal groups, in the sense that he loses the verbalizations which enable him to assign high status to men whose conduct has been considered "all right," even if "illegal" and "criminal."

It is my hypothesis that such success as has been experienced by Alcoholics Anonymous, Synanon, and even "official" programs like institutional group therapy and group counseling programs is attributable to the requirement that the reformee perform the role of the reformer, thus enabling him to gain experience in the role which the group has identified as desirable. "The most effective mechanism for exerting group pressure on members will be found in groups so organized that criminals are induced to join with noncriminals for the purpose of changing other criminals. A group in which criminal A joins with some noncriminals to change criminal B is probably most effective in changing criminal A, not B; in order to change criminal B, criminal A must necessarily share the values of the anticriminal members."[25]

This notion proposes that the same mechanisms which produce criminality be utilized in attempts to change criminals into noncriminals. The criminal has learned that he can gain desired status in one or more groups by participation in the use of verbalizations that enable him to perform in a manner our law defines as "criminal." Now he must learn that he can "make out" in a group by participating in verbalizations conducive to noncriminality. Further, this learning must be reinforced by arranging for him to be an "elite," one who knows the proper verbalizations and, therefore, the modes of conduct, and who, furthermore, attempts to enforce his conceptions of right con-

[23] L. Festinger et al., *Theory and Experiment in Social Communication: Collected Papers* (Ann Arbor, Mich., Institute for Social Research, 1951).

[24] D. R. Cressey, "Changing Criminals: The Application of the Theory of Differential Association," *American Journal of Sociology*, September 1955, pp. 116–20.

[25] *Ibid.*

duct among those beneath him in the status system. When these two things occur, he becomes more than a passive noncriminal; he becomes an active reformer of criminals, a true "square."

We now turn to the problem of avoiding the presentation, in the rehabilitation process, of verbalizations that inadvertently make criminals worse. In recent years, sociologists and social psychologists have displayed increasing concern for this problem, as reflected in the large numbers of studies of the detailed operations of rehabilitation organizations like mental hospitals and prisons. So far as criminology is concerned, the problem seems to have been first identified in 1938 by Tannenbaum, who wrote *Crime and the Community* with the help of two famous "symbolic interactionists," John Dewey and Thorstein Veblen. Tannenbaum's basic idea was that officially separating the delinquent child from his group for special handling amounts to a "dramatization of evil" that plays a greater role in making him a criminal than any other experience: "The process of making the criminal is a process of tagging, defining, identifying, segregating, describing, emphasizing, making conscious and self-conscious; it becomes a way of stimulating, suggesting, emphasizing, and evoking the very traits that are complained of."[26] This notion has been discussed more recently by Merton as "the self-fulfilling prophecy,"[27] and in 1951 Lemert gave the name "secondary deviation" to the outcome of the process.[28] The important point is that in attempting

to correct what Lemert calls "primary deviation" we sometimes give the deviants words which make their problems worse.

It is possible to carry this notion of "dramatization of evil" and "secondary deviation" so far that it can be erroneously deduced that the police and other official instrumentalities of the state are more important than informal interaction in producing criminality and other forms of deviancy. There seems to be a current tendency among social scientists to view police, prison workers, and parole officers as "bad guys" that are producing criminality while the crooks and other carriers of crooked values are the "good guys." This is absurd. Nevertheless, the current focus on both secondary deviation and primary deviation places our scientific concern exactly where, according to symbolic interaction theory, it needs to be placed—on the subcultures made up of verbalizations which inadvertently, but nevertheless inexorably, are presented to persons who adopt them and who, in adopting them, become criminals. To take a simple example from outside the field of criminology, speech experts have found that stutterers often are people whose parents have dealt with them severely in order to get them to speak correctly.[29] Similarly, others have shown that the male homosexual is often a person who has been stigmatized for effeminacy or who applies a verbalization like "queer" to himself when he recognizes in himself erotic responses to other males.[30]

Recent studies have indicated that the

[26] F. Tannenbaum, *Crime and the Community* (Boston, Ginn, 1938), p. 21.

[27] R. K. Merton, *Social Theory and Social Structure* (Glencoe, Ill., Free Press, rev. ed., 1957), pp. 421–36.

[28] E. M. Lemert, *Social Pathology* (New York, McGraw-Hill, 1951), pp. 75–76.

[29] W. Johnson, "The Indians Have No Word for It: Stuttering in Children," *Quarterly Journal of Speech*, October 1944, pp. 330–37.

[30] C. C. Fry, *Mental Health in College* (New York, Commonwealth Fund, 1942), pp. 139–40, 146–48; and L. Leshan, "A Case of Schizophrenia, Paranoid Type," *Etc.*, July 1949, pp. 169–73.

physician's attention plays a considerable part in bringing on the very symptoms which it is designed to diagnose. For example, Scheff points out that a false diagnosis of illness (made because the physician is obligated to suspect illness even when the evidence is not clear) often incapacitates the person being diagnosed:

Perhaps the combination of a physician determined to find disease *signs,* if they are to be found, and the suggestible patient, searching for subjective *symptoms* among the many amorphous and usually unattended bodily impulses, is often sufficient to unearth a disease which changes the patient's status from well to sick, and may also have effects on his familial and occupational status. . . . It can be argued that when a person is in a confused and suggestible state, when he organizes his feelings and behavior by using the sick role, and when his choice of roles is validated by physician and/or others, he is "hooked" and will proceed on a career of chronic illness.[31]

Consistently, a physician reports the case of a woman who began to suffer the symptoms of heart trouble only after she was informed that a routine chest x-ray revealed that she had an enlarged heart.[32]

From these observations in areas other than criminology, it may safely be concluded that official action by rehabilitators of criminals is important to producing a "vicious circle" of the kind described by Toby:

When an individual commits one crime, forces are set in motion which increase the probability of his committing others. When he uses alcohol to help himself cope with an unpleasant social situation, the reactions

[31] T. J. Scheff, "Decision Rules, Types of Error, and Their Consequences in Medical Diagnosis," *Behavioral Science,* April 1963, pp. 97–107.

[32] H. Gardiner-Hill, *Clinical Involvements* (London, Butterworth, 1958), p. 158.

of his friends, employers, and relatives may be such as to give him additional reason to drink.[33]

While the problem of "secondary deviation" is by no means solved when criminals are used as agents for changing other criminals or themselves, symbolic interaction theory hints that there might be an essential difference between situations in which "secondary deviation verbalizations" are provided by professional agents of change and those in which such verbalizations are presented by ex-criminals. When the former criminal presents verbalizations making secondary deviation appropriate, he is at the same time presenting verbalizations making it possible to move out of the secondary deviant's role. This is not true when the noncriminal, and especially a "professional" rehabilitator, presents the verbalizations. For example, I might easily be able to show a man signs that will lead him to a conception of himself as a homosexual, with resultant secondary deviation; but an ex-homosexual can show the same man the same signs, together with other signs (exemplified in his own case) that mark the road to abandoning both the primary deviation and the secondary deviation. Or, to take an easier example, in presenting anticriminal verbalizations to a criminal, I might inadvertently convince him that the life of a square is undesirable because there is no way for a square John to get his kicks; a criminal, however, could show the subject that there is a kick in just being square.

In this connection Volkman and Cressey have observed that addicts who go through withdrawal distress at Synanon, a self-help organization made up of ex-addicts, universally report that the with-

[33] Toby, *supra* note 15.

drawal sickness is not as severe as it is in involuntary organizations such as jails and mental hospitals.[34] The suggestion from theory is that much of the sickness ordinarily accompanying withdrawal distress is brought about by close familiarity with verbalizations making it appropriate to become sick when opiates are withdrawn. At Synanon these verbalizations are not available. A newcomer learns that sickness is not important to men and women who have themselves gone through withdrawal distress. He kicks on a sofa in the center of the large living room, not in a special isolation room or other quarantine room where, in effect, someone would tell him that he is "supposed to" get sick. In one sense, however, Synanon members do force newcomers into a "sick role," for a large part of the reception process is devoted to convincing newcomers that only crazy people would go around sticking needles in their arms. The important point, however, is that this "sick role" is not the one that addicts experience when drugs are withdrawn in a jail or hospital. It is a role that is learned at the same time a new "non-sick role" is being learned; the learning process is facilitated by the fact that the teachers are themselves persons who have learned the new "non-sick role." We have heard the following verbalizations, and many similar ones, made to new addicts at Synanon.[35] None of the comments could reasonably have been made by a rehabilitation official or a "professional" therapist. Each of them provides a route out of both addiction and the special sick role expected of newcomers to the organization:

[34] R. Volkman and D. R. Cressey, "Differential Association and the Rehabilitation of Drug Addicts," *American Journal of Sociology,* September 1963, pp. 129–42.

[35] *Ibid.*

"It's OK, boy. We've all been through it before."

"For once you're with people like us. You've got everything to gain here and nothing to lose."

"You think you're tough. Listen, we've got guys in here who could run circles around you, so quit your bullshit."

"You're one of us now, so keep your eyes open, your mouth shut, and try to listen for a while. Maybe you'll learn a few things."

"Hang tough baby. We won't let you die."

SUMMARY AND CONCLUSIONS

The theory of differential association and the more general "symbolic interaction theory" suggest that whether criminals are viewed as agents of change or targets of change when they are used as rehabilitators of other criminals, the concern must be for the fact that criminal conduct is *wrong.* "Guilt" and "shame" are contained in the verbalizations that make up a culture, and the problem of changing criminals is a problem of insuring that criminals become active members of intimate groups whose verbalizations make all criminality as guilt-producing, shameful, repulsive, and impossible as, say, cannibalism. Stated negatively, the problem is one of insuring that persons do not behave according to verbalizations which make criminality psychologically possible. Since reformed criminals have learned both to feel guilty and not to feel not guilty when they contemplate participation in crimes, they are élite carriers of anticriminal verbalizations and can be used effectively in the effort to prevent crime and reform criminals.

WORK RELEASE
AND THE MISDEMEANANT

Stanley E. Grupp

Work release as commonly employed and as used in this paper refers to the release of the prisoner from confinement during certain hours. Usually, though not exclusively, this release is for the purpose of employment. The prisoner returns to confinement at the close of the work day. Work release and other vehicles for mitigating the severity of punishment, such as halfway houses, weekend sentences, and home leaves are increasingly receiving favorable attention on the part of correctional authorities, legislators, and the general public. Although this favorable reception has not been without its critics, the trend is well entrenched.[1]

Work release is known by various labels. In California, work release is formally referred to as work furlough. Day parole is the common referent in Wisconsin. In Pennsylvania the term for work release practice is the outmate program.[2] Private prerelease work is the concept used in the United Nations' *Prison Labour* publication.[3] Taft and England use the phrase "extramural private employment."[4] Other referents include day work, daylight parole, free labor, free work, intermittent jailing, and in France, semi-liberté.

Today at least 24 states provide for some form of work release. The states and the respective years of the inauguration of work release are: Wisconsin (1913), Nebraska (1917), West Virginia (1917), Hawaii (1937), Massachusetts (1950), Virginia (1956), California (1957), Idaho (1957), Minnesota (1957), North Carolina (1957), North Dakota (1957), Wyoming (1957), Arizona (1959), Illinois (1959), Montana (1959), Oregon (1959), Missouri (1961), Washington (1961), Michigan (1962), Florida (1963), Indiana (1963), Maryland (1963), Pennsylvania (1963), and South

---

[1] The present paper is part of a continuing effort to describe and analyze work release. See, Stanley F. Grupp, "Work Release in the United States," *The Journal of Criminal Law, Criminology and Police Science*, Vol. 54, No. 2, September, 1963, 267–272 and "Work Release—Statutory Patterns, Implementation and Problems," *The Prison Journal*, Vol. 44, No. 1, Spring, 1964, pp. 4–25.

[2] See, for example, Alfred C. Alspach, "Lancaster County 'Outmate' Program," *Pennsyl-*

vania Bar Association Quarterly, Vol. 33, No. 3, March, 1962, 318–324, and *Trust, Tolerance, and Understanding—The Outmate Program*, Lancaster County Prison, Lancaster, Pennsylvania, 1962 (mimeographed).

[3] Department of Economic and Social Affairs, *Prison Labour*, United Nations (St/SOA/SD/5) (1955).

[4] Donald R. Taft and Ralph W. England, Jr., *Criminology*, The Macmillan Co., New York 1964, 4th edition, p. 462.

From *Federal Probation*, 29, 2 (June 1965), pp. 6–12. Reprinted by permission.

Carolina (1963).[5] The statutory and administrative provisions as well as the actual implementation are conspicuously varied. Statutory patterns, administrative provisions, implementation, and problems of work release have been dealt with elsewhere by this writer.[6]

Wisconsin's Huber Law of 1913 is commonly cited as the earliest use of work release in the United States. Earlier antecedents do exist, however. Prior to the inauguration of a formal work-release law in 1950 by Massachusetts, it was common practice to place women from the Massachusetts Correctional Institution at Framingham in the community under the indenture system. This system included not only the traditional indenture provision of releasing the prisoner to a citizen in the community, but release for day-work purposes as well. The latter provision existed at least as early as 1880.[7]

WORK RELEASE IN OTHER COUNTRIES

A number of countries abroad provide for some form of work release and closely allied procedures. They include Belgium, Denmark, Federal Republic of Germany, France, Great Britain, Italy, New Zealand, Norway, Scotland, Sweden, and The Netherlands. There are probably others. The practices in some of these countries are described elsewhere.[8]

Inspection of the available information suggests that a number of these programs are comparable to the halfway houses and prerelease guidance centers in this country and therefore depart somewhat from the concept of work release as it is considered in this paper. France is an exception to this generalization for the program includes persons serving short sentences of a year or less.[9]

Sweden may have been the earliest country to experiment with work release. Informal experimentations started there in 1937.[10] Informal work-release procedures seem to have antedated formal inauguration in other countries, too, for example, in Norway and France. And it appears that Germany under the Weimar Republic initiated procedures closely approximating work release.[11]

Sweden formally authorized work release in 1945. Formal inauguration in other countries followed: Scotland in 1947, Norway in 1958, Great Britain in 1953, and France in 1959. Of these countries, it appears that France is currently making the most active use of work release.

---

[5] Several other jurisdictions, Iowa, the Federal Government and the District of Columbia are currently considering work-release legislation and it seems probable work release will become a statutory reality for them in the not-too-distant future. See, for example, "Ask 'Outside' Employment for Inmates," *Des Moines Register*, November 24, 1964, p. 1; Federal Bureau of Prisons, *Federal Prisons, 1963*, 23; and "Bill Would Free Jailed During Working Hours," *Washington Post and Times Herald*, July 25, 1964, B-2.

[6] Grupp, "Work Release—Statutory Patterns, Implementation, and Problems," *op. cit.* supra note 1.

[7] Letter from Mrs. Betty C. Smith, Superintendent, Massachusetts Correctional Institution at Framingham, January 7, 1964.

[8] See Denyse Chast, "Quelques Aspects Nouveaux Du Régime De Semi-Liberté," *Revue de Criminelle et de Droit Pénal Comparé*, Tome XIX, No. 3, July-September, 1964, pp. 631–637. *Prison Labour, op. cit.* supra note 3 at 22–26; and *The Prison Journal, op. cit.* supra note 1 pp. 26–41.

[9] Jacques Verin, "Work Release in France," *The Prison Journal, op. cit.* supra note 1, pp. 28–34.

[10] Daniel Wiklund, "Work Release in Sweden," *The Prison Journal, op. cit.* supra note 1 at 35.

[11] James V. Bennett, S. Doc. No. 70, 88th Cong. 2d Sess., "Of Men Who Have Failed," *Of Prisons and Justice*, 1964, p. 53. Reprinted from *Federal Probation*, August–September, 1940.

PRESENT SITUATION IN THE UNITED STATES

Attempts to generalize about work release are difficult because of the rapid developments. The increase in recent years of the number of states providing for work release and the differences in the patterns thereof are evidence of this fact.[12] Since 1956, 18 states have added work-release provisions; 8 of these were added since 1960. And, changes in the substantive nature of the law and administrative provisions or regulations are taking place from year to year.[13]

The implementation of work release, however, is definitely not being pursued with equal vigor in the 24 states. In some its use is virtually nonexistent, while in others an aggressive effort is being made to extend the use of work-release procedures.

Those states with a well articulated program and which seem to be moving in this direction are relatively few. This situation stems in part from the fact that in most states work release is a sentencing procedure restricted to misdemeanants with responsibility for the implementation of the sentence resting on the local level, usually on the county sheriff. In terms of actual use of work release the most active states are Wisconsin, California, North Carolina, Maryland and, to a lesser extent, Minnesota, Michigan, and Arizona.[14] Not all of these have an organized work-release program at either the state or local county level. Stated another way, in most of the 24 states work release is a sentencing procedure for selected misdemeanants and felons, but beyond this provision no program exists.

At least nine states have rigid statutory limitations on the use of work release. Representative examples of these limitations follow. In Missouri it is limited to one county, in Florida to two counties. To be considered for work release in Oregon the sentence must be less than 6 months. In Illinois, West Virginia, and Indiana the work-release sentence may be considered for nonsupport cases only, while in Virginia the sentence is available only if the individual's dependents are potential public charges.

In seven states the provision applies to selected felons. The states are California, Hawaii, Maryland, Massachusetts, North Carolina, South Carolina, and Washington.[15]

Three of the four states considered to be the most active by this writer—California, Maryland, and North Carolina—extend their work-release provisions to felons and Wisconsin is currently considering this extension. Two of the four, Maryland and North Carolina, have a centrally administered program. California, although locally administered, does maintain a field representative in the Department of Corrections who functions in part as an adviser to counties.[16] Thus of the four most active states only Wiscon-

---

[12] For an extended analysis of statutory patterns see Grupp, "Work Release—Statutory Patterns, Implementation and Problems," *op. cit.* supra note 1, pp. 7–14.

[13] Witness, for example, the change in the Maryland law. Maryland's work-release law became effective June 1, 1963. At that time felons with sentences not exceeding 5 years were included. This upper limit was eliminated as of June 1, 1964.

[14] This conclusion is based in part on information collected by the writer during the summer of 1963. See Grupp, "Work Release—Statutory Patterns, Implementations and Problems," *op. cit.* supra note 1 pp. 14–21.

[15] In Maryland, Massachusetts, and South Carolina the current operation is virtually limited to felons.

[16] California is noteworthy because of the work being done in a few counties, namely Marin and Santa Clara. Six counties in California were actively engaged in utilizing work release in 1964. See, for evample, *Work-Furlough Program Procedure*, Santa Clara County Sheriff's Department, San Jose, California, no date.

sin with a long tradition of day parole operates without direct help from a central state agency.[17]

VARYING CONCEPTIONS ABOUT WORK RELEASE

Work release is variously conceived. Johnson refers to work release as "another form of disposition of offenders intermediate between probation and imprisonment."[18] Ruth Cavan refers to the Huber Law as "a unique plan of probation."[19] The California and Washington statutes include in their work-release provision the option of a work sentence "as a condition of probation for any criminal offense . . . ."[20]

As provided by statute and when it is implemented, work release is most commonly a sentencing procedure. In a few states it is the prerogative of the correctional authorities. In at least one state, North Carolina, work release may be initiated by either the court or the Prison Department.

Work release is sometimes thought of as a release procedure, as a means of assisting the inmate in making the transition from institutional life to life in free society. It is treated as such in a pre-release handbook issued by the American Correctional Association.[21] Similarly, George W. Randall, Director of the North Carolina Prison Department, while observing that work release has "been utilized as a bridge between probation and conventional imprisonment," also suggests that work release may be used for inmates who are "not yet ready for parole . . ." and observes that work release in North Carolina functions in part as a vehicle for "parole preparation and a pre-release program."[22] Sanger Powers, Director of the Wisconsin Division of Correction, has recently supported the latter view by suggesting that work release is useful for those who are not quite ready for release.[23] And with regard to the federal work-release proposal James V. Bennett has observed:

It seems to me to be a sensible sort of thing to do. That is another way of getting the fellow back into the community easily without all of this sudden change-over from the close regime of the institution, and get him back into useful work and on to a useful job. The sensible thing to do is let us put him back gradually through some kind of work furlough plan.[24]

[17] Wisconsin state correctional authorities, however, have actively supported work release. See, for example, Sanger B. Powers, "Day Parole for Misdemeanants," *Federal Probation*, December, 1958, 42–46. The Wisconsin Division of Corrections and the Wisconsin Legislative Reference Bureau have published several summary statements of work release in Wisconsin. For a list of these see Grupp, "Work Release—Statutory Patterns, Implementation and Problems," *op. cit.* supra note 1 at 8, f.n. 33.

[18] Elmer Hubert Johnson, *Crime, Correction, and Society*, The Dorsey Press, Homewood, Illinois, 1964, p. 647.

[19] Ruth Cavan, *Criminology*, Thomas Y. Crowell Company, New York, 1962, p. 372.

[20] California Penal Code, Section 1208 (b) (Supp. 1963). Washington Revised Code, Section 36.63.260 (2) (Supp. 1961).

[21] The Committee on Classification and Casework, *Handbook on Pre-Release Preparation In Correctional Institutions*, The American Correctional Association, New York, 1950, pp. 59–60.

[22] George W. Randall, Presentation to the Joint Meeting of the Association of Paroling Authorities and the Wardens' Association of America at the 93rd Annual Congress of Correction, Portland, Oregon, August 26, 1963, Reported in *American Journal of Correction*, Vol. 25, No. 3, September–October, 1963, p. 16.

[23] This observation was made by Mr. Powers in a presentation before a joint meeting of the Association of Correctional Administrators and the Association of Paroling Authorities at the 94th Annual Congress of Correction, Kansas City, Missouri, September 1, 1964.

[24] Hearing before the Subcommittee on National Penitentiaries of the Committee on the Judiciary United States Senate, 88th Congress, 2nd Session, January 22, 1964, p. 94.

This limited review clearly suggests that the conceptualization of work release by various writers, by state statutes, and in terms of actual implementation is quite varied. The stage has been set for the inclusion of a wide variety of penal-correctional measures under the banner of work release. In the remainder of this article I offer several suggestions which may assist in the conceptual clarification of work release and suggest a rationale for the continued use and expansion of work release.

WORK RELEASE AND THE HALFWAY HOUSE

Clearly some of the views on work release come very close to equating it to the halfway house concept. This is understandable when we recognize that comparable activities are being implemented under both of these labels, that interest in the two procedures has emerged more or less concomitantly, and that this interest has increased precipitously in recent years. It is my feeling, however, that we should retain and encourage the conceptual distinction of the two procedures. The following will make some suggestions to this end. The observations are not in any sense suggested as the final word and it is recognized that there will be some difference of opinion regarding most of the points mentioned.

The halfway house is appropriately conceived as a vehicle for assisting in the social-psychological adjustment of the individual in making the transition from institutional to free life. This function is an integral aspect of the halfway house concept. In contrast, work-release procedures may or may not be designed explicitly to assist in bridging the transition from prison to society.

Implementation of the halfway house procedure is commonly initiated following a period of institutionalization. Conceived thusly the halfway house is appropriately viewed as a postinstitutional procedure or at most a quasi-institutional operation. In contrast, work release is clearly institutional in the sense that the work release participant is a prisoner but one who engages in private employment and other approved activities outside the institution concurrently with confinement at nights and weekends. Work release is appropriately conceived as a punishment procedure in and of itself; this is especially true with regard to the misdemeanant. Halfway house procedures, in contrast, are appropriately viewed as one of a series of penal correctional measures in which the individual participates.

Professional staff are commonly accepted as an integral part of halfway house programs. The operation of work-release procedures, however, may be conducted with a minimum of professional staff.[25] It is this attribute which makes work release adaptable on the local level.

The financial expense of the halfway house usually prohibits its use on the local level, that is for misdemeanant prisoners in local or county jails. This is not true for work release; operating costs are not prohibitive. All that is needed for the implementation of work release on the local

[25] Not all will agree with this. Mr. Walter H. Busher, Work-Furlough Administrator in Marin County, California, believes that a person trained in the behavioral sciences is necessary for the proper screening of potential participants and that each work-release officer should have no more than 15 work-release prisoners under supervision at a given time. Observations by Mr. Busher were made in a presentation to the California County Supervisor's Association, November 16, 1962. It is apparent that Mr. Busher's view of work release calls for professional personnel and fairly intensive supervision.

level is a carefully contrived and well articulated work-release statute together with an imaginative willingness to make work release a reality.

One further distinction is apparent. Halfway houses may be public or private: as presently operated it appears that most halfway house programs are privately administered. Work release, however, is always implemented by the local county and state authorities. Work release is public and as such is a part of the formal punishment procedures promulgated and implemented by the state.

In summary, work release, as conceived here, is a public procedure implemented as a part of the state's formal punishment responsibilities. Work release involves private employment concurrent with institutionalization. Work release may be initiated at the beginning or early in the sentence of a prisoner. When it is initiated after an extended period of confinement, it is appropriate to view work release as an aid in making the transition to free society, and indeed, may be designed for this purpose. If, however, this program is such that extensive professional and supervisory personnel are an integral aspect of the work-release program then we have a situation which closely approximates a state operated halfway house.

The intent of the above effort to distinguish work release and the halfway house has been twofold: one, to contribute to the conceptual clarification of the two procedures and, two, to present part of the underlying rationale for implementing work release on the local-county level for misdemeanants.

WORK RELEASE AND THE MISDEMEANANT

Corrections on the misdemeanant level are a veritable wasteland in many areas,

characterized by an almost total absence of imaginative effort to implement sound penological practices. The situation in some areas is one approaching total apathy.[26] Work-release procedures are ideally suited to the short-term offender and can help to rectify some of the difficult problems confronting corrections on the local level. Although no panacea, work release has much to offer. This is not to suggest that there are no problems in the implementation of work release or that it should be given wholesale application irrespective of the type of prisoner or the conditions in the community.[27]

Work release is extended to misdemeanants in virtually all of the 24 states listed above. Available evidence suggests, however, that this extension is largely an artificial one. In many states it appears that little use is being made of the work-release provisions at the misdemeanant level. The fact that two of the currently most active states, North Carolina and Maryland, are actively extending their provisions to felons may serve to detract from the utility and potentialities of work release for the misdemeanant.

The major objectives and advantages of work release, whether or not the participants are misdemeanants or felons, may be summarized: the support of the offender as well as the support of his family and the potential rehabilitative

[26] Witness, for an example, the observations of Eugene Zemans, Executive Director of the John Howard Association, regarding several county jails in Illinois. See, "Rockford Jail 'Throwback' to 17th Century," *Chicago Daily News,* July 7, 1964, 3; and "Kennedy Asked To Investigate St. Clair Jail," *Belleville News Democrat,* Belleville, Illinois, July 11, 1964, p. 2; See also, "Iowa Jails: Dirty-Dangerous," *Des Moines Register,* August 9, 1964, p. 1.

[27] For a consideration of problems in the implementation of work release see the discussion in the references cited in note 1.

effect on the offender. Several additional advantages are apparent: the financial saving to the county or state and the increased possibility that the offender will have a job upon release. A latent function is served, that of mitigating the repressive features of local-county jail conditions as represented in the absence of activity and a work program. In 1960, 2,281 employed Wisconsin Huberites earned $633,000. Approximately 36 percent and 27 percent were spent for the support of the prisoners' dependents and the prisoners' board and room, respectively.[28] For the fiscal years 1957 through 1963, 1,593 work release prisoners in Santa Clara County, California, earned about $832,000; of this amount approximately 47 percent was spent for the support of the prisoners' board and room.[29] In 1962–1963, 177 work release prisoners in Marin County, California, earned about $47,000, of which approximately 47 percent was spent for the support of dependents and approximately 16 percent for reimbursement to the county.[30]

The financial saving is appreciable although the specific amount will vary depending on the nature of the program. The following examples give some idea of the financial return.

Direct financial savings to the governmental units are more clearly represented in recent California information. Summary data from four of five California counties actively implementing the work furlough law in 1963–1964 indicate that the program was self-supporting in all but one county. In this county, estimated administrative costs exceeded maintenance collected by a negligible $38.00. The remaining three counties received $2,000 to $10,000 in maintenance collected, over and above the estimated program costs. In addition, there are the appreciable savings represented by the family support money and aid to dependent children payments sustained by work-release prisoners.[31]

Defense of work release sentencing in terms of its rehabilitative potential must be largely speculative at the present time. Only limited data related to the question of rehabilitation are available.

George Randall has reported the recidivist rates for North Carolina work-release prisoners as 6 percent.[32] This seems amazingly low, particularly when we recall that the North Carolina program includes both misdemeanants and felons. Even if this were to increase appreciably, procedures which yield a recidivist rate this low bear close inspection.

Reported escapees from the program are not high. Wisconsin reports that in 1960, 8 percent of the employed Huber Law prisoners escaped.[33] Escapees from the North Carolina work-release program have been recently quoted as 5 percent.[34] Although escapes per se are not indicative of the rehabilitative potential of work release, they do give a perspective regard-

[28] Division of Corrections and Bureau of Research, *Day Parole and Employment of County Jail Inmates:* 1960 Survey of Wisconsin's Huber Law (Research Bulletin C-6, State Department of Public Welfare, Madison, February, 1962, pp. 5–7).
[29] Santa Clara County Sheriff's Department, *Work-Furlough Program Statistics,* San Jose, California, July, 1963.
[30] Information provided by Mr. Walter H. Busher, Work-Furlough Administrator, Marin County, San Rafael, California. Letter from Mr. Busher, September 30, 1964.

[31] Data provided by Mr. Murray Hannon, Field Representative, Department of Corrections, California. Letter from Mr. Hannon, October 15, 1964.
[32] *Op. cit.* supra note 22, p. 16.
[33] *Op. cit.* supra note 28, p. 9.
[34] Arturo F. Gonzalez, "They're Working Their Way Through Prison," *Family Weekly,* March 8, 1964.

ing the percent of work-release prisoners who successfully complete their sentences. Most of those successfully completing their sentences will be able to retain their jobs. To the former prisoner who is sincere in his desire to make it in society the importance of having work cannot be overemphasized.

It seems reasonable to assume then that a work release sentence will encourage consistent work habits and help the prisoner who does not have a sense of responsibility toward his dependents, to develop in this direction. In this regard George Randall, a man of considerable experience with work release, has observed that, "When a man supports his family, it gives him a degree of self-respect and is helpful in rehabilitation."[35]

Even if it is eventually determined that recidivism rates for work-release prisoners are as high as the rates for prisoners who serve conventional terms, and limited data indicate this will not be, work release is defensible. This defense has been in part suggested by the above discussion, namely, the financial return to the county and state. In and of itself, the potential financial saving should provide sufficient inducement to initiate work-release procedures. Ideally, financial considerations should not dictate penal-correctional policies, but when financial savings are known to accompany sound correctional procedures the usefulness of this unique fact in convincing skeptics should not be overlooked. Given this consideration, work release is especially applicable on the misdemeanant level, that is, to those prisoners confined in local-county institutions. This is true because work-release procedures can be achieved with a very minimum of specialized staff

and special housing facilities. On-going programs testify in this regard.[36]

The problems posed by punishment require that we seek those means for implementing punishment which potentially offer the greatest rewards for the least expensive, the least complicated, and the least specialized program. This is especially true at the misdemeanant level. Public concern for the misdemeanant in most areas is not such that it will sustain grandiose treatment projects. Neither are the qualified professional personnel available. Work-release procedures are, therefore, ideally suited to the pursuit of the objectives of punishment on the misdemeanant level. Indeed, work release may be one of few procedures if not the only sound correctional procedure which is both practically and economically feasible at the local level.

WORK RELEASE AND PUNISHMENT

Punishment today for both the misdemeanant and the felon involves working with him in such a manner that he can be reassimilated into the community. Simultaneously, punishment in contemporary society calls for working with the individual in such a manner as to effectively mitigate, though perhaps not com-

---

[35] "Prisoners Work in Outside Jobs," *New York Times,* August 18, 1963, p. 50.

[36] Professional opinion differs on the necessity of providing separate housing for work release prisoners. George Randall feels that work-release prisoners can be housed with minimum custody inmates who are not in the work-release program. Sanger Powers believes that an effective program must provide separate housing facilities for work-release prisoners. Observations made before a joint meeting of the Association of Correctional Administrators and the Association of Paroling Authorities at the 94th Annual Congress of Correction, Kansas City, Missouri, September 1, 1964. See *Wisconsin's Huber Law in Action,* Wisconsin Service Association, Milwaukee, 1958, pp. 13–14, and this author's discussion in "Work Release in the United States," *op. cit. supra* note 1, p. 271.

pletely satiate, the demand for retribution and further, "manipulating" him in such a manner as to serve as an effective deterrent to potential offenders. In summary, punishment in contemporary society involves the articulation and implementation of the integrative theory of punishment.

A strong case can be made for work release for the misdemeanant in terms of the integrative theory. The same rationale can be applied to selected felons. Although this remains to be empirically demonstrated, it is my feeling that work release is ideally suited to the implementation of the integrative theory.

The integrative or inclusive theory posits that it is possible to articulate a theory of punishment which will integrate the traditional functions of punishment, namely, retribution, deterrence, and rehabilitation. Further, the theory recognizes the reality of these multiple demands of punishment on the part of the public. These demands do not, of course, exist in a balanced proportion for all crimes and indeed they vary from case to case with a given type of crime. This is in part why Professor Robert G. Caldwell has referred to the implementation of punishment as an art.[37] In support of the integrative theory Professor Francis A. Allen has observed:

No social institutions as complex as those involved in the administration of criminal justice serve a single function or purpose. Social institutions are multi-purposed. Values and purposes are likely on occasion to prove inconsistent and to produce internal conflict and tension. A theoretical orientation that evinces concern for only one or a limited number of purposes served by the institution must inevitably prove partial and unsatisfactory.[38]

[37] Robert G. Caldwell, *Criminology*, The Ronald Press Company, New York, 1956, p. 403.

In what manner does work release assist in the implementation of the integrative theory of punishment on the misdemeanant level? If we may speak of the typical misdemeanant, it is observed that public wrath does not run high in his regard. The major exception to this is probably the minor sexual offender. Although he is no real threat to the community, it may be better to bar him from consideration for work release particularly if his inclusion will increase the risk of sacrificing the entire program. With regard to the typical misdemeanant it is suggested here that the retributive function of punishment *is* served by a work-release sentence. Surely it cannot be claimed that the state is not doing something. Spending one's nonworking hours in confinement is not exactly a luxury. With regard to misdemeanants, a relatively innocuous group of offenders, it is probable that most citizens will view the work-release sentence as adequately providing the requisite retributive function of punishment.

Similarly, it would appear that the deterrent function of punishment has not been damaged. The offender is a prisoner, he has a sentence to serve, and he must spend his nonworking hours in confinement. Violation of the conditions of the work release may incur revocation of the privilege. Potential offenders are given sufficient warning that work release is not a soft touch. Actively applied, work-release procedures may be sufficient warning to keep potential offenders, for example, the potential nonsupport offender, in line.

Do work-release procedures contribute to the rehabilitation of the offender? It

[38] Francis A. Allen, "Criminal Justice, Legal Values and the Rehabilitative Ideal," *The Journal of Criminal Law, Criminology and Police Science*, Vol. 50, No. 3, September-October, 1959, p. 227.

has been suggested above that this needs to be empirically verified; however, the limited data available and reasoned inquiry suggest that work-release procedures should contribute to this end. Presumably the program should contribute to the maintenance and development of self-respect. The prisoner is paying his way and he is helping to support his dependents; this in and of itself should contribute to the development of self-respect and a sense of responsible citizenry. The strongly increased probability of having employment following release should contribute appreciably to the individual remaining a law-abiding citizen.

$\mathcal{8}$

Juvenile Delinquency

DEFINING DELINQUENCY

In order to discuss any social problem meaningfully we must first define it. This is especially true of juvenile delinquency because it seems to mean something different to each person. As a legal concept, juvenile delinquency is an "umbrella category" that includes many types of behavior. On the one hand, most state statutes define as delinquent behavior any act committed by a youth under a certain age that would be considered criminal if committed by an adult. In addition, certain other behaviors applicable only to the juvenile may also be considered delinquent.

As an example, a typical state juvenile statute defines juvenile delinquency "as the commission by a child under eighteen years of age of any act which committed by a person of the age of eighteen or over would constitute: (a) A felony, high misdemeanor, misdemeanor, or other offense, or (b) The violation of any penal law or municipal ordinance, or (c) Any act or offense for which he could be prosecuted in the method partaking of the nature of a criminal action or proceeding, or (d) Being a disorderly person. . . ."[1] These refer to laws which also apply to adults. However, the statute goes on to say that juveniles under the age of eighteen may be classified as delinquents if they fall into any of the following categories or commit any of the following actions: habitual vagrancy; incorrigibility; immorality; associate with thieves, vicious, or immoral persons; grow up in idleness or delinquency; visit gambling places; idly roam the streets at night; truancy from school; and deportment endangering the morals, health, or general welfare of the child.[2] It appears, then, that the chief criterion for delinquency is age. The violation of criminal statutes by a youth under a certain age[3] is defined as delinquency rather than crime, but a series of acts applicable only to the juvenile are also defined as delinquent behavior.

Juvenile statutes have been subjected to criticism primarily because "certain categories or acts which are defined as delinquent are extremely broad and can be interpreted to include almost any type of deviant behavior by those under the age of eighteen."[4] Law enforcement officials are given much more latitude in dealing with youthful offenders than they are able to exercise on the adult level. The same type of criticism has also been leveled at the juvenile court. Since the 1899 founding of the first juvenile court in Cook County, Illinois, persons interested in the welfare of youth have been concerned that almost anything a juvenile does can be interpreted as delinquent by the court if it so desires.

Of course, the very idea of having a special court for juveniles infers differential implementation of the law. Juvenile court procedure is markedly different from adult criminal court procedure. There is seldom a trial for a juvenile, but only a hearing before a judge. It is unusual for a lawyer to be present on behalf of the child. Usually only a probation officer or a court official performs this function. He makes an investigation of the case and presents his findings to the judge. On the basis of the court's investigation, the judge may dismiss the case or commit the youth to a variety of treatment programs. Such commitments are for indeterminate lengths of time, depending upon the youth's ability to resume a law-abiding role in the community. These procedures reflect the very philosophy of the juvenile court: help, not punish, the child by doing what is best for him as an individual.

THE EXTENT OF DELINQUENCY

The national trend since 1940 has been a rise in the number of delinquents apprehended and brought to court each year, and, also, in the rate of juvenile delinquency. In other words, there has not only been an increase in the amount of delinquency, but there has also been an increase in the more accurate indicator of delinquency, the number of delinquent cases known to the courts per 1000 boys and girls between the ages of 10 and 17.[5] This upward trend, beginning with a 1940 rate of slightly less than 10, seemed to hit a peak in 1945 at 18 and came down somewhat during the next two years. However, in 1948 it went back up again and, except for 1961, it has been rising ever since. In 1963 the rate was just under 22. The most conservative estimates put the total number of cases which come to the attention of the juvenile court each year, excluding traffic violations, at around 600,000.[6] These cases involve approximately 2 percent of the children in this country between the ages of 10 and 17.

The magnitude of juvenile involvement in criminal behavior can best be seen by looking at the 1963 statistics pertaining to offenses committed by youthful offenders. Whereas offenders under the age of 18 accounted for 19 percent of the forcible rapes, 28 percent of the robberies, and 14 percent of the aggravated assaults, they also accounted for 52 percent of the burglaries, 52 percent of the larcenies or thefts, and 63 percent of the auto thefts.[7] The United States Children's Bureau reported that delinquency cases handled by juvenile courts increased 8 percent in 1963 over 1962. This represented a rate of increase twice that of the increase in the 10- to 17-year-old population.[8] Of course, as the chapter on crime pointed out, no delinquency statistics or records ever show the actual number of individuals who have broken the law. There are large numbers of concealed delinquencies just as there are large numbers of concealed crimes committed by adults. Hence, we are dealing with only a sample of the delinquent population and not with the total group of young people who have committed unlawful behavior.

Of those delinquencies who are known to the courts or to the police, the ratio of boys to girls is about 5 to 1.[9] That is, there are five male delinquents for every one known female delinquent. There are several reasons for this disparity in the number of boys and girls involved in official delinquency. One explanation is that the offenses usually committed by boys are the types that are most likely to be reported and most likely to be acted upon by the police and by the courts. The offenses committed by girls are what one criminologist has referred to as "masked crimes."[10] These are offenses which generally involve sex and do not come to the attention of the authorities. On the other hand, boys engage in many more offenses dealing with property—they steal a great deal more than do girls and, of course, those thefts are more often reported and acted upon. In addition, boys engage in more assaultive behavior than do girls and thereby expose themselves to greater official response by society's law enforcers.

A second reason why there are more boys involved in delinquency than girls is that girls are given more protection than boys. Girls are protected by the family, by neighbors, by the police, and by the courts as well. Despite the offense a girl has committed, there is much less likelihood that she will be reported to the authorities than a boy who has committed a delinquent act. A girl is shielded more than a boy because it is felt that her reputation is more important than is a boy's, and also because our society has traditionally attempted to protect its female members.

The third and last reason for the overrepresentation of boys is that they simply seem to be more delinquent than girls. This is primarily due to their social roles. Boys are socialized to be assertive, manly, "rough and tough," and ready for all types of adversities. Girls are socialized to play a very different role—a homemaking, a somewhat submissive, and passive role. As a result of this socialization process and the resulting social roles each sex is expected to play, girls do not become involved in acting-out behavior to the same extent as boys.

Despite the fact that the same act is not always defined as illegal in all countries of the world, thus making comparative crime statistics somewhat unreliable, many people believe that the United States has one of the highest rates of juvenile delinquency in the world. However, the United States is not alone in the problem of youthful law violators. It appears that most countries of the world are experiencing increasing rates of juvenile delinquency. England, for example, is having difficulty with "Teddy Boys," "Mods," and "Rockers," their equivalent to delinquent gang members. In Sweden 70 percent of all crimes known to the police are youth offenses.[11] Juvenile delinquency has been increasing in France, and it appears from unofficial reports that the Communist countries also are seeing a rise in the rate of juvenile crime. No one is yet ready to give a definitive answer to the question of why there is an increase in delinquency in the most affluent countries of the world. We do know, though, that the rate of juvenile delinquency is far outstripping the rate of juvenile population growth, and it appears to be climbing steadily upward.

TYPES OF DELINQUENTS

Juvenile delinquents have been categorized in several ways ranging from personality types to morphological types. Many of distinctions are more mythical than real, but there is one which does help us make basic distinctions. This distinction separates juvenile offenders into two types: the maladaptive type and the adaptive type.[12] The most important characteristic of the maladaptive delinquent is that he has some serious emotional problem. He is a delinquent primarily because he has an internal push or compulsion towards delinquent behavior. The maladaptive delinquent is a lone-wolf who does not become involved in delinquencies with other children. He usually starts his career very early in life and engages in malicious, destructive, and hostile behavior. He is, in essence, a miniature of the adult psychopath whose behavior is governed by neither external nor internal controls.

The maladaptive type accounts for a relatively small number of the known delinquents.[13] Because of the psychopathological basis of his deviancy, this type of delinquent comes from all social classes and environmental conditions. For the same reason, the maladaptive delinquent is very difficult to work with and to rehabilitate.

The adaptive delinquent is quite different and much more familiar to us. He is usually a lower-class boy who lives in a slum or high delinquency area. He is more often than not a gang member and his behavior is influenced greatly by his peer group. The adaptive delinquent's illegal acts are committed in the presence of his peers, the gang, because part of the reward for committing a delinquent action is having the other members of the peer group know of the activity. In this way the adaptive delinquent is able to gain status within his reference group.

Adaptive delinquents are not driven by the internal, emotional pushes which characterize the maladaptive delinquents. They are, in actuality, socialized delinquents. They are psychologically normal children who have learned how to be delinquent through membership in a gang or through the acquaintance of others who teach them how to do things that are illegal. This child, the adaptive delinquent, has both external controls and internal controls which influence his behavior. Unfortunately, the internal controls are not well developed, the most powerful external control is the peer group, and the peer group happens to be delinquent; hence, if certain of the external controls were changed, it is reasonable to believe that the adaptive delinquent could become a law-abiding citizen.

SOME EXPLANATIONS OF DELINQUENCY

As the discussion of the adaptive type delinquent indicates, most juvenile offenders are from the lower social class and reside in highly disorganized urban areas.[14] As a result, most prevailing explanations of causation focus upon lower-class delinquency. Sutherland's theory of differential association, discussed in the preceding chapter, implies that there is much more opportunity for the individual to have criminal associations in disorganized areas of high crime and delinquency rates than in areas that are socially integrated and stable. This helps explain the preponderance of lower-class boys among the delinquent population. But, by seeing delinquency as merely imitative behavior, the theory of differential association does not suggest any reasons which could provoke such norm violation. However, other theorists have directed their efforts to trying to understand the reasons for such norm violation.

Albert K. Cohen[15] has stated that gang delinquency is primarily a lower-class phenomenon and that certain working-class boys perpetuate a delinquent subculture because they are unable to function successfully in middle-class institutions. The inability of working-class boys to function successfully in institutions dominated by middle-class values results in their experiencing great frustration. The middle-class values to which they have not been strongly committed emphasize ambition, individual responsibility, skill, deferred gratification, rationality, manners, control of physical aggression, wholesome use of leisure time, and respect for property. Although working-class boys desire middle-class status, they do not find these values exemplified in their families and in their lower-class associates. Therefore, they do not adopt these values to the extent that they serve as controls over their behavior.

Cohen believes that there are at least three ways in which working-class boys may adjust to their status. They may simply accept their lower-class life and withdraw into a community of peers. This is the most common type of adjustment. They may, on the other hand, attempt to achieve middle-class status through education, the working-class boys' primary vehicle of upward mobility. Cohen calls those boys who accept their status "corner boys" and those who strive for middle-class status "college boys."

However, some working-class boys respond to their status frustration by turning to delinquency because they cannot make the adjustments of the "corner boy" or the "college boy." The delinquency response, which is best seen in lower-class gang behavior, rejects middle-class norms and values. In an attempt to strike back at what they believe to be the source of their frustration, working-class delinquents invert middle-class standards and legitimize aggressive and hostile behavior. More important, the delinquent subculture measures success and status in terms which working-class delinquents can meet.

According to Cohen the delinquent sub-culture has five outstanding characteristics: non-utilitarian behavior, malicious behavior, negativistic behavior, short-run hedonism, and group autonomy. In other words, he feels that (1) delinquents do not use or need what they steal, and illegal behavior is engaged in merely for the sake of doing it; (2) their behavior is destructive and discomforting; (3) they reject middle-class values and norms and adopt their opposites; (4) they are interested only in immediate satisfaction; and (5) they accept the authority only of their group.

Walter B. Miller has also made a contribution to the subculture theory of delinquency.[16] Miller asserts that a society may contain several value systems of unequal importance and that subscribing to a subordinate value system may evoke punishment from the agents of the dominant value system. In American society the subordinate value system is that of the lower-class.

There are three main points in the Miller thesis: (1) the lower-class is characterized by distinctive values; (2) these lower-class values differ from middle-class values upon which our legal codes are based; and (3) conformity with the lower-class values may in some cases mean automatic violation of the law.

The "focal concerns" or values of the lower-class are trouble, toughness, smartness, excitement, fate, and autonomy. Those who have internalized these values as a result of being socialized in the lower-class culture are especially prone to delinquency. On the other hand, the "focal concerns" of the middle-class are quite similar to those stated by Cohen. Just as the acceptance of lower-class values makes one vulnerable to delinquency, socialization in the middle-class values protects one against it. According to Miller, the rare middle-class delinquent is one who has not internalized the values of his culture.

One important difference in the Miller and Cohen theories of lower-class delinquency stands out. Miller does not believe as Cohen does that lower-class boys must be frustrated in their status desires before taking on the characteristics of the delinquent subculture. For Miller, delinquency is the expression of lower-class norms and the mere presence of boys in the lower-class culture is enough to produce it. However, he does admit that most juveniles in lower-class society are not delinquent because their aspirations are higher than those of the delinquents. Lower-class nondelinquency seems to depend upon the desire for and feasibility of upward social mobility.

Another theory of lower-class delinquency has been stated by Richard Cloward and Lloyd E. Ohlin who see it as the function of a limited opportunity system.[17] A basis for their view can be found in Durkheim[18] who believed that it was necessary to keep the goals of a society within the bounds of possible achievement. Later, Merton[19] claimed that although the many racial, ethnic, and religious groups in America have similar aspirations, there is great inequality in their ability to achieve their goals. When there is a breakdown in the relationship between goals and legitimate avenues of access to them, a condition of anomie, or a failure of regulative norms, will result. Under such conditions members of the society attempt to achieve the highly prized goals in whatever way possible. Thus, lower-class youth, aware of a very limited opportunity to achieve their aspirations, engage in delinquency more than youth in middle-class society who have greater success opportunities.

Specifically, Cloward and Ohlin contend that delinquency may be one result of a search for a solution to adjustment problems. They believe that pressures toward the formation of a delinquency subculture originate in inconsistencies between aspirations and means for achieving them in legitimate ways. Pressures for deviancy are produced by the unlimited aspirations which are a function of industrial society.

In American society, as in any industrial society, education offers the most immediate access to legitimate opportunity. However, different social class groups have differential access to education. Many youths in high delinquency areas or slums of American cities are restricted in occupational choices because of their lack of education; hence, for them there is no escape from poverty, and, consequently, they resort to illegitimate means of fulfilling their personal aspirations. In so doing, they legitimize the nonlegitimate norms which they believe will get them what they want.

How the deprived youth deals with his problems of blocked opportunity and unfulfilled aspirations depends upon what is available in his particular social setting. In an area where there is organized and professional crime, where adult criminals may serve as adult role models, and where youths aspire to the criminal role, a criminal subculture may develop around stealing. In a disorganized area where there is no tradition of professional or organized crime and where there are few criminal roles available for emulation, a conflict subculture may develop around violence and fighting. Lastly, individuals who can adopt neither of these behavioral patterns because of moral prohibitions or because they have already failed in the delinquent role may form a retreatist subculture which focuses on the use of drugs and alcohol. In short, Cloward and Ohlin feel that the type of deviant subculture that will develop is dependent upon the opportunities in the neighborhood.

The few theories of delinquency which have been presented here emphasize the role of the social structure in the development of deviant behavior. Rather than stressing individual abnormality or faulty personality development, these theories have seen the etiological factors as lying outside the individual in the social milieu which engulfs him. The environmental factors tend to serve as pressures on the individual which he is not able to handle adequately. The delinquent response is merely one way of adjusting to the problems that impinge upon the lower-class boy. This response, like all other responses, is learned in a process of interaction with others who are sophisticated in the delinquent response. This is the essence of the sociological explanations of lower-class delinquency and is the base upon which many intervention techniques have been built.

WHAT CAN BE DONE?

More solutions have been offered for the juvenile delinquency problem than for most of the other social problems considered in this book. These techniques of intervention fall into two broad categories: prevention of juvenile delinquency and rehabilitation of the delinquent. The first two readings examine some of the more promising attempts to prevent youthful law violation; the final reading shows how youths may be treated once they make the delinquency committment.

John M. Martin, in his article "Three Approaches to Delinquency Prevention: A Critique," concludes that the prevention of delinquency is actually a problem of social reorganization. In disorganized areas, characterized by a high disposition to delinquency, social change must be stimulated so that residents may be better able to control those environmental conditions conducive to delinquency. However, Martin feels that the local community must be organized for this effort. As in the Chicago Area Project, local residents should be utilized in a prevention program since they play a vital role in the socialization of the area children. Through the participation of qualified local residents in youth welfare organizations, both the area adults and juveniles become committed to the objectives of the program.

In the second reading the description of the Mobilization for Youth program in New York City emphasizes another dimension of the problem. This comprehensive delinquency prevention project based upon the Cloward and Ohlin theory of blocked opportunity is concerned with enhancing all of the individual's life opportunities. A multi-million dollar program, the largest of its kind, MFY has experimented with many innovative techniques that are designed to provide the lower-class youth with greater opportunities in the areas of employment, education, community action, and special individual, family, and group needs. Although some of these new techniques have aroused bitter controversy, they may well turn out to be the solution to the problem and must, in the long run, be evaluated on that basis. Unfortunately, no formal evaluation of this program is available at present.

One of the alternative ways in which a juvenile court judge may dispose of a case delinquency is to commit the youth to an institution. Traditionally, juvenile institutions have been little more than "reform schools" where emphasis has been placed on work and discipline with little attention paid to discovering and modifying the basis of the delinquent's deviant behavior. The Provo Experiment, described and analyzed in three sections by Empey and his associates in the third reading, is one of many new rehabilitation programs based upon sociological theory which attempt to change the delinquent values and attitudes that support lawbreaking. This program uses guided group interaction, a form of group therapy, as a technique to facilitate the boys' gaining insight into their behavior and helping each other find solutions to mutual problems.

There is little doubt that juvenile delinquency is an overt social problem in the United States. Unfortunately, we have not solved this problem and we probably will not solve it in the very near future. Although many programs designed to rectify it are being attempted at the present time, many more will undoubtedly have to be tried before our society finds a complete solution to the tragedy of wasted and misspent youth.

REFERENCES

1. Richard R. Korn and Lloyd W. McCorkle, *Criminology and Penology*. New York: Holt, Rinehart and Winston, Inc., 1963, p. 183.
2. Korn and McCorkle, p. 183.
3. In most states 18 years of age is regarded as the point differentiating juvenile from adult legal status. However, some jurisdictions have set the age at 16 and 17 years; see Harry M. Shulman, *Juvenile Delinquency in American Society*. New York: Harper & Row, Publishers, 1961, pp. 529–530.
4. Korn and McCorkle, p. 184.
5. *Juvenile Court Statistics–1963*. Washington, D.C.: The Children's Bureau, U.S. Department of Health, Education, and Welfare, Government Printing Office, 1965, Table 3, p. 11 and Table 9, p. 15; *Uniform Crime Reports–1963*. Washington, D.C.: U.S. Department of Justice, 1964, Table 20, p. 106; "Law Enforcement and the Administration of Justice," Presidential Message to Congress, March 8, 1965, *Indicators*. Washington, D.C.: U.S. Department of Health, Education, and Welfare, April 1965, p. 5.
6. *Juvenile Court Statistics–1963*, p. 1.
7. *Uniform Crime Reports–1963*, Table 21, p. 107.
8. *Juvenile Court Statistics–1963*, p. 1.
9. Albert K. Cohen and James F. Short, Jr., "Juvenile Delinquency," in Robert K. Merton and Robert A. Nisbet (eds.), *Contemporary Social Problems*. New York: Harcourt, Brace & World, Inc., 1966, p. 93.
10. Otto Pollak, *The Criminality of Women*. Philadelphia: University of Pennsylvania Press, 1950, pp. 1–7.
11. Clyde H. Farnsworth, "Youths in Sweden Form Car Fleets," *The New York Times*, March 21, 1965, p. 2.
12. Richard Jenkins, "Adaptive and Maladaptive Delinquency," *The Nervous Child*, 2 (October 1955), pp. 9–11.
13. Estimates of the size of the emotionally disturbed delinquent group have varied greatly, but the Kvaraceus and Miller estimate of not more than 25 percent appears most realistic. See William C. Kvaraceus and Walter B. Miller, *Delinquent Behavior: Culture and the Individual*. Washington, D.C.: National Education Association, 1959, p. 54.
14. Kvaraceus and Miller, p. 54; Albert K. Cohen, *Delinquent Boys*. New York: The Free Press of Glencoe, 1955; Richard A. Cloward and Lloyd E. Ohlin, *Delinquency and Opportunity*. New York: The Free Press of Glencoe, 1960;

Clifford R. Shaw and Henry D. McKay, "Report on Social Factors in Juvenile Delinquency," *Report on the Causes of Crime,* National Commission on Law Observance and Enforcement, Report No. 13, Vol. II. Washington, D.C.: Government Printing Office, 1937.
15. Cohen.
16. Walter B. Miller, "Lower Class Culture as a Generating Milieu of Gang Delinquency," *Journal of Social Issues,* 14, 3 (1958), pp. 5–19.
17. Cloward and Ohlin.
18. Cloward and Ohlin, pp. 77–83.
19. Robert K. Merton, *Social Theory and Social Structure,* Revised and enlarged ed. New York: The Free Press of Glencoe, 1957, Chap. 4.

ADDITIONAL READINGS

Bloch, Herbert A., and Frank T. Flynn, *Delinquency: the Juvenile Offender in America Today.* New York: Random House, Inc., 1956.
Cloward, Richard A., and Lloyd E. Ohlin, *Delinquency and Opportunity.* New York: The Free Press of Glencoe, 1960.
Cohen, Albert K., *Delinquent Boys.* New York: The Free Press of Glencoe, 1955.
———, and James F. Short, Jr., "Juvenile Delinquency," in Robert K. Merton and Robert A. Nisbet (eds.), *Contemporary Social Problems.* New York: Harcourt, Brace & World, Inc., 1966, pp. 84–135.
Martin, John M., and Joseph P. Fitzpatrick, *Delinquent Behavior.* New York: Random House, Inc., 1964.
Matza, David, *Delinquency and Drift.* New York: John Wiley & Sons, Inc., 1964.
Reckless, Walter C., *The Crime Problem.* New York: Appleton-Century, Inc., 1961, Chaps. 19, 20, and 21.
Robison, Sophia, *Juvenile Delinquency: Its Nature and Control.* New York: Holt, Rinehart, and Winston, Inc., 1961.

THREE APPROACHES
TO DELINQUENCY PREVENTION:
A CRITIQUE*

*John M. Martin***

Aside from punishment and strict repression, delinquency prevention is usually defined in these three different ways:

1. Delinquency prevention is the sum total of all activities that contribute

* Adapted from the author's book, *Juvenile Vandalism: A Study of Its Nature and Prevention,* published by Charles C Thomas, Springfield, Ill., 1961.

**Assistant Professor of Sociology, Department of Sociology and Anthropology, Fordham University.

From *Crime and Delinquency,* 7 (January 1961), pp. 16–24. Reprinted by permission of the author and the National Council on Crime and Delinquency.

to the adjustment of children and to healthy personalities in children.

2. Delinquency prevention is the attempt to deal with particular environmental conditions that are believed to contribute to delinquency.

3. Delinquency prevention consists of specific preventive services provided to individual children or groups of children.[1]

GENERAL DESCRIPTION

The logic underlying preventive activities of the first type is disarmingly simple: anything that contributes to the adjustment of children and to their healthy personality development prevents delinquency. Basically this approach links delinquency prevention with general improvements in the institutional fabric of our society, particularly as these affect child welfare. In large part this approach rests on a continuation and extension of measures, now commonplace on the American scene, which are designed to reduce the economic inequities of our social system. Such activities include procedures for raising the income levels of poverty stricken families, better low-rent housing, improving job tenure and work arrangements, and other means for reducing the rigors of poverty and economic insecurity. The approach also embraces attempts to reduce prejudice and discrimination against minority group people, increase the educational achievements of oncoming generations, improve marital relations by premarital counseling and family social work, and increase the impact of religious doctrines on both adults and children.

Preventive activities of the second

type, by and large, aim to overcome factors in the immediate environment of children that seem to contribute to their delinquency. Such activities include attempts at community organization, such as the Chicago Area Projects (to be discussed later in this article); work by "coordinating councils" for harmonizing the efforts of welfare and child care agencies in delinquency prevention; the work of recreational and character-building agencies of all types; and attempts to reduce the commercial activities of adults which are clearly illegal and detrimental to the welfare of children who may get caught up in such traffic as, for example, the sale of liquor to minors, dope peddling, and receiving stolen goods.

Preventive activities of the third type include probation and parole services to children and youths, the programs of residential institutions and special schools for delinquents, child guidance clinics insofar as they are concerned with the diagnosis and treatment of delinquents, direct work with antisocial street gangs, and a variety of other services whose principal purpose is the adjustment of individual children or groups of children.

RELATIVE MERITS

It would be enormously difficult, if not impossible, to measure the effectiveness of these three types of preventive activities in terms of their ability actually to reduce delinquency, and no attempt will be made to do so here. However, general comment will be made about the relative merits of the three approaches.

In the main it is correct to conclude that improvement in the collective welfare, particularly in the welfare of depressed minority people, will reduce delinquency. In areas such as metropolitan New York the reduction of

[1] H. A. Bloch and F. T. Flynn, *Delinquency: The Juvenile Offender in America Today*, New York, Random House, 1956, p. 512.

juvenile delinquency is most intimately linked with the successful assimilation of low-status groups, in particular the ever increasing number of migrant and uprooted Negroes and Puerto Ricans.[2] Whatever contributes to the welfare and assimilation of these people reduces the delinquency rate among their children and, correspondingly, in the communities in which they live; conversely, whatever impedes their progress inflates the delinquency rate in those areas.

But the relationship between delinquency and improvement in the general welfare is more complicated than it appears at first glance. For example, although it is tempting to claim that improved housing and the reduction of poverty will reduce both crime and delinquency, evidence that delinquency is highest during periods of extreme prosperity and *not* during depressions, as well as awareness of the variety and number of offenses committed by middle- and upper-class persons, should warn us against the facile assumption that the elimination of poverty is the Rosetta stone of crime prevention.

The relationship between delinquency, at least in terms of official statistics, and poverty and poor housing has, of course, long been noted by students of social problems. However, it is erroneous to conclude that the abolishment of these living conditions will also abolish delinquency among low-status children. As Bernard Lander pointed out in his study of differential juvenile delinquency rates by census tracts in Baltimore,[3] delinquency appears to be fundamentally related to social instability or *anomie* and not basically to poverty and poor housing.

It is within this context that we can best understand the disillusionment of those who expected too much by way of delinquency prevention from public housing. Their disappointment is well reflected in the pungent remark reportedly made by one student of New York's slums: "Once upon a time we thought that if we could only get our problem families out of those dreadful slums, then papa would stop taking dope, mama would stop chasing around, and Junior would stop carrying a knife. Well, we've got them in a nice apartment with modern kitchens and a recreation center. And they're the same bunch of bastards they always were."[4]

Emphasis upon *anomie* or social disorganization as a basic contributing factor to the high delinquency rates characteristic of some urban areas, with a concomitant de-emphasis of the obvious poverty of these areas as the underlying factor in their high delinquency rates, would, then, appear to be of cardinal importance for understanding and preventing delinquency in such places.

ANOMIE AND DELINQUENCY

Useful as Lander's statistical analysis of census tracts in Baltimore may be for destroying the myth that poverty and inadequate housing are the root causes of delinquency, the relationship between *anomie* and delinquency may also be more complicated than it seems. Lander emphasized the "internal" disorganization characteristic of high delinquency areas.

[2] For an excellent discussion of this point see O. Handlin, *the Newcomers*, Cambridge, Mass., Harvard University Press, 1959, especially chap. 4.

[3] See B. Lander, *Towards an Understanding of Juvenile Delinquency*, New York, Columbia University Press, 1954, especially p. 89.

[4] D. Seligman, "The Enduring Slums" in The Editors of Fortune, *The Exploding Metropolis*, Garden City, N.Y., Doubleday, 1958, pp. 111–132.

Yet relatively *stable* neighborhoods may also be characterized by comparatively high rates of delinquency. A good example of just such a neighborhood is the tightly knit Italian slum of "Eastern City" examined by William Foote Whyte in his classic, *Street Corner Society.*[5]

The existence of stable but delinquent neighborhoods suggests that there are at least two kinds of areas that produce delinquency:

One is the rapidly changing and thoroughly chaotic local area of the kind isolated by Lander, perhaps best illustrated by New York City's racially mixed and tension-ridden Spanish Harlem so well described by Dan Wakefield in *Island in the City.*[6]

The other is the rather well-organized neighborhood such as the Italian ethnic community studied by Whyte, "disorganized" primarily in the sense that the way of life there is judged "out of step" when contrasted with the essentially middle-class culture of the greater society.[7]

It is in the second kind of area particularly that well-developed relationships are likely to exist between criminally precocious adolescents, corrupt politicians, and the seemingly inevitable racketeers. These relationships go far in explaining the easy transition many delinquents make from juvenile misbehavior to the more sophisticated forms of adult criminality. It is in this type of area, too, that personality and family structures are less likely to split and disintegrate under the stresses and strains characteristic of more chaotic and tension-ridden neighborhoods.

But distinctions of this sort, important as they may be for understanding differences in the social structure of delinquency areas, must not obscure a more basic fact: quite aside from the stability or instability of social relations in delinquency-prone areas, the traditions, standards, and moral sentiments of such areas are notoriously delinquent and criminal in "complexion" and "tone." This peculiar cultural climate has long been recognized by students of urban life, particularly by the ecologists and social psychologists of the "Chicago School" of American sociology.[8]

Recently this recognition has linked up with a more general discussion of social class subcultures and particularly with more detailed analyses of lower-class culture as a breeding ground for delinquency. A good example of this is found in an article by Walter B. Miller which called attention to the delinquency proneness of lower-class culture in a discussion of the "focal concerns" of the urban lower-class way of life.[9] Miller's emphasis is not upon the so-called "subculture of the delinquent gang" as discussed by Albert K. Cohen,[10] but upon the content of the whole mode of existence of urban lower-class people. Miller believes that in the lower class, in contrast with the middle class, people are likely to have commitments to focal concerns such as physical

[5] W. F. Whyte, *Street Corner Society,* enlarged edition; Chicago, University of Chicago Press, 1955.

[6] D. Wakefield, *Island in the City,* Boston, Houghton Mifflin, 1959.

[7] For a further discussion of these two kinds of delinquency areas, see W. F. Whyte, "Social Organization in the Slums," *American Sociological Review,* February, 1943, pp. 34–39.

[8] For an excellent survey of studies in the "social ecology" of crime conducted during the past 150 years, see T. Morris, *The Criminal Area,* London, Routledge and Kegan Paul, 1958, chaps. I–VI.

[9] W. B. Miller, "Lower Class Culture as a Generating Milieu of Gang Delinquency," *The Journal of Social Issues,* Vol. 14, No. 3, 1958, pp. 5–19.

[10] See A. K. Cohen, *Delinquent Boys: The Culture of the Gang,* Glencoe, Ill., The Free Press, 1955.

"toughness," "smartness" interpreted as the ability to "con" or dupe others, and "excitement" in terms of seeking thrills, taking risks, and courting danger. When these commitments are combined with the intense need for 'in-group" membership and status or "rep" so characteristic of lower-class adolescents, Miller feels that conditions are especially ripe for the development of juvenile misconduct, particularly gang delinquency.

Thus the concept of social disorganization can be used to describe both stable and unstable delinquency areas. If we accept such disorganization as basic to an understanding of law violation in both kinds of areas, then we must question the value of other delinquency prevention methods besides those aimed at the reduction of poverty. In particular we should examine the limitations inherent in current attempts to prevent delinquency by the use of "individual-centered" techniques, such as social casework and related psychological-psychiatric services.

"INDIVIDUAL-CENTERED" TECHNIQUES

Practitioners of such techniques work toward individual adjustment, not social change. Seldom do they try to reduce the delinquency-producing features of the delinquent's environment, especially his extrafamilial environment; instead they emphasize adjustment to prevailing environmental conditions. For most delinquents, who are generally without emotional disturbance and who reflect the patterned deviancy so often found in their lower-class neighborhoods,[11] this means that they are expected to make a

[11] For a recent discussion of this crucial point, see W. C. Kvaraceus, *et al.*, *Delinquent Behavior: Culture and the Individual*, Washington, National Education Association of the United States, 1959, chap. 7.

non-delinquent adjustment to a highly delinquent life situation. Our recidivism rates testify that at best this adjustment is precarious. Furthermore—and this is perhaps the more basic point—because such efforts fail to come to grips with the underlying social and cultural conditions giving rise to delinquency, they do little to prevent the outcropping of delinquency in the first instance. Most try to take hold only after maladjustment, even delinquency itself, has become manifest in the lives of the youngsters they seek to help.

This, however, should not be taken as a rejection of probation and parole, of training schools and reformatories, of child guidance clinics, and of other kinds of institutions and agencies given over to the care and "correction" of delinquents. Far from abandoning this line of approach, we must work hard at improving existing facilities of this sort and act imaginatively regarding the "invention" of new ones. Furthermore, we must, as we have seldom paused to do in the past, rigorously test and verify the effectiveness of various approaches aimed at the rehabilitation of individual delinquents. In this regard the basic question still to be answered is: To what extent and under what conditions do our correctional agencies really correct?

But despite all of this, we must not be so carried away by our desire to rehabilitate delinquents that we fail to see individual treatment in a proper perspective, lose sight of its limitations, and ignore the fundamental proposition that *the prevention of delinquency should include both individual treatment and general or social prevention.* Unfortunately this is just what has happened. To a truly remarkable degree public and private delinquency-prevention agencies have spent comparatively little money or energy on community-centered programs of social prevention. For decades most of these agencies have put their effort into establishing various kinds of facilities for rehabilitating delinquents on a case-by-case basis, with the "model" and most prestigeful approach in recent years being that of the psychiatrically oriented child guidance clinic.

In sum, if we grant the primary role social disorganization plays in the development of delinquency, then the prevention of delinquency is not fundamentally a problem of bettering the general welfare of children or rehabilitating individuals, although the wisdom of continuing our attempts at both seems obvious. Nor for that matter is delinquency prevention essentially a problem of coordinating the activity of welfare agencies, although, like the application of "individual-centered" techniques, this too has an important role to play in prevention. (The coordination of agency activity is particularly valuable insofar as it enables accurate statistics on reported delinquency to be gathered in various jurisdictions, for it is only on the basis of such statistics that a community can determine the trend of its delinquency and measure the effectiveness of its preventive efforts. Agency coordination is even more valuable when it serves to bring various preventive programs and techniques to bear on potential delinquents before their deviancy becomes well established.)

Basically, the problem of delinquency prevention is a problem of social organization or reorganization and other approaches have merit only to the degree that they contribute to such reorganization.

SOCIAL REORGANIZATION

How can social reorganization best be accomplished? Although we may be both unable and unwilling to reduce substantially the drift toward *anomie* that Robert K. Merton[12] and others have suggested is a pervasive characteristic of American society, we may be able to make partial inroads upon such disorganization, particularly insofar as it is related to the problem of juvenile delinquency, if we focus directly on the local areas in which delinquency is most pronounced. The logic underlying this proposal is that a local area "does not need to control the entire culture of a nation (which would be impossible) in order to control its delinquency rate. The things that need to be done are local and relate to personal interaction rather than to the larger institutions."[13] The essence of this approach to social reorganization, then, is to stimulate social change in delinquency-prone neighborhoods.

Unfortunately we have no rich arsenal of tried and proven techniques for accomplishing such change. Much needs to be learned and many innovations need to be developed toward this end. Despite these difficulties, however, we do know much about stimulating change in delinquency areas. The framework within which the reorganization of such neighborhoods can be accomplished has been well described by Frederic M. Thrasher in his outline of a proposal for coordinating neighborhood activity for delinquency prevention.[14]

This proposal envisions that any attempt to prevent delinquency in local

[12] See R. K. Merton, *Social Theory and Social Structure,* Glencoe, Ill., The Free Press, 1949, chap. IV.
[13] E. H. Sutherland, "Prevention of Juvenile Delinquency" in A. Cohen *et al.* (eds.), *The Sutherland Papers,* Bloomington, Indiana University Press, 1956, pp. 131–140.
[14] F. M. Thrasher, "Some Principles Underlying Community Co-ordination," *The Journal of Educational Sociology,* March, 1945, pp. 387–400.

areas must fix responsibility for social change at the neighborhood level where such changes can be implemented by local community leaders assisted by experts. Implicit in this approach is the assumption that in even the most delinquency-prone neighborhoods not all the residents are criminals or delinquents, and that in such areas there is actually a duality of conduct norms—one favoring law-abiding behavior, the other favoring delinquency.[15]

Although Thrasher's plan utilizes, as subsidiary techniques, the best services offered by the usual community agencies —especially those of school, court, training institutions, and child guidance clinic —his proposal "represents a radical departure from the methods of social work and community organization as formerly conceived."[16]

This comment made almost three decades ago is nearly as applicable now as it was then. When one surveys current social work efforts at community organization, it becomes abundantly clear that, far from being focused in local areas, this activity is largely county- or city-wide in scope. Furthermore, all too often "community organization" in social work means that professional social workers meet with one another and with upper- and middle-class laymen for the purposes of mapping fund-raising campaigns, educating the public, coordinating agency activity, and similar objectives. Even when particular neighborhoods are the targets for such organization, seldom is the basic responsibility for such work placed in the hands of leaders who are truly representative of the people living in such areas.

Fundamentally the difference between the kind of plan outlined by Thrasher and traditional social work proposals for community organization is that in the former the real work is done by local residents who, banded together in a committee or council, act to (1) get the facts about delinquents and delinqency in their neighborhood; (2) organize existing preventive forces serving their neighborhood; (3) stimulate the development of new programs and services as required; and (4) in cooperation with professional agencies, look to the adjustment of their own delinquents, organize the leisure-time activities of their own children and young people, and improve the neighborhood environment, particularly by encouraging the enforcement of laws outlawing the activities of "slum landlords," petty racketeers, and other adults that are clearly detrimental to the welfare of their neighborhood and their children.

Other sociologists besides Thrasher have also foreseen the urgency of organizing the local community for delinquency prevention. Thus Edwin H. Sutherland, for example, endorsed local community organization as the most effective means for preventing delinquency, emphasized the need for placing responsibility for such organization in the hands of those whose children are the most likely to become delinquent, and cited the necessity of including juveniles themselves as participants in such organization.[17]

The inclusion of children and youths in neighborhood organizations for delinquency prevention is most vital. Too often

---

[15] For a discussion of the duality of conduct norms in delinquency areas, see S. Korbin, "The Conflict of Values in Delinquency Areas," *American Sociological Review,* October, 1951, pp. 653–661.

[16] F. M. Thrasher, *The Gang,* second revised edition; Chicago, University of Chicago Press, 1936, p. 538.

[17] Sutherland, "Prevention of Juvenile Delinquency," *op. cit.*

they are simply left out of the planning and management phases of such activity. As a result, the isolation of their adolescence is compounded and a real opportunity for establishing closer ties between the generations is overlooked.

CHICAGO AREA PROJECT

Perhaps the best known of the relatively few delinquency-prevention programs predicated on local community organization that are actually in operation are the Chicago Area Projects developed by Clifford R. Shaw and his associates.[18] Basically these projects aim at producing internal cohesiveness and conventional behavior in delinquency areas through the development of *indigenous leadership*. Outside professional leadership is minimal. Chiefly it is used to interest and develop local talent. Program activities are not ends in themselves but are used to achieve local unity. Some direct work is done with children and adolescents on a one-to-one counseling basis, and psychiatric and other types of referrals are made when needed. But the central aim is to draw local youngsters into various project activities so that they will identify with conventional rather than with delinquent groups and cultural patterns.

Outside leaders have a definite but limited role. This approach to area reorganization places principal emphasis on the role of natural community leaders who are carriers of conventional conduct norms. Not only do such leaders serve as nondelinquent models for emulation by youngsters attracted to programs offered

by projects of this type, but because these indigenous leaders have prestige in the local area, they easily attract adults, as well as children and youths, to project programs in the first instance. It is around natural community leaders, then, that legitimate social structures can be germinated and multiplied in delinquency-prone areas. And it is in relationship with such leaders and within such structures that youngsters can develop the close and intimate attachments with conventional models, achieve the satisfactions, and acquire the sense of personal worth and purpose necessary to counter the drift toward delinquency characteristic of their life situations.

SOME BASIC QUESTIONS

Two basic questions arise relative to preventive programs like the Chicago Area Projects: First, *can they be established, and once established will they last?* Second, *do they actually prevent delinquency?*

In regard to both parts of the first question, the answers seem to be definitely affirmative. Thus, in their recent evaluation of the Chicago Area Projects, Witmer and Tufts found that:

1. Residents of low-income areas can organize and have organized themselves into effective working units for promoting and conducting welfare programs.

2. These community organizations have been stable and enduring. They raise funds, administer them well, and adapt the programs to local needs.

3. Local talent, otherwise untapped, has been discovered and utilized. Local leadership has been mobilized in the interest of children's welfare.[19]

[18] For detailed descriptions of the Chicago Area Projects, see A. Sorrentino, "The Chicago Area Project After 25 Years," *Federal Probation*, June, 1959, pp. 40–45; S. Kobrin, "The Chicago Area Project—A 25-Year Assessment," *The Annals of the American Academy of Political and Social Science*, March, 1959, pp. 19–29.

[19] H. L. Witmer and E. Tufts, *The Effectiveness of Delinquency Prevetion Programs*, Children's Bureau, United States Department of Health, Education, and Welfare, Publication 350, Washington, Government Printing Office, 1954, p. 15.

A definite answer to the second question is much more difficult to obtain. However, two types of evidence tentatively suggest that it too may be affirmative. First, statistics from 1930 to 1942 indicate that delinquency rates declined in three out of four of the communities in which projects were then being carried on; second, in some of the projects, work with men and boys on parole from institutions has been very successful, with one project noting that out of forty-one parolees worked with between 1935 and 1944, only one was recommitted to an institution.[20] However, evidence such as this, without comparable controls, must obviously remain inconclusive. As has been remarked elsewhere, "the role of any preventive agency is likely to be most difficult to assess."[21] The Chicago Area Projects are no exception.

Another question that arises with respect to delinquency prevention programs geared to local leadership is: *How can they best be originated?* In this regard Walter C. Reckless has warned against waiting for the "spontaneous generation of experimental action"; outside help must get such programs started by stimulating local leaders to action.[22] Likewise it seems necessary that outside assistance should also include sufficient money, at least in the beginning, to help defray costs. Again and again programs of this type have foundered because the few hundred dollars raised by raffles, cake sales, thrift shops, and local donations were simply not enough to meet day-to-day expenses.

Who should provide such assistance? To this there are a number of answers. The potential role of private foundations, boards of education, fraternal organizations, and private industry and labor unions in supporting or initiating such activity is enormous. Of special significance is the potential but presently underdeveloped role urban churches can play in this field. The force of organized religion in the prevention of delinquency will be more fully realized if, and only if, more churches make realistic financial appropriations for such purpose and if, on the personal level, more churchmen base their approach to delinquency on love, direct service, intimate communication, and example, instead of on benign indifference, social distance, and exhortation.[23]

Assistance should also be available from other sources. For example, communities in states with Youth Authority plans might well call upon such authorities for help insofar as these state agencies actually make provision for realistic assistance to local communities; and in New York the new State Youth Division, one purpose of which is to stimulate communities to take action with regard to delinquency, should be a prime source of both money and advice, as should the Youth Board in New York City. Although the Federal Youth Corrections Act makes no provision for rendering assistance to local communities, the capacity of the federal government in this and other facets of community programs for delinquency prevention is tremendous. Finally, professional social workers themselves, as citizens, as agency representatives and educators, and as spokesmen for their

[23] For excellent descriptions of religious programs in which churchmen have established intimate relationships with gang members and other residents of delinquency-prone neighborhoods, see C. K. Myers, *Light the Dark Streets*, Greenwich, Conn., Seabury Press, 1957, and H. J. Rahm and J. R. Weber, *Office in the Alley: Report on a Project with Gang Youngsters*, Austin, University of Texas, Hogg Foundation for Mental Health, 1958.

[20] *Ibid.*, p. 16.

[21] Bloch and Flynn, *op. cit.*, p. 514.

[22] W. C. Reckless, *The Crime Problem*, New York, Appleton-Century-Crofts, 1950, pp. 524–525.

highly influential professional associations, might become less remiss about endorsing, inaugurating, and experimenting with community-centered crime prevention programs.

In any event, if neighborhood programs run by residents are to develop to their full potential, it seems almost axiomatic that outside assistance must be provided.

IN SUMMARY

Students of delinquency are becoming increasingly aware of the necessity of reaching out beyond the child and his family in their efforts at prevention. It is submitted that the most efficacious approach for modifying the operating milieu of the bulk of our delinquents is through the widespread establishment of community-centered programs of prevention. Supported by continued improvement in the collective welfare—particularly in terms of the successful assimilation of low-status groups—and incorporating the best of "corrections" and individual treatment, the community-centered approach offers the most hope for reducing law-violation by our children and adolescents.

MOBILIZATION FOR YOUTH

The years 1962 and 1963[1] were challenging and, in many respects, rewarding for the nation's first comprehensive action-research experiment based on a new theory of the causes of juvenile delinquency.

The total Mobilization (for Youth) effort is based on the belief that programs to prevent or control juvenile delinquency can succeed only if they provide young people with genuine opportunities to behave differently. Mobilization holds that

[1] The project was announced by President Kennedy and Mayor Wagner at the White House on May 31, 1962. As of the fiscal year beginning July 1st, Mobilization for Youth was to receive grants totaling $13.2 million for a time-limited attack on the roots of delinquency. Funding sources, and amounts, include the City of New York ($4.8 million), National Institute of Mental Health ($5.2 million), President's Committee on Juvenile Delinquency and Youth Crime ($1.9 million), and the Ford Foundation ($1.8 million).

obstacles to economic and social betterment are chiefly responsible for delinquency among low-income groups. And it contends that members of these groups, particularly those who are also members of minorities, must be given a stake in the future—a tangible reason for conformity—to prevent them from becoming alienated from the values of society.

An attack on poverty and discrimination is implicit in Mobilization's underlying theory. Action programs, in the same way, have been devised with these factors in mind. Thus, creative and exciting educational and work programs have been planned and put into operation, and local residents have been involved directly in efforts to improve the social and economic opportunities which their community affords to young people.

Mobilization for Youth, a non-profit voluntary organization, was formed in

From *Action on the Lower East Side*, Program Report: July 1962–January 1964. New York: Mobilization for Youth, Inc., 1964, pp. 1–30. (Editorial adaptations.) Reprinted by permission.

1958 by a group of welfare, civic and religious institutions and agencies located on the Lower East Side of Manhattan. It was born of a common concern about a staggering increase in the area's rate of juvenile delinquency—up 70 per cent in a three-year period. In an effort to find a solution to the problem, the support of the Research Center of the Columbia University School of Social Work was enlisted. Consultation and discussions led to the conclusion that a planning period would be essential for the development of a soundly-based action-research demonstration.[2]

The planning period involved fresh, new thinking about community problems, self-evaluation by agencies and institutions and give and take by all concerned in order to reach a concensus. The pivotal role of the City of New York in the launching of any comprehensive project also became apparent during this period.

Financial assistance from the City, as well as the participation of appropriate department and agencies was a necessary prerequisite to obtaining financial support from the Federal Government and the Ford Foundation for the project conceived by Mobilization for Youth, Inc. But the City's commitment and participation goes far beyond finance.

Problems have been posed by the project's mandate to focus on prevention while faced with an obvious need to advance remedial efforts, and over questions as to whether services and strategies should be focused on the most disadvantaged or the most disturbed among the project's "target population."

Some problems have also arisen, as a

result of the project's mandate to increase the responsiveness of conventional persons and institutions to the needs, wants and culture of low-income people.

Three methods have been employed in an effort to reach the project's objectives. One of these, demonstration, has already shown signs of effectiveness in several major areas. Programs advanced by Mobilization for Youth have been adopted or replicated, in New York City and elsewhere in the nation.

Some success has been achieved with the second technique—negotiation. One outstanding example is an agreement with the City's Department of Welfare affecting the earnings of families of youngsters in Mobilization's work program who receive assistance.

But the third involving attention-getting tactics, has sometimes resulted in misunderstandings or counter-pressure. All of these approaches are outlined in the Mobilization proposal.[3] At times they are interrelated and at times, in practice, they have conflicted with each other. A final word on this subject.

Unlike most experiments, Mobilization's activities are being conducted publicly in a 67-block area on the Lower East Side of New York.[4] Nevertheless, the project has proceeded as an experiment should—risking failure, and rejecting tendencies to "play it safe."

In the process, Mobilization has provided guidelines for more recent cam-

[2] A planning grant of $412,667 for the period extending from December 1, 1959 to November 30, 1961 was made by the National Institute of Mental Health on the basis of the project's potential contribution to the social sciences.

[3] *Mobilization for Youth: A Proposal for the Prevention and Control of Delinquency by Expanding Opportunities.* New York, A Publication of Mobilization for Youth, Inc., December 9, 1961.

[4] The project area, located in Manhattan, is bounded by East 14th Street, the East River, Brooklyn Bridge, St. James Place, Pearl Street, Park Row, Chatham Square, Division Street, Canal Street, Rutgers Street, East Broadway, Grand Street, Rivington Street, Clinton Street and Avenue B.

paigns against poverty. Its job training and remedial education programs have sought to alleviate today's poverty, especially among young people aged 16 to 21. And its educational and other programs have attempted to break patterns of dependency by providing young children with better opportunities. Early childhood enrichment, reading clinic, homework helper and other tutoring programs are among the vehicles employed.

Between October 1962 and January 1964, some 1,952 area youth applied to Mobilization's job center (the estimated total pool of unemployed youth in the MFY area is 3,280). The project was able to serve two-thirds of this number. This service spanned vocational counseling, work sampling and assessment, subsidized work groups, on-the-job training in private industry, scholarships for formal trade school education, remedial education and job placement.

Reading programs mounted cooperatively with the City's Board of Education have aided 2,374 pupils, almost one-half of the area's total who are reading below grade level. In addition, more than 2,400 children have been served in kindergarten and pre-school programs and over 875 in tutorial programs. During the period, a Mobilization "first-aid" program provided concrete services to approximately 1,900 impoverished families composed of 8,500 persons, through four neighborhood "helping stations," and a homemaking service.

The project also sought to clarify its responsibility to a "target population," deciding to provide 80 to 90 per cent of its time and resources for persons in the lowest 20 per cent of the economic bracket, most of them members of minority groups. Success in implementing this priority system is suggested by the fact families served by Mobilization were 57 per cent Puerto Rican and 17 per cent Negro, during the first 18 months, although these two groups comprise less than half of the area's families.

Mobilization has sought to offer services in different ways. And statistics reflect that, in most instances, the project was on the mark in defining the needs and wants of the community. As one staff member said, in describing a Neighborhood Service Center, "an oasis was planted in the desert."

YOUTH EMPLOYMENT AND TRAINING

Mobilization's work program, involving youth employment and training, is a pioneering effort. Started on October 15, 1962, it has significantly influenced the thinking and direction of other programs throughout the country.

The program's objectives are (1) to increase the employability of youths from low-income families, (2) to improve and make more accessible training and work preparation facilities, (3) to help young people achieve employment goals equal to their capacities, (4) to increase employment opportunities for the area's youths, and (5) to help minority group youngsters overcome discrimination in hiring.

A comprehensive approach to youth employment and training is designed to achieve these objectives, including: vocational counseling, work sample assessment, subsidized work experiences, on-the-job training, formal trade training, job placement, and a remediation program to overcome basic language deficiencies.

Youth Job Center

Ninety per cent of the young people who have applied at the Youth Job Center are school dropouts; 95% are Negro and

Puerto Rican, and many come from families on welfare. Eighty-five per cent of the applicants are sufficiently disadvantaged to be unable to obtain or hold jobs in private employment without work preparation. Each applicant is interviewed by a vocational counselor who assesses the most suitable type of work experience—direct job placement, assignment to a subsidized work crew, help in getting special training in industry, or in returning to school. Regardless of assignment, the vocational counselor continues to work with each youth as long as he needs service.

Urban Youth Service Corps

The Urban Youth Service Corps is a program of paid employment for unemployed out-of-school young people devoted to projects of social utility. Building trades projects at local settlements, churches and housing projects have taught youths to construct wall partitions, replace floor beams, lay new floors, install window sashes, tile floors, plaster, paint, and put in new sidewalks. A cooperative undertaking with the New York City Department of Parks calls for the construction of bleachers. Projects within hospitals have provided dietary and nurses' aide training. Other crews have been employed in clerical tasks, woodworking, food trades and sewing, to name a few. A cooperative program with the Shell Oil Company, from which Mobilization has leased a service station, and an automotive repair shop prepare young people for jobs in service stations and as auto mechanics.

Expansion of the Urban Youth Service Corps was made possible by additional funds granted by the Office of Manpower, Automation, and Training of the U.S. Department of Labor.

On the Job Training

Mobilization's youth employment effort has developed new forms of on-the-job training. As part of a Job Development Unit, the on-the-job training program has focused primarily upon hard-to-place youths. Young people are being placed in private industry, often in small businesses, with employers sharing the cost for initial training. Careful procedures have been devised, including field visits and telephone follow-ups, to insure the integrity of the placement for training purposes. Experience has indicated that on-the-job training is the most effective device for job upgrading.

Training and Remediation

Tuition payments for trade training on a full or part-time basis have been made possible by an additional grant from the Lavenberg Foundation. A "Second Chance" Tutorial Program, emphasizing the teaching of basic language and numbers skills, is made available to trainees. As a result of their experience in the work program, a significant number of youths have been encouraged to return to school.

While it is too early to assess the results of our employment efforts, one interesting fact has emerged. A large percentage of young people in the program have either been on probation or parole, and many are gang members. When given the opportunity, they have performed effectively. Disciplinary problems have been rare, even when members of unfriendly gangs have worked side by side on the same crew. Apparently, the commonality of the work situation reduced conflict.

EDUCATION

Mobilization for Youth has identified two broad substantive areas requiring new thinking, approaches or emphasis if the public schools are to serve low-income, minority-group children adequately. And its education program, advanced cooperatively with the New York City Board of Education, stresses action in these areas.

The first is educational technology, particularly in reading. Because the school program has a high degree of verbal content, scholastic accomplishment relates directly to reading comprehension, writing and speech fluency. The Mobilization for Youth program also seeks a reduction of the gap in understanding which exists between the educational system and its low-income clientele. In our view, the failure of some pupils to achieve in school has been too widely ascribed to their "inadequacies."

While it is true that lower income socialization gives a youngster poor preparation for managing the classroom environment, it is also true that insufficient attention has been given to determining how that environment contributes to education inadequacy.

These programs deal primarily with educational (reading) technology:

(1) *The Homework Helper*—enthusiastically received by pupils, tutors and teachers—tests the effectiveness of high school youths of similar class and ethnicity in tutoring elementary school youngsters badly in need of assistance, while at the same time providing incentives for the high school student to remain and achieve in school. Its participants include 570 pupils and 240 tutors in 11 schools.

(2) *The Early Childhood* program emphasizes materials and practices to enrich language and concept formation, attention-memory, and the development of awareness of one's self. It involves 20 kindergarten and 20 first-grade classes.

Four pre-school classes for four-year olds have also been organized.

(3) *The Therapeutic Curriculum*, an experimental program of the Institute for Developmental Studies, is operating on contract within the Mobilization area. It is designed to attack the problem of language impoverishment by intervening with rich experiences in listening, speaking, vocabulary building, and concept formation at the pre-first grade level. It is expected that the children in the experimental group will be able to achieve better in their academic subjects once formal schooling begins.

(4) Two *Reading Clinics* have been organized to serve Elementary and Junior High school children. They are engaged in intensive study of the reading interests of low-income youngsters, and hope to determine the extent to which current materials, in reflecting values and ways of life alien to underprivileged children, act as a deterrent in the motivation of these students. Classes for the parents of retarded readers have provided aid with simple, systematic, approaches to assisting their children in reading development.

(5) Nine *Mobilization Reading Teachers* in each of the area's 16 elementary schools serve approximately 90 moderately-retarded readers, with one day per week spent in workshops for the development of experimental material and approaches to the solution of reading problems.

Total involvement in efforts to attack reading retardation, during the first one-and-one-half years was 2,374 pupils, approximately 50 per cent of the number of area students requiring such assistance.

(6) *Guidance Teachers*, assigned by Mobilization to 14 elementary schools, have emphasized to a greater degree than

heretofore the guidance counselors' relationship to the instructional aspects of school life. The counselors' work with small groups of first grade youngsters who are showing difficulties in reading readiness, and small groups of third and fourth grade youngsters whose potential is high, but whose reading performance is low.

(7) A *"Second Chance" Guidance and Tutoring Program,* for school dropouts, serves the tutorial needs of Mobilization youngsters within the Work, Coffee House, and Social Reintegration Programs, particularly in basic language and numbers skills, as well as providing an educational guidance service to teenage youths.

(8) Two *Laboratory Schools,* one Elementary and the other Junior High, have been so designated to develop preservice training programs for teachers in low-income area schools in cooperation with teacher training institutions. These schools also serve as centers of experimentation with curriculum ideas and materials developed at Mobilization for Youth and the local colleges.

Programs which, in addition to emphasizing educational technology, aim to decrease gaps in understanding between the system and its clientele are also under way. These include:

(1) The *School Community Relations and Small Group Program,* which encourages home visiting by teachers of all youngsters in their classes—a practice which has gone out of style, yet which may be particularly valuable in low income areas, where many teachers are strangers to the community. Social workers within this program, in addition to conducting workshops on home visiting, serve as consultants to teachers on low-income life and style, and provide, on a modest basis, individual and group counseling to parents and school children.

(2) The *Curriculum Center* is geared to the location and development of materials, and the implementation of methods, which are specifically relevant to low-income minority group children. Content area priorities are the language arts and social studies, including material related to employment opportunities.

(3) *In-Service Training* emphasizes such courses as "The Lower East Side Community," "The Negro in the United States" and "Home and Family."

(4) The *Parent Education* program, which hopes to increase communication between the school and the community, is referred to in the "Community Organization" section of this report.

COMMUNITY ORGANIZATION AND DEVELOPMENT

Organizing the Unaffiliated

The "Organizing the Unaffiliated" program stems from Mobilization's community development approach, in which the community itself is the target for change, rather than the individual delinquent. Special attention is given to discrimination and other problems in education, employment, and housing.

The program hopes to increase the power of low-income people to effect community decision-making processes. A major rationale for this objective stems from the personal sense of powerlessness felt by many lower income people, who as a result, have little motivation to learn. If fate, luck, or chance controls one's destiny, attempts to improve one's lot are a waste of time. By supporting and encouraging opportunities for social action, organizing the unaffiliated hopes to counteract such self-defeating attitudes.

Such large-scale efforts as a *Voter Registration* campaign have been launched or enhanced as a result of the unaffiliated program. *Parent Education aides,* in addition to contacting newcomers to facilitate their best utilization of schools and other community resources, assist individuals and groups in discussing problems with school personnel and in taking action when their concerns are not heard or resolved. Organizing the Unaffiliated has strengthened existent lower-income groups, such as the Council of Puerto Rican Organizations, consisting of 26 groups representing 2600 people, and organized new groups, such as the Negro Action Group, with an active membership at the present time of 300 persons. *Casa de la Communidad,* a community organization storefront, has played a significant role in the initiation of new groups of unaffiliated persons.

In addition to professional community organizers, this program depends heavily upon the activities of indigenous community workers, themselves low-income persons.

Neighborhood Councils of the Lower East Side Neighborhood Association

The Lower East Side Neighborhoods Association includes the schools, public agencies, business concerns, religious organizations, civic groups, social agencies, and others predisposed to involvement in community matters. A contract with Mobilization for Youth strengthens their community coordination and planning efforts. It provides for the organization of neighborhood councils to support these attempts.

HOUSING SERVICES UNIT

Mobilization's housing services consist of housing clinics and apartment finding (Services to Individuals and Families), collective protest activities, such as rent strikes (Community Organization), and a Housing Services Unit.

The unit provides technical information to members of the Mobilization staff and to community groups interested in housing. It systematically collects data on housing violations, through a Central Informational File. Organized by landlord and building, the file compiles complaint and action reports from housing clinics in the area and from cooperating community organizations. It increases the effective processing of complaints, and enables the selection, for enforcement action and rehabilitation aid of those landlords who are responsible for the more distressing housing conditions in the area. The file also serves to document the inadequacy of current code enforcement efforts, pointing to the need for changes in housing procedures and laws.

The Housing Services Unit also acts in an advisory capacity to guide the agency in developing policy positions regarding housing problems.

Finally, the unit has shown itself to be uniquely suited to assist in formulating new housing rehabilitation strategies. By virtue of its commitment to the service of low-income groups and its community-based mandate, Mobilization for Youth can exploit facets of the housing problem which are apparent locally. As an experimental demonstration project, Mobilization can also be utilized by the regular agencies in their exploration of new programs.

Negotiations were under way as 1964 began with New York City housing agencies to develop a Rehabilitation Consultation Service, to provide landlords with advice on needed repairs and guide them through the several housing agencies, to facilitate the use of the municipal loan fund and tax abatement procedures. Also being negotiated, at the same time, was the organization of a Non-Profit Local Improvement Corporation to purchase buildings, demonstrate different rehabilitation tactics, and develop the role of tenant's representation.

LEGAL SERVICES

A Legal Service Unit, consisting of four lawyers, consultants, and an Advisory Committee of Columbia Law School faculty, was established in January, 1964, to mitigate inequalities of justice and help reduce the shortage of lawyers for poor people.

Mobilization's approach to legal services stems from the fact that the primary contact of poor persons with the decision-making of government is not in the courtroom (criminal or otherwise), but in the anteroom of a city, state, or federal agency office, as a determination of vital significance is awaited. In the project's view, the legal profession has thus far failed in its obligation to develop a rule of law within the administrative processes of welfare-type programs. To some extent, the failure has been in advancing a conception of *rights* which vest in those who fall within the legislative intent. To a more profound extent, it has been in an almost total failure to provide a source of legal assistance to complete the realization of rights which are quite clear under the relevant statutes, but which are observed more in the breach than otherwise.

Mobilization for Youth is only the third organization in the history of New York City to be granted the right by the courts to engage in legal aid assistance (the others are the Legal Aid Society and the local bar association). It has used this right to focus upon major areas of civil law, such as the Welfare Abuses (resident) Law of New York State, and housing, unemployment insurance, and consumer fraud problems. The Unit also provides legal representation in police stations, plays an active role in the disposition of convicted persons, and assists Legal Aid attorneys in the conduct of trials.

SERVICES TO INDIVIDUALS AND FAMILIES

Fast, visible, concrete assistance to impoverished slum residents is the goal of Mobilization's program of Services to Individuals and Families. This program, on the basis of new priorities, now focuses upon the following:

1. Increasing the use of existing institutional facilities by low income persons.

2. Accumulating data to document required policy changes in public agencies in order that they may be more responsive to the special needs of the poor.

3. Ameliorating the effects of poverty, such as alienation, tension, and psychological damage, where these exist.

Neighborhood Service Centers

Four neighborhood service "helping stations"—opened in 1962 and 1963—operate out of local stores. In addition to making referrals to Mobilization and other community programs, Neighborhood Center workers serve as "social brokers." Bureaucratic systems are, at best, difficult to manage, and low income persons, who need them most, are least able to manage them. The worker as broker intervenes in the client's behalf, and seeks to insure at least minimal redress. In addition, the Centers provide small emergency financial grants, legal help, homemaking services, baby-sitting, and other concrete services. A *Consumer Aid Clinic* was established in one center in December of 1963 to provide consumer advice of both a legal and non-legal nature. A *Welfare Clinic* planned for the spring of 1964 will provide assistance to residents receiving welfare by increasing their awareness of rights and responsibilities. *Housing Clinics* provide tenants with special help in coping with landlord and code enforcement problems. An *Apartment-Finding Service* also newly-established is geared to the reduction of discriminatory barriers in housing.

Visiting Homemaker

The Visiting Homemaker unit helps reduce the self-defeating attitudes and behavior of poor people by familiarizing them with available services, increasing communication between the persons served and the community, and by teaching the techniques of cooking, shopping, budgeting, and caring for children.

Fifteen neighborhood women serve as Visiting Homemakers. The program hopes to test the effectiveness, as well as assess the problems, of using people indigenous to the low-income minority group community in program roles.

Mental Hygiene Clinic

Two Mental Hygiene Clinics are testing the viability of classical treatment services with lower-class clients and experimenting with newer casework methods, such as family-centered treatment. Contracts have been drawn with two mental hygiene clinics at local settlements to conduct this program.

Narcotics Program

Drug addiction, called "the greatest public health problem since the plague," is the least accessible to direct intervention of the many problems which demand the attention of Mobilization for Youth. A meaningful approach to the problem of drug use and addiction requires eliminating the availability of drugs. Since this objective is hardly accessible to Mobilization's intervention, experimentation in ways of reducing or altering the drug traffic is a cornerstone of the Mobilization drug program.

A second major objective is to advance knowledge of prevention and treatment methods. Psychotherapy requires verbal skills not ordinarily possessed by low-income youth and an intensity of contact and relationship eschewed by the addict. Mobilization's efforts, therefore, have been increasingly directed to group and community approaches.

The Mobilization Narcotics program consists of:

1. Ambulatory care, including the maintenance dosage of drugs—a coalition of community resources, including a medical school, the New York City Department of Health, the Lower East Side Narcotic Information Center, a settlement, the local public health clinic, the National Association for the Prevention of Addiction to Narcotics and Mobilization for Youth, is preparing an ambulatory care research program, including maintenance dosage. While such a program has its political pitfalls and medical dangers, it does provide the opportunity for careful research of the circumstances whereby an addict will not be forced to go to the underworld for his drugs and will not be forced into a pattern of crime to obtain money to support his habit.

2. Group Abstinence—Serving a limited number of 12 addicts, this program will experiment with the use of group supports, i.e., "tough" group sanctions, work adjustment efforts, and cooperative living to achieve abstinence.

3. Community Oriented Service—To

limit drug experimentation on the part of those who may be susceptible to, but are as yet only peripherally involved in drug use, a neighborhood-based group and community organization program has been developed.

4. Referral and Concrete Social Services—The Narcotics Information Center's contract with Mobilization for Youth provides, in addition to some of the above mentioned programs, informational, referral, and specific concrete social services to reduce the tensions which are a consequence of the addict's life.

Social Reintegration of Juvenile Offenders

This program seeks to demonstrate and evaluate the effects of improving the social conditions faced by the returning parolee upon his chances of recidivating. Workers, responsible for after-care (parole) functions, are in contact with families at commitment and visit the youngsters monthly at the institutions. They provide job and school placement follow-up, as well as intensive family casework services.

SERVICES TO GROUPS

Group activities of a predominantly recreational nature are among the few programs in which the conventional world makes significant contact with older delinquent youngsters. Informal learning institutions and group-service activities are also uniquely able to exploit the positive features of the minority groups' cultural background. They offer an antidote to the insularity of slum youngsters who know no neighborhood other than the radius of a few city blocks. Techniques and programs are being used to maximize the development of work skills and attitudes, as well as of skills in urban living. Finally, they are giving youngsters an opportunity to express grievances and a channel for collective social action.

Coffee House

Two Coffee Houses, in attractive new facilities, symbolic of the style and mood of the youths themselves, have been opened. Serving as social and cultural centers, these shops cut across gang lines. The youths themselves play a large role in managing these facilities. One shop contemplates a Spanish "Living Theatre" workshop, offering members the opportunity of participating in their vast cultural heritage.

Young Adult Action Group

The Young Adult Action Group—established in the fall of 1963—gives a hearing to the largely submerged point of view of adolescents. It attempts to shift the hurt and deflected anger of minority group adolescents into actions for social change. An organizational model with socio-political and educational components, it is, in the present day, an untapped form for low-income youth participation.

Institutes on the Youth Employment Bill, education, problems with the police, civil rights and freedom rides, have been conducted. Funds have been raised by the group, community wide programs held, and a youth newspaper published. Seventy group members visited Washington in February to support the Youth Employment Act, and while there met with Secretary of Labor Wirtz, Attorney General Kennedy, and several members of Congress.

Detached Worker Program

The Mobilization Detached Worker program—another innovating activity—has required a shift of professional role emphasis. The worker is viewed as a "channel," concerned with relating the street gang to the major institutional orders that impinge upon it (school authorities, potential employers, the courts, the police, etc.). Previously, the primary functions of the gang worker were to develop a personal relationship with individual youngsters or to redirect the group's energies into socially acceptable types of leisure-time activities.

Fifteen workers serving approximately 30 groups, are under contracts to local settlements and the New York City Youth Board.

Adventure Corps

The Adventure Corps reflects the fact that lower-income youth prefer the rituals, symbols, and activities of a paramilitary organization to the soft, folksy styles of more traditional recreational programs. Fifteen squads of youngsters from 9–13 participate in the Corps, which emphasizes community projects, sponsorship by local agencies and indigenous organizations, and low income youth leadership. Its membership is 308.

Pre-Adolescent Program

To many youngsters in depressed communities, the teen-age delinquent exemplifies heroism, status, adventure, and power. The Pre-adolescent Program seeks to break the repetitive pattern whereby younger boys are recruited to gang life. Bulwark of the program is a group of highly skilled social workers, based in selected community centers, who try to shift pre-delinquents to a more positive identification with community life.

Leaders work with small groups of 8–12 year old youngsters. In addition to recreational activities, services range from remedial reading exposure to prevocational training. Parental participation in this, as in other group services programs, has been successfully encouraged. Three hundred and six youngsters are active in the program.

TRAINING

A key supportive role to the program is played by MFY's Training and Personnel Department.

Its functions include in-service training, developing study courses for MFY personnel, collecting and organizing social science techniques derived from Action programs, planning and supervising field work instruction for graduate students in social work, education and vocational counseling and administering a scholarship program for graduate students.

The Department also interprets the technical and theoretical base of the programs and collects and distributes professional literature for staff use and development.

In addition to collaborative efforts with Education on teacher training, MFY's training program has focused upon the recruitment, in-service training and professional preparation of future social workers and vocational counselors.

THE PROVO EXPERIMENT:

INTRODUCTION

LaMar T. Empey*

Most correctional programs have an uncertain ancestry. They have not been rationally conceived and deliberately created. They have evolved. Perhaps in no other area of societal life are ancient traditions having to do with such things as punishment and retribution been so intertwined and contrasted with modern concerns over organization, the law, professionalism and the social sciences. The consequence for these programs is a burden of conflicting and obscure objectives complicated by confusing and often contradictory mechanisms for realizing them.

The present trend is toward the community program. This trend has a faddish quality which results in many operations that are an interesting admixture of hopeful unreality and unanticipated difficulties. Some of the problems encountered in the early days of the Provo Experiment illustrate this point and suggest why considerable effort was eventually devoted, first, to the building of a theory of treatment and, second, to implementing it as systematically as possible.

GENESIS

The Experiment grew out of a program initiated originally by Monroe J. Paxman, Fourth Juvenile District Judge in Utah,

---

* In collaboration with Maynard Erickson, Max Scott, and Jerome Rabow.

and an advisory council of citizens. The objective of Judge Paxman and his advisory group was to develop a program for those delinquents who were not succeeding on probation and who might be incarcerated unless they were corrected. Incarceration was alien to the philosophy of the judge and he sought some community alternative.

This group did not have much money with which to work and sought to establish a largely volunteer program. They sought both professional and lay support and advice and eventually selected Dr. Ray R. Canning, who was then a professor of sociology at Brigham Young University, as its first director. It was Dr. Canning who bore the heavy responsibility, in addition to his full-time work at the University, of marshalling resources and setting up the initial program.

Dr. Canning had a free hand and did not have to be concerned with an established structure and solidified preconceptions as to what should be done. But the lack of any program structure whatsoever and a staff to manage it introduced liabilities of another sort. He had to struggle with the formidable task of building a system and providing a rationale by which to give it meaning. He was concerned, therefore, not only with the difficult task of deriving a change of strategy but with all the problems of a "grass

Previously unpublished material supplied by LaMar T. Empey.

roots" program: uncertain source of funds, the lack of a permanent meeting place volunteer help and resistant offenders.

After meeting in a series of temporary places, he eventually acquired an abandoned school as a meeting place. During the course of working, first with a group of 16–18-year-olds and later with a group of younger boys, Dr. Canning initiated a daily program consisting of a number of activities: remedial reading, handicrafts, athletic activities, periodic group counseling and a kind of on-the-job training in which a service station owner trained older boys as attendants and sought jobs for them among his competitors.

Boys continued to live at home and were required to meet each day in the late afternoon. Public school teachers assisted with remedial reading and handicrafts; Dr. Canning conducted group counseling sessions; college students provided the transportation each day to and from the boys' homes; and Brigham Young University made athletic facilities available.

On paper the program appeared to be a good one. It was the kind which, if described in a popular article, might seem to have all the necessary ingredients. But many of the time-worn problems were present which make it so difficult to work with delinquents. Dr. Canning was especially concerned with the resistance which the boys exhibited to any real involvement in the program. He was reluctant to accept that resistance as a given fact as many official agencies are forced to do. But there were other problems as well, an honest appraisal of which suggested the need for reflection before making them permanent fixtures in the project. Dr. Canning preferred to consider various alternatives before settling

upon any one approach. Unfortunately, however, because of ill health, he had to leave the program at this juncture. But it was these problems with which he was concerned, and which led eventually to a total reappraisal of the whole effort by those of us who replaced him.

ATTENDANCE PROBLEMS

Although the initiation of the community program was seen by authorities as beneficial, those offenders who were assigned to it were not overjoyed. The most obvious problem was their resistance to regular attendance. It was one thing, as in the past, to be ordered by a judge to report occasionally to a busy probation officer and quite another to have to attend a *daily* program.

Both the court and the program faced a dilemma on this issue. There was nothing sacred or rehabilitative about attendance for attendance sake. On the other hand, nothing could be accomplished unless offenders were present. Therefore, both court and program had to reconsider their commitment to a daily program. If it could not be beneficial, it should be discarded because once having been set up the integrity of both the court and the program were at stake. Unless effective sanctions—both positive and negative—could be found to insure attendance then its impact might be more harmful than useful. However, successful sanctions are not in plentiful supply. There are few programs in which delinquents—or anyone else for that matter— who are a semi-captive population will immediately buy the idea that there is something in it for them.

Quite the contrary. There is a great likelihood that the "captive" population either shares, or will develop, a collective resistance in which there is peer pressure both against cooperation and in favor of rewards for successful evasion and manipulation. The same characteristics which bring honor to prisoners of war for successfully avoiding collaboration with their captors are qualitatively similar in many ways to those which delinquents exhibit in their efforts to avoid involvement.

USE OF VOLUNTEERS

A second problem had to do with the use of volunteers. There is a rather pervasive and romantic notion that volunteers, banding together to deal with the complex problems of modern life, can somehow find solutions which heretofore have defied the "experts." Delinquency is one of the problems they might solve. But the matter is more complex than that.

Volunteers were very much a part of the Provo program. They contributed a great deal. Eventually the question arose, however, as to the kinds of tasks they should be asked to perform. How best could they contribute to a community program for delinquents? Should they be expected to do everything?

One function which volunteers performed was indispensable. It was that of service on the advisory council and other support groups. The volunteers on the council were very important in seeking funds and facilities, speaking to women's and service clubs and in exerting influence on their political representatives. They provided a bridge in some cases between the program and the school or potential employers. Later, as the Experiment developed, they worked in cooperation with the Women's Legislative Council, a most influential and responsible Council concerned with civic matters of all types. The Council provided a forum through which the pros and cons of the program

were debated; members of the Council appeared at County budget hearings in behalf of it; they invited state officials to appear and express their points of view. In many ways, the Council acted as a social conscience which was most helpful in explicating basic issues.

The participation of volunteers in the daily treatment program was another matter. There were problems in working out ways by which they might be made most effective. The various people who participated in the program—college students, after-hours teachers and so on—either volunteered their help or were paid a token sum. The result was not always a happy one. The director frequently had to substitute for absent volunteers, to mollify their injured feelings or even to act as a repair man for faulty plumbing and a worn-out furnace. Thus, while over-professionalized and expensive services may not be the answer, neither is the opposite extreme. The situation seemed to call either for a diminution in program size or the acquisition of funds by which volunteers could contribute to, but who would not be expected to play key roles in the change process.

UNCOORDINATED ACTIVITIES

A third problem had to do with the various segments of the program—counseling, handicrafts, athletics—which were included because of their seeming relevance to adequate adolescent adjustment. But a *potpourri* of activities does not a program make. Just as a host of hypothetically useful, but malintegrated and unfocused, activities in the community may fail to adequately socialize young people, so in a smaller program these same activities will not necessarily be functional. It seemed certain that the problems the program was having were not solely the result of delinquent depravity but of inadequate conceptualization and implementation. It was difficult to find a structure which could, first, *control* and then *involve* and then change offenders.

These are not uncommon problems. In fact, they are so common that three general types of reactions to them are familiar. The first is organizational where the needs to hold the operation together are so great that they supersede most efforts to change offenders. The major goal is to keep the lid on and the correctional organization becomes organized to that end.

The second is characteristic of treatment-oriented people who, in noting the apparent lack of anxiety and motivation among delinquents to change, either discard them as clients or tolerate untold chaos in the name of encouraging them to understand that, no matter what, the treaters *are* interested in them. But the anarchy that sometimes results is not an answer to the problem either.

The third is characteristic of institutions where offenders and authorities evolve a subtle, and often unrecognized, *rapprochement* in which issues are not resolved, only kept covert. People keep their noses clean, take care of their own jobs, do their own time. Problems are kept under control at the expense of seeing them solved. The wise inmate recognizes that it is to his advantage to avoid open conflict and cooperates to that end. But again the goals of rehabilitation are defeated.

An appraisal of these problems in the Provo program seemed to call either for a revision of aspirations downward regarding what could realistically be accomplished or the need to answer some hard questions: What were the specific goals of the program—to educate, to improve interpersonal skills, to become better workers? What relationship did these activities have to juvenile lawbreaking? How could offenders, first, be controlled and then motivated to change?

Obviously, there are no absolute answers to such questions. No one knows with certainty what forces lead to delinquency or how they can be altered. Nevertheless, the logic and methods of science can be applied more rigorously in seeking answers than they have in the past.

In the Provo instance, there was need for some theoretical guidelines, some kind of an intellectual map which would help to relate program activities both to the processes which lead to delinquency and to the variety of institutional forces which, quite apart from program operation itself, tend to inhibit the development of effective programs. Consequently, a conceptual structure comprised of three main building blocks was developed. The first was a series of theoretical postulates as to why adolescents become persistent offenders; the second a series of postulates as to what should be done to change them; and, the third, the development of a basic strategy for implementing change.

There was nothing sacred either about the postulates or the strategy that was developed. Given a different set of basic assumptions, a totally different strategy might have been derived. The important thing is that knowledge can be gained if program implementation is preceded by conceptualization and followed by evaluation.

THE PROVO EXPERIMENT
IN DELINQUENCY REHABILITATION[*]

LaMar T. Empey and Jerome Rabow

Despite the importance of sociological contributions to the understanding of delinquent behavior, relatively few of these contributions have been systematically utilized for purposes of rehabilitation.[1] The reason is at least partially inherent in the sociological tradition which views sociology primarily as a research discipline. As a consequence, the rehabilitation of delinquents has been left, by default, to people who have been relatively unaware of sociological theory and its implications for treatment.

This situation has produced or perpetuated problems along two dimensions. On one dimension are the problems engendered in reformatories where authorities find themselves bound, not only by the norms of their own official system, but the inmate system as well. They are unable to work out an effective program: (1) because the goals of the two systems are incompatible; and (2) because no one knows much about the structure and function of the inmate system and how it

might be dealt with for purposes of rehabilitation.[2] Furthermore, the crux of any treatment program has ultimately to do with the decision-making process utilized by delinquents in the community, *not* in the reformatory. Yet, the decisions which lead to success in "doing time" in the reformatory are not of the same type needed for successful community adjustment. Existing conditions may actually be more effective in cementing ties to the delinquent system than in destroying them.[3]

The second dimension of the problem has to do with the traditional emphasis

[2] Daniel Glaser maintains that the prison social system has not received the study it merits. Most writing about prisons, he says, is "impressionistic," "moralistic," "superficial," and "biased," rather than "systematic" and "objective." "The Sociological Approach to Crime and Correction," *Law and Contemporary Problems*, 23 (Autumn, 1958), p. 697; see also Gresham M. Sykes and Sheldon Messinger, "The Inmate Social System," in *Theoretical Studies in Social Organization of the Prison*, Social Science Research Council, March 1960, pp. 5–19; and Lloyd W. McCorkle and Richard Korn, "Resocialization Within Walls," *The Annals of The American Academy of Political and Social Science*, 293 (May, 1954), pp. 88–98.

[3] Sykes and Messinger, *op. cit.*, pp. 12–13; Richard McCleery, "Policy Change in Prison Management," *Michigan State University Political Research Studies*, No. 5, 1957; Richard A. Cloward, "Social Control in the Prison," in *Theoretical Studies in Social Organization of the Prison, op. cit.*, pp. 20–48; and Stanton Wheeler, "Socialization in Correctional Communities," in this issue of the *Review*.

[*] The inception and continuation of this experiment were made possible through the cooperation of the Judge (Monroe Paxman) and staff of the Third District Juvenile Court, a voluntary group known as the Citizens Advisory Council, and Utah County Officials. Evaluation is supported by the Ford Foundation. Grateful acknowledgment is made to all involved.
[1] Donald R. Cressey, "Changing Criminals: The Application of the Theory of Differential Association," *American Journal of Sociology*, 61 (July, 1955), p. 116.

From *American Sociological Review*, 26, 5 (October 1961), pp. 679–695. Reprinted by permission of the authors and the American Sociological Association.

upon "individualized treatment."[4] This emphasis stems from two sources: (1) a humanistic concern for the importance of human dignity and the need for sympathetic understanding;[5] and (2) a widespread belief that delinquency is a psychological disease and the offender a "*sick*" person.[6] If, however, sociologists are even partially correct regarding the causes for delinquency, these two points of view overlook the possibility that most persistent delinquents do have the support of a meaningful reference group and are not, therefore, without the emotional support and normative orientation which such a group can provide. In fact, a complete dedication to an individualistic approach poses an impasse: How can an individual who acquired delinquency from a group with which he identifies strongly be treated individually without regard to the persons or norms of the system from whom he acquired it?[7]

A successful treatment program for such a person would require techniques not normally included in the individualized approach. It should no more be expected that dedicated delinquents can be converted to conventionality by such means than that devout Pentecostals can be converted to Catholicism by the same means. Instead, different techniques are required for dealing with the normative orientation of the delinquent's system, replacing it with new values, beliefs, and rationalizations and developing means by which he can realize conventional satisfactions, especially with respect to successful employment.

This does not suggest, of course, that such traditional means as probation for dealing with the first offender or psychotherapy for dealing with the disturbed offender can be discarded. But it does suggest the need for experimental programs more consistent with sociological theory, and more consistent with the sociological premise that most *persistent* and *habitual* offenders are active members of a delinquent social system.[8]

This paper presents the outlines of a program—the Provo Experiment in Delinquency Rehabilitation—which is derived from sociological theory and which seeks to apply sociological principles to rehabilitation. Because of its theoretical ties, the concern of the Experiment is as much with a systematic evaluation and

[4] Cressey, *op. cit.*, p. 116.

[5] For example, see John G. Milner, "Report on an Evaluated Study of the Citizenship Training Program, Island of Hawaii," Los Angeles: University of Southern California School of Social Work, 1959, p. IV. Irving E. Cohen implies that anything which interferes with the establishment of "confidence, sympathy and understanding" between adult and offender interferes with the effectiveness of the individualized approach. See "Twilight Zones in Probation," *Journal of Criminal Law and Criminology*, 37, No. 4, p. 291.

[6] Michael Hakeem, "A Critique of the Psychiatric Approach to Juvenile Delinquency," in *Junvenile Delinquency*, edited by Joseph S. Roucek, New York: Philosophical Library, 1958. Hakeem provides a large bibliography to which attention can be directed if further information is desired. See also Daniel Glaser, "Criminality Theories and Behavioral Images," *American Journal of Sociology*, 61 (1956), p. 435.

[7] Cressey, *op. cit.*, p. 117. LaMay Adamson and H. Warren Dunham even imply that the clinical approach cannot work successfully with habitual offenders. See "Clinical Treatment of Male Delinquents: A Case Study in Effort and Result," *American Sociological Review*, 21 (June, 1956), p. 320.

[8] One program consistent with this premise is the Highfields Residential Group Center in New Jersey. Modern penology is indebted to it for the development of many unique and important aspects. See Lloyd W. McCorkle, Albert Elias, and F. Lovell Bixby, *The Highfields Story: A Unique Experiment in the Treatment of Juvenile Delinquency*, New York: Henry Holt & Co., 1958; H. Ashley Weeks, *Youthful Offenders at Highfields*, Ann Arbor: University of Michigan Press, 1958; and Albert Elias and Jerome Rabow, Post-Release Adjustment of Highfields Boys, 1955–57, *The Welfare Reporter*, January, 1960, pp. 7–11.

reformulation of treatment consistent with findings as with the administration of treatment itself. For that reason, research and evaluation are an integral part of the program. Its theoretical orientation, major assumptions, treatment system, and research design are outlined below.

THEORETICAL ORIENTATION

With regards to causation, the Provo Experiment turned to a growing body of evidence which suggests two important conclusions: (1) that the greater part of delinquent behavior is not that of individuals engaging in highly secretive deviations, but is a group phenomenon—a shared deviation which is the product of differential group experience in a particular subculture,[9] and (2) that because most delinquents tend to be concentrated in slums or to be the children of lower class parents, their lives are characterized by learning situations which limit their access to success goals.[10]

Attention to these two conclusions does not mean that emotional problems,[11] or "bad" homes,[12] can be ignored. But only occasionally do these variables lead by themselves to delinquency. In most cases where older delinquents are involved other intervening variables must operate, the most important of which is the presence of a delinquent system—one which supplies status and recognition not normally obtainable elsewhere. Whether they are members of a tight knit gang or of the amorphous structure of the "parent" delinquent subculture,[13] habitual delinquents tend to look affectively both to their peers and to the norms of their system for meaning and orientation. Thus, although a "bad" home may have been instrumental at some early phase in the genesis of a boy's delinquency, it must be recognized that it is now other delinquent boys, not his parents, who are current sources of support and identification. Any

---

[9] Richard A. Cloward and Lloyd E. Ohlin, *Delinquency and Opportunity: A Theory of Delinquent Gangs*, Glencoe, Ill.: The Free Press, 1960; Albert K. Cohen, *Delinquent Boys—The Culture of the Gang*, Glencoe: The Free Press, 1955; Albert K. Cohen and James F. Short, Jr., "Research in Delinquent Subcultures," *The Journal of Social Issues*, 14 (1958), pp. 20–37; Solomon Kobrin, "The Conflict of Values in Delinquency Areas," *American Sociological Review*, 16 (October, 1951), pp. 653–661; Robert K. Merton, *Social Theory and Social Structure*, Glencoe: The Free Press, 1957, Chapters IV–V; Walter B. Miller, "Lower Class Culture as a Generating Milieu of Gang Delinquency," *The Journal of Social Issues*, 14 (1958), pp. 5–19; Clifford R. Shaw, *Delinquency Areas*, Chicago: University of Chicago Press, 1929; Clifford R. Shaw, Henry D. McKay, *et al.*, *Juvenile Delinquency and Urban Areas*, Chicago: University of Chicago Press, 1931; Edwin H. Sutherland, *Principles of Criminology*, 4th ed., Philadelphia: Lippincott, 1947; Frank Tannenbaum, *Crime and the Community*, Boston: Ginn and Co., 1938; F. M. Thrasher, *The Gang*, Chicago: University of Chicago Press, 1936; William F. Whyte, *Street Corner Society*, Chicago: University of Chicago Press, 1943.

[10] Richard A. Cloward, "Illegitimate Means, Anomie, and Deviant Behavior," *American Sociological Review*, 24 (April, 1959), pp. 164–176; Cloward and Ohlin, *op. cit.*; Robert K. Merton, "Social Conformity, Deviation, and Opportunity-Structures: A Comment on the Contributions of Dubin and Cloward," *American Sociological Review*, 24 (April, 1959), pp. 177–189; Robert K. Merton, "The Social-Cultural Environment and Anomie," *New Perspectives for Research on Juvenile Delinquency*, edited by Helen Kotinsky, U.S. Department of Health, Education, and Welfare, 1955, pp. 24–50; Merton, *Social Theory and Social Structure, op. cit.*

[11] Erik H. Erikson, "Ego Identity and the Psycho-Social Moratorium," *New Perspectives for Research on Juvenile Delinquency, op. cit.* pp. 1–23.

[12] Jackson Toby, "The Differential Impact of Family Disorganization," *American Sociological Review*, 22 (October, 1957), pp. 505–511; and F. Ivan Nye, *Family Relationships and Delinquent Behavior*, New York: John Wiley and Sons, 1958.

[13] Cohen and Short, Jr., *op. cit.*, p. 24.

attempts to change him, therefore, would have to view him as more than an unstable isolate without a meaningful reference group. And, instead of concentrating on changing his parental relationships, they would have to recognize the intrinsic nature of his membership in the delinquent system and direct treatment to him as a part of that system.

There is another theoretical problem. An emphasis on the importance of the delinquent system raises some question regarding the extent to which delinquents are without any positive feeling for conventional standards. Vold says that one approach to explaining delinquency ". . . operates from the basic, implicit assumption that in a delinquency area, delinquency is the normal response of the normal individual—that the non-delinquent is really the 'problem case,' the nonconformist whose behavior needs to be accounted for."[14] This is a deterministic point of view suggesting the possibility that delinquents view conventional people as "foreigners" and conventional norms and beliefs as anathema. It implies that delinquents have been socialized entirely in a criminal system and have never internalized or encountered the blandishments of conventional society.[15]

Actually, sociological literature suggests otherwise. It emphasizes, in general, that the sub-parts of complex society are intimately tied up with the whole,[16] and, specifically, that delinquents are very much aware of conventional standards; that they have been socialized in an environment dominated by middle-class morality;[17] that they have internalized the American success ideal to such a degree that they turn to illegitimate means in an effort to be successful[18] (or, failing in that, engage in malicious, or retreatist activities);[19] that they are profoundly ambivalent about their delinquent behavior;[20] and that in order to cope with the claims of respectable norms upon them, they maintain a whole series of intricate rationalizations by which to "neutralize" their delinquent behavior.[21]

---

[14] George B. Vold, "Discussion of Guided Group Interaction and Correctional Work," by F. Lovell Bixby and Lloyd W. McCorkle, *American Sociological Review*, 16 (August, 1951), p. 460.

[15] As Glaser points out, sociologists have tended to be deterministic and to ally themselves with psychiatrists in the struggle against classical legalists and religious leaders over the free will versus determinism issue. He labels this struggle as a "phony war," involving polemics more than reality. However, he says the war is losing its intensity because of a declining interest in metaphysical issues and a recognition of the importance of voluntaristic rather than reflexive conceptions of human behavior. Contrary to their protestations, the determinists, for example, recognize that humans are aware of alternative possible courses of behavior and make deliberate choices between

them. See "The Sociological Approach to Crime and Correction," *op. cit.*, pp. 686–687.

[16] Sutherland, it will be recalled, maintained that "While criminal behavior is an expression of general needs and values, it is not explained by those general needs and values since non-criminal behavior is an expression of the *same needs and values*." *Op. cit.*, pp. 6–7, italics ours. The accuracy of the statement would hinge on the definition of "needs" and "values." See also David J. Bordua, *Sociological Theories and Their Implications for Juvenile Delinquency*, U.S. Department of Health, Education, and Welfare, 1960, p. 8, and Robin M. Williams, Jr., *American Society*, New York: Alfred A. Knopf, 1955, Chapter 11.

[17] Cohen, *op. cit.*, p. 133.

[18] Merton, *Social Theory and Social Structure*, *op. cit.*

[19] Cloward, *op. cit.*, and Cloward and Ohlin, *op. cit.* See also Robert Dubin, "Deviant Behavior and Social Structure: Continuities in Social Theory," *American Sociological Review*, 24 (April, 1959), pp. 147–164.

[20] Cohen, *Delinquent Boys, op. cit.*, p. 133; Cohen and Short, *op. cit.*, p. 21. See also John I. Kitsuse and David C. Dietrick, "Delinquent Boys: A Critique," *American Sociological Review*, 24 (April, 1959), p. 211.

[21] Gresham M. Sykes and David Matza, "Techniques of Neutralization: A Theory of Delinquency," *American Sociological Review*, 22, (December, 1957), pp. 664–670.

This suggests that delinquents are aware of conventional structure and its expectations. In many conventional settings they can, and usually do, behave conventionally. But it also suggests that, like other people, they are motivated by the normative expectations of their subsystem. Consequently, when in the company of other delinquent boys, they may not only feel that they have to live up to minimal delinquent expectations but to appear more delinquent than they actually are, just as people in church often feel that they have to appear more holy than they actually are.

If this is the case, the problem of rehabilitation is probably not akin to converting delinquents to ways of behavior and points of view about which they are unaware and which they have never seriously considered as realistic alternatives. Instead, the feeling of ambivalence on their parts might be an element which could be used in rehabilitation.

An important sociological hypothesis based on this assumption would be that the ambivalence of most habitual delinquents is not primarily the result of personality conflicts developed in such social *microcosms* as the family but is inherent in the structure of the societal *macrocosm*. A delinquent sub-system simply represents an alternative means for acquiring, or attempting to acquire, social and economic goals idealized by the societal system which are acquired by other people through conventional means.

If this hypothesis is accurate, delinquent ambivalence might actually be used in effecting change. A rehabilitation program might seek: (1) to make conventional and delinquent alternatives clear; (2) to lead delinquents to question the ultimate utility of delinquent alternatives; and (3) to help conventional alternatives assume some positive valence for them. It might then reduce the affective

identification which they feel for the delinquent subsystem and tip the scales in the opposite direction.

MAJOR ASSUMPTIONS FOR TREATMENT

In order to relate such theoretical premises to the specific needs of treatment, the Provo Experiment adopted a series of major assumptions. They are as follows:

1. Delinquent behavior is primarily a group product and demands an approach to treatment far different from that which sees it as characteristic of a "sick," or "well-meaning" but "misguided," person.

2. An effective program must recognize the intrinsic nature of a delinquent's membership in a delinquent system and, therefore, must direct treatment to him as a part of that system.

3. Most habitual delinquents are affectively and ideologically dedicated to the delinquent system. Before they can be made amenable to change, they must be made anxious about the ultimate utility of that system for them.

4. Delinquents must be forced to deal with the conflicts which the demands of conventional and delinquent systems place upon them. The resolution of such conflicts, either for or against further law violations, must ultimately involve a community decision. For that reason, a treatment program, in order to force realistic decision-making, can be most effective if it permits continued participation in the community as well as in the treatment process.

5. Delinquent ambivalence for purposes of rehabilitation can only be utilized in a setting conducive to the free expression of feelings—both delinquent and conventional. This means that the protection and rewards provided by the treatment system for *candor* must exceed those provided either by delinquents for

adherence to delinquent roles or by officials for adherence to custodial demands for "good behavior." Only in this way can delinquent individuals become aware of the extent to which other delinquents share conventional as well as delinquent aspirations and, only in this way, can they be encouraged to examine the ultimate utility of each.

6. An effective program must develop a unified and cohesive social system in which delinquents and authorities alike are devoted to one task—overcoming law-breaking. In order to accomplish this the program must avoid two pitfalls: (a) it must avoid establishing authorities as "rejectors" and making inevitable the creation of two social systems within the program; and (b) it must avoid the institutionalization of means by which skilled offenders can evade norms and escape sanctions.[22] The occasional imposition of negative sanctions is as necessary in this system as in any other system.

7. A treatment system will be most effective if the delinquent peer group is used as the means of perpetuating the norms and imposing the sanctions of the system. The peer group should be seen by delinquents as the primary source of help and support. The traditional psychotherapeutic emphasis upon transference relationships is not viewed as the most vital factor in effecting change.

8. A program based on sociological theory may tend to exclude lectures, sermons, films, individual counseling, analytic psychotherapy, organized athletics, academic education, and vocational training as primary treatment techniques. It will have to concentrate, instead, on matters of another variety: changing reference group and normative orientations, utilizing ambivalent feelings resulting from the conflict of conventional and delinquent standards, and providing opportunities for recognition and achievement in conventional pursuits.

9. An effective treatment system must include rewards which are realistically meaningful to delinquents. They would include such things as peer acceptance for law-abiding behavior or the opportunity for gainful employment rather than badges, movies or furlough privileges which are designed primarily to facilitate institutional control. Rewards, therefore, must only be given for realistic and lasting changes, not for conformance to norms which concentrate upon effective custody as an end in itself.

10. Finally, in summary, a successful program must be viewed by delinquents as possessing four important characteristics: (a) a social climate in which delinquents are given the opportunity to examine and experience alternatives related to a realistic choice between delinquent or non-delinquent behavior; (b) the opportunity to declare publicly to peers and authorities a belief or disbelief that they can benefit from a change in values; (c) a type of social structure which will permit them to examine the role and legitimacy (for their purposes) of authorities in the treatment system; and (d) a type of treatment interaction which, because it places major responsibilities upon peer-group decision-making, grants status and recognition to individuals, not only for their own successful participation in the treatment interaction, but for their willingness to involve others.

THE TREATMENT SYSTEM[23]

The Provo Program, consistent with these basic assumptions, resides in the

---

[22] McCorkle and Korn, *op. cit.*, pp. 88–91.

[23] Except for the community aspects, the above assumptions and the treatment system

community and does not involve permanent incarceration. Boys live at home and spend only a part of each day at Pinehills (the program center). Otherwise they are free in the community.[24]

HISTORY AND LOCALE   The Provo Program was begun in 1956 as an "in-between" program designed specifically to help those habitual delinquents whose persistence made them candidates, in most cases, for a reformatory. It was instigated by a volunteer group of professional and lay people known as the *Citizens' Advisory Council to the Juvenile Court*. It has never had formal ties to government except through the Juvenile Court. This lack of ties has permitted considerable experimentation. Techniques have been modified to such a degree that the present program bears little resemblance to the original one. Legally, program officials are deputy probation officers appointed by the Juvenile Judge.

The cost of treatment is financed by county funds budgeted through the Juvenile Court. So near as we can estimate the cost per boy is approximately one-tenth of what it would cost if he were incarcerated in a reformatory. Research operations are financed by the Ford Foundation. Concentrated evaluation of the program is now in its second year of a six year operation. Because both the theoretical orientation and treatment techniques of the program were in developmental process until its outlines were given final form for research purposes, it is difficult to make an objective evaluation of the over-all program based on recidivism rates for previous years, especially in the absence of adequate control groups. Such an evaluation, however, is an integral part of the present research and is described below.

Relations with welfare agencies and the community, *per se*, are informal but extremely co-operative. This is due to three things: the extreme good will and guiding influence of the Juvenile Court Judge, Monroe J. Paxman,[25] the unceasing efforts of the Citizens' Advisory Council to involve the entire county as a community, and the willingness of city and county officials, not only to overcome traditional fears regarding habitual offenders in the community, but to lend strong support to an experimental program of this type.

Community co-operation is probably enhanced by strong Mormon traditions. However, Utah County is in a period of rapid transition which began in the early days of World War II with the introduction of a large steel plant, allied industries, and an influx of non-Mormons. This trend, both in industry and population, has continued to the present time. The treatment program is located in the city of Provo but draws boys from all major communities in the county—from a string of small cities, many of which border on each other, ranging in size from four to forty thousand. The total population from

---

are similar to those pioneered at Highfields. See McCorkle, Elias, and Bixby, *op. cit.* The Provo Program is especially indebted to Albert Elias, the present director of Highfields, not only for his knowledge about treatment techniques, but for his criticisms of the Provo Experiment.

[24] The idea of a community program is not new. The Boston Citizenship Training Group, Inc., a non-residential program, was begun in 1934–36. However, it is for younger boys and utilizes a different approach. A similar program, initiated by Professor Ray R. Canning, in Provo, was a fore-runner to this experiment. See "A New Treatment Program for Juvenile Delinquents," *Journal of Criminal Law and Criminology*, 31 (March–April, 1941), pp. 712–719.

[25] Judge Paxman is a member of the Advisory Council of Judges to the National Council On Crime and Delinquency and is a member of the symposium preparing a work entitled, *Justice For the Child*, University of Chicago (forthcoming).

which it draws its assignees is about 110,000.

Despite the fact that Utah County is not a highly urbanized area, when compared to large metropolitan centers, the concept of a "parent" delinquent subculture has real meaning for it. While there are no clear-cut gangs, *per se*, it is surprising to observe the extent to which delinquent boys from the entire county, who have never met, know each other by reputation, go with the same girls, use the same language, or can seek each other out when they change high schools. About half of them are permanently out of school, do not participate in any regular institutional activities, and are reliant almost entirely upon the delinquent system for social acceptance and participation.

ASSIGNEES   Only habitual offenders, 15–17 years, are assigned to the program. In the absence of public facilities, they are transported to and from home each day in automobiles driven by university students. Their offenses run the usual gamut: vandalism, trouble in school, shoplifting, car theft, burglary, forgery, and so forth. Highly disturbed and psychotic boys are not assigned. The presentence investigation is used to exclude these people. They constitute an extremely small minority.

NUMBER IN ATTENDANCE   No more than twenty boys are assigned to the program at any one time. A large number would make difficult any attempts to establish and maintain a unified, cohesive system. This group of twenty is broken into two smaller groups, each of which operates as a separate discussion unit. When an older boy is released from one of these units, a new boy is added. This is an important feature because it serves as the means by which the culture of the system is perpetuated.

LENGTH OF ATTENDANCE   No length of stay is specified. It is intimately tied to

the group and its processes because a boy's release depends not only upon his own behavior, but upon the maturation processes through which his group goes. Release usually comes somewhere between four and seven months.

NATURE OF PROGRAM   The program does not utilize any testing, gathering of case histories, or clinical diagnosis. One of its key tools, peer group interaction, is believed to provide a considerably richer source of information about boys and delinquency than do clinical methods.

The program, *per se*, is divided into two phases. Phase I is an intensive group program, utilizing work and the delinquent peer group as the principal instruments for change. During the winter, boys attend this phase three hours a day, five days a week, and all day on Saturdays. Activities include daily group discussions, hard work, and some unstructured activities in which boys are left entirely on their own. During the summer they attend an all-day program which involves work and group discussions. However, there are no practices without exceptions. For example, if a boy has a full-time job, he may be allowed to continue the job in lieu of working in the program. Other innovations occur repeatedly.

Phase II is designed to aid a boy after release from intensive treatment in Phase I. It involves two things: (1) an attempt to maintain some reference group support for a boy; and (2) community action to help him find employment. Both phases are described below.

PHASE I: INTENSIVE TREATMENT

Every attempt is made in Phase I to create a social system in which social structure, peer members, and authorities are oriented to the one task of instituting change. The more relevant to this task the system is, the greater will be its influence.

SOCIAL STRUCTURE   There is little formal structure in the Provo Program. Patterns are abhorred which might make boys think that their release depends upon *refraining* from swearing, engaging in open quarrels or doing such *"positive"* things as saying, "yes sir," or "no sir." Such criteria as these play into their hands. They learn to manipulate them in developing techniques for beating a system. Consequently, other than requiring boys to appear each day, and working hard on the job, there are no formal demands. The only other daily activities are the group discussions at which attendance is optional.

The absence of formal structure helps to do more than avoid artificial criteria for release. It has the positive effect of making boys more amenable to treatment. In the absence of formal structure they are uneasy and they are not quite sure of themselves. Thus, the lack of clear-cut definitions for behavior helps to accomplish three important things: (1) It produces anxiety and turns boys towards the group as a method of resolving their anxiety; (2) It leaves boys free to define situations for themselves: leaders begin to lead, followers begin to follow, and manipulators begin to manipulate. It is these types of behavior which must be seen and analyzed if change is to take place; (3) It binds neither authorities nor the peer group to prescribed courses of action. Each is free to do whatever is needed to suit the needs of particular boys, groups, or situations.

On the other hand, the absence of formal structure obviously does not mean that there is no structure. But, that which does exist is informal and emphasizes ways of thinking and behaving which are not traditional. Perhaps the greatest difference lies in the fact that a considerable amount of power is vested in the delinquent peer group. It is the instrument by which norms are perpetuated and through which many important decisions are made. It is the primary source of pressure for change.

THE PEER GROUP   Attempts to involve a boy with the peer group begin the moment he arrives. Instead of meeting with and receiving an orientation lecture from authorities, he receives no formal instructions. He is always full of such questions as, "What do I have to do to get out of this place?" or "How long do I have to stay?", but such questions as these are never answered. They are turned aside with, "I don't know," or "Why don't you find out?" Adults will not orient him in the ways that he has grown to expect, nor will they answer any of his questions. He is forced to turn to his peers. Usually, he knows someone in the program, either personally or by reputation. As he begins to associate with other boys he discovers that important informal norms do exist, the most important of which makes *inconsistency* rather than *consistency* the rule. That which is appropriate for one situation, boy, or group may not be appropriate for another. Each merits a decision as it arises.

Other norms center most heavily about the daily group discussion sessions. These sessions are patterned after the technique of "Guided Group Interaction" which was developed at Fort Knox during World War II and at Highfields.[26] Guided

[26] See F. Lovell Bixby and Lloyd W. McCorkle, "Guided Group Interaction and Correctional Work," *American Sociological Review,* 16 (August, 1951), pp. 455–459; McCorkle, Elias, and Bixby, *The Highfields Story, op. cit.;* and Joseph Abrahams and Lloyd W. McCorkle, "Group Psychotherapy on Military Offenders," *American Journal of Sociology,* 51 (March, 1946), pp. 455–464. These sources present a very limited account of techniques employed. An intimate knowledge would require atendance at group sessions.

Group Interaction emphasizes the idea that only through a group and its processes can a boy work out his problems. From a peer point of view it has three main goals: (1) to question the utility of a life devoted to delinquency; (2) to suggest alternative ways for behavior; and (3) to provide recognition for a boy's personal reformation and his willingness to reform others.[27]

Guided Group Interaction grants to the peer group a great deal of power, including that of helping to decide when each boy is ready to be released. This involves "retroflexive reformation."[28] If a delinquent is serious in his attempts to reform others he must automatically accept the common purpose of the reformation process, identify himself closely with others engaged in it, and grant prestige to those who succeed in it. In so doing, he becomes a genuine member of the reformation group and in the process may be alienated from his previous pro-delinquent groups.[29] Such is an ideal and long term goal. Before it can be realized for any individual he must become heavily involved with the treatment system. Such involvement does not come easy and the system must include tech-

niques which will impel him to involvement. Efforts to avoid the development of formal structure have already been described as one technique. Group processes constitute a second technique.

Before a group will help a boy "solve his problems" it demands that he review his total delinquent history. This produces anxiety because, while he is still relatively free, it is almost inevitable that he has much more to reveal than is already known by the police or the court. In an effort to avoid such involvement he may try subterfuge. But any reluctance on his part to be honest will not be taken lightly. Norms dictate that no one in the group can be released until everyone is honest and until every boy helps to solve problems. A refusal to come clean shows a lack of trust in the group and slows down the problem-solving process. Therefore, any recalcitrant boy is faced with a real dilemma. He can either choose involvement or relentless attack by his peers. Once a boy does involve himself, however, he learns that some of his fears were unwarranted. What goes on in the group meeting is sacred and is not revealed elsewhere.

A second process for involvement lies in the use of the peer group to perpetuate the norms of the treatment system. One of the most important norms suggests that most boys in the program are candidates for a reformatory. This is shocking because even habitual delinquents do not ordinarily see themselves as serious offenders.[30] Yet, the tradition is clear; most failures at Pinehills are sent to the Utah State Industrial School. Therefore, each boy has a major decision to make: either

---

[27] Other goals relating to the emphasis upon group development, the role of the group therapist, and the nature of the therapeutic situations have been described briefly elsewhere. See *The Highfields Story, op. cit.,* pp. 72–80.

[28] Cressey, *op. cit.,* p. 119.

[29] Vold maintains that guided group interaction assumes that there is something wrong inside the individual and attempts to correct that. He is right in the sense that it emphasizes that an individual must accept responsibility for his own delinquencies and that no one can keep him out of prison unless he himself is ready to stay out. Vold, in our opinion, is incorrect if his remarks are taken to mean that the group does not discuss groups and group processes, what peers mean to a boy or how the orientations of delinquent groups differ from that of conventional society. *Op. cit.,* p. 360.

[30] Delinquents are like other people: The worst can never happen to them. See also Mark R. Moran, "Inmate Concept of Self in a Reformatory Society," unpublished Ph.D. Dissertation, Ohio State University, 1953.

he makes serious attempts to change or he gets sent away.

The third process of involvement could only occur in a community program. Each boy has the tremendous problem of choosing between the demands of his delinquent peers outside the program and the demands of those within it. The usual reaction is to test the situation by continuing to identify with the former. Efforts to do this, however, and to keep out of serious trouble are usually unsuccessful. The group is a collective board on delinquency; it usually includes a member who knows the individual personally or by reputation; and it can rely on the meeting to discover many things. Thus, the group is able to use actual behavior in the community to judge the extent to which a boy is involved with the program and to judge his readiness for release. The crucial criterion for any treatment program is not what an individual does while in it, but what he does while he is *not* in it.

The fourth process involves a number of important sanctions which the group can impose if a boy refuses to become involved. It can employ familiar techniques such as ostracism or derision or it can deny him the status and recognition which come with change. Furthermore, it can use sanctions arising out of the treatment system. For example, while authorities may impose restrictions on boys in the form of extra work or incarceration in jail, the group is often permitted, and encouraged, to explore reasons for the action and to help decide what future actions should be taken. For example, a boy may be placed in jail over the week-end and told that he will be returned there each week-end thereafter until his group decides to release him. It is not uncommon for the group, after thorough discussion, to return him one or more week-ends

despite his protestations. Such an occurrence would be less likely in an ordinary reformatory because of the need for inmates to maintain solidarity against the official system. However, in this setting it is possible because boys are granted the power to make important decisions affecting their entire lives. Rather than having other people do things to them, they are doing things to themselves.

The ultimate sanction possessed by the group is refusal to release a boy from the program. Such a sanction has great power because it is normative to expect that no individual will be tolerated in the program indefinitely. Pinehills is not a place where boys "do time."

AUTHORITIES   The third source of pressure towards change rests in the hands of authorities. The role of an authority in a treatment system of this type is a difficult one. On one hand, he cannot be seen as a person whom skillful delinquents or groups can manipulate. But, on the other hand, he cannot be perceived permanently as a "rejector." Everything possible, therefore, must be done by him to create an adult image which is new and different.

Initially, authorities are probably seen as "rejectors." It will be recalled that they do not go out of their way to engage in regular social amenities, to put boys at ease, or to establish one-to-one relationships with boys. Adult behavior of this type is consistent with the treatment philosophy. It attempts to have boys focus upon the peer group, not adults, as the vehicle by which questions and problems are resolved.

Second, boys learn that authorities will strongly uphold the norm which says that Pinehills is not a place for boys to "do time." If, therefore, a boy does not become involved and the group is unwilling or unable to take action, authorities will. Such action varies. It might involve requiring him to work all day without pay, placing him in jail, or putting him in a situation in which he has no role whatsoever. In the latter case he is free to wander around the Center all day but he is neither allowed to work nor given the satisfaction of answers to his questions regarding his future status.

Boys are seldom told why they are in trouble or, if they are told, solutions are not suggested. To do so would be to provide them structure by which to rationalize their behavior, hide other things they have been doing, and escape the need to change. Consequently, they are left on their own to figure out why authorities are doing what they are doing and what they must do to get out of trouble.

Situations of this type precipitate crises. Sometimes boys run away. But, whatever happens, the boy's status remains amorphous until he can come up with a solution to his dilemma. This dilemma, however, is not easily resolved.

There is no individual counseling since this would reflect heavily upon the integrity of the peer group. Consequently, he cannot resolve his problems by counseling with or pleasing adults. His only recourse is to the group. But since the group waits for him to bring up his troubles, he must involve himself with it or he cannot resolve them. Once he does, he must reveal why he is in trouble, what he has been doing to get into trouble or how he has been abusing the program. If he refuses to become involved he may be returned to court by authorities. This latter alternative occurs rarely, since adults have more time than boys. While they can afford to wait, boys find it very difficult to "sweat out" a situation. They feel the need to resolve it.

As a result of such experiences, boys are often confused and hostile. But where such feelings might be cause for alarm elsewhere, they are welcomed at Pinehills. They are taken as a sign that a boy is not in command of the situation and is therefore amenable to change. Nevertheless, the treatment system does not leave him without an outlet for his feelings. The meeting is a place where his anger and hostility can be vented—not only against the program but against the adults who run it. But, in venting his confusion and hostility, it becomes possible for the group to analyze, not only his own behavior, but that of adults, and to determine to what end the behavior of all is leading. Initial perceptions of adults which were confusing and provoking can now be seen in a new way. The treatment system places responsibility upon a boy and his peers for changing delinquent behavior, not upon adults. Thus, adult behavior which was initially seen as rejecting can now be seen as consistent with this expectation. Boys have to look to their own resources for solutions of problems. In this way they are denied social-psychological support for "rejecting the rejectors," or for rejecting decisions demanded by the group. Furthermore, as a result of the new adult image which is pressed upon them, boys are led to examine their perceptions regarding other authorities. Boys may learn to see authorities with whom they had difficulties previously in a new, nonstereotyped fashion.

WORK AND OTHER ACTIVITIES

Any use of athletics, handicrafts, or remedial schooling involves a definition of rehabilitation goals. Are these activities actually important in changing delinquents? In the Provo Experiment they are not viewed as having an inherent value in developing non-delinquent behavior. In fact, they are viewed as detrimental because participation in them often becomes criteria for release. On the other hand, work habits are viewed as vitally important. Previous research suggests that employment is one of the most important means of changing reference from delinquent to law-abiding groups.[31] But, such findings simply pose the important question: How can boys be best prepared to find and hold employment?

Sociologists have noted the lack of opportunity structure for delinquents, but attention to a modification of the structure (assuming that it can be modified) as the sole approach to rehabilitation overlooks the need to prepare delinquents to utilize employment possibilities. One alternative for doing this is an education program with all its complications. The other is an immediate attack on delinquent values and work habits. The Provo Experiment chose the latter alternative. It hypothesized that an immediate attack on delinquent values, previous careers, and nocturnal habits would be more effective than an educational program. Sophisticated delinquents, who are otherwise very skillful in convincing peers and authorities of their good intentions, are often unable to work consistently. They have too long believed that only suckers work. Thus concentration is upon work habits. Boys are employed by the city and county in parks, streets, and recreation areas. Their work habits are one focus of group discussion and an important criterion for change. After release, they are encouraged to attend academic and vocational schools should they desire.

[31] Glaser, "A Sociological Approach to Crime and Correction," *op. cit.*, pp. 690–691.

THE STARTER MECHANISM: PUTTING THE SYSTEM IN MOTION

There are both theoretical and practical considerations relative to the purposeful creation of the social structure at Pinehills and the process by which it was developed. The foregoing discussion described some of the structural elements involved and, by inference, suggested the means by which they were introduced. However, the following is presented as a means of further clarification.

The first consideration involved the necessity of establishing structure which could pose realistically and clearly the alternatives open to habitually delinquent boys. What are these alternatives? Since in most cases delinquents are lower-class individuals who not only lack many of the social skills but who have been school failures as well, the alternatives are not great. Some may become professional criminals but this is a small minority. Therefore, most of them have two principal choices: (1) they can continue to be delinquent and expect, in most cases, to end up in prison; or (2) they can learn to live a rather marginal life in which they will be able to operate sufficiently within the law to avoid being locked up. Acceptance of the second alternative by delinquents would not mean that they would have to change their entire style of living, but it does mean that most would have to find employment and be willing to disregard delinquent behavior in favor of the drudgery of everyday living.

Until these alternatives are posed for them, and posed in a meaningful way, delinquents will not be able to make the necessary decisions regarding them. The need, therefore, was for the type of structure at Pinehills which could pose these alternatives initially without equivocation and thus force boys to consider involvement in the rehabilitative process as a realistic alternative for them.

By the time delinquents reach Pinehills they have been cajoled, threatened, lectured, and exhorted—all by a variety of people in a variety of settings: by parents, teachers, police, religious leaders, and court officials. As a consequence, most have developed a set of manipulative techniques which enable them to "neutralize" verbal admonitions by appearing to comply with them, yet refraining all the while from any real adherence. For that reason, it was concluded that *deeds*, not *words*, would be required as the chief means for posing clearly the structural alternatives open to them.

Upon arrival the first delinquents assigned to Pinehills had every reason to believe that this was another community agency for which they possessed the necessary "techniques of neutralization." It was housed in an ordinary two-story home, and authorities spent little time giving instructions or posing threats. It must have seemed, therefore, that Pinehills would not constitute a serious obstacle for which they could not find some means to avoid involvement.

The following are examples of happenings which helped to establish norms contrary to this view. After attending only one day, a rather sophisticated boy was not at home to be picked up for his second day. Instead, he left a note on his front door saying he was at the hospital visiting a sick sister. Official reaction was immediate and almost entirely opposite to what he expected. No one made any efforts to contact him. Instead, a detention order was issued by the court to the police who arrested the boy later that evening and placed him in jail. He was

left there for several days without the benefit of visits from anyone and then returned to Pinehills. Even then, no one said anything to him about his absence. No one had to; he did not miss again. Furthermore, he had been instrumental in initiating the norm which says that the principal alternative to Pinehills is incarceration.

A second occurrence established this norm even more clearly. After having been at Pinehills for two months and refusing to yield to the pressures of his group, a boy asked for a rehearing in court, apparently feeling that he could manipulate the judge more successfully than he could the people at Pinehills. His request was acted upon immediately. He was taken to jail that afternoon and a hearing arranged for the following morning. The judge committed him to the State Reformatory.[32] Since that time there has never been another request for a rehearing. In a similar way, especially during the first year, boys who continued to get in serious trouble while at Pinehills were recalled by the court for another hearing and assigned to the reformatory. These cases became legendary examples to later boys. However, adults have never had to call attention to them; they are passed on in the peer socialization process.

Once such traditions were established, they could yet be used in another way. They became devices by which to produce the type of uncertainty character-

---

[32] Co-operation of this type between the Juvenile Courts and rehabilitative agencies is not always forthcoming. Yet, it also reflects two things: (1) the fact that Judge Paxman sentences only those boys to Pinehills who are habitual offenders; and (2) the fact that it is his conviction that rehabilitation must inevitably involve the Court's participation, both in posing alternatives for boys and in determining the effectiveness of various approaches.

istic of social settings in which negative sanctions should be forthcoming but do not appear. The individual is left wondering why. For example, not all boys who miss a day or two at Pinehills now are sent to jail. In some cases, nothing is said to the individual in question. He is left, instead, to wonder when, and if, he will be sent. Likewise, other boys who have been in serious trouble in the community are not always sent to the State Reformatory but may be subjected to the same kind of waiting and uncertainty. Efforts are made, however, to make it impossible for boys to predict in advance what will happen in any particular case. Even adults cannot predict this, relying on the circumstances inherent in each case. Thus, both ridigity and inconsistency are present in the system at the same time.

The same sort of structural alternatives were posed regarding work. Boys who did not work consistently on their city jobs, where they were being paid, were returned to Pinehills to work for nothing. At Pinehills, they were usually alone and had to perform such onerous tasks as scrubbing the floor, washing windows, mowing the lawn or cutting weeds. They might be left on this job for hours or weeks. The problem of being returned to work with the other boys for pay was left to them for their own resolution, usually in the group. So long as they said nothing, nothing was said to them except to assign them more work.

This type of structure posed stark but, in our opinion, realistic alternatives. It was stark and realistic because boys were still living in the community, but for the first time could sense the omnipresence of permanent incarceration. However, another type of structure less stringent was needed by which boys could realistically resolve problems and make choices.

Since, as has been mentioned, peer-group decision-making was chosen as the means for problem-resolution, attention was focussed upon the daily group meetings as the primary source of information. It became the focal point of the whole treatment system.

The first group, not having any standards to guide it (except those which suggested resistance to official pressures), spent great portions of entire meetings without speaking. However, consistent with the idea that deeds, not words, count, and that a group has to resolve its own problems, the group leader refused to break the silence except at the very end of each meeting. At that time, he began standardizing one common meeting practice: he summarized what had been accomplished. Of silent meetings he simply said that nothing had been accomplished. He did point out, however, that he would be back the next day—that, in fact, he would be there a year from that day. Where would they be, still there? The problem was theirs.

When some boys could stand the silence no longer, they asked the group leader what they might talk about. Rather than making it easy for them he suggested something that could only involve them further: he suggested that someone might recite all the things he had done to get in trouble. Not completely without resources, however, boys responded by reciting only those things they had been caught for. In his summary, the leader noted this fact and suggested that whoever spoke the next time might desire to be more honest by telling all. Boys were reluctant to do this but, partly because it was an opportunity to enhance reputations and partly because they did not know what else to do, some gave honest recitations. When no official action was taken against them, two new and important norms were introduced: (1) the idea that what is said in the meeting is sacred to the meeting; and (2) that boys can afford to be candid—that, in fact, candor pays.

The subsequent recitals of delinquent activities ultimately led to a growing awareness of the ambivalence which many delinquents feel regarding their activities. In the social climate provided by the meeting some boys began to express feelings and receive support for behavior which the delinquent system with its emphasis on ideal-typical role behavior could not permit.

Eventually, the meeting reached a stage where it began to discuss the plethora of happenings which occurred daily, both at Pinehills and elsewhere in the community. These happenings, rather than impersonal, easily speculated-about material, were urged as the most productive subject matter. For example, many boys had reached the stage of trying devious rather than direct methods of missing sessions at Pinehills. They came with requests to be excused for normally laudatory activities: school functions, family outings, and even religious services. But, again adults refused to take the traditional course of assuming responsibility and making decisions for boys. Boys were directed to the meeting instead. This not only shifted the responsibility to them, but provided the opportunity to develop five important norms: (1) those having to do with absences; (2) the idea that the place for problem-solving is in the meeting; (3) that everyone, not just adults, should be involved in the process; (4) that if a boy wants the meeting to talk about his problems, he has to justify them as being more important than someone else's; and (5) that any request or point of view has to be substantiated both by evidence and some relevance to the solution of delinquent problems.

It became obvious that even simple requests could be complicated. Boys found themselves using their own rationalizations on each other, often providing both humorous and eye-opening experiences. The climate became increasingly resistant to superficial requests and more conducive to the examination of pressing problems. Boys who chose to fight the system found themselves fighting peers. A stubborn boy could be a thorn in the side of the whole group.

The daily meeting summaries took on increased importance as the leader helped the group: (1) to examine what had happened each day; (2) to examine to what ends various efforts were leading—that is, to examine what various boys were doing, or not doing, and what relevance this had for themselves and the group; (3) to suggest areas of discussion which had been neglected, ignored, or purposely hidden by group members; and (4) to describe the goals of the treatment system in such a way that boys could come to recognize the meaning of group discussions as a realistic source of problem-resolution.

The structural lines associated with the meeting eventually began to define not only the type of subject matter most relevant to change, but the general means for dealing with this subject matter. However, such structure was extremely flexible, permitting a wide latitude of behavior. Great care was taken to avoid the institutionalization of clear-cut steps by which boys could escape Pinehills. Problem solving was, and still is, viewed as a process—a process not easily understood in advance, but something which develops uniquely for each new boy and each new group.

Finally, in summary, the Pinehills system, like many social systems, has some rigid prerequisites for continued membership. The broad structural outlines carefully define the limits beyond which members should not go. However, unlike most extreme authoritarian systems, there is an inner structure, associated with the meeting, which does not demand rigid conformity and which instead permits those deviations which are an honest expression of feelings.

The admission of deviations within the structural confines of the meeting helps to lower the barriers which prevent a realistic examination of their implications for the broader authoritarian structure, either at Pinehills or in society at large. Boys are able to make more realistic decisions as to which roles, conventional or delinquent, would seem to have the most utility for them.

This brief attempt to describe a complex system may have been misleading. The complexities involved are multivariate and profound. However, one important aspect of the experiment has to do with the theoretical development of, and research on, the nature of the treatment system. Each discussion session is recorded and efforts are made to determine means by which treatment techniques might be improved, and ways in which group processes can be articulated. All would be very useful in testing theory which suggests that experience in a cohesive group is an important variable in directing or changing behavior.

PHASE II: COMMUNITY ADJUSTMENT

Phase II involves an effort to maintain reference group support and employment for a boy after intensive treatment in Phase I. After his release from Phase I he continues to meet periodically for discussions with his old group. The goal is to utilize this group in accomplishing three things: (1) acting as a check on a boy's current behavior; (2) serving as a law-abiding reference group; and (3) aiding in the solution of new problems. It seeks to continue treatment in a different and perhaps more intensive way than such traditional practices as probation or parole.

Efforts to find employment for boys are made by the Citizens' Advisory Council. If employment is found, a boy is simply informed that an employer needs someone. No efforts are taken by some well-meaning but pretentious adult to manipulate the boy's life.

These steps, along with the idea that delinquents should be permitted to make important decisions during the rehabilitative process, are consistent with structural-functional analysis which suggests that in order to eliminate existing structure, or identification with it, one must provide the necessary functional alternatives.[33]

APPROPRIATENESS OF TECHNIQUES

Many persons express disfavor with what they consider a harsh and punitive system at Pinehills. If, however, alternatives are not great for habitual delinquents, a program which suggests otherwise is not being honest with them. Delinquents are aware that society seldom provides honors for *not* being delinquent; that, in fact, conventional alternatives for them have not always promised significantly more than delinquent alterna-

---

[33] Edwin M. Schur, "Sociological Analysis in Confidence Swindling," *Journal of Criminal Law, Criminology and Police Science*, 48 (September–October, 1957), p. 304.

tives.[34] Therefore, expectations associated with the adaption of conventional alternatives should not be unrealistic.

On the other hand it should be remembered that, in terms familiar to delinquents, every effort is made at Pinehills to include as many positive experiences as possible. The following are some which seem to function:

1.   Peers examine problems which are common to all.

2.   There is a recurring opportunity for each individual to be the focal point of attention among peers in which his behavior and problems become the most important concern of the moment.

3.   Delinquent peers articulate in front of conventional adults without constraint with regard to topic, language, or feeling.

4.   Delinquents have the opportunity, for the first time in an institutional setting, to make crucial decisions about their own lives. This in itself is a change in the opportunity structure and is a means of obligating them to the treatment system. In a reformatory a boy cannot help but see the official system as doing things to him in which he has no say: locking him up, testing him, feeding him, making his decisions. Why should he feel obligated? But when some important decision-making is turned over to him, he no longer has so many grounds for rejecting the system. Rejection in a reformatory might be functional in relating him to his peers, but in this system it is not so functional.

5.   Delinquents participate in a treatment system that grants status in three ways: (a) for age and experience in the treatment process—old boys have the responsibility of teaching new boys the norms of the system; (b) for the exhibition of law-abiding behavior, not only in a minimal sense, but for actual qualitative changes in specific role behavior at Pinehills, home or with friends; and (c) for the willingness to confront other boys, in a group setting, with their delinquent behavior. (In a reformatory where he has to contend with the inmate system a boy can gain little and lose much for his willingness to be candid in front of adults about peers, but at Pinehills it is a primary source of prestige.) The ability to confront others often reflects more about the *confronter* than it does about the *confronted*. It is an indication of the extent to which he has accepted the reformation process and identified himself with it.[35]

6.   Boys can find encouragement in a program which poses the possibility of relatively short restriction and the avoidance of incarceration.

7.   The peer group is a potential source of reference group support for law-abiding behavior. Boys commonly refer to the fact that their group knows more about them than any other persons: parents or friends.

RESEARCH DESIGN

An integral part of the Provo Experiment is an evaluation of treatment extending over a five year period. It includes means by which offenders who receive treatment are compared to two control groups: (1) a similar group of offenders who at time of sentence are placed on probation and left in the community; and (2) a similar group who at time of sen-

---

[34] Gwynn Nettler has raised a question as to who perceives reality most accurately, deviants or "good" people. See "Good Men, Bad Men and the Perception of Reality," Paper delivered at the meetings of the American Sociological Association, Chicago: September, 1959.

[35] Support for this idea can be found in a recently developed matrix designed to measure the impact of group interaction. See William and Ida Hill, *Interaction Matrix for Group Psychotherapy*, mimeographed manuscript, Utah State Mental Hospital, Provo, Utah, 1960. This matrix has been many years in development.

tence are incarcerated in the Utah State Industrial School. Since it is virtually impossible to match all three groups, random selection is used to minimize the effect of sample bias. All three groups are drawn from a population of habitual delinquents who reside in Utah County, Utah, and who come before the Juvenile Court. Actual selection is as follows:

The Judge of the Court has in his possession two series of numbered envelopes —one series for selecting individuals to be placed in the *probation* treatment and control groups and one series for selecting the *reformatory* treatment and control groups. These series of envelopes are supplied by the research team and contain randomly selected slips of paper on which are written either *Control Group* or *Treatment Group.*

In making an assignment to one of these groups the Judge takes the following steps: (1) After hearing a case he decides whether he would ordinarily place the offender on probation or in the reformatory. He makes this decision as though Pinehills did not exist. Then, (2) he brings the practice of random placement into play. He does so by opening an envelope from one of the two series supplied him (See figure 1 below). For example, if he decides initially that he would ordinarily send the boy to the reformatory, he would select an envelope from the *reformatory* series and depend upon the designation therein as to

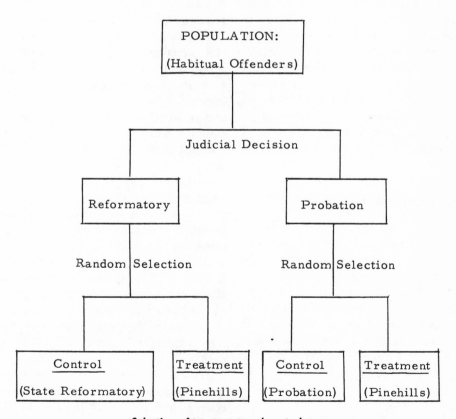

POPULATION:

(Habitual Offenders)

Judicial Decision

Reformatory

Probation

Random Selection

Random Selection

Control

(State Reformatory)

Treatment

(Pinehills)

Control

(Probation)

Treatment

(Pinehills)

Selection of treatment and control groups.

whether the boy would actually go to the reformatory, and become a member of the *control* group, or be sent to Pinehills as a member of the *treatment* group.

This technique does not interfere with the judicial decision regarding the alternatives previously available to the Judge, but it does intercede, after the decision, by posing another alternative. The Judge is willing to permit the use of this alternative on the premise that, in the long run, his contributions to research will enable judicial decisions to be based ultimately on a more realistic evaluation of treatment programs available.

In order to make the comparison of treatment and control groups more meaningful, additional research is being conducted on the treatment process. Efforts are made to examine the problems involved in relating causation theory to intervention strategy, the role of the therapist in Guided Group Interaction, and the types of group interaction that seem most beneficial. Finally, a detailed examination is being made of the ways in which boys handle "critical incidents"[36] after release from treatment as compared to the way they handled them prior to treatment.

SUMMARY AND IMPLICATIONS

This paper describes an attempt to apply sociological theory to the treatment of delinquents. It concentrates not only upon treatment techniques, *per se,* but the type of social system in which these techniques must operate. The over-all treatment system it describes is like all other social systems in the sense that it specifies generalized requirements for continued membership in the system. At

the same time, however, it also legitimizes the existence of a subsystem within it— the meeting—which permits the discussion and evaluation of happenings and feelings which *may* or *may not* support the over-all normative structure of the larger system.

The purposeful creation of this subsystem simply recognized what seemed to be two obvious facts: (1) that the existence of contrary normative expectations among delinquent and official members of the over-all system would ultimately result in the creation of such a subsystem anyway; and (2) that such a system, not officially recognized, would pose a greater threat, and would inhibit to a greater degree, the realization of the over-all rehabilitative goals of the major system than would its use as a rehabilitative tool.

This subsystem receives not only official sanction but grants considerable power and freedom to delinquent members. By permitting open expressions of anger, frustration, and opposition, it removes social-psychological support for complete resistance to a realistic examination of the ultimate utility of delinquent versus conventional norms. At the same time, however, the freedom it grants is relative. So long as opposition to the demands of the larger system is contained in the meeting subsystem, such opposition is respected. But continued deviancy outside the meeting cannot be tolerated indefinitely. It must be seen as dysfunctional because the requirements of the over-all treatment system are identified with those of the total society and these requirements will ultimately predominate.

At the same time, the over-all treatment system includes elements designed to encourage and support of the adoption of conventional roles. The roles it encour-

[36] John C. Flanagan, "The Critical Incident Technique," *Psychological Bulletin,* 51 (July, 1954), pp. 327–358.

ages and the rewards it grants, however, are peer-group oriented and concentrate mainly upon the normative expectations of the social strata from which most delinquents come: working- rather than middle-class strata. This is done on the premise that a rehabilitation program is more realistic if it attempts to change normative orientations towards lawbreaking rather than attempting (or hoping) to change an individual's entire way of life. It suggests, for example, that a change in attitudes and values toward work *per se* is more important than attempting to create an interest in the educational, occupational, and recreational goals of the middle-class.

The differences posed by this treatment system, as contrasted to many existing approaches to rehabilitation, are great. Means should be sought, therefore, in addition to this project by which its techniques and orientation can be treated as hypotheses and verified, modified, or rejected.

The Provo Experiment: Research and Findings

LaMar T. Empey*

It was felt that in order to test the theoretical postulates of the study and to determine something about its effectiveness, research would have to be concerned with three things: program *input*, describing the characteristics of the offenders assigned to the program; program *process*, a study of whether the theory of treatment had actually been implemented; and program *impact*, some measurement of program influence on clients, staff and community.

Examination of Input

The reason for collecting *input* data on offender characteristics is to determine wherein the basic assumptions of the study may be correct or incorrect. Such a collection of data is necessary because, if the basic assumptions about offenders have no basis in fact, then theoretically the treatment program would be relative-

* In collaboration with Maynard Erickson, Max Scott, and Jerome Rabow.

ly ineffective. It would be oriented to changing characteristics which in reality are unimportant.

Data which will reflect on basic causation assumptions have been gathered, not only from the experimental and control groups but from nondelinquents as well. In order to test postulates it is equally, or more, important to study differences between nondelinquents and delinquents. The reason is that the factors which distinguish delinquents from nondelinquents are those which are most crucial. It is those on which change should occur. At the same time such differences can also be used for testing the comparability of experimental and control groups. If they do not differ this is one method of assuring that samples are comparable, that the same types of people have been included in experimental and control groups.

Preliminary analyses on such variables as family adjustment, class level, school behavior, future aspirations, delinquent

Previously unpublished material supplied by the author.

history and friendship patterns have been made. Two papers describing the delinquent history of four delinquent and nondelinquent subsamples have been published.[1]

They present some striking findings. First, they indicate that the persistent offenders assigned to this study, as experimental and control groups, are far more delinquent than non- and one-time offenders. The selection process appears, therefore, to be valid.

Second, they indicate that the same kinds of differences do not exist between offenders from different status levels. Instead, boys on one status level seem to be no more nor no less delinquent than boys on another. There are instead rather distinctive patterns of delinquent behavior distinguishing different status groups.

Such findings are but a part of those that will be presented in the final report on the Experiment. They will indicate possible weaknesses in the basic assumptions and indicate ways in which they might be modified. Furthermore, they will provide information which will be useful in evaluating the impact of the treatment process. For example, changes in family and school adjustment, diminution of delinquent behavior and changes in friendship patterns will be useful indices in assessing outcome.

Examination of Process

GROUP DEVELOPMENT   During the whole course of the Experiment a taped

[1] Maynard Erickson and LaMar T. Empey, "Court Records, Undetected Delinquency and Decision-Making," *The Journal of Criminal Law, Criminology and Police Science,* 54 (Dec., 1963), pp. 456–469; Maynard L. Erickson and LaMar T. Empey, "Class Position, Peers and Delinquency," *Sociology and Social Research,* 49 (April, 1965), pp. 268–282; and LaMar T. Empey and Maynard L. Erickson, "Hidden Delinquency and Social Status," *Social Forces,* forthcoming.

recording and a research description of each group meeting was made. These materials were gathered in order to test experimental treatment assumptions, especially to relate the theory regarding the use of groups to what actually occurred.

The task of measuring group interaction is a monumental one. Very little empirical measurement has been carried out. Adequate tools have not been available. Because of these complex problems, the tape recordings and other research data were utilized primarily to provide a descriptive rather than evaluative analysis.

During the past year, the taped recordings and the research analysis have been examined in order to make a systematic analysis of the processual development and structure of the total treatment system and groups within it.

Although the analysis has not been completed, an examination of the process suggests the group development goes through a series of stages, from one in which involvement is minimal to one in which boys carry increasingly heavy responsibilities. Some groups develop more effectively than others. In those which do, the evolutionary process seems to be both theatening and rewarding, not only to boys but to staff.

On one hand, in order for boys to increase their capacity to take responsibility, power has to be granted to them by staff. Staff has to honor youthful participation in decision-making and other processes. It has to pay heed to differential perceptions and seek ways to change staff as well as delinquents if the two are to be successful in collaborating. It is not always easy for a staff to be willing to share power and responsibility.

On the other hand, problems face delinquent members of the group. They must decide whether they have more to lose than to gain if they do change. But, in addition, once having made an attempt to change, a group is still faced with community resistance. The question is not whether boys can assume responsibility, but whether the community is willing to *let* them assume it. Adults are often hypo-critical. On one hand, they are critical because delinquents are not responsible citizens. Yet, on the other, they are afraid of efforts which permit adolescents to make decisions, solve problems, or exer-cise control over one of their members. Nevertheless, the evidence seems to indi-cate that the capacity of a group of delin-quents to find new solutions or to deal with complex issues may exceed the will-ingness of authorities to let them exercise it.

The capacity to deal with such prob-lems varied somewhat from group to group. In general, however, the evidence seemed to be that most groups reached a stage in which the group as a whole be-came adept in isolating basic problems, in judging the performance of group members and in making decisions about individual members. The process depart-ed so far from traditional concepts of group therapy that it was these kinds of functions that encountered resistance from professional and community offi-cials.

WORK PROGRAM   The work program at the Provo Experiment involved a vari-ety of activities: work at the city ceme-tery, the building of a flood-control canal, minor construction on city streets or work at the city sewage disposal plant. Such work activities are generally seen by lay and professional people as having some inherent therapeutic quality. Ranches, in-stitutions, farms and youth camps utilize work programs on the premise that hard work will chance delinquent character-istics. Perhaps it was becauseof this orien-tation that our community work program was reluctantly, but nevertheless eventu-ally, accepted and supported by local and state funds. Two interesting conse-quences resulted.

On one hand, our experiences during the first two years of the Experiment caused us to question the rationale ex-pressed above. We wondered whether, by having delinquent boys work together, we were perpetuating rather than chang-ing delinquent behavior. There was con-tinual friction between the boys and the adult supervisors who were hired to direct them. These supervisors tended either to take an unbending authoritarian stance with the boys, or to be seduced by them, succumbing in the last case to manipulations in an apparent desire to be accepted by the boys. The result was that the responsibility for work failures and delinquent acts on the job were shifted from the boys and their supervisors to the group leaders at the Experiment. It fell to them to try to maintain control and prevent outbursts. Consequently, rather than work becoming a productive and positive experience, it became a thorn in the side.

These circumstances served primarily to reinforce rather than diminish delin-quent perceptions. Any difficulties were blamed by boys upon adults. The gap be-tween offenders and adults remained as wide as ever. There was no mechanism by which to bridge this gap and to share responsibility for that which occurred. This led, in the third year of the Experi-ment, to a rather drastic change.

In an attempt to locate responsibility for difficulties on the job, adult work supervisors were fired and members of the work crews themselves were appoint-ed as supervisors.

Initially, the change resulted in anxiety and confusion. Boy supervisors now found themselves in the role of adults attempting to exercise control over their peers. Such conditions provided an insightful experience. Boys began to recognize for the first time some of the pressures that they had put previously upon those who had attempted to control them

Fortunately, the work activities did not degenerate but tended to improve. A different attitude began to develop among the work crews. When mistakes were made, the boys rather than adults, had to bear the responsibility. There was no adult present upon which to levy blame. It was much easier in the group meetings, therefore, to examine realistically what the problems were on the job: who the poor workers were, what kind of delinquent manipulations were taking place, what it meant to be an adult rather than a child. The change seemed to provide an opportunity for boys to experiment realistically with new adult roles. Furthermore, the work output increased.

The second major observation relative to the work program has to do with the kinds of problems that were generated in providing work opportunities for the delinquent boys. A city government or a private business is not always organized to employ young people, even if they have a contribution to make. Child labor laws often create difficulties and young people competing for jobs may even be seen as a threat to the job security of older people.

Thus, although there seemed to be considerable work that needed to be done in Provo, and, although wages paid to the delinquent work crews were small, it was not always possible to have work projects outlined in advance. In addition, it was difficult for city foremen to accept the notion that the boys in the work crews could become supervisors. Not only were foremen concerned about legal responsi-

bility, but the age, mode of dress, and mode of speaking of many of these offenders. It was difficult to have the work crews accepted as a part of the daily operation.

It seems unlikely that such problems can be overcome on a permanent basis. Instead, they must be dealt with on a day-to-day basis. In order to do this, a mechanism must be set up and nourished which will permit differences to come into the open. Only after they are made explicit and examined is it possible to work out an accommodation which will result in the perpetuation of adolescent work programs. There was some evidence that this finally developed in Provo.

The role of work crews at the Experiment gradually became that of trouble shooter; that is the crews were used in a variety of places wherever the need was greatest. One summer they built a flood-control ditch in a particularly dangerous area. During the winter they worked to maintain a city skating rink. In the spring they worked at the cemetery and other places, cleaning them up after the winter's debris. They were able to perform a useful and productive function.

As some evidence of this, Provo City eventually expanded its work program to include adolescents other than those at the Experiment. In so doing, they sought the assistance of the staff at the Provo Experiment in terms of the best means for obtaining insurance coverage, determining pay scale and procedures, controlling adolescent workers and the best means for selecting and employing supervisors. The most unique thing of all was the fact that the City hired former delinquents from the Experiment as supervisors for both the delinquent and nondelinquent work crews. These adolescent supervisors were carefully selected and seemed to be able to deal well with the problems which they encountered. This use of former delinquents seems very important in light of contemporary efforts to find work opportunities for out-of-school youth. Not all graduates of the Experiment could perform the functions but several could.

COURT RELATIONS The Judge of the Juvenile Court, Monroe J. Paxman, played a vital and indispensable role in the Experiment. Without his active and consistent support, it could not have occurred. Yet, a number of problems were generated which should be considered in any future experimentation.

The first has to do with the Court staff itself. They could not escape its impact. One very obvious reason is that the Experiment design put them in competition, in one sense, with the Experiment. The boys who were members of the probation control group were members of probation officer case loads. Consequently, it was impossible for the Chief Probation Officer and his deputies to ignore the possibility that those for whom they were responsible might do more poorly than boys who attended the experimental program. No amount of discussion regarding the scientific need to try different methods or to recognize that the treatment approaches were vastly different could do away with a sense of competition.

A second problem had to do with differences in treatment philosophy. For example, the intervention strategy of the Experiment called for intense efforts to promote anxiety and to pose alternatives clearly for delinquents. If boys who were assigned to the program failed to attend or continued to get into trouble, requests were sometimes made to the Court that they be placed in detention. The effort was then made to use their position in detention as a means of involving them more effectively in group discussions. The idea was to use negative sanctions more

effectively, to utilize them as means for change rather than as means for punishment. Such practices and philosophy differed, of course, from the practices and philosophy of many professionals and organizations now in the field.

But there are not many happy alternatives to the use of occasional short-term detentions for the serious offender. Unless short-term detention along with other activities in the community can be utilized to change these offenders, then the only alternative is to incarcerate them permanently. This paradox was discussed on several occasions with opponents. It was never resolved.

Another problem seems in retrospect to be that of a failure on the part of the Experimental staff to devote long periods of time with the Court staff in discussing philosophy and experimental findings. One problem was that research takes many years to accomplish. Its results cannot be made immediately available. Nevertheless, greater efforts should have been made.

All of these problems placed the Judge of the Juvenile Court in a difficult position. Efforts to bridge the gap on his part may have only served to broaden the rift. The Judge found himself in a difficult position of trying to support both his own staff and the Experiment as well. His position was made even more difficult because of the publicity accorded the Experiment, both locally and nationally.

On a local level the Experiment gained considerable attention because of the efforts of the Experiment staff to gain the support of political, citizen and bureaucratic officials. Court staff could not but feel left out because of all the attention the Experiment was getting.

On a national level, the Judge found himself in a position of explaining and supporting the Experiment's theoretical design, methodology and techniques. But while doing so, he again may have appeared to be ignoring the efforts of his own staff. Regardless of what probation officers did, it may have been perceived by them as being insignificant in the eyes of the Judge when compared to what the Experiment was doing.

When these problems were added to the feeling of the Court staff that their own work was being evaluated and researched, a situation was created which was not easily resolved. However, there are some fascinating findings which may have resulted from these tensions. They will be explained in the statistics on recidivism.

The problems with the Court, especially the Chief Probation Officer, had direct influence on the treatment program during the last few months of operation, particularly, in terms of the availability of detention facilities. Eventually the pressure became so great that all use of detention facilities was discontinued. This seriously hampered efforts to control boys who were continuing to get in trouble, and although new methods were devised to cope with the problem, it placed considerably more demands upon the treatment staff in terms of time and energy. In our opinion, these other methods were not so successful as the use of detention. It remains, however, for the research analysis to indicate whether or not this was in fact the case.

THE SCHOOLS   In the initial phases of the Provo Experiment, it was felt that some delinquent boys who had had a long history of school failure might better be encouraged to leave school. We felt that, given some support to find jobs, a job might diminish some of the tensions felt by the boys. However, as the discussion groups began to develop it was with some surprise that we discovered that most of the boys in the groups did not share this opinion. They seemed to feel that despite all problems, the best place for adolescents to be was in school. Consequently, the emphasis changed. Considerable effort was made by the groups to help boys remain in school.

School problems became a matter of great importance in group meetings; school progress was used by group members as a criterion for judging progress and release; and, a more effective liaison between experimental staff and school officials was established. A system for exchanging progress reports in both agencies was developed. In addition, a tutorial program was added to the Experiment.

The result was the development of an exceptionally cooperative relationship between the Experiment staff and school officials. We are not sure yet as to the basic reasons for the success of this relationship. Some boys who otherwise would have dropped from school have remained in. However, until research analyses are made, we are not sure that their staying in school was because of a better academic performance on their part or because their attitude and behavior had changed markedly.

We suspect that part of the reason they seemed to get along better in school was because they became much less a conduct problem. School officials were delighted because boys who previously had caused a great deal of trouble were now much less trouble. School principals, counselors and teachers, therefore, expressed considerable concern that the treatment program would end once the original experimental period was over. They were among those who most actively supported the notion that the program should become a community fixture.

COMMUNITY RELATIONSHIPS   Support by the community for the Experiment was mixed. On one hand, the support of citizens and organized groups in developing the Experiment was indispensable. There was virtually no opposition to having a special program for delinquents in the community. Local groups vigorously supported the use of County funds by which to run the program.

On the other hand, it was extremely difficult to obtain the support of key County and State officials. During the early years of the program, before it was formalized as an Experiment, Utah County provided a small amount annually with which to run it. When a research grant was obtained, County funds, approximately $12,000 per year for treatment purposes, was matched by funds from the Ford Foundation. (In addition, Ford funds financed the research operation.) But, when, in the elections of 1960, political control of the County Commission changed hands, strong opposition was raised to any further County financing.

During that year, and for two subsequent years, County funds were budgeted only after a running battle between the County Commission and supportive citizens' groups. County officials contended, and with some justification, that since both the Juvenile Court and probation systems in Utah are state systems, the State, not the County, should finance the program. State officials, on the other hand, demurred, arguing that since the program was started on a local level it should be financed on the local level.

The Speaker of the Utah House of Representatives attempted to intercede, feeling that the State had some investment in seeing the Experiment completed since it was much less expensive than total incarceration and might be equally or more successful. On one occasion he arranged a meeting involving the Utah County Commission, the Utah State Welfare Commission and legislative representatives from Utah County. The goal was to see if the State and County could not cooperate in providing the small amount of funds needed for the experimental program. His suggested solution was a matching of State and local funds but state officials were unwilling to support the suggestion, even though funds would have come from a separate bill which would not have endangered their regular appropriation. The irony, of course, was that the amount needed per year was very small. The program was being run in an ordinary home, required only two full-time staff members, a secretary and incidental expenses.

Insofar as the program staff was concerned, the struggle to obtain local financing grew so great that the treatment and research aspects of the Experiment were being slighted. After careful study, it was determined that the original design of the 6 year Experiment could be carried out if funds were carefully expended and, therefore, that the political and bureaucratic battles would not be waged any longer. If the program were to continue after Experimental funds were exhausted, new solutions would have to be found.

Several articles appeared in the newspapers indicating that the program would close unless local funds could be found. The result was that numerous meetings were held with citizens' committees and the program's budgetary needs made public. The Utah County Mental Health Association offered $10,000 if this money would insure continuation of the program. This offer was especially meritorious because the Mental Health Association itself was under considerable financial stress and its own future was uncertain. But because the amount would not have been adequate for a single year's operation, the treatment staff of the Experiment could not be expected to stay on so uncertain a future. Therefore, after the fifth year of the Experiment, treatment was ended and the remaining time devoted to research matters.

The fact that the program has discontinued is a lesson in Community and organizational failure. As will be seen from subsequent findings, the Experiment did seem to provide a marked increase in success with delinquents. It was a pioneer effort in the search for alternatives to incarceration. Yet, it failed for precisely the same reason that correctional and mental health programs have had such difficulty in the past: key decision-makers in the community would not commit themselves to experimentation and innovation.

There is no doubt that those who operated the Experiment contributed to some of its problems. The most glaring fault was the lack of effort at the very outset to involve state officials. So much attention was devoted initially to the difficult tasks of conceptualizing and implementing the Experiment, that the necessary organizational steps were not taken. Perhaps if state officials had been involved, they would have supported the Experiment and incorporated the better parts of it in the State system or have been willing to try it out further. But this is speculation without empirical evidence as to just what strategy should be adopted in attempts at innovation. It may well be that bureaucratic resistance at the outset would have prevented the Experiment's ever beginning. Certainly, strong early resistance, coupled with other problems could have spelled the end of the effort without any program ever having been developed. The Experiment departed sufficiently far from tradition that continuing differences over them could, and

eventually did, block an extended testing of them.

Research on Outcome

It will be recalled that, in order to evaluate *impact* on offenders, an experimental design was created in which delinquents assigned to the program could be compared to two control groups: one group which was left in the community on probation and a second which was incarcerated in the Utah State Industrial School.

The initial experimental design was set up with the idea that all three groups could be drawn randomly from a common population of persistent offenders residing solely in Utah County. However, some modifications had to be made. The reasons were these:

The population of persistent offenders to be included in the Experiment was restricted to only 15 per cent of all cases coming before the local juvenile court. This small proportion was not always adequate to fill one experimental and two control groups. But, in addition, Judge Paxman has always been disinclined to commit boys to a state institution. Consequently, the *reformatory* control group was not adequately filled. Too few boys, in Judge Paxman's mind, seemed to warrant institutionalization. Consequently, it became necessary to select a similar, rather than a random sample from the Utah State Industrial School and to determine if, and on what characteristics, it might differ from the experimental control groups from Utah County.

Statistical comparisons among the three groups on a large number of variables—offense history official and undetected amount and type of undetected delinquency, family characteristics, education, and future aspirations—have not revealed many significant differences. It was felt, therefore, that some confidence might be placed in comparisons. Nevertheless, the comparison between the experimental program and the incarcerated group will be affected by the change.

SIX MONTHS SUCCESS RATES   A very stringent measure of recidivism was used, namely, the filing of an arrest report on a boy. This measure was used in an attempt to avoid all of the formal and informal decisions that are made once an offense is detected; that is, to handle the offense informally without court hearing, to return the arrestee to court or even to revoke probation or parole. Once these factors enter the picture it is almost impossible to establish any consistent criterion of success or failure unless the same procedure and persons are used in all cases—a condition which rarely, if ever, exists.

Prior to the introduction of the Experiment in Provo, only about 55 per cent of the kinds of persistent offenders who were eventually assigned to it were succeeding on probation. In order to see if improvement could be made for this hard-core group, the Experiment was introduced and treatment and control groups were selected. The evidence is strong that improvement did occur.

Six months after release, 73 per cent of those who were assigned to, and 84 per cent of those who completed the experimental program, had not been arrested. The remainder had been arrested only once and none had been incarcerated. But this possibly was not the most impressive finding.

During the same period, the success rate for the control group under regular probation had gone up almost as precipitously. From its original success rate of 55 per cent the Probation Department developed a success rate of 73 per cent for those assigned to regular probation and 77 per cent for those who completed it.

Apparently the introduction of the Experiment and the research which accompanied it had some influence on the Probation Department itself. Improved efforts, perhaps a sense of competition with the Experiment, and some alteration in techniques seems to have resulted. In addition, the community struggled with and helped to provide a daily work program and other facilities as aids both to the Experiment and to the Probation Department.

On the other hand, the second control group, made up of incarcerated offenders, was not nearly so successful as the experimental and probation control groups. Six months after release, only 42 per cent of the incarcerated offenders had remained unarrested. Of the remaining 58 per cent, half had been arrested two or more times.

This finding, of course, must be tempered by the fact that random selection from a common population broke down and thus the incarcerated, comparison group had to be selected on another basis. Yet, if the differences are due to factors other than treatment, our research cannot indicate what they are. As mentioned above, a statistical comparison of the incarcerated group with the experimental and community central groups, over a long list of variables, did not isolate any differences. Other than differences in recidivism rates, the three groups did not seem to differ. If there is any validity to the figures, therefore, the community programs not only resulted in significantly less recidivism but they cost only a fraction of the money. However, the follow-up is continuing and final figures may change somewhat.

COMPARATIVE COSTS OF DIFFERENT TREATMENTS INVOLVED   The experimental program was considerably cheaper than different kinds of residential programs. For example, a California State Youth Authority School at Whittier, California, had an annual expenditure per boy which was approximately 4 times as great as that of the Experiment, the Federal youth institution at Inglewood, Colorado, an expenditure which was 3 times as high and the Utah State Industrial School an expenditure which was over twice as high.

The cost for the probation control group was lower than any of the above. Some estimates run as low as $200 per boy but these are inexact figures because this is an average cost which overlooks the extra time usually spent on persistent offenders. We do not at this time have an exact figure on the matter.

Another cost estimate was based on the cost of treating one boy at the Experiment and at the Utah State Industrial School. The average stay at the Utah State Industrial School in 1962 was 9½ months and cost approximately $2,015. The average stay at the Provo Experiment was approximately 7 months (although it will be recalled that a boy continued to live at home) and cost about $609 per boy. This would mean roughly a saving of $1,406 per boy plus 2½ months of his time.

In addition to basic recidivism figures, other *outcome* analyses are being conducted: before-and-after psychological changes, school performance, work behavior, changes in peer relations, and predictions of success and failure by both boys and staff members. These data will be presented at a later date.

9

Drug Addiction

DEFINING DRUG ADDICTION

Drug addiction has been defined by the World Health Organization as "a state of periodic or chronic intoxication detrimental to the individual and to society, produced by the repeated consumption of a drug (natural or synthetic)."[1] It is not known when man discovered that drugs could intoxicate, but the earliest known record is found in the language of the Sumerians who lived in Mesopotamia some five or six thousand years before Christ. Homer and Virgil refer to the "sleep-bringing poppy" and Hippocrates recommend the juices of the opium poppy for certain illnesses. Later, in the ninth and tenth centuries, products prepared from the poppy were widely used in India and China.

In the early nineteenth century, a German pharmacist separated the main ingredient of opium, perhaps the most common narcotic drug, and named it morphine after the Greek god of sleep, Morpheus.[2] With the isolation of other natural alkaloids of opium, the use of opium and its derivatives spread widely. In the United States these were inexpensive and used for practically every kind of human ailment without limitation. Freely prescribed by physicians and contained in numerous patent medicines prior to World War I, "the use of opium and its derivatives was generally less offensive to Anglo-American public morals than the smoking of cigarettes."[3] Although not all persons using these drugs did so for their psychological effects, many became addicted and physicians gradually became aware of this danger. Heroin, first produced in 1898, was originally thought to be a solution to the addiction danger, producing the same satisfactory results in patients but none of the addictive ones. By 1914, however, the habit-forming qualities of heroin were also widely recognized but by this time its high potency and easy adulteration made it the underworld's most merchandisable drug commodity.[4] This was only to increase after the passage of restrictive federal legislation.

The Harrison Act of 1914, passed by Congress to regulate the sale, use, and transfer of opium and coca products, provided for the registration of all legitimate drug handlers and the payment of an excise tax on drug transactions. The original intent of this act was to control the domestic use of drugs but, in effect, it redefined the addict as a criminal since it made it illegal for him to buy or possess the narcotic drugs. Although the act did not forbid the legitimate treatment of addicts by physicians, in 1919 the Narcotics Division of the Treasury Department charged several medical practitioners who had prescribed opiates for addicts with law violation. Although these physicians had written prescriptions for addicts on a wholesale scale without regard for medical responsibility and flagrantly abused their medical role, their convictions were interpreted as a denial of the physician's legitimate right to prescribe drugs to addicts in the course of medical treatment.[5]

Even though a 1925 Supreme Court decision upheld a physician's right to prescribe drugs in the course of medical treatment, it was too late to counter the popular interpretation of the Harrison Act which persists to this day. The Federal Bureau of Narcotics has fostered the misinterpretation and restricted the medical treatment of addicts by ignoring the 1925 court decision, discouraging physicians from treating addicts and, in some cases, by outright harassment. Other federal legislation has effectively prohibited the import or export of most narcotics and has banned the sale or possession of even some nonaddictive drugs, primarily marihuana.

Medical and psychological definitions of drug addiction are quite different from the legal definition. Three characteristics must be present for true drug addiction: tolerance, physical dependence, and habituation. Tolerance refers to the lessening effect of the same amount of a drug. As the body adapts to the drug, consistent users soon find that they need increasing amounts to get the original "kick" and to feel normal. In addition, the body develops a dependency upon the drug and needs it to prevent acute discomfort known as the abstinence syndrome. The degree and extent of the physical symptoms of abstinence depends upon the drug used, dosage, length of use, and frequency of use. Unlike physical dependency, habituation refers to the user's emotional or psychological need for the drug. Such emotional dependency develops to the point where he needs the drug to function on a day-to-day basis and to handle the stresses and problems of life.

The most significant of these characteristics of drug addiction is habituation. When any of the opiates are taken, the addict feels pleasantly intoxicated, relaxed, and euphoric. As tolerance and physical dependency increase, the effects of the drug become less pleasurable and it is taken primarily to prevent the physical anguish of withdrawal.[6] However, both of these physical characteristics of addiction can be overcome comparatively easily. Within as little time as a week (abrupt withdrawal) or as long as several months (prolonged withdrawal) the symptoms of abstinence disappear and the addict no longer has a physical need for drugs. Unfortunately, the user's emotional dependence on the drug is not so easily overcome.

Physical dependence and tolerance result only from the use of opium and its products, including morphine, heroin and codeine, morphine substitutes, and barbiturates. Other narcotic drugs, such as bromides and marihuana, and stimulant drugs like cocaine and benzedrine, do not create the same physical needs for their users.[7] However, all of these addicting drugs usually cause an emotional dependence and the user feels that he cannot stop taking them. Habituation does not end with disuse or withdrawal but only with a realization that drugs do not solve problems and a subsequent change of attitude. As many of the readings in this chapter indicate, such change is very difficult to effect.

What is drug addiction, then, a crime, an illness, or both?[8] Perhaps the latter is closest to reality. Drug addiction is a physical and psychological condition rather uniquely defined as criminal. If a drug addict is registered as such with the federal authorities, it is not illegal to be an addict. If he does not register, his very status, not an overt act of law violation, is illegal. It is also illegal for him to possess drugs, but the unavailability of legal sources of supply forces him to break the law by purchasing the drugs from illegal sources at exorbitant prices. In order to finance his habit and to avoid detection and public stigma he often engages in further deviant behavior, finally becoming part of a drug subculture where he is understood and accepted by fellow addicts and where a new criminal self-image is developed.[9]

THE EXTENT OF DRUG ADDICTION

It has been claimed that prior to the passage of the Harrison Act in 1914, hundreds of thousands of people used opiates freely. The number actually addicted at that time has been estimated to be around 100,000. With the exception of relatively brief periods of increase, this number has declined since then to where it is now estimated that there are approximately 60,000 addicts in the United States. Because of the legal and social sanctions involved in addiction, it is assumed that there are many more addicts than enforcement agencies know of. Nevertheless, drug addiction cannot be considered a numerically important problem.

In 1964 there were 37,802 arrests made for narcotic law violations, a rate of 28.5 per 100,000 persons[10] and a rise in this figure of 3.3 since 1961. Since this data includes many nonaddicts, it is not an accurate index of actual addiction. Perhaps a more reliable one is a permanent register of active addicts in the United States kept by the Federal Bureau of Narcotics. In 1961 there were 46,798 names contained in this register.[11] Although this figure is not overwhelming when compared with other forms of personal deviance, it remains significantly larger than those for most European countries, many of which have fewer than 1000 known addicts.

Earlier in this century the "typical" addict was a lower-class white person living in the South or in a few big cities. The representative addict of the 1930s was white, an itinerant worker, about 33 years of age and very poorly educated.[12] In many respects today's drug addict is quite different. Prior to the Harrison Act female drug users outnumbered male users at a rate of 3 to 1. Since then the ratio has shifted drastically to the point where male addicts now outnumber female addicts 9 to 1. In 1964, six times as many males were arrested for narcotic drug law violations as females.

The register of active addicts indicates that Negroes comprise 56.1 percent of all those listed, Puerto Ricans 10.2 percent, Mexicans 7.1 percent, other whites 25.3 percent, and all others 1.3 percent. The Negro population at the Federal Narcotics Hospital in Lexington, Kentucky, has grown in recent years from 10 to 40 percent. Although minority group members are more likely to be arrested and institutionalized for their addiction, the use of drugs has obviously increased in these groups. Another shift that can be seen in the characteristics of the known addict population pertains to age. In Chicago between 1928 and 1934 only 8 percent of 2439 known addicts were under 25 years of age whereas by the early 1950s nearly one-half of 5000 known addicts were under 25.[13] From the late 1930s to the early 1950s admission data from the Lexington Hospital show that the under 25-years-of-age group rose from 10 percent to more than 33⅓ percent. Turning again to information supplied by the Narcotics Bureau's register of active addicts, 10.6 percent are over 40 years of age, 35.8 percent between 31–40, 49.8 percent between 21–30, and 3.8 percent under 21.

The incidence of drug addiction is highest in lower-class, poorly educated, occupationally unskilled groups. There are exceptions to this, two of the most interesting being physicians and jazz musicians. It is estimated that approximately 1 percent of all practicing physicians are drug users. Although this has often been attributed to their easy access to drugs, one writer points out that pharmacists also have easy access to drugs but not nearly as much addiction as among doctors. He goes on to say that this is ". . . probably because the kind of person who becomes a pharmacist is likely to be quite different from the kind of person who becomes a physician."[14] Jazz, a form of musical protest, has long attracted those who define themselves as "different." In such a group unconventional values are emphasized and rewarded, including the search for "kicks" through the use of marihuana. New members of the group, desiring acceptance and searching for the same "kicks," soon learn to behave like the others, and thus perpetuate the high usage of drugs among jazz musicians.[15]

For some years drug addiction has been an urban problem concentrated mainly in our largest metropolitan centers. Again, of the 46,798 registered addicts, 46.6 percent resided in New York State (almost all in New York City), 16.2 percent in California (Los Angeles and San Francisco), 14.8 percent in Illinois (Chicago), 4.2 percent in Michigan (Detroit), and 18.2

percent in the other 46 states and Washington, D. C. Arrests for drug law violations are also concentrated in our largest cities. Within the urban areas, drug use, peddling, and enforcement activities occur largely in the transitional areas marked by slums, unemployment, minority groups, and people who are generally alienated from the conventional society. This is so because the great bulk of drug addicts lived in such areas prior to their addiction and because many nonresidents gravitate to transitional areas once they become addicted. The laissez-faire attitude and mobility of area residents permits the addict to engage more easily in and without observation of his deviant behavior.

Today's "typical" addict, then, is unlike the "typical" addict of the 1930s or earlier. Although he, too, is more likely to be a lower-class person with relatively poor education, there are important exceptions and the general elevation in educational attainment characteristic of most Americans is probably true for the addict as well. He is apt to be a member of a racial or ethnic minority group living in the most deteriorated sections of a few large cities. Above all, he is younger, and considerably so, than his counterpart of the past. But, why is he addicted to drugs?

SOME EXPLANATIONS OF ADDICTION

Like other forms of personal deviance, drug addiction cannot be explained by one theory. As one recent classificatory scheme indicates, there are at least three types of addicts, the accidental or medical, the emotionally disturbed, and the socially processed, and each has been explained by different etiological theories.[16] Although some drug users are accidental addicts, that is, they became addicted as a result of medical treatment and continued taking narcotics after their cure, they account for only a small proportion of the addict population. The great bulk of addicts are thought to be the products of psychological or social processes.

Psychologists and psychiatrists generally see addiction as a symptom of some emotional disorder and believe that certain personality types are more prone to drug use. Addicts have been described as emotionally immature, hostile, and aggressive persons who are fraught with inner tensions and seek relief in a "chemical adjustment" to the world. They are motivated by an immature hedonism and a need for pleasurable or exotic experiences. With drugs the addict can evade his responsibility and eliminate conscious discomfort. Another group of addicts may be seen as neurotic persons whose anxiety and obsessive or compulsive symptoms are abated by drug use. Hence, drug use is seen as only another step in a marginal and unsatisfactory adjustment to life.

Gerard and Kornetsky, who investigated the social and psychiatric characteristics of addicts in the 17–20 age group at Lexington, believed that their subjects were seriously maladjusted.[17] They felt that these patients displayed a pattern of characteristics consisting of (1) near depression accompanied with feelings of futility and expected failure, (2) sex identity problems, and (3) a disturbance of interpersonal relationships. Later, when these researchers compared their group of addicts with a control group of non-addicts, they concluded that the addicts significantly exceeded the controls in personality deviation.

Chein and his associates, after a major study of youthful addiction in New York, have concluded that:

> The evidence indicates that all addicts suffer from deep-rooted, major personality disorders. Although psychiatric diagnoses are apt to vary, a particular set of symptoms seems to be common to most juvenile addicts. They are not able to enter prolonged, close friendly relations with either peers or adults; they have difficulties in assuming a masculine role; they are frequently overcome by a sense of futility, expectation of failure, and general depression; they are easily frustrated and made anxious; and they find both frustration and anxiety intolerable.[18]

Alfred Lindesmith has criticized this approach to the problem on several grounds.[19] Basically he has objected to its overemphasis on the supposed gratification the addict gets from drugs, its inability to explain why some "normal" people become addicted, the cultural and group differentials in addiction rates, and the methodology of many of the psychologically-oriented studies. He pointed out that all of these studies have focused on those already addicted, so that the personality traits attributed to addicts may be the result of addiction rather than its cause.

Actually Lindesmith believes that most addicts were psychologically normal before they became addicted. For him it is the physical dependence on the drug which develops over time that is the crucial factor in addiction. If, when the drug user attempts to withdraw, he does not see the relationship between his physical distress and anguish and the drug, he will escape addiction. However, once he realizes that his discomfort results from the lack of drugs and he continues to use them to alleviate this condition, he becomes addicted. "Addiction is generated in the process of using the drug consciously to alleviate withdrawal distress."[20] The fear of withdrawal means that the addict is "hooked" and drug use takes on a new and important meaning. The original reasons for use now become quite secondary to the prevention of withdrawal.

Becker has also emphasized the learning process in becoming an addict.[21] In his study of marihuana users, he discovered that they come to enjoy the effects of the drug only after they learn to conceive of it as a pleasurable experience. This process includes learning how to smoke "reefers" so as to produce maximum effects, learning to recognize the effects and connecting them with the drug, and, since the effects are not in themselves enjoyable, learning to define them as such. As in the process described by Lindesmith, the motivation for use changes as the addict learns to redefine the experience as a pleasurable one.

At this point in the learning process, the addict's self-definition and behavior change and he begins to play a new role, that of "drug addict." His need for a constant supply of drugs demands that he associate with others who have similar needs and who can help him obtain his supply. But the addict culture does more than that, because he is now a social pariah and it provides him with a group of like people to which he feels he belongs. In this group he learns a new status system, a new language, and, above all, new techniques and skills for acquiring the needed drugs.

The socially processed theory of addiction leaves many questions unanswered. It does not account for those who have access to drugs but do not use them or why certain individuals find drugs pleasurable and continue to use them. As we shall soon see, there are those who experiment with drugs and others who use drugs occasionally without becoming addicted. Perhaps the most feasible explanation of addiction is found when we put certain psychological and social factors together, which by themselves cannot explain this phenomenon. Three assertions based on much research seem warranted at this point: (1) excessive drug use is a condition found overwhelmingly among deprived, minority people and in transitional, disorganized neighborhoods; (2) drug addiction may be associated with certain personality characteristics, but is not the inevitable result of these characteristics; and (3) the use and proper effects of drugs must be learned before the individual considers himself addicted.

Urban slum dwellers, especially adolescents, are faced with many adjustment problems. Confronted with poverty, discrimination, segregation, blocked opportunity, and countless other frustration-inducing conditions, they tend to seek "kicks" or escapes.[22] Some may become delinquents, others develop neurotic or psychotic conditions, and still others may use drugs. This latter adaptation depends upon the availability of drugs and the subcultural prohibitions against such behavior. Finestone, in his study of youthful Negro drug users in Chicago, found that they were sensitive to the values and norms of the larger, conventional society but did not feel a part of it.[23] Their drug use represented an attempt to handle the problems of status and identity which they felt. The boy who experiences these same pressures and frustrations but is able to withstand the appeals to become a "cat" is one who has an inner strength, a strong sense of identity, and positive support from adults. Cloward and Ohlin see drug use as "retreatist" behavior used by lower-class boys to solve their status dilemma.[24] However, since it is not widely accepted behavior even within delinquent subcultures, this form of adaptation is used only by the "double failures," those who cannot achieve their goals legitimately and at the same time are unable to use illegitimate success routes.

Under such life conditions and in an environment where drugs are available, the young person has sufficient motivation to experiment with drugs and to learn the needed prerequisites for addiction. But, since all persons exposed to these conditions do not use drugs, it would appear that another factor is needed to round out the etiological picture. Chein and his associates believe that this factor is the individual personality. Addicts in their study were raised in a family milieu which contributed to "the development

of weak ego functioning, defective super-ego, inadequate masculine identity, lack of realistic levels of aspiration with respect to long-range goals,
and a distrust of major institutions."[25] Such personality tendencies are not
necessarily abnormal and are not the unique property of addicts, but when
they are combined with certain social, economic, and environmental conditions, especially the availability of drugs, addiction is a likely response.

STAGES IN DRUG USE

Using drugs does not mean that one will necessarily become addicted,
since for every true addict there are many who try drugs but do not become
habitual users. Chein and his associates distinguish four stages in involvement with drugs: experimentation, occasional use, regular or habitual use,
and efforts to break the habit.[26] A drug user may progress through all of
these stages, or stop at any one. Therefore, there are four possible types
of users: those who try drugs once and quit, those who use drugs on occasion but do not become addicted, those who do become addicted but somehow are able to break their addiction, and those who become addicted and
remain so.

In the Chein study of heroin use among teen-agers in New York, the
investigators found that most of the users had had prior experience smoking
marihuana cigarettes. Although first use of heroin usually started when the
boys were about fifteen, they had heard of it long before that. The first
chance to try it came about casually, at the suggestion of a friend or in a
small group at the initiative of the group. In such situations the boys were
initially interested in experimenting with the drug.

Experimental use of this kind is most prevalent in neighborhoods with
high drug use. Chein and his associates found other neighborhoods in which
the suggestion to try heroin never came up. Similarly, they found youths
who refused to experiment. In a control group of 50 nonusing delinquent
teen-agers, two-thirds had a chance to use drugs, but only four accepted
and they did not continue. Among nondelinquent controls, only 40 percent
had a chance to try, but none of them did. In the high drug use neighborhoods, contrary to the popular stereotype, neither peers nor "pushers" put
pressure on the boys studied to try the drug other than offering the drug
for use. The lack of outer constraint and inner restraint made use possible
on the first try which later became true addiction in three-fourths of the
cases. On the other hand, those who refused use were generally younger,
had negative views of drug use, and were aware of how "significant" adults
felt about its use.

Those who experienced euphoria on the first try were more apt to repeat
the experience. Of those, two-thirds continued immediately, compared with
only two-fifths whose initial reaction was unfavorable. Within a year of the
first experience 90 percent were regular users and the remainder became so
within two years. Much like Becker's marihuana users, some of these heroin

users indicated that initially they did not know what to expect, saying "if you don't know about it, you don't know how the kick goes."[27] Users such as these required some tutelage before they could fully appreciate their drug use.

It is generally believed by experts that experimentation invariably leads to habituation. Yet Chein and his associates found a small group of occasional users who did not become addicts. They used drugs at parties, on week-ends, and when they felt low. Use made them feel good, they seemed to experience no side effects, and apparently enjoyed the so-called "honeymoon stage." After a few years of this occasional use, they stopped using drugs entirely.

By contrast, others went on to greater use accompanied by increased tolerance, habituation, and dependence. These regular users were thought to have either a strong need for the effects of narcotics or little desire to control their impulses. Regular users were characterized by those situational, family, and emotional factors described earlier. However, the vast majority of regular or confirmed users expressed concern about their drug habit. Some 75 of 100 users studied made at least some effort to stop, and half of them tried even more than once. The reasons mentioned most often by those having some desire to quit were that they felt drug use was wrong, they worried about the money needed to sustain a habit, that heroin made them feel "sick," and that they worried about becoming really "hooked." But, for most, actually stopping was extremely difficult and out of 94 gang users studied, only 14 had actually stopped while another 20 had reduced their intake. The authors of this important study of drug users concluded that young regular users were better able to break the habit when family cohesion was strong, other significant people in their lives disapproved of their behavior, and, contrary to popular opinion, delinquent gangs disapproved of drug use.

WHAT CAN BE DONE?

Since the Harrison Act the drug problem has received a great deal of public attention, perhaps more than it numerically deserves. For a number of reasons a "drug fiend mythology" has developed and we have tended to see the problem as one demanding strong police action for prevention and control. In recent years, however, attitudes have been changing and this has been reflected in the techniques of intervention devised to handle the problem. Preventive measures still lag far behind attempts at rehabilitation (their success notwithstanding) because prevention is viewed in most quarters as impossible without altering all of the personal and cultural factors contributing to drug use. As with many other problems of personal deviancy, it is somehow "easier" to wait for the addiction to develop and then try to change the individual's behavior.

As reported in the first reading, New York City's Lower Eastside Information and Service Center for Narcotics Addiction, Inc., is actually attempting a prevention program by changing adolescents' values toward experimenting with drugs. By working directly with adolescents and through the family and community structures in an area of great drug use, it is hoped that highly susceptible adolescents will be dissuaded from resorting to this form of adjustment. Although it is too early to demonstrate the effectiveness of such an undertaking, it seems reasonable to assume that it, coupled with the other activities of Mobilization for Youth (see Chapter 8), is a most logical preventive attempt.

In 1935 the U.S. Public Health Service opened a hospital in Lexington, Kentucky, designed to treat drug addicts and this is described in the second reading. In this drug-free environment, both voluntary and committed patients undergo treatment consisting of two general phases: withdrawal and rehabilitative therapy. After withdrawal, the rehabilitation program includes vocational training, recreational activities, and some form of individual or group therapy. The Lexington hospital experience has been successful in reducing the addict's tolerance and physical dependence (indeed, some addicts commit themselves for just this reason), but because most patients return to the same posthospital environments and few are followed up in the community, the number who remain free of drugs is assumed to be small.

Since 1958 Synanon House (reading 3) has enabled a number of addicted persons to remain free of drugs and its methods have thus been spreading. In Synanon addicts live with former drug users in a program of work, group sessions, and informal interaction. After the addict withdraws from drugs, his peers attempt through a variety of techniques to help him understand his problems and change his attitudes toward drug use. The group meetings are an essential element of this program, but "the basic therapeutic force is the overall Synanon social system." This system provides for individual involvement in the program, an achievable status system, a new social role for the addict, an opportunity for social growth, social control exercised by the addict's peers, and the development of empathy and new self-identity. In such a social setting addiction and its social and psychological prerequisites and consequences can be understood by the addict.

Reading 4 describes another new and unique, but quite different, approach to drug addiction. Providing drug addicts with daily, massive doses of methadone, a drug long used to ease the pains of withdrawal, appears to satisfy their craving for other narcotic drugs but has none of the harmful side effects of these drugs. The daily maintenance doses of methadone seem to permit the addict to lead a "normal" life, just as a diabetic who must use insulin is able to lead a "normal" life. Although this program is still highly experimental and is not claimed to be a "cure" for addiction, it certainly shows promise in controlling some of the personally and socially detrimental aspects of addiction.

Other countries have responded to the drug problem differently. In the last reading Edwin M. Schur describes the British system of narcotics control. Under this system addiction is seen as a medical problem, addicts are not treated as criminals, and they do not have to register with any legal agency. Physicians are permitted to dispense maintenance doses of drugs and to treat addicts as they would any other patient, thereby eliminating the need for an illegal drug traffic or addict crime. Although few people, including Schur, would advocate our adopting the British system in its entirety, it does provide us with a different model from which we can learn a great deal about controlling the drug problem.

REFERENCES

1. John A. Clausen, "Drug Addiction," in Robert K. Merton and Robert A. Nisbet (eds.), *Contemporary Social Problems.* New York: Harcourt, Brace & World, Inc., 1966, p. 195.
2. Nathan Eddy, "The History of the Development of Narcotics," *Law and Contemporary Problems,* 22 (Winter 1957), p. 4.
3. Rufus King, "Narcotic Drug Laws and Enforcement Policies," *Law and Contemporary Problems,* 22 (Winter 1957), p. 113.
4. Clausen, p. 201.
5. King, pp. 122–123.
6. Harris Isbell, "Manifestations and Treatment of Addiction to Narcotic Drugs and Barbiturates," *The Medical Clinics of North America,* 34 (March 1950), pp. 426–428.
7. Victor H. Vogel and Virginia E. Vogel, *Facts About Narcotics.* Chicago: Science Research Associates, Inc., 1951, p. 10.
8. For enlightened discussions of this issue, see: *Drug Addiction: Crime or Disease?* Interim and Final Reports of the Joint Committee of the American Bar Association and the American Medical Association on Narcotic Drugs. Bloomington, Ind.: Indiana University Press, 1960; and Edwin M. Schur, *Crimes Without Victims.* Englewood Cliffs, N.J.: Prentice-Hall, Inc., 1965, Chap. 4.
9. Schur, p. 163.
10. *Uniform Crime Reports, 1964.* Washington, D.C.: U.S. Department of Justice, Federal Bureau of Investigation, 1965, p. 107.
11. This figure and all subsequent references to the Federal Bureau of Narcotics register of active addicts are for the year 1961 and can be found in Russel R. Dynes, Alfred C. Clarke, Simon Dinitz, and Iwao Ishino, *Social Problems: Dissensus and Deviation in an Industrial Society.* New York: Oxford University Press, 1964, pp. 514–518.
12. Charles Winick, "The Drug Addict and His Treatment," in Hans Toch (ed.), *Legal and Criminal Psychology.* New York: Holt, Rinehart and Winston, Inc., 1961, pp. 372–373.
13. Clausen, p. 207.
14. Winick, p. 373.
15. Howard S. Becker, *Outsiders: Studies in the Sociology of Deviance.* New York: The Free Press of Glencoe, 1963, Chaps. 3 and 4.
16. *Drug Addiction: Crime or Disease?,* pp. 50–59.
17. D. L. Gerard and C. Kornetsky, "Adolescent Opiate Addiction: A Study of Control and Addict Subjects," *Psychiatric Quarterly,* 29 (April 1955), pp. 457–486.

18. Isidor Chein, Donald L. Gerard, Robert S. Lee, and Eva Rosenfeld, *The Road to H: Narcotics, Delinquency, and Social Policy*. New York: Basic Books, Inc., 1964, p. 14.
19. For a discussion of Lindesmith's critique of psychiatric explanations as well as of his theory of addiction see *Opiate Addiction*. Bloomington, Ind.: Principia Press, 1947; "A Sociological Theory of Drug Addiction," *American Journal of Sociology*, 43 (1938), pp. 593–613.
20. Lindesmith, "A Sociological Theory of Drug Addiction," p. 599.
21. Becker, Chaps. 3 and 4.
22. John A. Clausen, "Social Patterns, Personality, and Adolescent Drug Use," in Alexander Leighton, John A. Clausen, and Robert Wilson (eds.), *Explorations in Social Psychiatry*. New York: Basic Books, Inc., 1957, p. 269.
23. Harold Finestone, "Cats, Kicks and Color," *Social Problems*, 5 (July 1957), pp. 3–13.
24. Richard A. Cloward and Lloyd E. Ohlin, *Delinquency and Opportunity*. New York: The Free Press of Glencoe, 1960, pp. 178–186.
25. Chein and others, p. 268.
26. Chein and others, pp. 149–176.
27. Chein and others, p. 157.

ADDITIONAL READINGS

Becker, Howard S., *Outsiders: Studies in the Sociology of Deviance*. New York: The Free Press of Glencoe, 1963, Chaps. 1–4.
Chein, Isidor, Donald L. Gerard, Robert S. Lee, and Eva Rosenfeld, *The Road to H*. New York: Basic Books, Inc., 1964.
Clausen, John, "Drug Addiction," in Robert K. Merton and Robert A. Nisbet (eds.), *Contemporary Social Problems*. New York: Harcourt, Brace & World, Inc., 1966, pp. 193–235.
Clinard, Marshall, "Drug Addiction," *Sociology of Deviant Behavior*. New York: Holt, Rinehart and Winston, Inc., 1963, Chap. 10.
Drug Addiction: Crime or Disease? Interim and Final Reports of the Joint Committee of the American Bar Association and the American Medical Association on Narcotic Drugs. Bloomington, Ind.: University of Indiana Press, 1960.
Lindesmith, Alfred, *Opiate Addiction*. Bloomington, Ind.: University of Indiana Press, 1947.
Narcotic Drug Addiction, Mental Health Monograph 2. Washington, D.C.: U.S. Department of Health, Education, and Welfare, 1963.
Schur, Edwin M., *Crimes Without Victims*. Englewood Cliffs, N.J.: Prentice-Hall, Inc., 1965, Chaps. 4 and 5.

PREVENTION OF ADDICTION
BY CHANGING THE VALUES
OF ADOLESCENTS TOWARD
EXPERIMENTATION WITH DRUGS

Lower Eastside Information and Service Center for Narcotics Addiction, Inc., Edward Washington, M.S.W., and Staff

I. Mobilization for Youth has requested the Lower Eastside Information and Service Center for Narcotics Addiction to develop new ideas for combatting the problem of drug addiction among adolescents. One of the requests that was made in their reviewing the 1963 contract is to project a program for changing the values of adolescents toward experimentation with drugs. An exploration of this approach has led us to the following proposal for enacting such a program.

II. PROPOSAL FOR ENACTMENT OF PROGRAM

A. Working Directly with the Adolescent

1. Soft Sell—"Drug Addiction is an Illness."
   a. Posters
   b. Pamphlet
2. Hard Sell
   a. Comic Books
   b. Other adolescent material
3. Small group education

4. Channelling hostility
5. Sex education

B. Working through Family To Alter Adolescent Attitudes

1. Family response to drug problem
2. Identifying and correcting environment that is predisposing to addiction.
3. Every day and common place familial interaction.

C. Working through Community Structures

1. Organizing relatives of addicts
2. Provision for an educational network composed of agencies, and schools for education of parents.
3. Public school health education in classes

III. DESCRIPTION OF PROPOSALS

A. Working Directly with the Adolescent

1. SOFT SELL   It is proposed that the "soft sell" will promote the idea that drug

This paper, written by Edward Washington, M.S.W., was based on staff discussions including Edward Brown, B.D., Executive Director, Yves Kron, M.D., Medical Director, Aleathea Griffin, M.S.W., Supervisor, Raya Kowarsky, M.A., Psychologist, Herbert Barish, M.S.W., Sylvia Davis, M.S.W., Carmen Osorio, M.S.W., Antonio Torres, and Robert Watkins in connection with a contract grant from Mobilization for Youth, Inc., with funds provided by the United States Department of Health, Education and Welfare.

addiction is a mental illness. The implication through postering would then be that the individual who uses drugs is mentally ill. This is considered a workable deterent because in our past experiences addicts have resisted referrals to state hospitals for detoxification because of the inference that they are crazy. The gains of this proposal would be two-fold. While the "soft sell" executes its purpose of educating youth to the nature of the problem, it also *undercuts the value of experimentation with drugs as a "hip" means of expressing anti-social attitudes.* In other words seeing drug addiction as an illness should remove the illusion of glamour that it might hold for some youth. Such posters would headline *"Drug Addiction Is an Illness"* or *"Drug Addiction Is a Mental Illness,"* depending upon how soft or hard one wants to carry the message.

The "soft sell" campaign can be carried out through the use of posters, pamphlets and other vehicles of mass media. Campaigns of other public health problems such as venereal disease and smoking should be thoroughly investigated for the purpose of exploring what ideas if any may be translated to the campaign against drug addiction. This campaign has the *additional virtue of educating the community and altering adult values toward drug addiction as a medical problem rather than a criminal or punitive problem.*

2. HARD SELL—COMIC BOOK   The comic book would seem to be a good vehicle for graphic portrayal of the real life experiences of an addict. Through this medium we could *hit hard at those properties of drug addiction that an adolescent is mostly likely to reject.*

Through characterization we could depict the emotional immaturity of an addict, how his difficulties in relating to

women would implicate him as being a fairy. We can show how he uses drugs to run away from daily problems. We would also show that not only does the addict end up with no girl, but also ends up with no money because all funds eventually go for the acquisition of drugs and he just isn't "boss." We can emphasize his consequent lack of ambition, lack of physical energy and his accompanying loss of esteem. Other important things to highlight would be the numerous summers that addicts spend in hospitals while others in the community are enjoying themselves. We would show how he ends up by being the "fall guy" and sucker for pushers who profit from his discomfort. Finally we would show how rather than becoming more independent and adult, he becomes more dependent on his parents for he progressively loses the ability to function independently of parents, and to exert authority of his own. In the final analysis he ends up being a mama's boy or a sissy.

3. SMALL GROUP EDUCATION   Utilizing the rehabilitative and educational process of group work in the prevention and control of delinquent acts is not a new concept; however we need to explore new methodology and strengthen old processes to increase the effectiveness of this method. Experimentation with narcotics often is one avenue of gang activity, and acts as a media for adolescent rebellion. *Much of what was learned from the treatment of delinquent gang members can and should be translated into work with the addict-prone adolescent.*

Early and decisive identification of the addict-prone youth is a necessity. Schools and social agencies are in a position to make this kind of identification; however the early school dropout, the youth who soon loses contact with all formal institutions, needs to be picked up by detached workers operating on the street. Frequently these youngsters lack mobility. The world for them does not extend beyond a few blocks' radius of their living quarters. *Horizons of these youth must be extended* so that they have the opportunity to be exposed to the values that exist outside of their immediate sub-culture. In thinking of programming material for these youth, it should not be overlooked that many have probably never seen the bright lights of Broadway.

Availability and physical presence of a worker on the street is extremely important, for the need for acceptance and belonging will make a youngster support and go along with activity of the group although these activities often conflict with the immediate personal interest and wishes of the individual. *The worker's presence affords the youth the opportunity of a choice of whom he will turn to for acceptance and support.* Of no lesser importance is the fact that the worker's presence also affords an excuse for the youth who does not want to participate in a particular activity.

The youth's ability to use the worker depends foremost on the skills and insight that the worker brings to the setting. Let us explore the more significant skills and understanding that we suggest are necessary for working with delinquents or addict-prone groups which we observe to be often missing in workers.

Initially the worker must conscientiously present himself as an individual whom the youngsters can imitate. Identification rather than mere imitation is the long range goal. It should be understood that youth and adolescents are going through an exploratory stage; they imitate personalities of the movies, sports and neighborhood, and try and disgard them with the regularity of the ease of a woman trying on shoes in a store. The warm and understanding face-to-face contact of the worker with the youth gives him a decided advantage over the other personalities to whom the youth responds. The continuity of the contact helps the worker become the object of true identification. The skills in this area referred to in the beginning of this discussion revolve around the worker's ability to *conceive what the youngsters are looking for and adapt himself to this within his own life style with comfort and ease.*

The youth themselves have not been inarticulate in their concept of whom they would want to identify with. Translated from the colloquialism of the street, youth look foremost for a strong male figure. They seek the toughness and authority of a television detective, without the interpreted oppression, the con artist's knowledgeability of the street culture without being involved in it, the movie gangster calmness and reserve without the coldness, the father's concern for his boy's welfare without ambivalence.

Ambivalence in a worker can lead to his rejection and the manipulation of him on the part of the youth. Youngsters are keenly aware of their own ambivalence toward socially accepted activity and delinquent behavior. They look to the worker to set the kinds of limits that will help control this ambivalence. In the area of gang activity, youth could carry around weapons with the terrifying knowledge that in case of conflict they might feel compelled to use these weapons. The conflict that many of them had over this was resolved for them when the worker would set limits on their carrying weapons when in a center or in his presence. They were thus relieved of the burden of deciding whether or not to respond to their own distaste for using weapons or going along with what they thought to be the generally accepted behavior and motivation of the group. No good worker would tolerate a youth's carrying a zip gun or switchblade while in his presence. The worker would clarify this position with the group, interpret the significance and, if tested, then carry out his threat to report the incident to the proper authority. The same limits must be carried out in the area of experimentation with drugs.

Too often workers do not carry over to narcotics those same limits they set about gang fighting, whether it is merely in discussion or involves direct observation of an occasional "bag" or "set of works." Limits may be set directly. Patterns of behavior can evolve in a group because no one thinks to question the direction they are going. The worker's role as the catalyst for more democratic procedure can lead the group into developing limits and pressures of their own. We cite a specific example again in the area of gang hostility. There was a particular gang group that had been involved in numerous conflict situations. Completely caught up in the excitement of these hostilities, they would respond immediately to an individual report of being insulted or assaulted by another group. On one occasion this occurred during the worker's presence with the group. Without telling the group that they should not go to their member's assistance, the worker merely casually asked about the specifics of this member's report. The group picked up on this and began to find uncomfortable contradictions in the story. They then made the decision on their own not to respond to this call to battle. *The worker, by educating the group with honest arguments against drug usage, can make calculated comments on the subject whenever it comes up, combined with a positive statement of his opposition and rejection of this behavior by the group members.* The

worker's continued esteem for them as individuals provides an indirect means of setting limits by influencing the change in value within the group.

It is important to establish definite limits for adolescents where acting out is detrimental to the physical health of an individual or society. Just as the good group worker handles guns or knives he can, when drugs are mentioned, clarify his position with the group, interpret his reasons and give warning that he would report their activity and then carry it out if he were tested further. *We propose that common community-wide approach by group workers would go far towards altering the teen-age values about drug use.* A program to develop this common approach using all lower eastside institutions is needed.

It is of equal importance, however, for the worker to respect and tolerate the adolescent need for healthy exploration, even should this exploration extend beyond the worker's own limits of social propriety. The worker might seek to effect change, but he can not arbitrarily limit these activities as we would do in the area that would endanger health, life, limb and/or property.

4. CHANNELLING HOSTILITY   The hostility and anxiety that sustain adolescent rebellion can be channelled to produce social change. Hostility can be handled on the one hand to avoid retreatism and on the other hand constructively to prevent guilt or isolation. Constructive organization of this hostility for positive action will increase both the self-esteem of the adolescent, and the esteem for the potential of youthful productivity in the eyes of the adult. More activity like youthful leadership being demonstrated in the racial issue is necessary. Discussion and demonstrations can develop around a racial issue, the issue of more job train-

ing with school dropouts, more realistic vocational training in public schools and more funds to increase staff and facilities of recreational and social service agencies.

5. SEX EDUCATION When we consider devaluing experimentation with narcotics, we have to ask what other activity could possibly replace it. The adolescents who become addicts have deep unfulfilled needs which must be consummated so that rechannelling of their energy is as important as thwarting drug experimentation. Consultants have pointed out that *only one activity can really replace drug experimentation—sex.* In the final analysis sex may be the most important factor in terms of resolving the problem of drug addiction growing out of the experimentation. We find the mother, in an overwhelming number of case histories, infantalizing the drug addict or potential drug addict. The result is the stunting of the normal maturation process. These inadequacies become most prominent during adolescence when the youth are first exploring normal co-educational relationships. Many addicts speak of feelings of inadequacy in relating to members of the opposite sex, or in competing for their attention. Some even admit to feeling sexually incompetent, and so state that they look to drugs to build their confidence. The fact is that addiction generally eliminates sexual strivings along with the feeling of inadequacy. The difficulties in this area are both the result of personality disorders, and a common ignorance about factual material on sex.

There are discrepancies between facts and corresponding beliefs and attitudes because there is a lack of availability of facts. Individuals tend to create fantasies when their environment does not provide facts or when the needs of the individuals are frustrated. Thus the adult fears and indifferences to sex education support and perpetuate the misconceptions that youth develop from unsupervised group discussions and exchange of experiences, with the experience being more fantasy than actual. *Honest and factual material on sex must be presented to our adolescents under the supervision of social workers and public health personnel.* Take sex out of the murky environment of the back streets and hushed parlor discussions, place it in the enlighten environment of society-based institutions, lessen the guilt and anxiety around the mere curiosity, and show tolerance toward healthy exploration. The emergence of sex is one of the primary forms of adolescent insecurity. Adolescent competition which is so strong often first focuses on competition for girls. Fantasies need to be replaced by knowledge.

Community-wide social work in this area is often hampered by the difference between the middle class sexual standards of the worker and the sub-cultural values of the neighborhood. Any differences between value systems must be actively overcome by the worker's tolerance and ability to openly discuss the problem with the teen-agers.

B. Working through the Family

Parents must be alerted to recognize the type of familial environment that can produce the potential drug user. Through small group and individual counseling parents must be educated to know debilitating effects of the exercise of excessive control and strictness as well as excessive indulgence and absence of discipline. *Parents must be helped to work through the confusion that can culminate in the above response.*

Earlier in the proposal we spoke of the infantalizing of youth; parents must be made aware of the dangers of their own seductiveness toward youth that can be demonstrated through such things as excessive petting and babying of a child, also improper sleeping arrangements. Parents must also be educated towards early identification of the potential addict to recognition of such trouble areas as difficulties relating to school, difficulties with authorities such as teachers, bosses, etc. They must know that the very quiet or withdrawn and very pliant youngster has just as much potential toward drug experimentation as the so-called "trouble maker."

It should be understood that the addict takes drugs to relieve himself of inner tension caused by hostile and aggressive feelings that he can not successfully cope with. Family counseling agencies should be alert to recognize such family problems peculiar to drug abuse as the neglect of children whose parents are addicted to drugs. Supportive help must be given to the mother who is concerned about an addicted member of the family who is destroying the total family unit. The agency must be alerted to and call attention to the potential of other siblings' becoming involved in drugs when the parents are spending all of their energy and attention on a particular problem child.

Parents also must be helped to interpret the problem to other siblings. Finally there can be such concrete safeguards against the problem of experimentation by removing the opportunity to temptation by not giving the youth too much money, knowing and showing some concern about the youth's activities and peer group, and developing an on-going communication with the youth so they can express their concern. Parent education programs of all kinds are needed.

C. Working through Community Structures

Much of what can be done with the community structure has already been developed in the preceding pages. We feel that the remainder of the outline is self-evident.

THE LEXINGTON PROGRAM
FOR NARCOTIC ADDICTS

John A. O'Donnell, Ph.D.

The treatment program of the United States Public Health Service Hospital at Lexington, Kentucky, and the characteristics of the addict as they are seen at that

[1] James V. Lowry, M.D., "Hospital Treatment of the Narcotic Addict," *Federal Probation,*

hospital, were described by Dr. James V. Lowry[1] in *Federal Probation* 5 years ago. The characteristics of addict patients have not changed substantially since that

December 1956, pp. 42–51.

From *Federal Probation,* 26 (March 1962), pp. 55–60. Reprinted by permission.

time and will be touched on only briefly in this article.

The general philosophy of the treatment program is also unchanged, but there have been administrative changes in the procedures followed. These will be described. The main purpose of this article is to furnish information to probation officers so they can make more effective use of the hospital for persons under their supervision. Effective working relationships have been achieved between the hospital and federal probation officers over the years, but there could be much improvement in the relations between the hospital and probation officers from other jurisdictions who frequently use the hospital for "voluntary" patients.

THE HOSPITAL AT LEXINGTON

Located about 5 miles from Lexington, Kentucky, the USPHS hospital for narcotic addicts was opened in 1935. The present functional capacity of the hospital is about 1,050 patients. This represents a reduction in capacity of about 150 patients in the 5 years since Dr. Lowry's article. This reduction in capacity was the result of converting some dormitory space to additional or expanded treatment facilities. About 240 of these beds are in medical, surgical, intensive psychiatric, and withdrawal units. The rest of the beds are in continued treatment units; 440 of the beds are in single rooms, another 220 beds are in double rooms, and the remainder in multiple rooms none of which has more than six beds.

Since its opening the hospital has handled about 70,000 admissions. Roughly 60 percent of these have been first admissions, and a large part of the readmissions are accounted for by a relatively small number of persons. In recent years, the average number of addict admissions has been about 3,500 per year. This figure is about twice as high as it was in the first 10 years the hospital was open, but is much less than it was in the early 1950's. Slightly over 10 percent of admissions are accounted for by federal prisoners, and 50 to 60 admissions a year are accounted for by federal probationers. To the extent that beds are available after eligible prisoners and probationers have been admitted, voluntary patients are admitted at their own request. They account for almost 90 percent of all addict admissions.

The essential eligibility requirement for admission is that the patient has been addicted to narcotic drugs as defined in the federal law. These include: Cocaine, Coca Leaves, Codeine, Dihydrocodeinone (Dicodid, Hycodan), Dihydromorphinone (Dilaudid), Heroin, Indian Hemp (marihuana), Laudanum, Meperidine (Demerol, Isonipecaine), Methadon (Dolophine), Metopon, Morphine, Opium, Pantopon, Paregoric, Peyote (mescaline), and NU-2206 (3-Hydroxy-N-Methyl-Morphinan). Persons addicted to barbiturates, alcohol, or other drugs not listed above are not eligible for admission unless they are also addicted to a narcotic drug.

While federal prisoners represent only about 10 percent of admissions, they account for about half of the patients in the hospital on any given date because they remain longer. These prisoners are not necessarily persons who have violated one of the federal laws concerning drugs. Many, for example, were sentenced for stealing from the mails, transporting cars across state lines, etc. They are sent to the hospital rather than one of the Bureau of Prisons institutions because they happen to be addicts and require treatment.

Those selected for commitment to Lexington actually form only a small percentage of federal addict prisoners, many of whom are committed to reformatories and penitentiaries because they have marked antisocial records prior to addiction, are escape risks, or for other reasons are unsuitable for the treatment program at Lexington.

Federal probationers are committed to the hospital as a condition of their probation and would normally be regarded as violating probation if they demanded release and left the hospital before the staff felt they had completed the period of treatment indicated for them.

The voluntary patient applies for admission and may leave the hospital against medical advice at any time. Many of these patients come to the hospital under a great deal of pressure, perhaps from their families or physicians. Quite frequently the voluntary patient is on probation from a county or city court. There are two chief differences between such a patient and the federal probationer. One is that the hospital is not required to accept him as a patient. He must go through the usual admission procedures for voluntary patients, sometimes including a fairly long waiting period. Another difference is that if a person on probation from a nonfederal court demands his release, the hospital cannot notify his probation officer or anyone else without the patient's consent.

Voluntary patients are required to pay for the cost of hospitalization if they can afford to do so. This cost has varied over the years. At the present time it is $9.50 per day. The determination as to ablility to pay is made by the medical officer in charge of the hospital and is based on information the applicant furnishes on his application. In practice, few voluntary patients can afford to pay the cost of hospitalization.

LENGTH OF HOSPITALIZATION

A prisoner can be kept under treatment for the full length of his sentence, or may be transferred to a penal institution after whatever treatment period seems adequate to the medical staff. For probationers and voluntary patients there is no fixed length of hospitalization, though normally a period of about 5 months is considered the minimum. Treatment considerations may require extending the period of hospitalization to a year or even more, and in unusual cases a shorter period may be considered sufficient.

ADMISSION POLICIES

The admission policies and procedures are simple. Federal prisoners and probationers must be admitted. Voluntary patients will be admitted when beds are available for their treatment. A person desiring to be admitted as a voluntary patient may obtain an application form from the hospital, complete it, and mail it directly to the hospital. He will be notified by letter that he is to report to the hospital by a certain date, that his name is being placed on a waiting list and that he will be notified when a bed is available, or that he is not eligible for treatment.

Admissions are authorized in the order in which the applications are received, though the hospital reserves the right, during periods when a waiting list is established, to give priority to applicants who have not been treated before. The Lexington hospital accepts women from any state and men from east of the Mississippi River. Men from west of the Mississippi usually are treated at the

United States Public Health Service Hospital at Fort Worth, Texas. There are minor exceptions to this rule. Others may be made when waiting lists exist.

TREATMENT PROGRAM

The treatment program consists of four phases. For voluntary patients, the first phase is usually the withdrawal of narcotics. Methadone is substituted for the various narcotics used by patients and reduced gradually but rapidly in amount. If a patient is also addicted to barbiturates, a similar but slower gradual reduction is carried on simultaneously. The average time for withdrawal is about a week, but may range from a day or two to 3 or 4 weeks. The withdrawal procedure varies from individual to individual, the time required depending on many factors, most important of these being the drug used, the quantity used, and the physical condition of the patient. Prisoners and probationers have usually been withdrawn from drugs before they arrive at the hospital.

The second phase begins when withdrawal has been completed, or when it has been determined that withdrawal is not necessary. The patient is transferred to an Orientation and Evaluation Unit. The time spent in this ward will vary from about 2 weeks to 1 month. During this time patients are seen, in groups and individually, by a psychiatrist, a psychologist, a social worker, a vocation and education officer, and a psychiatric aide. As the name of the unit implies, these contacts have two purposes: The patient is familiarized with the hospital program in terms of what is expected from him and of what kinds of treatment facilities are available. Simultaneously, the professional personnel of the hospital are engaged in the study of the patient, each focusing on the area of his specialization. The purpose of this study is to evaluate the nature of the psychiatric disorder and the patient's readiness for the different kinds of treatment available. When presentence investigation reports are available, they are extremely valuable in the study of the patient.

When the study is completed the staff members meet, discuss the case, and agree on a hospital program for the individual patient.

The third phase of treatment begins with the patient's transfer from the Orientation and Evaluation Unit to a Continued Treatment Unit. Normally he is first assigned to a ward where supervision is quite close, with the understanding that he can be transferred later to medium or minimum supervision wards as he demonstrates his ability to function with less supervision.

The psychiatric staff of the hospital consists of eight staff psychiatrists and 10 to 12 psychiatric residents in the first or second year of their training. While these numbers seem high to those who are familiar with the staffing of correctional institutions, they are low for the number of annual admissions and the number of patients who are potential candidates for psychotherapy. During 1960, a total of 263 addict patients were carried in psychotherapy, 156 in individual psychotherapy, and 117 in group psychotherapy. (These figures total more than 263 because some patients were in both individual and group psychotherapy.) In 1960 a total of almost 8,000 hours was spent by these patients in psychotherapy.

In most cases of individual psychotherapy the patient is seen a minimum of 1 hour per week on a regular basis. Some are seen more frequently. In 1960 two were being seen five times a week. The usual pattern of group psychotherapy is one 90-minute session per week, but several groups meet twice a week. Group therapy is normally conducted by a therapist-observer team.

Whether or not a patient is assigned to formal psychotherapy, he continues under psychiatric supervision throughout his hospital stay. To each continued treatment area, of approximately 200 patients, there are assigned one or more psychiatric residents, a staff psychiatrist, and a social worker. Together with the psychiatric aides in these areas they are responsible for the clinical management of the patients.

The hospital emphasizes the vocational assignment of patients as one of its major treatment methods. In many cases, particularly when the patient has no work skill, as occurs frequently in the Youth Corrections Act cases, a major treatment objective is training in a skill. As examples of the jobs for which formal training programs are available, the agricultural industry trains patients in the fields of dairying, meat packing, equipment operation and maintenance, greenhouse operation, truck gardening, landscaping, office record management, and others. The needletrades industry has six training units aimed at developing specific vocational skills required in the garment industry. The printing and woodcrafts industries similarly prepare patients for specific skills in these industries. Patients can be assigned as helpers to the skilled tradesmen represented in the maintenance and housekeeping areas for job training in these specialties. These job assignments are by no means a complete listing.

Some of these assignments are also used for women patients who, in addition, can receive training in a microfilm unit as chairside dental assistants and as office personnel.

While this vocational training can obviously be of value in itself, the skills learned often are conceived as a secondary goal. The primary aim is therapeutic and arises from the relationship between the patient and the work supervisor. Many of the patients admitted to Lexington are not good candidates for any form of psychotherapy because this type of relationship has no meaning for them. A relationship with a work supervisor, however, has usually been part of their background and quite frequently is a troublesome relationship for them. With the training and consultation he receives from the psychiatric staff, the work supervisor can frequently establish a relationship with a patient which is potentially more therapeutic than would be a relationship with a therapist. This is true to the extent that frequently the work assignments are made not so much on the basis of the skill which the patient may be able to learn, as the personal characteristics and abilities of a given work supervisor who may have demonstrated that he works unusually well with patients of a certain type.

In some cases, of course, patients show little motivation for vocational advancement. Training in work habits may be the highest goal that can be set. Such patients are usually assigned to jobs which must be done to keep the hospital operating, for example, kitchen work, cleaning, and messenger service. In no case, however, is a patient given a meaningless task simply to keep him busy. He can always feel that he is doing something useful and constructive.

In addition to psychiatrists, the hospital staff includes specialists in surgery and internal medicine and a dental unit.

There are many recreational activities,

both of the spectator and participant types, under the supervision of recreational therapists. Church services and pastoral counseling are provided by part-time chaplains. Patients also are encouraged to assume some responsibilities for their own management and treatment, through such devices as Patients' Councils, publication of a patient newspaper, and through Addicts Anonymous.

In summary, this third phase of the treatment program is not a single program, alike for all patients. Rather, there is an indefinite number of possible programs, ranging from those in which only physical and custodial care in a drug-free environment are of significance, to those where intensive treatment, perhaps along several different lines, is provided. The determination of which program a patient will follow depends partly on his needs, and partly on his desire to participate in treatment. The patient himself determines to a large extent whether his period of hospitalization is to be a matter of "doing time" in an institution, or of active treatment. When a patient complains, as some do, that the hospital is really not a hospital but a prison, it is made because the patient makes it so.

Whatever the specific program, the hospital tries to establish a therapeutic environment in which the patient's attitudes and personality can be modified. As one example, many addict patients see authority as an irrational, unpredictable, and hostile force to be placated, to be seduced, and to be out-maneuvered by those who are clever enough to find its weak spots. To the extent that the hospital succeeds in being firm and consistent, but kind and reasonable in its handling of patients, it presents the patient with a new situation, and forces him to find new ways of relating to authority.

The fourth phase of treatment, in some respects the most important, is unfortunately the least well developed. This is the followup help a patient can use from agencies in his home community. Treatment of addiction which does not include this followup is inadequate, and in this sense few addicts receive adequate treatment. At the present time, this followup help is, in effect, available only for those prisoners and federal probationers who are discharged under the supervision of a federal probation officer, and in a few cases of voluntary patients, where community agencies exist and are willing to work with addict patients.

RESULTS OF TREATMENT

The most obvious criterion of success of treatment is the patient's abstinence or relapse to drug use after he leaves the hospital. There is no logical reason to expect a high rate of abstinence in patients who receive only the first three phases of treatment—those which are accomplished in the hospital. To date there have been no formal attempts to provide the fourth phase, for Lexington patients, and to evaluate the results.[2] Suggestive material, however, may be found in the case records of Lexington patients released on parole.

Diana was admitted to the hospital in February 1958, less than a month after her twenty-first birthday. A white, married woman, she was sentenced under the Youth Corrections Act for illegal importation of narcotics. She and her husband were ap-

[2] Studies based on addicts released from other institutions, who receive specialized followup care, are in progress. See Meyer H. Diskind, "New Horizons in the Treatment of Narcotic Addiction," *Federal Probation*, December 1960, pp. 55–63. Similar studies by the Illinois Division of Narcotic Control and by the California Department of Corrections have not yet been reported.

prehended in an attempt to bring heroin and amphetamine into this country from Mexico.

This patient had been in difficulties since age thirteen, when she began running away from home. Use of marihuana, and quite quickly of heroin, dated from about age fifteen. She had a ninth grade education, and no employment history except for very brief periods as a waitress. She had been married twice and her second husband was an addict.

In the hospital she adjusted well, and was given training in developing X-ray films. She was an excellent worker, learned quickly, and her supervisor felt she had the ability to become an X-ray technician. She obviously had difficulty in getting along with other people, not in the sense of any overt misbehavior, but in letting herself feel close to them. She was seen in individual therapy weekly for a period of about 4 months. While in therapy she moved toward a decision that she would not reunite with her husband. During her hospitalization her parents moved to a different state, and the probation officer who interviewed them felt that they were sincerely interested in helping her make a fresh start. She was released on parole in October 1959.

In April 1961 her probation officer reported a good adjustment under supervision. The plans for training as an X-ray technician had fallen through but she had completed training as a beauty operator and was employed at this work. The probation officer felt her adjustment warranted a recommendation that her supervision be terminated in November 1961. There was no indication of any relapse to drug use or of other offenses.

Robert was a 28-year-old Negro admitted to the hospital in December 1953 with a sentence of 40 months to 10 years for sale of narcotics. His drug use dated back 5 years, but prior to that he had had a fairly stable home environment, a period of satisfactory adjustment in the Army, and had completed high school and about half of a training course as a dental technician. He was married once, but separated from his wife and then had a series of "common law" relationships.

In the hospital the patient was not in psychotherapy, but was given a training assignment as a shipping clerk in the printing industry where he did quite well. Parole was granted in March 1957.

He returned to an eastern seaboard city where he lived with his sister. For the first several years he was out of the hospital he had a great deal of difficulty finding employment, and when he did succeed the jobs did not last long and were at menial work. With the support and encouragement of his probation officer, he managed to get through this period without getting into any difficulty and finally in January 1960 was able to get a job with the Federal Government as a messenger. Within a year after that he received two grade raises because of his fine work. He never reunited with his wife, but at the time of the last report in March 1961 was courting a girl of good character and reputation, her influence being one of the factors which the probation officer considered largely responsible for his "striking" improvement. Again, there was no hint of any further drug use or of any further difficulty with the law.

Any probation officer who has worked with a number of addicts can match these cases with others in which the person relapsed to drug use almost immediately after leaving the hospital or after a period of very marginal adjustment. What accounts for the success in these cases, and the failure in others? What proportion of cases could be classed with the cited ones as successful, and what proportion as failures in the sense of relapse to drug use?

No satisfactory answer can be given to these questions at the present time, because the research necessary to answer them has not yet been done. The early stage of a followup study of Kentucky addicts presently being conducted by the author of this paper suggests that the percentage who remain off drugs, at least in the area being studied, may be much higher than most people would have expected, perhaps in the range of 40 to 50 percent, even among persons with long histories of addiction and repeated relapses. Other studies, and clinical impressions, suggest that the relapse rate may well vary geographically, with higher rates of relapse in the metropolitan centers like New York and Chicago where the number of addicts is higher. Studies by Pescor[3] and Diskind[4] indicate that supervision, and particularly intensive supervision, produces lower relapse rates at least for the periods of supervision. This appears to be more true for persons released on parole than for those being supervised on probation,[5] but it also seems possible that this difference may be accounted for in terms of the different selection process of patients for the two types of supervision.

Clinical impressions (still not corroborated by research) also suggest that, for at least some patients, success in abstaining from drugs is associated with a move away from the area in which the person was addicted. If this turns out to be correct, it will probably be explainable not as a simple function of availability of drugs, but rather as removal of the person from all of the cues and reminders of previous drug use. Probation officers could contribute greatly to answering these questions by papers reporting on their successful and unsuccessful cases.

[3] Michael J. Pescor, M.D., "Follow-Up Study of Treated Narcotic Drug Addicts," Public Health Reports, Supplement No. 170, 1943.
[4] Diskind, *op. cit.*
[5] In an unpublished pilot study of probationers and parolees, based on a small sample, the author found the parolees to have significantly lower relapse rates. See also, Morris Kusnesof, "Probation for a Cure," reprinted in U.S. Senate, Committee on the Judiciary, Hearings on S. Res. 67, *Illicit Narcotics Traffic*, 84th Cong., 1st Sess., 1955, pp. 2091–2110.

PREPARATION OF ADDICTS FOR HOSPITAL TREATMENT

The probation officer interviewing an addict who is to be sent to the hospital can assist the hospital, and greatly facilitate his own later supervision of the patient on return to the community, in several ways. The following suggestions are especially applicable to nonfederal probation officers who send addicts to the hospital as voluntary patients.

Plans for followup care should begin at the time the patient is admitted to the hospital, or even earlier. Probation officers should feel free to communicate with the social work service of the hospital which will cooperate with them and with the patient in formulating plans to assist the patient on his return home. Presentence reports or other information about the patient are most valuable to the hospital if they are received before, or immediately after, the patient's admission.

Nonfederal probation officers should be aware that the law which permits the hospital to treat voluntary patients also forbids it to release any information on the patient. The hospital adheres to this rigidly, except when the patient, in writing, asks us to give information to outside agencies. It is therefore advisable for the nonfederal probation officer, before sending the patient to the hospital, to have the patient sign a statement in which he clearly authorizes the hospital to release information to the probation officer about his hospitalization and discharge. This statement need not be notarized, but should be witnessed by the probation officer or another member of the staff. It should name the hospital, and clearly authorize the hospital to release information to the probation officer, or even better, to the probation office as an agency, rather than the officer as an individual. This statement signed by the patient should be sent to the hospital as quickly as possible so the hospital can notify the probation officer of the patient's arrival, and later of plans for his discharge.

When the patient is being admitted as a voluntary patient, the probation officer should be aware of, and should discuss with the patient, the fact that voluntary patients may leave the hospital at any time they choose to demand their release against medical advice. Remaining in the hospital until discharge is approved by the medical staff and can be made a condition of probation just as is done in the federal courts. If this is a condition of probation, the probation officer should make it clear to the patient that he will be returned to court as a violator if he leaves the hospital against medical advice. It is also helpful if the probation officer will state this definitely in a letter to the hospital so that the social worker will be in a strong position to reinforce this motivation if the patient begins to wonder if he can get away with leaving the hospital.

It would also help if the probation officer would discuss with the patient some of the negative aspects of the hospital. There seems to be a tendency on the part of some persons who work with addicts before they come to the hospital to describe the hospital in glowing terms, to give a sales talk to patients in which the hospital is presented as a very pleasant place, a "country club." When the patient gets to the hospital he is struck by the less pleasant aspects of hospitalization, and in many cases this contributes to his leaving, against medical advice, before he completes treatment. If he is prepared for the negative aspects of hospitalization before he comes, his initial adjustment will be easier, and the probability of discharge against medical advice will be lessened.

One factor which bothers many patients is the lack of freedom in the hospital. There are many restrictions on patients, even voluntary patients, and there is little difference between the handling of prisoners and voluntary patients. These restrictions are necessary not only because some patients are prisoners, but even more so because of the security provisions to prevent the introduction of drugs and other contraband. Mail is censored; there are limits on the number of letters a patient may send, and on the number and frequency of visits he may receive. Except in unusual circumstances, a patient is not given leave from the hospital before discharge, he may not make phone calls, and he may receive packages from home only after receiving prior permission for specific items.

Almost half of the hospital population consists of Negro patients, and there is no segregation of races. This is sometimes a problem to white patients. There is no segregation of prisoners from voluntary patients, or by age groups, or in general, any segregation except of the sexes.

The patient should know this in advance. He can also be told, however, that the addict population covers the entire range of personality types, and of educational and cultural backgrounds. The period of adjustment to this situation can be difficult, but the patient can be assured that it will not be impossible, and that he will have the support of a trained staff which understands the problems of adjustment. Further, he can be assured that many patients like himself have been able to go through this period and to profit from treatment. As he becomes familiar with other patients, he will meet those whose backgrounds and interests are closer to his own, and almost any patient can be sure of finding a group of persons much like himself, with whom he can live quite comfortably in the hospital.

During the withdrawal phase, the patient is physically ill and uncomfortable. The patient can be assured that he will be withdrawn slowly enough so that there will be no danger, and so that the discomfort is minimized. However, he should also know that the medical staff will withdraw him as rapidly as possible and that he is bound to suffer some discomfort.

We have found no good reasons to minimize these difficulties to a prospective patient. It seems desirable to call these facts to the patient's attention if he has not already given thought to them. This may keep some applicants from coming for the treatment they need, but if this happens it is almost certain that the patient would have left very soon after admission anyway. It will make it more probable that those who do come will remain for the treatment they need. Difficulties which have been foreseen are much less frightening when they appear than those which arise unexpectedly.

THE ANTICRIMINAL SOCIETY: SYNANON

Lewis Yablonsky, Ph.D.

A reader of the *Terminal Island News* of April 12, 1962 would be somewhat surprised to note an unusual statement called "Breaking the Invisible Wall" authored by a former criminal and inmate of the Federal Correctional Institution at Terminal Island, Calif., the U.S. Public Health Service Hospital at Fort Worth, Texas, the State Prison of Southern Michigan, and various juvenile reformatories. James Middleton, the writer of the statement, had served a total of 15 years in these institutions. He has currently been clean of his past lengthy addiction and criminal history for almost 3 years. Middleton is one of a group of seven ex-offenders and former prisoners who go to the Terminal Island institution once a week to run group counseling sessions with about 25 addict inmates. This is the way Middleton described this project in the *Terminal Island News:*

As a former using addict and inmate of Terminal Island and other prisons, having been free from the use of drugs for the past 2½ years by being a resident of Synanon House, I have been aware of the lack of communication between inmates and all those in positions of authority. Perhaps the most difficult problem to overcome for penologists, prison officials, and others dealing with the socially rejected group, the criminal, is the problem of establishing an area of communication, some feeling of rapport. The convict, criminal, or any rebellious delinquent has a defiance of all authority. This he carried to such an extent that he will refuse to even talk to a person in any position of authority whom he considers his enemy. He takes the attitude that "If you are not on my side, you are against me."

On November 26, 1961, six members of

From *Federal Probation*, 26 (September 1962), pp. 50–57. Reprinted by permission.

the Synanon Foundation were invited to the Terminal Island correctional institution by Chief Parole Officer Frank E. Saunders who believed that the Synanon approach might have something to offer the prisoners who had an addiction history.

Of paramount significance perhaps is the effect synanon has had in bridging this gap in communication between prisoner and official. This has been accomplished by the prisoners being encouraged to verbalize their problem, frustration, attitudes, opinions, etc., in the synanon.

Synanon is a form of intense group interaction. In these meetings synanites and inmate addicts are encouraged to break down this wall and see their problems in a more realistic light. Part of the success of these meetings can be attributed to the fact that an inmate can often lie to the officials and get away with it, however with his fellow inmates, those who know him intimately, and can identify with his problems and his unsatisfactory reaction to them, he can't get away with as much. They see him as he is. Once a person has admitted his failures and inadequacies to others, and as an eventual consequence, to himself, he finds that he can discuss these things with almost anyone.

They are no longer deep, dark secrets which he must hide from others and himself. As Dr. Yablonsky, U.C.L.A. criminologist said, "This is the most significant breakthrough in the field of criminology in the past 50 years."

It is conceivable to me as an ex-inmate myself that someday Synanon could become an established part of the prison program throughout the United States.

THE BACKGROUND OF SYNANON

The Synanon organization,[1] of which Middleton is a significant member, has been in operation about 4 years. As a result of exposure to this unique social system approximately 100 persons, most with long criminal and addiction records,

[1] The name Synanon was derived from the slip-of-the-tongue of a confessed addict attempting to say seminar. It was adopted because it is a new word for describing a new phenomenon.

no longer find it necessary to use drugs or commit crimes. Some Synanon residents have been clean of these deviant patterns for periods of up to 4 years.

This antiaddiction society originated with Charles E. Dederich, a former business executive, who had worked through an alcoholic problem and was motivated to transmit the forces which had led to his own recovery. A strong personality with characteristics of a charismatic leader, Dederich attracted to his residence by the beach in Ocean Park a coterie of alcoholics and drug addicts who found stimulating and interesting the lengthy philosophical discussions which he led. Many of these persons had no roots and moved into Dederich's "pad." Within a short time a small colony of about 15 addicts moved into the various apartments in the immediate area and emerged as the early core of the Synanon movement. At this point, about 6 months after its inception, there emerged an idealized assumption that no one was using drugs; although this fact was only true for about half the residents at the time.

Two incidents sharply changed the nature of this unusual collectivity and projected the evolution of a clean Synanon community. One was what later became known as the "big cop-out." This involved the open admission of occasional use by several key residents. Shortly after this episode the balance of power shifted over to a community with a majority of *clean addicts*. This new situation gave strength and credence to an antiaddiction, anticriminal ethos. To my knowledge, it was the first time anywhere that a group of nonprisoner ex-addicts could be found in one location.

By the summer of 1959 about 40 to 50 men and women, not using drugs, were living in a Synanon colony in one large building. The Synanon movement had become more established and aroused the interest of many significant professionals. *Time* magazine in its April 7, 1961 issue published an extensive description of the Synanon organization at that time.

S. S. HANG TOUGH

Early in August 1959, homeowners along the stylish Pacific Ocean beaches in Santa Monica, Calif., were dismayed to get a new set of neighbors: a bedraggled platoon of half a hundred men and women, who moved into a run-down, three story, red brick building that once was a National Guard armory. White and black, young and middle-aged, criminals and innocents, artists and loafers, the unlikely assortment shared one trait: they were narcotics addicts determined to kick their habit for good.

Scrounging lumber, paint and old furniture, the group converted the top floor of the armory into a barracks-style men's dormitory. They turned the second floor into offices, kitchen, dining hall and living room, and the main floor into women's sleeping quarters. Over the doors in the living room they hung their emblem: a life preserver with the words "S. S. *Hang Tough*," slang for "don't give up." . . . .

Such was the formal dedication of Synanon House a self-run, haphazardly financed experiment in human reclamation whose success has been hailed by Dr. Donald Cressey, University of California at Los Angeles sociologist, as "the most significant attempt to keep addicts off drugs that has ever been made." . . . . The technique was patterned roughly after the group-therapy methods of Alcoholics Anonymous. . . . . Dr. Cressey describes the psychology: "A group in which Criminal A joins with some noncriminals to change Criminal B is probably most effective in changing Criminal A."

In the often brutally frank personal exchanges, the addicts slowly reveal themselves . . . and through daily contact with similarly beset persons are reinforced in their determination to quit narcotics permanently. Says the founder of Synanon House, 48-year-old Charles E. Dederich . . . , once an alcoholic but never a drug addict: "It is something that works."

The Synanon curriculum is divided into three stages. During the first phase, the emotionally shaken, physically weak addict gradually adjusts to his new surroundings. . . . During the second stage, the ex-addict works at a regular job on the outside, contributes part of his wages to the group, continues to live at the house . . . . In its final stage, Synanon sends its member out into society.

Interestingly, the potential of this type of an anticriminal society for modifying difficult offenders had been forecast by Professor Cressey in an article published in 1955 in *The American Journal of Sociology*.[2] His projection of the need for this treatment approach was based upon Sutherland's causal theory of criminal "differential association." Cressey logically speculated that, "if the behavior of an individual is an intrinsic part of the groups to which he belongs, attempts to change the behavior must be directed at groups."[3]

Cressey, utilizing "differential association" theory as a diagnostic base, projected the necessity for an anticriminal society to modify deviant behavior.

The differential association theory of criminal behavior presents implications for diagnosis and treatment consistent with the group-relations principle for changing behavior and could be advantageously utilized in correctional work. According to it, persons become criminals principally because they have been relatively isolated from groups whose behavior patterns (including attitudes, motives, and rationalizations) are anticriminal, or because their residence, employment, social position, native capacities, or something else has brought them into relatively frequent association with the behavior patterns of criminal groups. A diagnosis of criminality based

[2] Donald R. Cressey, "Changing Criminals: The Application of the Theory of Differential Association," *American Journal of Sociology*, September 1955, pp. 116–120.
[3] *Ibid.* p. 117.

on this theory would be directed at analysis of the criminal's attitudes, motives, and rationalizations regarding criminality and would recognize that those characteristics depend upon the groups to which the criminal belongs. Then if criminals are to be changed, either they must become members of anticriminal groups, or their present pro-criminal group relations must be changed.[4]

Life in the Synanon anticriminal society revolves around a set of educational and apparently group therapeutic procedures developed by Dederich and the group of ex-addict leaders he had personally trained. Synanon by this time had many characteristics of an extended father-dominated family. As Dederich himself described it in an address before The Southern California Parole Officers Association:

We have here a climate consisting of a family structure similar in some areas to a primitive tribal structure, which seems to affect individuals on a sub-conscious level. The structure also contains overtones of a 19th century family set-up of the type which produced inner-directed personalities. It is the feeling of the Synanon Foundation that an undetermined percentage of narcotic addicts are potentially inner-directed people as differentiated from tradition-directed people. A more or less autocratic family structure appears to be necessary as a pre-conditioning environment to buy time for the recovering addict.

. . . The autocratic overtone of the family structure demands that the patients or members of the family perform tasks as part of the group. As a member is able to take direction in small tasks such as helping in the preparation of meals, housecleaning and so forth, regardless of his rebellion of being "told what to do," his activity seems to provide exercise of emotions of giving or creating which have lain dormant. As these muscles strengthen, it seems that the resistance to cooperating with the group tends to dissipate.

[4] *Ibid.* p. 118.

SYNANON GROUP THERAPY

The daily program for the Synanon resident includes some type of work, a noon educational seminar, the synanon (a form of leaderless group therapy in which all residents participate three times a week), and daily interaction and communication with hundreds of "squares" (nonaddicts) from all walks of life who visit the building regularly.

The synanon, a form of group interaction vital to the overall approach, tends to be a unique form of aggressive leaderless nonprofessional group psychotherapy, directed by what Dederich has referred to as a Synanist. According to Dederich:

The Synanist leans heavily on his own insight into his own problems of personality in trying to help others find themselves, and will use the weapons of ridicule, cross-examination, and hostile attack as it becomes necessary. Synanon sessions seem to provide an emotional catharsis and trigger an atmosphere of truth-seeking which is reflected in the social life of the family structure. The Synanist does not try to convey to another that he himself is a stable personality. In fact, it may very well be the destructive drives of the recovered or recovering addictive personality embodied in a Synanist which makes him a good therapeutic tool—fighting fire with fire.

This form of group therapy is ideally suited for the overall Synanon community. The group sessions do not have any official leader. They are autonomous; however, leaders emerge in each session in a natural fashion. The emergent leader tells much about himself in his questioning of another. Because he is intensely involved with the subject or the problem in the particular session he begins to direct, he is in a natural fashion the "most qualified" session leader for that time and place. In short, the expert of the moment may be emotionally crippled in many personal areas, but in the session where he is permitted by the group to take therapeutic command, he may be the most qualified therapeutic agent.

Synanon, as a side effect, trains persons to become a new brand of therapeutic agent in the correctional field. The system provides the opportunity for offenders to modify their own deviant behavior and then work with other offenders. In this context I view the phenomenon of Synanon at Terminal Island as a major breakthrough in the field of correction.

Although ex-offenders have been randomly used over the years in the processes of correction, Synanon provides a unique contribution. One can view the seven 2-year-clean Synanon participants in the Terminal Island project as a new type of "therapeutic agent" for dealing with the crime problem. Unlike most professional or ex-offender workers in the field the trained synanist has three levels of experience which uniquely qualify him for work with other offenders.

1. He has a lengthy history of criminal experience. He himself has made the "scene." He knows the crime problem in its many dimensions—at first hand.

2. At Synanon, this individual has deeply experienced the emotional upheaval of rejecting one way of life for another. He has "in his gut" gone through a resocialization process and knows something about the set of experiences and the pain involved in the transition.

3. He knows the Synanon social system. He has a subconscious conception of the processes at work for helping others and he is himself a functional part of this organization. He has been trained at "the Synanon College" for working with recalcitrant offenders.

This triad of experiences qualified the Synanist uniquely for the task at hand. Terminal Island inmates in the Synanon project know they are encountering in the Synanist a new breed of "treatment man." The Synanist is difficult to con or juggle out of position. The Synanist cannot easily be out-maneuvered from his zeal to point up a new direction in life to replace the roles of crime and addiction which he now views as wasteful and stupid behavior. This point of view of the Synanist seems to get across to the inmate seeking a noncriminal mode of existence.

Although the synanon form of group therapy is an important aspect of the method, the basic therapeutic force is the overall synanon social system. The best way to reveal this overall dynamic is to examine its impact on one successful resident.

FRANKIE: A CASE STUDY OF THE SYNANON SYSTEM[5]

Frankie, a 2-year-clean Synanon resident, first came to the author's attention in an unusual fashion. While listening to some tapes being played on the Egyptian King gang killing (an incident studied intensively by the author), Dederich detected a familiar voice. Hearing one King comment, "I kicked him in the head, it was the least I could do," Dederich remarked, "That sounds like Frankie." It was later confirmed that Frankie was this Egyptian King gang member's older brother. It was also determined that Frankie's early case history and violent gang life pattern paralleled his younger brother's. Frankie later turned to using and pushing drugs, a criminal career, which carried him to the

[5] This section is partially derived from a recent volume by the author, *The Violent Gang* (New York: The Macmillan Company, 1962).

Federal Correctional Institution at Danbury, Conn., New York City's Riker's Island Penitentiary, and finally Bellevue Hospital in New York City. As a result of his experience at Synanon, Frankie was at the time free and clear of drugs and violence for over 2 years.

"Frankie would never use a knife; unless he had to. Mostly with his fists he would beat a guy down and try to kill him right there. They pulled him off this big guy one time—he wouldn't stop punching him in the face." This was a casual observation made by Frankie's ex-"crime partner," the girl with whom he had lived for 5 years in New York. (She is also currently a successful resident at Synanon.)

Frankie's first reaction to Synanon was confusion. "The first thing they hit me with flipped me. This tough looking cat says to me—'there are two things you can't do here, shoot drugs or fight.'" Frankie said, scratching his head, "I was all mixed up—these were the only two things I knew how to do."

Frankie first came West at the insistence of his parents "to try a new way of life." "The family chipped in, gave me a plane ticket, and told me to straighten out or drop dead." He accepted the plane ticket they gave him and came West under the assumption of continuing his old way of life. In the Los Angeles situation he had trouble getting a good drug connection and stealing enough money to supply his habit. He heard about Synanon, and decided to try it. His initial motives were not pure. His thought was "to get cleaned up a little" and either get organized for a new onslaught on Los Angeles or steal enough to return to New York and his old criminal pattern. Something happened at Synanon to make Frankie stay "clean" for 2 years and later

assume the administrative role of "coordinator" at Synanon.[6]

The Synanon environment was interesting and exciting for Frankie. There were, in the addicts' jargon, "lots of hip people." Jimmy the Greek, who at 48 had been an addict for 20 years and a criminal and con-man for over 30 years[7] and Jimmy Middleton, who now ran the kitchen at Synanon. In the kitchen Frankie received his first job scouring pots and pans and mopping floors. According to Frankie, Jimmy M. could not be conned or manipulated out of position like the therapist Frankie had encountered at Riker's Island Prison. Jimmy M., of course, knew the score and to him Frankie with all his exploits was a "young punk," who could give him no trouble. "I've met

[6] A coordinator works a 4-hour shift, answering phones, catering to visitors and generally handling the House's business as it emerges. It requires some ingenuity and administrative ability.

[7] Jimmy's personal statement in the *Synanon Issue* of the *Terminal Island News* further reveals his criminal background and current view of life: "My addiction history goes back to when I was 12 years old (I am close to 50) but up until the time I came to Synanon, 31 months ago, I never knew what it was to be "clean" on the streets. I have done just about everything illegal to obtain money; work was not a part of this life, for I could not support a habit working. I have spent almost 10 years in county jails, the Lewisburg federal penitentiary, and chain-gangs. I can go so far as to say that I had never met a 'clean' dope-fiend until I came to Synanon. . . .

I have been a resident of Synanon for 31 months. I plan on staying for some time to come. For the first time in my life I like what I am doing—Synanon is growing and I am part of it. There is a group from Synanon attending meetings at Terminal Island every week, for the past 4½ months; I am project director of this group. There are plans in the making to start Synanon meetings on the women's side at Terminal Island—and eventually, men and women together. I am sure with the cooperation we have been getting this plan will come about in the near future."—James (Greek) Georgelas.

kids like this all my life—in and out of the joint."

According to Frankie, "I hated this '. . . .' for no good reason. I used to sometimes sit and plan ways to kill him." When Frankie wanted to fight Jimmy over a disagreement about work (no fighting allowed at Synanon) Jimmy laughed and told him if he wanted to fight he would be thrown out of Synanon.

The usual prison situation was reversed and confusing to Frankie. In the "joint" (prison) if Frankie got in trouble confinement became increasingly severe with the "hole" (solitary confinement) as an end point. At the Bellevue Hospital psychiatric ward where Frankie had also "done time" it was a straight-jacket. What made Frankie remain, even behave in order to stay at Synanon with its open door?

The fact that Frankie was exported from New York to Los Angeles was a significant force initially in keeping him at Synanon, as he stated it: "At times I felt like splitting (leaving), then I thought it will be hard to make it back to New York. I didn't know Los Angeles and I was afraid to make it out there—cause I didn't know the people. Synanon was better than anything else I could do —at the time."

Also, Synanon House was on the beach. The meals were good. In the evening many ex-addict top musicians would play cool jazz.[8] Also there were, according to Frankie, "broads to dance with and get to know." But highly important in this antiaddiction, antidelinquency society there were others who understood him, had made the same "scenes" and intuitively knew his problems and how to handle him. He respected people he could not

con. He belonged and was now part of a "family" he could accept.

At Synanon Frankie could also make a "rep" without getting punished or locked up. In prison, the highest he could achieve in terms of the values of "his people" was to become "King" of the sociopathic inmate system, acquire a "stash" of cigarettes, obtain some unsatisfactory homosexual favors, and land in the "hole." In the "inmate system" of Synanon he could achieve any role he was "big enough of a man" to acquire and this carried the highest approval of his fellows. He could actually become a *director* in this organization—which was now in the national spotlight.[9] Articles on Synanon had been published in national magazines like *Time, Life,* and *Nation,* and were coming out daily in the press. For the first time in his life, Frankie was receiving status for being clean and nondelinquent.

Of course, when he first arrived at Synanon, Frankie attempted to gain a "rep" by conniving and making deals in accord with his old mode of relating. He was laughed at, ridiculed and given a "hair-cut" (a verbal dressing down) by other "old-time con men" members of the organization. He was accused of "shucking and sliding" (simply not performing adequately). The old-time Synanists were ferocious about keeping the organization, which had literally saved their lives and given them a new life status, operating smoothly.

Frankie found that "rep" was acquired in this social system (unlike ones he had known) by truth, honesty, and industry. The values of his other life required reversal if he was to gain a "rep" at Synanon. These values were not goals *per se*

---

[8] The Synanon Band recently produced a widely acclaimed professional record album, appropriately called: *Sounds of Synanon.*

[9] There are currently 8 directors of the Synanon Foundation. This is the highest and most respected status level of achievement in the organization.

which someone moralized about in a meaningless vacuum; they were means to the end of acquiring prestige in this tough social system with which he now intensely identified.

In the small *s* synanons, three nights a week Frankie participated in a form of leaderless group psychotherapy. In these synanons the truth was viciously demanded. Any system of rationalizations about past or current experience were brutally demolished by the group. There was an intensive search for self-identity.

In the process the individual attempted to learn what goes on beneath the surface of his thoughts. For Frankie this was the first time in his life that he discovered others had some idea about what he was thinking underneath. He had individual group therapy in prison—but there he could "con" the therapist and most important, "I said what I thought they wanted to hear so I could hit the street sooner."

Most important Frankie began to get some comprehension of what others thought in a social situation. The fact of empathy or identifying with the thoughts and feelings of others became a significant reality.

Frankie was at first empathic in his usual pattern of sociopathic self-centered manipulation. However, a new force was introduced into the situation—he began to care about what happened to others at Synanon. This was at first selfish. Synanon was for him a good interesting way of life. He had identified with the system and learned "gut level" that if any Synanon member failed, he too was diminished and failed. In Cressey's words which Frankie learned to quote (since after all Professor Cressey was a friend of his) "When I help another guy, it helps me personally."

In the status system, Frankie's rise to the role of coordinator was not quick nor easy. He moved from the "dishpan" to serving food at the kitchen counter.

After several months he was allowed to work outside on a pickup truck which acquired food and other donations. With two other individuals who worked with him on the truck a group decision was made one day "that one shot wouldn't hurt." One individual knew a "connection" on the route. They went to his home. All they could get were some pills.

When they arrived back at Synanon their slightly "loaded" appearance immediately became apparent to the group ("they spotted us right away") and they were hauled into the main office and viciously (verbally) attacked to tell all ("cop-out") or get out of the building. A general meeting was called and they were forced to reveal "all" before the entire group.[10] Frankie was back at work on the dishpan that evening.

Such "slips" often come out in the synanon. In a sense, in addition to other forces of growth from the synanon it serves as a form of "first-aid" therapy. If anyone reveals a minor "slip," the personal wound is examined and cleaned up by the group before a serious act of misbehavior occurs. (The synanon situation has some of the characteristics of an underground organization operating during wartime. If any member "falls," it may entail the destruction of the entire organization.)

The norms of synanon society are the reverse of the criminal code. On one occasion Frankie, with two other members

---

[10] This process known as a "fireplace" may be called at anytime, day or night. The "transgressor" is placed at the fireplace in the main living room in front of all other residents. He is ridiculed into an open-honest revelation of his "offense." The group may then decide to evict or give the individual another chance.

of Synanon, went for a walk into town. One individual suggested buying a bottle of wine. (No drinking is permitted.) The other two (including Frankie) smashed the idea. However, no one revealed the incident until 2 days later it came up in a synanon. The group jumped hardest on Frankie and the other individual who did not reveal the potential "slip," rather than on the transgressor who had suggested the wine. Frankie and the other "witness" were expected to report such "slips" immediately, since the group's life depended on keeping each other "straight." For the first time in his life Frankie was censured for *not squealing.* The maxim "thou shalt not squeal" basic to the existence of the usual underworld criminal culture was reversed at Synanon and just as ferociously sanctioned. An individual could get "kicked out" of Synanon for *not* being a "stoolie."

The rule of no physical violence was at first extremely difficult for Frankie to grasp and believe. Since his usual response to a difficult situation would be to leap fists-first past verbal means of communication into assault. As a result of the synanons and other new patterns of interaction, Frankie's social ability for communication increasingly minimized his assaultive impulse. Although at first he was controlled from committing violence by the fear of ostracism, he later no longer had a need to use violence since he now had some ability to interact effectively. He could express himself with a new form of communication on a nonviolent, verbal level.

On occasion Frankie would regress and have the motivation for assault—but the system had taken hold. In one synanon session I heard him say, "I was so . . . mad yesterday, I wished I was back at Rikers (prison). I really wanted to hit that bastard Jimmy in the mouth."

Frankie had a sketchy work record prior to Synanon. Other than gang fighting, "pimping," armed robbery, pushing heroin, and some forced work in prison, he seldom acted in any role resembling formal work. His theme had been "work was for squares." He learned how to work at Synanon automatically as a side effect of his desire to rise in the status system. He also learned, as a side effect of the work process, the startling fact "that talking to someone in the right way made them do more things than belting them."

Frankie's most recent position involves the overall supervision of Synanon's number two building. Here 12 mothers (ex-addicts) in residence at Synanon live with their children. Frankie supervises a budget, the care and feeding of the establishment and the inevitable daily counseling of his "wards." Although it is not apparent on the surface of his efficient administration, Frankie beneath maintains a state of personal amazement about his new social role in society.

As a consequence of living in the Synanon social system, Frankie developed an increasing residual of social learning and ability. His destructive pattern of relating to others withered away because it was no longer functional for him within this new way of life. Synanon developed his empathic ability, produced an attachment to different, more socially acceptable values, and reconnected him adequately to the larger society within which Synanon functioned as a valid organization.

PRINCIPAL FORCES AT WORK IN THE SYNANON SOCIETY

INVOLVEMENT   Initially, Synanon society is able to involve and control the offender. This is accomplished through providing an interesting social setting comprised of associates who understand him and will not be outmaneuvered by his manipulative behavior.

AN ACHIEVABLE STATUS SYSTEM   Within the context of this system he can (perhaps, for the first time) see a realistic possibility for legitimate achievement and prestige. Synanon provides a rational and attainable opportunity structure for the success-oriented individual. He is no longer restricted to inmate status, since there is no inmate-staff division. All residents are staff.

NEW SOCIAL ROLE   Synanon creates a new social role which can be temporarily or indefinitely occupied in the process of social growth and development. (Some residents have made the decision to make Synanon their life's work.) This new role is a legitimate one supported by the ex-offender's own community as well as the inclusive society. With the opening of new Synanons and increasing development of projects like the one at Terminal Island, Synanon trained persons are increasingly in demand. Since the Synanon organization is not a hospital or an institution, there is no compulsion to move out of this satisfying community.

SOCIAL GROWTH   In the process of acquiring legitimate social status in Synanon the offender necessarily, as a side effect, develops the ability to relate, communicate and work with others. The values of truth, honesty, and industry become necessary means to this goal of status achievement. After a sufficient amount of practice and time, the individual socialized in this way in a natural fashion develops the capability for behaving adequately with reference to these values.

SOCIAL CONTROL   The control of deviance is a by-product of the individual's status-seeking. Conformity to the norms is necessary in order to achieve. Anomie, the dislocation of goals and means, becomes a minimal condition. The norms are valid and adhered to within this social system since means are available for legitimate goal attainment.

Another form of control is embodied in the threat of ostracism which becomes a binding force. After being initially involved in Synanon, the individual does not at the time feel adequate for participation in the larger society. After a sufficient residue of Synanon social living has been acquired the individual no longer fears banishment; however, at the same time he is then better prepared for life on the outside (if this is his choice). He no longer fears ostracism and may remain voluntarily because he feels Synanon is a valid way of life for him. In Synanon he has learned and acquired a gratifying social role which enables him as a "coordinator" or a "director" to help others who can benefit from Synanon treatment.

Other forms of immediate social control include ridicule ("hair-cuts," the "fireplace") and the synanon sessions. The individual is required to tell the truth in the synanon. This also regulates his behavior. Real life transgressions are often prevented by the knowledge that the individual's deviance will automatically, rapidly, and necessarily be brought to the attention of his community within the synanon session. He is living within a community where others know about and, most important, are concerned with his behavior.

EMPATHY AND SELF-IDENTITY   The constant self-assessment required in his daily life and in the synanon sessions fosters the consolidation of self-identity and empathy. His self-estimation is under constant assessment and attack by relevant others, who become sensitive to and concerned about him. The process provides the opportunity for the individual almost literally "to see himself as others do." He is also compelled as part of this process to develop the ability to identify with and understand others. A side consequence is the development of self-growth, social awareness, the ability to communicate and empathic effectiveness. When these socialization processes are at work and take hold, the youth becomes reconnected with the legitimate society and no longer finds it necessary to use drugs or assume a deviant role.

SYNANON'S FUTURE

From its unusual beginnings the Synanon Foundation has emerged as a highly efficient organization. The Foundation has federal tax exempt status and is a corporate entity in the State of California. The State Legislature passed and the Governor signed into law The Petris Bill on June 15, 1961, officially sanctioning Synanon as a "Place" for rehabilitating drug addicts.[11]

[11] The Petris Bill especially passed for Synanon is here presented in full:
Assembly Bill No. 2626 (State of California). An act to amend Section 11391 of the Health and Safety Code, relating to narcotic addiction.
The people of the State of California do enact as follows:
Section 1. Section 11391 of the Health and Safety Code is amended to read:
11391. No person shall treat an addict for addiction except in one of the following:
(a) An institution approved by the Board of Medical Examiners, and where the patient is at all times kept under restraint and control.
(b) A city or county jail.
(c) A state prison.
(d) A state narcotic hospital.
(e) A state hospital.
(f) A county hospital.
This section does not apply during emergency treatment or where the patient's addiction is complicated by the presence of incurable disease, serious accident, or injury, or the infirmities of old age.
Neither this section nor any other provision

Synanon, over the past year, as a partial consequence of donations and the earning power of its residents, has rented four buildings with a total rental of over $1500 a month. Although its budgeting is tight, comparable to other nonprofit organizations, it has met all of its financial obligations as a result of community support. The organization over the past year has sustained approximately 85 residents in food and clothing, and has entertained approximately 19,000 guests (mostly professional visitors). In addition to the Terminal Island project a Synanon educational and addiction-prevention program has involved most of the 100 Synanon members in over 400 speaking engagements delivered to business, professional, religious, youth, and college and university groups. One evening a week about 40 nonaddicts from all segments of society participate in the so-called "Square

of this division shall be construed to prohibit the maintenance of a place [Synanon] in which persons seeking to recover from narcotic addiction reside and endeavor to aid one another and receive aid from others in recovering from such addiction, nor does this section or such division prohibit such aid, provided that no person is treated for addiction in such place [Synanons] at reasonable times and, if it con-ing, or prescribing of narcotics. The preceding sentence is declaratory of pre-existing law. Every such place [Synanon] shall register with and be approved by the Board of Medical Examiners. The board may inspect such places [Synanons] at reasonable times and, if it concludes that the conditions necessary for approval no longer exist, is may withdraw approval. Every person admitted to such a place [Synanon] shall register with the police department of the city in which it is located or, if it is outside of the city limits, with the sheriff's office. The place [Synanon] shall maintain its own register of all residents. It shall require all its residents to register with said police department or sheriff's office and, upon termination of the residence of any person in said place [Synanon], it shall report the name of the person terminating residence to said police department or sheriff's office.

Synanons." Here the variety of human problems are examined through utilization of the Synanon method involving Synanon residents mixed with "squares." This interaction and cross-fertilization of ideas and insights appear to be of benefit to all.

As a social science research center Synanon is unique. In this open-door environment run by ex-offenders themselves, persons with long addiction and criminal background freely provide important data unavailable in the usual custodial setting. Synanon thus enables the systematic gathering of much useful information about crime, addiction, and the solution of these problems.

The Synanon approach which has emerged under the creative and capable leadership of Dederich and his uniquely trained staff of directors as an effective anticriminal and antiaddiction society, also involves an organization of distinguished citizens from all walks of life called "S.O.S." or Sponsors of Synanon. This supportive organization has a national membership of over 600 persons who donate money, goods, and services. They are currently launching a building program for an ideal Synanon community.

The organization is naturally committed to expansion. Synanon-trained personnel of the type carrying out the program at Terminal Island will no doubt shortly be utilized as the core staff for Synanon Houses planned for other communities. Each new establishment has the potential for "cleaning-up" another hundred offenders.

As viewed by its founder, Charles Dederich, Synanon is still in its infancy. The fact of 100 individuals with long addiction and criminal histories currently clean attests to its effectiveness. However, Synanon, as a social movement or community way of life, appears to have possibilities beyond exclusive application to the addiction problem. As Middleton commented at the outset: "It is conceivable to me as an ex-inmate myself that someday Synanon could become an established part of the prison program throughout the United States."

NEW HOPE FOR DRUG ADDICTS

Roland H. Berg

The 52 addicts speak reverently of the program as if it were a religious movement instead of a scientific research study of narcotics. Each patient has been a "mainliner" (one who injects a narcotic drug into a main vein), a confirmed user of heroin for two to 16 years; most have spent years in prisons for crimes related to drug addiction. In hospitals or prisons, they had submitted willingly or unwillingly to gradual withdrawal treatments or abrupt "cold-turkey" cures. None of

From *LOOK Magazine*, 29, 24 (November 30, 1965), pp. 23–24. Copyright © 1965 by Cowles Communications, Inc. Reprinted by permission.

the attempts succeeded, and after every failure, all of the addicts climbed back on the same narcotic treadmill.

But not this time. Now it's different. Their craving for heroin has vanished. The euphoria they once sought from drugs with a zeal blotting out all else is only a blurry memory. The hard knot in their stomachs has unraveled. Now, they no longer think only of where the next "fix" is coming from. No longer are they forced to steal to support a habit that daily had become more expensive. For the first time since they've been on narcotics, they dare to believe there is a future for themselves and their families.

What makes the difference to the 52 addict-patients under treatment at the Manhattan General Division of Beth Israel Medical Center in New York City is one or two teaspoonfuls of a bitter brew taken daily in a cup of orange juice to mask the taste. A daily dose of this maintenance medicine for one addict-patient costs less than ten cents.

The medicine is called methadone. It is no new miracle drug. Actually, it has been around for nearly 25 years, and as drugs go, it has been a useful medication but never a front-page success. The manufacturers seldom even bother to advertise it to doctors anymore.

During World War II, German chemists synthesized the drug while searching for inexpensive morphine substitutes. As a pain-killer, methadone is not as effective as morphine, but a lot cheaper. At war's end, the United States Government seized the methadone formula—with thousands of others—as spoils of war to be turned over to American drug manufacturers as an "open patent." Methadone's effects are not quite as potent as morphine's, but they last longer. For that reason, until now the medicine has had

its chief use in this country as a substitute narcotic in the unsuccessful withdrawal treatment of heroin addicts.

The classic method of withdrawing addicts is to substitute a smaller dose of another drug, such as methadone, for the one the addict is using, and, in daily diminishing doses, wean him away from dependence on narcotics. The process takes about two weeks of giving smaller and smaller amounts of the substitute until the addict is getting no drugs at all. During this period, he suffers some withdrawal symptoms—nausea, cramps, sweating, chills and vomiting—but the reaction is not nearly as violent as it would be were he suddenly deprived of all narcotics.

Unfortunately, withdrawal treatment, or detoxification, is neither a cure nor even a successful treatment. Studies at a variety of treatment centers, including the Federal hospital at Lexington, Ky., indicate that more than 90 percent of addicts subjected to withdrawal programs return within a few days or weeks to the use of narcotics.

Addicts often voluntarily seek withdrawal treatment. It isn't that they want to be cured permanently; they're just anxious to get their habit down to a level they can afford. For an addict to feel "high," he must continually increase his shot of heroin. Finally, the amount he needs to get high is so expensive, he can't even steal enough to pay for it. It's not unusual for a junkie to work up to a $100-a-day habit. And at the prices fences pay, a junkie would have to steal more than $500 worth of merchandise a day to net about $100 in cash. But after a two-week withdrawal treatment, he can get high for perhaps $10 a day, at least for a while. Then the cycle of bigger and bigger doses resumes.

Methadone's new role as a cinderella drug began quietly nearly two years ago at the Rockefeller Institute in New York City, where Doctors Vincent P. Dole and Marie Nyswander started their current research on narcotic addiction. Dr. Dole, a member of the Institute, is a dark-haired, 52-year-old, quiet-spoken physician who has earned a distinguished reputation in metabolic research. Dr. Nyswander, slim, blonde and younger-looking than her 46 years, is a psychiatrist and analyst who, for more than 15 years, has sought an effective treatment of narcotic addiction.

The two researchers were looking for a "maintenance medicine" that would enable addicts to live normally without illicit drugs. Was there a medicine, they wondered, that would do for addicts what insulin does for diabetics? Back in 1957, the Council on Mental Health of the American Medical Association had pondered the question and concluded that earlier evidence was insufficient to prove or disprove the maintenance theory. And although, since 1957, many medical and legal committees had urged that studies be undertaken, no one had made the search.

Drs. Dole and Nyswander began their research modestly with two users of heroin who volunteered and were hospitalized at the Rockefeller Institute. One was 31 years old, a mainliner since he was 18; the other was 22, "hooked" for six years. Both had police and prison records.

At the start, the doctors tried to satisfy the two addicts' craving for a fix with shots of morphine. But because morphine's effects do not last long, it became necessary to give the addicts bigger and bigger doses many times a day. Soon, the two volunteers, who were enjoying an addict's paradise, were getting larger shots of narcotic than they had ever dreamed about. But the addicts were no better off than when they were on the street. True, they didn't have to steal to get high, but they were lethargic, apathetic and needed a fix every few hours. Obviously, morphine was not the ideal maintenance medicine the doctors were seeking.

Then the question was: How to reduce the huge daily doses of morphine without making the men suffer severe withdrawal symptoms? Drs. Dole and Nyswander resorted to the usual methadone. But because of the amount of morphine the men were getting, it was necessary to start them on doses of methadone more than twice as large as usual to prevent acute withdrawal symptoms. And to insure their comfort for the next few days, the addicts were given bigger and bigger daily methadone drinks instead of the smaller shots given in classical—and unsuccessful—withdrawal treatment.

About 72 hours after the two addicts were taken off morphine and put on the massive substitute quantities of methadone, a remarkable change occurred. "Their color improved, their appetites were hearty," Dr. Nyswander recalls. "They were more alert. The two men even started talking about getting jobs and going back to school; and for addicts, that's really something."

Sensing the promise of this accidental discovery, Dr. Nyswander recruited four more addicts who were on heroin and put them through the same treatment. Again, the miracle change occurred. The switch to massive, daily maintenance doses of methadone produced an alert, normally thinking and functioning individual. At the same time, she and Dr. Dole ran an elaborate series of blood and urine tests to determine what ill effects the substitute drug was having on the addicts.

There were none. Methadone in large amounts was harmless; its only side effect was constipation.

The six addicts continued taking heavy, daily maintenance doses of methadone in cups of orange juice, and for nearly a year, the remarkable physical and emotional changes persisted. Then, Drs. Dole and Nyswander decided, it was time for the challenge. What would happen, the doctors wanted to know, if their addict-patients, who were now successfully weaned to methadone, were given a big shot of their favorite narcotic? Would they get high again? And would the taste of heroin rekindle the flame of addiction?

The doctors injected large doses of the illicit narcotic into their patients' veins. Quietly, the doctors awaited some changes in their patients' attitudes or behavior. Nothing happened. Heroin had no effect; the addicts did not get high on it, nor did they crave more. By a strange pharmacological trick, methadone had blocked the effects of heroin. With a daily dose of methadone, the addicts were free of the craving for heroin.

Tests on only six subjects are far too few to convince scientists. To prove their findings were no fluke, the two doctors had to test more addicts, but there was no space at the Institute's hospital. Dr. Dole went to see Dr. Ray Trussell, then New York City's Commissioner of Hospitals.

The city's narcotics problem is huge and costly. As many as 60,000 addicts roam the streets of New York, committing crimes that cost a quarter of a billion dollars a year. Although the city operates several withdrawal treatment centers in a number of hospitals, it has been unable to diminish, let alone solve, its narcotics problem.

After listening to Dr. Dole's account, Dr. Trussell studied the researchers' meticulous case histories. He was impressed.

Realizing that the methadone-maintenance program might be the answer to New York's narcotics crisis, the Commissioner immediately went to see Mayor Robert F. Wagner at City Hall. The Mayor was about to leave for a speaking engagement, so Dr. Trussell rode along in the Wagner limousine long enough to explain what Drs. Dole and Nyswander had stumbled upon. "It will cost $80,000," the Commissioner told the Mayor, "to expand this program enough to determine whether it's worth doing on a big scale. I can find that much in my hospital budget, if you will okay it." The Mayor agreed, and in March, 1965, the city opened an expanded methadone program at the Manhattan General Division of Beth Israel Medical Center. Drs. Dole and Nyswander took charge.

When the new unit opened, there was no need to search for more patients. Word had already spread among New York's junkies that something good was going on at the hospital. Each day, addicts showed up asking to get on the program. Soon there were 20 patients; now, there are 52, as many as the limited space can handle.

Upon acceptance, the addicts are hospitalized in the 15-bed ward unit for six weeks. They get exhaustive blood, urine and other tests to determine metabolic function. They also go through psychological examinations, including intelligence-grading, aptitude and vocational tests. And in the early weeks of hospitalization, doctors in the unit find out how much methadone each patient needs daily to block his addiction and get him to think and act normally. After the first two weeks, hospital rules may be relaxed, with addict-patients allowed to leave during the day and return at night to sleep. Some visit families they haven't seen for months; others take jobs or go to school.

After hospitalization, the ex-addict is discharged to the out-patient clinic, which he visits once a day to drink his daily cup of orange drink spiked with methadone, and to leave a urine sample. The urine is tested regularly to determine the effects of methadone. (Another purpose of the testing: to check for traces of heroin residue, evidence that the man is secretly taking illicit drugs.) He sees one of the unit's doctors once a week for a chat and a checkup. If he needs help in getting a job or going back to school, he can talk to the unit's social worker.

Psychotherapy is not a regular part of the methadone-maintenance program, although Dr. Nyswander is a psychiatrist and has used the therapy extensively in previous attempts to treat addicts. She points out that, with methadone, the need for supportive psychotherapy appears to be minimal. Only two of the 52 thus far treated have shown a need or desire for such help. "Maybe," she reflects, "the psychological factors in narcotic addiction have been overemphasized."

More than half of the 52 addict-patients now under treatment—some for only a month, others for nearly two years —are either working or going to school. There have been no failures in the group,

and no dropouts. Two addicts were quickly removed from the program as soon as the doctors discovered they were addicted to barbiturates and alcohol as well as narcotics. There have been two arrests among the group, but both were for offenses committed before the addicts joined the program.

The two original addict-patients from the Rockefeller Institute days are still on the program. The older man is working as a gardener and going to landscaping school at night. The younger, who is a high-school dropout, went to night school, passed his high-school equivalency test with straight A's and has entered college on an academic scholarship. He wants to be an engineer. Both men are making it on daily doses of methadone.

New York City authorities are enthusiastic over methadone's performance. To give the maintenance program the chance to prove itself fully, they are allocating $1,380,000 to treat 250 addicts at four hospitals. Next year, a team of experts selected by Columbia University's School of Public Health and Administrative Medicine will evaluate the results and render a verdict. Until then, doctors and scientists, who are bound by scientific principles, must withhold official judgment.

But not so the 52 addict-patients. They are convinced. With methadone, they are men again.

BRITISH NARCOTICS POLICIES

Edwin M. Schur

INTRODUCTION

There has been developing in recent years an increased interest in possible modifications of the current American narcotics policies. In this regard the British practice relating to drug addiction has been mentioned as a model which might be worthy of imitation. Although at least two authoritative descriptions of the British approach to this social problem recently have been published in the United States (one written by a British medical practitioner, the other by an American sociologist),[1] a considerably distorted picture of the British policies seems to continue to enjoy fairly wide circulation. The object of this paper is to throw some additional light on a few points of contention regarding such policies. The conclusions reached here are based on two years' research in England studying British addiction policies in operation.[2]

Since the aforementioned articles described fully the relevant legal provisions, it should suffice here merely to summarize briefly the basic elements of British addiction law. Under provisions of the

---

[1] Bishop, *A Commentary on the Management and Treatment of Drug Addicts in the United Kingdom,* in Nyswander, The Drug Addict as a Patient, 148 (1956); Lindesmith, *The British System of Narcotics Control,* 22 Law & Contemp. Prob. 138 (1957).

[2] As well as examining various official documents, the writer gained useful information through the following: personal interviews with officials of the Dangerous Drugs Branch of the Home Office, and with physicians, psychiatrists and pharmacists having experience in cases of addiction; questionnaire responses of thirteen British medical specialists having experience in over four hundred cases of addiction encountered in a variety of settings; information about twenty-one "representative" addict-patients, provided by these specialists; detailed case studies of five addicts, four through lengthy personal interviews; a questionnaire survey of all general practitioners registered with the National Health Service in one Greater London borough; and a sample survey of 147 21-year-olds in the same borough —inquiring into contact with narcotic drug use, knowledge of the drug laws and attitudes towards addiction. See Schur, Drug Addiction in Britain and America: A Sociological Study of Legal and Social Polices (1959) (unpublished doctoral thesis, University of London). In the present article it is not possible to deal at any length with the American narcotics situation. Readers unfamiliar with the American policies may wish to consult Cantor, *The Criminal Law and the Narcotics Problem,* 51 J. Crim. L., C. & P.S. 512 (1960); Nyswander, *op. cit. supra* note 1; the symposium on *Narcotics,* 22 Law and Contemp. Prob. (1957); *Narcotics Regulation,* 62 Yale L. J. 751 (1953); Anslinger & Tompkins, *The Traffic in Narcotics* (1953), as well as other general works on narcotics addiction. A particularly pungent critique of American policy was provided by Lindesmith, *"Dope Fiend" Mythology,* 31 J. Crim. L. & C. 199 (1940); for an opposing view see Michelson, *Lindesmith's Mythology,* 31 J. Crim. L. & C. 375 (1940).

Dangerous Drugs Act,[3] stringent control is placed on the possession and supply of such drugs as opium, heroin, morphine, pethidine (Demerol), methadone (Amidone), and cocaine.[4] Persons authorized to handle such dangerous drugs are required to keep careful records of all drugs received and supplied, and these records are routinely examined by the Home Office and by special Ministry of Health inspectors. Dangerous drugs must be kept in locked receptacles and prescriptions for such drugs are subject to special rules. Although the Government urges doctors to exercise great caution in the supplying of narcotics to patients, physicians may in fact (if certain broad conditions are met) legally supply narcotics to addicts.[5] Doctors who improperly divert narcotic supplies to their own use, or who otherwise violate provisions of the drug laws, are subject to fine or imprisonment; furthermore, the Home Secretary may, on conviction for an offense against the Act, withdraw a doctor's authority to possess, prescribe or distribute dangerous drugs. There is no formal state registration of addicts, but doctors are requested to inform the Home Office of any addicts who come under their care. There is no provision for compulsory treatment of drug addicts in the United Kingdom, and "There are no State institutions specialising in the problems of drug addiction, but treatment can be obtained at a number of public hospitals; a small number of private nursing homes most of them primarily concerned with alcoholics, also accept drug addicts."[6] Finally, and crucially, it should be noted that, "to be a drug addict has never been and is not now illegal in this country. The addict is committing an offence only if drugs found in his possession have been unlawfully obtained."[7]

To combat American expressions of interest in this non-punitive medically-oriented approach, defenders of current drug policies in the United States promote two views of the British policy. Either it is argued that the British approach essentially is no different from that in this country, or, alternatively, it is maintained that the British approach is too different, too radical, that it has had bad results in Britain and should not even be considered as a possibility here. It may be useful to consider these views in the light of actual British practices regarding the control and treatment of addiction.

---

[3] 14 & 15 Geo. 6, c. 48 (1951). This statute repealed several previous Dangerous Drugs Acts, consolidating the provisions of all such prior laws.

[4] Cannabis, or marihuana, is also subject to control under this law, but as in the United States it is not commonly used in medical practice. The key differences between British and American narcotics policies relate to the prescription of the distinctly addictive opiates and opiate-type drugs and (occasionally) cocaine.

[5] The guiding principle in this regard continues to be that laid down by a Departmental Committee in 1926: ". . . morphine or heroin may properly be administered to addicts in the following circumstances, namely, (a) where patients are under treatment by the gradual withdrawal method with a view to cure, (b) where it has been demonstrated, after a prolonged attempt at cure, that the use of the drug cannot be safely discontinued entirely, on account of the severity of the withdrawal symptoms produced, (c) where it has been similarly demonstrated that the patient, while capable of leading a useful and relatively norman life when a certain minimum dose is regularly administered, becomes incapable of this when the drug is entirely discontinued." Ministry of Health, Departmental Committee on Morphine and Heroin Addiction, Report, 19 (1926). This statement is reprinted in the circular distributed by the Home Office, The Duties of Doctors and Dentists under the Dangerous Drugs Act and Regulations, 14 (D.D. 101, 6th ed., 1956).

[6] Home Office, Report to the United Nations on the Working of the International Treaties on Narcotic Drugs for 1957, 4.

[7] Bishop, *op. cit. supra* note 1, at 150.

THE BRITISH APPROACH IS DIFFERENT

An anonymous mimeographed statement about the "British Narcotics System"[8] contains the claim that, "The British system is the same as the United States system."[9] Similarly, the 1956 Senate investigation of narcotics traffic elicited testimony that, ". . . the English system is, for all practical purposes, the same as our own in this continent, in the United States and Canada."[10] In the same hearings, Mr. J. H. Walker, the United Kingdom delegate to the U.N. Narcotic Commission, was quick to stress that, ". . . dangerous drugs are subjected in the United Kingdom to a wide degree of control and the exacting standard de-

manded by the international agreements to which . . . the United Kingdom is a party. The indiscriminate administration of narcotics to addicts would be incompatible with those obligations and is not now, and never has been, a feature of United Kingdom policy."[11] Testimony before the Canadian Senate, reprinted in a recent report on the British system distributed by the U.S. Federal Bureau of Narcotics, includes the statement: "the authorities advise that they are quick to take appropriate action whenever a case comes to their attention that a doctor is supplying drugs to an addict."[12]

Assertions that British and American drug policies are the same are totally misleading. It is true that in Britain drugs are subject to "a wide degree of control," that there is no "indiscriminate" prescribing for addicts, and that the authorities take "appropriate action" where necessary. But what these statements mean in practice is determined by the general tenor of British narcotics policy, and this overall outlook is sharply divergent from that which determines American policy. The major point on which the two approaches differ is the degree of freedom accorded the medical profession as regards the treatment of addiction. Within broad limits, the British doctor has almost complete professional autonomy in reaching decisions about the treatment of addicts. When a responsible medical practitioner determines that an addict needs drugs, it is very unlikely that this prescribing will be considered to be "for the mere gratification of addiction." This follows from the fact that in Britain addiction is

---

[8] Distributed by, and presumably prepared by, the Federal Bureau of Narcotics. This pamphlet was circulated at the 1954 meeting of the American Prison Association. For further discussion of this statement see Lindesmith, *op. cit. supra* note 1, at 151–52.

[9] In support of this claim reference is made to the Home Office's statement that, "The continued supply of drugs . . . solely for the gratification of addiction is not regarded as a medical need." See Home Office, The Duties of Doctors and Dentists, *op. cit. supra* note 5, at 2. It is quite true that the British authorities serve up this warning to medical practitioners, but it is highly misleading to quote this statement by itself as an indication of the general tenor of British policy. This statement must be read in the light of the principle quoted in note 5, *supra.* As will become clear later in this article, the British basis for determining what constitutes "medical need" for the administration of narcotics differs strikingly from the basis for such determination in the United States.

[10] Statement of Dr. G. H. Stevenson, director of drug addiction research in the University of British Columbia. *Hearings Before the Subcommittee on Improvements in the Federal Criminal Code of the Senate Committee on the Judiciary,* 84th Cong., 1st Sess., pt. 5 (hereafter referred to as *"Daniel Hearings"*). A more complete statement of Stevenson's views may be found in a reprint circulated by the Narcotics Bureau. Stevenson, *Arguments For and Against the Legal Sale of Narcotics,* reprinted from 31, No. 4 Bull. of the Vancouver Med. Ass'n.

[11] *Daniel Hearings, op. cit. supra* note 10, at 1770.

[12] Excerpt from statement of Hon. Paul Martin, in "Advisory Committee to the Federal Bureau of Narcotics, The British System," July 3, 1958, mimeo, p. 9.

officially recognized as a medical problem. As the Home Office recently stated in a report on addiction, "In the United Kingdom the treatment of a patient is considered to be a matter for the doctor concerned. The nature of the treatment given varies with the circumstances of each case."[13] This writer recently asked a Dangerous Drugs Branch official how often legal proceedings are instituted against doctors for improper prescribing of drugs to addict-patients. The official could recall only two or three cases where there were prosecutions for what was felt to be overprescribing. But he stated that these prosecutions were unsuccessful because the courts are unwilling to convict the doctor in such instances; if the doctor states that the patient needed the amount prescribed, the court ordinarily will uphold his professional judgment. Apparently most of the checking-up on doctors who are found to be prescribing narcotics regularly is undertaken with a view to uncovering doctor-addicts who are prescribing for fictitious patients.[14]

[13] Home Office, Report to the United Nations, *op. cit. supra* note 6, at 5.
[14] Even when such instances are discovered the doctor is treated leniently. Usually he is prosecuted, but the typical sentence is a fine (and ordinarily he will lose his authority to possess, prescribe or supply Dangerous Drugs; he may, however, continue to practice medicine). The Dangerous Drugs official could think of no case in which a doctor-addict had been sent to prison. The doctor's broad responsibility in the treatment of addicts is not enjoyed by his American colleague. While there is no provision in the basic federal narcotics law (the Harrison Act) which specifically prohibits doctors from treating addicts, the U.S. Narcotics Bureau persistently has interpreted the Act to have that meaning. Treasury Department regulations require that prescriptions for narcotics be for "legitimate medical purposes" only, and state further that, "An order purporting to be a prescription issued to an addict or habitual user of narcotics, not in the course of professional treatment but for the purpose of providing the user with narcotics sufficient to

A related point of importance is that in Britain the medical profession and law enforcement officials are in general agreement concerning the proper approach to the addiction problem: addicts are patients, not criminals. An early and influential expression of this view—which is held in common by almost all those who are professionally concerned with addiction—was provided in 1926 by the Departmental Committee on Morphine and Heroin Addiction. The committee asserted that, "With few exceptions addiction to morphine and heroin should be regard-

keep him comfortable by maintaining his customary use, is not a prescription within the meaning and intent of the act; and the person filling such an order, as well as the person issuing it, may be charged with violation of the law." U.S. Treas. Reg. No. 5, Art. 167, as reprinted in Bureau of Narcotics, Prescribing and Dispensing of Narcotics Under Harrison Narcotic Law (1956). The same pamphlet also contains the warning that, "This Bureau has never sanctioned or approved the so-called reductive ambulatory treatment of addiction for the reason that where the addict controls the dosage he will not be benefited or cured." *Id.* at 8. At least one legal critic contests this interpretation—stating that the Bureau has substituted its own views for the real intent of the Act (which had nothing to do with addicts), and that it has acknowledged only those court decisions favoring its position while ignoring other, less favorable judicial holdings. See King, *Narcotic Drug Laws and Enforcement Policies,* 22 Law and Contemp. Prob. 113 (1957); and *The Narcotics Bureau and the Harrison Act: Jailing the Healers and the Sick,* 62 Yale L. J. 735 (1953). Additional stringent federal legislation (including the Narcotic Control Act of 1956) and a vast array of anti-narcotics measures in the various states (some of which have now made addiction, *per se,* a crime) further support the Bureau's approach to the addiction problem. *Ibid.* The practical consequences of these measures and interpretations are that: *American physicians have been prevented from prescribing drugs for addicts, even in (ambulatory) withdrawal treatment. In Britain the doctor has the freedom to undertake withdrawal treatment, and also in many cases may legally prescribe drugs for addicts not currently undergoing such treatment.*

ed as a manifestation of a morbid state, and not as a mere form of vicious indulgence."[15] My own research and observations in Britain lead me to believe that Bishop is quite right in maintaining that, "There is a very real spirit of cooperation between the medical profession and Government and Police authorities which has helped a great deal to keep this country free from organised drug trafficking."[16] Although United States narcotics policies have at times coincided with the views of the American medical profession, recent developments, which are described below, suggest that medical approval of such policies is definitely waning. At any rate it is well known that (in contradistinction to the British situation) the keynote of American policy has been punitiveness. Despite official efforts to "cure" addicts, the addict has been treated primarily as a criminal, not as a patient. In some instances the punitive nature of American policy imperils even modest efforts at medical evaluation of addicts.[17]

[15] Departmental Committee on Morphine and Heroin Addiction, *op. cit. supra* note 5, at 31.

[16] Bishop, *op. cit. supra* note 1, at 153.

[17] "[I]t is our feeling that use of our clinic by the Narcotics Court was not motivated by any clear understanding of the problem; frequently punitiveness, exhibitionism, and at times confusion in regard to guilt of the patient were the motivating causes for referral. Something of this is understandable from the fact that apparently the whole narcotics drive had many aspects of immaturity itself—it was an impulsive gesture designed to rid the city *at once* of a problem which is deep-rooted in the very nature of our western culture.

"The function of a court clinic in a 'drive' such as this is a difficult one. Normally the function of a court clinic is fairly well-defined —but under the extreme pressures brought to bear upon us by the Court, the Police Department, the newspapers and interested lay groups during such a drive, it is a struggle to preserve professional integrity, and not to become involved in legalistic and political maneuvering." McFarland & Hall, *A Survey of One Hundred Suspected Drug Addicts,* 44 J. Crim. L., C. & P.S. 317 (1953).

BRITISH POLICY SUCCEEDS

The recent assessment of British policy distributed by the Federal Bureau of Narcotics includes a reference to, "The unfortunate narcotic situation in the United Kingdom."[18] The present writer is unable to see any factual basis for such an assertion. At no time since the passage of the original Dangerous Drugs Act in 1920 has the amount of recorded addiction risen to an alarming level. Current estimates place the number of addicts between 300 and 500. It is particularly significant that the estimated prevalence of addiction actually has decreased over the years; in 1935 the Government estimated a total of 700 addicts whereas in 1957 the estimated number was 359.[19] Undoubtedly these official figures on known addicts somewhat understate the actual number of addicts, but there is no evidence of any large number of addicts besides those receiving their drugs through legal channels. As Lindesmith has pointed out,[20] one reason for believing that there are few concealed addicts is the fact that few addicts are sent to prison; assuming competent police work, addicts relying solely on black market drug sources would invariably incur prosecution and imprisonment. It is easy to understand why there

[18] "Advisory Committtee to the Federal Bureau of Narcotics," *op. cit. supra* note 12, at 14.

[19] The former estimate is reported in Adams, Drug Addiction 37 (1937); for the latter see Home Office, Report to the United Nations, *op. cit. supra* note 6, at 5. Recent reports indicate that known addicts now number about 700. This may represent partly an actual increase and partly an improvement in official reporting methods over those employed at the time this article was originally published. There is no significant increase reported in either illicit traffic in opiates or in addict-crime.

[20] Lindesmith, *The British System of Narcotics Control, op. cit. supra* note 1, at 141–42.

are few illegally-supplied addicts. Previous accounts of the British drug policies have stressed the fact that legal provision of drugs at a nominal cost under the National Health Service has taken away the economic incentive which supports illicit narcotics traffic. Why should the addict pay for drugs, at the same time risking liability for narcotics violations, when usually he can obtain them legally from a doctor? All the available evidence supports the claim that there is hardly any illicit traffic in opiates. A Home Office official told the writer that he could not even recall a case involving heroin trafficking in recent years. According to several British addicts, the small illicit traffic which does exist supplies mostly "joy poppers" and other experimenters who could not obtain drugs through medical channels, as well as some recently-addicted persons who are afraid of contact with "the law." And probably this small black market is limited geographically as well as numerically. One London addict informed me that, "—— Street is about the only place. You can't get it anywhere else. Leave —— Street, you leave it all behind."

Some critics of the British approach to addiction have alleged that, "There is a very considerable black market for hashish (marihuana) in the United Kingdom. . . ."[21] Quite apart from the fact that the rate of marihuana use may not be directly relevant to a discussion of policies toward opiate addiction, there is no real evidence to back up this charge. There may be a minor trend toward increased use of marihuana in certain cir-

cles.[22] But the overall prevalence of such drug use is not high. In 1955 only 115 persons were prosecuted for offenses involving marihuana; in 1957 the number was 51. Some findings from the present writer's survey of a sample of 21-year-olds in a Greater London borough may also be relevant to this question. When presented with the statement, "A 'reefer' looks like (check one) —— A Pipe —— A Cigarette —— A Hypodermic Injection —— Don't Know ——", only 76% were able to state the correct answer. Twenty-one per cent checked "Don't Know." Of 147 respondents, only seven (5%) reported having seen someone using a reefer and only one had tried to obtain a reefer for himself. While colored persons were probably underrepresented in my sample, these results still suggest that knowledge of and contact with marihuana has not in fact spread widely throughout the population.

Just as lack of economic incentive inhibits the development of a large-scale illicit traffic in drugs, low-cost provision of drugs means that the addict need not turn to criminal activities in order to finance his habit. Already noted has been the significant fact that very few addicts are imprisoned for any sort of offense. According to a Home Office official, those addicts who do go to prison usually have committed "minor violations of the narcotics laws in order to get a bit more drug than the doctor was providing." In 1957 the few addicts convicted of drug offenses either had obtained drugs from chemists by forged prescription or had

---

[21] "British Narcotics System," *op. cit. supra* note 8, and adjoining text.

[22] Bishop, for example, refers to a group of drug users who "are often coloured dance band players but may also be white English men

and women. These are the adolescents who frequent the cheap dance halls. They smoke a 'reefer' in an attempt to show off in a daredevil spirit or because they have been told it will make them more 'sexy.'" Bishop, *op. cit. supra* note 1, at 158.

gotten supplies from more than one doctor.[23] Addicts then do not often become criminals, and by the same token underworld and criminally-prone elements are not particularly likely to come into contact with addiction. It is especially noteworthy that juvenile delinquency and addiction have not become intermeshed, as they have to a considerable extent in the United States. Dr. T. C. N. Gibbens, a leading British forensic psychiatrist, has studied 200 boys aged 17–21 sent to Borstal institutions from the London area (one hundred in 1953—every other lad sent to Borstal in the Metropolitan Police Area for about nine months—and a similar number in 1955). He has also seen about 700 wayward girls aged 14–17 in a London remand home between 1951 and 1958. Among the boys, "there were no cases with any experience of addiction." As to the wayward girls, "about 1% claimed to have had a reefer offered to them, usually by U.S. service boy-friends, or sometimes in clubs, and there were no cases approaching addiction. . . ."[24] All the available evidence supports the Government reports that most of the British addicts are over 30 years of age. The experience of medical practitioners who have treated addicts attests further to the general separation of addiction and criminality in Britain. In response to the question, "How many of the addicts you've seen do you think likely to have close friends in the criminal underworld?", none of the thirteen specialists questioned by the writer thought that either "practically all" or even "many" of the addicts had such underworld connections. Seven specialists answered "a few," and four answered "none." Two said "about half." Similarly most of these specialists indicated that only "a few" or "none" of the addicts they had observed seemed to identify themselves with a criminal role and way of life. It would seem that the policy of refusing to label the addict a "criminal" has in fact had the effect of helping to insulate addicts from criminal contacts and activities. The fact that there is little addict-crime in Britain lends strong support to the mass of American evidence showing that addicts in the United States commit crimes mainly to obtain funds to support their habit. One certainly finds in Britain nothing to uphold the argument that most addicts are basically criminals anyway, that criminality precedes addiction rather than stemming from the peculiar situation of the American addict.[25] The lack of crimi-

---

[23] Home Office, Report to the United Nations, *op. cit. supra* note 6, at 8.

[24] Dr. Gibbens writes further: "One psychopathic girl recently, a lesbian and prostitute and approved school absconder, claimed to have taken reefers a fair bit and to need them, and another similar girl seen in 1952 was followed up in prison recently and she had had a spell of 'drug-taking' but had passed on to other matters with no trouble. That's really the lot, at least of any gravity. These 700 represent nearly all the seriously wayward girls in London of 14–17 who came before the juvenile courts in need of care or protection." Personal letter to the writer. I am grateful to Dr. Gibbens for permission to reproduce these unpublished data.

[25] This latter argument is stated with regularity by American narcotics officials. *E.g.*, "In addition to suppressing the traffic in narcotics, police activity against drug addicts is a very essential part of general police operations. The great majority of addicts are parasitic. This parasitic drug addict is a tremendous burden on the community. He represents a continuing problem to the police through his depredations against society. He is a thief, a burglar, a robber; if a woman, a prostitute or a shoplifter. The person is generally a criminal or on the road to criminality before he becomes addicted. Once addicted he has the greatest reason in the world for continuing his life of crime." Anslinger & Tompkins, *op. cit. supra* note 2, at 170.

nality among British addicts also seems to contradict the argument that legal dispensing of drugs will not really curb criminality because addicts will never be content with the legally-provided drugs.

The British approach furthermore has limited the emergence of a distinct addict subculture. Albert Cohen has written that, "The crucial condition for the emergence of new subcultural forms is the existence *in effective interaction of a number of actors with similar problems of adjustment.*"[26] Unlike what happens in America, addicts in Great Britain are not completely cast out of respectable society, and there is no special likelihood that ordinarily they will find themselves "in effective interaction" with one another. And while they may have certain "similar problems of adjustments"—in the sexual and occupational realms for example—the problems they encounter more often call for individual rather than group solutions. They are not subjected (as are the American addicts) to a constant struggle for economic survival, for drug supplies, and for anonymity in the face of relentless police action and a hostile public. British addicts are not, *ipso facto*, members of an addict subculture.

POSSIBILITIES FOR REFORM IN AMERICA

Several important proposals for reforming American addiction laws have embodied the spirit if not the letter of the British approach. One of the first of these proposals appeared in the report of a committee of the New York Academy of Medicine in 1955.[27] The committee stated

that, "There should be a change in attitude toward the addict. He is a sick person, not a criminal. That he may commit criminal acts to maintain his drug supply is recognized; but it is unjust to consider him criminal simply because he uses narcotic drugs. . . . The Academy believes that the most effective way to eliminate drug addiction is to take the profit out of the illicit drug traffic. . . ." To this end the Academy proposed a program for the legal dispensing to addicts of low-cost drugs, at federally controlled dispensary-clinics throughout the country. Such clinics, it was felt, also would provide a setting within which intensive efforts to treat addicts could be made and would afford opportunities for the collection of much useful information about addiction. As the late Dr. Hubert Howe, author of the plan, testified: "We are not saying to give the addicts more drugs. We are simply advising a different method of distribution. The Government says he cannot get it legally; therefore, he has got to steal and rob, and so on, in order to get it. . . . But every addict gets his drug right now . . . why not let him have his minimum requirements under licensed medical supervision, rather than force him to get it by criminal activities, through criminal channels?"[28] Thus the force of some collective professional opinion gave added weight to the earlier calls by influential individuals (including Judge Jonah J. Goldstein and Magistrate John M. Murtagh in New York) for some change in our narcotics laws.

In 1958 a joint committee of the American Medical Association and the Ameri-

---

[26] Cohen, Delinquent Boys: The Culture of the Gang 59 (1955).

[27] New York Academy of Medicine, Subcommittee on Drug Addiction, *Report*, 31 Bull. N.Y. Acad. of Medicine 592 (1955); see also Nyswander, *op. cit. supra* note 1, at 162–70.

[28] Hubert S. Howe, M.D., in *Daniel Hearings, op. cit. supra* note 10, at 1332. For another statement of Dr. Howe's views see his article, *An Alternative Solution to the Narcotics Problem*, 22 Law and Contemp. Prob. 132–37 (1957).

can Bar Association released a report expressing grave dissatisfaction with current American addiction policies.[29] The core of this committee's proposals was that a small "experimental" clinic program should be set up. Presumably this procedure would offer an opportunity of testing (without the risk of any widespread adverse consequences) how well a carefully run system of dispensing low-cost narcotics might work. It would also enable researchers to discover, under experimental conditions, the administrative problems which would have to be considered in the development of any larger program. This proposal followed the important 1957 report on addiction of the American Medical Association's Council on Mental Health.[30] The Council's report contains an extensive review of the whole problem of drug addiction, and includes a brief consideration of the British practice. The Council was not prepared to approve proposals for the establishment of clinics "at this time." It was not sure that such a program would curb all illicit traffic, and it noted the considerable expense and administrative problems involved. However the Council did recommend greatly modified penalties for narcotics law violations; civil rather than criminal commitment of addicts for treatment where possible; extension of opportunities for voluntary admission to treatment facilities; more treatment facilities; and more research. It also asserted both that "There is nothing in the federal narcotic law which prohibits a physician from treating an addict," and that the American Medical Association itself was largely responsible (see below) for the

current state of addiction policies. Although recognizing the many difficulties involved in implementing the British approach in the United States, the Council clearly was interested in that possibility. It recommended that the Association revise its earlier policy statements on addiction, and considered including in such a revised statement "a plan endorsing regulations somewhat similar to those currently in force in England."[31]

Despite these signs of increasing professional acceptance of the British outlook on addiction, there remain a number of serious obstacles to reforming the American laws. In the first place there may be some feeling that the British policy does not place enough emphasis on the treatment and cure of addiction.[32] It is true that there is no provision in Britain for compulsory treatment of addicts, and there are no special institutions comparable to the Lexington and Fort Worth hospitals in this country. But this may well represent a realistic recognition of the considerable limitations of withdrawal treatment, and may constitute a humane alternative to a policy aimed at compulsory confinement. As the Ministry of Health committee noted in 1926, in

---

[29] Reported in N.Y. Herald Tribune, June 25, 1958.

[30] A.M.A., Council on Mental Health, *Report on Drug Addiction*, 165 A. M. A. J. (Nov. 30, 1957; Dec. 7, 1957; Dec. 14, 1957).

[31] *Id.* at 1973 (Dec. 14, 1957). The assertion that "nothing in the federal narcotics law" prohibits a physician from treating an addict refers to the fact that such prohibition (which actually is in effect today) stems primarily from current interpretation of legal provisions and not from the provisions themselves. See discussion *supra* note 14.

[32] Thus physicians testifying before the Daniel Committee expressed the view that the Howe plan and similar proposals amounted to an admission of defeat in the battle against addiction. Similarly, note the following statements: "I think it is fair to say that it [the Howe plan] sort of represents throwing in the sponge." (then N.Y. Attorney General Javits) "It would seem to me that was a defeatist attitude. You just throw up your hands and give up on the problem." (Sen. J. M. Butler) *Daniel Hearings, op. cit. supra* note 10, at 1446, 1449.

addiction cases, "Relapse, sooner or later, appears to be the rule, and permanent cure the exception. . . ."[33] There is no way of estimating the degree of success achieved in British attempts at curing addicts; almost always there is difficulty in maintaining a satisfactory follow-up on the patient. Probably most British specialists would content themselves with very cautious appraisals, like the one provided the present writer by the nursing sister in charge of a home for alcoholics and addicts: "We are in touch with a number of ex-patients in whom there has been no relapse over a period of years." There is no reason to assume that American officials, who place such great stress on cure, can legitimately claim much more than this.[34] At any rate, there is no way of

ensuring that an addict who has undergone withdrawal treatment will remain abstinent. As the Lexington doctors themselves have stressed, the withdrawal process is "the least important step in the treatment of narcotic addiction. . . ."[35] There are several reasons for thinking that the British approach holds out a fair hope of effecting meaningful cures. The British policy recognizes that you cannot really force an addict to be cured against his will; treating the addict as a human being, as a troubled person who merits some consideration, may increase the chances of obtaining his cooperation in treatment efforts. (As one British addict assured the writer, compulsory confinement simply won't work: "They can lock you up. All nonsense. Shouting, beating you up, won't get anyone anywhere.") Similarly, the general social situation of the addict in Britain may work to decrease the dangers of relapse, where the addict seriously wishes a permanent cure.[36]

---

[33] Departmental Committee on Morphine and Heroin Addiction, *op. cit. supra* note 10, at 17.

[34] Medical officers at Lexington stated some years ago, with regard to addicts treated at that hospital, "Follow up reports indicate that over 16 per cent of these patients have remained abstinent over a seven year period, and probably at least an additional 20 per cent have remained abstinent for extended periods of time." Vogel, Isbell & Chapman, *Present Status of Narcotic Addiction,* 138 A.M.A.J. 1025 (1948). Probably these estimates are optimistic. The high rate of relapse may indeed call into question the entire treatment program in the federal hospitals. Dr. Herbert Berger testified before the Daniel Committee: "It is quite probable that the individual who stays for a full course of treatment might well cost the United States Government $2000 to $4000. I am sure these are minimal figures. . . . No one knows the exact rate of relapse. It has been estimated, and I emphasize these are estimates, as being anywhere from 70 to 95 percent. If the rate approaches 90 percent, and most addicts seem to think it exceeds that figure, then that $4000 that we spend for the treatment of one patient becomes $40,000 for cure. Now this is an astronomical figure.

"We in medicine do not accept with equanimity any treatment that fails to achieve cure in even 5 per cent of the cases of any specific disease. Yet the United States Government is committed to a plan of action which fails more than 90 percent of the time." Herbert Berger,

M.D., in *Daniel Hearings, op. cit. supra* note 10, at 1372.

For a recent assessment of the Lexington and Fort Worth treatment efforts see Winick, *Narcotics Addiction and its Treatment,* 22 Law and Contemp. Prob. (1957). The hospitals take both voluntary and mandatory (narcotics law violators) patients, and the treatment program includes physical withdrawal from drugs (with gradually decreased doses of methadone), vocational and recreational activities, and some kind of psychotherapy. Winick states that, "Every attempt is made to re-educate the patient in a therapeutic environment, and his other ailments are treated. Most patients do not receive effective psychotherapy because of limitations of personnel and time."*Id.* at 24. While most doctors associated with these treatment efforts appear to be generally interested in helping addicts, their efforts may be foredoomed by the overall negative and punitive attitude toward the addict in this country.

[35] Vogel, Isbell & Chapman, *op. cit. supra* note 34, at 1026.

It might also be claimed that the British approach represents merely a grand give-away program, that anyone can walk into a doctor's office and get drugs, and that therefore drug addiction is positively encouraged. Apparently it is difficult even for well-meaning students of addiction fully to accept the non-punitiveness which is implied in recognizing that the addict is a troubled person.[37] Actually there is no need to consider "allowing everyone free access to the drug" the only alternative to a punitive anti-addict policy. It is not the case that in Britain anyone can walk into a doctor's office and get narcotics. Except in rare cases of effective deception, the non-addict cannot get drugs in this way (for regular administration that is—we are not considering here short-term administration for relief of pain). Even the diagnosed ad-

dict does not get whatever amount of drugs he desires. As Bishop has stated, "physicians do not *supply* drugs; they try to cure the addict."[38] Except in the small number of cases where the addict is felt to be definitely incurable and where the doctor may be willing to sustain him with a regular dose, most doctors will make some effort to cut down gradually the prescribed dosage. Often this continuing process may reach a point at which either the patient or the doctor will seek to make new arrangements. As one (non-doctor) addict described it, doctors tend to "get fed up" with addicts. Even if the doctor does not get fed up with the addict, the addict may get fed up with the doctor. Often the non-doctor addict will only be content to "stretch" the prescribed dosage so far. Once the real straining point is reached, and unless he is fully dedicated to trying to be cured, the addict may look for a way to supplement the dose or he may try to find a new doctor who will agree to provide a somewhat larger amount of his drug than that to which he has been reduced. This points up a limitation of the British approach (which makes no adequate provision for the addict "between doctors"), but at the same time it makes clear that the approach does not constitute a mere catering to the whims of addicts. There are addicts, on the other hand, who remain under medical supervision for long periods of time—sometimes under a single

[36] As one psychiatrist has pointed out, ". . . environmental pressures generated by addiction itself help drive the released drug addict on the road to relapse. Back in his home community, a social outcast, frequently with no home, and doubtful prospects of finding legitimate employment, he easily falls under the influence of his former addict associates. The first step toward resumption of addiction is almost invariably precipitated by renewed interpersonal contacts with drug users." Ausubel, Drug Addiction: Physiological, Psychological, and Sociological Aspects, 90 (1958). In Britain, where the ex-addict need not be a social pariah, and where interpersonal contacts between individual drug users may be limited, the chances for a real recovery may be enhanced.

[37] "It is difficult to appreciate the logic or consistency of regarding the chronic alcoholic as an ill person and drug addict as a criminal. There is a marked difference, however, between *not* regarding drug addiction as a crime and legalizing the practice, that is, allowing everyone free access to the drug. The suggestion advanced by certain well-intentioned but misinformed persons that the habit be legalized for present known addicts only is unsatisfactory, because it would provide legal and moral sanction for the habit and thus encourage its spread." *Id.* at 15. As is made clear by the British experience, there is no reason to assume the validity of this latter claim.

[38] Bishop, *op. cit. supra* note 1, at 158. This refers primarily to the non-doctor addict. But it is likely (considering the fact that their records are subject to inspection at any time) that even such undisclosed doctor-addicts as may exist carefully limit the amounts of drugs they use. Doctors comprise a high proportion of the known addicts in Britain; such known doctor-addicts ordinarily are under the care of fellow practitioners and are thus receiving carefully limited dosages.

doctor's care. And it is noteworthy that the "between doctors" situation has not led to any large-scale illicit traffic.

Another obstacle to acceptance of the British view is the notion that "public opinion" is opposed to any leniency toward drug addicts.[39] Findings in some American studies do suggest widely held punitive attitudes toward addiction and drug peddling.[40] But it is one thing to recognize this likelihood and another to suggest, as some critics of the British approach seem to do, that drug addiction is so intensely repulsive to all right-thinking people that there is something inherently wrong about a non-punitive addiction policy. Presumably Britons are no less right-thinking than Americans, yet they appear able to accept without great difficulty a humane approach to the addict's problems. This was brought out in the present writer's survey of attitudes among 21-year-olds. In response to the question, "Would you say a drug addict is primarily a sick person or primarily a bad person?," only 2% of the sample said the addict is primarily bad; 80% said addicts are primarily sick, 12% said "both sick and bad" and 6% answered "don't know." When asked, "What should be done with drug addicts? Should they be sent to prison, put in hospital, or merely be left alone?," 93% suggested they be put in

hospital, 2% said addicts should be left alone, 5% answered "don't know." *Not one respondent* said that addicts should be sent to prison. It is particularly striking that while (in response to another question) 50% of the sample felt that "Prison is too good for sex criminals; they should be publicly whipped or worse," not even one person prescribed prison for the drug addict. Not having been subjected to a prolonged barrage of invective against addicts, the British public has not developed intense hostility towards them. Even to the extent that this might be because British addicts are actually (as compared with American addicts, for example) relatively harmless, one is still led back to the addiction policies as the key factor. These policies in part determine the behavior of addicts, and they can also directly shape "public opinion" toward addicts.

Sometimes supporters of current American policy cite the very fact that proposed reforms would require legal revision as indicating the undesirability of such reform. This sort of argument, of course, is begging the question—which is, or should be, whether current policies are effective or whether they need changing. Narcotics laws and regulations are not immutable entities, but rather should be subject to rational scrutiny when circumstances demand it. Connected with the call for adherence to (current) "law," is the argument that, ". . . to conform to the clinic idea, it would be necessary to abrogate the treaties into which the United States solemnly entered along with sixty-four other nations of the civilized world."[41] This argument cannot

[39] The recent A.M.A. report, for example, included the statement that, "If the Association did approve a proposal to legitimize dispensing of opiates to addicts, changes in federal, state, and local laws would be necessary before the plan could be put into operation. It seems very unlikely that such changes can be effected without a marked shift in public opinion." A.M.A., Council on Mental Health, *op. cit. supra* note 30, at 1969.

[40] See Rose & Prell, *Does the Punishment Fit the Crime? A Study in Social Valuation*, 61 Am. J. Soc. 247 (1955); Gilbert, *Crime and Punishment: An Exploratory Comparison of Public, Criminal and Penological Attitudes*, 42 Mental Hygiene 550 (1958).

[41] Anslinger & Tompkins, *op. cit. supra* note 2, at 191. Critics of reform frequently link the British approach with the American clinic experiment between 1912 and 1925, which it is claimed was markedly unsuccessful. But it is

validly be applied to the British approach. Apart from the fact that Britain has no "clinics," Britain also is a signatory to the various international agreements in question. Her insistence on treating addiction as a medical problem does not appear to contradict the provisions of such agreements.

The foregoing material suggests some of the ways in which American statements have conveyed what this writer considers to be misleading impressions about the British approach to addiction.[42]

Another aspect of the official reaction to interest in the British drug policies has been the persistent resort to vituperative epithets in describing the proponents of reform. Typical was the reference to a leading sociologist as "a self-appointed expert on drug addiction"; this was followed by the statement: "The professor followed the method used by dictators to 'make it simple, say it often'; true or false, the public will believe it. 'Adopt the British system' is now urged by all self-appointed narcotic experts who conceal their ignorance of the problem by ostentation of seeming wisdom."[43] It seems likely that the growing interest in reform exhibited by various professional bodies is going to make it more and more difficult for the Narcotics Bureau to rely on this name-calling. It will have to present solid evidence to back up its point of view if it wishes to prevent revision of the current policies. Particularly significant could be pressure for change from the medical profession. A 1924 resolution of

---

not really clear that these clinics, which provided low-cost drugs for addicts in some forty American cities, were a failure. Accounts of the clinic experience vary considerably, and some writers assert that the government closed the clinics largely on evidence about the New York clinic, which was the least efficient clinic and the least successful. The 1957 A.M.A. report concludes that, "Reasons for closing the clinics are obscure." A.M.A., Council on Mental Health, *op. cit. supra* note 30, at 1709. The Narcotics Bureau's view of the clinics is set forth in the official publication, Narcotic Clinics in the United States (1955). For an objective analysis of the various reports see Nyswander, *op. cit. supra* note 1, at 6–13. The clinic and British approaches have at times been linked in the present article because they do reflect the same general outlook.

[42] Unfortunately there have even been some statements by British officials which contribute to these misunderstandings. For example, a Home Office spokesman is quoted as writing to the Federal Bureau of Narcotics, "we make it clear that there is not in fact any such thing as a 'British System' which is an invention of certain Americans who wish to prove a particular point of view." "Advisory Committee to the Federal Bureau of Narcotics," *op. cit. supra* note 12. When the present writer inquired at the Home Office about such statements, an official pointed out that it is misleading to speak of a British "system" since that suggests a distinct plan decided upon and put into effect at a particular time. Actually the current "practice" or "approach" has evolved slowly through developing medical procedures and outlooks. Then too, the *laws* (in the narrow sense—including only statutes) in the United States and Britain *are* essentially the same. Both of these points are correct, strictly speaking, but they

seem insufficient reason for creating the impression that American and British policies are the same. Very likely the desire to avoid publicizing any startlingly different approach to addiction stems in part from the avoidance of sensationalism which characterizes British drug policy generally. Also the writer has the impression that British officials are eager not to be put in a position where they seem to be criticizing their law enforcement colleagues in America. Unfortunately, this leads to implicit endorsement of an approach they would not accept in their own country.

[43] "British Narcotics System," *op. cit. supra* note 8, and adjoining text. Similarly, note the following statements attributed to a Narcotics Bureau representative at a recent New York City Youth Board conference: "Mr. Levine denounced 'lime-light-seekers, sensationalists and public speakers' who regard the addict as 'a poor, sick individual.'"

"He quoted excerpts from a book by Chief Magistrate Murtagh that he said were examples of 'false, vicious statements' being spread by 'pseudo-experts.'" N.Y. Times, Oct. 29, 1959.

the American Medical Association called on "both federal and state governments to exert their full powers and authority to put an end to all manner of so-called ambulatory methods of treatment of narcotic drug addiction whether practiced by the private physician or by the so-called 'narcotic clinic' or dispensary." This resolution is still cited in support of current American drug policy.[44] If action is taken on the recent recommendation of the Association's Council on Mental Health that this resolution be revised, the impact may be considerable.

CONCLUSION

There are no available empirical data on the basis of which one can determine whether or not narcotics policies patterned along British lines would work in this country. It is doubtless true, as critics of reform proposals point out, that the addiction "problem" in America is now quite different from that which exists in the United Kingdom. The American problem is enormously larger than that in Britain. (It should be stressed, however, that prior to legal control of narcotics, addiction was widespread in the United Kingdom.) Historical differences may have operated to help create, in America more than in Britain, the image of the

drug addict as an underworld type. Very likely the detection and prevention of narcotics smuggling is much more of a problem in the United States than in the United Kingdom. And there may be other relevant differences between the situations in the two countries. But it does not necessarily follow from the fact that such differences may exist that the British approach will not work in America. When one considers the interrelationship between policy and problem, one can see that these differences may actually stem in large measure from the different policies in force in Britain and in the United States. One also becomes aware that current American policies cannot help but fail. The policy of withholding legal satisfaction of the demand for narcotics inevitably leads to a profit-motivated and socially-dangerous illicit market in drugs. There is no need to elaborate here on the evils of the current narcotics situation in the United States; the profiteering in contraband drugs, the high rate of addict criminality, and the special problems of juvenile addiction are well known. These problems are crucially *inter*related with our current policies. As Rufus King has stated, "It is precisely our law enforcement efforts, and nothing else, that keep the price of drugs, nearly worthless in themselves, so high as to attract an endless procession of criminal entrepreneurs to keep the traffic flowing."[45] It would seem foolhardy indeed to dismiss out of hand a policy which accords with common sense and humane feeling, and which has proven its effectiveness in Great Britain.[46] An exprimental test of

---

[44] This resolution was instrumental in the closing of the clinics referred to in note 41, *supra*. Of the resolution, the Daniel Committee has stated: "The Bureau of Narcotics received a mandate from the medical profession to do what it has done, namely, suppress the clinics. This policy has never been withdrawn by the American Medical Association after its verbatim acceptance by the house of delegates in 1924. . . ." *Daniel Hearings, op. cit. supra* note 10, at 1459 n. 1. The resolution also is quoted with approval in the Narcotics Bureau's pamphlet for doctors, Prescribing and Dispensing of Narcotics Under Harrison Narcotic Law 8 (1956).

[45] Rufus King, in *Daniel Hearings, op. cit. supra* note 10, at 1379.

[46] The writer has not intended to create the impression that the British policy is foolproof. Addicts occasionally succeed in getting extra drugs through forgery or by managing to get

such an approach, as suggested by the AMA-ABA committee, seems the very least that can be done in the interests of uncovering a workable drug policy.

At the heart of the controversy over proposals for a more medically-oriented addiction policy in America lies the question: Should addiction be treated as a crime? The evidence from Britain suggests the considerable extent to which the addict's behavior is determined by the social reaction to his addiction. Keeping this in mind, it is difficult to see how addiction, as such, can properly be labelled a criminal form of behavior. Hermann Mannheim has suggested that only behavior which is anti-social should be treated as a crime.[47] The only real ground on which one could label addiction, as such, anti-social is that addicts tend to lead socially-unproductive lives. Even

conceding this point, one would still have to ask whether addicts are *sufficiently* anti-social to be considered criminals. Above all it should be clear that addiction as such may not be as anti-social as are the types of addict behavior which a punitive approach to addiction tends to produce.

A last-ditch objection may assert that even if the addict is not overtly anti-social the preservation of certain basic social values requires anti-addiction laws. Thus one writer on addiction states: "It is morally indefensible for society to legalize a vice simply on the grounds that restrictive legislation creates an illicit market and hence a profit motive for racketeers."[43] It is difficult to reconcile the description of addiction as a "vice" with the generally accepted view (expressed even by Ausubel elsewhere in his book) that it is an illness. But probably there is no way of proving or disproving the claim that a type of human behavior is a "vice." The present writer, however, prefers to approach the problem of addiction not from a position based upon abstract moralizing, but rather from the standpoint of examining the specific social consequences of various addiction policies. If one proceeds along this latter path, the importance of the British experience becomes obvious.

---

narcotics from two doctors at once. Some doctors abuse the system by diverting drugs to their own use. But all the evidence indicates that abuses are not widespread. It may also be worth noting that the British Government is far from complacent about the success of their drug policies. On the contrary, these policies are under almost constant review. For example, see the recent report, Ministry of Health, Central Health Services Council, Report of the Joint Sub-Committee on the Control of Dangerous Drugs and Poisons in Hospitals (1958). A review of the entire addiction question (by an expert committee established in 1958) has just been completed. The report is not yet available.

[47] Mannheim, Criminal Justic and Social Reconstruction 5 (1946).

[48] Ausubel, *op. cit. supra* note 36, at 79.

10

Alcoholism

DEFINING ALCOHOLISM

Unlike drug use, the consumption of alcoholic beverages in any quantity is not illegal. Indeed, drinking has become a generally accepted part of the American way of life. Contemporary culture is not unique in this respect since the use and misuse of alcohol can be traced to prehistoric times. Among the ancient Egyptians, Babylonians, Greeks, Romans, and Chinese alcohol was widely used and intoxication was a problem of notable concern. More recently the American colonists brought their beverages and drinking customs with them to the new land. Originally beer and wine, but later distilled spirits as well, played an important role in the religious, medical and dietary habits of the colonists.[1] Drinking was a part of family and community life and was well regulated by familial and religious norms.

Although the drinking of the colonists was primarily moderate, its nature began to change with the population. As greater numbers of unattached males migrated to and settled in the colonies, the use of distilled spirits increased and drinking began to lose its family significance. Drinking took on new meaning to this large group of settlers and "may have served to compensate for the absence of the gratifications, responsibilities, and stability of family living. The frequent use of alcohol to produce intoxication became particularly characteristic of life on the ever expanding frontier and among the less stable segments of communities during the several decades following the Revolutionary War."[2]

Today drinking alcoholic beverages is viewed by most people as being socially useful and even necessary. Alcohol is used to celebrate holidays and special events, to help negotiate business deals, and to entertain friends. In many cases the predinner cocktail is as much of the meal as the food itself. Having a "good time" at a social event is often synonymous with drinking as much as possible. Drinking by teen-agers and college students is a common part of their social life and is often seen as a *rite de passage* from adolescent to adult roles. Family and religious sanctions which once served to control this activity are hardly meaningful any longer. Such new and widespread drinking patterns are not in themselves problematic, except for those who view all consumption of alcoholic beverages as morally objectionable. They do, however, indicate that drinking is largely done in situations and under conditions which may foster excessive use. The excessive use of liquor may, under certain conditions, develop into alcoholism which creates great social concern because of its detrimental effects on the alcoholic and his social world.

The many definitions of the term "alcoholism" indicate that the concept is far from precise and clear-cut, and that the phenomenon itself is yet to be fully understood. Within the last few decades the thinking about alcoholism has changed greatly so that it is now thought of as a sickness or disease[3] constituting a major public health problem. This conception of alcoholism is embodied in the following definition:

Alcoholism is a chronic illness, psychic or somatic or psychosomatic, which manifests itself as a disorder of behavior. It is characterized by the repeated drinking of alcoholic beverages, to an extent that exceeds customary dietary use or compliance with the social customs of the community and that interferes with the drinker's health or his social or economic functioning.[4]

On the basis of this definition it might be said that an alcoholic is a person whose excessive drinking interferes with his family relationships, job, health, or general welfare. Although alcoholism requires drinking and usually drunkenness, not all those who drink or become drunk are alcoholics. The distinguishing characteristic is the true alcoholic's addiction to alcohol and his inability to control intake once he has begun to drink.[5] The occasional or even habitual excessive drinker does not share these features of alcohol use.

Alcohol has both a physiological and psychological effect on man.[6] After intake alcohol requires no digestion and is absorbed directly into the blood stream. In this way it is carried to the brain where it acts as a depressant and tends to reduce inhibitions. Depending upon the concentration of alcohol in the blood, various parts of the central nervous system are affected with resulting disturbances in behavior. The person may appear drunk—thick speech, clumsiness, sagging knees—because the alcohol has served to depress the brain's control over these functions. The greater the concentration of alcohol reaching the brain, a condition dependent upon factors other than sheer volume of intake, the more levels of brain functioning become depressed and the more symptoms of intoxication become evident.

In addition to physical reactions, alcohol may also induce psychological effects which vary, among individuals, with the amount ingested and at different times. Taken moderately, it acts as a tranquilizer to reduce anxiety and tension and to lessen depression. The individual may feel relaxed and warm, less concerned with minor irritations, and have a sense of general well-being. In less moderate quantities it will definitely impair reasoning power, discrimination and judgment and often give the user the feeling that he is more competent and able than he actually is.

American society has always been ambivalent about alcoholic beverages, using them but never feeling quite comfortable about it. At various times attempts have been made to suppress their use entirely. According to one writer,[7] this attitude toward alcohol use and the attempts at suppression have been legitimized by three American values: (1) each individual should be completely responsible for what he does and its consequences and he should do nothing to cause a loss of self-control; (2) any behavior designed solely to achieve ecstasy or pleasure is disapproved of; and (3) the humanitarian belief that alcohol users benefit when they are unable to give in to their weakness. In the past these typically American values have given rise to the temperance movement and the Prohibition Amendment of 1919.

Originally, the American temperance movement was concerned only with the use of distilled spirits and not with the moderate use of beer and wine. By 1840, however, the movement became more radical and all alcoholic beverages were condemned. In succeeding years the temperance organizations were influential in achieving prohibition in many rural states. However, there were some states that tried it and then abandoned it. It was not until 1919 that sufficient pressure was brought upon Congress to pass the Eighteenth Amendment to the Constitution, national prohibition. From January 1920 until December 1933, when Prohibition was repealed, the United States was a "dry" nation.

The period of Prohibition did not mean an end of drinking. Bootleggers flourished and criminal syndicates became rich and powerful from selling illegal alcohol. Drinking took on a romantic quality and appealed to many who used it under conditions conducive to excess and drunkenness. It soon became evident that Prohibition was a failure. With repeal the temperance movement all but vanished from the American scene and the government became content with attempting to control the importation, manufacture, and sale of alcoholic beverages through a system of duties, taxes, licensing, and state regulatory commissions. Thus, decades after the most dramatic attempt to abolish alcoholic drinking, the use of liquor is as prevalent as it ever was and alcoholism or chronic, excessive drinking is still an issue of social concern.

THE EXTENT OF ALCOHOLISM

In the absence of a national census of drinking behavior, estimates of how many people drink are based upon local or national sample surveys. Although these estimates vary, most indicate that approximately two-thirds of the population over 21 drink alcoholic beverages. One recent study shows that 71 percent of the adult population, about 80 million people, drink to some extent.[8] When this figure is added to the 8 to 10 million youth between 16 and 20 who drink, it indicates that perhaps as many as 90 million Americans over 15 years use alcoholic beverages.[9]

There are also other indicators of the extent of alcoholic drinking.[10] In 1959, 9.6 billion dollars were spent on alcoholic beverages and in 1960 the Treasury Department collected $3,193,714,000 in excise taxes on liquor, more than was collected on gasoline, tobacco, or automobiles. Also in 1960, the per capita consumption of distilled spirits was 1.90 gallons; of wine, 1.32 gallons; and of beer, 21.95 gallons, for a total per capita consumption of 2.07 gallons of absolute alcohol. Interestingly, this latter figure has hardly changed at all since 1850, inasmuch as the consumption of spirits has decreased in that time while the use of wine and beer has grown.

Of the large number of adult drinkers, there are approximately 5 million alcoholics or excessive drinkers. This figure is derived from a formula which holds that for every alcoholic dying from cirrhosis of the liver (a frequent ailment among excessive users), three are without fatal complications. Hence, the number dying with complications multiplied by four determines the number of alcoholics.[11] Using the same formula, the 1955 rate per 100,000 adults aged 20 and over was estimated as 4360.

The social consequences resulting from the excessive use of alcohol give an even better picture of the extent of the problem. It is estimated that yearly losses due to alcoholism total 765 million dollars in the United States, with wage, crime, and accident losses comprising the bulk of this figure.[12] Incalculable are the less tangible effects of alcoholism, the millions of family members who are influenced by the alcoholic's behavior, the broken homes, the harm done to others in highway accidents, and, perhaps above all, the alcoholic's own loss of self-respect and self-confidence and his slowly slipping into a way of life revolving completely around "the next drink."

Drinking patterns are found to correlate with certain social characteristics, including sex, age, social class, religion, ethnic group, and where one lives.

SEX   In a 1947 study,[13] Riley and Marden found that 75 percent of adult males drank whereas only 56 percent of adult females did so. Of the regular drinkers (three or more times a week), 27 percent were men and 8 percent women. A more recent study also shows that men use alcohol with greater frequency than women. Mulford's data reveal that 79 percent of the men and 63 percent of the women drink alcoholic beverages.[14] Although many women drink alcohol, and some with great frequency, the nearly 6:1 ratio of male to female alcoholics has not changed significantly since 1940.

AGE   The Riley and Marden national survey also showed that drinking declines with age. About 75 percent of those between 21 and 35 years of age drink, somewhat more than 60 percent of those between 36 and 55, and about 50 percent of those over 55.[15] Drinking is very prevalent among high school and college students.[16] One study reported that 90 percent of the students 16 and over in a New York county drink on some occasions; a second study, in Michigan, reported that 23 percent drank regularly while a much larger number had tasted alcohol; and a third study showed that about half of the high school students in Kansas use alcohol. Although high school students do not drink often, nor do they consume very much, college-age students drink about as much and as often as the general population. Straus and Bacon report that 74 percent of students at 27 colleges studied drank in some regular pattern.

SOCIAL CLASS   Drinking appears to be most prevalent in the upper-class, associated with high income and greater education. In this class drinking is an important part of business and social life and is not seen as a moral issue. The middle-class contains the greatest number of total abstainers and those who do indulge do so sparingly. Drinking is often viewed as a moral issue and may be completely forbidden by some. Alcohol use and even drunkenness are more acceptable in the lower-class. The greater tendency for lower-class people to become involved with the police when drinking and their overrepresentation among skid row derelicts has created a somewhat distorted image of the extent of alcohol use in this class.

RELIGION AND ETHNICITY   The prevalence of drinking varies greatly with religious affiliation and ethnic group membership. Jews report the highest incidence of drinking, Catholics next, and Protestants last, with percentages of 87, 79, and 59, respectively.[17] The high incidence rates for Jews and Catholics are not surprising since these groups are composed largely of people for whom drinking is institutionalized in the dietary, ceremonial, and religious customs. Especially among Jews drinking is frequent but moderate and the rate of Jewish alcoholics is infinitesimally low.

The Irish and Italians probably have higher incidences of drinking than other ethnic groups. In both cultures virtually all adult males drink but the alcoholism rates are quite different. Alcoholism among Italian-Americans is low while among Irish-Americans it has always been high. In both World Wars Irish-American draftees were rejected for alcoholism more often than members of any other ethnic group.[18]

RESIDENCE   Drinking also varies according to where one lives. Over two and one-half times as many people drink in the mid-Atlantic states than in the eastern south-central states.[19] Rural people are more abstemious than urban dwellers, residents of small cities more so than residents of large cities. Obviously, these differences are closely associated with such factors as religion and ethnicity which we have discussed.

There are other social correlates of drinking behavior. Nevertheless, they too lead to the conclusion that how much one drinks, when, where, and under what conditions is greatly determined by the groups with which he identifies. One who identifies with his ethnic, religious, or occupational group will more than likely drink or not drink as other members of the group do. Why some people go beyond group sanctions and become excessive drinkers is not entirely known, although current etiological statements present some clues.

SOME EXPLANATIONS OF ALCOHOLISM

Although we are primarily interested in the sociocultural explanations of alcoholism, it must be pointed out that physiological and psychological factors have also been used to determine causation. Physiologically, alcoholism has been attributed to biochemical defects of various kinds which produce a craving for alcohol, to a lack of nutrition, to the defective functioning of the endocrine glands, and to a masked food sensitivity. These defects are usually assumed to be genetic and their correction should allay the alcoholic condition. Unfortunately, this has never been demonstrated.[20]

The typical psychological explanations attribute alcoholism to faulty personality development and emotional problems. Alcoholics have been viewed by psychologists and psychiatrists as feeling inadequate, being latently homosexual, desiring self-destruction and self-punishment, attempting to escape from their inner guilt and conflicts, or being insecure and dependent upon others for support. These personality traits resulting from certain childhood experiences and interpersonal relationships create enormous tension and anxiety which is overcome with alcohol. As relief is found through alcohol use, the individual's dependence upon it grows greater and alcoholism results.

Many critics have pointed out at least three shortcomings in this approach: (1) to date evidence does not indicate that there is an "alcoholic personality" with distinguishing traits shared by all alcoholics; (2) those personality characteristics that are found in alcoholics may be the result of alcoholism and not the cause of it; and (3) personality characteristics found in alcoholics are also found in nonalcoholics. As Straus concluded:

Knowledge about the psychological effects of alcohol in alleviating anxiety and providing a sense of well-being helps explain why alcohol is attractive to and functional for persons with deep feelings of emotional insecurity, but psychological theory cannot tell us, for example, why, of the people with a so-called alcoholic personality, only some become alcoholics, while others do not.[12]

Sociocultural explanations of alcoholism have generally emphasized the role of drinking customs and the social circumstances under which drinking occurs. Bales, after observing the differences between Irish and Jewish drinking customs and rates of alcoholism, has suggested that the extent of alcoholism is determined by several aspects of the culture.[22] First is the amount of tension which the culture induces within the person; second are the attitudes toward drinking as a legitimate means of releasing these tensions; and third is the extent to which the culure provides alternative ways of resolving tension. Among groups with a high prevalence of drinking behavior, Irish, Jews and Italians, for example, these cultural factors are believed to account for the differential rates of alcoholism.

Irish immigrants migrating to the United States brought with them an institutionalized means of dealing with psychic tension, drinking. Because of the custom of inheritance in Irish society and the meager productivity of their farms, men could not assume adult roles until their fathers died or gave up the farm. Sexual activity, marriage, an independent income, and the raising of a family were dependent upon the control of land which usually came late in life. As a result, great tension and frustration developed and found release in drinking and intoxication which were supported by the culture as acceptable outlets. New tensions and frustrations resulting from a low socioeconomic position developed after migration to the United States. After escaping the oppression of the Old World culture, many Irish males found the expectations of the new culture just as anxiety producing. Unlike many other immigrants who experienced similar anxiety, Irish customs and attitudes permitted and encouraged drinking as a means of adjusting to the situation.

Jews and Italians, on the other hand, have extremely low rates of alcoholism even though the prevalence of drinking is great in these cultures.[23] For most Jews drinking is not associated with tension management. Moderate consumption is traditional, an integral part of religious symbolism, and Jewish children learn early in the socialization process that the purpose of drinking is not to produce intoxication or to provide temporary relief from stress. Similarly for Italians, drinking is not used as an escape but is a part of traditional dietary habits. Alcohol, usually wine, is ingested, sometimes in great quantities, at meals beginning quite early in the individual's life. Drinking under these conditions is sanctioned and supported by the culture and when intoxication does take place it is viewed in the same way as overeating. Under such conditions alcoholism is infrequent.

The stress and pressures which individuals experience and seek solutions to may be produced by a number of factors. Today, as was the case with the preimmigration Irish, problems associated with adult role assumption play an increasingly important role in drinking behavior.[24] Alcoholism rates are high in groups which do not introduce their youth to drinking until adolescence, when it becomes a *rite de passage*, a symbol of new independence or "manliness." The groups which introduce their youth to alcohol at an early age, like the Jews and Italians, maintain a low rate of alcoholism. In such groups drinking is usually related to family and ritual and is not seen as a way of helping the young bridge the difficult period between adolescence and adulthood.

These examples lend support to Bales' contention that certain cultural norms determine the extent of alcoholism. Jews and Italians probably experience as much stress and psychic tension as do the Irish or any other group. The difference lies in the culturally sanctioned means of handling such problems. Alcoholism is most common when excessive drinking and intoxication are a part of the culture's drinking customs and, in the absence of meaningful alternatives, alcohol is seen as a way of coping with the problems of social existence.

BECOMING AN ALCOHOLIC

Although there are differing types of alcoholism, the most common in the United States is that which develops progressively over a period of time, perhaps from 5 to 15 years. On the basis of over 2000 histories of male alcoholics who had lost control over their intake, Jellinek has delineated four phases in the development of the alcoholic condition: the prealcoholic symptomatic phase, the prodromal phase, the crucial phase, and the chronic phase.[25] Not all alcoholics go through each of these phases, nor necessarily in the sequence indicated, but it apears that the majority do and experience the symptoms characteristic of each stage.

In the first or prealcoholic symptomatic phase the socially motivated drinker experiences rewards in the form of tension relief. Associating relief with drinking, he begins to seek out situations in which he might drink. As his tolerance for tension decreases he begins to drink daily, not to the point of intoxication but until he no longer is bothered by his emotional stress. Although the drinking is not yet noticeable to others, increasing amounts are needed to produce the desired effects.

The second phase is characterized by frequent blackouts and the inability to remember activities and conversations occurring while drinking. The prospective alcoholic begins to sneak drinks, gulping the first few rapidly, and develops a preoccupation with alcohol. Another symptom generally occurring during this phase is the self-realization by the drinker that somehow he is abnormal. Guilt feelings develop and he begins to "cover-up" so as to protect himself from friends and family members.

When the drinker loses the ability to control the amount of his intake once he has started to drink, he has passed into the crucial phase. In this phase the drinking behavior becomes conspicuous to others and the drinker begins to build a system of rationalizations to counter social pressures and to convince himself that he has not lost control. Despite his rationalization he loses self-esteem and gradually isolates himself from others, experiencing persistent remorse. Drinking becomes all-important and once-important aspects of the drinker's life are pushed into the background as his entire existence becomes focused around drinking. As the symptoms increase and physical and social deterioration become more evident, the alcoholic begins to drink in the morning to face the day ahead.

Regular morning drinking marks the end of the third phase and the beginning of the chronic phase. In this phase the alcoholic experiences prolonged intoxications, impairment of thinking, indefinable fears, tremors, and the loss of certain psychomotor skills. He now drinks at any time and, in the absence of liquor, may resort to such things as rubbing alcohol or shaving lotion. He has now reached bottom and feels that he is utterly defeated. Many experts feel that the alcoholic who has reached this stage is now accessible to treatment, but in the absence of such intervention obsessive drinking continues.

WHAT CAN BE DONE?

An attitude of hopelessness seems to characterize the prevention and control aspects of the alcoholism problem. This is especially true of prevention since so many preventive experiments have failed. Many authorities feel that the prevention of pathological drinking leading to alcoholism, like other social problems examined in this book, can be achieved only if and when the social structure is significantly altered. Short of creating a structure completely without stress-producing situations and expectations, impossible in a heterogeneous, complex society such as our own, alcoholism might be averted by developing behavioral controls which eliminate the possibility of drinking as a means of adaptation.

In the first reading Edwin Lemert examines four such models of social control of alcohol use. These models—prohibition, education, government regulation of consumption, and substituting other activities for drinking—are derived from experience and have not been very successful. Lemert indicates the strengths and weaknesss of each and shows how they might be made into better working models. Although it is unlikely that any one model of control will work in a heterogeneous society, it is necessary that drinking not "disrupt crucial social integrations." The lack of success of state control plans leads Lemert to conclude that various groups in the society must work together to control drinking behavior at the "grass roots level." Although this type of control, like others, can have only limited effectiveness, it is probably the most potentially useful method of controlling alcohol use.

In his article "Prevention Can Be More than a Word," Seldon D. Bacon singles out cultural attitudes toward alcoholism as the target for effective prevention. Typical attitudes toward alcoholism not only hinder the acceptance of therapy by those experiencing the problem, but they also serve to increase its incidence. He believes that most cases of alcoholism originate and persist as a result of social interaction favorable to it, and that without such interaction it would not occur or, at least, be easily stopped. Bacon proposes that prevention will be enhanced by "the modification of selected areas of value and social action in selected segments of the existing community." However, as he indicates, much research must be done to determine just what values and patterns of action must be modified and, most crucially, how such modifications can be achieved.

Despite only modest success at best, programs designed to rehabilitate the alcoholic abound. In the third reading Thomas F. A. Plaut examines some of the treatment programs carried on by both general and specialized "helping" agencies. He indicates that the extent of alcoholism would seem to warrant great interventive efforts on the part of the general agencies. Instead, most professional workers in such settings react negatively to the alcoholic and his problems, feeling that he could solve his own problems if he really wanted to. Needless to say, what services they do provide are rarely effective. Specialized programs, such as special programs in mental hospitals, alcoholism clinics, and half-way houses, do not provide the entire answer either, although their orientation is generally more conducive to helping the alcoholic patient. Rather, Plaut believes that the answer might lie in a more comprehensive and united approach by the various community agencies that come into contact with the alcoholic and his many problems.

The work of Alcoholics Anonymous in rehabilitating alcoholics is widely known and has been subjected to much study. In the fourth reading Harrison M. Trice describes this popular self-help program which claims to have restored thousands of alcoholics to sobriety. Founded and led by alcoholics, this program demands that members admit that they have "reached bottom" and be willing to turn to others, including a "power" greater than themselves, for help. Through spiritual experiences and group processes the alcoholic's conception of himself changes and individual behavior is altered. For those able to adjust to the casual, informal group life, Alcoholics Anonymous provides the member with an alternative way of satisfying his emotional needs which led to his compulsive drinking.

REFERENCES

1. Robert Straus, "Alcohol," in Robert K. Merton and Robert A. Nisbet (eds.), *Contemporary Social Problems*. New York: Harcourt, Brace & World, Inc., 1966, p. 245.
2. Straus, p. 245.
3. This idea is fully discussed in E. M. Jellinek, *The Disease Concept of Alcoholism*. New Haven, Conn.: Hillhouse Press, 1960.
4. Mark Keller and Vera Efron, "The Prevalence of Alcoholism," *Quarterly Journal of Studies on Alcohol*, 16 (1955), p. 621.
5. E. M. Jellinek, "Phases of Alcohol Addiction," in David J. Pittman and Charles R. Snyder (eds.), *Society, Culture, and Drinking Patterns*. New York: John Wiley & Sons, Inc., pp. 356–368.
6. Leon A. Greenberg, "Intoxication and Alcoholism; Physiological Factors," *The Annals*, 315 (January 1958), pp. 22–30.
7. Howard S. Becker, *Outsiders*. New York: The Free Press of Glencoe, 1963, p. 136.
8. Harold A. Mulford, "Drinking and Deviant Drinking, U.S.A., 1963," *Quarterly Journal of Studies on Alcohol*, 25 (December 1964), pp. 634–650.
9. Straus, p. 251.
10. See Marshall B. Clinard, *Sociology of Deviant Behavior*. New York: Holt, Rinehart and Winston, Inc., 1963, pp. 332–333.
11. Mark Keller, "Alcoholism: Nature and Extent of the Problem," *The Annals*, 315 (January 1958), pp. 1–11.
12. George N. Thompson, *Alcoholism*. Springfield, Ill.: Charles C Thomas, Publisher, 1956, p. 453.
13. John W. Riley and Charles F. Marden, "The Social Pattern of Alcoholic Drinking," *Quarterly Journal of Studies on Alcohol*, 8 (September 1947), pp. 265–273.
14. Mulford, p. 637.

15. Riley and Marden, p. 268.
16. Straus, pp. 250–256.
17. Riley and Marden, p. 270.
18. Reported in R. R. Dynes, A. C. Clarke, S. Dinitz, and I. Ishino, *Social Problems.* New York: Oxford University Press, 1964, p. 528.
19. Mulford, p. 640.
20. Keller, p. 10.
21. Straus, p. 263.
22. Robert F. Bales, "Cultural Differences in Rates of Alcoholism," *Quarterly Journal of Studies on Alcohol,* 6 (March 1946), pp. 480–499.
23. Morris E. Chafetz and Harold W. Demone, Jr., *Alcoholism and Society.* New York: Oxford University Press, 1962, pp. 80–88.
24. Albert D. Ullman, "Ethnic Differences in the First Drinking Experience," *Social Problems,* 8 (Summer 1960) pp. 45–56.
25. Jellinek, "Phases of Alcohol Addiction," pp. 359–367.

ADDITIONAL READINGS

Bales, Robert F., "Cultural Differences in Rates of Alcoholism," *Quarterly Journal of Studies on Alcohol,* 6 (March 1946), pp. 480–499.

Chafetz, Morris E., and Harold W. Demone, Jr., *Alcoholism and Society.* New York: Oxford University Press, 1962.

Jellinek, E. M., *The Disease Concept of Alcoholism.* New Haven, Conn.: Hillhouse Press, 1960.

Lucia, Salvatore P., (ed.), *Alcohol and Civilization.* New York: McGraw-Hill Book Company, Inc., 1963.

Pittman, David J., and Charles R. Snyder, (eds.), *Society, Culture and Drinking Patterns.* New York: John Wiley & Sons, Inc., 1962.

Snyder, Charles R., *Alcohol and the Jews: A Cultural Study of Drinking and Sobriety.* New Haven, Conn.: Yale Center of Alcohol Studies, and New York: The Free Press of Glencoe, 1958.

Straus, Robert, "Alcoholism," in Robert K. Merton and Robert A. Nisbet (eds.), *Contemporary Social Problems.* New York: Harcourt, Brace & World, Inc., 1966, Chap. 5.

"Understanding Alcoholism," *The Annals of the American Academy of Political and Social Science.* 315 (January 1958).

FOUR MODELS OF SOCIAL CONTROL

Edwin Lemert

A reasonable working assumption is that the objective of social control over alcohol use generally is to minimize the costs of intoxication and drunkenness. For purposes of determining whether and how such an objective can be reached, it is

From *Society, Culture and Drinking Patterns,* David J. Pittman and Charles R. Snyder, eds., New York: John Wiley Sons, Inc., 1962, pp. 560–571. Reprinted by permission.

helpful to formulate a number of hypothetical models of social control. These are drawn from the experiences of whole societies and also from the ideologies and programs of power elites which at different times and places have actively sought to bring alcohol use under control.

MODEL I

The Costs of Intoxication and Drunkenness Can Be Reduced by a System of Laws and Coercive Controls Making It Illegal to Manufacture, Distribute, or Consume Alcoholic Beverages

This, of course, is a familiar model—prohibition. It has been tried in several forms, for long and short periods of time, in Aztec society, ancient China, feudal Japan, the Polynesian Islands, Iceland, Finland, Norway, Sweden, Russia, Canada, and the United States. The well-documented failures of the model can be attributed to its high costs, the instability of power elites favorable to prohibition, the limitations of power and available means of control, and the growth of resistance unresponsive to coercion.

The prohibition model in effect sacrifices all of the values of moderate drinking as well as those associated with intoxication, plus the vested values of those who earn a livelihood or receive investment returns from the production and distribution of fermented drinks and liquor. In order for such high costs to be willingly paid a large number of power elites must either see positive value gains in prohibition laws or see them as a means of protection against threatened value losses (24). Consequently the prohibition model most likely can be established only through a social movement during periods of rapid social change, culture conflicts, conquest, or nationalistic movements.

Reform movements, from which prohibition springs, tend to be ephemeral in nature because new issues supplant the old, undermining or destroying the alignments of elites suporting them. Disillusionment of their individual adherents and defection of groups through changing policies are speeded by difficulties of enforcement and consequences of resistance.

Resistance can be predicted for any model of control requiring the abandonment of values deeply held by large segments of a population. In the case of prohibition the problem of enforcement is augmented because it is a form of sumptuary legislation which affects the more personal aspects of human behavior and individual choice making in intimate or private behavior. In the absence of a reinforcing public opinion the application of coercive controls seldom has succeeded. Even the most severe punishments, such as death among the Aztecs and exile to Siberia in Russia, failed to abolish bootlegging in those societies (28).

In large, complex societies a control model which prohibits a highly desired item increases its scarcity value and also the probabilities that collective enterprise will grow up to supply it. The large variety of foods which can be converted into alcohol and the ease and cheapness of its production and its movement make bootlegging and smuggling inevitable. The costs to the state of discovering and stamping out such illegal industry can reach a point where governing elites are unable or unwilling to pay them. The organization of evasion poses threats to other values such as respect for property and life, and even the value of government under law. This contributes further to resistance and reaction against prohibition.

The power of a given state to enforce prohibition may be insufficient if the economic and political values of other states are threatening thereby. In 1841, France intervened under threats of bombardment and compelled the reigning monarch of the Hawaiian Islands to end prohibition there (46). France, Germany, Russia, and Spain at different times variously applied pressures to Finland, Norway, Iceland, and Turkey in order to prevent interference with liquor imports and smuggling (5).

It may be more profitable to speculate on the conditions under which the prohibition model can succeed rather than to inventory the reasons for its failure. Probably it would require conspicuously high costs of drunkenness on one hand and on the other a positive replacement of the drinking values or substitution of new means for achieving the old values. A precondition of this would be relatively complete geographic isolation, similar to that found on islands, where behavior deviations have a high visibility. A social structure in which power is concentrated and little affected by public opinion or is upheld by supernatural sanctions perhaps would make for successful prohibition. Needless to say, conditions such as these are increasingly anomalous in the world of the present.

MODEL II

The Costs of Intoxication and Drunkenness Can Be Reduced by a System of Indoctrination of Information about the Consequences of Using Alcohol—Thus Leading To Moderate Drinking or Abstinence

The assumption behind this control model is that a causative relationship holds between controlled presentation of information and change in attitudes and values. The general idea is favored by some research on attitudes in specified areas of behavior. The findings, however, are not altogether consistent and where giving information has been found to modify attitudes and values the change is not always in the anticipated direction (4). In general it would be hard to say whether exposure to information leads people to change specific values or whether the reverse is true—that is, whether the adherence to certain values stimulates people to inform themselves of pertinent facts. Currently there is no conclusive research from which judgments can be made about the kinds of information or educational content best calculated to achieve the goals of abstinence or moderation in drinking.

In the absence of data, the content of alcohol education has tended to be influenced by values and policies of temperance groups. This has been especially true of alcohol education in the schools of countries where forms of this model have been tried. Those whose values are more directly involved—parents—are not inclined to resist the inclusion of special curricula on alcohol education in the schools because many believe that some guidance is needed, especially in the United States where education is apotheosized as a solution for social problems. On the other hand some evidence from England and America speaks of indifference to or lack of sympathy with the alcohol curriculum on the part of teachers who do not subscribe to temperance values. This may reflect a failure to reconcile religious and scientific orientations in the recommended curricula (29). Resistance from these sources, of course, need not necessarily be fatal to the working of this model.

A more serious flaw in the educational model of alcohol control lies in the probability that values surrounding drinking and embedded in drinking patterns are primarily shaped by experiences in the family and in peer groups rather than by formal educational agencies (29, 42, 45). No problem is created for the society relying upon the educational model if it is homogeneous with reference to its drinking or abstinence habits. In the absence of such homogeneity, educators are faced with discontinuity between the learning process in the schools and what goes on in primary groups outside. Examples set by parents at home or pressures to conform in friendship groups easily cancel out the abstinence or moderation precepts of the school.

Education for restraint in drinking might be directed to parents instead of youth, through agencies outside or peripheral to the school. Yet prospects for this kind of enlightenment are not promising. Family-life education generally considered has yet to prove its worth (13). Other programs, such as those promoted by state mental hygiene departments or by local alcoholism committees, or by citizens' committees as in Russia, are still largely untested by research or extensive empirical trial. In some places it has been shown that mental hygiene education can have effects opposite to those intended (9, 10).

The means which can be made to work for alcohol education have not been well adapted to the ends sought. Pamphlets, charts, movies, and lectures which dwell upon the results of excessive drinking often seem to run afoul of the ambivalence underlying popular reactions to alcohol. The arousal of fears, implied warnings, or threats as to what will happen if one drinks too much have been noted to provoke avoidance reactions towards further propaganda. There also seems to be an unwillingness of audiences to particularize such propaganda. This is very apt

to be true if the educational materials are pointed to alcoholism as an end result of drinking.

Research into the factors which account for the long history of Jewish sobriety makes it fairly certain that the indoctrination of values is significant. It has not yet been settled what the values are, nor whether they are generalized or specific in nature. Furthermore there is a good possibility that such values may be functional only in a special context of ongoing social control represented by the Jewish community (12, 44). Comparable research into drinking by Italian Americans and Italians concludes that valuation of wine as a food is an important part of their relative sobriety (30). Yet this scarcely seems to be a complete explanation, and even if it were, there are no investigations to clarify the process by which such a value is inculcated or maintained in the ethnic population.

A final necessary comment on the educational model of control is that in a mobile, culturally diversified society which changes rapidly it becomes difficult to predict what pattern of values indoctrinated in children will best serve to adjust them as adults. To the extent that drinking is a response to situations, to adventitious groupings, and to stresses generated by role conflicts or social isolation, reliance upon a preconceived pattern of drinking values to control excessive use of alcohol may fail. Attention must be directed to the controls functioning in the drinking situation.

MODEL III

The Costs of Intoxication and Drunkenness Can Be Reduced by Legal Regulation of the Kinds of Liquor Consumed, Its Pecuniary Cost, Methods of Distribution, the Time and Place of Drinking, and Its Availability to Consumers according to Age,

Sex, and Other Socio-economic Characteristics

This model rests upon the conviction that the state or its agencies can determine what amounts and what forms of drinking have costly consequences. In most comprehensive form the model defines drinking as a privilege which, if abused, can be withdrawn from the individual; corollary to this is withdrawal of privileges, such as that of driving an automobile, which are affected by drinking. Archetypes of this model are found in the history of Scandinavian countries —particularly Sweden, home of the Gothenberg and Bratt systems of liquor control. Examples also come from the temperance orders of medieval Germany, possibly including the apocryphal *jus potandi,* the drinking code of orders given to heavy drinking (41).

Government regulation of alcohol consumption grew up historically largely from non-moral considerations. Among these were popular agitation that governments make fermented beverages equally available to localities and demands that the quality of such drinks be insured against fraud. The willingness of populations to accept taxes on alcohol production as a revenue measure has been an enticing path to regulation for financially hard-pressed governments (5). This last possibility has caused a persistent dilemma for governing officials who have to choose between raising money the "easy way" and at the same time taking steps to diminish heavy drinking which has the effect of decreasing revenue. The dilemma has been conspicuous in the history of Russia, where, under the Tsar's *kabak* system, and subsequently under the "farming out" system of vodka monopoly, the government abetted or encouraged widespread drunkenness (11, 17). The dilemma still lives today in muted controversies over the respective merits of licensing versus monopoly and trust systems of alcohol distribution.

Effective alcoholic beverage control may strike heavily at the economic values of producers and distributors even when it does not threaten drinking values of the population. If these elites are numerous and well organized, their resistance may well nullify efforts at regulation. A well-documented case in point is France, whose parliaments passed a series of regulatory laws after the First and Second World Wars. Yet the great power of the wine industry there has prevented anything beyond token enforcement of the laws. The presence of approximately a third of the electorate who are either workers in the wine industry or their family members does much to explain this phenomenon (34). The so-called *bouillers de cru,* home distillers, who are entrenched in certain areas of France seem to openly defy regulation, protecting their traditional privileges largely through sheer power of numbers at the polls.

In the latter part of the nineteenth century, in some countries pressures from temperance groups exerted a mounting influence on government regulation. The result has been that regulation more and more reflected a power conflict between temperance organizations and those of the liquor industry. Regulations formulated by legislative bodies have been the incorporation less of consistent policy and designed control than of compromises, special concessions, exceptions, and arbitrary requirements. The atmosphere of mutual distrust between the two power alignments, of which these have often been the products, is not conducive to enforcement.

As other power elites, such as health, welfare, and law-enforcement people, researchers, and tax officials, become more professionalized and articulate their values, regulatory laws can become more symmetrical. Administrative rule making also permits a more rational adaptation of means of control to ends. If the regulatory model is to work efficiently, however, conflicting elites must be able to believe that their values can be realized or preserved through regulation. Those persons and groups who have to bear the heaviest sacrifice of values must be able to find alternatives.

The organization and jurisdiction of regulatory agencies present as yet unsolved problems of this control model. In large, heterogeneous societies like our own and perhaps that of Russia, a high level of uniformity in regulations coupled with centralized control over alcohol use carries a strong probability of resistance. On the other hand extreme decentralization of control and dependence upon purely local agencies invite connivance and circumvention of rules where they deviate from local drinking customs or run counter to interests of local power elites.

Although this model is not designed to liquidate values associated with drinking or even drunkenness, it may nevertheless have this effect through regulations which significantly alter the form or pattern of drinking. In areas where public opinion does not support such regulations or the actions of the enforcing agencies, the result often is simply to add extraneous behavior to the form of drinking without appreciably modifying it. Thus a rule specifying that children and youth may not enter a liquor establishment unless food is served there may do nothing more than cause proprietors to install a bare minimum of restaurant equipment. Requirements that wine and liquor can only be served with meals may simply have the effect of adding the cost of a meal to the liquor bill.

Where lawyers or legal-minded elites set the policies of regulatory agencies there may be little understanding of the functions and values of drinking groups and related institutions. Historical studies and research reports both have shown a significant relationship between drinking groups and the persistence of primary groups' values (20, 29, p. 25 f.). Ignorance or disregard of such facts easily vitiates regulation. In this country many states have regulations against extending credit in bars and taverns. Yet frequently the success of such a place depends upon personal ties between customers and barkeepers. Hence many of the latter put drinks "on the tab" or "hold" personal checks as a means of giving credit. Not only does the regulation often fail in its purpose, but it also plays a part in many bad-check offenses.

The chief means for implementing regulatory rules are suspensions and withdrawal of distributors' licenses or, in the case of monopoly systems, manipulating the number of outlets and their hours of sale. Along with these are the withdrawal of ration cards or "buyer surveillance" (23), techniques aimed at errant individual drinkers. Behind all of these is the possibility of police action for persistent and flagrant violators.

Distributors and retailers unquestionably can be hurt economically and made more receptive to rules by suspension or revocation of licenses. Furthermore, experiments in rural Finland have shown that placement of sales outlets does have some limited effects upon the kinds of alcoholic beverages consumed in certain population categories (21). No workable methods yet have been invented to control the individual drinker or drinkers who want to "beat the system." If motivation is strong enough such persons will find ways of circumventing the regulations. Furthermore, controls focused upon the excessive drinker often inconvenience or alienate persons who comply with the form and meaning of the regulations. Even in Scandinavian countries, where a strong tradition of government paternalism prevails, ration cards and "buyer surveillance" have not been popular (23).

This underscores the importance of public opinion in securing cooperation necessary for regulatory control. The cooperation of local law-enforcement officials is equally important. A broad area of responsibility for dealing with consequences of drinking must always remain with the local community because it must deal with disturbances of public order, offenses against the family, and juvenile offenses, which in varying degrees involve drinking and drunkenness. Legal procedures and coercive controls, such as fines and jail sentences, are poor methods for handling such cases because the consequences of punishment often are worse than the offense.

MODEL IV

The Costs of Intoxication and Drunkenness Can Be Reduced by Substitution of Functional Equivalents of Drinking

This model has received most attention in England where it has been the subject of investigation under the heading of "moderating influences" and "counter attractions" (29). It has interested those who see excessive drinking as a symptom of some kind of "deprivation" of human beings due to defects or omissions in social structures (2, 39). It carries the assumption that values satisfied through drinking or drunkenness can be fulfilled through other activities. It calls for an engineering-type reorganization of community life so that time, money, and interests devoted to drinking will be redirected into sports, games, gardening, radio listening, motion picture, travel, and similar diversions. Improved housing to make family life more attractive and building of community centers also are envisioned as part of this model.

In certain kinds of internally controlled or isolated community situations where boredom and apathy or social isolation have reached critical proportions, diversionary activities may very well decrease the extent of drunkenness. This has been observed in military encampments and isolated outposts (36). Comparable data are also at hand in the history of a missionary system of control among Salish Indians of British Columbia where religious pageantry organized by Catholic Oblates for a time, at least, successfully replaced whiskey feasts and decreased other forms of drunkenness (26).

It is, of course, naive to expect to convert urban communities into analogues of military camps or missionary societies. Short of this the best that can be done is to introduce new programs, such as recreation, into situations where many other variables cannot be controlled, and to look for changes in the amount and forms of drinking. This is a crudely empirical procedure and can be very costly. Where heavy economic costs must be met, as in housing development, business and governing elites will not easily support the programs.

Despite these reservations this model may have usefulness in many situations which occur in contemporary societies. Here we think of logging camps, long-term construction projects in sparsely settled areas, technical research teams, and diplomatic corps in foreign countries, as well as of military installations throughout the world. Wherever there are situations in which centripetal social integration operates, manipulation of social participation may be significant in reducing drunkenness.

This model has an appeal to the researcher because in the kinds of situations which have been specified it may lend itself to rigorous testing. An important task in such research would be to ascertain whether in given cultural contexts drinking is inescapably associated with attaining certain value satisfactions. The obverse of the question is whether drinking or drunkenness is symptomatic for societies in the same way that some psychiatrists hold it to be for individuals. This also merges into a query about the influence of values on the selection of narcotics, stimulants, and sedatives by societies, similar to the problem of "symptom choice" in psychiatry.

CONCLUSION

As yet, no model of social control has been evolved which has been greatly effective for diminishing the costs of excessive drinking. Research is complicated by the fact that the adoption of control programs and a decline in drunkenness both may be functions of changes in larger value systems. In general, those societies and groups which place a high value on sobriety and a low value on intoxication do not have a need for extensive social control. This is subject, however, to the qualification that drunkenness among a small number of persons whose roles express basic values of the society or drunkenness at vulnerable junctures in an industrial system magnifies the need for control. Presumably the necessary controls are more easily established under such conditions.

Societies which place a high premium upon the pleasures of drink and which have the greatest need for control are inclined to reject programs of control or to sabotage them if they are established. Members of these societies who do not share the drinking values or who perceive their high costs may be unable to make their voices heard in the arena of government or in community councils. If they do, they risk unpopularity and ostracism. France is an almost classic example of this situation.

Large societies with mixtures of ethnic minorities, diverse locality, and occupational groups make it unlikely that any one model will suffice to eliminate socially harmful drinking. The problem of choice of a model is complicated by the fact that drinking may be, in turn, a culture pattern, a symptom of psychic stress, a symbolic protest, or a form of collective behavior. Yet a technologically oriented society inexorably demands that drinking, whatever its form, not be permitted to disrupt crucial social integrations which cut across many groups. Formulation of these requirements in the areas of industry, communications, health, and family life probably can only be done by controlling elites "from above." Achievement of these minimum conformities in drinking behavior can best be implemented at the "grass roots" level in particular groups where resources for control at the level of informal interaction can be tapped and brought into play (23).

An example of the possibilities in such a process was the decision of English labor groups and associations in the nineteenth century to remove their meetings from public houses. According to some writers (41), this was important among other influences bringing about a decline in drunkenness during this period. Returning to our present-day situation, there is little hope that state officials or police can directly control such indigenous cultural growths as office parties at Christmastime, New Year celebrations, "martini luncheons," "beer-bust" picnics, and general weekend and holiday drinking behavior. It does seem possible, however, that employers' groups, professional groups, unions, clubs, and civic associations which are close to drinking phenomena can assume a larger share of responsibility for such control.

The problem of establishing communication between these groups and responsible control agencies is formidable, and it requires more than legal instrumentation. When drinking takes place adventitiously or when it is a form of protest or alienation from society—as with much teenage drinking and with "bottle gangs" in Skid Row—control through the cooptation of groups is difficult if not impossible. It is here that direct regulation, unsatisfactory though it may be, must be applied.

Control of any kind is a marginal influence in social and cultural change—a consideration no less true of action to reduce the costs of intoxication and drunkenness. Control cannot create behavior *de novo*, but it can strengthen existing tendencies by articulating unspoken values and by organizing the unorganized dissidents in a population. Further, it can define programs of action in a way to minimize resistance or gain the support of otherwise opposed or indifferent groups. Whether this can be done best at the local, regional, or national level is a question best left to research and open-minded experimentation.

No effort has been made here to devise and discuss a model of control for the addictive drinker. Models suitable for limiting drunkenness in whole societies most assuredly will not apply to the alco-holic. The nature and ordering of values in these persons is such that they usually are unmoved or even made hostile by symbols of control which have an effect upon other drinkers. The extreme tensions under which they labor and their disturbed social interaction distort their value systems in complex ways which preclude the communication necessary for control. Such pathological drinkers presumably can be made responsive only through specially invented therapeutic models of control.

REFERENCES

1. Bacon, Selden D., "Alcohol and Complex Society," in *Alcohol, Science and Society*, New Haven, Conn.: Journal of Studies on Alcohol, 1945, pp. 190–193.
2. Bales, Robert F., "Cultural Differences in Rates of Alcoholism," *Quart. J. Stud. Alc.*, 6:482–498, 1946.
3. Benedict, Ruth, *Patterns of Culture*, New York: New American Library (Mentor Books), 1958, pp. 78–82.
4. Bonner, Hubert, *Social Psychology*, New York: American Book Company, 1953, pp. 185–192.
5. Catlin, George, *Liquor Control*, New York: Holt, Rinehart and Winston, 1931.
6. Cherrington, Ernest H., *Standard Encyclopedia of the Alcohol Problem*, Westerville, Ohio: American Issue Publishing Company, 1925, pp. 5–7; 37–39.
7. Chittenden, Hiram M., *The American Fur Trade of the Far West*, Vol. 1, New York: Frances P. Harper, 1902, Chapter IV.
8. Cottrell, W. F., *Research for Peace*, Amsterdam: North Holland Publishing Company, 1954.
9. Cumming, Elaine, and John Cumming, *Closed Ranks: An Experiment in Mental Health Education*, Cambridge, Mass.: Harvard University Press, 1957.
10. Davis, Kingsley, "Mental Hygiene and Class Structure," *Psychiatry*, 1:55–65, 1938.

11. Efron, Vera, "The Tavern and Saloon in Old Russia: An Analysis of I. G. Pryshov's Historical Sketch," *Quart. J. Stud. Alc.*, 16:484–505, 1955.

12. Glad, D. D., "Attitudes and Experiences of American-Jewish and American-Irish Male Youths as Related to Differences in Adult Rates of Inebreity," *Quart. J. Stud. Alc.*, 8:406–472, 1947.

13. Goode, William J., "Social Engineering and the Divorce Problem," *Ann. Amer. Acad. Pol. Soc. Sci.*, 272:86–94, 1950.

14. Haggard, H. W., and E. M. Jellinek, *Alcohol Explored*, Garden City, N.Y.: Doubleday, Doran and Company, 1942.

15. Horton, Donald, "The Functions of Alcohol in Primitive Societies: A Cross-Cultural Study," *Quart. J. Stud. Alc.*, 4:199–319, 1943.

16. Howay, F. W., "The Introduction of Intoxicating Liquors Amongst Indians of the Northwest Coast," *British Columbia Hist. Rev.*, 6:157–169, 1942.

17. Johnson, W. E., *The Liquor Problem in Russia*, Westerville, Ohio: American Issue Publishing Company, 1915.

18. Kelbert, M., and L. Hale, *The Introduction of Alcohol into Iroquois Society*, unpublished manuscript, Department of Anthropology, University of Toronto, no date.

19. Kluckhohn, Clyde, *Navaho Witchcraft*, Papers of the Peabody Museum, Vol. 22, No. 2, Cambridge, Mass.: Harvard University, pp. 52–54.

20. Kolb, John H., *Emerging Rural Communities*, Madison, Wis.: University of Wisconsin Press, 1959, p. 60 f.

21. Kuusi, Pekka, *Alcohol Sales Experiment in Rural Finland*, Helsinki: Finnish Foundation for Alcohol Studies, 1957.

22. Landis, Benson Y., "Some Economic Costs of Inebriety," in *Alcohol, Science and Society*, New Haven, Conn.: Journal of Studies on Alcohol, 1945, pp. 201–221.

23. Lanu, K. E., *Control of Deviating Drinking Behavior*, Helsinki: Finnish Foundation for Alcohol Studies, 1956.

24. Lee, Alfred, "Techniques of Social Reform: An Analysis of the New Prohibition Drive," *Amer. Sociol. Rev.*, 9:65–77, 1944.

25. Lemert, Edwin, *Alcohol and the Northwest Coast Indians*, Publications in So-ciety and Culture, No. 2, Berkeley, Calif.: University of California Press, 1954, pp. 303–406.

26. ———, "The Life and Death of an Indian State," *Hum. Org.*, 13:23–27, 1954.

27. ———, "The Use of Alcohol in Three Salish Indian Tribes," *Quart. J. Stud. Alc.*, 19:90–107, 1958.

28. ———, "An Interpretation of Society's Efforts to Control the Use of Alcohol," in *Alcoholism—Society's Responsibility*, Berkeley: California State Department of Health, 1958.

29. Levy, Hermann, *Drink: An Economic and Social Study*, London: Routledge and Kegan Paul, 1951, pp. 136–141.

30. Lolli, Giorgio, et al., *Alcohol in Italian Culture*, Glencoe, Ill.: Free Press, 1958.

31. MacLeod, William C., *The American Indian Frontier*, London: Kegan Paul, French, Trubner and Company, 1928, chapter III.

32. Mead, Margaret, "Public Opinion Mechanisms Among Primitive People," *Pub. Op. Quart.*, 1:5–16, 1937.

33. Meighan, Clement, Personal Communication, Department of Anthropology and Sociology, University of California, Los Angeles, 1952.

34. Mignot, André, *L'Alcoolisme: Suicide Collectif de la Nation*, Paris: Cahiers des Amis de la Liberté, 1955, p. 83 f.

35. McIlwraith, T. F., *The Bella Coola Indians*, II, Toronto: University of Toronto Press, 1948.

36. Moore, Merrill, "The Alcohol Problem in Military Service," *Quart. J. Stud. Alc.*, 3:244–256, 1942.

37. Myerson, A., "Alcohol: A Study in Social Ambivalence," *Quart. J. Stud. Alc.*, 1:13–20, 1940.

38. Nordhoff, Charles B., and J. N. Hall, *Pitcairn's Island*, Boston: Little, Brown and Company, 1934.

39. Poirier, Jean, "Les Sources de L'Alcool," *Alcool en Oceanie*, Paris: Mission des Iles, No. 66, 1956.

40. Salone, Emile, "Les Sauvages du Canada et les Malades Importées de France au XVIIIe Siècle: La Picote et l'Alcoolisme," *Journal de la Société des Américanistes*, 4:1–17, 1904.

41. Samuelson, James, *The History of*

Drink, London: Trubner and Company, 1878, chapter VIII.

42. Sáriola, Sakari, *Drinking Patterns in Finnish Lapland,* Helsinki: Finnish Foundation for Alcohol Studies, 1956.

43. Smith, Adam, *The Wealth of Nations,* London: Methuen and Company, 1950, pp. 456–457.

44. Snyder, Charles R., *Alcohol and the Jews,* Glencoe, Ill.: Free Press, 1958.

45. Straus, Robert, and Selden Bacon, *Drinking in College,* New Haven, Conn.: Yale University Press, 1953, chapters 6 and 9.

46. Thursten, Lauren A., "The Liquor Question in Hawaii . . . ," Manuscript Collection, University of Hawaii Library, no date.

47. *Translation of the Laws of the Hawaiian Islands Established in the Reign of Kamehameha III* (manuscript), Hawaiian Missionary Children's Society Library, Honolulu, 1842.

48. White, Leslie, *The Pueblo of Santa Ana,* Pub. *Amer. Anthrop.* New Series, 44, 1942, p. 69.

49. Wraxall, Peter, *An Abridgment of the Indian Affairs, Contained in Four Folio Volumes, Transacted in the Colony of New York, From the year 1678 to the year 1751* (edited by Charles H. McIlwain), Cambridge, Mass.: Harvard University Press, 1915.

PREVENTION CAN BE MORE THAN A WORD

Selden D. Bacon, Ph.D.

What is prevention, what are we doing about it, and what could we be doing? If I had only heard yesterday for the first time about the new American movement against alcoholism, my guess would be that almost nothing of a planned, disciplined nature was being done about the prevention of alcoholism. The reason for such a guess would be this: movements concerned with health and behavioral problems don't start off with prevention of the problem phenomena as a major goal. The typical progress of such a movement begins with recognition and labeling of manifest symptoms, alleviation of the worst symptoms; moving to the attack on earlier stage symptoms, to study and experimentation with techniques of control, to study of measurable causes; and then, if the problem continues to hurt people, on to preventive action. Planned, disciplined, significantly supported and activated work on the level of prevention tends to come late in the history of such a movement.

There are various sorts of prevention. Furthermore, each of these preventions might be put in one of two categories: those whose emergence occurs largely as an unexpected by-product and those whose emergence is related to organized planning and activity.

From *Realizing the Potential in State Alcoholism Programs,* Hartford, Conn.: Connecticut Commission on Alcoholism, 1959, pp. 5–18. Reprinted by permission of the author and Alcoholism Division, Connecticut Department of Mental Health.

PREVENTION THROUGH THERAPY: A BY-PRODUCT

I would like to cite one example to illustrate, first, one of the various types of prevention, and second, that what is defined, long after the fact, as prevention may have been a secondary, tertiary or even non-existent motive of those activating the process.

There is a widespread belief, and it has at least some illustrative material to back it up, that alcoholism is a progressive and long-lasting condition, that once the alcoholic has passed the point of "loss of control" he will continue as an alcoholic, getting progressively sicker, until he dies. Only if there is an interruption can the condition be halted. I do not say this

will stop the progression and eliminate the symptoms of an alcohol ingestion nature) has frequently and convincingly been shown.

These therapeutic successes have not in and of themselves cut down the incidence of alcoholism, that is, the number or rate of new cases per year. This is true by definition. However, they have cut down the prevalence of alcoholism; that is, the total number of cases existing in any one year, in a most significant fashion; this is so *if* the belief in inevitable continuity until death is wholly, largely or even only partly true.

For example, let us assume 1,000 cases of recovery or persistent arrest of the condition in 1940, with the following 9 years showing the vast increases generally reported, as in Table 1.

TABLE 1   ESTIMATED NUMBER OF YEARS OF NONALCOHOLISM IN RECOVERED ALCOHOLICS SINCE 1940

Date of Therapy	No. of Cases	Years of Recovery for Each	Total Years of Nonalcoholism
1940	1,000	× 10	10,000
1941	2,000	× 9	18,000
1942	4,000	× 8	32,000
1943	7,000	× 7	49,000
1944	15,000	× 6	90,000
1945	25,000	× 5	125,000
1946	40,000	× 4	160,000
1947	50,000	× 3	150,000
1948	60,000	× 2	120,000
1949	70,000	× 1	70,000
1950	274,000		824,000

belief has been verified in disciplined fashion; it very definitely has not. I do say that this is a widespread belief, that there is illustrative case material which tends to reinforce it, and that its converse (i.e., that therapeutically oriented attempts

With such figures, and they are not unreasonable, we can say, quite accurately and legitimately (if the inevitable continuity hypothesis is correct) that from 1940 to 1950, if none of these cases died, 824,000 years of alcoholism were prevented. If just these cases remain nonalcoholic and alive through 1959 and their life expectancy prior to treatment was 1960 or beyond, then we will have added a further 2,740,000 years of prevention. And we still, by the direct effect of our therapy, will not have prevented the appearance of one new case. Lest anyone feel that these figures are an exaggeration, let me add that, if the underlying belief of inevitable continuation until death is 50 per cent or more true, the figures are almost certainly a gross understatement. This example demonstrates a type of prevention enormously significant for what may be termed the public health problem of alcoholism. It is, however, only one type of prevention and, paradoxical as it may sound, prevention (viewed in a different light) did not operate in a single one of these cases; by definition they all became alcoholics.

FOLLOW-UP

The other aspect of this illustration to which I would draw attention is that the individuals and organizations active in the therapeutic process described above were little concerned with the idea of prevention. As a matter of fact, they aren't too much interested in 1959. Follow-up studies are the bare, minimal essential by which one could find out if there was any persistence to the therapeutic interruption. Without concrete statements of the nature of the condition at the time of presentation, the nature of the interruption and the nature of comparable conditions at the time of follow-up, there is not even the possibility of follow-up. I know of only one organization dealing with a good number of cases over a period of 4 or more years that has followed up in any disciplined fashion even 30 percent of

those cases from each of 4 or 5 years for as much as 4 or 5 years.

However, even if the facts didn't so obviously show this lack of interest, it would be fairly obvious from the statements and activities of the therapists, whether psychiatrists, clinics, A.A.'s as groups or as individuals, missions, or others. With the partial exception of A.A., all seem to view alcoholism much as an individual, time-bound, predominantly physiological illness. A.A. has both practices and sayings indicating their belief that the condition is not time-bound. However, A.A. has a philosophy which makes any recordkeeping practically impossible; nor would I for a moment suggest that they attempt to get into this field. To almost all the groups concerned alcoholism would seem to be a condition which is located inside an individual. Therapy would seem to be a process directed at that individual and for the most part it is, as far as the therapist is concerned, completed in less than 6 months, often in a much shorter time. Rarely are cases actively carried for longer periods, certainly less than 10 percent of the whole, and frequently the individual is to be labeled as a particularly dependent person who is substituting the therapist for his bottle.

There are some exceptions to this. A.A. attempts to create an additional, new group life for the individual and also, and this is most important for the present consideration, attempts to find new individuals for the sake of others. They define those others as individuals but those others can be defined as a group. And this group is intended to last through time, longer than the therapy, longer even than the life of the individual. We know that this happens; it may well be an unintended by-product.

GROUP THERAPY

Group therapy will jump to the forefront of some minds, but group therapy is in fact a misnomer. What is called group therapy is obviously individual therapy which is conducted in a group setting. The group is not expected to persist; its life is judged entirely in terms of the therapist's convenience or the progress of a given number of the members in other settings. Group therapy refers to a time-bound, individual-bound perception of alcoholism.

Group work with the husbands and wives of alcoholics is an exception in a different direction. Often it starts as a reaction to the perception that alcoholism is partly a product of a relationship between husband and wife. I say that such a therapeutic action often *starts* with such a perception; this often leads to the insight that the wife or husband is another individual with a different individual sickness. Then a second individual therapy pattern is commenced. Sometimes groups of husbands or wives or both are convened for therapeutic purposes; here again, it is individual therapy utilizing a group situation.

I have extended my remarks on the individual-bound and time-bound philosophy of these therapies for alcoholics because the subject is so pertinent for the major subject I wish to discuss. You might call it therapy for alcoholism instead of therapy for alcoholics. Being an optimist I call it prevention. It is another sort of prevention from that described earlier. Let me recapitulate on the first type: it affected prevalence, not incidence; it has probably been of tremendous importance quantitatively as a direct preventive; it was largely unplanned; it has not been of great interest to therapists or therapy organizations as can be seen both in their failure even to check on its reality and in their philosophy of treatment which is to view the alcoholic as an isolated individual who will or will not be a successful case within a matter of months.

Prevention of alcoholism can be greatly helped, I believe, through the sort of prevention I have just described. In other words, all this prevention of prevalence may indirectly have an impact on incidence. If so, it is an untested and surely an unplanned impact.

PLANNED PREVENTION

I would like to turn to planned prevention of alcoholism. At first glance this might seem an impossible sort of goal in terms of any sort of realizable achievement. If we don't know the trend in annual incidence, how could we ever know whether it was decreasing or increasing, whether any efforts we were to make were having the desired effect, the opposite effect or any effect at all? I think the aspect of impossibility is perfectly reasonable. It is, however, only one aspect. As I will point out later it rather clearly indicates two areas for realistic work toward the alcoholism prevention goal.

SOME ETIOLOGICAL FACTORS

There are other ways for working toward the prevention of alcoholism. I wish to speak of some ways which might be termed etiologic rather than epidemiologic. Because we don't have an adequate epidemiology, we can hardly expect our analysis of causes to be perfect. We do, however, have far more adequate perceptions of cause today than were available 20 years ago.

At our present level of knowledge and disciplined opinion, what are the chief causes of alcoholism? I will present my own list. The relevance of this list is to be found in the process of looking at areas of what are roughly termed cause, measuring them in terms of their extent, of their importance for the emergence of the condition, and of their susceptibility to change or reversal by organized, planned activity. I have selected five causes: (1) Alcohol itself, especially its pharmacological properties as they affect the central nervous system. (2) The possibility of physiological differences in individuals making for greater or less susceptibility. (3) Psychological deviation, imbalance, or anomaly which, if not essential prior to the alcoholism, is almost necessary to explain its persistence. (4) The drinking culture and its activation through social mechanisms. (5) The culture and its activation through social mechanisms as it relates to chronic drinking deviation, especially that deviation known as alcoholism.

I am hypothesizing that these five, or at least four of them, are essential factors in the emergence of alcoholism in that if you knock one of them out or significantly modify its nature, action or strength, then you will knock out alcoholism or significantly modify its nature, action or strength. If our notions of cause are even generally in the right direction and if we can significantly attack one of those causes, then we will note impact on both prevalence and incidence even without much exact or society-wide epidemiologic knowledge. This very sort of effort, if it progresses even in the smallest way, will greatly add to our techniques for developing a better epidemiology.

ATTACKING THE CAUSES

ALCOHOL　　To evaluate and categorize the possibilities of preventive action for alcoholism which might stem from direct attack on one or more of the hypothesized areas of cause, we may readily start with that labeled number one—alcohol. This attempt has been made on a very wide basis in our country. There have been several trials, each lasting for 10 years or so. The trials failed. There can be no questioning of the proposition that in the absence of alcohol there can be no alcoholism. However, we do not live in an isolated logical abstraction. There are undoubtedly many reasons to explain the failure of Prohibition to eliminate alcoholism. For purposes of this presentation many of them are irrelevant. I would draw your attention, however, to the following. Alcohol as a beverage has many physiological, psychological and sociological functions other than those related to or causative of alcoholism. It would seem rather obvious that alcoholism only follows upon the use of alcohol in a small, small minority of cases. As a target of attack this area of cause is, in view of the many other functions of alcohol, an uneconomical target. When one attacks this target, one immediately takes on a wide variety of other targets that are not only irrelevant to alcoholism but also have values and organizations which will resist.

PHYSIOLOGICAL FACTORS　　The physiological target, if it exists, and to the extent that it may be crucial for the emergence of the condition, is a most economical target. But it is a tremendous gamble. Even if ever discovered it may not be crucial in 30 or 60 or 90 percent of the cases. I firmly believe that action for prevention should proceed along these lines.

The type of action will be laboratory research followed by testing along lines to be developed by an emerging epidemiology. We can all hope for progress and support the work of those in this line of prevention.

PSYCHOLOGICAL FACTORS   The psychological target is that which has received the greatest amount of verbal attention in recent years. I am referring to etiological orientation. Alcoholism is discussed and dealt with primarily in terms of psychological imbalances or deviations and of concrete manifestations of individual drinking behaviors. This orientation has moved out from research and therapeutic circles to dominate discussion and presentation in the world of mass media. The more sophisticated approaches, such as those of most clinics and of A.A., heavily emphasize the importance of the general psychological factors, viewing the concrete behavioral deviations as signs of or results of this individual psychological imbalance or anomaly. This orientation perceives alcoholism as arising from and as existing within an individual.

Unfortunately, for purposes of attack of a preventive nature on alcoholism (and this is to be contrasted with attack of a therapeutic nature on one alcoholic) this area is at least as broadly pervasive as was the first, that of alcohol itself. No single psychological mechanism, process or pathology has been found unique to alcoholism. Every such pathology asserted to be of key significance for alcoholism is found widely in nonalcoholics, both among nonalcoholic drinkers and among teetotallers.

To attack mental ill health in order to prevent alcoholism is, to the extent that alcoholism stems from mental ill health, a logical step. It becomes even more logical if, in addition, some mental ill health stems from alcoholism. Furthermore, distinguishing this area of cause from that of alcohol itself, practically everyone will agree that attacking mental ill health is in itself a good thing. I think it must be perfectly clear to all, however, that this would be an attack on an area vastly greater than that of alcoholism, and on an area whose own causes are as diffuse and ill defined, if not more so, than those of alcoholism itself. This is not an economical area for those specializing in alcoholism to take as a major target for specific attack. It is a closely related area. However, the specialists in alcoholism will accomplish more for both fields by emphasizing their own competencies. That they should cooperate perhaps even integrate with those in mental health is probably a wise undertaking.

THE DRINKING CULTURE   To my own way of thinking the culture and social activation of drinking forms, together with alcohol itself, the crucial factor in the emergence of alcoholism; I do not feel, however, that this is the best target for those concerned with the prevention of alcoholism. The culture and social activation of drinking cover a far, far wider field than that of alcoholism. The impact of an attack in this area will require a long, long time before it can be measured. Many values only distantly related to alcoholism will be involved, and the attempts to change such values may instigate conflicts which would seem pretty irrelevant and hardly worth the effort to those concerned specifically with alcoholism. Preventive work on this level is in some ways analagous to preventive work concerned with mental health. Unless changes occur, alcoholism will presumably continue. Certainly preventive work on alcoholism will aid preventive work in the field of social and cultural disorganization related to the use of alcohol. Cooperation, perhaps integration, with any working on those problems would probably be a wise step.

THE TARGET OF CHOICE

Cultural Attitudes toward Alcoholism

And so we come to the fifth area, the one I believe to be the target of choice: That part of the culture and its social activation which relates to chronic deviations from the drinking culture, especially the deviations called alcoholism. The phenomena referred to are those behaviors and expressed attitudes both of individuals and groups which repeatedly occur in patterned fashion as responses to what is called alcoholism. In addition, for purposes of more extensive and more intensive understanding, one should consider repeated, patterned responses in the society to other deviations and irritations which are in any way similar to alcoholism. This will allow us to see the cultural items and social mechanisms which are available but which are not recognized or at least are not used in this particular situation.

I will not attempt more than a brief, oversimplified and, for purposes of exposition, perhaps exaggerated recapitulation of these phenomena. The most obvious response is perhaps that of avoidance, both an intellectual and a physical avoidance. Individuals, families, unions, business management, insurance companies, the military, the healing and health professions, and on and on have been avoiding perception of the problem. Much of this is passive avoidance; some of it is active avoidance. By "active" I mean that positive steps requiring money, time, energy and personnel are utilized to block recognition or action.

A second phenomenon occurs after recognition of the fact of chronic irritating deviation directly related to alcohol usage in an individual can no longer be avoided. This phenomenon is the use of mislabeling. It may be conscious or unconscious, based upon ingenuity or ignorance. The label may be the common cold, "nerves," emotional instability, sowing wild oats, grief, accident or kidney disease. The label may be applied on a death certificate, in a disciplinary hearing, in a cocktail conversation or by an alcoholic himself in utilizing some alibi which he all too shrewdly perceives will be accepted by many in the society.

A third phenomenon, one which also appears after recognition can no longer be avoided, but which accepts the idea that deviant consumption of alcohol is an important factor in the situation, is to fall back on archaic and useless responses such as cursing, ridiculing, beating, hiding, covering with maudlin sympathy, arguing with, lecturing at, pleading with, firing, fining, imprisoning, ostracizing, shaming, and putting into operation all the quack-therapy activities temporarily available in the society.

This is enough to indicate what is meant by repeated and patterned responses to the occurrence of chronic painful deviation related to consumption of alcohol in a given individual. If going to alcoholism clinics, to physicians active and able in this field, and to A.A. is a more satisfactory response, then it is very doubtful if as much as 10 percent of the estimated number of alcoholics has shown this response in the last 20 years, doubtful that 1 per cent show it any one year.

INFLUENCE OF ATTITUDES ON THERAPY

I would first like to indicate the impact of the typical responses and typical attitudes on the therapeutic process. A study by Trice[2] on acceptance and rejection of A.A. is directly relevant to this subject. Mr. A and Mr. B, both alcoholics, come to the alcoholism clinic or to a physician or to an A.A. group. Let us state that they each have made four visits during a period of 10 days. Each has a wife, each has a close friend, each has a relationship with another individual who is a supervisor or close associate on the job. These three people are emotionally and behaviorally significant others. This, of course, puts them in a remarkably different spot than that occupied by the therapist who is not only a stranger but a threatening stranger, one who is going to steal from the alcoholic his great satisfaction in life and who is going to analyze him as if he were a bug on a pin and who is going to try to ram some esoteric philosophy, perhaps called religion or psychiatry or an adjusted life, down his gullet.

If Mrs. A and A's buddy and A's workaday associate or boss all agree that the clinic or A.A. group or that a doctor or an individual A.A. are no good, hypocritical, stuffed-shirt meddlers who can't do Mr. A any good and if they further indicate that Mr. A is a weakling, a sissy and no friend of theirs if he continues visiting these people, there is a very good chance that Mr. A will not be a good bet for recovery through the clinic, the physician or the A.A. approach. Let me postulate that Mr. B is psychologically, socially, physically and drinking experience-wise as identical with Mr. A as possible, but that Mrs. B, B's buddy and B's business associate or supervisor think that his new therapeutic venture is just about the smartest thing he ever did, that it is pretty sure to work and that he has

[2] Trice, H. M. A study of the process of affiliation with Alcoholics Anonymous. Quart. J. Stud. Alc. 18: 39–54, 1957.

gained new and significant respect from them because of this action. Then I think there is a very good chance for Mr. B's recovery.

This example relates to the social mechanism as it directly affects the individual alcoholic after he has been recognized as a chronic problem drinker. Now let us turn to the cultural setting and the social mechanisms on a less direct level. From this level we may get insight into the factors lying behind and supporting the positions of the two sets of wife, buddy, business associate and the accepting target of their actions. Mr. A's church, the druggist or old gentleman down the street or popular columnist or even doctor who serves as Mr. A's fountainhead of health knowledge, Mr. A's dear old mother and Mr. A's one-time social drinking cronies implicitly or explicitly agreed that a drunk was a weak-willed or weak-witted excuse for a human being or was inevitably a particularly nasty type or was someone who "inherited bad blood and that was that" or who was a strong-willed sinner. Or they may have quite clearly expressed the belief that a great many men were "that way" and it wasn't particularly surprising and only nosy-Parkers and cops bothered about it anyway: Why shouldn't a man get plastered and throw his weight around a bit every once in a while?

These are common responses in our society. They reflect social values and they reflect perceptions of cause and effect in human behavior which are directly in conflict with current therapies for achieving recovery from alcoholism. These general responses can be strongly backed up by incidents and by the reporting of incidents which are interpreted in ways harmonious with the theory or value. They can be further reinforced by the absence of counter-values, counter-explanations and counter-incidents, especially when such counter-views are present and are active and are recognized in closely related problems. However, when there are doctors and nurses and clinics and when there are chronic cases who have gotten well through their advice and service and when industry, unions, management, and the armed forces and the church effectively spread these counter-values, explanations and their success, when the druggists and popular cartoonists and columnists and movie stars express these counter-views, then the power of the attitudes and behaviors which block acceptance of therapy are reduced.

I am emphasizing by indirection a definition of alcoholism which goes beyond the usual orientation suggested, if not, indeed, explicitly posed by usual psychiatric explanations. I am saying that alcoholism, at least its persistence through time, is a product of social interaction. This does not deny, nor is it incompatible with, descriptions of alcoholism given in terms of individual psychic or emotional process. However, I will go out on a limb and state that I believe in 90 percent of what is called alcoholism that without the social interaction favorable to its origination and persistence, alcoholism will not occur, or, if it should start, will be easily stopped. I will pick out another limb and state that social interaction and cultural settings with only the most minor and fleeting psychic maladjustments are the major factor in perhaps 25 percent of all those conditions commonly called alcoholism. Let me add that in this case, I would fully expect larger psychic problems to emerge later in many instances, but not all.

This means that only when the cultural values and social interaction patterns are favorable, will individual therapy direct-ed towards psychological problems be frequently effective. As a precondition, alcohol consumption by the affected individual must cease.

CULTURAL ATTITUDES AND PREVENTION

Just as mental health in general lies behind the psychic healths relevant to alcoholism, so do the cultural and social mechanisms related to use of alcohol lie behind the cultural and social mechanisms related to chronic deviation from drinking. Preventive work in the field of alcoholism will necessarily approach both these fields. But the economical target for the specialist in alcoholism will rest in the areas of immediate and directly related phenomena. In relation to therapy, this may be equally divided between attack on the psychic causes and attack on the social interaction and cultural causes. In relation to prevention, however, cultural and social factors will be the significant point of attack.

I am proposing that this can occur as an unconscious by-product and that it also can be rationally planned, organized and activated. It is my belief that insofar as it is presently occurring, this sort of process is largely unplanned or, when recognized as an important function, is so recognized on a verbal level, is given little in the way of time, money, personnel, organized effort, or measurement of effectiveness. Whether in service or research, to put it conversely, the lion's share of those resources goes to individual therapy. It is commonly stated by social workers, by physicians and by A.A. members, that a crucial factor in therapy is "the readiness" of the alcoholic candidate; they define readiness as a state of affairs internal to the candidate. I am proposing that "readiness" is only in part internal to the individual, that it is almost always, perhaps always, a function of social interaction and cultural values.

Three different methods of meeting the problems of deviation from cultural values and social interaction patterns have been attempted. One of these is to change the individual so that he can rejoin the preferred cultural and social setting. This could be attempted through intensive psychotherapy.

A second way is to add an additional group existence with pertinent cultural values and social interactions to the individual's store of memberships. This can be attempted through Alcoholics Anonymous. Again, the individual's past cultural values and systems of interaction must be fairly compatible with the demands and philosophy of the additional group and so must be his other current activities and memberships because, pertinent as the new group may be, it is only an addition to the past and present, not a substitute for them.

A third mode of attempt, one being experimented with in some of the halfway houses, is the development of a new form of association which will not be just an addition but will cover the larger part of the individual's life. As Rubington[3] has pointed out, this new form must be related in many significant ways to the socially constructive and rewarding ways of the older life (with alcohol taken out) or it is unlikely to succeed.

MODIFYING CULTURAL ATTITUDES

There is, however, a fourth way or set of ways to meet these problems of social value and social interaction. It is the

[3] Rubington, E. The chronic drunkenness offender, Ann. Amer. Acad. Polit. Soc. Sci. 315: 65–72, 1958.

mode of attack I am proposing. It is the modification of selected areas of value and social action in selected segments of the existing community; it is the attack upon those typical patterned and repetitive reactions of nonalcoholics to the facts of alcoholism. This mode of attack, like the previous three, will aim directly at more effective therapy but will in addition aim at prevention.

We have heard a good deal about desocialization in the development of individual alcoholics and a good deal about resocialization in individual therapy. I am suggesting that we have been explaining both processes and attacking both processes almost entirely in terms of one aspect of or one party to this interactional phenomenon; that for purposes of therapy this has frequently been ineffective; and that for purposes of prevention it has been close to irrelevant.

Only very briefly will I suggest the structuring of rational, organized action requisite for such a goal. I am not unmindful of the difficulties to be faced by any group which attempts to move in the proposed direction. Many such groups evaluate themselves and request the public to evaluate them in terms of numbers of alcoholics who are helped. Many social workers have turned themselves into individual therapists and have gained real gratification in this work. Alcoholics, their families and friends want help for the individual who bothers them; they may well object to time, energy, money, and personnel being withdrawn from helping alcoholics to be used in attacking alcoholism. They too would like to visualize alcoholism as being something inside abstracted individuals.

Let no one interpret my remarks as

suggesting that therapeutic efforts should be given up or that therapeutic efforts with individuals have no preventive value. I consider that approach to be essential. I also believe, however, that if 80 percent or more of an alcoholism service's efforts are directed towards this individual therapeutic goal, it is an unbalanced and inadequate type of program.

Furthermore, the broadcasting of speeches and pamphlets, the holding of occasional conferences for unspecified audiences or for unspecified purposes, the repeated announcement of slogans or appeals for general sympathy do not form in my estimation a rational program for the modification of attitudes and behaviors. They are a start in that direction, perhaps a necessary start. They are quite crude, however, and may have unfortunate results. For example, the simple statement that hospitals should open their doors to alcoholics and the achievement of that simple goal—without analysis of the quite realistic factors which caused the original door closing and without careful preparation which will allow different results from those of the past—is likely to increase not decrease unfavorable attitudes and behaviors.

METHODS OF ATTACK

Attack along these lines will call for expert description and analysis of the existing values and patterns of action related to the facts of chronic drinking deviators. There will then be assessment of the more and less significant of these values and patterns as they block therapeutic processes or block recognition of the facts. There will be assessment also of the probable susceptibility of these negatively significant attitudes and behaviors to planned modifying action. There will

then be description of the attempted modifying action itself, followed by measurement at timed intervals to record such changes as may have occurred in the phenomena which were attacked. It might prove efficient to have a total community attack on all the undesirable values and behaviors, but this would be a very difficult approach to utilize in any undisciplined, measurable fashion in this problem in the setting of large and complex communities. In any event, a more limited attack on specified goals is clearly available and, if successful, makes a later attempt at total approach all the more likely to be useful.

I take it for granted that those organizing such work will recognize that in relation to the various values and behavior patterns which block recognition of cases and block effective therapy, there are different categories of alcoholics, different strata of people in the community, and different classes of individuals in each stratum.

EFFECTS OF ACTION

Any modification of these negative values and practices will not only result in more effective therapy for a given alcoholic, but will also make possible recognition and therapy for alcoholism generally. This is one reason why this target is more economical for prevention than the target of rehabilitating individual alcoholics. Another reason for choosing this target is that it will help to cut down incidence as well as prevalence. This is because attitudes and actions, such as avoidance, mislabeling and the use of archaic, ineffective reactions to alcoholism, not only serve to protect and reinforce the already developed case, they also bring cases into being. Attitudes and practices towards drinking deviations do not function solely after alcoholism or chronicity of deviation has been established. They go into operation when the deviation occurs, whether it be an isolated instance, a first instance, or the 21st instance in a series. To change the nonalcoholic side of the interaction which results in alcoholism will be in many, I happen to believe the majority, of cases as effective as dealing with the other side of that interaction.

Furthermore, limiting the attack on attitudes and practices to those which concern responses to deviation will increase the motivation to accept the proposed changes and there will be comparatively little antagonism toward such changes. The opposite may well be the case if changes are directed toward alcohol, toward all drinking customs or toward all the targets involved in the area of mental health. In these instances the targets are so broad that specific motivation is hard to oragnize and many, many toes will necessarily be stepped on, resulting in organized antagonism.

SUMMARY

Finally, let me return to the proposition that there are many types of prevention and perhaps many ways of achieving each. I am selecting one type and deliberately arguing that it is more needed than the others. I am deliberately challenging those present on two fronts: first, there isn't much real interest in prevention anyway and second, what interest does exist is of a narrow, individualistic nature which can at best affect prevalence alone and probably prevalence in one or two types of alcoholism only.

In attempting to challenge, I may have overstated the case for one mode of prevention and thus belittled the other modes. To avoid this belittling, may I conclude by stating that the epidemiological approach is in my estimation an essential for eventual increasing control and prevention, that attack on the problematic role of physiological susceptibility must not be dropped, that work on psychological processes and alcohol and on cultural and social processes related to drinking is necessary for eventual success. Individual therapy has, albeit in unplanned fashion, already contributed to the very possibility of these other attacks and it will continue to be an essential for the continuation of these other attacks. The role, for example, of Alcoholics Anonymous in making possible the eventual development of prevention can hardly be overestimated, although as you are all aware, this was not and is not its purpose and is probably hardly recognized by the membership as a significant fact.

So, although I will defend the thesis that the outstanding direction for achieving future potential lies in modification of the negative attitudes and practices of the relevant nonalcoholic public, I will also plead for preventive activity of all sorts, planned or unplanned, organized by laymen or by specialists, directed toward long range and general or toward short range and specific goals. The future potential of our field, however, is above all to be expressed not in terms of individual therapy but in terms of social prevention.

ALCOHOLISM AND COMMUNITY
CARETAKERS: PROGRAMS AND POLICIES*

Thomas F. A. Plaut, Ph.D., M.P.H.

Persons with alcoholism and other problem drinkers constitutes a significant proportion of the clientele of most community helping agencies. However, usually such agencies prefer not to deal with these patients and few have given any particular attention to them. In recent years health and social welfare agencies have begun to develop new approaches and special programs in providing care and treatment for problem drinkers.[1]

The magnitude of alcoholism and other types of problem drinking virtually precludes the establishment of a special network of services for this cate-

gory of patients. The burden of providing care necessarily then falls on the general community agencies. The challenge is to overcome the continuing neglect by the bulk of these general caregivers and to develop adequate services at the community level.

Impact of Problem Drinkers on General Helping Agencies

Large numbers of problem drinkers are in contact with various helping agencies. While these persons often are even identified as problem drinkers, in many instances they receive little or no treatment for their drinking problems.

The impact of problem drinkers on major American care-giving agencies is illustrated by the following statistics. In 1963 over 70,000 men were admitted for the first time to the nearly 300 state mental hospitals in the U.S. Twenty-two percent (15,957) of these patients were given an alcoholic diagnosis.[2] Among women patients the proportion with alcoholic diagnoses was far lower—only 5.6%. Because problem drinkers generally have

* This is a revision of a paper presented at a conference, "Treatment Methods and Milieus in Social Work with Alcoholics," sponsored by the Social Welfare Extension, University of California (Berkeley), in cooperation with the Institute for the Study of Human Problems, Stanford University, at San Francisco, December 3, 1965.

I am deeply grateful to Sidney Cahn (Stanford University) and Thomas Scheff (University of California – Santa Barbara) for their careful and critical review of this paper.

[1] At the Federal level there has been greatly increased interest and activity. Several bills have been introduced to establish alcoholism programs; an Intra-Departmental Committee on Alcoholism has been meeting regularly in the Department of Health, Education and Welfare; President Johnson specifically referred to alcoholism in his 1966 Health Message; and a center on Alcoholism is being established by the National Institute of Mental Health.

[2] *Patients in Mental Institutions, 1963: Part II—State and County Mental Hospitals*, U.S. Department of Health, Education and Welfare. National Clearinghouse for Mental Health Information, Public Health Service Publication No. 1222, Washington, D.C., 1964, p. 21.

a short duration of stay in mental hospitals (in California averaging less than two months), the proportion of *resident patients* with an alcoholic diagnosis is far lower—generally under 6% of all patients.

In nine states alcoholic disorders lead all other diagnoses in mental hospital admissions. The majority of these patients are not psychotic, and in many states most are admitted on a voluntary rather than a committed basis. Most still have some ties to their families, and the majority are upper-lower class or lower-middle class.

The number of psychiatric wards in general hospitals is rapidly increasing, and currently more patients are admitted annually to these wards than to the state mental hospitals. The proportion of the patients who are alcoholic is virtually identical to the figure for mental hospitals. In 1963, 23% of the men and 5.9% of the women admitted to the community-based psychiatric facilities were diagnosed as alcoholic.[3] In these facilities too, the duration of stay for the alcoholic patients is short—often lasting for only a few days, i.e. until the "detoxification" is completed.

Over 500,000 adult patients are seen each year in general psychiatric clinics.[4] While the proportion of these patients diagnosed as alcoholics is very small, only 3% to 4%, the total number is between 15,000 and 20,000.[5] The total number of patients seen annually by the approximately 135 specialized alcoholism clinics probably also is under 20,000.

The impact of problem drinkers on the medical-surgical wards of general hospitals is illustrated by the following study.[6] The extent of drinking problems among one hundred consecutive male admissions to a general hospital was determined. No preselection was made in terms of the diagnosis of the patient, and the hospital did not have a psychiatric service. The admitting physicians identified twelve of the one hundred men as problem drinkers, and seventeen additional cases of "probable alcoholism" were uncovered by the researcher, making a total of 29%. Case-finding of problem drinkers in this population is, then, relatively easy.

The relation between economic dependency and drinking problems has been much discussed. However, only a few studies have been made of the incidence of drinking problems in welfare case-loads, and there is little information on the causal relation between the problem drinking and dependency.

The Federal Welfare Administration reports that alcoholism was found in 14% of closed A.F.D.C. cases.[7] In 1964 the Westchester (New York) Department of Public Welfare undertook a study of the frequency of various social and health problems in public assistance case-loads. Alcohol problems were found in 26% of the households. However, "emotional instability" was reported for 75% of the households, marital problems in 69%, children out of wedlock in 27%, and chronic health problems in 40%.[8] The Wyoming De-

[3] *Ibid., Part III—Private Mental Hospitals and General Hospitals with Psychiatric Facilities*, p. 41.

[4] Rosen, B. M., Bahn, A. K., and Kramer, M. "Demographic and Diagnostic Characteristics of Psychiatric Clinic Outpatients in the U.S.A., 1961." *American Journal of Orthopsychiatry,* 34: 455–465, 1964.

[5] Bahn, A. K., "Outpatient Psychiatric Clinic Services to Alcoholics, 1959." *Quarterly Journal of Studies on Alcohol.* 24: 213, June, 1963.

[6] Pearson, W. S., "The Hidden Alcoholic in the General Hospital: A Study of 'Hidden' Alcoholism in White Male Patients Admitted for Unrelated Complaints." *North Carolina Medical Journal,* 23: 6–10, 1962.

[7] Unpublished study of the American Public Welfare Association.

[8] *Monthly Report Bulletin,* County of Westchester, Department of Public Welfare, Vol. 4, No. 10, October, 1964.

partment of Public Welfare reported the proportion of cases in different categories where alcohol was a "factor contributing to need"; in O.A.A. 6% were so designated, in A.D.C. the figure was 11.5%, and in General Welfare 25% of the cases.[9] The Massachusetts Department of Public Welfare reported that 14% of 2,359 cases requesting disability assistance were suspected of having a drinking problem.[10] The Edmonton (Alberta) welfare agency examined its various case-loads and found the occurrence of severe drinking problems ranged from 10% to 17%.[11]

Welfare agencies, in addition to having different policies about acceptance of clients, also vary in what they label as a "drinking problem." Variations in this "labelling" process result, at least in part, from differences in the attitudes about drinking on the part of the staffs. While the relationship between drinking problems and the onset and persistence of the dependency is not demonstrated by these studies, it is clear that problem drinkers frequently are found in welfare families.

Many arrests involve alcohol-related offenses. The impact of problem drinking on the American police-legal system is graphically illustrated by the following figures. In 1963, out of 4,438,000 arrests in the U.S. for all offenses, over 1,515,000 were for public drunkenness (34%). In addition, there were 218,000 arrests for driving while intoxicated. Another 490,-000 individuals were charged with disorderly conduct—which some communities use in lieu of the public drunkenness charge. Thus approximately 40% of all arrests are for being drunk in a public place or being drunk while driving.[12] A word of caution must be added here. Many persons arrested for public drunkenness are no more intoxicated than countless other individuals who escape arrest because they are not as exposed and "vulnerable" to police detection as "Skid Row" men. The public is more likely to insist on police removing the unshaven, toothless, poorly clothed man than an equally drunk visiting businessman!

Low Priority of Assistance to Problem Drinkers in American "Helping" Agencies

In view of the large numbers of problem drinkers in the U.S.A., and the extent to which these people are among the clientele of virtually all helping agencies, it is rather striking how little focus there has been on this area by the major professional associations. Psychiatric, medical, social service, or public welfare agencies generally also have not taken the responsibility for ensuring appropriate attention to these patients. For example, despite substantial improvement in recent years, medical care for the acute effects of excessive drinking still leaves much to be desired. The fact that a man's condition is due to the intake of large amounts of alcohol has a great impact on how he is handled by hospitals—or by physicians in private practice. One of the factors influencing the medical care is the appearance and "stance" of patients as they present themselves to the physician.[13]

However, the neglect of the behavioral aspects, i.e. the drinking problem itself,

[9] *Public Assistance Cases Where Alcohol is a Factor Contributing to Need*, 1965, Wyoming State Department of Public Welfare, Cheyenne, Wyoming.

[10] *Massachusetts Mental Health Planning Project Report*, Massachusetts Department of Mental Health, 1965.

[11] Wass, D. K., "Public Welfare and the Drinking Problem," *Progress*, The Alcoholism Foundation of Alberta, Vol. VI, No. 4, pp. 64–68, June, 1964.

[12] *Crime in the United States—Uniform Crime Reports—1963*. Federal Bureau of Investigation, U.S. Department of Justice, Washington, D.C., 1964.

[13] Wolf, I. Chafetz, M. E., Blane, H. T., and Hill, M. J., "Social Factors in the Diagnosis of Alcoholism: II. Attitudes of Physicians," *Quarterly Journal of Studies on Alcohol*, Vol. 26, No. 1, March, 1965.

is even more striking. Few physicians are interested in or feel qualified to help a patient overcome his drinking problem. The same can be said of psychiatrists, who generally believe that problem drinkers cannot be helped by the same methods used for other psychiatric patients. Problem drinkers constitute only a small fraction of total case loads in psychiatric clinics. While few clinics have explicit policies excluding problem drinkers, generally the staff feel unable to help these patients, and as a result, most alcoholic patients get "screened out." Other community agencies, often aware of the lack of interest in psychiatric clinics, do not make referrals. Most mental hospitals are ambivalent in their attitude towards the many problem drinkers admitted to their wards. The short duration of stay and frequent absence of any real treatment for these patients are indicative of this attitude.

Let us compare the reaction of mental hospital staff to three patients: The first is a schizophrenic man admitted to the hospital for the third time in a two-year period. The staff will be concerned about him, will wonder how the treatment could be improved this time. Second is a man admitted for the third time in the same period because of a suicide attempt. Again the hospital staff will be concerned, but also puzzled, perhaps a bit disappointed, and they may consider keeping the man in the hospital longer. The third returning patient is a problem drinker. Here, the reaction is more likely to be one of irritation, anger, and even punitiveness. Comparison with the suicidal patient is particularly instructive, because "self-inflicted" elements also are clearly present in that condition. However, the negative reaction to the alcoholic patient is likely to be far stronger—and less sympathetic.

Individual and cultural responses to problem drinking cannot be understood without examining certain characteristics of "normal" drinking practices. Alcohol use in our society is surrounded with many ambivalent attitudes and ambiguous norms. Serving drinks is an intrinsic part of being a good host—of contemporary hospitality patterns. Yet it is unclear how much one should drink, and considerable guilt and discomfort may accompany over-drinking. Drinking is associated with pleasure, with indulgence of impulses in a culture that still retains strong elements of a Protestant ethic stressing the importance of hard work, of self-control and of personal responsibility. Because most Americans get pleasure from their drinking, and are able to control it adequately, there is a tendency to feel that the problem drinker should also be able to control his drinking. The complicated feelings that most Americans have about their own and other persons' use of beverage alcohol, probably have delayed the development of more adequate services for problem drinkers. Despite the increasing awareness that problem drinkers need help, there remains a strong belief that the condition is self-inflicted, i.e. that the man could stop his destructure drinking if he "really" wanted to. The heritage of Prohibition and the long history of moral and religious controversy about drinking have contributed to the mixed attitudes, lay as well as professional, towards persons with alcohol problems.

Further difficulty has been created by confusion of the medical and behavioral aspects of the condition. Because problem drinkers may require medical attention for immediate (or long term) consequences of drinking, there is a tendency to stress the importance of the medical management to the exclusion of the psycho-social management. This is demonstrated in the almost universal isolation, at least in the U.S.A., of detoxification services from services of a psycho-social nature. Few alcoholism clinics or psychiatric clinics have any working relationship with medical facilities providing care and treatment for acute intoxication.

Until very recently—and it is still substantially true—there were three major step-children of the mental health field. All three are problems affecting many persons, and all are areas where psycho-social understanding is essential for the care and treatment of the affected persons. The three are: (1) mental retardation, (2) problems of old age, and (3) problem drinkers. There probably is more potential for interrupting destructive life styles and improving functioning in alcoholism than in either of the other two conditions.

Some Characteristics of Services for Problem Drinkers

Currently there are three major types of services for problem drinkers. These are: special programs in mental hospitals, alcoholism clinics, and half-way houses. Over 10% of the 286 state mental hospitals have special programs for problem drinkers. Most programs consist of separate wards for these patients; others, however, just have special activities for these patients. Often admission to the programs is restricted to voluntary patients. Generally the wards are open, but off-hospital ground privileges are rarely granted. Most programs make some use of didactic procedure—group discussions, lectures or movies. Formally scheduled individual psycho-therapy is extremely rare. The major form of treatment almost always is group therapy. Recovered alcoholics generally are part of the staff, and often exert

a great influence on the treatment philosophy. A sort of "anti-alcohol" culture often is created in the hospital wards, with the staff encouraging almost continuous discussions among the patients. These discussions often are extensions, in only slightly altered form, of what goes on in the more formal group therapy sessions.

Almost without exception, the alcoholism programs prefer patients with better levels of social functioning, i.e. those who are still members of intact families and have recently held a job. Skid Row men are rarely found in these special programs. A sizable minority of the programs have fixed periods of stay with regularly scheduled activities for each week. The length of these fixed-duration programs ranges from three to six weeks.

Often the alcoholism unit is located in an older, somewhat isolated part of the hospital. Professionally too, the programs generally are isolated; psychiatric residents and hospital social work trainees do not spend time on the alcoholism unit. Often the units receive little help from the hospital social service staff or from other specialized personnel. A striking shortcoming is the almost universal inadequacy of after-care arrangements. Rarely are arrangements made for any post-hospital treatment. Referral to local A.A. groups is the extent of the after-care program in many hospitals. No models for the treatment of problem drinkers have as yet been established in the community mental health centers. Current plans include special services for problem drinkers within some of these centers, such as a small number of specially designated beds as part of the in-patient service or a separate out-patient clinic for these patients and attaching of special personnel to the center.

At present there are approximately 135

specialized alcoholism clinics in the U.S.A.; however, only a minority of these clinics are open on a full-time basis. Many function in a manner similar to psychiatric clinics, with the staff usually consisting of psychiatrists, social workers, and psychologists. Public health nurses are included more often than in general psychiatric clinics. Most treatment is provided by non-medical personnel, especially social workers. Many clinics are directed by social workers and psychologists, more so than in the general psychiatric field. However, all clinics do have psychiatric consultation available. While many clinics do suggest to patients that they attend A.A. meetings, few recovered alcoholics are on the staff of these clinics.

While generally the clinic staff members are psychodynamically oriented, there usually is emphasis on "confrontation," supportive therapy, and dealing with reality problems rather than "insight." Patients generally are seen weekly, and while the use of group therapy is growing, the primary modality still is individual treatment. The clinics often try to involve families in the treatment program. Many clinics use some tranquilizing drugs and antabuse, and often rely heavily on such medications. Only a small proportion of the patients initially appearing at these clinics eventually enter the treatment program. (This, of course, is also true for general psychiatric clinics.) Most alcoholism clinics have a screening process which often eliminates those patients not suited to the particular treatment regime offered by the facility. Generally the clinics serve primarily lower-middle class patients with a few from a slightly higher socio-economic group. Most patients are still with their families and most men have recently been employed or are employeed at the time of treatment. Usually there are three to four times as many men as women patients. Homeless, "Skid Row" men are practially never found in the alcoholism clinics.

While the alcoholism clinics tend to be more in the mainstream of psychiatric practice than the special mental hospital programs, even the clinics are usually rather isolated from other psychiatric services. Where alcoholism clinics do have working relationships with other agencies, it often is on a "one-way" basis. That is, the other agencies refer cases to the clinics, but there is little subsequent referral from alcoholism clinics to such agencies.

Half-way houses (or recovery homes) for problem drinkers are found in many areas of the country. The name "half-way house" often is a misnomer, because most residents do not come directly from a mental hospital or a correctional institution. These facilities, almost always small (under 30 beds), have been established outside the system of community helping agencies. The majority have been developed through the efforts of A.A. members. Residents are expected to obtain employment in the community and to contribute regularly towards their room and board. Other than A.A. meetings, there usually is little treatment, although some facilities are beginning to work with professional agencies. The "staff" of the homes generally are recovered alcoholics. The financial status of the homes often is very precarious and many have not survived. Strict rules exist about sobriety, and admission and discharge policy usually is in the hands of the resident manager. Residents rarely are long-time Skid Row men, but often they have had very uneven employment histories, particularly in recent years, and generally they are separated from their families. There are few half-way houses for women. The "anti-alcohol" norms of these houses are very striking. The men spend a great deal of time talking about their drinking problems, and the A.A. "sobriety" ideology is constantly being stressed.

Half-way houses have arisen to fill a void in community services. There clearly is a need for the development of these "intermediate" types of facilities. However, half-way houses should be brought into a better relationship with the other helping agencies.

The Issue of Motivation

In most agencies providing treatment for problem drinkers, the key screening criteria is the patient's motivation (or sincerity). Often it is assumed that motivation is an all-or-none affair. If present, the patient can be "worked with"; if absent, nothing can be done until the patient "really" wants to control his drinking. The impact of Alcoholics Anonymous on the thinking of professional workers is reflected in this view of motivation.

The former attitude of rejecting all problem drinkers has now been shifted to an acceptance of those who are "motivated," and a rejection of the remainder. There also often is the belief that there are very clear-cut stages through which problem drinkers pass before becoming "true" alcoholics.[14] In some clinics considerable staff time is spent in determining whether a patient is a "true" alcoholic—even though the treatment implications of such labelling are unclear.

To dismiss a large proportion of problem drinkers as "unmotivated" is an abdication of professional responsibility. If current approaches and techniques are ineffective with many patients, then new methods and approaches must be developed. Evidence is accumulating that

changes in operation and treatment philosophy can have a substantial effect on an agency's ability to work with "unmotivated" patients. Recent work at the Massachusetts General Hospital[15] has demonstrated that such changes can radically increase the proportion of those patients referred from an emergency service who subsequently come to an outpatient clinic for treatment. A similar experiment has recently been reported in improving the utilization of alcoholism clinic services by women released from a correctional institution.[16] The use of "motivation" as a criteria for screening also often excludes patients from variant cultural backgrounds, particularly from the lower socio-economic strata, who may not be comfortable with the style of operation of middle-class clinics. The expectations that one will talk about one's problems, that other family members should be involved, and that one must come at a fixed time every week are alien to many lower class persons. The need to overcome excessive reliance on certain types of therapeutic approaches is not, of course, restricted to alcoholism clinics. It applies equally to most general psychiatric agencies and many other helping services.

ALCOHOLICS ANONYMOUS AND PROFESSIONAL PROGRAMS

Alcoholics Anonymous has had an immense impact on public attitudes and professional programs. However, there are some elements of Alcoholics Anonymous, its orientation, and the attitudes of many members that bring it into conflict with professional workers. Many persons

---

[14] See Jellinek, E. M., *The Disease Concept of Alcoholism*, College and University Press, New Haven, Conn., 1960.

[15] Chafetz, M., *et al.*, "Establishing Treatment Relations with Alcoholics," *Journal of Nervous and Mental Diseases*, 134: 395, 1962.

[16] Demone, H. W., Jr., "Experiments in Referral to Alcoholism Clinics," *Quarterly Journal of Studies on Alcohol*, 24: 495, September, 1963.

in A.A. feel there is little place for professional services (except for medical care) in the rehabilitation of problem drinkers. The success of A.A. and the widespread knowledge of its work have led the public and many professional community "care-givers" to expect A.A. to shoulder major responsibility for the rehabilitation of problem drinkers. "Since A.A. does such an excellent job, why do we need alcoholism clinics?"

A.A. has operated differently than most other mutual-aid groups, because of the "all-purpose" function it seeks to fill for many problem drinkers. However, many A.A. groups, and individual members, are now less antagonistic towards persons in A.A. seeking additional help from professional agencies. It should be kept in mind that the principles of A.A. have only limited applicability to the operation of professional services, and that probably A.A. will never be able to work with more than a tiny fraction of all problem drinkers.

CHARACTERISTICS OF ADEQUATE COMMUNITY SERVICES FOR PROBLEM DRINKERS

Below are listed some essential characteristics of services for problem drinkers:

(1) A range of different services must be provided—emergency, in-patient, out-patient, and intermediate. These services must be inter-related to ensure continuity of care and optimal utilization.

(2) The services must be of sufficient magnitude to meet the need. For example, one ten bed half-way house in a city of 500,000 is inadequate to the needs for this type of care.

(3) Services for problem drinkers should be staffed primarily by personnel skilled in assisting patients with psychological and social problems.

(4) Medical facilities serving problem drinkers should be equipped to deal with behavioral as well as medical aspects. Medical treatment of the acute and chronic effects of excessive drinking only rarely influences basic drinking problems.

(5) Facilities must serve a wide range of different problem drinkers. Different agencies will have to offer services to different types of problem drinkers. Since agencies prefer clients from higher socioeconomic groupings,[17] there should be services of equal quality for different social class groups—and each will have to be attuned to the particular characteristics of that sub-culture.

(6) Services for problem drinkers must be coordinated with the major "care-giving" services in the community—mental health, public health, medical care, public welfare, etc. Large numbers of problem drinkers are known to these agencies, and they will have to provide much of the help and treatment for these patients.

The Special Problem of Skid Row

The current police handling of persons found drunk on the streets is generally acknowledged to be archaic, ineffective, and inhumane.[18] The bulk of the persons arrested are homeless, isolated men, and thus the public drunkenness problem must be seen in the context of Skid Row. However, Skid Row is not primarily an

[17] Pittman, D. J., and Sterne, M. W., *Alcoholism: Community Agency Attitudes and Their Impact on Treatment Services*. National Clearinghouse for Mental Health Information, National Institute of Mental Health, U.S. Department of Health, Education and Welfare, U.S. Government Printing Office, Washington, D.C., Public Health Service Publication No. 1273.
[18] Two recent court decisions barring the criminal imprisonment of "chronic alcoholics" for public intoxication have focussed public attention on this issue. (*Easter* vs. *District of Columbia*, U.S. Court of Appeals, D.C., No. 14365, 1966 and *Driver* vs. *Hinnant*—F, 2nd—Fourth Circuit Court of Appeals, 1965.)

alcohol problem. Because Skid Row men live outside the larger society, special facilities probably are needed to assist these persons with their economic, social, and psychological problems. They generally do not "fit" into the existing structure of helping agencies.

Leadership in providing care for homeless men and women will probably have to come from public welfare departments. The health and social problems of these persons are so interwoven with economic difficulties that public assistance agencies are logical foci for such services. However, welfare departments alone cannot undertake this task. They need assistance from traditional professional care-givers, as well as from new agencies, such as the Office of Economic Opportunity and the Department of Housing and Urban Development.

Is It Desirable to Establish Separate Services for Problem Drinkers?

It has often been suggested that adequate treatment for problem drinkers can only be provided if a special network of services is established. However, there is increasing agreement that establishing any substantial number of specialized services is neither feasible nor desirable. Many of the services needed by problem drinkers already exist in American communities. The objective should be to ensure that these services are strengthened, supported and made available to problem drinkers on an equal basis with other patients. The establishment of specialized services could weaken rather than strengthen the activities of the key "care-givers" is assisting problem drinkers. There is evidence that the general care-giving agencies will "dump" problem drinkers on such specialized services. That is, a special alcoholism clinic in a community may provide an additional

"excuse" for psychiatric clinics to reject these patients. Or, if there is a specialized in-patient unit in a city, general hospitals are even less likely to admit alcoholic patients.

There is also a danger that specialized services will operate in isolation from the community helping services—thus weakening the effectiveness of these agencies with alcoholic patients and re-enforcing the belief that problem drinkers are very, very different from other patients. The presence of even limited special alcoholism facilities may also create the erroneous impression that much is being done for this patient group, that the problem is being handled.

There are three major reasons why treatment for problem drinkers should be provided through the basic "helping" services: (1) Drinking problems are of such magnitude that sufficient funds and manpower probably could not be mobilized for a special network except by "robbing" other needed programs; (2) Drinking problems do not exist in isolation from other social, psychological and health problems. It is inconceivable that any system of specialized facilities could be established to deal adequately with all these associated problems. (3) Large numbers of problem drinkers are already known to major care-giving agencies, and often are obtaining some kinds of help from these agencies. The separation of this type of help from assistance for the problem drinking would be unfortunate and possibly even disastrous.

Ensuring Appropriate Attention to Problem Drinkers—The Role of Specialized Personnel and Programs

Until work with problem drinkers becomes fully assimilated into the activities of agencies such as mental hospitals, community mental health centers, general hospitals, welfare agencies, health departments, etc., there will be an important role for special alcoholism staffs. The long neglect of this area makes essential reliance on specially trained and oriented personnel. However, such specialists should work primarily in educational, catalytic, supervisory, and consultative capacities, rather than solely in direct treatment relationships with alcoholic pa-tients. These specialists can: (1) provide consultation to community care-giving services, and (2) stimulate the development of needed mechanisms for the planning and coordination of programs for ensuring continuity of care.

There must be some means of ensuring proper emphasis in alcoholic-related services, lest problem drinkers become lost or "buried" within the larger structure of the agency and the neglect of alcoholic patients continue. The alcoholism specialists seek to bring about social change, to influence agency operations and policy. Their knowledge of the needs of problem drinkers, of the existing services, and their skills in community organization should enable them to assist agencies in providing better services to problem drinkers.

Specialized services for problem drinkers will be needed for certain purposes; to demonstrate that problem drinkers can be helped, to provide a training opportunity for personnel who subsequently will work in other generalized agencies, and to undertake research studies.

ALCOHOLICS ANONYMOUS

Harrison M. Trice

Alcoholics Anonymous is a fellowship of compulsive drinkers, both men and women, who join with each other in a mutual effort to remain sober. It was started by alcoholics themselves in their despair and hopelessness and has apparently achieved a success as great as, if not greater than, professionally directed therapies.

At both "open" meetings to which the public is invited and at "closed" meetings for alcoholics only, its members frankly narrate their drinking histories—their "stories"—and explain how the A.A. program enabled them to gain sobriety. State-wide "retreats" to some outdoor spot widen the scope of associations. Members travel in small groups to adjacent communities to tell their "stories" and share their program for sobriety at A.A. meetings there. Often two or three members will hold meetings in prisons or hospitals where they explain the A.A. program to alcoholic inmates.

From *The Annals of the American Academy of Political and Social Science,* 315 (January 1958), pp. 108–116. Reprinted by permission of the author and American Academy of Political and Social Science.

The fellowship, however, is more than this. Local groups sponsor dances, parties, and picnics. Families of members who attend such events together often form family auxiliaries with scheduled meetings. Individual members get together to eat lunch, drink coffee; they meet after work, to bowl, fish, and play cards. These informal contacts between members extend the relationship developed at the formal meetings. In this network of interpersonal relations, the "Twelve Steps," listed below, are the core of the joint effort to remain sober.

Membership in A.A. depends solely upon whether or not an alcoholic says he is a member. New members are sought through "Twelfth Step Work," that is, carrying the message to other alcoholics. According to the society's definitions, an A.A. group exists whenever two "drunks" join together to practice the A.A. program for sobriety. There are no officers, no hierarchy, no dues. Local secretaries are necessary, but tenure is short.

Although A.A. is not organized in the usual sense, a common body of tradition underlies the movement. The "Twelve Traditions" set forth the policies that have been effective guides for the society in the past. One of them is a statement of A.A.'s single purpose: to help alcoholics remain sober. Another is to refrain from embracing any cause except the one of aiding alcoholics. Its Traditions keep A.A. apart from any temperance or political movements and allow it to concentrate solely on rehabilitating alcoholics.

This is A.A. in broad outline. It is a group endeavor on the part of alcoholics themselves to find a solution to their crippling compulsion. Out of their face-to-face associations with each other there arises a network of group controls for sobriety that is not present in the usual doctor-patient situation. Members refer to this encompassing experience as a "way of life"—an apt phrase since A.A. is, in essence, an emotionally satisfying alternative to chronic drinking.

A DESCRIPTION OF THE FELLOWSHIP

On a Friday night in a small Midwestern city numerous persons are parking their cars outside a large brick house in the University district. Some of them are wearing casual sport clothes and some are dressed more conservatively; their cars are of all makes and models. Other persons, obviously still in work clothes, are walking from the bus stop toward the house. This is the A.A. clubhouse, and the meeting is scheduled for eight o'clock. But, as one member put it, "We never start then; we have to do some 'coffee-clatching' first."

Inside the meeting hall many more people are standing around and talking in small groups. One man is describing his reaction to telling his "story" last week at the mental hospital, "I saw myself as I used to be, sitting right there in the front row." To others recapitulating last Saturday night's party, a woman is saying, "We had fifty-eight people here. I had a hilarious time and all of it without any booze."

Approximately sixty persons have assembled. A man at the speaker's stand announces that this is the regular Friday night "open" meeting of A.A., and he calls for a moment of silence to be used as each person sees fit. "My name is Jim P. and I am an alcoholic," he begins and explains the general nature of the fellowship. As chairman for this meeting, he has invited two members of a new group in a nearby community to speak this evening. He calls on the first one.

"My name is Dave L. and I am an alcoholic." Dave's "story" is a series of anecdotes embellished with frank humor. Laughter from the group interrupts him frequently. Someone whispers, "If he made it, anyone can. What a lush he used to be!" His excessive drinking landed him in a mental hospital five times. In the process of his alcoholism he went from manager of a chain grocery store to itinerant laborer. His family had forsaken him, and numerous times he heard the ward doctors brand him hopeless. He "hit bottom" after his third attack of delirium tremens. Twice he almost died from them.

Dave had scorned the idea of A.A. when a member came to him during his fourth commitment. "I thought the guy was shooting an angle, but when I finally went to a meeting during the fifth time I was at the hospital, I discovered he wasn't." He repeats several times that he was surprised to learn from A.A. that he was "sick," but that as such he could still be respectable. The idea of a "higher power," a God, was difficult for him to accept. He finished dramatically, telling the group that he has found in A.A. a "bunch of real friends—twice as good as those drinking buddies who pumped me for every cent I had."

The second speaker is a woman. She starts with the customary introduction, "My name is Grace B. and I am an alcoholic." She observes that her "story" is different from Dave's in almost every respect but stresses the common denominator of alcoholism.

Her drinking began in college. After her marriage to a prominent lawyer she gradually became a confirmed alcoholic. There were no mental hospitals, no jails, no "drying out" places for her; but there were large medical bills for politely labeled illnesses. Her father was convinced that she was not capable of caring for her two children and urged her husband to divorce her. Instead, her husband asked his law partner, an A.A. member, to send a "Twelfth Stepper" to see her. Grace had no difficulty in accepting the program as described to her by this woman. "I had been looking for some way to admit to myself and to others that my drinking had defeated me. I found the spiritual emphasis something I had yearned for, but could not find alone."

When she finishes her talk, the chairman comments on his own alcoholic history. His concluding remarks concern anonymity. Alcoholics Anonymous, he explains, makes every effort to protect the names of its members; and it is one of the Traditions to insist on anonymity at the level of the press, radio, and television. After these remarks he asks everyone to stand and say the Lord's Prayer. The meeting is over and the "coffee-clatching" starts again.

At "closed" meetings of fewer members, there is more informal discussion of how the program works—that is, how the members "live this program for twenty-four hours at a time rather than face the hell of living and the rest of our lives without the stuff." Members intimately confess their drinking escapades and often disclose personal problems. A point frequently made to newcomers is, "We did it, so can you."

HISTORY OF A.A.

The society of A.A. has its roots in the Oxford Groups, a religious movement which operated informally through small discussion groups, emphasizing confessions, honesty, talking out of emotional problems, unselfishness, and praying to God as personally conceived. Both cofounders of A.A. had been exposed to the movement and for a short time worked within its framework.

In 1934, Bill W., a New York broker and an alcoholic, had been introduced to the Oxford Groups by an alcoholic friend who was staying sober by attending their meetings and following their precepts. Impressed by the effects, the broker attended their meetings and he, too, was able to remain sober after what he termed "a spiritual awakening."[1]

He promptly tried to convert other alcoholics to his method but failed due to what his doctor called "too much preaching." The physician told him to first convince his prospects that they suffered from a physical allergy and a mental obsession, and mention the spiritual aspects later. Early in 1935 Bill W. tried this approach on a physician in Akron, Ohio, Dr. Bob S., and it worked. They tried it on other alcoholics in Akron, and the first A.A. group grew from these efforts.

Bill W. started another group in New York City, using a modification of the Oxford Group technique. By this time A.A.'s main strategy had been determined; they met in small groups, admitted they were alcoholics, prayed to some conception of God, and sought other sufferers with whom to share their method.

In its efforts to raise money the New York group formed a tax-free charitable trust, the Alcoholics Foundation, with a board of trustees composed of both alcoholics and nonalcoholics. As part of this drive the early members wrote and published their "stories" and their "program" in a book entitled *Alcoholics Anonymous*.[2] Favorable publicity about it created a wave of interest in A.A. during 1939 and 1940. An article in the *Saturday Eve-*

ning Post in 1941 accelerated the sale of the book and a flood of inquiries. Using the book as a guide, groups of alcoholics throughout the country began to hold meetings. The trustees of the Foundation established a headquarters in New York City to answer inquiries and stimulate the growth of the movement.

Without organizational mechanics to guide this sudden expansion, the society experienced a period of confusion. From the policies evolved through trial and error from 1942 to 1946, the headquarters staff formulated the Twelve Traditions to guide local groups. During the late forties when expansion continued, especially internationally, the cofounders and headquarters staff became concerned about linkage of these far-flung developments. The trustees authorized an experimental plan for elected representatives to attend a General Service Conference each year. This gave A.A. more, but very loose organization.

The Conference has no authority over any individual group; it expresses to the trustees the opinion of A.A. groups throughout the movement and in its debates to reach consensus it, in turn, influences local groups. After a five-year trial, the Twentieth Anniversary Convention in 1955 recognized this body as "the voice of the group conscience of our entire Fellowship, and the sole successor of its cofounders, Dr. Bob and Bill."

EXTENT OF A.A. ACTIVITIES

In 1938 there were three A.A. groups and approximately 100 members. By 1944 the movement had 10,000 members in 300 groups in America and Canada. In 1950 there were 90,000 members in 3,000 groups spread throughout the world. The 1957 estimate was 200,000 members and 7,000 groups.

---

[1] *Alcoholics Anonymous Comes of Age: A Brief History of A.A.* (New York: Alcoholics Anonymous Publishing, 1957), p. 63.

[2] *Alcoholics Anonymous* (New York: Works Publishing Company, 1939).

The movement has spread to sixty countries; in all, there are 710 foreign groups with 15,000 members. Although many members are Americans living abroad, the majority are natives. Problems of translating A.A. literature have arisen and there are numerous variations on the A.A. theme.

Alcoholics Anonymous groups hold meetings in institutions in both the U.S. and abroad. In 1957 there were 257 hospital groups with 6,000 members and 296 groups with 15,000 members holding meetings in jails, reformatories, prisons, and workhouses. Approximately 1,000 seamen and "lone" members in remote areas maintain a contact with each other by mail. Al-Anon Family Groups number approximately 1,000; these are relatives of alcoholics who have banded together to overcome the difficulties of having an alcoholic in the family.

Other facets of A.A. activity are the operations of its General Service Board. Alcoholics Anonymous Publishing, Inc. makes available to local groups a wide variety of booklets, pamphlets, and articles on A.A. subjects. General Service Headquarters with a staff of twenty corresponds with groups, institutions, "loners" and answers general inquiries. Members of A.A. throughout the movement contribute their case histories, group discussions, personal impressions of A.A., and group problems as articles in the *Grapevine,* a monthly journal.

THE TWELVE STEPS

The "Program," as A.A. members call it, consists of twelve suggestions for recovery from alcoholism. They originated in the process of writing *Alcoholics Anonymous* when the early members listed specific steps they took to reach sobriety.

1. We admitted we were powerless over alcohol—that our lives had become unmanageable.
2. Came to believe that a Power greater than ourselves could restore us to sanity.
3. Made a decision to turn our will and our lives over to the care of God as we understood Him.
4. Made a searching and fearless moral inventory of ourselves.
5. Admitted to God, to ourselves, and to another human being the exact nature of our wrongs.
6. We were entirely ready to have God remove all these defects of character.
7. Humbly asked Him to remove our short-comings.
8. Made a list of all persons we had harmed, and became willing to make amends to them all.
9. Made direct amends to such people wherever possible, except when to do so would injure them or others.
10. Continued to take personal inventory and when we were wrong, promptly admitted it.
11. Sought through prayer and meditation to improve our conscious contact with God as we understood Him, praying only for knowledge of his Will for us and the power to carry that out.
12. Having had a spiritual awakening as the result of these steps, we tried to carry this message to alcoholics and practice these principles in all our affairs.

One of the most bitterly debated points in the development of the Steps concerned the spiritual references. Atheist and agnostic members challenged the concept of God, and other members objected to doctrinal implications. Slowly, discussion forged a common agreement on the phrases "a power greater than ourselves" and "God, as we understand him." Thus the Steps rest on a broad spiritual base, allowing members practically any conception of spiritual power.

In recognition of the fact that an alcoholic will resist pressure in any form, the Steps were labeled "suggestions." In the permissive tone that has come to pervade

A.A., the Steps are phrased in terms of "we did" rather than "you must."

From the psychological standpoint, the Steps create attitudes that are therapeutically effective for the alcoholic. Step 1 relieves the alcoholic of the need to demonstrate that he can drink like others. Instead of grudging compliance to sobriety, this Step advocates complete surrender. Steps 2 and 3 enable the alcoholic to realize that to remain sober he needs help from outside himself. Alcoholics Anonymous offers the emotional support of the group and of God "as you understand him" as a way to meet this need.

Step 4 recognizes the fantastic rationalizations that the typical alcoholic has constructed to justify his drinking and encourages a constant effort to see these for what they really are. Step 5 helps the alcoholic reduce anxiety by sharing his emotional problems, and Step 8 helps him reduce guilt by making restitutions.

Step 12 proposes that the member continue to see himself as he was in the past by seeking another alcoholic who is not a member and telling him about the program. He makes himself available to the novice for consultation and companionship, reteaching himself in the process.

TYPES WHO ARE ATTRACTED TO A.A.

Alcoholics Anonymous is effective for the alcoholic who can affiliate with it because it gives him a new conception of himself. This change is due to Twelfth Step Work, A.A.'s insistence upon alcoholism as an illness, and the feeling of group solidarity that provides a sense of belonging. He does not feel alone in his efforts to remain sober; all around him are living, breathing examples that the group purpose is within his individual reach. He has become a part of a group that has "found a way out," and this

group stands apart from the rest of the alcoholics even though it constantly seeks their affiliation. A network of mutual obligations, shared emotional problems, and reciprocal aid between members engenders an "in-group" feeling. Finally, this "we" attitude is cultivated in an informal, often casual, atmosphere. Each member is accepted at face value, no questions asked, no censure raised.[3]

Unfortunately, this group therapy takes place *after* an alcoholic has affiliated with A.A. How he came to affiliate with the society in the first place is another matter. Thousands of alcoholics are exposed to A.A. but do not affiliate with it. Many join upon first exposure. What basic differences exist between these two types?

One detailed study[4] of the affiliation process with A.A. found that those alcoholics who affiliated with it differed significantly from those who did not in that: (1) they regarded themselves as persons who could easily share their basic emotional reactions with others, and (2) they also believed that they easily adapted themselves to the casual give-and-take that develops before and after A.A. meetings. Other research shows that affiliates had considerable experience with informal, small groups.[5, 6]

Why does this outgoing, sociable type of alcoholic align himself with a group

[3] Some observers have doubted this "accepting" nature of A.A. See Alan D. Button, "Psychodynamics of Alcoholism," *Quarterly Journal of Studies on Alcohol*, Vol. 17, 1956, pp. 443–60. He states, "A.A. is by no means as 'accepting' as it is advertised."

[4] H. M. Trice, "The Process of Affiliation with A.A.," *Quarterly Journal of Studies on Alcohol*, Vol. 18, 1957, pp. 39–54.

[5] Eugenia Hanfmann, "The Life History of an Ex-alcoholic," *Quarterly Journal of Studies on Alcohol*, Vol. 12, 1951, pp. 405–43.

[6] Joan Jackson and Ralph Connor, "The Skid Row Alcoholic," *Quarterly Journal of Studies on Alcohol*, Vol. 14, 1953, pp. 468–85.

whose chief norm is sobriety? It is quite probable that only those who regard their drinking behavior as symptomatic of a "problem" do so. Affiliates in this study saw few social rewards in the results of heavy drinking. They visualized them as a threat to home, job, and community esteem. They had developed greater emotional conflict about their drinking behavior than had nonaffiliates. They were "ready" to do something about it. Nonaffiliates, on the other hand, associated the pleasures of living with their drinking experiences. "Blackouts," "shakes," even delirium tremens, were not, to them, indicative of an "illness." This was the price paid for a "good time." Furthermore, their drinking behavior brought them prestige among their drinking friends.

Aids and Impediments to Affiliation

Within the broad type just sketched, specific experiences acted to aid or impede affiliation. Nonaffiliates had, in contrast to affiliates, significantly more esteemed friends and relatives who, they thought, had stopped drinking by their own volition. When they went to their first A.A. meeting they were faced with a choice between an unknown A.A. group and acting like their "will-power model." Affiliates, on the other hand, were not faced with such a choice.

Furthermore, nonaffiliates had heard A.A. members described as insincere, and this prejudiced them even more against A.A. Also, nonaffiliates were still actively drinking in well-defined drinking groups as the time they first went to a meeting. Consequently A.A. faced stiff opposition.

The way A.A. groups received newcomers created, at times, further obstacles. Although sponsorship is a vital part of the A.A. technique, the evidence indicates that nonaffiliates were not spon-

sored in the full A.A. meaning of that word. Often they were not sponsored at all; and if they were, it was only a superficial relationship. Whenever the sponsor, however, brought the newcomer beyond their own close relationship to over-all contact with the whole group, the newcomer was more likely to affiliate with the society. Moreover, field observations during this study indicate that some A.A. groups overlook the newcomer; forget his doubts, confusions, and false expectations; and at times decide in advance that "he can't make it."

After attending meetings for a few weeks the probability of affiliating with A.A. was further improved if the wife or girl friend attended the meetings and supported what she saw and heard. Nonaffiliates were not fortunate in this respect. Often their wives presented them with a hard choice; drink with the woman you love or abstain with a group of strangers. Another aspect of family life influenced affiliation. If an alcoholic during the first few weeks of attending A.A. experienced a great deal of support from relatives in his drinking behavior and in the problems deriving from his drinking, he was less apt to become affiliated.

This research also developed a definite hypothesis about the temporary nature of nonaffiliation for many alcoholics. Large numbers of those who turned away from their first contact with A.A. later returned in desperation after trying other methods without success. At this point the individual realized it was literally a question of "do or die." Under these conditions A.A. may be accepted where it had been initially rejected.

These points show that, although there were many A.A. successes, there are also many factors operating against affiliation. Alcoholics Anonymous has been eulogized and analyzed, but seldom have its "negative instances" been scrutinized. Further, specific study of them may reveal how more alcoholics can be brought to sobriety via A.A.

Adaptation to American Society

Since A.A. has been largely an American development certain dominant themes, relatively unique to American society, have influenced it. Individualism, suspicion of established authority, lack of class consciousness, pragmatism, and simplified spiritual experience can be seen as American values to which A.A. has adjusted itself; however, there is only partial adaptation to any one of them.

Alcoholics Anonymous is most ambivalent about individualism. On the one hand, it suggests that the alcoholic admit he is powerless, that his life is unmanageable. This is in opposition to the American norm of "standing on your own two feet," but it is essential if sobriety is to be achieved. On the other hand, members perform many A.A. activities in an individualistic manner. Even though they emphasize group action, they put it in this kind of framework. Thus a recipient of a Twelfth Step call is merely told the member's story and left to decide on any further action himself. Alcoholics Anonymous speakers constantly state, "every one gets this program in a different way— it's up to the individual himself," or, "this is just my story and my opinion; it might not fit you."

When suspicion to establish authority is considered, A.A. has demonstrated a closer relation to the American norm. Even the smallest group retains its autonomy. Alcoholics Anonymous attempts to lodge final determination in the individual groups who, in turn, tend to emphasize the rights of specific members. Even here, there is no complete expression of this value. Informal controls and

guidance form the very stuff A.A. therapy is made of. It has avoided centralized authority, as the structure of the General Service Conference shows, but it has developed a standardized program with authority through its Steps and Traditions. It has never given its cofounders any definite "office" or status; on the other hand, these men have exercised a personal influence that clearly sets them apart.

The same partial adaptation to the American ideal can be seen in A.A.'s lack of class consciousness. Compared to other societies, class differences are minimized in America and A.A. reflects this characteristic. It can do it more effectively than many groups because there is a common malady linking upper, middle, and lower class members. Again, however, the agreement between value and action is not complete. Alcoholics Anonymous groups often divide along class lines. Class factors operate in aiding or blocking affiliation.

Other central values in American life are likewise operative in A.A. behavior. Alcoholics Anonymous is quite pragmatic, paying scant attention to theories about alcoholism and in this respect it mirrors the American emphasis on "practicality," on "doing something." Alcoholics Anonymous' simplified approach to spiritual experiences is compatible with the behavior of many Americans who seek such experiences outside formal churches. However, this parallel is blurred by the fact that members tend to return to their church organizations in response to the spiritual content of A.A. The important point is that A.A., like other face-to-face groups in American life, never fully expresses any one specific theme. American values are too complex, too heterogenous for that. So, although A.A. is composed of deviants as far as drinking is concerned, it is characteristic of the general American scene from which it emerged.

IMPLICATIONS FOR MEDICAL SOCIOLOGY

In addition to physiological therapy techniques are needed in treating degenerative illnesses such as heart trouble, mental illness, and alcoholism. Therapeutic methods extending beyond the purely clinical and into the everyday life of the patient are essential. In this context, A.A. shows the therapeutic potential available in groups of patients assuming responsibilities for their own recoveries. For many alcoholics, medical treatment has joined with A.A. for long-range treatment success. Similar combinations have aided mental patients, tuberculosis victims, the aged, and drug addicts. These extensions of A.A. type therapy indicate that successful follow up in degenerative illnesses may be substantially increased by group processes similar to A.A.

The Al-Anon Family Groups—composed mainly of wives, husbands, and children of A.A. members who hold meetings patterned after the A.A. program—indicate that involvement of close relatives in follow-up therapy is a valuable treatment adjunct. Since these relatives may have developed their own emotional problems because of living with and attempting to adjust to the alcoholic, they may be helped therapeutically by participating in such an auxiliary A.A. group. This, in turn, creates a more favorable environment for the recovery of the alcoholic himself.

Finally, formal group psychotherapy might profitably recognize that A.A. has succeeded because it encouraged the alcoholic to take the active role of therapist through Twelfth Step work. He is not in the subordinate role of "patient" with an "expert" analyzing him. Rather he is playing a protective, helping role toward one who is "still in his cups." It seems reasonable that group therapy in a clinic or hospital setting might incorporate this approach by encouraging patients of some different illness categories to seek out others with similar diagnosis in Twelfth Step fashion, informing them of such group effort and offering hope, support, and guidance on this nonprofessional level.

CONCLUSION

Alcoholics Anonymous is not the only pioneering effort to do something constructive about alcoholism. It was, however, in the forefront of the trend to regard alcoholism as a treatable condition. Rather than moral condemnation or therapeutic hopelessness, A.A. has shown beyond the slightest doubt, that an alcoholic can be rehabilitated.

On the other hand, its therapy tends to be limited to those who can adjust to the intense group life of its program. Consequently many alcoholics are not treatable via its approach. Despite this limitation, A.A. remains one of the chief ways of dealing with alcoholism. As a follow-up method it is unexcelled and, for thousands of alcoholics, it constitutes the main hope for a life free from the compulsive use of alcohol.

11

The Professionalization
of Problem Solving

One of the dominant responses to the many social problems in our society, such as those that have been considered in this book, has been the emergence of a wide variety of new occupations and new occupational groups which have as their major goal the application of human skills and resources to the prevention or amelioration of these problems. For example, urban renewal, community development, housing, transportation, and poverty program specialists, city planners, social workers, guidance counselors, psychologists, city managers, and a whole new variety of law enforcement, rehabilitation and corrections, and public health officers are just a few of the many new occupational skill categories which have emerged in response to the problems of an urban-industrial society. Also, many older and better established occupations such as teaching, psychiatry, the ministry, and architecture have responded by expanding their focus, or by producing new subspecialties within their ranks. For want of a better term, skill groups such as these will be referred to here as *problem solving* professions.

As these problem-oriented occupations emerge, expand, proliferate, and become more visible in contemporary society, it is increasingly clear that they are becoming more and more professionalized. Indeed, increased professionalization may be viewed as an inevitable result of urbanization and industrialization, and as part of a general tendency for almost all occupations to seek some sort of professional status. The motives for this are obvious, for the well-established professions stand at the apex of the occupational prestige structure, their members receive higher incomes than most workers, and they exert greater power by occupying a high proportion of the governing posts in our society.[1]

The traditional view of the professions sees them as tightly organized, autonomous and independent, highly specialized, high in prestige, and monopolistic in their controls over their respective fields of practice.[2] Yet, a contemporary glance at some of the newer, less well-established occupations such as those mentioned earlier would suggest that as a result of rapid social and technological changes now taking place, it may be more accurate to view modern professions as operating in the context of increasingly more complex organizational environments over which they only have very limited control.[3]

As a result, it may no longer be possible for emergent occupations aspiring to higher professional status to take on all of the characteristics of the traditional model of professionalism. For as sociologist Harold Wilensky has suggested, "it seems certain that many occupations will assert claims to professional status and find that the claims are honored by no one but themselves."[4] William J. Goode has further referred to the struggle of many occupations for the benefits of professional status as a zero-sum game, in which the relative position of some occupations inevitably moves down on the power-prestige hierarchy as the position of other occupations moves up. Each occupation that rises does so at the expense of others which it surpasses, and when many occupations are rising, their net gain, in terms of power and prestige, is low relative to one another.[5] Thus, Wilensky's conclusion that perhaps no more than thirty or forty occupations are now fully professionalized probably does represent the maximum achievable limits of full professional status.[6]

In one important sense, then, the professionalization process may be viewed as a continuous struggle, in which the occupations aspiring to professional status are engaged in competition for relatively higher positions of power and prestige in the occupational hierarchy. This tendency is one of the most significant aspects of occupational life in the United States, for it has serious implications concerning the nature and distribution of many vital skills and services, which are currently in great demand and short supply. For example, the amount and type of controls that professional groups exert in regulating the flow of recruits into their respective fields of practice, in setting standards for training and performance, and in providing ethical foundations for professional practice are crucial to the task of providing the full range of services needed and demanded by the larger society.

It will be the task of the rest of this chapter to explore these potential implications of the professionalization process and to assess both their positive and negative consequences for the professionals themselves, for the organizations or agencies that employ them, and for the communities they serve.

THE PROFESSIONAL ASSOCIATION AND PROFESSIONAL STATUS

One essential characteristic of a profession is that its members are formally organized as a professional association. Such an association is necessary, because it is the major instrument for formulating the policies and goals of the profession and developing the procedures for their implementation. Thus, no true profession can exist without such an association.

In the broadest sense, the professional association may be described as a *categoric* unit of social organization. A categoric unit, according to Amos Hawley, is one made up of members occupying a single status category, who unite in a collective attempt to meet common external threats: or to put it another way, to maintain the *status quo*.[7] Hawley's discussion of the function of categoric organizations is particularly pertinent:

Categoric units emerge only in those occupations that have been confronted by challenges which, if unattended, might impair or eliminate the sustenance base of the individuals involved. These are usually the most highly skilled occupations which are often so specialized that the individuals committed to them cannot readily shift to other occupations. The medieval guild and the modern professional association are illustrative of highly developed categoric units.[8]

Professional groups which are well established tend to be protective and conservative in their basic functions. But paradoxically, there may be situations where these functions can best be served by the active promotion of change. This is especially true for occupations in their emergent stages, which are not yet well established. Therefore, when aspirant professional groups emulate the more protective and conservative patterns of professions such as medicine or law, this may in fact serve as a barrier to their further professional development. This is a dilemma that will be considered more fully later in this discussion.

Actually, there are two major kinds of goals which are representative of any ascendent professional group. They include: (1) enhancing the prestige of the organization and its members; and (2) acquiring a high degree of social control over its professional field of practice. These goals may be seen as highly related to one another in the sense that more prestige may give the professional group a higher degree of social control, and vice versa. For example, William J. Goode has analyzed the functional relationships between social control and prestige, at least for the well-established professions, as follows:

Typically a profession, through its association and its members, controls admission to training and requires far more education from its trainees than the containing community demands. Although the occupational behavior of members is regulated by law, the professional community exacts a higher standard of behavior than does the law. Both of the above characteristics allow the professions to enjoy more prestige from the containing community than can other professions.[9]

It thus can be implied from the above that professions hold power in the community as a result of both their prestige and the legal and social controls they acquire. Although it is the values of the larger society which give rise to the power of the professional community, Goode further suggests that no such power would be given if there were not a professional community to demand it and be responsible for its utilization. For as a consequence of the rewards given by the larger society, the professional association is able to demand higher talents in its recruits and require that they go through a considerable adult socialization process.[10]

The internal dynamics of the drive for greater prestige and power within emergent professions can also be understood more clearly by viewing a profession as an occupational "system" consisting of several interrelated parts or dimensions. In this context, the professional association is by no means the only source of professionalization, for it is only one part of a larger occupational complex. The occupational system, to be properly understood, must also include these important dimensions: (1) the work agency, which is the organizational environment in which the profession is practiced; (2) the professional schools, which socialize and train recruits; (3) the informal group of colleagues, which creates and promulgates occupational norms, ideologies, and expectations; and of course, (4) the formal professional association.

Within the framework of the system spelled out above, the informal colleague group is the major link which supplies the dynamics of change between the remaining occupational components. In other words, the colleague group provides the linkages between what goes on in the work agencies, the professional schools, and the professional association. It is the experience of members of the colleague group as they move through the professional schools and into the various service agencies that sets the pattern of professional expectations, professional careers, and professional norms. In turn, the demands of job security and advancement, increased professional identification and recognition grow out of the conditions experienced by members of the colleague group as they proceed through their careers, and these demands give rise to many of the policies and goals of the professional society.

Thus, whenever their professional aspirations appear to be threatened or frustrated in any way, the members of a profession will collectively demand that their representative professional association provide a solution to the problem, through protective controls, lobbying and public relations, or other devices designed to enhance the status of the occupation. At the same time, the alternatives open to the professional association in protecting or advancing the professional standing of the occupation are to a certain extent limited and shaped by factors peculiar to its own membership. Some of the more significant kinds of perceived threats to the professional status of problem-solving occupations and their collective responses, as reflected in activities of their representative associations, will be considered below.

THE QUEST FOR LEGAL STATUS AND EXCLUSIVE
JURISDICTIONAL CONTROL

For many of the emergent problem-solving occupations, the interprofessional struggles and competition with rival occupations are perceived as among the greatest threats to their professional growth and development. For example, the executive of one association has described the threat to his profession in this way:

The increased stature of the profession leads to greater expectations and stronger public images as to its performance and abilities, at the same time that we become the targets for significant public attacks upon our existence and achievements. Similarly, greater acceptance of the role of planners by many professionals in the overlapping fields of related physical design, law and public policy, and the social sciences likewise has led to scurrilous interprofessional attacks and irresponsible attempts to limit our field.[11]

Competition between rival problem-solving professions is rendered particularly complicated by the fact that the boundaries of their service areas are overlapping and blurred. This is largely due to the fact that the problems to which these professions aim their services are themselves overlapping and highly interdependent in their causes, consequences, and treatment. For example, city planners, transportation planners, social workers, housing specialists, and architects or civil engineers may all play important roles in urban renewal, but where the responsibilities of one occupation end and the others begin in the urban renewal process is not very clear in actual practice. Also, most of the emergent professions that work at solving social problems tend to define their own service areas rather broadly so as not to unduly limit their own growth potentials. Very often, they equate their professional work roles with the entire work programs of the organizations which they serve. What these agencies do, in effect, is what each of the service occupations claims as its own job territory. This tendency is most marked in those cases where the administrative-agency and skill group lines of development historically have been closely related and overlapping, as in the case of social work, city planning, and urban renewal, but similar tendencies have also appeared among the various mental health professions. Such conditions lead to many jurisdictional disputes and conflicting claims to exclusive technical competency between the competing professions working in the same general problem areas.

Perhaps the most common response to the threats of interprofessional rivalry have been the attempts by many occupations to establish exclusive legal jurisdiction over their alleged fields of practice, through devices such as licensure, registration, or certification. Such status has been sought by many occupations working in common social problem areas including teaching, social work, and city planning, and, of course, it has already been achieved in some states by some of the better established occupations. Wilensky has described this strategy as one of the phases that nearly all professions go through, and he describes this stage of the professionalization process as follows:

There will be persistent political agitation in order to win the support of law for the protection of the job territory and its sustaining code of ethics. Where the area of competence is not clearly exclusive, legal protection of title will be the aim; where the definition of the area of competence is clearer, then mere performance of the act by someone outside the fraternity will be declared a crime.[12]

But the real value of licensure to a profession or to the larger society is not entirely clear, for it varies according to the purpose for which it is intended, how it is structured, and how well and by whom it is administered. The major significance in the trend toward this aspect of professionalism probably lies in the amount and type of controls that the professional groups exert in providing necessary services to the larger society. Such controls are often functional in that they tend to provide levels and standards of service that are higher than might be the case where occupational groups do not have the power to regulate themselves or to resist the interference of uninformed lay groups. But when such controls in the hands of a professional group become excessive, they may lead to an imbalance between the supply, quality, and demand for services, which is a condition that may be profitable in the short run for members of the professions involved, but which is also dysfunctional for the larger society.

Efforts to obtain legal monopolies over their respective fields of practice are especially unjustified for newer problem-solving professions, which are in a much too fluid stage of growth and change to "freeze" at their present level of development. Also, legal efforts to curb jurisdictional disputes and interprofessional debates over who is best qualified to do the work at hand are unfortunate, because much of this debate has positive value. That is, it forces each profession involved into a re-examination of its own values, standards, and techniques, and in this way it provides continuous pressure toward improvements in the quality of the services offered by each separate profession. Self-criticism, which often stems from such competition and debate, is perhaps one of the more important characteristics of a healthy and growing profession.

One of the consequences that must be faced by an emergent professional group aspiring to a legal monopoly over its alleged field of practice is that this aspiration is often attacked by rival professionals and other critics as "protectionism," or "unionism," rather than as "professionalism," and charges such as these have often been made against associations representing a wide variety of both newly emergent and well-established professions. Of course these charges tend to obscure the differences between collective actions designed to regulate and control a field of practice, presumably in the public interest, and those kinds of actions such as strikes, walkouts, or collective bargaining more clearly designed to advance an occupation's own narrow self-interests. Nevertheless, a professional group may expose itself to attack by pursuing either type of control, when it appears to outsiders that occupational self-interests are pursued at the expense of the public interest.

Some occupations, such as teaching and social work, have often assumed a form of professionalism that can best be characterized as "unionism." While unionism may have provided some short-run gains, there is no real evidence to suggest that this approach has necessarily increased the prestige of these occupations, or that in the long run it has gained for them the power of self-regulation.

The main point here is that the importance of legal controls as a source of professionalism for some of the problem-solving occupations has probably been over-emphasized at the expense of other alternatives which may in the long run be more beneficial in enhancing their status and prestige. It is further suggested that efforts to obtain exclusive jurisdiction over their stated fields of practice may be unattainable and unrealistic, given the functions of these occupations and their bureaucratic setting. In the broadest sense, only a very limited amount of power may be attainable by any of the emerging modern professions which operate primarily in the complex organizational setting of urban government. Under such conditions, the major function of the professional association is to assist the employing organizations to recruit, train, socialize, and channel the appropriate personnel into the appropriate positions. But they only share a limited amount of responsibility with the hiring agencies for establishing the conditions of professional work within the organizational setting. At worst, when it does not do its job well, the status and power of an occupational association may be so low that it will not ordinarily be consulted by the hiring agencies with respect to the placement of its members; that is, the agency itself determines its own job specifications within given skill areas, independent of the recommendations of the representative occupational associations. At best, the occupational associations do enhance their prestige and standing within the organizations they serve by seeing to it that the appropriate skills are fed into the bureaucratic machinery. When a professional society performs this function well, it will be consulted by the organizations it serves, and thus may be given a certain amount of control over the flow of personnel in and out of the professional job market, and over the training and socialization of recruits. Whatever self-interests may be served by this functional relationship is incidental, of course, to the larger task of providing essential professional services demanded by the public.

THE PROBLEM-SOLVING PROFESSIONS AND PUBLIC POLICY

In the structure of urban governments and agencies, the professions occupy an intermediate and indeterminate status somewhere between the routinized technical positions at the bottom of the organizational hierarchy, which require minimum skills and training, and the managers of policy makers of the organizations which they serve. This causes no serious conflicts for those professionals who define their roles in purely technical terms, or for those who do not view the service structures in which they operate as the most crucial aspect of their work. In other words, professionals who serve the personal needs of individuals and who view the individuals they serve—not the organizations which hire them—as their clients are probably most often found in this category; for example, many case workers or psychiatrists.

But the nature of the tasks performed by many of the newly emerging problem-solving professions would suggest that these occupations also include many individuals occupying professional roles which are directly concerned and involved with policy formulation and decision-making processes at the highest organizational levels. Most of the technical decisions which are made in city planning, for example, are by their nature closely tied to and affected by public policy. Zoning decisions affecting future land use patterns, the adoption of housing density standards, and long-range facilities and capital budget programming are all part of the professional city planner's technical work role, but it is imposssible to perform these tasks without regard to public policy.

Therefore one finds in many service agencies what Wilensky calls the "program professionals."[13] These are the problem-solving professionals whose commitments to particular programs and policies are as great as their commitments to the techniques and procedures of their professional field. According to Wilensky, the program professional exhibits the following characteristics:

By virtue of his technical prowess, he makes himself indispensable as a policy advisor. In his job moves—between government and private agencies, civic organizations, foundations, universities—he follows the programs to which both his skills and his social philosophy are bound. . . . End products of social reform, these men combine professional standards of work with programmatic sense and constitute an important link between professional and civil culture, the man of knowledge and the man of power.[14]

Program professionals play an indispensable role in service organizations with rapidly changing and expanding functions, and they are in growing demand at strategic points in the urban service structure. For example, the community action and work-training programs of the "war on poverty," and the many new kinds of educational programs aimed at the culturally deprived in urban communities are illustrations of some of the newer users of the program professional variety.

Perhaps it is more accurate to view many of the program professionals as organizational "innovators"—that is, as individuals whose major role is to create new organizational machinery for getting a wide variety of urban "housekeeping" done. At the very least, program professionals serve to coordinate existing programs in more meaningful and orderly ways. Innovating program professionals have had great impact on the structure and policies of urban governments and private urban service agencies in recent years, and many of these innovators have been quite successful in achieving their program goals through some combination of personal effectiveness and situational factors which have made this possible.

But the role of the professional program innovator does involve some inevitable strains and stresses which may significantly reduce its impact, and this is problematic for the professional groups involved. One major reason for this strain is that the efforts of the program innovators are often blocked by pre-existing power structures which may include better established professional groups, lay governing board or commissions, legislative bodies, or elected and appointed political officials. Social workers, teachers, and city planners, for example, are among professionals whose work is ordinarily controlled and dominated by combinations of politicians and lay governing bodies of one sort or another. Thus, the innovators in these occupations often come into direct conflict with the preexisting authority structure over matters which cannot be clearly differentiated according to a technical-policy dichotomy. In such cases, the professionals often view the "politicians" as major sources of obstructionism in blocking the achievement of program goals which meet their own standards and expectations. Part of the frustration that results is, of course, also due to the fact that the large-scale and complex programming and reorganization that is so often a part of the program professional's procedures and objectives may take a good many years to get under way. Thus, public rejection of their proposals, or sharp opposition by elected political officials, after years of hard work and effort, can be especially discouraging and disillusioning to the program innovators.

A second major source of role strain is that the program innovator not only is in frequent conflict with the officials for whom he works, but also frequently finds himself at odds with his own professional colleague group.

In the earliest stages of professionalization, a newly formed professional association takes on the social movement characteristics of its members, and so there is a great deal of organizational support for experimentation and innovation. In fact, these may be important sources of prestige and recognition for the occupation, especially if they are successful. This is to say that new occupational groups attempting to get themselves established have a stake in producing a visible impact in their areas of specialization. For example, the activities of the earliest professional city planners in getting planning programs established as legitimate functions of local governments actually did advance the status and prestige of the newly emerging city planning profession.

But for professions which have already found some niche in the occupational hierarchy, innovation become less important as a source of status, and in fact, it may then be viewed by the professional society with caution or suspicion. In well-established professions, there have been many instances where innovators have been viewed with alarm as radicals or charlatans and expelled from membership from their formal associations. Also, some innovators refuse to affiliate with the professional organizations as a matter of choice, which may be a matter of embarrassment to the professional society, especially when such individuals have made prominent and acknowledged contributions to the larger society. To a certain extent this has already begun to occur in some of the problem-solving professions, where prominent innovators who are forced, or choose, to remain outside the formal colleague associations are labeled as outsiders, radicals, or non-professionals.

When it reaches the stage where the innovator must become a maverick to his own technical profession, it may be said that the professional society has reached the stage where its self-conserving and protective functions have become dominant, at the expense of other important professional objectives and considerations. Of course, it is difficult to determine with any degree of precision the point at which an occupation ceases to be "innovative" and becomes "conservative." However, the point here is that in the advanced stages of professionalization, *professionalism* in the conservative sense and *innovation* are two processes that may be partially incompatible, both for the professional society and for individual practitioners. Therefore, whether the innovator role in urban government can ever be fully professionalized in the traditional sense depends to a large extent on the degree to which the professional society is willing and able to reconcile the two incompatible roles.

Failure to reduce this source of role strain may produce several unfortunate outcomes. First, many program professionals may retreat from the somewhat complex and difficult to maintain mixed, technical policy-making orientation to a simpler and less difficult occupational stance. For example, they may retreat either to a strictly technical orientation, which stresses the procedural aspects of their work rather than the policy aspects, or to a form of provincialism or "localism" which allows them to become a compliant part of the local power structure and to adopt the prevailing policies and goals as their own. As another alternative, the program professional may retreat to a "careerist" orientation which stresses job advancement, security, and the symbols of professional status, rather than either the technical or policy aspects of his work.

All of the forms of professional retreatism mentioned above are probably motives for the legalistic kinds of protectionism described earlier, but, more important, they serve as barriers to the maintenance of innovating and mixed types of technical policy roles for the problem-solving professions. In the fluid and rapidly changing social context in which these occupations function, such retreatism ought to be viewed as among the pathologies of professionalism, rather than among its essential characteristics.

PROBLEM-SOLVING PROFESSIONALS AS GENERALISTS

One of the most important barriers to full professional status for many of the newer problem-solving occupations is that they are largely dependent on a variety of other disciplines for the development of their own body of knowledge and techniques. Although some of these occupations focus on problems of organization while others are most concerned with problems of human relations and/or personal pathologies, the fact is that virtually all of them borrow their skills from a full range of previously existing professional areas and disciplines. For example, city planning borrows heavily from architecture, engineering, law, economics, geography, public administration and sociology, while social work is rooted in sociology, psychology, psychoanalysis, and some aspects of public administration. In particular, most of the problem-solving occupations would appear to be especially well grounded in the social science disciplines.

What many of these occupations have attempted to do is to carve out job territories which represent unique and distinct combinations of some of the above skill areas. At the same time, they have attempted to avoid specialization within new kinds of narrow limits. What seems to be emerging, at least among the program-oriented professions, is a "generalist" orientation. This orientation is reflected in their self-images and self-definitions, as illustrated by a city planner in the following image of his own occupation:

The man most likely to succeed and to be happy in the planning profession is the one who possesses foresight; social consciousness; ability to analyze broad situations, and to synthesize multitudinous details in order to grasp common elements; the broadest sort of imagination and interests; and the ability to engage in constructive and creative efforts involving relationships between the problem and factors of modern living . . . .[15]

It would appear that a generalist approach is essential to the program professions if they are to have a significant impact on the communities they serve, but such an orientation has been extremely difficult to achieve and maintain, given the prevailing trends toward increased specialization in almost all aspects of urban living. In fact, the professions themselves are usually defined as technical, or "functionally specific," within limited and well-defined areas of specialization. Carr-Saunders has stated the problem of the more generalized occupations this way:

Where the technique is specialized, the rise of a profession is unescapable. Where it is generalized, its coming must wait upon the growth of a sense of a common responsibility in order that the loose bond, created by the possession of a common but ill-defined technique, may be drawn more tightly.[16]

For one thing, the generalist orientation tends to obscure the diversity of approaches and "schools" that exist within each of the separate professions, so that the forces which continually threaten to fragment each profession into splinter-groups or subspecialties cannot be adequately regulated or controlled. A second barrier to the maintenance of a generalist orientation includes the educational tendencies which favor increased specialization in the numerous fields of knowledge upon which the problem-solving professions are based. The specialization of the source disciplines in turn has led to increased compartmentalization and competition within the education framework, and of course, this is not an appropriate training background for a generalistic orientation. Some professional schools have attempted to create and maintain a generalist approach by creating a variety of inter-disciplinary programs, but these programs are relatively few and their status in relationship to the professional schools from which they stem is often precarious and marginal. Also, most of the interdisciplinary programs (urban studies, for example) are not primarily designed to train profes-sional practitioners in the conventional sense. Thus, the professional schools (the field of city planning is probably the major exception here) to date have not been major contributors to the development and maintenance of a generalist orientation among practitioners.

The hiring agencies are still another barrier to a generalist approach. Modern personnel and civil service procedures have increasingly fragment-ed the division of labor into more and more specialized positions and job specifications within public and private agencies. Very little room is left open in the service agencies for the generalist, and there is no well-estab-lished niche for this kind of professional, except perhaps as an outside consultant. Perhaps some professionals who have become administrators near the top of the organizational hierarchy actually do play a generalized role, but this is usually only after long careers as technical specialists in some more limited aspects of the agency's work.

It may be that as new programs and institutional arrangements develop in response to increasingly more complex urban problems, there will be more room and opportunities created for professionals to function as gen-eralists, but within the existing maize of established agencies and depart-ments of urban government, the resistance to such change is still great.

SUMMARY

The professionalization of the problem-solving occupations has had both positive and negative consequences for the occupations themselves, for the agencies in which they are employed, and for the communities they serve. Some of the positive contributions of professionalization, at least in its ear-liest stages, include the introduction of expertise and innovation into the service structure, the upgrading and broadening of the skills and perfor-mance of agency staffs, and the creation of new and attractive career oppor-tunities for service professionals. But the active search for the material and psychic benefits of professional status has also unduly emphasized occupa-tional self-interest and interprofessional rivalry, which detract from the potential value of the services offered by these occupations. For those ser-vice occupations which already have become reasonably well established, conservatism and protectionism have become forces which impede their value as the source of bold and comprehensive new approaches for dealing with social problems.

The capacity to innovate, within sensible limits, is essential if urban communities are to respond successfully to the forces that threaten their future growth and development. That is, they must be capable of abandoning those programs and policies which are ineffective or obsolete and be willing to create and adopt more promising alternatives. Urban service occupations have aided this process in the recent past, as illustrated by many of the more successful innovations in city planning, urban renewal, community development, public health, social welfare, mental health, corrections, and urban education. But more effective approaches still need to be developed in these areas, and the program professionals are among the vanguard of those best equipped to bring about such changes. Much of the responsibility for creating sufficiently broad and imaginative approaches rests with the professional training schools and professional associations that provide the necessary skills and attitudes. Perhaps this can best be achieved by establishing closer ties than is currently the case between the training schools and the professional associations, on the one hand, and the agencies which employ them, on the other hand. In this way, a better fit can be provided between the skills and performance actually needed by responsive urban communities, and the skills, ideology, and career expectations that are produced in the schools and associations.

Finally, the whole area of interprofessional relations between rival service occupations needs to be improved, because excessive jurisdictional battles designed to establish legal monopolies over their respective fields of practice reduces the possibility of coordinating and integrating their professional contributions into a more effective and meaningful service package. In the long run, interprofessional cooperation is more likely to enhance the status and prestige of these occupations than the protective jurisdictional disputes that are central to many current strategies for professional growth and development.

The selections to follow, unlike those in previous chapters, do not all necessarily offer solutions to the problems that have been discussed here, primarily because the problems inherent in the professionalization of problem-solving occupations are themselves too recent, or heretofore unrecognized, to have been adequately dealt with in this way. Instead, these selections are intended to explore still further the complexities and consequences of the professionalization process, to more specifically identify some of the difficulties faced by particular problem-solving professions, to delineate more clearly the relationship of these occupations to their clients or to the social problems they hope to solve, and to consider more fully the complex service structures in which the problem-solving professions operate. The final selection speculates on some future problems and prospects for the problem-solving professions.

REFERENCES

1. Wm. J. Goode, "The Librarian: From Occupation to Profession?" in P. H. Ennis and H. W. Winger, *Seven Questions about the Profession of Librarianship*. Chicago: University of Chicago Press, 1962, pp. 8–9.
2. See Alexander M. Carr-Saunders and A. P. Wilson, *The Professions*. New York: Oxford University Press, 1933; Talcott Parsons, *Essays in Sociological Theory*, 2d. ed. New York: The Free Press of Glencoe, 1954, p. 38; A. Maude and R. Lewis, *Professional People*. Chicago: Phoenix House, 1952, pp. 55–56; Robert C. Stone, "The Sociology of Bureaucracy and Professions," in Joseph S. Roucek, *Contemporary Sociology*. New York: The Philosophical Library, 1958, p. 496; and Wm. J. Goode, "Community within a Community: The Professions," *American Sociological Review* (April 1957).
3. This observation, plus much of the discussion which follows, is based on a previous work by the author. See Harry Gold, "The Professionalization of Urban Planning," unpublished Ph.D. dissertation, University of Michigan, 1965.
4. Harold L. Wilensky, "The Professionalization of Everyone?" *American Journal of Sociology* (September 1964), p. 142.
5. Goode, "The Librarian: From Occupation to Profession?" p. 8.
6. Harold L. Wilensky, "The Dynamics of Professionalism: The Case of Hospital Administration," *Hospital Administration* (Spring, 1962), p. 12.
7. Amos H. Hawley, *Human Ecology*. New York: The Ronald Press Company, 1950, p. 218.
8. Hawley, p. 218.
9. Goode, "Community within a Community: The Professions," p. 195.
10. Goode, p. 196.
11. From a memorandum by the Executive Director, The American Institute of Planners, November 25, 1964.
12. Wilensky, "The Professionalization of Everyone?", pp. 142–46. This is from the author's more comprehensive discussion of the natural history of professionalization.
13. Wilensky, p. 158.
14. Wilensky, p. 158.
15. From a policy statement by the American Institute of Planners, "The Content of Professional Curricula in Planning," October 1947 (mimeographed).
16. Carr-Saunders, p. 287.

ADDITIONAL READINGS

Carr-Saunders, A. M., and P. A. Wilson, *The Professions*. New York: Oxford University Press, 1933.
Clark, Burton R., *Educating the Expert Society*. San Francisco: The Chandler Publishing Company, 1962.
Davis, F. J., and others, *Society and the Law*. New York: The Free Press of Glencoe, 1962.
Garceau, Oliver, *The Political Life of the American Medical Association*. Cambridge, Mass.: Harvard University Press, 1941.
Gouldner, Alvin W., and S. M. Miller, *Applied Sociology*. New York: The Free Press of Glencoe, 1965.

Hughes, Everett C., *Men and their Work*. New York: The Free Press of Glencoe, 1958.

Lieberman, Morris, *Education as a Profession*. Englewood Cliffs, N.J.: Prentice-Hall, Inc., 1956.

Maude, A., and R. Lewis, *Professional People*. Chicago: Phoenix House, 1952.

Perloff, Harvey S., *Education for Planning: City, State, and Regional*. Baltimore: The John Hopkins Press, 1957.

Rushing, William A., *The Psychiatric Professions*. Chapel Hill, N.C.: The University of North Carolina Press, 1964.

Schwartz, Edward E. (ed.), *Manpower in Social Welfare*. National Association of Social Workers, 1966.

Shostak, Arthur, *Sociology in Action*. Homewood, Ill.: The Dorsey Press, 1966.

Wilensky, Harold L., and Charles N. Lebeaux, *Industrial Society and Social Welfare*. New York: Russell Sage Foundation, 1958.

THE SOCIAL SERVICE CRISIS

The Dilemma—Success for the Agency or Service to the Needy?

Martin Rein

The social services are, in the 1960's, becoming the major means by which many more persons can hope to "participate in prosperity"—an early slogan for the "war on poverty." Therefore, the organization and distribution of the social services, critical now, will become a crucial problem in the next decade or two. The Negro protest is already exerting heavy pressure for more equitable distribution and better organization. Emphasis must increasingly shift from "stabilization" and individual security to the overall expansion of individual opportunity and general economic growth. "Who gets what and how" will become an important political, as well as technical issue.

By social services I mean those forms of collective intervention which are outside of the market place and which include education, medical care, recreation, guidance, mental health, and social work. In a period of rapid social change such as ours, we must examine afresh the fabric of our social service network. "We need to consider," as Richard Titmuss, professor at the London School of Economics, so pointedly observed, "not only embarking on new social services but reform of existing ones." This paper examines some of the more glaring deficiencies in the local social services.

Almost every reader knows of people who have fallen into trouble that did not fit into any social service's individual definition of its function, and who were therefore in effect, when all the buckpassing was finished, deprived of help. What is not so often mentioned are the trials of those who became involved with

From *Trans-action*, 1, 4 (May 1964), pp. 3–8. Reprinted by permission of the author and the publisher.

too many social services, each with different values, goals, and systems of classification. If these conflicts get settled at all, it is all too often in line with precedent or the relative powers of the agencies, rather than according to what the recipients actually need. In addition to all his other problems, the recipient must make such adjustments as he can between several authorities each of whom has different ideas of who he is, what his problem is, and what should be done with him.

Each agency in a local social service network functions as an autonomous unit, and acts according to its own interpretation of what its mission is. Each has different aims and different approaches. Coordination is poor and accountability almost absent. Social policy's attention has been riveted on problems of case integration, program coordination, and gaps in services. Attempts at better cooperation have been numerous, although historically they have met with small success. By contrast, the need for more basic social reform has been, until recently, almost completely neglected.

The dispensers of services themselves decide a recipient's problems, needs, and the appropriate moral attitude to take. A fatherless family is likely to get financial help if the mother applies to public welfare—and substitute child care if she goes instead to a child welfare agency. Agency function, and not necessarily the client's situation, determines the nature of the services dispensed.

Often agencies negate each other's work. In one community we studied, the Society for the Prevention of Cruelty to Children sharply reduced the percentage of its cases sent to court, consistent with the standards of good professional practice. The other community agencies, apparently disagreeing with SPCC's man-

agement referred SPCC's cases to court, and the net effect on the community was nil.

In the end agencies generally do what they want within the limits of their power. D. Donnison, professor of the London School of Economics and Political Science, notes that voluntary service projects "arise from a wish to serve rather than from a problem to be solved." Projects favored by agencies are those which lend prestige, attract public support, and avoid controversy. The situation is comparable to Dr. Mandeville's famous doggerel about the bees which prospered as a community because each bee pursued its own individual task with vanity, envy, vice and waste.

Competing Views

The work of community agencies can be viewed in four competing ways: as a form of supply designed to meet a consumer demand; as assistance in self-actualization; as help for the helpless; or as promotion of adjustment and conformity.

Accordingly, recipients may also be viewed by the dispenser of the service in four different ways:

1.   as customers purchasing a service for which they have been solicited or recruited—for instance, for the use of recreation or group work services;

2.   as clients or patients—if the service dispenser is considered to be a therapist of some kind, assisting others to understand and realize themselves;

3.   as victims of circumstance or society, deprived and relatively helpless, aided by the dispenser to win access to resources and rights previously beyond reach;

4.   or as deviants who have broken moral and legal rules and whom the ser-

vice network must bring into line. This pressure toward conformity takes place in a supposedly pluralistic society in which variety is officially considered a virtue, and in which professionals are themselves not clear where acceptable variation ends and dangerous deviancy begins.

Services may therefore be "sold," offered, provided as rights, or imposed as obligations.

Customers and clients are supposed to have more control over their fates than victims or deviants. (Customers, in turn, are presumably more individually responsible than clients—"let the buyer beware" is not considered an acceptable slogan for therapy." Customers are "sold," clients "treated," victims "cared for," and deviants "controlled." "Sales and therapy" imply personal responsibility; "care and control" mean community responsibility.

Great confusion results when different dispensers hold different views of the same classes of individuals. How, for instance, should an illegitimate birth be defined? To many professionals it is a psychological symptom, an outcome of internal emotional stresses—the mother must therefore be treated as a client or patient. But morally she may be a deviant—and there are frequent movements to abolish, or severely limit, welfare payments to mothers who continue to have illegitimate children—the hope being that this may also limit immorality. But socially and economically the illegitimate mother may be a victim. Many studies have established a strong relationship between illegitimacy and inequality. Raymond T. Smith of the University College of the West Indies has shown that when steady incomes are available to Negro families in the Caribbean there is greater family stability, less male desertion, and fewer illegitimate births.

From this view effective help is a matter of reducing inequality and expanding opportunity. In short, how we define "illegitimate birth" determines the fate of mother and child—and, in practice, the fates of many mothers and children.

To wrongly label a victim a client can have the unintended effect of "cooling the mark out"—that is, disposing of the case without disposing of the cause, and keeping the victim from seeking further help (or from demanding it) by impressing on him that the fault lies only within himself rather than in outside circumstances.

Prestige and Reward

Those who serve "clients" and provide "therapy" enjoy the highest professional prestige; but those who "care" for "victims" have the lowest prestige—in fact, they are sometimes blamed by the public for what the victim is and does. Therefore, each dispenser tries to improve his social status by calling what he does "therapy," and by trying to reclassify his recipients as "clients"—or at least by excluding those who stand little chance of becoming clients. There is always a tendency for deviants, victims, or customers to be transformed into "patients" and for their problems to be treated as "sickness."

As social service comes to be dominated by the concepts of clients and customers, care and control as explicit goals become more and more unpopular—are considered less "worthy" pursuits. Professionals shun working in such places as welfare departments, prisons and reformatories. Delinquency and dependency come increasingly to be considered malfunctions or flaws of personality—with less and less emphasis on changing the conditions in which they occur.

In the end, the decision about which

label to attach to a recipient can become a political decision. Is public relief a form of public subsidy for low wages in an economy which cannot keep all its labor force working? Or is there more political advantage in calling welfare cases personal failures with low intelligence, low motivation, and high pathology—that is, the poor have only themselves to blame for their poverty?

Neglecting Those in Greatest Need

The service network is so organized that many in extreme need cannot find their way to it. If they do manage the tortuous, badly lighted path, they often find themselves ineligible for help; or, if eligible, their own ideas of what their problems are can differ strongly from what the professionals tell them. Services originally designed to act as a doorway and a mirror for community needs often act instead as a barrier.

Agencies neglect those in greatest need because there is pressure to accept "good" clients who will deliver all the rewards that professionals and agencies need or want. A "good" client is cooperative, motivated to use what is offered, capable of improvement, and eventually able to express gratitude. The lower the social class the less likely that individuals will be able to meet the standards of the "good" client. In short, it is preferable, and nicer, to work with cases amenable to easy change than with so-called "hopeless" persons and families.

The labels for the hard cases, many of whom are in extreme need, vary—they may be called "multi-problem," "chronic," or "unreachable." But such labels highlight the specialization, differentiation, and narrowing of services offered by agencies rather than the problems of the service recipients. In our study of SPCC, it was found that the more often a case was referred for help, the less likely that help was to be given. Many reasons account for this rejection—professionals claim that little can be done for such "hopeless" families, and time and money are better spent where they can do more good. Yet some agencies—all too few—specifically concentrate on helping the most rejected. Many non-professional organizations like the Salvation Army, and some professional organizations like the Pavinstedt Clinic in Boston, take as their main tasks the care of the discarded and ignored.

Richard A. Cloward describes this rejection as "planned disengagement." He notes that the number of cases deliberately closed out "at the end of the first interview increases rapidly as social class declines." He accurately concludes that there is "something in the nature of professional technology that exerts pressure for disengagement whatever the setting." He describes how private agencies pass on their rejects to public agencies:

> Private residential treatment institutions for juvenile delinquents . . . pass on their difficult cases to the public training schools; settlements and community agencies arrange to have the more difficult gangs worked with by public detached street workers; family agencies abandon so-called multi-problem families to public welfare; private hospitals shrug off the chronically ill to the back wards of public custodial hospitals.

Professional Rigidities

The rise of "professionalism" and of "professional organizations" among social service workers is itself a hazard for those in greatest need. When a group of persons who perform a service band together to control the body of persons who may legitimately perform that service, certain inevitable consequences follow: a striving to raise their own prestige and rewards;

a tendency to overdefine the skills needed to do the work; a limit on those who may do it, and to whom it may be done; a growth of fringe technicians for the dirty parts of the job; and an increasing concern with "professional standards," personal satisfaction, and income. The danger, as noted, is that the interests of the recipients can easily become subverted to serve the interests of the dispensers.

Individualistic Bias

Barbara Wooton in her incisive analysis of "Social Science and Social Pathology" notes: "We prefer today to analyze the infected individual rather than to eliminate the infection from the environment." When we meet maladjustment, we propose individual therapy; when confronted with expanding delinquency, we ask for more probation officers; when we see widespread ill health we call for more physicians. We assume that the expert has the magic competence to cope with a problem by dealing only with the individual.

In our study of protective services in one community, we were given many strong moral and psychological opinions and judgments about how to handle neglectful parents, but the families were judged in isolation from their environments. Professional workers did not even have systematic information about occupations, incomes, or integration of families into their neighborhoods. The professional strategy of separate, individual treatment seems to screen out basic background information that they agency needs to treat the individual as part of a social milieu.

Very many cases, of course, do call for separate, personal treatment. On the other hand, something like mass unemployment creates such a destructive atmosphere that the social structure itself requires treatment before much can be done for the individual. It is like trying to solve rush hour traffic jams by concentrating on making each car and driver—more precisely, those cars and drivers who encounter problems and are picked up by repairmen or police—as efficient as possible, all the while scolding the drivers to obey all laws and drive right, or trying to rehabilitate them by sending them to driving schools. But clearly, more efficient automobiles and more responsible drivers will not solve traffic jams.

Criticism and Change

One of the more encouraging developments of this decade is the rising chorus of criticism of the social service network. Most of this criticism has come from the outside—from James B. Conant on American education, from O. L. Peterson on health, from Alvin W. Gouldner on social services, and from Robert Morris on social planning.

Historically, pressure for reform has usually started from the outside—institutions seldom seriously criticize or reform themselves.

But what will really bring reform? The symptoms of illness are blatant; but are the doctors—or critics—sure of what causes the disease?

Some critics see the basic fault in the great numbers of independent agencies and in the lack of central standards or control. Social service is in many ways the last bastion of free enterprise. Any time that two people come together in the name of good works, they can start a welfare agency and scramble around for funds, personnel, and clients. They can even claim to be coordinating the work of other agencies, who in turn have the right to ignore them. This lack of focus is often defended as basic to our democratic way of life. It is helped along by the lack of positive national goals.

Other critics see the trouble in "institutionalization"—the pioneering institutions of yesteryear become the conservators of today, interested in surviving and repelling invaders of their entrenched fortresses. They respond less and less to the social problems for which they were designed—often at the very times that needs are greatest.

Some scholars criticize increasing specialization by both professionals and agencies, with longer and narrower training required, and with increasing splintering of functions.

Finally, some critics think that the fault goes down to the root; that social welfare services are primarily concealed devices for distributing, preserving, and multiplying advantages and privileges, rather than for reducing inequality. It is inevitable, from this view, that the most underprivileged should be ignored.

Planning Goals

Planning organizations trying to remedy the situation select one or another of the defects of the social service network against which to concentrate their main thrusts. Three general action programs are emerging:

1. redefining agency boundaries,
2. servicing rejected populations,
3. reducing concentration on the individual only—the "individualistic Bias."

The redefinition of boundaries has actually been proceeding for some time. The shift from caring for people in some central "warehouse" institution, to caring for them in their own homes or in the community, is fundamental and historic. Almshouses have given way to public welfare; hospitals send chronic patients to nursing homes, and mental hospitals allow extended home visits where possible. Children have moved out of orphanages and into foster homes.

One form that planning to redefine boundaries may take is illustrated by the federal regulations governing grants to states for construction of mental health centers. To make sure that no major break in patient care occurs within or outside the hospital—a critical problem at present—federal regulations attempt to secure as a condition for federal grants more than a vague promise of cooperation between in-patient, out-patient, and after-care services. They want a firm contract assuring smooth transition of patients from one service to another. The goal is ambitious; the problems to overcome are formidable.

The Fringe Groups

Every agency develops a marginal group of people it is supposed to serve but doesn't want. Courts and reformatories acquire chronic repeaters; hospitals house alcoholics who keep returning though their alcoholism is not helped; and schools worry what to do about dropouts. All such unpopular groups have one quality in common: the agencies that serve them believe they have little chance to improve.

Planning for reform therefore must concentrate first on encouraging institutions to keep trying to serve these unwanted persons, providing extra money and services to improve effectiveness.

In an effort to correct the "individualistic bias," some service planning is explicitly directed at changing institutions. Plans to reduce delinquency—including those of the President's Committee on Juvenile Delinquency and Youth Crime—are taking as a major assumption the fact that our social institutions themselves throw up barriers that effectively wall off the poor from access to dominant values and satisfactions, and that slum youths often turn delinquent because they find no other way to acquire them. Therefore, these programs are aimed at providing such access, and changing the institutions accordingly.

New Bottles, Old Wine

These are the new approaches and attacks on the old problems. How effective are they?

As might be expected, they are encountering trouble. Each community approaches the job of redefining agency boundaries afresh, as if no one else had ever had the same problem. As with local efforts toward reform in the past, the danger is that there will be a busy juggling of boundaries and shunting back and forth of recipients, but no comprehensive approach involving fundamental change. A major reduction in agency independence must occur to assure continuous flow between resident and community organizations. Enforceable plans that would actually assure an accountable meshing of pre-care, institutional, and after-care services are at present notable by their absence—though, as mentioned, mental health programs which want federal money in the future will have to assure such continuing care. A cynical view would hold that the main difference between the new reform programs and the old may lie only in the sources and amounts of money.

New plans to "reach the rejected" continue to "cream off" the most able and fluff off those who most need help. For instance, California developed an elaborate program to train minority members to find jobs in the aerospace industry—but the standards grew so rigid that the target population was missed. The Labor Department recently reported that retraining programs generally catch the younger and better educated workers, and leave untouched the hard-core unemployed.

Change the System

In practice, planners still avoid changing the system in favor of changing the individual. This is not always conscious; it may proceed by small and almost imperceptible steps; but it occurs when the program is specifically designed to bring about fundamental change.

"Citizen action programs" is an example. Purportedly, these groups are supposed to change institutions. Immediately and primarily they aim to shake urban dwellers from apathy, to try to get them concerned and involved in the larger community. The actual results are less impressive. Ends and means become subtly blurred: the promotion of groups that encourage participation and concern about the psychological health of the individuals in the groups, comes to replace the goal of institutional change.

We are leaving the institutional edifice as it is. The gardens are beautified while the mansion is untouched. We shovel on remedial programs while neglecting to modify architecture. We build around existing institutions, and parallel them, but do relatively little to change the basic structures of the social services and their interrelationships. The entrenched interests of bureaucratically encrusted and feuding departments and agencies are not seriously attacked or dislodged.

Perhaps in desperation, the emphasis may shift to creating new institutions rather than reforming old. New youth training centers spring up—but there is little attempt to change the vocational high schools in the same towns. In one metropolitan city the Mayor's office, the

Ford Foundation, and other sources are supporting a new agency organized by Negro leaders which in effect attempts to set up a separate school system parallel to the public vocational schools. The reason given for such duplication is that the new may improve the old by serving as model and pilot; presumably small programs affecting small populations for short times may eventually arouse pressures and set patterns for major overhaul. How this may be done has not been clearly thought through. The result can easily be the illusion of change.

Demonstrations

How can we account for these failures —the neglect of comprehensive overall planning, the "creaming off" of the most able, the avoidance of real institutional change? I believe that equating social planning with "demonstration programs" is one major cause.

The "demonstration-research" project may well be the major instrument which planning organizations employ in their efforts to promote social planning in America today. Although not all the evidence is in, and not all demonstration programs are the same, growing indications are that many are not turning out as planned, and may actually contribute to the neglect of the aims for which they were set up.

The severest critics blame this on the concept itself: they say that demonstrations by their very nature lead to the crippling of overall planning—they are fragmented, narrow in focus, and serve to act as stop-gaps, interfering with realistic attempts to come to grips with major mass social problems. Harvey Perloff has argued that programs like Mobilization for Youth, which serves a limited group in a small corner of New York and costs more than $12,000,000, is essentially misplaced do-goodism distracting attention from the major job that needs to be done.

Further, as S. M. Miller points out, demonstration projects, too, eventually become committed to success, and come to concentrate on the "good risk client." The result is not fewer "poor risk" cases but more—those who cannot adjust to society, those who cannot adjust to the social services, and those who cannot adjust to the new demonstration.

For a variety of reasons, original purposes become undermined. One reason is that federal money is often supposed to be matched by local money, on the ground that only communities willing to put up their own money are really interested in change. This results, however, in political horsetrading in which often only the "safe-thing" survives. Local community agencies tend to support projects which will not challenge the established distribution of power and influence, and which will more likely result in "success."

There are many other complex reasons why the new programs are not accomplishing their goals, but all are related somehow to the nature of the society in which we live. The failures in the social services reflect the basic character of our society—a private economy in which specialized service can easily become fragmented, tradition-bound, and bureaucratic; and in which vested interests leave intact or strengthen present inequalities. Local planning organizations, developing programs of limited scope, often fighting for their own survival, cannot really dent such a well-supported structure. Perhaps major national programs capable of modifying the operation of an unfettered market system, such as the Social Security Act of the 1930's, could accomplish something fundamental; but nobody is suggesting them today.

Telling the "Non-Success" Story

If planning organizations cannot really effect much change, they can at least confront the public with the facts, and thus pave the way for more fundamental planning for the late 1960's and 1970's. In the meantime, what is needed are at least some "non-success oriented" demonstration programs which probe basic policy issues and structure, which ask the tough questions and refuse to concentrate on looking for proof that all is well. Some researchers suggest that the deeper they probe the public assistance system the more they become convinced that what is needed is not more tinkering with it, but abolishing it altogether, and substituting something like a "negative income tax."

This suggestion may not hold up under further analysis; but whatever its conclusions or future, non-success research is at least research in the service of social criticism rather than in the service of social apology.

PROJECT CAUSE, THE FEDERAL
ANTI-POVERTY PROGRAM,
AND SOME IMPLICATIONS
OF SUBPROFESSIONAL TRAINING

Jesse E. Gordon

The Federal Anti-Poverty Program has brought home an awareness of a developing problem in our national life, that of youth unemployment. The magnitude of the problem can be sensed from the following statistics. The rate of unemployment for those in the age range of 16 to 21 years is approximately 15%, three times the national average of 5.7%. There were 1.2 million jobless youth in 1963, not counting those who were in school. This unemployment is not evenly distributed over all youth; it is heaviest among nonwhites. Twenty-seven percent of nonwhite youths within the 16- to 21-year age range are jobless. This is double the rate of unemployment for white youth. Further, the unemployment rate for nonwhites is rising twice as fast as the rate for whites, a trend which has existed at least since 1955. That these differences between whites and nonwhites in unemployment are not only a product of differences in educational attainment is indicated by the fact that when education is comparable (i.e., comparing nonwhites with high school diplomas with high school graduated whites), the unemployment rate for the nonwhites is still twice that of the whites.

From *American Psychologist* (May 1965), Reprinted by permission of the author and the American Psychological Association.

These problems will further multiply in the immediate future. Between 1964 and the end of this decade, 17 million youth will reach labor market age. Current estimates indicate that 7 million will have quit school before the twelfth grade. These 7 million are very likely to include the 3.5 million young people growing up in poverty families (i.e., families earning less than $3,000 a year) containing five or more children to be supported by this inadequate income.

We know what tends to happen to out-of-work and out-of-school youth. They concentrate in slums where they can find "something" to do—as reflected in crime statistics. Eighty-eight percent of all car thefts are committed by people under 25 years of age. For crimes of homicide, rape, robbery, burglary, aggravated assault, larceny, and auto theft, 46% of all arrests are of young people 18 years or younger.

To make matters worse, the national trends are for an increasing loss of entry level jobs. While there are increasing needs for older, skilled technical personnel, farm employment which has functioned as an introduction to the world of work for young people has declined. Automation tends to displace the least skilled, the least trained, the least educated, the youngest workers.

The evolution of societies and cultures is highly coordinated with the kinds of economic situations within which the societies and cultures exist. Linton and Kardiner (1952) showed us how the culture of Tanala-Betsileo changed in response to the change from dry to wet rice cultivation. It is no less true that the subculture of America in which unemployment has been most chronic, and indeed, has become hereditary, has made its adaptations. Where work has traditionally not existed, there is little achieve-ment motivation. Where opportunity does not exist, there is disbelief in the rewards for work. We thus have a growing group of young people who do not value work, who do not believe in the rewards of work, and who therefore have no skills appropriate to the labor market. Even if they would, they do not know how to apply for a job, they do not know how to behave in the social role of an employee, and thus they do not know how to keep a job. As this group grows in size, it will constitute an ever-increasing danger to the larger society; the irony of it is that the subculture of chronically unemployed youth has evolved to the point at which even the availability of work is insufficient by itself to end the unemployment. Making jobs available to people who have little interest in work, little belief in its rewards, and no skills, produces the paradox of continued unemployment together with labor shortage. We are thus in the unfortunate position of sitting on a powder keg and not knowing how to defuse it.

If the availability of jobs is no longer sufficient to solve the problem, then perhaps job availability plus vocational counseling, guidance, and employability development is what is needed. Indeed, it seems to be the only possible solution and it is the one which forms the organizing principle for several aspects of the Federal Economic Opportunity Program. But in many ways this may seem to be a most unpromising solution. The very existence of masses of chronically unemployed and unemployable youth testifies to the continued failure of counseling and guidance as professions and as a body of social institutions to meet the need. And this failure is as deeply rooted and structural as is the problem of chronic unemployment. I would like to discuss quite briefly some of the dynamics which have prevented counseling and guidance, psychology, and social work from dealing effectively with this problem in the past. Much of what follows may be generalized from the field of vocational counseling to other aspects of the helping professions which may be involved in the several anti-poverty programs, such as teaching, casework and group work, family counseling, child guidance, programs for the aging, etc.

PROFESSIONAL UNPREPAREDNESS

1. Lack of Techniques

The counseling process and its array of associated techniques as represented in the standard textbooks and educational curricula is one which has been evolved through decades of practical experience and research with middle-class clients and subjects, most in both categories being students. The techniques which have been developed are therefore specifically appropriate to well-motivated applicant-clients who are verbally expressive and quite accepting of middle-class values relative to work and achievement. They are accustomed to accepting the kind of role assigned to a student-client vis-à-vis a counselor, social worker, or psychologist, and to working within that role.

While some experimental and demonstration agencies in recent years have tried various new procedures for making contact with disadvantaged youth, for motivating them, counseling them, and training them, these techniques have not yet been collected into a coherent body of principles and methods, they have not been adequately communicated to the profession, and they have not found their ways into university programs of counselor preparation, into textbooks, and into the repertories of counseling agencies by and large. Some idea of the in-appropriateness of the standard techniques can be gathered from the difficulties faced by the Selective Service Rehabilitant Program. The program was started last February 17 to help disadvantaged youth, mostly school dropouts and unemployed, to find employment and a place in society. The program hoped to do this by guiding draft rejectees into state employment offices for interviews, counseling, and job placement, in the traditional model of vocational counseling.

Underemployed and unemployed rejectees were invited by letter to visit employment service counselors in their offices to talk about jobs and career planning. Of the 234,000 rejectees so invited, of whom 78,000 were unemployed, only 42,000 showed up for interviews, and of these 32,000 were unemployed or underemployed. Thus the majority of the unemployed and underemployed who received letters—46,000—failed to respond. And of the 42,000 who did respond, fewer than 13,000 were referred to jobs; fewer than 7,000 of these hired, and some for only a few days. One-third of these invited Selective Service rejectees had less than an elementary education; 80% were school dropouts. It is apparent from this experience that arranging for an office appointment for counseling services is an unsuccessful way of making counseling services available to these youth, and that the services available for those who do respond are inappropriate and relatively nonproductive. The United States Employment Service recognizes this now, and has begun a program of stationing Employment Service personnel in the induction centers themselves; they are going to where the clients are instead of waiting for these unemployed to come to them.

2. Class Bias in Recruitment and Training of Professionals

Whether it is cause or effect of the middle-class orientation of counseling techniques and procedures, it is true that counselor education, and even more so, clinical psychology, devotes almost all its resources to the preparation of counselors and psychologists for middle-class secondary schools, middle-class agencies, and for universities, thus missing entirely the body of needy, out-of-school non-middle-class people. The result has been that almost 90% of the graduates of counseling and guidance training programs find employment in schools and universities. The figures for psychology are comparable in indicating an overwhelming orientation toward serving the educational and counseling needs of the middle class. A number of factors contribute to this state of affairs:

a. Students of counseling and guidance, psychology, and social work typically come from marginal middle-class backgrounds. Their need to confirm and enhance their social status leads them to a preference for the accoutrements of a professional identity, such as office work, the use of verbal and conceptual skills, connection with solidly respectable social institutions such as schools, job security, and a public identity which, if not outright prestigeful, is at least considered respectable. They prefer to work with people who will enhance their identities, and they tend to feel threatened by association with the milieu from which the marginal middle class is so anxious to separate itself. Thus social psychological factors within the personnel available for the helping professions incline them towards school counseling with college-bound youth.

b. When such candidates for training find themselves in a professional training program, their inclinations are reinforced. The prestigeful role models most available to them are their professors, the conditions of whose employment (teaching and research, publish or perish) result in staff selection factors which emphasize research, theorizing, scholarship, verbal-conceptual skills, and the enjoyment of theoretical and academic discussion with peers. These available role models thus omit reference to actual counseling, to actual contact and involvement with disadvantaged youth, to familiarity with the culture of poverty, and with lower-class orientations and values. Within such a faculty, processes take place which maximize the rewards of grades, honors, and scholarships for those students who most completely incorporate the characteristics of their models. These are the students who are most highly recommended for the most prestigeful job placements upon completion of training. These organizational factors within the university thus operate to further move students away from work with disadvantaged youth. The university community thus tends to further attract students whose interests and attitudes are consonant with the university ethos and which are therefore inappropriate for work with disadvantaged youth, and to repel the action oriented who thus do not gain access to the profession. While these action oriented may possess some of the skills and characteristics necessary for counseling with disadvantaged youth, they may not possess the skills and characteristics most frequently rewarded in training programs ostensibly designed to prepare them for service work. This is a reflection of a situation in which the skills required for successful completion of training are different from, and perhaps even negatively correlated with, the skills needed for successful performance on the job.

It is worth noting here that those professionals who rise to the top of their professions are often those who best exemplify some of the factors described above. These are the people who constitute the professional leadership and who help to define the profession for the public and for potential recruits to it.

3. Inappropriateness of the Model for Personal Help

Another related factor which has rendered the helping professions inappropriate for meeting the problems of current youth unemployment is in the nature of the professional model for helping work which has been developed and amplified through the course of the class-restricted history of the helping professions. This model is one in which a fully qualified professional person takes all responsibility for the counseling. He carries out personally all aspects of the process, including public information, motivating of clients, intake, testing and diagnosis, interviewing, referral, and follow-up and evaluation. A fully qualified professional practices in all areas. As new knowledge has been created concerning each of these functions, there is a press to increase the length of training and preparation to acquire more and more information about all of these aspects, and no one may be graduated with a professional degree who has not mastered all of them. This lengthening of the training process further restricts and limits the supply of professional counseling personnel, and so further intensifies the self-selection of lower middle-class students and increases the time in which

the conformity pressures within the training institution can operate.

This model of the professional as the "compleat clinician" and the implied model of the helping process are based on implicit acceptance of the transference hypothesis which sees personal counseling as evolving and moving forward only in the context of a continued personal and intimate relationship between client and counselor. It is assumed that the intimate concerns and life activities of a client can only be exposed where there is an intimate personal relationship. I would like to suggest the possibility that this assumption is valid for the middle class, but may not be valid in lower-class culture. Middle-class children are raised within an ethic of modesty. They are taught that there are spheres of their own activities, mostly those involving biological functions of toileting, eating, and sexuality, which may not be shared or made public to anyone outside of the immediate family, and may even be entirely private within the family. The possibilities for such privacy hardly exist in crowded tenements in which several families live together and share inadequate facilities. I suspect that one of the results of these living conditions is a reduction in the demand for intimacy as a precondition for "exposing" personal matters. Furthermore, the dynamic bases for transference are attenuated in lower-class culture in which children are brought up by a variety of other people, a shifting group of adults, neighbors, temporary parents-consorts, and whatever siblings happen to be around at the moment. There is thus less investment of affect in a single reliable person, and there may also, therefore, be a greater readiness to relate to the *roles* of others rather than to the individual characteristics of the individuals filling those roles. For these reasons I suggest that there is less need for a transference relationship as a precondition of counseling, less readiness to develop transference attitudes, and a smaller demand for intimacy with a particular counselor, in lower-class culture. Thus the professional model of counseling as a one-to-one relationship may not be necessary or even desirable for working with disadvantaged youth.

One consequence of the primacy of this "transference model" of counseling is that it makes no room for subprofessionals, and it therefore makes no demand for professionals to be skilled in supervision of subprofessional roles or in training people for subprofessional roles. I shall return to this point in another section of this paper.

4. Shortage of Professionals

Even without these social and psychological dynamics, the helping professionals are ill fit to cope with the problems of youth unemployment by the severe shortage of trained professional workers. The current demand for psychologists, social workers, and counselors far exceeds the supply, and the demand is growing at a much greater rate than the student bodies in these professions. For years we have been telling ourselves that we were not turning out enough qualified professionals to meet the social needs, and some of the leading universities have even abdicated from any attempt to meet the needs by concentrating their efforts on turning out theoreticians and researchers and leaving others to turn out practitioners. The others, of course, attempt to emulate the leaders, and in the scramble for academic prestige few concern themselves with whether anybody

has picked up the responsibilities of which the leaders have divested themselves.

TWO SOLUTIONS

Two solutions to the problem of providing services to the disadvantaged have been offered. The first is akin to the phenomenon studied by Festinger (1956) in his *When Prophesy Fails*. If the existing structuring of the professions is failing to meet the need, then increase the dosage. Thus pleas are made for more federal aid for faculty and for student support so that more professionals can be trained. But, of course, if the middle-class orientation of the professions is not altered, or the structural or dynamic factors responsible for this orientation are left undisturbed, there is no reason to think that an increased supply of professionals would result in more effective counseling with the disadvantaged, or a greater quantity of such counseling, particularly as middle-class affluence grows and makes it increasingly capable of absorbing more of the services of the trained professionals being produced. This is, then, a solution which does not solve anything except the problem of enhancing and protecting the traditional identities of the professions which have evolved, by a total preservation of the models on which their activities are based.

Until recently, this was the only solution offered by the helping professions, and as the problems of youth unemployment grew, it remained for the federal government to step in and take political action. The Department of Labor's Project CAUSE was one of the actions taken. In the summer of 1964, Project CAUSE recruited almost 1,900 people for intensive 8- to 10-week training courses conducted by 27 universities around the country, designed to prepare these recruits for subprofessional roles in Youth Opportunity Centers, conceived of as specialized branches of existing employment services.

Despite intensive intraprofessional discussions about subprofessional training in the recent past, the major thrusts have been away from terminal MA training in psychology, from a 1-year MA to a 2-year MA in counseling and guidance, and to the 2-year MSW as a minimum requirement in social work. Thus none of the helping professions have made room for subprofessional roles of the kind for which Project CAUSE recruits were to be trained. This led inevitably to ambiguity and uncertainty regarding the roles for which they were being trained. Nevertheless, the character of the training made it clear that the successful trainees, designated as Counselor Aides and Youth Advisors to discriminate them from the fully qualified professionals, would be some kind of a cross between social workers and vocational counselors, and would work under the supervision of qualified professionals. Thus the solution to the problem of the shortage of professional personnel who can deal with disadvantaged youth posed by Project CAUSE is one in which a new subprofession has been created by federal action. The recruitment, selection, and training, as described by Kranz (1964), were intended to create a subprofession which would be particularly appropriate for the needs of disadvantaged youth. Project CAUSE, while the largest, is just one of many programs designed to produce subprofessionals, such as pilot projects in training retirees to supervise sheltered workshops, training of tutors for literacy training

projects, psychiatric aide training, job retraining counselors, and many others.

The helping professions are thus faced with a fait accompli, and they are unprepared for it. In the absence of any other viable solution to the shortage of counselors for disadvantaged youth, the professions must either adapt to this new subprofession and include it within their structures, or leave the field of counseling with the disadvantaged to an entirely independent and potentially rivalrous subprofession.[1]

I believe that subprofessional training can be a most appropriate and effective solution to the problems described above, and that Project CAUSE presages a new and exciting day of development and revision in the helping professions which will add considerable vitality to them. It poses some challenges which, if met, will involve exciting growth and development in the helping professions which have had so much success in meeting other challenges in the past. The consequences of not meeting the challenges include the further restriction of psychology, counseling, and social work to more and more limited ranges of activities, to increasing concentration on minutia and esoterica, and to an early senescence.[2]

[1] Many of the projects with vocational orientations which have excited the most interest, because of their inventiveness and willingness to break out of traditional molds—projects such as Mobilization for Youth, JOIN, JOBS, Haryouth-Act, the Los Angeles Youth Opportunity Board —are heavily staffed by social workers, with almost minimal participation by professionals in vocational counseling and guidance. These agencies make extensive use of personnel with varieties of academic and special training, but without specific professional identities (in the sense of having the usual degrees); they are "home grown" to meet the specific needs of the projects, have developed exceptional competence, and have made some of the most original contributions to the field.

[2] In one leading graduate department, al-

IMPLICATIONS FOR THE PROFESSIONS

I see the challenges posed by Project CAUSE as falling into five general areas:

1. How can the counseling process be subdivided into roles which can be filled by subprofessionals operating in a team under the direction of a qualified professional?

2. How are subprofessionals to be supervised, and how can students in professional training programs be trained for supervision?

3. If some part of subprofessional training is to take place in service agencies, how can the professional staffs of these agencies develop skills in training methods and techniques?

4. If much of the service work is done by subprofessionals, shall they be administered by a professional person who does not provide direct service to clients, or should agencies be administered only by those who are intimately and experientially familiar with the services to be provided by the agency?

5. Given the already overburdened staffs of university departments, where is subprofessional training to be located and by whom conducted?

I would like to make some brief comments about each of these challenges in the remainder of this paper.

1. Job Specifications and the Counseling Team

The most important challenge faced by the helping professions today is that of attempting to break down the professional role into subprofessional classifications or subroles, each of which may be filled by people with less than complete professional training and whose training is specific to the roles. I must admit that I cannot think of how this might be done; however, I have no doubt that it can be done. I can conceive of a team, operating under the direction of a professional, in which each member of the team bears a responsibility for one part of the total helping process. Thus one might be an outreach person whose job it is to make contact with the youths to be served. A second might specialize in dealing with other community agencies. A third might play a "big brother" role in such matters as teaching a young man how to fill out an application, or going with him to his first job interview. Still another member of the team might be the one who specializes in home visits, and yet another might be the test administrator. Intensive psychological interviewing can probably only be done by a professional person, but intake work could well be done by a subprofessional, which in many agencies would be an improvement over the secretary-receptionist who fulfills this function.

Thus far, such a breakdown into subroles has not been developed, except in medicine, which makes use of practical nurses, nurses' aides, nurses, laboratory technicians, and medical technologists, all of whom can be trained at less than the BA level. It was the absence of such a breakdown which produced the ambiguity and confusion concerning the job specifications for Counselor Aides and Youth Advisors in Project CAUSE, and may pose similar difficulties for the VISTA volunteers and the staffs of Job Corps Centers and Camps, Neighborhood

---

most all the students in clinical psychology receive the bulk of their training in agencies serving moderately disturbed out-patient middle-class adults. Few of the students are interested in hospitalized people; none are interested in lower-class youth.

Youth Corps, and other such eleemosynary programs. Without such job specifications which can fit the subprofessional into a structure for providing appropriate and high quality services, and which can make the training of the subprofessionals specific to their roles, the training programs must opt for a generalized introduction to the professional field, thus turning out junior professionals who know a little bit about everything the professional knows a lot about, and who therefore can be expected to do a little bit of everything the professional does. With the continued shortage of personnel, it is no wonder that agencies rapidly come to use their subprofessionals as if they were fully qualified, thus producing lowering of professional standards. But the fault for such a development lies not with the concept of subprofessional training, or with the Governmental agencies which are specifically responsible for taking action in the interests of the public welfare; the fault lies with the professions which, lacking a clear mechanism which requires responsiveness to the needs of the public, have done little to meet the needs, and have not prepared themselves to use and incorporate subprofessionals in their structures. It is no use to demand that subprofessionals trained by the Government must be supervised, and must not simply be ill-trained junior professionals, if the professions take no steps to develop valid subprofessional roles, and to train their members for using and supervising those who fill the roles adequately and appropriately. In brief, the lowering of standards which the professions fear so much as a consequence of subprofessional training is more likely to occur as a result of the professions' unpreparedness than it is a necessary consequence of the use of subprofessionals. And each restric-

tive step taken by the professions to protect and enhance standards increases the pressures which lead to Government action in creating subprofessionals who must then operate without clearly defined roles and without appropriate supervision, thus ultimately further threatening the professional standards. We recognize such self-defeating defensive reactions to perceived threat as neurotic in clients. The cure lies in making adaptations of the needs, skills, and goals of the professions to the realities; such an adaptation can be much more enhancing than blind resistance, defense, and denial.

There are some attractive advantages to a team model. The specialized training for each of the roles can probably be done in short intensive training programs which could probably recruit from indigenous personnel and from other groups such as the early retired, married women, etc., for whom long-term academic work is either inappropriate, unavailable, or unwanted. Thus the helping professions can tap a much larger pool of potential workers who can be trained fairly rapidly and with much less expense than is required for full professionals. The fully qualified professional can probably head up two or more such teams, since he would be spending much less time in activities which can be handled by the subprofessionals. Thus each professional person could service a greater number of clients, effecting a needed economy in the use of scarce professional resources.

For example, the problems of the Selective Service Rehabilitant Program, described above, indicate that counseling with disadvantaged youth requires that steps be taken actively to contact clients, rather than waiting for the clients to come to the agency. Counseling personnel cannot sit in an office and wait; they must go out to where the clients are. Further, counseling with such clients poses some additional problems which require that counseling personnel work directly in the living environment of the clients. Relatively nonverbal, nonexpressive, and educationally disadvantaged clients, unlike the middle-class patients in psychotherapy which forms the model for counseling services, cannot reproduce verbally within an interview all of the factors and events which exist in their life spaces. Nor can they carry back to their home environments the processes and events which took place during the interviewing and counseling and translate them into actions in their homes and neighborhoods by converting the verbal dialogue into appropriate specific actions. In dealing with this population, the professional must go to the client's home and talk to him there; he must meet him at work; he must hold family conferences in the client's home; he may have to meet with the client and his peers in the neighborhood gathering places. He may have to visit the client's school, his employer, the police, and other social agencies. Such visits outside the agency office are essential, but they are also incredibly costly of time and money. Considering the present and future shortage of fully qualified professionals, I do not see how they can justify the time and money which will be eaten up in city traffic jams, in public transportation systems; a counselor with a 2-year master's degree who spends 2 or more hours a day between here and there is far too expensive. Out-of-office work may be essential, but much of it can be done by subprofessionals who may even be stationed in the communities and neighborhoods being served.

A second major advantage of the helping team is that it may include workers from the same milieu as the clients served by the team, and these workers could well be much more successful than the fully qualified professional in making contact with potential clients, in motivating them, and in interpreting the agency to the client. Where they have been well trained and well supervised, indigenous leaders have made important contributions which cannot be made by anyone else. There are dimensions of expression, voice inflection, gesture, body language, which are almost instantly recognizable as signs of class and ethnic origin. The indigenous leader can communicate instantly to the suspicious and distrustful client, avoiding noblesse oblige, in a way that many middle-class professionals cannot do when dealing with disaffected, hostile, anomic youths who see the middle-class agency worker as part of the system against which he is fighting. In the long run, disparities between the class castes of counselor and client might make no difference in the outcome of the counseling, if the long run is long enough and the counseling approaches psychotherapy in its depth and intensiveness. But the kind of work which will be most common in the various phases of the Anti-Poverty Program is not likely to use the long run, and, in brief contacts, first impressions can be all important in determining whether the client will be relaxed and receptive, or on his guard and defensive. Indigenous personnel who "speak the client's language" can form an extremely effective bridge between the milieu of the client and the milieu of agency; they can make important contributions to the counseling team in contacting the clients to be served, in maintaining them through their agency contacts, and may be particularly effective in follow-up work with the clients in their home, community, and on the job. A client is more likely to be able to report continuing difficulties, after his counseling contacts, to an indigenous worker, than he is to the professional interviewer toward whom the ethic of mutual cooperation and courtesy requires that he affirm the success of the counseling and deny continued problems.

2. Supervision

If we are going into subprofessional training, perhaps using a team concept such as that suggested above, then the second challenge to the helping professions involves training for supervision. In the current model of counseling, the worker "on the line" requires no skills in supervision, since there is no one present to supervise. In graduate training programs it is generally assumed that as the recent graduate acquires more and more experience, he will begin to move up in the organizational hierarchy. He will gradually take on supervisory responsibilities and will develop his skills in supervision by emulating those who supervise him. Even with the current model of counseling, this assumption is false. Many graduates find that their very first job is that of head of an agency or a service. They are immediately expected to supervise, with no prior training in supervision. Typically, they fall back on the kinds of supervision they experienced as graduate students. But this kind of supervision is specifically appropriate to highly verbal, academic, intelligent, professionally trained personnel. It is not appropriate for subprofessionals. But if a counseling team is going to work effectively, much will depend on the quality and competence of the supervision it receives, supervision which is designed for subprofessional roles. Recognition of this important function in professional train-

ing is long overdue, and the renewed recognition of the importance of supervision which was stimulated by Project CAUSE and similar programs may be listed as among the achievements of these programs. It is of no use for the professions to seek guarantees that subprofessionals will be given adequate supervision if the professions do not produce people who are trained to provide it.

3. Training Skills

A third challenge posed by subprofessional training is concerned with training methods. While subprofessionals might be trained for varying periods of time in academic settings, it seems likely that such training will serve best as a prologue or introduction to the professional field, while the major portion of the skill training for the specific roles to be filled by the subprofessionals can best be handled by representative agencies in which the subprofessionals will be employed. The local community agency is likely to be the best place in which to train indigenous leaders, but the task of providing such in-house training for subprofessionals is a large one, and is one for which most agencies are ill equipped. When the notion of using indigenous personnel was first developed in the lower East Side of New York, the very first problem which had to be faced was that of providing suitable training within the agency, and with the only available models of training being those derived from academic education, the burden for innovation and creativity fell on the training agencies. When asked to do training, many agencies automatically fall back on the patterns established by their own professional training, and so they institute workshops, lectures, and seminars. Such procedures, as imitations of university education, can just as well be done at a university which is experienced with them. They fail to capitalize on the distinctive contributions which can be made by an operating social agency. It is the agency's work setting which must be involved if the agency is to do the kind of training for which it is best suited.

Training of residents and interns has been a standard part of the tasks of many agencies for years. However, there is a certain amount of arrogance implied by the fact that despite this traditional role, little or no training in methods of education is given to the students in the profession who man these training agencies. Is our level of insight into human behavior so complete and deep that we have nothing to learn from the specific studies and skills of educators? Thus I suggest that increased demand for agencies to do role-specific training implies a recognition of training functions as part of the role of a fully qualified professional person. This recognition further implies the building into professional training of courses in training methods and procedures.

4. Who Shall Administer?

The picture which emerges from the above discussion is that of a fully qualified professional person more highly trained in supervision and in training methods than in the past; he heads a team or teams of subprofessionals, trains people for the team, and supervises the activities of the team members. In brief, the professional person functions as an administrator. But where is he to learn agency administration? If he is a social worker, he may have learned it in the course of his graduate training. If he is a vocational counselor or a clinical psychologist, he will have learned it only by

imitation of university professors who operate captive agencies which function very differently from those serving the disadvantaged poor. This indicates still another implication of subprofessional training.

I think it worth noting that there are some psychological factors which impinge on supervision and administration in the helping professions. It seems to me as if people in the helping professions as a group are reluctant to supervise and administer. They seem to dislike being in superior-subordinate relationships. This may be connected with the antiauthoritarianism which is so characteristic of those in the helping professions, or it may come from a variety of other sources about which one could speculate. The point is simply that there does seem to be an avoidance or reluctance which must be overcome if supervision and administration are to be institutionalized as part of the professional's function and as elements in his training.

One problem in connection with administration should be mentioned. The age-old question involved here is of whether an agency ought to be run by people specifically trained in supervision, or whether it should be run by professionals who are completely experienced in the function being administered. If the fully qualified member of the team devotes himself to administration, supervision, and training, there is the danger that he will become so far removed from the realities of actual work with the clients as performed by the subprofessionals that his supervision and administration may become unrealistic. This problem has not been solved in the schools, in the universities, in business, or in Government; it is unlikely to find its completely adequate solution in the helping professions. Nevertheless, it is a problem which needs to be recognized, and it is part of the challenge posed by the broadening of counseling to include subprofessionals.

5. Who Shall Train?

The last problem I would like to discuss here concerns the locus of subprofessional recruitment and training. In Project CAUSE, the training was located in universities and was dominated by academic instruction. As indicated earlier, the success of such instruction rests heavily on the academic skills and the verbal-conceptual orientation of the trainees. It was also suggested earlier that these skills may be different from those which are required for successful performance in subprofessional roles. One is not likely to find many indigenous leaders, for example, who will be able to fit themselves into the academic mold even for brief, intensive training. Furthermore, the very concept of an indigenous leader is destroyed when one thinks of sending such a person to a university distant from his neighborhood, and away from his milieu. On the other hand, there are no other institutions which can marshal the intellectual and professional resources for providing such training. It is possible that local community colleges and junior colleges may be able to play a role in subprofessional training, especially if they are able to make use of personnel from higher institutions and community agencies.

Such training will demand an interdisciplinary approach, if it is specifically designed for workers with the disadvantaged. Skill and technique instruction will have to come from experienced clinicians, workers, and/or counselors, but the limitations in their experience to middle-class populations will require

supplementation from sociologists, economists, criminologists, housing authorities, community action specialists, jurists, and others who have devoted their attentions to problems of the poor. It was the experience of many of the universities which participated in Project CAUSE training that contact with these other fields proved to be a source of renewed excitement and stimulation to the members of the counseling and guidance departments. Continued interaction of this sort can do much to invigorate counseling and guidance both as a profession and as a field of scholarship.

To recapitulate: There are overwhelming social needs requiring increased professional attention. There is a shortage of professional personnel, and the models which underlie the structures of the professions as presently constituted are inappropriate for meeting the social needs. One solution to these problems lies in subprofessional training, to implement a team concept which may provide services more appropriate to the population needing them and which can compensate for the shortage of fully qualified professionals. The establishment of subprofessional training requires attention to ways in which helping work can be subdivided into subprofessional roles which are effective and economical, the development of techniques for supervision, the training of professionals in supervision, attention to methods of in-service training and the development of training skills in professional personnel, the use of the fully qualified professional person as an administrator of services, and attention to the location and institutionalization of subprofessional training. The helping professions must attend to these problems if they are to remain responsive to the changing nature of the social needs, and if they are to continue to make the kind of contributions to society for which they are the most appropriate social institutions currently available. Failure to meet these challenges through a rigid clinging to methods no longer appropriate to the needs could render these professions so inappropriate that new ones may have to arise to fill the gap.

PROFESSIONAL STANDARDS AND RESISTANCE TO CHANGE

I would like to make a final comment about professional standards. As I see it, the development of subprofessional roles involves both a lowering and a raising of traditional standards. The establishment of specific subprofessional roles affords an economy of training which many will see as a lowering of professional standards (Odgers, 1964). On the other hand, the inclusion of these roles within the professional structures, as suggested above, requires that the fully qualified professional develop new and more advanced skills than those which are currently included in his repertoire. In this sense, we have a call for higher standards. There are those who criticize Project CAUSE and other similar programs as an attack on professional standards. I believe this to be a short-sighted view which implies a refusal on the part of the professions to adapt to the current needs, with the standards-enhancing implication of such an adaptation. The appeal to standards is traditionally the socially accepted defense against disturbance of the established status quo. Segregation in the neighborhoods has been defended by reference to standards of neighborhood care and upkeep; the exclusiveness and hegemony of medieval guilds was defended by reference to craftsmanship standards; the segregation of school children has similarly been justified. I see little use for high and restrictive standards for professional treatment if, because of those standards, treatment is completely denied to those needing it. And the data clearly indicate that effective and appropriate treatment is being denied to the disadvantaged youth of today. While such denial may not be willful or intended, its reality testifies that opposition to an expansion of appropriate services in the service of a defense of standards is in the interests of maintenance of the establishment rather than in the interests of those needing help.

REFERENCES

Festinger, L. *When prophecy fails.* Minneapolis: Univer. Minnesota Press, 1956.

Kranz, H. A crash program to aid disadvantaged youth. *Guidepost,* 1964, 6, 3–6.

Linton, R., and A. Kardiner. The change from dry to wet rice cultivation in Tanala-Betsileo. In G. E. Swanson, T. M. Newcomb, and E. L. Hartley (Eds.), *Readings in social psychology.* New York: Holt, 1952. Pp. 222–230.

Odgers, J. Cause for concern. *Counselor Education and Supervision,* 1964, 6, 17–20.

THE PLANNER AS A BUREAUCRAT

Norman Beckman

This column is motivated by the apparent attitude of many planners and other observers of the urban scene that: (a) little progress has been, or is likely to be, made toward acceptance or implementation of sound urban planning; and (b) the cause of this failure to achieve rational, orderly urban development is "politics" and politicians—the elected officials that run our local governments. This distrust and dislike are often returned in kind. Indications that this malaise does exist are the sometimes high rate of reversals of staff planning and zoning recommendations; the extensive use of private consultants for public business rather than the building of strong institutional planning staffs in our local governments; and the high turnover and mobility rate of the planning profession.

A recent letter written by a local planner who was trying to form a panel to speak to an AIP chapter on the subject of professional and political obligations of the planning profession summarizes the situation. Expressing concern with the lack of effectiveness of planning programs in the Washington region, he observed that:

Probably the best example I can give as food for thought is the fact that every planning director in the Washington metropolitan region has either resigned or has been replaced within the last 24 months.

This indicates to me that there must exist a fairly wide gap in philosophy between political goals and planning goals.

In seeking solutions to the problem of improved planner-politician relationships, one could approach the subject in terms of improving public relations techniques, identifying the local power structure, or improving the tools of the planning profession. The orientation used here, however, is that of public administration and the possible contribution of that academic and professional field to the problem at hand.

This column is addressed both to planners who are identified as politically controversial figures and to those who see themselves as planning technicians. In the long run, both may do harm to the causes and profession they serve—the former by his loss to the community in a change of administration or because he becomes "expendable," and the latter by the sterility of his efforts. I shall seek to examine the similarity of the roles of the politician and the planner and the conflict thereby engendered; the vulnerability of the planner if he challenges the elected official for community leadership; the unique capability of the planner to serve the chief executive, whether governor, county board, mayor, or manager; the special character of government employment and the place of the public ser-

From *Journal of the American Institute of Planners,* 30, 4 (November 1964). Reprinted by permission of the author and the American Institute of Planners.

vant in a responsible bureaucracy; and finally, some advice by experts on how to survive and be effective in the public sector.

In speaking of these problems, emphasis will be placed on certain fundamentals of our system of government that are often given lip service but not fully understood or applied in the particular situation. These fundamentals are: *one,* the dominant role of the politician in our governmental system; and *two,* the inevitable involvement of planners and other administrative generalists in the political process.

THE CASE OF THE CONFLICTING IDENTITIES

The public esteem of those who seek elected office, especially local office, is not always high. Neither, it should be noted, is the public esteem of the civil servant. Indeed the popular image of the politician is often heavily tinged with venality and hypocrisy, if not outright dishonesty. This is not an encouraging or healthy situation at a time when all levels of government are being called upon to provide expanded public services and play an increasingly influential role in all our lives. One can only speculate as to whether the attitude of the average planner is much different from that of the general population with respect to elected officials.

What are the traditional definitions of the function of a politician and political party? The role of politics has been defined as: *one,* coordinating diverse and antagonistic interests; and *two,* sublimating the private interests by furthering principles that merge them with the general interest. A useful working theory of politics defines the politician's role as that of a "broker-mediator." Under this approach, the typical party leader is a person concerned primarily in mediating, adjusting, and pulling views into sufficient harmony for action. Elected officials are assigned the difficult task of working toward decisions by bringing together the judgment of the expert and the "will of the people." Other roles of the party have been identified.[1] However, the broker-mediator theory seems to come closest to explaining the observable phenomenon of many interest groups, each seeking to influence action by government. Indeed, one of the rapidly growing industries of the National Capital area has been the opening of offices by interest-group associations.

No doubt many planners would favor having a planner for President just as businessmen, scientists, and economists would like to see their profession represented in the office of Chief Executive. Perhaps some of the nostalgia and idealization surrounding the depression-born National Resources Planning Board is derived from the identification of the planning profession with the Presidency. (Technocracy was also in vogue about the same time.) A reassuring fact, however, is that none of the professions is likely to consider turning over our political leadership at the national level—or at the local level—to groups other than their own, except to politicians.[2]

One must keep in mind that the objective of a political party is to win elections and remain in office. Once the elected official obtains his position, his reelection is dependent upon how successfully he reconciles and integrates the many competing demands that we, as citizens and members of groups, place on him. A basic reason why our governmental system has been so durable is its capacity to meet many of the demands made by any one group in a manner that is consistent with the public interest. One of the major qualities of the successful politician is the ability to understand and adjust to these constant but ever changing demands. The competition in this occupation is keen, however, and the turnover rate is high—much higher than for the heads of even the largest private organizations. So much for the politician.

Now let us examine the role and function of the planner as described in a recent statement of the profession's roles and purposes and relate it to the above definitions of politician.

As men who have specialized in the general, the truly effective city planners have functioned as catalysts for the developmental plans of the more specialized groups in government. By bringing representatives of public and private agencies together, they have helped to synthesize new amalgams that better reflect both the separate and the mutual goals of the various participants. Individual plans for components have been reframed to accord with criteria established by the plans for the next-larger systems of components that, in turn, conform to more comprehensive overviews of the future and of the community's objectives.[3]

Note the similarity of terms—"coordinate," "working harmony," "reconcile," "integrate," "public interest," "adjust," "synthesize," "next larger systems," "comprehensive overviews." Both the politician and the planner see themselves as responsible for integrating the independent development decisions with their attendant social and economic effects that are made in the community and for providing leadership in achieving the good life generally. Thus we are faced with a problem of conflicting identities. The conflict between some planners and some politicians arises because each believes that he is best fit—through training, experience, and institutional expectations— to serve the public as broker-mediator,

coordinator, and goal-maker. *This conflict of identity can best be resolved, and the planner's effectiveness enhanced, if he is willing to accept the vital but more limited role that our system assigns to the public employee.*

In this role of assisting and serving the elected policy-maker, the tools of the planner's trade and his heritage of comprehensiveness give him a special competence, perhaps above all other public service professions. To quote further from the statement on the profession's roles:

Improved data systems will permit planners continuously to meter the states of affairs of the various population groups, the economy, the municipal fisc, the physical plant, and other aspects of the city. Improved theory, describing and explaining the processes of city life and city growth, will permit us more sensitively to identify those crucial points of public intervention that are appropriate to accomplishing specified objectives.[4]

Indeed, what is that *sine qua non* of the planner's profession, the land use map and the master plan, but an attempt to express a multitude of public and private decisions affecting a given political jurisdiction. Perhaps most important, "the city planner's realistic idealism, his orientation to the whole city, and his focus upon future conditions have placed him in a position of intellectual leadership,"[5] in serving as key staff in the cause of effective political leadership.

It may be argued that the planner's bias toward the long-range and the politician's equal bias toward the immediate establishes a situation of continuing conflict. The politician faces frequent elections before an existent constituency, with a resultant need for short-range performance, while the planner may be more concerned about the provision of services in the still unpopulated areas of suburbia. But is concern with the broad geographic area, the interdependence of decisions, the future population, and the long-range interest inconsistent with providing answers to immediate issues? Until all basic questions concerning long-term development and goals—such as patterns of growth and industrial and residential character of the community—are dealt with, it is difficult to determine the most effective means of providing any given function. Surely the alternative of uncoordinated development, conflicting land uses, and resultant depreciation of property values and uneconomical public facilities, is not good politics.

This concern for "future conditions" is not unique to planners. Government exists because there is public concern for the long-term, for the citizen at large, and for the public interest. From agriculture to water resources, long-range planning is being carried on by competent professionals at all three levels of government. Perhaps the planner's main contribution is his concern for the interrelatedness of more specialized long-term planning.

THE VULNERABILITY OF THE PLANNER

The planner is vulnerable in any competition with the politician. Primarily this is because it is in the nature of his job to become deeply and inevitably involved in politics and the political process. In the field of government, every administrative action, from surly behavior of a licensing clerk to a health department decision to prohibit individual wells and septic tanks in an urban area, is weighed on a political scale. Those actions which benefit or hurt individuals produce a reading on that scale. It is difficult to anticipate what actions will be elevated to

public attention. In my own community, a single zoning decision to permit construction of an apartment house along the Potomac resulted in the unseating of several members of the county board of supervisors. Planning agencies help to determine "who gets what, when, and how" and to do that means to function politically.

The commission form of organization and the professionalization of the occupation are presumably designed to "remove planning from politics." Yet the operating relationships of planning agencies with other local, state, and federal agencies and the effect on, and exposure to, large numbers of citizens inevitably means that the planner is politically involved and subject to political attack. Planning agencies, by having to operate on the cutting edge of politics and administration —concerned with the "obstetrics of public policy"—are especially vulnerable to such attack. The planner's main stock in trade are his professional skills, the merit of his ideas, and his ability and willingness to serve as a conduit for exchange of information with other governments and agencies.

The planner's place in the structure of local government differs from that of most other public employees. Instead of being held directly accountable to the elected executive, he is more commonly responsible to a lay or ex-officio planning commission.[6] Such boards have the inevitable effect of insulating the planner from the politician and the chief executive who most needs his help in moderating special interest demands. Too often, relatively independent commissions can operate to obscure public accountability, provide an excuse for delay, and produce a "lowest common denominator" kind of decision too early in the political decision-making process. The bulk of local planning activities today are executive or operational in nature and as such should be headed by a single executive. The use of boards and commissions to carry out local government planning activities might better be limited to the performance of certain quasi-legislative planning functions, such as zoning actions. The problems of regional planning agencies may be unique. Here the desire for representation by the various jurisdictions may require a board form, but this governing body should be chosen by, or made up of, responsible elected officials rather than by other subregional or local planning agencies.

Despite the facade of autonomy and independence behind which planning agencies seek to achieve the heavenly city of the twentieth century, it must constantly be kept in mind that planning agencies have almost no levers, no gifts, no grants, no weapons, no operating programs, no strong base of independent political support. It is, therefore, imperative to stick close to (and serve to the extent possible as key management staff) responsible officials who do have executive powers—the mayor, the county council, or the city manager.

The problem is especially acute for the metropolitan agency, since it has no single political jurisdictional counterpart. New Jersey's Department of Conservation and Economic Development properly advocates that areawide planning agencies be headed by decision-makers:

To create regional planning boards based solely upon the theory of impartial-disinterested citizen participation and to assign them the job of coping with area-wide long-range issues is to invite an unnecessary excursion beyond reality. What regional planning needs is the participation of decision-makers. While this may or may not include participants other than elected officials, it must include the executive officials of those governments taking part in specific regional planning operations.[7]

Politicians, even lay planning commission members, are often only too glad to let planning staffs serve as advocates for new development proposals. If the public reaction (that is, interest group reaction) is adverse, well, it's back to the drafting board to devise a new formula for growth and redevelopment and perhaps to initiate efforts to recruit a new planning director. Getting very far ahead of commission members and elected officials is a dangerous game for any bureaucrat, especially a vulnerable one.

It is an occupational hazard of the professional public employee (and planners perhaps are especially susceptible on this score) to become absolutely convinced not only of the rightness of his "plan," but that the plan, the zoning ordinance, and the zoning decision, is an end in itself. A public servant can never indulge that kind of faith without bad results. Much of the sense of frustration from which too many planners suffer springs from the expectation of immediate, measurable, and conclusive influence. He finds it hard to understand why responsible officials, and the public generally, do not do what he is satisfied is the best thing to do. He tends to forget that his is the more limited function of seeking to blend, to synthesize, and to adjust programs to the hopes and fears, likes and dislikes, of the politician he serves.

SURVIVAL IN A BUREAUCRACY

It is fundamental to our system of government that public employment "does not require partisans of a particular general outlook, whether Republican or Democrat, conservative, progressive, or socialist, but it does require specialists who know their job and will, therefore, *effectively execute the general rules decided upon by executive or legislative leadership in accordance with popular preferences.*[8]

Max Weber's idealized construct of bureaucratic organization still has validity today: (a) the head of the organization owes his authority and position to election; (b) the remaining staff under such authority are organized in a defined hierarchy of office; (c) they are selected on the basis of technical qualifications; (d) such an appointment constitutes a career, including promotion based on seniority and achievement as judged by superiors; (e) the person filling the office works entirely separately from ownership or the means of administration; (f) he is subject to strict and systematic discipline and control in the conduct of the office.

Large scale public and private organizations are similar—except in the important things. The public servant must remember that the character of *government* employment is different—first in its breadth of scope, impact, and consideration; second, in the public accountability to which he will be held; and third, in the political character of his work which requires him to ask before making any decision: "Who is going to be mad? How mad? Who is going to be glad? How glad?"[9]

The planner, frustrated or disheartened by the decisions made by his superiors—elected or otherwise—must constantly remind himself that he serves in an official rather than a personal capacity. General Dawes, first Director of the United States Bureau of the Budget, explained how the system works: "If the President wants us to spread garbage around the White House, it is our job to figure out how to pile it deeply

and uniformly and at the least possible cost."

Not every one is built for the bureaucratic life, and for those planners whose "idealism" and "professionalism" make life in an institutional setting intolerable, perhaps the role of the academic, researcher, or technician is appropriate. However, the rest of the government bureaucracy will continue whether or not planners participate, and in the long-run, planners' contributions to administration will be best achieved by formal participation in the governmental hierarchy.

AN ILLUSTRATION: THE BUREAU OF THE BUDGET

Let us examine briefly the experience of a staff agency generally considered successful—the Bureau of the Budget. The Bureau has responsibility for developing the President's executive budget, for coordinating the executive branch legislative program, and for serving as an extension of the President to see that Presidential programs are supported by the often decentralized departments, agencies, and bureaus. How many of these politically charged personnel in the Bureau were replaced when Mr. Eisenhower took over from President Truman? Perhaps five. A similar number were affected when President Kennedy took over after eight years of Republican Administration. Indeed, the present Deputy Director has served at the directorate level under four Presidents. Several years ago he was given a present by Budget Bureau staff—a large seat cushion with a donkey on one side and an elephant on the other.

Let me summarize and paraphrase some of the orientation literature given to the new Bureau of the Budget employee, as it contains some clues to why the Bureau has had success in serving elected officials and affecting public policies indirectly. The advice is applicable elsewhere.

The employee has a difficult role to play. He must be humble, self-effacing, and quietly loyal. He will have little or no opportunity to use pronouns in the first person singular. He must be self-effacing because his role is institutional. He is a team player. His loyalty to the politician must be that of the disciplined soldier in combat who has been trained to know that while his commanding officer will protect him to the extent possible, he is nevertheless expendable, both as an individual and as part of a unit. This means that the staff member must develop his instinct for self-preservation to the highest possible point. He cannot afford to make many mistakes. The consequences to himself, his agency, and the elected official may be much too serious.

The administration to be served at any given time represents a point of view so far as public policy is concerned. The staff member's job is to understand this point of view and assist the public official in achieving his objectives. Above all, obstacles are not to be put in the way of the public official. What this comes down to is that every professional is expected to keep his personal notions about public policy in check. He should resist revealing strong attitudes which might raise doubt about his objectivity and, therefore, about his agency's goals. Proposals can often usefully be presented as a range of alternatives, the strengths and weaknesses of each (including the probable political ramifications) identified, and a staff preference stated.

Is this intellectually dishonest? We are here to give public service to all the people. We do not have to compete for our jobs on a political basis. As Harlan Cleveland, Assistant Secretary of State, has recently noted, this does not mean the avoidance of controversy within the agency or the government generally or finding out what the boss thinks before you give him your opinion:

The decisions that "work" are not produced by the pliant collaboration of yes-men, but by loud and cheerful argument among colleagues who know they are all trying to catch a glimpse of the same moon from different parts of the forest.

The job of the top administrator is not primarily to make peace within his own organization. It is to tighten the web of tensions he deliberately creates, weighing the options revealed by the arguments among his staff, and then to elicit the loyalty of these same people to the wider public interest as expressed in his decisions.[10]

Planning agencies, like other institutional staff (the Bureau of the Budget, the city manager, the school superintendent), must be sensitive to shifts of public policy. A professional should be able to weather any political transition. Once the staff advisor has lost the confidence of his political superior his usefulness is finished. Those too closely identified with the ideals and aims of the previous administration must be expected to depart quietly, or not so quietly. This kind of adaptability is the hallmark of the professional bureaucrat at any level of government.

Even without a change of administration, bureaucrats must keep the way open for modification and adjustment. The ability to revoke or modify decisions on important issues becomes an important criterion of the successful administrator. The land use map has the unfortunate connotation of irrevocability, infallibility, and inviolateness. Emphasis should be on "the planning process" rather than on "the plan."

PLANNING IS THE ART OF THE POSSIBLE

Constant attention must be paid to problems and implications of implementation. No "unseen hand" will bring about orderly urban development. Action is needed to insure that urban expansion occurs in the "right areas." *The Year 2000 Plan* for the National Capital Region devotes 108 pages to proposals and three pages to implementation—one page for the District, one for the metro center, and one for the region. The *Wedges and Corridors* plan prepared by the Maryland National Capital Park and Planning Commission, designed to translate part of the *Year 2000* sketch plan into more detailed proposals, properly devotes almost half the report to zoning, tax policies, and controls to implement the plan.

Planning commission publications can no longer be limited to general development plans. They must also come up with sound proposals for governmental cooperation and restructuring where necessary to carry out carefully drawn plans. Planners today must not only be sewer, water, air pollution, highway, and recreation experts; they must also have legal, organizational, and economic competencies available to them. They must also be political pragmatists with a good public relations sense.

Chester Barnard, a long-time practitioner in public and private administration, has laid down four conditions that must be met before a proposal is accepted. These conditions may serve as a guide to making major land use proposals. The person receiving the proposal (the politician, the public) will accept it as authoritative if: (a) he can and does understand the communication; (b) he believes that it is not inconsistent with the purpose of the organization; (c) he believes it to be compatible with his personal interest as a whole; and (d) he is able mentally and physically to comply with it.[11]

Planners, above all others, cannot afford to be called dreamers or ivory tower types. To put out proposals that clearly have little chance of acceptance and accomplishment inevitably reduces the planner's always limited supply of public confidence and makes acceptance of subsequent proposals less likely, regardless of their merit.

Richard Neustadt, in his book *Presidential Power,* makes two observations of direct relevance to planners. First, the fact that the President issues an order does not necessarily mean that it will be carried out. Resistances all along the line can frustrate the President's wishes. Second, every defeat that a President suffers reduces the prestige and effectiveness of subsequent efforts, even in unrelated fields. If this is true for the Presidency, it is also true for lesser executive positions.

CONCLUSION

Influence on public policy is achieved within the bureaucracy through competence. Planners and other staff advisors have influence only as they can *persuade* their political superiors; their power is the power of the idea.

Given the high turnover rate of elected officials, continuity and accumulated experience are valuable assets to the bureaucracy. A number of small victories can be as important as a major victory. "As trifles make the sum of human things, so details make the substance of public affairs." To those discouraged by the failure to establish bold planning goals or to prompt resolute action to achieve these goals, perhaps the views of William James, given toward the end of his life, are appropriate. James commented that he was "done with great things and big things, great institutions and big success," and was rather "for those tiny, invisible, molecular moral forces that work from individual to individual, creeping through the crannies of the world like so many soft rootlets, or like the capillary oozing of water, yet which, if you give them time, will rend the hardest monuments of men's pride."

Planners, like all professionals, are overly pessimistic about the status and recognition of their own field. The increasing reliance on planning requirements in federal grant-in-aid legislation, the availability of "701" and Community Renewal Program funds, the swelling membership rolls of the Institute, the expanding budgets for planning agencies, the emergence of the planner—development coordinator as a key staff advisor to a number of big city mayors—all indicate acceptance of the role of planning in the administration of the public business.

Planners in government are involved in the political process. If this conclusion appears to exalt planning, it must be remembered that in our system of government politics subordinates the public employee, grants responsibility and power to the politician, and vests ultimate authority in the voter.

REFERENCES

1. See Neil A. McDonald, *The Study of Political Parties* (Garden City, New York: Doubleday & Company, Inc., 1955), pp. 8–36, for a useful summary of the literature on the functions of political parties.
2. For a development of this thesis see Paul Appleby, *Policy and Administration* (University, Alabama: University of Alabama Press, 1949), p. 47.
3. Melvin M. Webber, "Comprehensive Planning and Social Responsibility: Toward an AIP Consensus on the Profession's Roles and Purposes," *Journal of the American Institute of Planners,* XXIX (November, 1963), 236–37.
4. *Ibid.*
5. *Ibid.*, p. 238.
6. On the subject, see the article by Peter H. Nash and Dennis Durden, "A Task-Force Approach to Replace the Planning Board," *Journal of the American Institute of Planners,* XXX (February, 1964), 10–22.
7. New Jersey State Department of Conservation and Economic Development, *The Setting for Regional Planning in New Jersey* (December, 1961), p. 86.
8. Carl J. Friedrich, *Constitutional Government and Democracy* (Boston: Ginn and Co., 1950), p. 409. Italics added.
9. Paul Appleby, quoted in Harlan Cleveland, "The Case for Bureaucracy," *New York Times Magazine,* October 27, 1963.
10. *Ibid.*
11. Chester Barnard, *The Functions of the Executive* (Cambridge, Massachusetts: Harvard University Press, 1938), p. 165.

SOCIAL CHANGE:

Implications for Welfare Manpower

Louis H. Orzack*

An appraisal of changes in the patterns of our national institutions and specifically in social welfare institutions indicates both drift of the course and heading on the compass. It includes an assessment of the effects and consequences of accustomed daily practices and behaviors, and an analysis of desired targets and goals. It incorporates an effort to understand how the various environmental forces that impinge upon a single institution, social welfare, affect both its structure and its functioning.

This discourse on changes in process in American society and their relationships to prospective events and policies in social welfare is rooted in the realism of the present-day organization of American society and is tied to the future through a series of projections and predictions. An element of fantasy, a mood of whimsy and of imagination, is present in the visualization of what might be and what might happen. What ought to happen also needs a portrayal and so the projections from the present to the future include statements of how our social, economic, educational, and other resources

* Louis H. Orzack, Associate Professor of Sociology, Department of Sociology and Anthropology, Boston University, Boston, Massachusetts.

can better than at present be made available to individuals in the last third of the twentieth century. How, we ask, can these ample resources be utilized so as to enhance the opportunities they provide for social and psychological growth?

If we think of the year 2000 A.D., for example, we are forced to assume that institutional lags will continue, that conflict among interest groups will remain, that resources will still be less than needs and certainly less than either demands or expectations. Identity crises will still be features of our future patterning of individual growth and development. The transitions to adult status, to marriage and family obligations, to careers and to jobs, and the adjustments required by geographic migration and social mobility will still occur and will still often threaten the individual. Dependency will still be forced upon many of the handicapped and underprivileged; children of the divorced or separated, or of parents affected by illness or by accidents, and perhaps by unemployment, will still require a variety of forms of support and counsel. Such problems will continue, although their frequency and import will undoubtedly change. Finally, the city as the larger environment for most social relationships will remain, but the city as

Reprinted with permission of the author and from *Manpower in Social Welfare: Research* of Social Workers, 1966), pp. 17–30. of the National Association of Social Workers, *Perspective* (New York: National Association a social form will be even more complex, more highly paced, more challenging, more impersonal, and conceivably more confusing and threatening than at present.

How can these developments be accommodated? What new obligations will confront welfare personnel? For what social welfare tasks will we have to educate how many recruits in the world of the future toward which we now look? What will be the manpower requirements in social welfare?

An idealized description of the future internal organization of the social welfare field might be as follows: Intellectually and technically equipped men and women, selected and screened through appropriate achievement tests, move smoothly into work roles that are graded appropriately to require varying amounts of responsibility in accordance with their experience, capabilities, and potential. These positions yield them the rewards they have come to expect, rewards of social recognition and prestige, of money, and of leisure. These rewards also serve as motivational forces to elicit additional expenditures of energy and ever higher levels of expectations regarding performance through direct service to others, and through supervision of subordinate, competent, and willing personnel in their provision of service to others. Other role tasks are: (1) informed consultation to administrative policy-makers, (2) direct administration of complex, formal organizations concerned with, or having an impact on, social welfare, (3) teaching newcomers in the social welfare field and teaching others in allied fields who can benefit from social welfare instruction, and (4) conducting or sanctioning behavioral science research in areas of knowledge relevant to the organization of social welfare services. In this idealized scheme the social system will provide qualified welfare workers in numbers sufficient to perform the necessary services.

Can this organization of the social welfare field be realized? Will it be realized? Should it be realized?

This presentation cannot pretend to answer all these questions. It aims at a description of changes to be expected in selected aspects of American society and in welfare needs, and to make conjectures relevant to how some aspects of the social welfare manpower picture may develop.

CULTURAL THEMES AND SOCIAL CHANGE

Several key patterns of change seem likely and may be noted at the outset.

First, the general devotion of more and more time to formal education now evident will continue. Greater proportions of young men and women can be expected to be graduated from high schools, colleges and universities, professional schools, adult education programs, junior and community colleges, and various specialized programs.

Second, our population will concentrate more heavily than at present in cities, in larger, more dense, and even more sprawled metropolitan regions.

Third, changes in technology will continue to occur at the same rapid and hectic rate at which they are now taking place, especially in the fields of industrial production but also increasingly for tasks now handled by white collar, administrative, supervisory, managerial, and professional personnel. These changes can be expected to affect, and to be related to, changes in themes and assumptions in our cuture. Some of these themes can be here specified, if somewhat tentatively.

1. *An ever greater stress on achievement as the avenue to status can be expected.* In a formal sense, certain factors of ascription of status, although not all, will have lost or be losing the functions they perform today in limiting entry to desirable social positions. In the 1960's, race, for example, is clearly under massive social attack as a barrier to achievement. That this attack will have eliminated the consequences for life careers of the decades-old discrimination and prejudice practiced in both North and South in the areas of education seems doubtful indeed. To expect that Negroes and persons from other minority groups will soon be able fully to qualify for achievement-stressing positions in systems of government, education, and industry is unrealistic because of the grave handicaps and educational deficits of most persons in minority groups except the very young. The suggestion here is that efforts in the direction of remedial and special education for older members will have to be made by our social welfare agencies, both public and private, during the next several decades.

The stress on achievement as the route to status and to recognition is complicated by other social factors. Sex is an interesting example. Alice Rossi has observed that inequality between the sexes is still a paramount feature of American society and that no ideology of equality concerning the sexes has in fact taken hold.[1] In the context of anticipated revolutionary changes through automation in modes of

[1] Alice S. Rossi, "Equality Between the Sexes: An Immodest Proposal," in "The Woman in America," *Daedalus*, Vol. 93, No. 2 (Spring 1964), pp. 607–752.

industrial production, what can be expected with regard to a separation of work from sex? Many white collar and professional positions are not sex linked; at the same time, a smaller proportion of women are in the labor force than men and their career spans are shorter. If work achievement continues in the decades ahead to have the dominant status-bearing value it now has and if more work can be done by fewer people than at present, a formal re-emphasis on sex as a discriminatory factor may appear, and women may be discouraged from entering the labor market.

Longer life expectancy and more years of education may be accompanied by greater overt attention to age-graded groups in many aspects of social organization. Careers, after all, are graded by age and to some extent so are neighborhood residential patterns and geographic mobility patterns, political preferences, and religious beliefs. One out-on-the-limb prediction is that age will in fact be a more important status-determining factor than at present.

On an over-all basis, then, achievement or its social recognition will no doubt remain as a dominant cultural pattern, but with some limits that in part will accent those of the present day.

2. *Impersonality in many important social relations will be accented even more than at present.* As organizations grow in size and expand in functions, both of which can be expected in the next decades, the necessity of dealing with others in categorical terms will, not surprisingly, be maximized rather than mitigated. A contributing factor is the expected increase in rapidity and ease of travel and transport as one gets beyond the bounds of cities. The expected increase in mobility of populations for

vacation and leisure travel as well as for more permanent changes of residence will underscore such impersonality and the stress often found associated with it.

3. *Individuality will be enhanced and will be obtained, contrary to many appealing and alarming predictions, through participation in large, complex, and formal organizations.* Lipset, Hughes, and Kerr *et al.* all contend that bigness does not of necessity breed conformity and a reduction of creativity, but rather leads to the opportunity in time for the individual to liberate himself.[2] The exercise of personal choice will occur in more extensive arenas of decision and options than were or are now available.

4. *A change in the social ethic of work may be expected, although the exact dimensions of the change are difficult to isolate.* Reductions in the hours of a standard work week for manual workers and to a lesser extent for white-collar workers will be followed, probably a few decades later, by similar reductions for most professionals, especially those whose work is primarily organizationally located. Independent professionals apparently lag furthest behind in the reward of weekly clock hours for leisure, although other rewards—money and prestige—clearly come to them in greater abundance than to manual and white-collar workers and to "organization" professionals.

One wonders what will be the new social ethic presented to the young. Will

it be a new Protestant ethic focused on leisure rather than on work? Perhaps the concern that many have about leisure—that it should not be wasted, that it is a mounting social problem, that it should be used creatively and constructively so that personal satisfaction is maximized—is the new dramatic enactment of the Protestant ethic. Doing nothing when at leisure violates the moral norms of those who feel that a void exists. American society seems now to confront the paradox that one of the great rewards of advancing civilizations—freedom from drudgery and toil—gets doled out in greater supply to culture consumers than to culture creators, innovators, professionals, teachers, and the like. A confounding factor is that the choice made by many with time for leisure away from work is a second job; 3,900,000 persons held more than one job in May 1963, an increase of 600,000 over the year before.[3]

Forecast

To sum up, one may forecast at least some of the following changes in our social system: Our population will continue to increase. The complexity and the size of formal organizations will be greater. Opportunity for personal expression may expand. Manual work of a routine sort in the factory may be a memory while nonroutine work will continue, although the necessity of work for some segments of what is now the labor force may continue only in residual form. The tasks of persons performing services, such as those in the professions, will proliferate. Prejudicial discriminations and exclusions on the basis of race, religion, age, sex, and nationality may, ac-

[2] *See* Seymour Martin Lipset, *Political Man: The Social Bases of Politics* (New York: Doubleday & Co., 1963), p. 452; Everett C. Hughes, "Professions," in "The Professions," *Daedalus,* Vol. 92, No. 4 (Fall 1963), p. 452; Clark Kerr, John T. Dunlop, Frederick Harbison, and Charles A. Myers, *Industrialism and Industrial Man: The Problems of Labor and Management in Economic Growth* (New York: Oxford University Press, 1964), pp. 221–222.

[3] Forrest A. Bogan and Harvey R. Hamel, "Multiple Jobholders in May 1963," Special Labor Force Report, No. 39, *Monthly Labor Review,* Vol. 87, No. 3 (March 1964), p. 249.

cording to some, be expected to dwindle in significance; at the same time, our society may in fact be more rigidly organized into groups segregated on the basis of age and sex, and on the basis of achievement of both intellectual and occupational varieties, and the effects of discriminatory exclusions from occupational roles because of race, religion, and nationality, although diminished, may persist as the result of continuing educational and other deficits. Our communities will have the appearance of megalopolis—long urban stretches still probably largely unplanned. Finally, our society will remain one with many juxtaposed and fantastic contrasts of housing, industry, transportation, recreation, and educational facilities.

THE BEHAVIOR OF BEHAVIORAL SCIENTISTS

Assertions about the features and promontories of the body of scientific knowledge, about the distribution of knowledge among scientists, and about the range of their influence or of their prominence are as risky as those concerning general cultural and social change.

Robert Merton's observation that ". . . it cannot be assumed that all social and cultural changes will automatically and promptly induce or reinforce interest in a particular field of inquiry" commands our attention.[4] However, he states that a necessary condition for the development of scientific interest is the definition of societal changes as "social problems" and the occurrence of acute social conflicts.

According to Marvin Sussman in his presidential address to the Society for the

Study of Social Problems in 1963, the "social problem" area has acquired growing acceptance as a legitimate focus of interest at least for the sociologist.[5] He attributes this to the crisis in international relations and the occurrence of social ills, and remarks that the interest reflects a change in the pendulum from an earlier disallowance of social problems as a matter of significant concern for behavioral scientists. Accordingly, he appraises the emergence of the newer roles of consultant and administrator for sociologists along with the more traditional roles of teacher and researcher.

Harry Alpert recently defined the major contemporary features of sociology as follows: rigorous methodology, empirical emphasis, behavioral orientation, and conceptual consciousness.[6] He pointed to the sociologist's concern for social structure, group and institutional analysis, value orientations and social ethos, for the forms and patterns of social control, and for social roles and positions including deviant roles that induce social change. Subfields of the discipline, he noted, in which a reflection of the major features occurs are urban and rural sociology, race and ethnic relations, demography, communications, public opinion and attitude studies, collective behavior, occupations, the sociology of medicine and social psychiatry, social disorganization and deviant behavior, industrial sociology, family sociology, and the sociology of science, along with others.

The behavioral sciences and not simply sociology are, according to Robert Mer-

[4] Robert K. Merton, "Notes on Problem-Finding in Sociology," in Robert K. Merton, Leonard Broom, and Leonard S. Cottrell, Jr., eds., *Sociology Today* (New York: Basic Books, 1959), p. xxxiii.

[5] Marvin B. Sussman, "The Social Problems of the Sociologist," *Social Problems*, Vol. 2, No. 3 (Winter 1964), pp. 216–221.

[6] Harry Alpert, "Sociology: Its Present Interests," in Bernard Berelson, ed., *The Behavioral Sciences Today* (New York: Harper & Row, 1964), pp. 52–59.

ton, "the distinct possession of our own time," and he adds that "some 90 to 95 percent of all behavioral scientists who have ever lived are now alive."[7] Moreover, the numbers double every ten to fifteen years. Some verification of this growth may be found in Matilda Riley's description of membership in the American Sociological Association; from 3,500 in 1950, the membership jumped to 6,300 in 1959.[8] Merton, indeed, refers to this as an age of behavioral science, just as it is, of course, an age of the atom and an age of automation.

The social organization of the fields themselves may affect who works on particular problems and for how long. The development of experimental centers, research stations, and institutes in the social sciences, and the linking of behavioral science units with professional schools, with government, and with agencies will delineate career lines that will provide incentives for social scientists and may thereby stimulate greater attention to social problems and to the needs of professional groups.

Organized links beween university departments and both professional and governmental organizations and agencies will open up applied fields to more rigorous scientific investigation. Programs for consideration of such links are increasing. An instance is the 1964 conference sponsored by the National Association for Retarded Children that brought together institutional directors and university faculty from medical schools and from departments of psychology, sociology, and the like. The aim was to further the establishment of research departments at

institutions for the retarded and the budgeting of funds for part-time or full-time institutional positions for personnel with research as the vital core of their jobs.

The development and acceptance of subfields means subgroups and competition among them. Merton's observation that the sociologist's special raison d'être is his ability to analyze man's institutions and their dysfunctions as well as latent functions is pertinent.[9] As our scientific institutions change, we may expect newer achievements and also greater likelihood of negative consequences, at least for certain existing behavior patterns, such as perhaps a diminution of interest in general explanations and general sociological theory. Organizational settings for behavioral science research will increasingly be operating in standard-setting agencies and independent research institutes, in addition to the conventional university settings. Behavioral scientists, wherever they may be, will share in advancing knowledge of individual social institutions and social behavior. Their specific roles may include participation in the education and training of professionals and technicians in the helping fields of health, education, and welfare. The methods stressed will also include quantification for certain kinds of problems. Careful design will utilize computational techniques, and there the fields are likely to see re-formation of methodologies and less certainly the expanded use of mathematics per se.

The number of behavioral scientists is increasing, their output is increasing, and career patterns are changing, with a smaller proportion of academics and with greater numbers involved in service and

[7] Robert K. Merton, "The Mosaic of the Behavioral Sciences," in *ibid.*, pp. 249, 268.

[8] Matilda White Riley, "Membership of the American Sociological Association, 1950–59," *American Sociological Review*, Vol. 25, No. 6 (December 1960), p. 915.

[9] Robert K. Merton, *Social Theory and Social Structure* (Glencoe, Illinois: Free Press, 1949), pp. 65–68.

welfare agencies. Some blurring of lines between behavioral science specialties and practitioners' roles may be expected, especially as consultation increases. A survey conducted for the Eastern Sociological Society's Committee on the Profession in 1963 resulted in the finding that an increasing proportion of the membership works outside academic settings or, if the academic institution is the employer, earns outside consultation income.

Although we can be optimistic about such developments as more sensitive prediction models and more powerful data-processing technology, it is difficult to be equally sanguine about other more intriguing matters. At least, the crystal ball clouds over. Will we be able to spot value conflicts at their inceptions? Or anticipate patterns of normative deviation? Or predict instabilities in career patterns and role discontinuities?

Behavioral science practitioners can often handle short-run predictions, especially with limited variables. However, data collection is difficult and the range is cumbersome, sometimes even for computers, and the delays in attainment of results are long. Will we be better able to determine when institutional lags thwart human development? Will we have a much more viable and abstract body of established theory in the behavioral sciences than we now have? Can we expect great fruits from our search for methods necessary for the exploration and testing of sociological propositions about complex organizations? Will, for example, a proposed "miniature replica model" permit formulation of significant propositions about behavior in organizations?

We are thus seeing an expansion of the use of methods and techniques in the behavioral sciences. As important for the future growth and development of these fields is a major change in the kinds of opportunities sanctioned for sociologists with completed and attained degrees. Mental hospitals, community centers, institutions for the retarded, and welfare agencies are increasingly available for research, for training, and ultimately for professional affiliation by behavioral scientists. In an earlier era, they would have found such career chances wanting and would have considered them outside the groves of academe. In the future, along with sanction for positions in academic organizations, sanctions will exist for such varied affiliations, and we may expect even closer collaboration between the groups, now largely separated, of behavioral scientists and social welfare personnel.

SOCIAL CHANGE AND SOCIAL POLICY FOR THE FUTURE

What will be the nature of societal change? Clark Kerr, John T. Dunlop, Frederick Harbison, and Charles A. Myers describe the evolving pattern as pluralistic industrialism. Individuals, they argue,

. . . will identify themselves more closely with their occupation, particularly if it involves a formal training period for entry, and mobility will follow more the lines of the occupation than the lines of the industry or the job possibilities of the immediate geographical area. In terms of identification, the orientation will be more nearly that of the member of the guild than of a class or of a plant community. Mayo will turn out to be as wrong as Marx. . . . The occupational interest group will represent the employee in his occupational concerns and the occupation will draw his allegiance.[10]

"Bureaucratic gamesmanship" is the waxing enterprise, yet leisure rather than work commands man's excitements. Kerr

[10] Clark Kerr *et al., op. cit.,* p. 236.

and his associates suggest that "the areas closest to technology will be the most conformist; those farthest from the requirements of its service, the most free." They conclude that "outside his working life the individual may have more freedom under pluralistic industrialism than in most earlier forms of society." Their prediction is that man's great new freedom "may come in the leisure-time of individuals." The world, they say, will be for the first time a totally literate world, an organization society but not one that will be peopled by "organization men."[11]

Dramatic support for this view comes from the theme that increasing education leads to higher status and, in terms of the "Triple Revolution," greater freedom.[12] Charles Killingsworth has testified as follows: the United States is now in a stage of mass consumption; the slow shift from production of goods characteristic of that stage is accompanied by declines in demands for employees in older industries; the new technology will result in extensive displacements; and the most rapidly growing parts of the growing service sector of our economy are health care and education. He notes the decrease in unemployment rates for college graduates in the period from 1950 through 1962. A 36 percent decrease in the rate of unemployment for those with sixteen or more years of education has occurred, compared with a 9.5 percent increase in unemployment rates for those with seven or fewer years of education.[13] Demand

patterns are rapidly leading to a labor market "twist." Fewer of the less educated participate in the labor force—a drop of 22 percent from 1950 to 1962 for those with four or fewer years of education, compared with an increase of 0.2 percent for those with sixteen or more years completed.

Killingsworth argues that many of the less educated have been squeezed out of the labor force, and that unemployment among the less educated is resistant to general improvements in employment in the economy. He calls finally for "investment in human beings" to stimulate economic growth. This includes basic literacy training and provision of sufficient numbers of those able to train and motivate those in need of educational uplift. The training programs started under the Economic Opportunity Act and the Manpower Act are one major step in this direction.

Robert Davis has stated that "contemporary poverty . . . is strikingly immune to economic growth," and he attributes this to a combination of social, psychological, and economic factors, in particular personal disabilities, depressed aspirations, dependency, and lacks in formal education. Interestingly, he reports from a University of Michigan study that public welfare programs do not reach the majority of poor families. Poverty, he asserts, is a major current phenomenon, despite general economic growth, that is not handled adequately by welfare and related programs. Any "programmatic attack," he states, on the problems of the poor will require attention to "the social psychological as well

[11] *Ibid.*, pp. 237–239.

[12] "The Triple Revolution," Report of an Ad Hoc Committee, shortened version, *The Correspondent*, No. 31 (March-April 1964), pp. 24–30.

[13] Charles C. Killingsworth, "Automation, Jobs and Manpower," *Reprint Series, 1963–64* (East Lansing: School of Labor and Industrial Relations, Michigan State University), reprinted from Senate Committee on Labor and Public Welfare, 88th Congress, First Session, *Nation's*

Manpower Revolution, Part 5, Hearings before the Subcommittee on Employment and Manpower (Washington, D.C.: U.S. Government Printing Office, 1963), pp. 1461–1483.

as economic aspects of the culture of poverty."[14]

The 1964 *Report on Manpower Requirements* by Secretary of Labor Wirtz listed an impressive and challenging set of areas of major concern: productivity, changing technology and employment, improper preparation for work, the decline in rural workers and the movement away from farms, Negro workers, and older workers.[15] To this list one may add the mentally retarded, mental patients and their families, and women.

Raising or changing levels of expectations, coupled with the vast gains in energy resources from the atom, are bounded only by the scope of human imagination and ingenuity. But prestige and status distinctions will remain, the status war will continue as an energizer and as a mode of reward, and thus, the abundance of our economy will be unequally distributed.

Along with the abundance theme must be an awareness of the continued necessity for work, but work in a different form. Its pace and content, the requirements and qualifications for performance, and the impact on man's other roles may be different from what can now be visualized.

We may yet see a return in urban settings to the fusion of the places where man works and where he lives. Community mental health centers may be one early indicator of the trend toward the decentralization of large specialized organizations and the location of their facilities and services in closer proximity to the populations to be served. Mass transportation facilities may permit the goods of automated factories to be distributed more effectively than formerly to points of demand. The growth of our cities may be such that foci of work and residence may be spotted around the terrain, separated physically from each other but in touch through modern transportation and communication technology. The drain in time and the cost in psychological strain that result from extensive commuting, coupled with the rising economic costs that come from delay, may lead to the urgent redefinition of what are the socially acceptable roles for adults in our society.

We are faced with an overwhelming challenge. It was expressed as follows by Herbert E. Striner and Henry Holmquist, especially with regard to the urban problem:

If we remember that, in a relatively few years, close to 80 per cent of the population of this country will dwell in urban areas, and that the current outlook in these areas is one of racial friction, transportation chaos, and economic strangulation, then the necessity for planners and social scientists to recognize the critical reasons for each other's existence is paramount. The scientist —in the "natural" and physical as well as the social sciences—must produce the knowledge and techniques by means of which the planners and policy makers can arrive at good solutions to metropolitan problems.[16]

At the same time, the city must also be recognized as the prime haven for the innovators, the deviant, and the creative individuals of our society.

[14] Robert C. Davis, "Poverty in the Affluent Society: A Review Article," *The Sociological Quarterly*, Vol. 4, No. 4 (Autumn 1963), pp. 335–343.

[15] U.S. Department of Labor, *Manpower Report of the President* and *A Report on Manpower Requirements, Resources, Utilization, and Training, by the U.S. Department of Labor*, Part II, March 1964 (Washington, D.C.: U.S. Government Printing Office, 1964). *See also, Manpower Report*, March 1965.

[16] Herbert E. Striner and Henry E. Holmquist, "Social Science and Community Problems," in Leonard J. Duhl, ed., *The Urban Condition: People and Policy in the Metropolis* (New York: Basic Books, 1963), p. 308.

Can these and other challenges be met? The American Association of Junior Colleges recently observed that the system of higher education in the United States is moving away from what the association described as its Victorian style and is moving ahead through the "almost fantastic" development of the junior and community college "toward a real democratization."[17] This points to a major shift in our opportunity structure.

Conflict will nevertheless continue in a democratic society, according to Seymour Lipset.[18] A democratic society is not simply a society of equals who enjoy common rewards for common achievements. It is rather a society with equal opportunity for participation and for striving to attain and to influence, and thus a society of conflict. The individual required is one with adaptability, who can move into a variety of roles, who derives satisfaction from conflict rather than pleasure from security.

How will our society tolerate and adjust to conflict? How can institutions be arranged so that satisfaction from conflict can be accommodated along with demands for achievement? The realities of our social structure call for a tempering of any conclusions we reach about the manner in which institutions will accommodate a clash of expectations and fulfillment. Robert Weaver observed that "pragmatic and proximate adjustments rather than comprehensive remedies" dear to the hearts of professional students of urban problems may be necessary in that area.[19] He questioned the assumption of a direct relationship between the severity of social problems and the degree of popular interest and action toward effective solutions. He noted, for example, the centrifugal process of separation of races and classes within metropolitan areas comprised of numerous municipalities as well as a central city. Minority groups find it difficult to move to more satisfactory housing in better neighborhoods; local prejudice tends to limit low-rent public housing programs to already congested and run-down neighborhoods.

Training and education need to be provided, Weaver observes, to permit the underprivileged to qualify for improved jobs and careers. Either jobs, however, have to be provided wherever they can be, or consideration of newer centers of combined work, residence, and recreation may come to the fore, with the conjugal family again operating as a multifunction institution and the whole extended family being revived.

In an essay written in 1956, Daniel Bell wondered about the effect of that joining of Arcadia and Utopia represented by automation. With this arises a "new concept of work . . . man as creator and regulator of delicate and precise machines."[20] But he concluded, ". . . what will happen when work and workers are displaced by the machine?" as he repeated Freud's observation that "work . . . is the chief means of binding an individual to reality." Against this view is Bell's assertion that "the tendencies to evade work . . . so characteristic of the American factory worker . . . today obsess all workers."

Hard, physical, manual work may be

[17] Norman C. Harris, *Technical Education in the Junior College: New Programs for New Jobs* (Washington, D.C.: American Association of Junior Colleges, 1964).

[18] Lipset, *op. cit.*, p. 439.

[19] Robert C. Weaver, "Major Factors in Urban Planning," in Leonard J. Duhl, ed., *The Urban Condition: People and Policy in the Metropolis* (New York: Basic Books, 1963), p. 99.

[20] Daniel M. Bell, *The End of Ideology: On the Exhaustion of Political Ideas in the Fifties* (rev. ed.; New York: Collier Books, 1961), Chapter 11, "Work and Its Discontents: The Cult of Efficiency in America," p. 256, pp. 264 ff.

destined for replacement through machine systems controlled by computers that regulate production through information flows. The manual or blue collar worker in an assembly operation needs or will need retraining for other work tasks or resocializing for other nonwork activities. White collar work may be next in line; the middle managers and executives may now work at tasks that in large part will in time be hard hit by technological change.

Some exceptions exist even in physical work and certainly in the nonphysical realm. Prefabrication of a house is one thing; its installation on a site is another. Heavy construction, as of bridges, highways, tunnels, need machine directors for operations as well as engineers and planners. Personal services must, it would seem, need personal handling. Professional work also, one may say, can hardly ever be replaced, although patterns of professional behavior are subject to change.

In the area of employment, a main question stands out. Will the economic-technological system develop to a point of such increased productivity of material goods that the number of jobs relevant to those tasks will permanently be greater than the number of persons who wish to work?

We know that white collar occupations are increasingly predominant, that more and more jobs and professions include tasks that are primarily service-oriented and require interpersonal skills as well as administrative and organizational abilities. Our economic-technological system may be moving in this direction, but perhaps it will not accommodate the increasing numbers of men and women actively interested in work. A source of trouble is the mounting educational requisites for initial employment and possibly for continuance in jobs.

Alice Rossi, commenting on the inequality between the sexes, notes the difficulties faced by women who return to the labor market after several years' withdrawal during marriage and childbearing. Much greater difficulties obviously confront members of minority groups who have been blocked from educational opportunities during generations of discrimination. It does not appear likely that significant changes in the distribution of Negroes, for example, through the entire spectrum of professional, white collar, administrative, and supervisory positions that require extensive technical ability can be induced in the short span of years available to the current generations. One may doubt that quick programs, not matter how desirable in the current context of civil rights and no matter how much social thrust supports them, can break down in the short run all the lasting effects of historic patterns of exclusion. Technical specifications for performance in high status jobs preclude this.

Support for this comes from Herman Miller who has shown with convincing data that income differentials between whites and nonwhites are almost identical for 1947 and 1962, and that occupational differentials in income are not decreasing. The income gap between the unskilled and the skilled, which at one time was diminishing, has now started to widen again. Miller also reports that "the income gap between white and nonwhite *widens* [his italics] as education increases."[21] Clearly, this tokens an area of discrimination in which current improvements in access to formal education alone will not by themselves yield removal of race as a significant determining

[21] Herman P. Miller, *Rich Man, Poor Man* (New York: Thomas Y. Crowell Company, 1964), pp. 60, 63, and 163.

factor in life chances for generations of adults who are already handicapped.

Career channels are shifting, if perhaps more slightly than sometimes stated: By 1975, 25 percent of the labor force will comprise professional and managerial workers, compared with 22 percent today; semiskilled workers will decline from 18 percent to 16 percent; laborers from 6 percent to 4 percent; and farmers and farm workers from 8 percent to 5 percent. The increasing industrialization and professionalization of the labor force is apparent. This trend is complicated by the relatively small proportion of the labor force that enjoys the accumulation of status and rewards entailed in careers.

The very patterning of careers appears, furthermore, to be undergoing change. The term "careers" as used here is defined as those sequences of work roles in which movement from role to role is significantly greater than chance, occurs throughout the work-life cycle, and brings to the participating individuals increasing rewards of prestige, status, income, leisure, and the like. In this sense, it appears that technological change and the growing size of organizations foreshorten the period of work life during which education and training will ensure continued vertical improvement or ascent in career ladders. Thus, periodic advanced education and retraining are increasingly required for career ascent; simple persistence or staying power means less and less. What may be called skill careers become more significant than simple career lines. This suggests that movement among skill career patterns is likely to be a more dominant pattern in the future, and that even more emphasis will be placed, in the social welfare fields and in most other professional and technological areas, on re-education and re-training as the requirements for continued career ascent.[22] Harold Wilensky estimated, however, that only a minority of the labor force participates in career sequences during their working lifetimes.[23] The protection of career systems, perhaps even in the social welfare fields, is thus not available to the majority of the working population, unless re-education and retraining occur even more often and for more groups in the labor force than at present.

Another basic question is that of entry position. For young grade school or high school graduates or dropouts who are not skilled or are semiskilled, entry positions have been hit hard by the changes in the kinds of skills needed in modern industry. Business-run training programs now concentrate on white collar tasks necessary for service positions, leaving to the government the task of providing initial training for production workers. The current increases in jobs for education, health, government, and consumer services may require vast increases in government investments in training programs, for business is unlikely to pay the costs of efforts to provide initial training for the performance of work tasks.

Leaving aside this problem of changes in the initial requirements of education and training for the world of work, we must also be aware of a shift in the style of operation of business organizations,

[22] An unpublished paper on "The Implications of Manpower Trends for Career Patterns," by Louis H. Orzack and Jeffrey Salloway (presented at Manpower Research Section, Population Association of America, April 1965, Chicago) develops further the analysis of how career *patterns* are undergoing systematic change in the contemporary United States.

[23] Harold L. Wilensky, "Work, Careers, and Social Integration," *International Social Science Journal*, Vol. 12, No. 4 (Fall 1960), p. 554.

and the decreasing vitality of the traditional job-climbing ladder in business and industrial organizations.

The definitions of the core composite of tasks required in jobs in such organizations clearly include both technical behaviors and social attitudes. Many observers incline to the conclusion that core tasks of jobs have more typically in the past than at present involved what Robert Dubin calls "technological behaviors," that is, those that are mainly physical, that require dexterity in finger, hand, foot, and body movements.[24] A further contention is that the core tasks at the center of many jobs increasingly demand social skills. In the past, the guild system institutionalized a mechanism for learning both kinds of core tasks that required movement through a step system, a ladder upward from apprentice to journeyman to master. As our factory and industrial systems have evolved, there was a time when the very narrow specialization was primarily technological. We now link jobs through promotional systems, through both formally and nonformally patterned connections. However, Froomkin argues that movement from the jobs at the bottom of status systems is largely blocked at present.[25]

Industry, government, education, health and welfare agencies now require specialized preparation in technological and social skills for entry to middle-rank positions. Movement from the bottom to the middle or top of status ladders occurs by meeting educational requirements, by seniority systems, by the grouping of positions into seniority families, and by

[24] Robert Dubin, *The World of Work* (Englewood Cliffs, New Jersey: Prentice-Hall, 1958), pp. 62 ff.

[25] Joseph Froomkin, "Jobs, Skills and Realities," *Columbia University Forum,* Vol. 7, No. 2 (Spring 1964).

the extensive specializations that may require organizations and agencies to look to universities even more than at present for the hiring of supervisory and administrative personnel.

These developments can paradoxically lead both to heightened achievement and reduced flexibility. Whether in the long run we can expect a more nearly perfect match between the capabilities of the men and women actively interested in work and the types of skills that the labor market will demand is difficult to predict. An informed guess, however, for the social welfare field and for the many other areas of work is that a perfect fit is rather unlikely.

CONCLUSION AND SUMMARY

Let us make an attempt to tie these forecasts together and to arrive at predictions about manpower trends in the welfare fields. What are the likely over-all social-cultural trends? How will these trends generate demands for welfare manpower? What expectations will exist for social welfare workers at all professional levels?

This is difficult territory where we have to think about the unknowable or the unthinkable. The parameters are barely discernible; the way they will affect the dependent variables too obscure. The precise nature of our social structure, its descriptive outlines, and the dynamics of the era can hardly be predicted with great confidence.

Several observations, nevertheless, can be made. It seems likely that the following will occur at various levels of social reality:

1. Social welfare personnel will have much broader roles than at present, including what Wittman recently sum-

marized as "preventive social work,"[26] and thus will be engaged in work that will cut across class and across crisis, and will run throughout the age cycle of man.

2. The enhancement of the environment for the psychosocial development of man will be the focus of social welfare efforts, rather than the much more limited, though currently more extensive, emphasis on relationships between income and personal morality, as Mencher observes.[27]

3. Trends toward professionalism and professionalization will no doubt continue, and probably at an accelerating rate, with concurrent expansion of educational programs and a proliferation of educational requirements for top level social workers as well as for social service technicians.

4. What may come to be described as the "affluent" or the "automation" or the "leisure" society will continue to pose choice and adjustment problems for individuals, including the use of leisure time.

5. The organization of cities to provide satisfactory and challenging social environments for our populations will probably not be accomplished in the next few decades, and this will still mean the occurrence of the alienated and anomic individuals who are not incorporated in or do not participate effectively or satisfactorily in social units.

6. Expectations concerning educational achievements as conditions for entry into the social and occupational orders will continue to rise.

7. Cultural deprivation may still be a

[26] Milton Wittman, "Preventive Social Work: A Goal for Practice and Education," *Social Work*, Vol. 6, No. 1 (January 1961), pp. 19–28.
[27] Samuel Mencher, "Perspectives on Recent Welfare Legislation, Fore and Aft," *Social Work*, Vol. 8, No. 3 (July 1963), pp. 59–65.

vital factor, because of the inherent complexity and variability of our modern urban, industrialized and technological society and because of the continued acceptance of individual choice as a vital element in our culture.

8. Mental retardation and mental illness will still occur, whether through genetic processes, socially caused accidents that injure the human organism, or as the result of continuing social variability; the current association of these conditions and social stigma, while more problematic, may survive.

9. Greater skill in social prediction by behavioral scientists, and their far greater use in applied settings and in preparation institutions for health, education, and welfare roles, seem inherent in current trends.

A view, therefore, of our society of the future can be portrayed as follows: It will be a society with contrasting elements of equalitarianism and élitism, with status ladders, with placement still based in part on ascription and in part on achievement; an age graded society; a working society, with the nature of work transformed and with an increase in the range and number of opportunities for leisure; an affluent society, with many continuing pockets of poverty left over from earlier categorical discriminations on the basis of race, national origin, and geographical location; an urban society, with continued congestion and sprawl, and with the likely concurrent development of multi-functional communities; an organizational society; an occupational and professional society, with many competing specialties; and an educationally oriented society.

The scope of social welfare manpower needs seems obviously to be expanding, with increases in planning, prevention, amelioration, and the offering of positive services in many new areas of social life. Over all, we may expect great increases in demand for diverse kinds of social welfare professionals and for facilities to enhance the over-all social welfare. No one can categorically state that our future economic and community institutions will function more adequately to satisfy human expectations than they now do. Given that and given rising expectations, an expansion of the numbers and the uses of social welfare personnel may confidently be foreseen.

Here an element of urgency enters and calls for positive actions to hasten that expansion of numbers and of uses and to permit the social welfare professionals to join the others who will meet the challenges of the future. For, as President Johnson's Council of Economic Advisers concluded in their 1965 Report,

The steps we take during the next few years will help to determine the quality of life in the year 2000. . . .

Most important is the need to develop the potential of human beings. . . .

With more education, better health, greater incentives, and equality of opportunity, the number of disadvantaged will decline. And the Nation's greatly enlarged resources will permit the diminished numbers of the disadvantaged to share more fully in the prosperity of the society.[28]

[28] *Annual Report of the Council of Economic Advisers* (Washington, D.C.: U.S. Government Printing Office, 1965), pp. 169–170.

Index

NAME INDEX

Wooton, Barbara, 530
Wortis, H., 268, 272
Wraxall, Peter, 482

Wyle, Clement J., 306
Yablonsky, Lewis, 431, 432
Yinger, J. Milton, 314

Zemans, Eugene, 337

SUBJECT INDEX